SOUTH-WESTERN

ECONOMICS

THE SCIENCE OF COST, BENEFIT, AND CHOICE

THIRD EDITION

J. HOLTON WILSON
Professor
Business Economics and Marketing
College of Business
Central Michigan University

J. R. CLARK
Tom E. Hendrix Professor
  of Economics and Free
  Enterprise
University of Tennessee / Martin

SOUTH-WESTERN PUBLISHING CO.

Acquisitions Editor: Robert E. Lewis
Developmental Editor: Nancy A. Long
Production Editor: Melanie A. Blair
Designer: Nicola M. Jones
Marketing Manager: Donald H. Fox

ISBN: 0-538-61400-5

Library of Congress Catalog Card Number: 91-61756

3 4 5 6 7 8 9 Ki 9 8 7 6 5 4 3

Printed in the United States of America

PREFACE

Today, more than ever before, economics plays a vital role in society. Trade and exchange seem to reach every aspect of our lives through the choices we make in the marketplace and voting booth. Relationships between nations are likely to revolve as much around economic matters as around everyday political affairs of state.

The increasing role that economics appears to play actually is nothing new or different. We have always made choices, and choices have always been the essence of economics. It is true, however, that in the past 35 years or so we have become increasingly aware that much of our decision making is highly economic in nature. The primary goal of *Economics: The Science of Cost, Benefit, and Choice,* 3d Edition, is to explain in simple terms the role that economics plays in understanding and improving the quality of the choice-making process.

This text is designed along guidelines suggested by the Joint Council on Economic Education's *Master Curriculum Guide. Economics: The Science of Cost, Benefit, and Choice,* 3d Edition, provides you with a primer on economics in its most basic form.

CONTENTS

Part I, "Making Economic Decisions," initially examines the choice process from an individual viewpoint. A five-step decision process that you can use in making personal choices is presented. If followed closely, this process enables you to make informed and relevant choices in the marketplace, the voting booth, and your own social life. The text teaches you to identify the opportunity costs of any choice and to evaluate these costs against the expected benefits. Part I then expands the choice process from individual to social choice.

Once the role of choice in economics is firmly established in Part I, Part II, "Microeconomics," explains the choices made by individual consumers and producers in the marketplace. Part II shows how these individual choices affect supply and demand. It describes the organization of individual business firms and markets, ways to improve the market system, the labor market and individual income, and the importance of agriculture in the economy.

Part III, "Macroeconomics," explains the choices made by the whole economy, as reflected in aggregate demand and supply. Topics explored include GNP, unemployment, inflation, the money supply and the banking system, and monetary, tax, and fiscal policies.

Part IV, "The United States and the World Economy," explores economic topics related to the world economy. These include alternative economic systems, international trade, and problems of the less-developed countries. Again, the role of choice is applied to these topics. The economic choices of what, how, and for whom goods will be produced are examined under the economic systems of capitalism, socialism, communism, and government-assisted capitalism.

THE CROSS-REFERENCE INDEX SYSTEM (CRIS)

One of the helpful features of *Economics: The Science of Cost, Benefit, and Choice,* 3d Edition, is the Cross-Reference Index System (CRIS). CRIS was developed to supplement the standard textbook presentation with a set of learning keys and guideposts for you to follow as your individual learning needs dictate. CRIS provides a clear organizational skeleton for the material, guides you to greater explanations and detail, if necessary, and gives assistance in answering the chapter-end questions. CRIS is designed to help you gain a clear understanding of the factual material as well as to develop the ability to reason in "the economic way of thinking."

How the CRIS System Works

There are six major elements of the CRIS system in each chapter of the text:

1 — Learning Objectives

The first page of each chapter presents clearly defined learning objectives for each major concept covered in the chapter. The learning objectives are competencies you will acquire and be able to demonstrate after completing the chapter. The learning objectives are numbered sequentially by chapter and concept, and they form the starting point for the CRIS system. For example, the third objective in Chapter 1 is to "Explain the concept of economic scarcity" and is numbered "1–3." These numbers are referred to as the "CRIS numbers."

2 — Key Terms

Key economic terms are highlighted in bold type and defined in the margins where they first appear. All marginal terms refer to the first learning objective in each chapter. For example, all marginal terms in Chapter 1 are keyed to CRIS number 1–1, "Define terms related to the economic way of thinking."

3 — Text Material

Within the text material, CRIS numbers appear in the margins next to the concepts to which they refer. For example, in Chapter 1, CRIS number 1–3 appears in the margin beside the text material which introduces the concept of economic scarcity.

4 — Chapter Summaries

One- or two-sentence-long summaries of the main concepts are included at the end of each chapter in a section entitled "Reviewing the Chapter." Each summary item is preceded by a CRIS number linking it to its respective learning objective.

5 — End-of-Chapter Questions

Two end-of-chapter sections entitled "Reviewing Economic Concepts" and "Applying Economic Concepts" include questions directly related to each learning objective. A CRIS number preceding each question indicates the learning objective to which the question relates. This provides you with a significant hint as to which major economic concept to apply in answering the question as well as where to look in the text for the answer.

6 — Student Supplement

You can continue the CRIS process in the *Student Supplement* as well. The same cross-references are provided for each question, problem, or project. If you have difficulty, you can return to the objective or the chapter summary of main points. The true/false and multiple choice items in the *Student Supplement,* as well as the vocabulary reviews, will reinforce your recognition and understanding of the material and help you to develop better economic reasoning.

How to Use the CRIS System

As you begin each chapter, first read the learning objectives, then the text presentation and the chapter summary of main points. When answering the chapter-end questions, the CRIS numbers will help you to answer those with which you have difficulty. Look at the CRIS number of the question and return to the chapter objective with the same number. If you still have difficulty, return to the appropriate cross-referenced text location.

Your teacher may place emphasis upon some objectives while skipping over others. Also, after a chapter or part test, your teacher will be able to pinpoint the objectives and concepts in which you are weak. Take a close look at the diagram on the following pages to see more clearly how the CRIS system can help you learn faster and remember longer.

CROSS REFERENCE INDEX SYSTEM (CRIS)

CRIS NUMBERS
Keyed to the learning objectives, CRIS numbers appear in the margins next to the concepts to which they refer.

PART I: MAKING ECONOMIC DECISIONS

Economics Makes Us More Effective Citizens

As a citizen in this country, you have the opportunity to vote. You can help decide the future course the economy will take. Do you want to pay higher taxes for more new roads and schools? Or do you want to pay lower taxes and accept poorer roads and schools? The candidates will have to make these economic choices, and you must decide which candidates to vote for. As you cast your vote, you should understand what these choices will mean to you.

You might even want to become a political candidate yourself. However, before you could take a position on an issue, you would need to understand how it affects the economy. Perhaps you would favor a tax cut that would reduce unemployment. But what if the tax cut also increased inflation? Would you favor free trade with other countries, or would you expect us to buy only American-made products? These and many other questions would be an important part of your life.

The study of economics helps people and societies make better choices. An understanding of economics is vital to your success in the workplace, the marketplace, and the voting booth.

A SCIENCE OF CHOICES

When a person thinks of the term *economics*, many impressions come to mind. Students often associate the term economics with money, the stock market, inflation, taxes, and unemployment. But economics is much more. It is a scientific body of knowledge that can analyze, explain, and in many cases predict people's economic behavior. This behavior is centered around the basic economic problem.

The Basic Economic Problem: Scarcity

The basic economic problem is scarcity. **Scarcity** is the condition that occurs because people's wants and needs are unlimited, and the resources needed to produce goods and services to meet these wants and needs are limited.

There are two sides to the scarcity problem. One of the basic human characteristics is that people are never fully satisfied. Psychologists say that as soon as the basic needs for food, clothing, and shelter are met, the mind creates new needs, such as physical security. When this need is fulfilled, the mind finds even more new needs. This need creation and fulfillment process has no end. Every time a need is satisfied, a new need is created. No matter if

1-2

1-2

1-1
scarcity
The condition that occurs because people's wants and needs are unlimited, and the resources needed to produce goods and services to meet these wants and needs are limited.

1-3

CHAPTER 1

THE
ECONOMIC
WAY
OF
THINKING

Learning Objectives

1–1 Define terms related to the economic way of thinking.

1–2 Discuss why you should study economics.

1–3 Explain the concept of economic scarcity.

1–4 Understand the opportunity cost and the opportunity benefit of an economic choice.

1–5 Explain how individual and social choices relate to microeconomics and macroeconomics.

1–6 List three basic economic choices that must be made in all societies.

1–7 Explain why economic theory is important in economic decision making.

2

KEY TERMS
Key economic terms are highlighted in bold type in the text and defined in the margins where they first appear.

LEARNING OBJECTIVES
Clearly defined, individually numbered learning objectives for each chapter form the basis of CRIS.

16
PART I: MAKING ECONOMIC DECISIONS

REVIEWING THE CHAPTER

1-2 1. An understanding of economics is important to your everyday life. Economics helps you make more informed decisions as a consumer, worker, and citizen.

1-3 2. Economics is a social science concerned with the basic economic problem of scarcity. Scarcity arises because limited resources are available to satisfy unlimited wants and needs.

1-4 3. Because of scarcity, we must allocate our limited resources among our unlimited wants and needs. This requires us to make individual and social decisions. With every decision, there is an opportunity cost and an opportunity benefit.

1-5 4. Economics is divided into two major types of theory. Microeconomics is concerned with individual producing or consuming units and generally involves individual decisions. Macroeconomics is concerned with the economy as a whole and generally examines social economic decisions.

1-6 5. Economies operate under various systems of economic decision making. Some economies are ruled by social decisions, while others operate mostly by individual decisions. Regardless of structure, all economies must decide on the three basic economic questions of what to produce, how to produce, and for whom to produce.

1-7 6. Economic theory is a broad description that simplifies reality. Theory acts as a guide to (1) understanding or (2) taking informed action in a particular situation. Economic theory, unlike mathematical or physical theory, is not always precise in all situations. It is, however, extremely useful and relevant when correctly applied.

REVIEWING ECONOMIC TERMS

1-1 Supply definitions for the following terms:

scarcity
unlimited wants and needs
limited resources
allocation
economics
opportunity cost

opportunity benefit
microeconomics
macroeconomics
theory
budget constraint

Name _____

CHAPTER 1

THE ECONOMIC WAY OF THINKING

STUDY GUIDE

Part 1 • Vocabulary Review (1-1)

DIRECTIONS: Fill in the blank in each of the following sentences with the word or words from the list below that best complete the sentence.

allocation	macroeconomics	social cost
budget constraint	microeconomics	the economic problem
economics	opportunity benefit	theory
individual choice	opportunity cost	three basic economic questions
individual cost	scarcity	unlimited wants and needs
limited resources	social choice	

1. Because we never feel that all our wants and needs are satisfied, economists say that we have _____
2. Scarcity is _____
3. Individual selection of one alternative over another is referred to in economics as _____

CHAPTER 1 • THE ECONOMIC WAY OF THINKING

Part 2 • True/False Review

DIRECTIONS: Place a check mark (√) in the proper Answers column to show whether each of the following statements is true or false.

	Answers		For Scoring
	True	False	
1-3 1. Scarcity comes about because although resources are unlimited in this world the wants and needs of individuals are highly limited.			1.
1-3 2. Scarcity is the major reason why it is necessary to allocate our resources among our wants and needs.			2.
1-5 3. Microeconomics is concerned primarily with individual producing or consuming units such as one person or one business firm. It deals mostly with individual decision making.			3.

17
CHAPTER 1 THE ECONOMIC WAY OF THINKING

REVIEWING ECONOMIC CONCEPTS

1-3 1. What is the basic economic problem?

1-3 2. Why does scarcity occur in a society?

1-3 3. What is the solution to the basic economic problem?

1-5 4. Name the two kinds of choices that we must make in a society.

1-5 5. Give an example of a microeconomic choice and a macroeconomic choice.

1-6 6. What are the three basic economic questions?

1-6 7. In the United States today, why is coal produced by a capital-intensive process instead of a labor-intensive process?

APPLYING ECONOMIC CONCEPTS

1-4 1. If you had to choose between going swimming and raking your neighbor's lawn for $10, which two economic concepts would enter into your decision? What would you decide and why? If the opportunity to swim were lost, but the offer from the neighbor remained, would this change your decision?

1-3 2. If you had an income of $1 million a year, would you escape the basic economic problem of scarcity? If so, how? If not, why not?

1-4 3. If you were a highly skilled brain surgeon, and your brother or sister were a school teacher, which of you would have the larger opportunity cost by being drafted into the army? Why?

1-6 4. Would you rather live in a country that made most of its decisions socially, or one in which individuals made most of the decisions? In which of those countries would there be more freedom of choice?

1-3, 1-4, 1-5 5. Candidates for political office often speak of what their administration will give voters if they are elected. Candidate *A* promises more roads, new schools, more public parks, and new fire trucks. From what you have learned in this chapter about scarcity, choices, and cost, what are the obvious questions for you to ask Candidate *A*?

1-7 6. Can you develop a simple theory about how much water people drink in the summer relative to how much they drink in the winter? Will your theory always be correct for all people? If not, does that mean your theory is worthless in describing human behavior? Is your theory better than trying to observe how much water each human drinks in each season? Why or why not?

Name _____

CHAPTER 1 • THE ECONOMIC WAY OF THINKING

Part 3 • Multiple Choice Review

DIRECTIONS: For each item below, select the choice that best completes the sentence. Print the letter identifying your choice in the Answers column.

	Answers	For Scoring
1-2 1. A knowledge of economics is vital to students because (A) it directly affects the course of our everyday lives (B) it helps us make informed decisions in both the marketplace and the voting booth (C) it makes us more effective citizens (D) all of these.		1.
1-1 2. Economics is a science which analyzes (A) how people get rich (B) how to hit it big in the stock market (C) how the government spends our tax dollars (D) how individuals and societies make choices.		2.
1-1 3. Economics is one of the (A) physical sciences (B) social sciences (C) mathematical sciences (D) theological sciences.		3.
1-3 4. Scarcity is the basic economic problem. Scarcity comes about because (A) people's wants and needs are limited while the resources to fulfill those needs are unlimited (B) human beings always want more money (C) people's wants and needs are unlimited while the resources to fulfill those needs are limited (D) sometimes there is not enough of everything to go around.		4.

vii

ADDITIONAL FEATURES

This text offers many other special features which will help enhance your study of economics.

Special Sections

Special sections entitled "Leaders in Economic Thought" highlight the lives of people who have influenced the areas discussed in the chapters. "Thinking About Economic Issues" sections present information on relevant economic topics, such as the value of an education and the salaries of professional athletes.

Full Color Illustrations

Graphs, tables, and maps, in full color, break up the narrative and provide graphic illustration of the concepts presented. In addition, the many color photographs illustrate important concepts. The photographs often portray people in everyday situations to reinforce the idea that economics is important in everyday life.

Appendixes

Appendix I, "Economic Measurement Concepts," introduces measurement concepts helpful to understanding the text material. This appendix should refresh your understanding of the many key arithmetic relationships frequently used to present and analyze economic information. Appendix I was designed to accompany Part I of the text.

Appendix II is included to give you the opportunity to apply the concepts of supply and demand to a real-world industry. Appendix II, "Supply and Demand Forces at Work: Health Care in the Economy," could be covered after completing Chapters 6–8 on supply and demand concepts.

Glossary

A complete glossary of all important economic terms defined within the text is provided at the end of the text. The terms are also defined in the margins next to the text material in which they are introduced. Thus, you will have easy access to definitions of any terms you do not understand.

Bibliography

A bibliography of suggested readings is included for each chapter so that you may expand your economic understanding beyond the text presentation. These readings were selected for both relevancy and appropriate level of difficulty for high school students.

Index

A detailed index is provided at the end of the text. The in-depth nature of this index will be a valuable aid to you in looking up locations of particular concepts given in the text.

THE WHOLE PACKAGE

Included in the package are a *Student Supplement* workbook, student audiocassette tapes, a complete testing package, a *Teacher's Manual,* a *Teacher's Resource Package,* a *Teacher's Edition,* and four-color overhead transparencies.

Student Supplement

The *Student Supplement* (Stock No. HB29CD) provides a number of student activities to reinforce learning. For each chapter, the *Student Supplement* provides the following:

1. A skeleton outline of the chapter with space for students to write in their own study notes.
2. A vocabulary exercise for reinforcing the meaning of new terms. These exercises take various forms, including crossword puzzles, word search games, matching, and fill-in exercises.
3. A section of true/false questions about chapter concepts.
4. A section of multiple choice questions about chapter concepts.

The true/false and multiple choice questions are of the type teachers are likely to use in their testing programs. In general, it is reasonable to expect that students who have successfully completed the *Student Supplement* exercises will be more likely to succeed in the testing program than those who have not.

Student Audiocassette Tapes

The student audiocassette tapes (Stock No. HB29CM) are designed to provide students with important information from each chapter in an alternative learning format. Each chapter of the text is reviewed in a separate segment of a tape. Some students might wish to listen to these tapes prior to reading the corresponding chapter of the text. The tapes may also be useful for reinforcing the main ideas of a chapter after students have studied the text. These tapes are not meant to be used as a substitute for reading the student textbook. There is information in the textbook that is not included in the tapes.

Testing Package

A booklet of *Achievement Tests* (Stock No. HB29CG) is available from the publisher. The tests are also available as *MicroExam,* an easy-to-use menu-driven microcomputer testing package. *MicroExam* is available for the Apple® IIe, IIc, and IIGS® computers[1] (Stock No. HB29CH73T). It is also available for IBM® computers[2] (Stock No. HB29CH81T). Each booklet or diskette provides a 20-question multiple choice test for each chapter. In addition, a 20-question test for each part may be used individually or combined to provide semester exams.

Teacher's Manual

The *Teacher's Manual* (Stock No. HB29CX) is a valuable resource for teachers of this economics course. Answers are given for end-of-chapter activities, *Student Supplement* exercises, and test questions. In addition, 126 transparency masters are included.

Teacher's Resource Package (TRP)

The *Teacher's Resource Package* (Stock No. HB29C8) contains the following individual items: the videotape *Whose Debt Is It?* and its Teacher's Supplement; instructional objectives and outlined instructional strategies; stock market game; solutions to end-of-chapter activities; ideas for developing critical thinking skills; answers to the *Student Supplement* overprinted on the student copy; correlations between this text and the text-workbook *Economic Experiences,* the videotape *Whose Debt Is It?,* and the *Economics U$A* videotapes; 126 transparency masters; references; answers to the *Achievement Tests* overprinted on the student copy; enrichment activities; and instructor's audiocassette tapes. The *TRP* is packaged in an easy-to-carry briefcase-style container that keeps all support materials organized and ready to use.

Teacher's Edition

New this edition, the *Teacher's Edition* (Stock No. HB29CW) of the textbook is an exact copy of the student textbook overprinted with valuable marginal notes.

---

[1]Apple is a registered trademark of Apple Computer, Inc. Any mention of Apple refers to this footnote.

[2]IBM is a registered trademark of International Business Machines Corporation. Any mention of IBM refers to this footnote.

Four-Color Overhead Transparencies

The four-color overhead transparency package (Stock No. HB29CL) consists of 50 transparencies.

ACKNOWLEDGMENTS

In preparing the third edition of *Economics: The Science of Cost, Benefit, and Choice,* the authors have benefited from feedback received from teachers and students who have used the first two editions. Their comments and suggestions have helped to make this edition of the text even better than the first two editions. While we believe this is the best high school economics text available, we welcome your comments and suggestions as we look toward making future editions meet all your needs.

The authors would also like to thank Leslie Wolfson, Judy Sandefer, Fonda Gamlin, and Tara Phillips for their helpful contributions to the manuscript. Jan Eddleman should also be recognized both for her assistance in controlling the reading level, as well as contributing helpful hints and teaching suggestions.

Finally, the generous support of Tom E. Hendrix, founder and chairman of the board of Henco Corporation, should be recognized. His dedication to improving the teaching of high school economics has contributed to the development of this text.

J. Holton Wilson

J. R. Clark

CONTENTS/PART I

MAKING ECONOMIC DECISIONS

PART II

MICROECONOMICS

PART III

MACROECONOMICS

PART IV

THE UNITED STATES AND THE WORLD ECONOMY

Figures

Figures (continued)

Tables

Tables (continued)

PART I

MAKING ECONOMIC DECISIONS

CHAPTER 1

THE ECONOMIC WAY OF THINKING

Learning Objectives

1-1 Define terms related to the economic way of thinking.

1-2 Discuss why you should study economics.

1-3 Explain the concept of economic scarcity.

1-4 Understand the opportunity cost and the opportunity benefit of an economic choice.

1-5 Explain how individual and social choices relate to microeconomics and macroeconomics.

1-6 List three basic economic choices that must be made in all societies.

1-7 Explain why economic theory is important in economic decision making.

ECONOMICS IS IMPORTANT

Why should you study economics? What will you gain from learning about it? Lately, almost everyone has heard something about economics. It is difficult to pick up a newspaper, watch television, or have contact with the world outside your home without encountering some economic information. In order to understand the economic information you hear every day, you will need to become familiar with the economic way of thinking.

1–2

Economics Affects Our Everyday Lives

Economic concerns are the topics of many newspaper headlines: "Teen Unemployment Rate Remains High," "U.S. Auto Makers See Brighter Times Ahead," "College Tuition To Rise," "Concern About Inflation Remains High." You can see that these are topics that affect your everyday life—cars, school, jobs, and so on. Economics not only identifies economic problems for us. Economics also provides us with a logical, effective decision-making process. This process helps us to make the most of our resources and to satisfy many of our wants and needs every day.

1–2

Economics Helps Us Make More Informed Decisions

As a worker and a consumer, you will have to make many economic decisions. You will have to decide how to spend your income. The cost of all the goods and services you would like to buy will most likely be greater than your income. So, you will have to choose them carefully. You also will have to choose a career for yourself, and this choice will surely affect your lifetime income, personal happiness, and success. You will make decisions about working, learning, earning, and spending. All these decisions can be made more effectively with a basic understanding of economics.

1–2

Illustration 1–1
Economic news reaches all of us and has daily impact on our lives.

Economics Makes Us More Effective Citizens

1–2 As a citizen in this country, you have the opportunity to vote. You can help decide the future course the economy will take. Do you want to pay higher taxes for more new roads and schools? Or do you want to pay lower taxes and accept poorer roads and schools? The candidates will have to make these economic choices, and you must decide which candidates to vote for. As you cast your vote, you should understand what these choices will mean to you.

You might even want to become a political candidate yourself. However, before you could take a position on an issue, you would need to understand how it affects the economy. Perhaps you would favor a tax cut that would reduce unemployment. But what if the tax cut also increased inflation? Would you favor free trade with other countries, or would you expect us to buy only American-made products? These and many other questions would be an important part of your life.

1–2 The study of economics helps people and societies make better choices. An understanding of economics is vital to your success in the workplace, the marketplace, and the voting booth.

A SCIENCE OF CHOICES

When a person thinks of the term *economics*, many impressions come to mind. Students often associate the term economics with money, the stock market, inflation, taxes, and unemployment. But economics is much more. It is a scientific body of knowledge that can analyze, explain, and in many cases predict people's economic behavior. This behavior is centered around the basic economic problem.

The Basic Economic Problem: Scarcity

1–3 The basic economic problem is scarcity. **Scarcity** is the condition that occurs because people's wants and needs are unlimited, and the resources needed to produce goods and services to meet these wants and needs are limited.

There are two sides to the scarcity problem. One of the basic human characteristics is that people are never fully satisfied. Psychologists say that as soon as the basic needs for food, clothing, and shelter are met, the mind creates new needs, such as physical security. When this need is fulfilled, the mind finds even more new needs. This need creation and fulfillment process has no end. Every time a need is satisfied, a new need is created. No matter if

1–1
scarcity
The condition that occurs because people's wants and needs are unlimited, and the resources needed to produce goods and services to meet these wants and needs are limited.

you are rich, poor, or in between, you probably can think of many things you need right now. **Unlimited wants and needs**, then, is the human characteristic of never feeling that all wants and needs have been satisfied.

Fulfilling most needs requires goods and services of one kind or another. To produce goods and services, resources or the raw materials of production are needed. For example, building houses to fulfill the human need for shelter requires wood, glass, concrete, steel, copper, and the services of builders. However, there is only so much lumber, glass, concrete, steel, and labor available. There is a limit to resources. **Limited resources**, then, means that there are never enough resources to fulfill all wants and needs.

Limited resources available to satisfy unlimited wants and needs creates *scarcity*, the basic economic problem. The solution to the problem of scarcity is allocation.

Allocation is the process of choosing which needs will be satisfied and how much of our resources we will use to satisfy them. We must choose which needs to neglect and just how much to neglect them. This allocation process requires making *trade-offs* or choosing among alternatives. When we allocate, we choose among alternatives or make trade-offs in deciding how to use our resources.

Definition of Economics

Economics, then, is the science of making effective choices or decisions by examining the alternatives. As a social science, economics studies how people interact in their society in an economic way. Broadly defined, **economics** is the social science that deals with how society allocates its scarce resources among its unlimited wants and needs.

1–1

unlimited wants and needs
The human characteristic of never feeling that all wants and needs have been satisfied.

1–1

limited resources
There are never enough resources to fulfill all wants and needs.

1–1

allocation
The process of choosing which needs will be satisfied and how much of our resources we will use to satisfy them.

1–1

economics
The social science that deals with how society allocates its scarce resources among its unlimited wants and needs.

Illustration 1–2
Building a house satisfies this family's need for shelter. The resources required in constructing the house (such as wood, cement, and glass) are limited.

COSTS AND BENEFITS

You have learned that economics is the science of making choices. However, in order to make effective choices, you must understand the costs and the benefits of any given choice. When you make a purchase decision, you weigh the price you must pay against the satisfaction or use you believe you will get from the purchase. There is more to cost, however, than just the dollar price. Economists consider the *opportunity costs* and *opportunity benefits* in making each decision.

Opportunity Cost

1-4

1–1

opportunity cost
The value of any alternative that you must give up when you make a choice.

Opportunity cost is the value of any alternative that you must give up when you make a choice. In short, the opportunity cost is the value of the opportunity lost. If you choose to study for a test rather than to ski, the opportunity cost is the skiing time you must give up to study.

Let's develop another example of opportunity cost and use some of the tools that an economist would use to make a decision. Assume for the moment that you have a weekly income of $30 and that you spend that income on only two different goods: movies and T-shirts. We will keep the numbers very simple and assume that T-shirts sell for $10 each and movies cost $5 each. Table 1–1 shows how many of each item you can buy with your income.

Obviously you could spend all of your income on three T-shirts or on six movies. However, you may wish to have some of both goods. In that case, you would spend some of your income on movies and some of your income on T-shirts. Of course, how much you spend on movies will determine how much income you have left to spend on T-shirts. Now look at the graph in Figure 1–1 on page 7 which illustrates the information in Table 1–1. Let's look at two cases to see clearly the opportunity cost of two alternatives from which you may choose.

You may choose to go to four movies and use the remaining income to buy one T-shirt.

$$
\begin{array}{ll}
\text{4 movies @ \$ 5 = \$20} & \\
\underline{\text{1 T-shirt @ \$10 = \$10}} & \text{Combination } A \\
\text{TOTAL = \$30} &
\end{array}
$$

Another choice is to go to two movies and use the remaining income to buy two T-shirts.

$$
\begin{array}{ll}
\text{2 movies @ \$ 5 = \$10} & \\
\underline{\text{2 T-shirts @ \$10 = \$20}} & \text{Combination } B \\
\text{TOTAL = \$30} &
\end{array}
$$

TABLE 1–1

USE OF INCOME TO BUY T-SHIRTS AND ATTEND MOVIES

T-Shirts You Can Buy	Price	Total Cost	Your Total Income	Income Left Over
1	$10	$10	$30	$20
2	$10	$20	$30	$10
3	$10	$30	$30	$ 0

Movies You Can Attend	Price	Total Cost	Your Total Income	Income Left Over
1	$5	$ 5	$30	$25
2	$5	$10	$30	$20
3	$5	$15	$30	$15
4	$5	$20	$30	$10
5	$5	$25	$30	$ 5
6	$5	$30	$30	$ 0

Either choice is possible since you have $30 to allocate. How, then, will you decide which alternative to choose? Will you choose Combination *A* or *B*? The best way to make that choice is to look at the opportunity cost of each alternative. Suppose you are presently considering Combination *A* with four movies and one T-shirt. What, then, will you have to give up to move to Combination *B*,

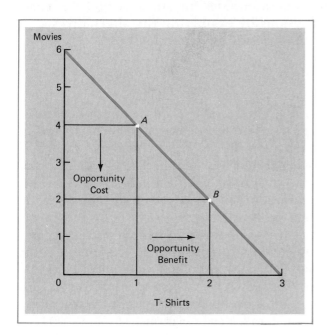

FIGURE 1–1   THE OPPORTUNITY BENEFIT AND OPPORTUNITY COST OF TWO ALTERNATIVES
As you move from Combination *A* to Combination *B*, you gain one T-shirt (opportunity benefit) and give up two movies (opportunity cost).

Illustration 1–3   To choose a T-shirt is to miss out on two movies.

which allows you two T-shirts and two movies? As the graph in Figure 1–1 shows, to get the additional T-shirt in Combination B, you will have to give up two of the four movies you would have had in Combination A. The opportunity cost now becomes quite clear. In this case, to get one additional T-shirt you have to give up two movies. Therefore, the opportunity cost of one T-shirt is two movies.

You should make your decision based on how much you like movies compared with how much you like T-shirts. You need to decide if you like one T-shirt enough to give up two movies. On the other hand, you also can consider whether you like two movies enough to give up one T-shirt. What, then, is the opportunity cost of two additional movies? It is one T-shirt.

1–4   We can now add the concept of opportunity cost to the definition of economics. Economics includes the study of how we make effective choices or decisions by examining the alternatives and considering the opportunity cost of each alternative.

Opportunity Benefit

1–1

opportunity benefit
What is gained by
making a particular
choice.

1–4   Another way of making choices is to look at the opportunity benefits of the alternatives. The **opportunity benefit** is what is gained by making a particular choice. If, in the above case, the opportunity cost of moving from Combination A to Combination B is two movies, then the opportunity benefit is one T-shirt. In the case of choosing to study rather than to ski, the opportunity benefit is receiving a better grade on your test.

1–4   Every economic choice has an opportunity benefit and an opportunity cost. When you make an informed choice, you compare the opportunity benefit (what you gain) with the opportunity cost (what you lose). This simple concept will serve as a good guide as you further your knowledge of economics. It will also be useful as you make more complicated individual and social decisions.

8

INDIVIDUAL AND SOCIAL CHOICES

There are at least two kinds of choices that we must make in a society. These are individual choices and social choices.

First, individuals must make choices every day in trying to satisfy their own needs. Individuals might make choices about how to divide time among study, leisure, physical exercise, and work. Other examples are choices about spending individual income on clothing, entertainment, or tuition.

Second, society must make social choices to try to satisfy the needs of society as a whole. Some social choices determine how much of society's income is spent on national defense, roads, schools, or cultural affairs for citizens.

Obviously individual and social choices play a large role in the functioning of the economy. To analyze this, economics is divided into two separate branches that deal with these two basic types of choices.

Individual Choices and Microeconomics

Microeconomics is the branch of economics that examines the choices and interaction of individuals concerning one product, one firm, or one industry. It is concerned primarily with individual decision making. The unit of analysis is one person, one product, one firm, or one industry. An example of a microeconomic choice would be how individual beef farmers respond to higher beef prices in the market. Each farmer must decide whether to supply more, less, or the same amount of beef to the market at the new price. Individual consumers of beef must decide whether they wish to buy more, less, or the same amount of beef at the new, higher price. Each individual, both on the buying and selling sides, will make an individual choice.

1–5
1–1
microeconomics
The branch of economics that examines the choices and interaction of individuals concerning one product, one firm, or one industry.

Illustration 1–4
If beef prices rise and a farmer decides to produce more beef, that is a microeconomic choice.

Social Choices and Macroeconomics

1-5   **Macroeconomics** is the branch of economics that examines the behavior of the whole economy at once. Thus, the unit of analysis is the whole economy. Macroeconomics asks: How much total output is the economy producing? Are the resources of the economy fully employed? How high is the rate of inflation in the economy?

1-1

macroeconomics
The branch of economics that examines the behavior of the whole economy at once.

An example of a macroeconomic choice is how the government of a country deals with inflation. The government could cut back its spending, make credit more difficult for consumers to get, and encourage consumers to cut spending by raising taxes. This is a social decision made by government to deal with a macroeconomic problem such as inflation.

THREE BASIC ECONOMIC CHOICES

Some societies make many more *social* decisions than others because of how their system of government is designed. Some other societies conduct most of their economic affairs through *individual* decision making. Regardless of the relative amounts of

1-6   social and individual decision making in an economy, all societies use some combination of these decisions to answer three basic economic questions:

1. *What* will be produced with the limited resources?

2. *How* will the goods and services be produced?

3. *For whom* will the goods and services be produced?

What to Produce

All societies try to produce certain basic goods like food, clothing, and shelter. The real questions are: How much food? How much clothing? How much shelter? Remember, if more food is produced, there will be an opportunity cost of this additional food. The society must give up some shelter or clothing or something else that is being produced.

The questions get more difficult if you consider other essentials such as national defense, roads, and schools. If members of society are to be well protected and secure, then they may not, at the same time, be as well dressed or well fed. If education takes top priority, then perhaps the roads used to get to the schools will not be repaired as often. The society must decide exactly what mix of goods and services to produce. In the United States, this decision is made mostly by the interaction of individual buyers and sellers. In some societies, the decision is made in quite different ways. You will study these ways of decision making in later chapters.

How to Produce

There are many different ways to produce most goods and services. For instance, a highway can be built using large bulldozers and earth movers. A highway of equal quality can be built with thousands of individual workers using wheelbarrows, picks, and shovels. In America, we are accustomed to the use of heavy machinery. This does not mean that the use of many laborers and smaller tools is less effective. Decisions about how to produce take into account the resources that are available. A country with a large population and very few machines may decide that the best road-building method is *labor intensive.* That is, using more laborers and fewer machines costs less. Here, the opportunity cost of machines is higher than the opportunity cost of labor.

A historical example of this concept is the coal industry. Several decades ago, coal mining in the United States was a relatively low-paying profession with many dangers. About one million miners worked with picks, shovels, and drills to remove coal from the ground. These coal miners eventually organized and demanded higher and higher wages. Thus, it became much cheaper, in many cases, for coal companies to develop and use huge machines rather than laborers to aid in mining coal. Today the coal output of the United States is much greater than it was in the 1940s; yet only half a million workers are employed in mining. Why is coal produced with a *capital-intensive* (use of many machines) process now, when the process used to be labor intensive? Because the opportunity cost of labor (workers) relative to capital (machines) went up.

For Whom to Produce

Once goods and services are produced, all economies must decide who will use them. Will every citizen get the same quality and amount of goods and services or will there be differences? In America, who gets what is decided by consumers and the price system in the market. Anyone who can pay the price for a Rolls Royce may have one. On the other hand, a person may spend a smaller amount on a Ford Escort in order to allocate the remaining income to other uses. How individuals choose to spend their income varies according to their personal preferences as well as their income levels. In our economy, the question of for whom to produce is primarily an individual choice.

Other societies allocate goods and services by other means. Some societies provide housing for all workers which, by and large, is identical in design, space, location, and even color. Individuals can't make many choices in this situation. They may choose any

Illustration 1–5
Harvesting fruit crops was once a labor-intensive activity. The use of new capital equipment adds great speed to the process. The sloping surface cherry harvester shown above can shake the fruit from a tree in 15 seconds.

Illustration 1–6
In our society, individuals make product choices based on personal preferences and the size of their incomes.

housing they desire, but only from the location, design, or color that is provided. Here, the social decision to provide identical housing for the whole society takes away much of the *individual* choice as to which kind of house a person can live in.

THE IMPORTANCE OF ECONOMIC THEORY

1–1

theory
A simplified description of reality.

All economic systems are guided in their economic decision making by the use of economic theory. A **theory** (also called a *model*) is a simplified description of reality. Theory is not always perfect, however. Sometimes economic decisions do not produce the results that theory might have predicted. Why, then, is it important to understand economic theory? To answer this, we will return to a previous example.

1–1

budget constraint
The mix of goods that can be purchased, given a limited amount of income.

Earlier we discussed the concept of opportunity cost as applied to buying T-shirts or going to the movies. This case used a theoretical tool that economists call a budget constraint. A **budget constraint** is the mix of goods that can be purchased, given a limited amount of income. The budget constraint in the earlier example was that you had $30 to spend on T-shirts and movies. The choices were limited to only two goods. In reality, an individual can, and usually does, choose among many goods. Why, then, do we use these simplified theoretical tools? Can they tell us anything about the real economic world? The answer is a definite yes! Remember, theory is merely a simplified description of reality.

Economic Theory Simplifies Reality

To describe reality in detail would be an endless task. If we tried to consider every thought and action an individual has in making choices about all goods and services, there would be no end to the process. The description would be so complicated that we could not draw any meaningful conclusions from it.

Theory, on the other hand, is like a road map. A road map is a relevant guide to be used for a specific purpose. It does not show *every* street or even every small town. Trees, rocks, mountains, and fields are not generally part of the road map because they do not affect the decisions of a driver. A road map is helpful to a driver because it simplifies reality.

A hiker, on the other hand, would benefit more from a relief map showing mountains, fields, streams, and landmarks. This kind of map simplifies reality as needed for a hiker. Streets are not much help and are, therefore, unnecessary information. A theory must include only the useful data. In simplifying reality, it is important to develop the right theory for the problem to be solved.

Economic theory is very much like the map example. To study how individuals make decisions (microeconomic theory), we may need a different theory from the one we use to study how whole societies make decisions (macroeconomic theory). The theory we use to understand problems such as inflation and unemployment is different from the theory we use to understand gasoline prices. Before we simplify our description of reality, we must know what we are trying to describe.

With the budget constraint for T-shirts and movies, we were trying to simplify the process that individuals use in making informed choices between two alternatives. We *assumed* that there were only two choices. This assumption told us under what conditions our theory was valid. We could have used much more complicated theories and not needed this assumption. However, the concept of opportunity cost might not have been as clear.

Illustration 1–7
If an aerial map showed every rock and bush on the ground below, it would only confuse the pilot. In the same way, a theory must include only useful and relevant data for the problem to be solved.

Economic Theory Is Relevant

As you go through life, you will make economic decisions as a consumer, as a worker, and as a citizen. An understanding of economic theory will be relevant to your everyday life. It will help you to make the most informed decisions possible on every economic issue you will face.

1–7

Look for the relevance in every economic theory you learn in this book. Ask yourself how and under what conditions each concept applies. As you do this, you will train your mind in the economic way of thinking.

THINKING
ABOUT ECONOMIC ISSUES

Insurance is a means by which people protect against a possible large loss by paying a smaller cost. The large loss, such as theft of a car or a house destroyed by fire, is uncertain. Such large losses are not frequent, but when they occur they can mean financial ruin for a family. Rather than risk this result, you can protect yourself by paying a smaller amount, called a *premium*, to an insurance company. The insurance company would then cover the large loss should the unlikely event occur.

To help you understand how insurance works, consider the following situation. If your bicycle is stolen you might have to pay $100 to replace it. Your bicycle probably won't be stolen, but there is some risk that it will be. If you and the other people who own bicycles decided to share that risk, the cost to you of a loss would be less.

Suppose you have 50 people who agree to share the risk. If two bikes are stolen each year, you would pay $4 per year. (The cost of replacing two bikes would total $200. Dividing the $200 cost among 50 people would be $4 each.) This $4 would be a small cost to protect against the possibility of having to pay $100 to replace your stolen bicycle. And if you are all more careful with your bikes, perhaps only one bike would be stolen each year. Then the risk of loss would fall and your insurance cost would fall to $2.

The major types of insurance you have to think about as you enter adult life are described on the following page. For some of those kinds of insurance, personal decisions are limited by laws or other factors. For example, state laws usually require that car owners have insurance to cover costs to other people in the event of an accident. Also, when a bank lends people money to buy a house or a car, the bank will usually require the borrower to carry insurance. Then if the car or house is damaged due to an accident or fire, the loss will be covered by the insurance company.

**Insurance:
An
Individual
Choice**

MAJOR TYPES OF INSURANCE
PEOPLE CHOOSE TO BUY

Car insurance protects against large losses resulting from owning and/or driving a car. There are three major types of car insurance:

1. Liability insurance covers losses to others such as bodily injury or property damage;

2. Collision insurance covers losses to the owner's car;

3. Medical payments insurance covers the cost of medical care to the policyholder and family members if they are hurt in a car accident.

Life insurance protects families from financial loss when a family member dies. The two most common forms are term life insurance and whole life insurance. The cost of *term insurance* is lower, but one can get money from the insurance only at death. With *whole life insurance* you can get money (called a cash value) from the policy prior to death.

House insurance protects against loss related to damage to your home or property. Policies are available for both home owners and for renters. The insurance covers repair or replacement of the home and contents when damage is caused by fire, lightning, or vandalism. *Personal liability coverage* is often included as well. This protects against losses related to injury to others or damage to other people's property caused by you or your family.

Health insurance protects against loss related to sickness or injury. Some employers provide **group health insurance** plans to workers. You can also buy *individual health insurance* but usually at a higher cost. The health insurance pays the costs of doctor bills, hospital bills, and sometimes the costs of medicines. Often the patient pays a part of the cost as well.

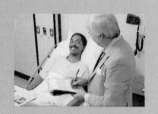

Income insurance protects against a loss of income due to disability or unemployment. Many employers provide *disability insurance,* and most states have an *unemployment insurance* program. Such policies provide some income during a period when a worker is disabled or unemployed. The amount is normally less than the income earned while the person is working, but it does help provide the basic needs. Part of the Social Security program provides disability insurance as well.

REVIEWING THE CHAPTER

1-2   1. An understanding of economics is important to your everyday life. Economics helps you make more informed decisions as a consumer, worker, and citizen.

1-3   2. Economics is a social science concerned with the basic economic problem of scarcity. Scarcity arises because limited resources are available to satisfy unlimited wants and needs.

1-4   3. Because of scarcity, we must allocate our limited resources among our unlimited wants and needs. This requires us to make individual and social decisions. With every decision, there is an opportunity cost and an opportunity benefit.

1-5   4. Economics is divided into two major types of theory. Microeconomics is concerned with individual producing or consuming units and generally involves individual decisions. Macroeconomics is concerned with the economy as a whole and generally examines social economic decisions.

1-6   5. Economies operate under various systems of economic decision making. Some economies are ruled by social decisions, while others operate mostly by individual decisions. Regardless of structure, all economies must decide on the three basic economic questions of what to produce, how to produce, and for whom to produce.

1-7   6. Economic theory is a broad description that simplifies reality. Theory acts as a guide to (1) understanding or (2) taking informed action in a particular situation. Economic theory, unlike mathematical or physical theory, is not always precise in all situations. It is, however, extremely useful and relevant when correctly applied.

REVIEWING ECONOMIC TERMS

1-1   Supply definitions for the following terms:

scarcity	opportunity benefit
unlimited wants and needs	microeconomics
limited resources	macroeconomics
allocation	theory
economics	budget constraint
opportunity cost	

REVIEWING ECONOMIC CONCEPTS

1-3 1. What is the basic economic problem?

1-3 2. Why does scarcity occur in a society?

1-3 3. What is the solution to the basic economic problem?

1-5 4. Name the two kinds of choices that we must make in a society.

1-5 5. Give an example of a microeconomic choice and a macroeconomic choice.

1-6 6. What are the three basic economic questions?

1-6 7. In the United States today, why is coal produced by a capital-intensive process instead of a labor-intensive process?

APPLYING ECONOMIC CONCEPTS

1-4 1. If you had to choose between going swimming and raking your neighbor's lawn for $10, which two economic concepts would enter into your decision? What would you decide and why? If the opportunity to swim were lost, but the offer from the neighbor remained, would this change your decision?

1-3 2. If you had an income of $1 million a year, would you escape the basic economic problem of scarcity? If so, how? If not, why not?

1-4 3. If you were a highly skilled brain surgeon, and your brother or sister were a school teacher, which of you would have the larger opportunity cost by being drafted into the army? Why?

1-6 4. Would you rather live in a country that made most of its decisions socially, or one in which individuals made most of the decisions? In which of those countries would there be more freedom of choice?

1-3, 1-4, 1-5 5. Candidates for political office often speak of what their administration will give voters if they are elected. Candidate *A* promises more roads, new schools, more public parks, and new fire trucks. From what you have learned in this chapter about scarcity, choices, and cost, what are the obvious questions for you to ask Candidate *A*?

1-7 6. Can you develop a simple theory about how much water people drink in the summer relative to how much they drink in the winter? Will your theory always be correct for all people? If not, does that mean your theory is worthless in describing human behavior? Is your theory better than trying to observe how much water each human drinks in each season? Why or why not?

CHAPTER 2

MAKING PERSONAL DECISIONS

Learning Objectives

2–1 Define terms related to individual decision making.

2–2 Explain how the three basic economic questions are answered in a market economy.

2–3 Discuss the role of individual self-interest in a market economy.

2–4 Describe the effects of social choice on individuals and society.

2–5 Explain the five-step decision-making model.

2–6 Apply the five-step decision-making model.

INDIVIDUAL AND SOCIAL DECISIONS

Because of scarcity, economics is a science of choices. Economic decisions are made either by **individual choice** (individuals acting separately) or by social choice (the whole society acting together). To make intelligent choices, individuals and whole societies must carefully consider the costs and benefits of each choice.

Economic Questions and the Market Economy

A society must answer the **economic questions** of what, how, and for whom to produce. Some economies rely much more on individual decisions than on social decisions to answer these economic questions. An economy in which economic questions are decided mostly by individuals in the marketplace is called a **market economy**. *Capitalist economy* is another name for a market economy. The American economy is an example of a market, or capitalist, economy.

People's actions in a market economy result from their motives or incentives for personal gain. **Economic incentive** is the increase in our personal satisfaction that may result from some economic activity. This increase in satisfaction may be the result of having more money income.

But money is not all that is important as an economic incentive. **Psychic income** is the nonmonetary reward we get from some activity. For example, we may feel a sense of pride from having done a job well. We are happier because of that pride and so have some personal gain. We will see that this economic incentive of personal gain is very important in how economic questions are answered in a market economy.

In a market economy, *what to produce* is decided by consumers voting in the marketplace with their dollars. If a great many individual consumers decide to buy a good or service, the product succeeds in the market. The producers earn money by providing more of those products consumers want.

However, if many consumers individually choose not to buy a product, the product fails in the market. The producer then faces loss and individually chooses not to produce the item. Thus, the product disappears from the market. This process of individual choice by consumers and producers in a marketplace determines what will be produced.

How to produce is also decided by individual choice in a market economy. Assume that you are an individual producer in a highly

2–1
individual choice
Decisions made by individuals acting separately.

2–1
economic questions
Decisions a society must make on what, how, and for whom to produce goods and services.

2–2
2–1
market economy
An economy in which the economic questions are decided mostly by individuals in the marketplace.

2–1
economic incentive
The increase in our personal satisfaction that may result from some economic activity.

2–1
psychic income
The nonmonetary reward we get from taking some action.

2–2

2–2

Illustration 2-1
In a market economy, *what to produce* is decided by consumers voting with their dollars in marketplaces like this modern shopping mall.

competitive industry such as wheat production. The market price for wheat might be $3.50 a bushel. How will you produce the wheat so that you can make a profit? There are many ways to grow wheat. For instance, you can employ hundreds of farm workers who use hand tools, or you can employ fewer workers and more machinery (tractors). How will you choose between these two methods? You will choose the one that produces the greatest amount of wheat at the lowest cost.

It might take 100 hours of plowing with a tractor to cultivate the crop. The tractor might cost $75 an hour to rent and operate. Your cost of plowing with the tractor will then be $7,500. You could do the same amount of plowing in 100 hours with 100 workers who each earn $3.25 an hour. Then your plowing cost is $32,500 (100 hours × 100 workers × $3.25 an hour = $32,500). You would probably choose the method that costs less—using the tractor.

Hundreds of other production decisions would be made the same way. You, as an individual producer, would choose as effectively as you could with the best information you could find. Your incentive is personal gain. You want to maximize your income from the production of your product.

2-2   *For whom to produce* also is answered in a market economy by individual choice. Anyone who has enough money can buy any product.

Individual Choice, Self-Interest, and the Invisible Hand

The issues of individual choice and personal gain are important in understanding market economies. During the past 50 years,

American capitalism has produced a standard of living unparalleled in the modern world. One reason for this is that individuals directly benefit from their decisions in a market economy. Their individual decisions are guided by self-interest. In some other kinds of economies, individuals do not necessarily benefit from their own decisions.

In a market economy, if you do not seek out the correct information — and therefore choose poorly — your costs will rise and your profits will decline.

Economic profit is the difference between the money you obtain from selling a product and the cost of producing the product. For example, in the production of wheat, you might have chosen to use laborers instead of a tractor. Your profits would have been $25,000 more if you had chosen the tractor. You will pay a price in a market economy for choosing poorly.

2–1
economic profit
The difference between the money you obtain from selling a product and the cost of producing the product.

The power of self-interest cannot be overstated. It is the driving force behind market economies. Self-interest is not merely an advantage to individuals. It is what makes individual choice influence the marketplace. Many economists believe that self-motivated individual choice does the greatest good for society as a whole. Adam Smith stated the importance of self-interest more than 200 years ago (see page 22).

2–3

When the producer and the consumer meet in the marketplace, they pursue their own self-interests. The producer wants to maximize profits, and the consumer wants to minimize costs. The bargain that is struck must benefit both producer and consumer, or they would have no reason to trade or exchange. The incentive that guides individuals to choose in the best interest of society by pursuing their own self-interests is called the **invisible hand**. This role of self-interest is best explained in Adam Smith's description of the invisible hand:

2–1
invisible hand
The incentive that guides individuals to choose in the best interest of society by pursuing their own self-interest.

> An individual neither intends to promote the public interest, nor knows he is promoting it. . . . He intends only his own gain, and he is led by an invisible hand to promote an end which was no part of his intention. . . . It is not from the benevolence of the butcher, the brewer, or the baker that we expect our dinner, but from their regard to their self-interest. We address ourselves not to their humanity, but to their self-love and never talk to them of our necessities, but of their advantages.[1]

2–3

---

[1]Adam Smith, *An Inquiry Into the Nature and Causes of the Wealth of Nations,* ed. Edwin Cannan (Chicago: University of Chicago Press, 1976), 18.

ADAM SMITH

Adam Smith was born in Scotland in 1723. He became a professor of logic and moral philosophy at the age of 28. His concept of the *invisible hand* remains a key principle in modern economic theory.

In the late 1700s, Europe was marked by a period of substantial social decision making. Governments heavily regulated trade with foreign countries as well as much of the behavior of individuals. Citizens were discouraged and, in some cases, prohibited by law from buying foreign goods. Government encouraged and supported trade guilds. This government support forced workers to join guilds if they wished to work, and forced people to buy from these guilds rather than from individual merchants. Individual freedom and, therefore, individual decision making were not major forces in the economy.

In 1776, Smith published *An Inquiry Into the Nature and Causes of the Wealth of Nations,* which is considered to be the first systematic study of economics. Smith said that self-interest would encourage individuals to do the job they did best and which produced the greatest benefit for themselves. Thus, human and material resources of the society would be put to the most productive use, and the whole society would benefit.

Smith was clearly a proponent of individual choice. He had a low opinion of the government of his time. Also, he observed that government decisions, which were supposed to benefit the whole economy, often benefited individuals of power or wealth instead of the whole society. He felt that if individuals were allowed to make their own economic choices, those choices would be made more carefully than if they were made by government.

Smith considered the proper role of government to be that of encouraging free trade and individual freedom and providing some limited public goods such as roads, bridges, military defense, and a court system. He saw self-interest to be in harmony with a thriving economy and a wealthy nation.

Smith's philosophy was radically different for its time. Historians have credited him with causing a change in the political and economic thinking of generations.

Costs and Benefits of Social Choice

As did Smith, many present-day economists believe that individual choice in most economic matters is far superior to social   2–4
choice. Social choice implies that the benefits and the costs of a choice will affect the whole society. If a society chooses to have free public education, all workers will be taxed to pay for it. People who do not have children will receive no direct benefit from free schooling but still must pay the tax. In this case, a social decision has placed a cost on some members of the society to whom it gives no direct benefit. Overall, however, the benefits to families with children probably far outweigh the somewhat unfair costs to families without children. The point is that social choice benefits some members of the economy at the expense of *all* members.

Individual Incentives and Social Choice

Social choice can reduce the incentive of direct self-interest   2–4
and therefore, at times, discourage individual productive efforts. Let's consider the case of a wheat producer again. This time, however, assume the farm is owned by the government. Workers are expected to work eight hours each day, and everyone is paid equally. What if you, a worker on this farm, work very hard, put in extra hours, and spend your off hours thinking of ways to improve output? As a result of your efforts, the farm increases output by 1,000 bushels. You, however, receive only the same pay and rewards as your co-workers who do not try to produce as much. You have no incentive to produce more than your co-workers. The social decision that the whole society should benefit from the farm equally overrides the value of any individual decisions you might make. It is highly likely that you will choose in your own self-interest not to work as hard but to enjoy the same benefits as your co-workers. From the view of productivity, social decisions are generally not as effective as individual decisions.

Illustration 2–2
The costs that result from the social choice to have free public education are shared by all taxpayers.

FOCUS ON INDIVIDUAL DECISIONS

As both consumers and producers of goods and services, our individual or personal decisions affect our own satisfaction as well as the satisfaction of others. Making a correct decision the first time around is always better than trying to correct a poor decision once

2–5 it has been made. A logical, well-reasoned approach to individual problem solving involves five separate steps:

1. Define the problem.

2. List the alternatives among which you must choose.

3. List the criteria by which you must evaluate the alternatives.

4. Evaluate the alternatives based on the criteria you have chosen.

5. Choose the alternative that best meets the criteria you have chosen.

2–1

model

A simplified form of reality which shows the relationship between different factors.

These five steps make up the personal decision-making model. In economics, a **model** is a simplified form of reality which shows the relationship between different factors. For example, a model airplane shows you what a real airplane looks like but does not show every detail. A model decision-making process shows you the general idea of how to go about making well-informed decisions. However, it does not show you every specific detail you have to consider in making every decision.

1 — Define the Problem

In Lewis Carroll's *Alice's Adventures in Wonderland*, the Cheshire Cat tells Alice:

> If you don't know where you are going, any road will take you there.

Decision making by individuals is often clouded by emotion and misinformation. Instead of plotting a straight path to solve a problem, individuals might take *any road* and hope it is the right one. 2–5 But *any road* might lead to the wrong solution! Therefore, the first step is to define exactly what the problem is.

Economic decisions generally start as a problem of scarcity or the need to allocate. For example, consider the problem of a football team that has more players than can fit on the team bus. This problem can be defined as how to allocate the available spaces to team members. How do we decide who will travel and who will not?

As another example, consider the following allocation problem. You have just received a tax refund check for $350. You have many uses for this money, and you want to make the best decision you can. You have defined the problem as: "Given this income of $350, how can it best be allocated to fulfill my needs?"

2–6

Similar decisions concerning allocation could involve how to allocate your limited free time among studying, work, and leisure. Or you might have to choose how to spend your income or your energy. Before you can make these choices, you must first define each individual problem.

Be Objective. **Objectivity** means ruling out aspects of a problem which seem important only because of strong emotions or feelings about them. In defining the problem, you should be as objective as possible. You should weigh each aspect of the problem in regard to the role it plays. Let's return to the case of the football team and the bus. What is the real problem here? Is the bus too small? Or is the team too large? The third-string guard may feel that the bus is too small. The starting quarterback, however, may feel that the team is too large.

Both of these problem definitions are affected by the emotions involved with how sure an individual player is of getting a seat on the bus. If the star quarterback's throwing hand had been broken recently, the quarterback's definition of the problem might change. The quarterback would not be so sure of getting a seat on the bus and might agree that the bus is too small.

Focus on the Issue. After ruling out emotional involvements, you must focus your thought on the true issue. For example, individuals without emotional involvement in the problem of the football team's bus will view the issue differently. The school principal may feel that the team is too large. The coach, however, may argue that the team needs to carry as many players as possible in order to train young talent. The problem should be defined objectively and clearly. Buses are limited in size, and most teams usually have more players than seats. The problem definition then becomes how to allocate the limited seats among a larger number of players.

2–1
objectivity
Ruling out aspects of a problem which seem important only because of strong emotions or feelings about them.

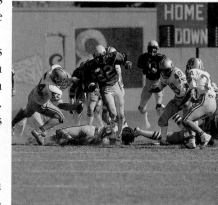

Illustration 2–3
Objectivity means thinking about a decision apart from emotion or personal motives.

2—List the Alternatives

2–5

2–1
alternative
A possible course of
action.

An **alternative** is a possible course of action. Once the problem has been defined, the next step in the personal decision-making model should be to list the alternatives.

You have already defined the tax refund problem as, Given this income of $350, how can it best be allocated to fulfill my needs? Next, you should make a list of the alternative uses for this income. Remember that your problem is limited by your income. Let's assume that you consider the following four items to be your most important choices:

2–6

1. A new stereo receiver

2. A one-week vacation to Florida during spring break

3. A new electric guitar

4. A new moped

Limit Your Alternatives. There are probably many other items that you have considered and ruled out. Remember, you could consider every item in the world before making your choice. However, that would take more time and effort than you are willing to spend. So, you must list a reasonably small number of realistic alternatives among which to choose.

Be Realistic. While you might like a new car, the $350 you have to spend makes this an unrealistic alternative. On the other hand, you might be able to buy a used car for $350. But a car bought for that price might not be something you could depend on. Obviously Step 2 requires that you come quickly to a small but realistic set of alternatives.

Illustration 2–4
Buying a stereo receiver is one of four realistic alternative ways you can spend your $350 tax refund.

3 — List the Criteria Used to Evaluate Your Alternatives

Now that you have defined the problem and listed your alternatives, you need to evaluate the alternatives. The characteristics of a group of alternatives that will be judged to make a choice are called **criteria**. Ask yourself the following question: Given these alternatives, on what criteria should I base my choice? Should you consider cost, or usefulness, or product life, or some other aspect of the product? The answer will vary from person to person, but you should select your criteria objectively and realistically.

Let's assume that the important criteria in this case include the following:

1. *Durability* — How long will the goods or services last?

2. *Acceptability to authority figures* — Will your parents, police, school authorities, and others accept your choice? Another way of looking at this criterion is: How will a given choice affect your relationship with others?

3. *Other expenses* — What other costs, such as maintenance, will there be to each alternative? What other things will you need to make use of the alternative, such as fuel for the moped, records for the stereo, or a camera for your vacation?

4. *Salvage or trade-in value* — When you no longer desire to own the good, will it have any remaining value? Will you be able to get that value for yourself?

Having decided on your criteria, you may also want to rank them in order of importance. For example, you might feel that product durability is more important to you than acceptability to parents. That might sway your final choice to the moped. However, you may find out that your state has a law requiring that mopeds be licensed at a cost of $60 per year. The weight you place on the criterion of acceptability to authority figures may then change.

4 — Evaluate the Alternatives

You have now defined the problem, listed the alternatives, and selected some criteria on which to decide. The next step involves evaluating each alternative using the criteria. To do this, set up a table of alternatives and criteria, such as Figure 2–1. This is sometimes called a decision matrix. A **decision matrix** is a table showing comparisons of alternative decisions.

Each alternative listed in this decision matrix is weighed according to its costs and benefits. Thus, it gives a clear comparison of the

2–5

2–1
criteria
The characteristics of a group of alternatives that will be judged to make a choice.

2–6

2–5

2–1
decision matrix
A table showing comparisons of alternative decisions.

value of each alternative relative to each criterion. In our example, each alternative is ranked on each criterion from most desirable (1 point) to least desirable (4 points). After the points for each alternative are totaled, final ranks are figured. The lower the number of total points, the more desirable the alternative is. Thus, the stereo receiver is ranked first because it has the lowest total points.

This example uses hypothetical information about each alternative. Your individual evaluation may be different. Every individual places a different and unique value on each good or service in the world. You may enjoy one T-shirt as much as two movies. One of your friends may feel just the opposite. Your friend may like one movie as much as two T-shirts. Both of you are entitled to your preference, and both of you are right.

2–1

utility

The satisfaction one receives from the consumption, use, or ownership of a good or service.

2–1

util

The unit of measurement for utility.

Economists have developed a term to describe the strength of your preference. They call it utility. **Utility** is the satisfaction one receives from the consumption, use, or ownership of a good or service. The unit of measurement for utility is the **util**. In the above example, for instance, each T-shirt has twice as many utils (units of use value or satisfaction) for you as going to a movie.

Wise choices are those that maximize the utility of the choice. A related concept economists use is psychic income. As you learned earlier in this chapter, psychic income is the nonmonetary satisfaction received by taking some action. Psychic income is also called *psychic utility.* For example, volunteer work at a hospital may not pay anything, but those who do it receive psychic income. They receive personal satisfaction or utility from doing such work.

You may feel that owning a moped would give you status, peer acceptance, or the attention and admiration of your friends. That choice might hold some psychic income for you beyond its utility as transportation. This is another criterion you may want to use to evaluate your alternatives.

Remember, the utility each individual receives from a particular good, service, or action varies from person to person. The important point here is not how you feel about each choice. Instead it is important that you develop an organized, logical approach to making choices.

5 — Choose the Best Alternative

2–5

2–6

From our example decision matrix (Figure 2–1), we can see that our best alternative is the stereo. It has the lowest total score, which means that the individual ranks for this alternative were lower overall than those of the other alternatives. Remember, however, that your final choice depends on the criteria you choose and on your own preferences. If you live only for today, then product

		STEREO RECEIVER	FLORIDA VACATION	ELECTRIC GUITAR	MOPED
PRODUCT DURABILITY AND PRODUCT LIFE		Ten years or more	One week; memories good or bad, one lifetime	Five years	Five years
Rank of Alternative		1	3	2	2
ACCEPTABILITY TO AUTHORITY FIGURES		Highly acceptable	Moderately acceptable	Acceptable with volume control	Highly questionable; possible danger, laws, etc.
Rank of Alternative		1	3	2	4
RELATED EXPENSES		Moderate and flexible; new records	Some, but flexible; entertainment, shopping, etc.	None or minimal; strings, earplugs, electricity	High; fuel, insurance
Rank of Alternative		3	2	1	4
SALVAGE OR TRADE-IN VALUE		Relatively high	None	Moderate	Very low
Rank of Alternative		1	4	2	3
Final Rank of Alternative		6 points 1st choice	12 points 3rd choice	7 points 2nd choice	13 points 4th choice

(Column heading: ALTERNATIVES; Row heading: CRITERIA)

FIGURE 2–1   A DECISION MATRIX

The four alternatives are listed at the top of the last four columns. The four criteria for evaluating the alternatives are listed in the first column. Note the final rank shown for each alternative.

durability may not be important to you. Therefore, your choice might well be the vacation. If you can get lots of utility from your music, the guitar may be a better choice for you. There is an important issue here. If you make your personal decisions in the logical, organized, and effective way described, the utility you get probably will be greater than a choice made another way. This will be true no matter what individual preferences enter into your evaluation.

Individual Choice and Opportunity Cost

It is also important to remember that every time you make a choice, you must pay an opportunity cost. That is, you give up some alternative that you could have chosen. By using the five-step decision-making model in your choices, you can make comparisons between your opportunity costs.

For example, if you choose the stereo, your opportunity costs are the alternatives you have given up—the vacation, guitar, and moped. But by using the decision-making model, you have chosen the alternative that will give the most satisfaction. Thus, you also have the lowest possible opportunity costs.

In Figure 2–1, the stereo was the clear-cut first choice. It is possible that prices of stereos may rise quickly. You might find that you cannot buy the stereo for $350 anymore, and you may have to make a second choice. From the decision matrix, note that the electric guitar follows as a close second choice. Therefore, you may not suffer greatly if you settle for the guitar. Also, note that the vacation and the moped, while rated lower than the guitar or stereo, were almost equal choices. They were rated only one point apart. If both the guitar and the stereo became unavailable, you might have to carefully consider your choice between the vacation and the moped. You might even want to add more criteria.

APPLYING THE DECISION PROCESS TO REALITY

The decision-making process described here may seem very complicated. It seems like a lot of work just to make a choice. In reality, the first few times you try the process, it may take some time. After a few times, however, you get accustomed to using the five-step process, and things move more quickly. In the first few attempts, it might be wise to write out a decision matrix like Figure 2–1. After a few times, this should not be necessary. Just think through the process:

1. Define the problem.
2. List the alternatives.
3. List the criteria.
4. Evaluate the alternatives.
5. Choose the best alternative.

REVIEWING THE CHAPTER

2–6

2–5

2–2   1. Economies must make choices because of scarcity. Some economies rely more on individual decisions than on social decisions to make these choices.

2–2, 2–3   2. In a market economy, the economic questions of what, how, and for whom to produce are decided mostly in the marketplace by individual producers and consumers. Self-interest guides these individual choices. Correct choices result in individual benefits, and incorrect choices produce costs.

2–4   3. When social choices are made in an economy, some members of society benefit at the expense of all members.

2–3   4. Adam Smith, a Scottish economist, made the first systematic study of economics in 1776. Smith said that self-interest and individual choice would produce the greatest benefit for the individual and, therefore, the whole economy.

2–5 5. Individual choices play a major role in a market economy. Therefore, it is important to know how to make effective individual decisions.

2–5 6. To make better personal choices, five steps can be followed:
1. Define the problem.
2. List the alternatives.
3. List the criteria.
4. Evaluate the alternatives.
5. Choose the best alternative.

REVIEWING ECONOMIC TERMS

2–1 Supply definitions for the following terms:

individual choice	model
economic questions	objectivity
market economy	alternative
economic incentive	criteria
psychic income	decision matrix
economic profit	utility
invisible hand	util

REVIEWING ECONOMIC CONCEPTS

2–2 1. How are the economic questions of what to produce and how to produce decided in our economy?

2–2 2. Why are personal decisions important in a market economy?

2–3 3. What is the guiding force behind individual decisions in a market economy?

2–4 4. What is the effect of social choices on individuals?

2–5 5. List the five steps in the decision-making model.

2–5 6. What two things should you do in order to clearly define a problem?

2–6 7. How do we choose alternatives?

2–6 8. How do we select criteria on which to base our decisions?

2–6 9. How do we evaluate the alternatives based on our criteria?

2–6 10. How can you get the most satisfaction from any personal decision you make?

APPLYING ECONOMIC CONCEPTS

2–3   1. "Self-interest is selfish, greedy, and not in the best interest of our market economy." Do you agree or disagree with this statement? Why?

2–4   2. In a modern society, government should decide what should be produced and how so that the goods and services that everyone needs are produced. Do you agree or disagree? Why?

2–6   3. Assume that you have just broken off your present dating relationship and now have six more hours of free time per week. You can allocate this time among studying, working, dating others, or spending time with your family. Set up a decision matrix. Select your own criteria, and use the five-step decision-making process to decide logically how you will spend your time.

2–4   4. Suppose your school passes a conduct code (makes a social decision) that prohibits dating. Would this represent your preferences? If so, do you think that it would represent all the individual preferences of the student body? If not, why not?

2–4   5. Which do you prefer: an economy based primarily on individual choice or on social choice? Why? You will be asked this question again after you have completed Chapter 3, so think carefully about your answer.

PERSONAL JOB DECISIONS AFFECT YOUR ECONOMIC FUTURE

Many personal decisions will affect your own economic future. One of these is your career selection. It is clear that the level of education you obtain will influence your earning power. On average, college graduates earn twice as much each year as people who do not complete high school and about 1.7 times as much as those who stop going to school after graduating from high school.

In considering a career, some of the issues you need to think about are (1) What do you do well; (2) What do you enjoy doing; (3) How much education is required; and (4) How will economic trends affect your choices. Your school counselors can probably help you with the first two of these items. Library research and your study of economics will help you with the last two items.

As you think about different jobs, be sure to include the idea of opportunity costs in your thinking. The decision-making process discussed in Chapter 2 will help you with your job decisions.

CHAPTER 3

MAKING SOCIAL DECISIONS

Learning Objectives

3–1   Define terms related to social decision making.

3–2   Explain how the three basic economic questions are answered in a
       social economy.

3–3   Discuss the place of personal incentives under social choice.

3–4   Explain the conditions under which social choice is preferable to
       individual choice.

3–5   Apply the five-step decision-making model to making social
       decisions.

ECONOMIC QUESTIONS AND SOCIAL ECONOMIES

Some economies in the world operate through mostly *social* decision making. An economy in which the major economic questions of what, how, and for whom to produce are determined by the government representing the interests of the entire society is called a **social economy**. A social economy is sometimes called a *command economy*.

What to Produce

The question of what to produce with a nation's given stock of resources presents an interesting problem of economic choice. While market economies operate mostly through individual choice, social economies use committees of experts who pool their knowledge. These committees work out elaborate plans as to what the economy will produce.

Social economies are guided by a central planning committee. This committee decides which goods and services should be produced in the best interest of the whole society. Individuals do not directly make these decisions. Rather, the goods and services are produced by order of the planning committee and appear in the marketplace when completed. The varieties and choices of goods and services in the market are limited to what the central planning committee feels will benefit the whole society. The goods and services produced do not have to pass the difficult test of individual market choice. If they did, many might not survive.

This lack of individual choice in a social economy greatly affects the consumer and producer. When only one kind of product is made to fill a given need, the consumer still must choose. But the choice is highly limited. The consumer can either buy the available product or completely do without it. Producers do not have profit incentives. However, it is extremely difficult for their products to fail in the marketplace, since there are few competing goods.

3–1
social economy
An economy in which the major economic questions are determined by the government representing the interests of the entire society.

3–2

Illustration 3–1
In the Soviet Union, the central economic planning committee convenes in Moscow at the Kremlin, the country's administrative center. Recently the Soviet Union has moved to allow more private economic decisions to guide the economy.

The main idea in social economies is that the government rather than individuals decides what to produce. This decision-making structure implies that individuals may not be capable of choosing for themselves as well as their government can. **Social choice**, then, is decision making by government in the interest of society.

How to Produce

3–2   The question of how to produce is decided in social economies primarily by government decree. Central planning authorities decide which producers will produce what goods and services. Quantities of resources are allocated to those producers only. Usually output quotas are set, but the producer does not risk market failure since there are few competing goods. Of course, if resources are used wastefully, there is concern. But with government support, producers cannot incur losses and eventually go out of business.

   In a social economy, there is little difference in reward to the producer who is very efficient and to the producer who is only moderately efficient. Profits are not a major goal, and self-interest

3–3   is not a socially acceptable incentive. Therefore, there is no profit incentive. Producers decide how resources are to be used by what is allocated to them, not by what individuals will choose to buy in the marketplace. Producers do not have the guidance of an extremely accurate resource price system to guide their choices. The incentive for producers to achieve excellence is not very strong.

Illustration 3–2
In China, which has a social economy, the economic question of *how to produce* is determined by government decree.

KARL MARX

Throughout history, many economists and philosophers have strongly advocated socialism and social decision making. Karl Marx is probably the best known. He certainly had the most influence on the development of socialist ideals.

Marx was born in 1818 and attended the Universities of Bonn and Berlin. He received a doctoral degree from the University of Jena in 1841 and wrote widely about his views on social decision making. Marx believed that the State (entire society) should own the factors of production and guide decisions about the production and distribution of wealth. He openly advocated violent revolution by the working class (proletariat) to overthrow the capitalist ruling class (bourgeoisie).

Marx saw communism as a natural evolution of capitalism. He felt that capitalism and individual decision making would lead to the development of a few very wealthy and all-controlling people who would produce nothing. They would live on the labors of the working class. The evolution of a nonproductive bourgeoisie would lead to violent revolution. Then the power and ownership of the society would revert to the common people.

Marx envisioned a classless society of equals. In this society, all people would contribute to the society according to their ability and take from the society according to their needs. He wrote that once the bourgeoisie was overthrown all power would be in the hands of the State. The State would then gradually distribute power to the people, and the population would make cooperative decisions in the best interest of the society.

Marx's most famous writings were *The Communist Manifesto*, written with Friedrich Engels in 1848, and *Das Kapital*, part of which was published in 1867. These books laid much of the groundwork for socialist philosophy, but Marx was not really the author of communism. After Marx's death, Vladimir Lenin elaborated on Marx's works and formed the guiding philosophies of today's communism.

For Whom to Produce

3–2

3–1
equity
Equality of opportunity.

The question of how goods are distributed in a social economy is made primarily in an effort to provide equity. **Equity** means equality of opportunity. The fruits of the entire economy's labor are intended to give all members of the society a fair share. Equity, however, is a difficult objective. What *you* think is fair or equitable probably is different from what your neighbor thinks is equitable. There are probably as many different opinions of what is equitable in any society as there are citizens.

Social economies try to provide equitable goods and services. This, however, means that individuals do not have the right to choose among many significantly different goods and services. If everyone gets an equitable house, for instance, there certainly cannot be any significant differences between houses. You can choose any house you want, but they may be all alike.

SOCIAL CHOICE AND PUBLIC GOODS

In the United States, we make most of our economic decisions in the marketplace (individual choice). It is important to note, however, that we also make a number of important choices as a society (social choice).

The Public Goods Rationale

3–1
public goods
Goods and services available to the whole society.

3–4

3–1
economies of scale
The concept that some economic activities become more efficient when done on a large scale.

As a society, we choose to provide public goods. **Public goods** are goods and services available to the whole society. Roads, schools, national defense, and police and fire protection are examples of public goods.

There are several important reasons for using social choice to provide public goods. One reason, however, is clearly more valid than the rest. We provide public goods through social choice simply because sometimes it is cheaper to do so. This illustrates the concept of economies of scale. **Economies of scale** is the concept that some economic activities become more efficient when done on a large scale. Many people can enjoy a large public park at a lower cost per person than if individuals tried to provide their own parks, for example.

Consider a public road. Everyone who uses the road benefits from it. Each individual pays for only a very small part of the total cost of the road. If each of us had to buy or build a road to wherever we wanted to go, no one could afford to travel by road.

Illustration 3–3
If individuals had to buy or build their own roads, our transportation system would not be as efficient as it is today.

By joining together, we can realize an economy of scale, by spreading the cost of expensive goods like roads over everyone in the society. The road is there for everyone to use. In economics, this is referred to as the public goods rationale (reason) for social choice. The **public goods rationale** is the argument that some public goods can be produced more efficiently by social choice. Even Adam Smith agreed that government could provide some public goods more efficiently than could individuals.

The public goods rationale can be applied to police protection or any other public good. For instance, suppose you need a police officer to guard your home from burglars. You could hire a guard to walk around outside your house all day. This would be expensive, however. The mere presence of the officer would probably frighten burglars away from your home and your neighbor's home. The officer might even be protecting the whole block. Unfortunately you would be paying the bill individually, but your neighbors would benefit as well. How could this situation be improved? You and your neighbor could split the bill. You might extend this effort to everyone in the neighborhood if they would cooperate. One officer could patrol 50 homes, and each home owner could pay 1/50 of the expense. All would share in the benefit, and the cost to each individual would be much less. Services like these are provided more efficiently by a group or society than by an individual.

3–4
3–1

public goods rationale
The argument that some public goods can be produced more efficiently by social choice.

The Free Rider Problem

When whole societies make decisions, these decisions must be enforced with the power of law. Suppose the society were going to build an army to protect itself. If individuals were left to make this choice, there would be a problem. Even if individuals banded together to pay for the army, some persons would not agree to pay. A person who benefits from a public good without sharing its cost is called a **free rider.**

It would be impossible to protect those who did pay without also protecting those who did not pay. Thus, in order to eliminate free riders, it is necessary to back social choice with the power of law. Eliminating free riders is also efficient in spreading the cost of the public good over the whole society.

3–1

free rider
A person who benefits from a public good without sharing its cost.

SOCIAL CHOICE IN REPRESENTATIVE GOVERNMENT

Now that you know why we have social choices, let's look at how social choice works in our society. Representative government implies that individual citizens, through their votes, elect government officials. These officials are expected to make social choices for the voters they represent. Therefore, you should vote for the candidates who most closely represent your views on social issues. If your elected officials choose differently from how you would have, you have the right to vote for other candidates.

Unfortunately representative government, just like social choice, reduces the number of alternatives you have to choose from. A candidate must vote for or against an issue. You must choose with your vote among two or three candidates. There is little chance that any candidate would vote just as you would on every social choice.

Illustration 3–4
In our system of representative government, individual citizens support the candidates who will represent their views.

MAKING EFFECTIVE SOCIAL CHOICES

Representative government and social choice concentrate the power to choose in the hands of a very few people. These choices by a few public officials affect the lives of everyone in a society. Therefore, such social choices should be made very carefully.

To better understand social issues, you must know the choices involved. It is important to clarify the benefits and the costs of each choice. You learned to apply the five-step decision-making model to make better individual decisions. Apply that same five-step process to guide the choices you make on social issues.

Let's look at an example of a social decision which might affect your life at school. Assume that enrollment at your school has increased during the last five years. The parking lot is no longer big enough to hold the cars of all the students who drive to school. Students park on nearby streets once the lot is full. Now residents of the neighborhood are starting to complain. The town police chief has notified the school that student cars parked on residential streets will be towed beginning next Monday. Students are arguing among themselves about who should get to use the school parking lot. The social issue here is that members of the society (the students) want to use a public good (the parking lot). That public good, at present, cannot meet the needs of all the students.

You and five other students have been elected by the student government to deal with the problem. You are now a public official, and you must guide the public (the student body) in its choices. You must choose for them.

In making your social choice, you will want to follow the five-step decision-making model:

3–5

1. Define the problem.

2. List the alternatives.

3. List the criteria.

4. Evaluate the alternatives.

5. Choose the best alternative.

1—Define the Problem

3–1
distribution effect
The way the inconvenience of a social issue is distributed among the members of the society.

Presently there are more cars than spaces available in the parking lot. Students are distributing the burden of the shortage to private home owners nearby. Thus, residents cannot park in front of their own homes. Residents are being inconvenienced. This is called a distribution effect in economics. A **distribution effect** is the way the inconvenience of a social issue is distributed among the members of the society. Presently the burden is being distributed from students to home owners.

Is the parking lot too small? Or is the number of cars too large? The town cannot afford to build another parking lot for student cars at this time. Therefore, the "small parking lot" definition of the problem is not workable. The problem then becomes how to allocate the available spaces among the large number of cars.

In every choice, both individual and social, an allocation of resources is involved. Public officials vote every day on projects and laws. They allocate public money for public projects. More money for one project means less money for other possible projects. Laws define what choices we, as a society and as individuals, can and cannot make. Laws allocate the power to choose. If we pass a law that prohibits nonresident parking on residential streets, that choice or alternative is no longer available. All choices require us to allocate something. In the case of the parking lot, we have defined the problem as: How will we allocate the limited space among the larger number of students who drive?

3-5

2—List the Alternatives

3-5   What are some alternatives to the parking situation? The current alternative is allocation of spaces on a first come–first served basis. This presents some problems. If students drive to school, they will not know in advance if they can park in the school lot. They would either have to return home and leave their cars, or continue to break the law. Some students would leave home hours earlier just to get a space. This would be a great waste of time. Still, other students who drive parents, brothers, sisters, or others to their destinations before coming to school probably would never get a space. If students who live close to school leave home at the same time as students who live farther away, the students who live close will arrive earlier, quickly filling the available spaces. Students who live too far away to walk or who might not have access to bus transportation might need the spaces most. However, they might be the very students who suffer the most under the first come–first served rule.

A second alternative might be to allocate the spaces by selling expensive school parking permits. Those who could afford the permits could drive, and those who could not afford them would have to walk or find other transportation. This alternative would allocate the spaces, but it also has problems. Many students work to earn money for college or simply to meet everyday expenses. These same students frequently drive to school, since they must go to work after school. Charging high fees to park would eliminate the ability of these students to drive and therefore to work. The fee system would take the parking privilege away from those who need it the most.

A third alternative might be to allocate parking spaces by seniority. Seniors could have first choice. This would, no doubt, be popular among seniors. But juniors who drive might think it was unfair. Juniors and seniors could alternate days for using the lot. However, this would probably be more an inconvenience than a solution. Everyone would have to be constantly concerned with what day it was, and their needs for transportation might not fall on the days they had use of the lot. Also, enforcing this rule and sorting out which cars belonged to which students might be difficult.

Finally, the available spaces could be allocated by need. Students who worked, traveled long distances to school, or were the only drivers in their families might be given use of the lot. Students who had no access to bus service or other transportation would fall into this category. This might be considered fair, but just who fits into each category of need would have to be determined for each individual. Some person or group would have to judge each student's need, and this might not be easy.

3 — List the Criteria (Social Goals)

Obviously there are advantages and disadvantages to each alternative. In order to evaluate the alternatives, we need to set up some criteria. In social decision making, the criteria are social goals. **Social goals** are the goals of an entire society.

What goals are you trying to attain with your choice? Some societies strive for social goals which include equality, justice, freedom, and efficiency. What are the goals of this particular choice on the use of the school parking lot?

Clearly your choice should be fair or just. It should not give one group of students advantage over another without a very good reason. *Equity* might also be a part of your considerations of justice. Everyone should have an equal chance to use the parking lot. Remember, however, that equity is a difficult goal, as you will see later.

Social costs of the rule and its enforcement also might be a consideration. **Social costs** are the costs to a society of a social choice. The more efficient the rule is to administer, the less costly it will be to the society. If the rule is easy to understand, more students will probably feel that it is fair.

Freedom of choice also might be an important goal. **Freedom of choice** is the individual power to choose and receive both the

3–4

3–1
social goals
The goals of an entire society.

3–1
social costs
The costs to a society of a social choice.

3–1
freedom of choice
The individual power to choose and receive both the costs and the benefits of a choice.

3–1

social benefits

The benefits received by a society from a social choice.

costs and the benefits of a choice. Your rule might want to offer students an individual choice rather than simply dictate a course of required action.

Social benefit might be another goal. **Social benefits** are the benefits received by a society from a social choice. You might want to guide your choice by trying to produce benefits for the largest part of society. Here, a plan which shares the benefits of the choice among many people or groups would be preferable to one benefiting a few individuals or groups. You are trying to do the most good for the most people. In any case, a clear understanding of the goals you are trying to achieve will aid in your social choice.

4—Evaluate the Alternatives

3–5   Having defined your problem, determined your alternatives, and established your criteria (social goals), you now must evaluate each alternative. Through evaluation, you will get a clear idea of the costs and benefits (advantages and disadvantages) of each possible choice. Let's set up a decision matrix like the one in Chapter 2.

In Figure 3–1, each of the four criteria (social goals) is listed in the first column. The four alternatives are in the first row. Beginning with Alternative 1, compare that alternative with the other three on the basis of each criterion. Notice that the parking fee alternative in Figure 3–1 ranks first in social costs, second in freedom of choice, third in social benefit, and third in equity. This alternative is good because the people who get the benefit of parking spaces are the ones who pay the fees; and it permits some individual freedom of choice. In this way the policy would function a lot like the marketplace. It is weak in equity because it discriminates against those who cannot pay the fee. The social benefits are also received only by those who pay the fee. Given its strong and weak points (costs and benefits), this alternative ranks second among the four alternatives.

The first come–first served alternative is the best social choice of the four. This alternative is strong on individual freedom and equity since everyone has an equal chance to try for the available spaces. Students could also choose how early they are willing to leave home each day. Enforcement costs are zero, since when the available spaces are taken no one else can occupy them.

The real shortcoming of this rule falls under another criterion that we did not consider. What happens if you try for a space and the lot is full? Are the unlucky individuals supposed to take their cars home or do something else with them? Under such a situation, it is likely that some people would park on the streets again and eventually be towed away. This is an example of how difficult it may

	ALTERNATIVES			
CRITERIA (Social Goals)	**(1) FIRST COME— FIRST SERVED**	**(2) PARKING FEE**	**(3) NEED**	**(4) SENIORITY**
EQUITY (equal opportunity)	Everyone has an equal chance.	Limited to those who can afford the fee.	Different treatment for individuals with different needs.	Somewhat limited; not everyone makes it to their senior year.
Rank of Alternative	1	3	2	4
SOCIAL COST (cost to administer and enforce)	No costs — no more room when spaces are full.	Very low; pays for itself through fees.	Difficult to measure and classify individual needs.	Low cost; seniors easily identified.
Rank of Alternative	2	1	4	3
SOCIAL BENEFIT (greatest good for the greatest number)	Benefits only those who get there first.	Limited; only those who can pay can benefit.	Limited to those who need it the most.	Benefits seniors only.
Rank of Alternative	2	3	1	4
FREEDOM OF CHOICE (individual choices)	Individuals can choose how early they want to arrive.	Some choice allowed; individuals can choose to pay to drive.	Not much choice; individuals could only change their needs such as moving farther from school.	No choice
Rank of Alternative	1	2	3	4
Final Rank of Alternative	6 points 1st choice	9 points 2nd choice	10 points 3rd choice	15 points 4th choice

FIGURE 3–1   A DECISION MATRIX FOR THE PARKING LOT CASE
In this decision matrix, the criteria are the social goals.

be to include every possible consideration in the social decision-making process. This is probably why some social decisions do not always work out as planned.

Illustration 3–5
No matter how you solve this social issue, some students will be excluded from the parking lot.

There is another relative weakness to this alternative. Only those who can regularly get to school early will receive the benefits of the choice.

Alternative 3, allocating space by need, ranks highly on equity and social benefit. At first glance, it may seem very fair to let the people who have the greatest need for parking use the spaces. This does the greatest good for as many people as there are parking spaces available. However, need is very difficult to determine. If I am handicapped, I have an obvious need to park near the building. On the other hand, what if I live a half mile closer to school than you do? Do I have less need than you for transportation? This is a matter of judgment. The individual case of every student would have to be considered separately and would require large amounts of time and effort. Individual circumstances would change with time, and the judgment process would have to continue for as long as the parking rules were in force. Considering all the criteria, this alternative ranked third.

Assigning space by seniority ranked poorly on almost all social goals. Such a rule would provide no individual choice. All seniors could drive, but no one else would have the privilege. The social benefit would go to seniors only. Since all students do not stay in school until they are seniors, not everyone would have an equal chance to park in the school lot. Actually such a plan would discriminate against students with academic problems, since this group might not be as likely to survive to the senior year. This alternative turned out to be the worst choice, based on the social goals that were established.

5 — Choose the Best Alternative (Social Choice)

3–5   After evaluating the alternatives in regard to the social goals, the first come–first served rule is the best choice. Don't forget, however, that the outcome is based on the alternatives you have considered and the value the society places on each of the social goals. If there were a social goal of trying to provide convenience for student drivers, the outcome might have been different. If the certainty of getting a parking space were very important to students, this might have been a criterion. Then another rule may have been chosen. As the values of a society change, its social choices will reflect those changes.

The quality of the social choice will depend on being able to weigh carefully the costs and benefits of each alternative. Following a logical and well-organized method of decision making will improve your ability to understand and participate in the social decision-making process.

YOUR ROLE AS A SOCIAL DECISION MAKER

Once you have decided which alternative is in the best interest of the student body, your work is just beginning. You have only worked out the costs and benefits in an understandable form. Your next and most important task is to clearly communicate the costs and benefits of each possible alternative to your constituents. **Constituents** are the individual citizens or voters in a democracy who are represented by a particular public official.

You must be able to explain your stand on the issue and support it with facts. Obviously you should try to convince the student body that your decision was based on how each possible alternative measured up to the social goals that were considered. (The social goals reflect values which most of the students have in common.) This process should also protect you from student criticism regarding your own self-interest. For example, if you had chosen the alternative of allocating space by seniority, students would quickly check to see what class you were in. If you are a senior, you would have to present clear evidence that your choice was not based only on personal gain.

Once you have communicated the costs and benefits of each alternative to the student body, you should measure the responses. You might try to get an overall impression of how the student body feels about the best alternative. Since an individual ballot is not often used to decide issues, you must choose for your constituents. You must reflect what you think the majority wants. Obviously your choice cannot reflect the individual preference of every single student. Some individuals will almost always have opinions different from the majority. Whether you like it or not, your social choice will override the individual choices of these individuals. Your action, by necessity, will take away the power of their individual choice.

With this in mind, your task is twofold. First, you must convince as many students as possible that your choice is the best for the society. And second, you must exercise your power of social choice with the greatest of care. You must be mindful that when you choose for others, they may not agree with your choice. Thus, in the long run, they may choose some other social decision maker who more closely represents their views. For this reason, you might want to try to include the possibility of providing some individual choice in any alternative you choose.

APPLYING SOCIAL DECISIONS TO REALITY

Remember how the individual decision-making process seemed very complex at first? After several tries, however, you probably

3–1
constituents
The individual citizens or voters in a democracy who are represented by a particular public official.

3–5

learned to use the process quickly and efficiently. The social decision-making process may also seem complex. If you repeat the process with several different issues, however, you will quickly come to understand its value. The five-step decision-making model will not give you a specific answer to any problem. But it will help you organize your thinking and more effectively develop your own solutions to problems involving choices. The selection of social goals and the value your society places on each goal is up to you to determine.

The five-step decision-making model is in some respects more important in making social decisions than it is in making individual decisions. When you choose only for yourself, you usually do not have to justify or explain your choice to others. Your criteria reflect your own values. With social choices, however, you will not only have to make careful decisions. You will also have to clearly communicate to the society how and why you made these decisions.

3–5   The five-step decision-making process clarifies your decisions and makes it much easier to communicate the *why* and *how* of your decision to the society. It also gives you the opportunity to see if your ranking of the criteria (goals) agrees with that of the society. You may have overlooked a major consideration. Through discussions with voters, you might change the outcome of your decision. Finally, if you can communicate the five-step decision-making process to the society, each individual may be able to make more effective decisions in the future. All these outcomes will be to the benefit of the society and to the individuals who belong to it.

REVIEWING THE CHAPTER

3–2   1. Social economies answer the three basic economic questions of what, how, and for whom to produce mostly by government decree. Central planning committees decide which resources (and in what quantities) will be used to produce the goods and services selected for production. This process limits the amount of individual choice given to the citizens of such an economy.

3–3, 3–4   2. Personal incentives are not as strong in a social economy as they are in a market society. Even in a market economy, however, there are significant numbers of situations where social choice is more efficient and more equitable than private choice. Public goods such as roads, schools, and national defense are examples of situations where public choice may be superior to individual choice.

3-4   3. In cases where public choice is preferable to individual choice, the power of law is frequently necessary to deal with the free rider problem. The free rider problem refers to providing a public good to those who do not share in the cost of the good. Laws taxing everyone in a society (regardless of their preference) in order to provide for national defense is an example of such a situation. It is difficult or impossible to defend the society and yet not defend some of its citizens. With this in mind, everyone is taxed by law, whether they wish to be defended or not.

3-5   4. A society can make more efficient social choices by applying the five-step decision-making model to its choice process: (1) Define the problem. (2) List the alternatives. (3) List the criteria or social goals. (4) Evaluate the alternatives in regard to the criteria. (5) Choose the best alternative that meets the criteria (social choice).

3-5   5. A logical, organized, and effective decision-making process may be even more important in making social decisions than in making individual decisions. Social decision makers must clearly communicate the costs and benefits of each alternative to the society and explain the reasons for their choices. The five-step decision-making model clearly presents these costs and benefits.

REVIEWING ECONOMIC TERMS

3-1   Supply definitions for the following terms:

social economy	distribution effect
social choice	social goals
equity	social costs
public goods	freedom of choice
economies of scale	social benefits
public goods rationale	constituents
free rider	

REVIEWING ECONOMIC CONCEPTS

3-2   1. How are the major economic questions of what, how, and for whom to produce answered in a system of social decision making?

3-3   2. What personal incentives exist for the producer of goods or services under social choice?

3–4   3. Under what conditions is social choice preferable to individual choice?

3–5   4. How can the five-step decision-making model be applied to social choice?

3–5   5. Why is an effective decision-making process often more important in social choices than in individual choices?

APPLYING ECONOMIC CONCEPTS

3–3   1. If you were a producer or worker in a social economy, what personal incentives would motivate you to strive for excellence or efficiency? If you were in the same position in a system of primarily individual decision making, would your incentives be any different? If so, how? If not, why not? Which kind of system do you prefer?

3–4   2. What do you feel is the strongest argument in favor of social decision making? In what types of situations do you feel social decision making would be better or more efficient than individual decision making?

3–4   3. Karl Marx's dream of a communist society was a state in which individuals would contribute to society to the fullest of their abilities and take from society only what they needed. Do you believe this to be a workable reality? If so, why? If not, why not?

3–5   4. If social decision makers make choices that do not agree with your preferences, what is your recourse under representative government? Does representative government have the ability to make social decisions which completely reflect your individual preferences? If so, how? If not, why not? What would you suggest as an alternative form of government?

3–5   5. As president of the student council, you and your fellow council members must decide how the council's social events budget will be spent this year. There are sufficient funds for only one event. Alternatives include a junior/senior prom, an all-school picnic, a recognition banquet for this year's football team, or a senior trip to Washington, D.C. Your criteria or goals might be equity, social benefit, and any other two you feel are important. Use the five-step decision-making process to develop your position on this issue. Once you have made up your mind, clearly communicate your decision and supporting reasons to the class. Do other students agree or disagree and why? Can someone else offer a better choice? Can others communicate the logic of their decision to the class as well as you have?

CHAPTER 4

PRIVATE SECTOR DECISIONS: CONSUMERS AND BUSINESSES

Learning Objectives

4–1 Define terms related to the private sector.

4–2 Explain how economic decisions are made in the private sector.

4–3 Discuss the major differences between the private sector and the public sector.

4–4 Describe how competition improves efficiency in the private sector.

4–5 Discuss how markets benefit consumers and producers.

4–6 Discuss the role of profits in the private sector.

4–7 List the three major pitfalls associated with the market system in the private sector.

WHAT IS THE PRIVATE SECTOR?

4-1

private sector
The part of an economy which is owned by private individuals and operated for their personal benefit.

The **private sector** is the part of an economy which is owned by individuals and operated for their personal benefit. It is made up of private citizens. You are a member of the private sector.

PRIVATE OWNERSHIP—PRIVATE BENEFIT

4-1

private goods
Goods that are privately owned and used to benefit only their owners.

In the private sector, individuals own and operate businesses for their private gain. If you own a house, you have the right to reside in it alone. It is not public property, and you can exclude the public from using it. You may even sell your house at a profit. As the owner, you, not the public, benefit from the sale. **Private goods**, then, are goods that are privately owned and used to benefit only their owners.

Of course, there is a public sector in our economy as well. The *public sector* is that part of an economy which is owned by and operated for the benefit of the whole society. All public goods are found in this sector. All members of the economy own and share the public goods, and no individual can exclude anyone from their use. As a citizen, you are part owner of such public goods as roads and schools. You share your classroom with your classmates. You

Illustration 4–1
Private goods are for private use only. Anyone can swim in a public pool. But only invited guests may use the pool in your backyard.

share the use of highways with other drivers. Neither you nor others can exclude anyone from lawful use of the roads and schools.

Members of the private sector produce private goods and services mostly for the benefit of private owners. For example, General Motors is a private firm that produces automobiles which it owns and then sells to earn profits. These profits are private benefits paid to owners of the company. If you buy a GM car, you own it privately and can use it to your benefit. You control the rights to your private property. General Motors controls the rights to the private property it owns.

Private institutions are also designed to produce private benefits. If individuals form a private country club, it is only for members who bear the cost and enjoy the benefits. The private club, the private auto, and the private company are all private properties which benefit their owners. In general, they are not meant to benefit everyone in society.

PRIVATE SECTOR — PRIVATE CHOICE

The private sector is controlled by individual or private choice. You individually choose which house or car to buy. Companies, which are owned by one individual or a group of individuals, decide what to produce and how to produce it. Private institutions decide not only who will receive their benefits but also how. Individuals decide how to allocate their time among study, leisure, and work so that they receive the maximum benefit.

4–2

All these individual choices will be guided by one important principle of economics. Individuals will choose the alternative that produces the maximum private benefit or the minimum private cost to them. This principle is important because it guides the whole private sector. The private sector today produces the majority of all the income in our economy. Therefore, it is reasonable to say that the American economy is primarily an economy of private ownership.

Economic activity involves exchanges. An **exchange** is the giving of one thing in return for some other thing. In economic terms, a voluntary exchange occurs only when both parties benefit from the exchange. In America, most property is privately owned. Therefore, most of the economic activity involves the exchange of private property between private individuals, businesses, and institutions. Because private sector decisions involve exchanges, they generally are made in some kind of a market situation. Two parties exchange something of value, and both parties are better off because of the exchange.

4–1
exchange
The giving of one thing in return for some other thing.

Efficiency and Individual Choice

4–3

4–1

efficiency

Using a given amount and combination of resources to get the maximum amount of benefit.

In the private sector, there is the possibility of gaining private benefits. Therefore, private choices try to maximize benefits or minimize costs. This makes the private sector very efficient. You might say that efficiency is the primary concern of the private sector. **Efficiency** is using a given amount and combination of resources to get the maximum amount of benefit.

For instance, suppose you have a one-pound jar of peanut butter and a loaf of bread (24 slices). You can make up to 12 sandwiches. Each sandwich can have 1⅓ ounces of peanut butter. If you are not efficient in spreading the peanut butter, however, you may not get 12 sandwiches. If you drop slices of bread on the floor and spoil them, your output (sandwiches) will be less than it could have been (12). Some sandwiches could have lots of peanut butter, others less, and still others might have none. Your output would be inefficient and not uniform.

Efficiency is not a negative word! In the private sector firms must try to be efficient to stay in business. When a firm tries to produce at the lowest cost, it is not trying to cheat customers. For example, you buy a pair of jeans because you are willing to pay the price in exchange for the benefit you receive from having the

Illustration 4–2
Given a loaf of bread and a jar of peanut butter, the number of sandwiches you could produce would depend largely on your level of efficiency.

jeans. If the company that makes your favorite jeans reduces the quality of its jeans, you would notice. You would then reevaluate whether the price you must pay is worth the benefit you receive. You might decide to buy another brand of jeans. If another company provides better jeans at the same price, that company is more efficient.

Competition Improves Private Sector Efficiency

The existence of many individual jeans producers and many individual consumers of jeans contributes to the efficiency of that industry. Levi's, Lee, Wrangler, and all other jeans companies must compete with each other for the consumer's buying decision.

Competition is the rivalry between two or more parties to gain benefits from a third party. Competition forces producers to aim for efficiency. A local tailor shop may not be able to produce jeans which you feel are equal to the major brands at a competitive price. This leaves only two possibilities for that local tailor shop if it wants to compete with such firms as Levi's at the same price. The shop must improve its ability to produce an equal or better pair of jeans at an equal price. The alternative is to go out of the jeans business. Competition not only encourages customers to be more efficient, but also forces weaker, less efficient companies out of the industry.

Competition in the marketplace works to the consumer's advantage. However, there is also competition among consumers. If everyone in the United States wants a pair of Levi's jeans right away, it is doubtful that Levi's could produce rapidly enough the amount consumers wanted. Prices would rise, and only those willing and able to pay the higher price would get the Levi's jeans. Some consumers would be priced out of the market. If the Levi's jeans cost $45, fewer consumers would buy them. Only consumers wealthy enough to pay $45 would get those particular jeans. The competition among consumers for the available jeans might mean that you must purchase some other brand of jeans instead.

Competition on the consumer side exists all the time, just like competition among producers. Suppose you wanted to buy tickets for a particular concert. However, at the ticket counter you found that there were no tickets left. Because of a limited number of tickets, not everyone who wanted one received one. Some people settled for less than exactly what they wanted. For example, you may have bought tickets for some other concert.

This competition process causes all of us to choose so that we get the maximum benefit for a given sacrifice or opportunity cost. It makes us more efficient consumers. If the sold-out concert had

4–4

4–1

competition
The rivalry between two or more parties to gain benefits from a third party.

Illustration 4-3
Up against stiff competition in the hamburger business, Burger King has developed a more efficient, creative outlet for its products. The consumer benefits most from innovations such as this in the marketplace.

been more important to you, you might have bought your tickets earlier. However, you decided that the benefit was not worth the cost to you of getting there earlier. Therefore, you were forced out of the market for this concert, just as inefficient producers are forced out of their markets. Competition improves the efficiency of both producers and consumers.

PRIVATE SECTOR MARKETS AND ENTREPRENEURS

Most individual decisions in the private sector are exchanges between private parties. These exchanges usually take place in a market setting. The term **market** refers to the exchange activities between buyers and sellers of goods and services. Goods and services of value are exchanged in the market, and all buyers and sellers benefit from the exchange. If you did not benefit from an exchange, you would not participate in it. For exchange to take place, both parties must be willing and able to give up what the other wants in return for the benefits received.

4–1

market
Exchange activities between buyers and sellers of goods and services.

Markets Give Us Price Information

4–5   Markets give us important information on which we make our exchange decisions. First of all, markets establish and provide price information. You make your buying decisions based on the price of the item and its benefit to you. A market quickly establishes prices through competition. It takes only a minute to find out the market price of a pair of jeans. A quick call to several stores will give you this information. If one seller's price is much higher, you may buy somewhere else. If the market price for a pair of jeans is more than you are willing to pay, you might check the market price of other types of pants.

Markets Provide Many Choices

The second important function of markets is that they usually provide many choices. Not only can you get price information, you can also find substitutes to fill your need rather quickly. If competitive markets did not exist, there might not be a large variety of goods and services from which to choose. There also might not be a range of prices from which to choose.   4–5

Suppose you needed a means of transportation to get to school. A quick look in the Yellow Pages will give you references to buses, taxis, trains, airplanes, dealers of automobiles, motorcycles, bicycles, and many other alternatives. However, even if you consider just one of these substitutes to fill your needs, the market is still very large. For instance, assume you decide to buy a bicycle. The market for bicycles offers you everything from a simple one-speed model to racing bikes, three wheelers, dirt bikes, and motorized bicycles.

Markets usually provide you with many choices to satisfy your needs. You make those choices based on what has the greatest private benefit for you relative to the market price you must pay. Markets provide information through advertising, public relations, promotions, and demonstrations which enables you to make more efficient private choices.

Markets Benefit Entrepreneurs

So far, you have learned mostly about the consumer's view of the private sector. Consumers obviously benefit from market information. Using that information, they make choices that maximize their satisfaction or minimize their costs. Let's now consider the situation from the producer's point of view.

Profits benefit producers. Therefore, producers in the market   4–6
try to maximize profits. The success of producers depends on satisfying the wants and needs of consumers more efficiently than others. Therefore, producers must find out what consumers want or need. Once the consumer's needs are identified, producers must decide what resources to use and in what quantities to make a product that satisfies these needs. Resource prices guide producers just as final goods prices guide consumers' choices. For example, what if the price of metal buttons rises? Levi's might then change to plastic buttons or some other substitute. Then they could earn the same profit without raising their prices.

This is one major difference between consumer choices and producer choices. Producers take greater risks in making their decisions. Individuals who organize a company to produce a

4-1

entrepreneurs
Individuals who organize a company to produce a product for a profit.

4-1

private enterprise
A system in which private individuals take the risk of producing goods or services to make a profit.

Illustration 4-4
Clipping and using coupons is one way to allocate your income efficiently among the products and services you purchase.

product for a profit are called **entrepreneurs**. Entrepreneurs bring together the inputs of production (raw materials, workers, machines, etc.) and produce a product to satisfy consumer wants and needs. While consumers can see the products that they can buy to satisfy their needs, entrepreneurs cannot see their product until it is produced. Therefore, entrepreneurs must take the risk that their finished product will satisfy a need and be attractive to consumers. The entrepreneur takes the risk that the product will produce profits.

Sometimes our economy is referred to as a private enterprise economy. **Private enterprise** is a system in which private individuals take the risk of producing goods or services to make a profit. An entrepreneur engages in private enterprise. In private enterprise, an entrepreneur is willing to take risks or try something which has not been done before. If entrepreneurs did not risk producing new products, we would not have the variety of choices we have today. If reasonable profits were not possible, entrepreneurs would not risk producing new and better products. The market rewards successful entrepreneurs with profits.

On the other hand, the market punishes with large losses entrepreneurs who produce products that consumers do not want. In the early 1980s, Adam Osborne identified the need for a small portable computer. At first his idea was very successful in the marketplace. His company, Osborne Computer Corp., became one of the best-known names in technology. However, the company failed to keep up with current market trends. New products introduced by Apple, IBM, and others were favored by consumers. The Osborne computers failed in the eyes of consumers. Osborne Computer Corp. filed for bankruptcy.

The market rewards consumers with the benefits of new and better products to fulfill their wants and needs. Consumers who choose carefully and allocate their incomes efficiently through the market increase their satisfaction. Consumers who choose poorly do not receive the same satisfaction per dollar spent.

In summary, the private sector functions primarily through markets. Markets give power to both producer and consumer through competition. The market encourages producers to take risks and to produce new and better products. Markets help producers and consumers to make more efficient decisions and to maximize their own well-beings.

MARKET PITFALLS

The system of private enterprise in our markets has produced one of the highest standards of living in the twentieth century. The efficiency of the private sector can take much of the credit for the

large assortment of goods and services we enjoy today. You should   4–7
be aware, however, that this market system in the private sector
does have three major pitfalls:

1. *Reduced Competition:* Much of the efficiency of the private sector is brought about by competition among buyers and sellers. However, sometimes competition is not as strong as it
   could be.

2. *Goods for Public Use:* Several factors outside of the private
   sector also help it to function well. For example, roads, which
   are public goods, increase the efficiency of shipping goods
   to markets. Schools train individuals in the skills which can
   someday make them efficient participants in the market
   system. Both of these public goods help the private sector to
   be more efficient. The problem is that, to some extent, the
   public sector is supporting the efficiency of the private sector.

3. *Costs Outside the Market:* The private sector passes on some
   production costs to citizens beyond the prices of the goods
   produced.

Reduced Competition

Competition makes private sector markets efficient. However,   4–7
competition can be reduced both by producers and consumers,
thus making markets less efficient.

How Producers Reduce Competition. Competition makes producers
try to produce the goods consumers want at the lowest possible
cost. Competition among buyers indicates that producers will be
able to offer their goods to many buyers and sell to the highest bid-
ders. Both consumers and producers have alternative choices and
usually can get a fair deal in the market.

Sometimes, however, producers try to swing the forces of the
market in their favor. Perhaps all the producers of milk might get
together and agree to set a uniform price higher than the existing
market price. If no producer will sell below the agreed-upon price,
consumers must pay the higher price. The choices available to consumers are reduced. If they want milk, they must pay the price.
The producers gain at a cost to the consumer. These same producers can use their extra profits to build larger and more efficient
plants, and thus further reduce their costs. They now are able to
produce milk at lower costs because of these large plants. Newer
and smaller milk producers cannot afford such large plants. They
cannot produce milk at as low a cost as the large companies can,
and therefore, they cannot enter or succeed in the market. Competition is reduced.

How Consumers Reduce Competition. Consumers sometimes agree not to buy a particular item from a particular producer. Assume that a dairy is charging the fair market price for milk. However, consumers band together and refuse to buy from that dairy until it lowers its price. Consumers then benefit at the cost of the dairy.

The action of milk producers or the consumers working together to reduce competition destroys the efficiency of the market. It enriches one party in an exchange at the cost of another. Eventually it leads to inefficient production on the part of producers and inefficient buying decisions on the part of consumers.

The private sector has a definite interest in keeping markets competitive. Both producers and consumers stand to benefit from competitive markets. Unfortunately neither group is really in a position to force competitive behavior from the other. So far, the only partial solution to the problem has been public laws against noncompetitive behavior. This moves the solution to the problem from the private sector to the public sector. You will learn how the public sector deals with this problem in the next chapter.

Goods for Public Use

4–7   Many aspects of the private sector depend on public goods to operate efficiently. To see this, assume that in a farming area no roads exist. There are just dirt paths and trails that people use. This would be much like things were when our country was first settled. Farmers would drive their pigs, cattle, or sheep to market on foot through these crude trails and paths. The animals would lose a great deal of weight on the long journey. This would cause producers to earn a smaller profit on their product. Consumers would receive smaller animals in poorer physical condition in return for the price paid. In this situation, producing a public good such as a road would be in the interest of both producers and consumers.

Once roads were built, the exchange of private goods between producers and consumers would be more efficient. Because the trip to market was not as long, animals would not lose as much weight, and the farmers would get a better price for them. Also, the consumers would get a better quality animal. In addition, producers, consumers, and the whole public could use the roads for many other purposes besides bringing animals to market. You can see that in this case private sector exchange was made more efficient through public goods.

Public goods, however, do cause problems for the private sector. Public goods cannot easily be provided by the private sector. Private benefits usually would be less than private costs. For example,

Illustration 4–5
Many private companies depend on the U.S. postal service to ship their products to consumers. The postal service is a public good which contributes to the efficiency of the private sector.

if only farmers had paid to have a road built, the cost to each farmer would have been very large. Their individual use could not justify such a cost. Also, it would be very difficult to keep the public from using the road if it were private property. The use of guards or expensive fences would only increase the cost of the road. There would be no easy way to exclude those who did not pay to have the road built. If it were difficult to exclude nonpayers, some farmers might even refuse to pay, but would use the road anyway.

Private goods yield benefits only to their owners. They are goods which exclude the public from their use. Goods such as roads or schools surely contribute to the efficiency of the private sector, but they also benefit the whole economy. Public goods cannot be provided as effectively by the private sector, since individuals cannot keep all the benefits for themselves.

Costs Outside the Market

4–7

When producers provide goods and services to the market, sometimes there are side effects. For example, air and water pollution are often by-products of the production of goods and services. Or a new apartment building may be built across from your home on a lot now occupied by a flower garden. When the building is finished, your view will be a concrete wall instead of the flower garden. Your satisfaction or well-being will be reduced by the construction of the building. In effect, a cost will be passed on to you. This is not a cost in dollar terms, but a reduction of your satisfaction. Costs or benefits passed on outside of the market system are called **externalities**. Another term for externalities is *spillover effect*.

4–1
externalities
Costs or benefits passed on outside of the market system.

The garbage produced at a local restaurant is another example of costs outside a market. It costs money to clean up and carry away the garbage. The restaurant would save money by cutting back to two garbage pickups a month. As a result, there could be either lower food prices or larger profits. However, the garbage would accumulate and pass a cost on to residents of the neighborhood in terms of smell and unsightly appearance. Again, this is not a dollar cost, but a reduction of satisfaction. It is an externality, a cost passed on to others outside of the market system.

One solution to the restaurant's garbage situation is to have the garbage collected more often and the additional cost passed on to consumers through higher food prices. Getting rid of the garbage is then a true part of the cost of the food. Those who benefit from eating in the restaurant would pay the full cost of the benefit. If garbage collection is reduced to keep food prices low, consumers are not paying the full cost of the food. Local residents are paying part of the cost by enduring the smell and mess.

Externalities can also be positive. They can pass on benefits as a by-product of some action. If your neighbor buys a very large dog, it may frighten burglars away from your house, too. You receive a benefit for which you did not have to pay.

In the business world, a positive externality might occur when one company hires guards to patrol its offices and grounds. Other businesses in the area would receive some benefit, because the patrol might keep some criminals away from the whole area. Fewer burglaries would benefit all companies in the area, not just the company that hired the guards. Whether externalities are positive or negative, they are not reflected in market prices. Therefore, they are a true problem for the market system.

CONSUMERS AND BUSINESSES MUST MAKE DECISIONS ABOUT INSURANCE

Insurance is a type of protection. It is protection against financial loss. When you buy insurance, you pay a relatively small amount to protect yourself from a big, but uncertain, loss. Life insurance can replace income lost when a wage earner dies. Health insurance provides protection against the huge costs that can result from severe illness and may provide income when someone cannot work because of an injury. Car insurance protects against potential losses due to damage related to the use of a car.

The cost of insurance is based on the average level of risk for the group being covered. That is why car insurance is usually more expensive for teenaged drivers. Overall, teenagers have more accidents than do middle-aged drivers. Thus, the cost of insurance is higher for teenagers. Similar comparisons can be made for all types of insurance. A business in a high-crime area would pay more for business insurance than one in a safer area.

THINKING
ABOUT ECONOMIC ISSUES

Crime is a social problem that we hear about everyday in the news media. Like other social scientists, economists have turned their attention to analyzing and attempting to deal with this problem, using the scientific tools within their discipline. Economists contend that the decision to commit a crime against property is an economic choice. Potential criminals weigh the costs of committing the crime against the benefits.

Suppose a laborer who earns $8,000 a year notices several color television sets on a loading dock next to the construction site where he works. These TVs sell for about $400 each. When the worker gets home, he might read in the newspaper that a local judge has just sentenced a thief in the town to three years in jail. The article also mentions that in this year alone, 150 thieves have been apprehended (that is, caught and arrested), but only 15 were convicted and sentenced to three years in jail. If the worker steals the TV, he would gain a piece of property worth $400. However, his decision to steal is not without its costs.

The worker realizes that approximately 15 out of 150 or 10 percent of the thieves that are caught are convicted and sentenced to three years in jail. Three years in jail would cost him three years of lost wages at $8,000 per year, or a total of $24,000. If he has a 10 percent chance of being convicted, then he might think his "cost" is 10 percent of the $24,000 or $2,400. So, from an economic standpoint, it would be a bad idea to steal the TV. The costs to him exceed the benefits.

People rationally choose to do things for which their benefits are greater than their costs (Benefits > Costs). In the case of our worker, $400 is less than $2,400, so he realizes the benefits are not worth his costs. He can attain the TV at a lower cost to himself by working and buying it legally.

Suppose that the next day the laborer notices in the newspaper another article on crime in the city. In this article, he learns that the police apprehend only one out of every ten thieves (10 percent) that commit acts of theft. The worker now realizes that the arithmetic of his decision was

wrong. He overestimated his costs since the chances that he will have to serve three years in jail are not as high as he thought. If only 10 percent of the thieves get caught, and of those 10, only one (10 percent of the original 10 percent) is convicted, then his chances of being caught, convicted, and sent to jail for three years is only one chance in 100. Using this new information, we now see that his "cost" of stealing the set is only $240 or ($24,000 $\times$ 10% $\times$ 10%). Because the value of the TV ($400) is greater than $240, from a purely economic standpoint, it would be rational for him to risk stealing the TV.

Remember that we are only discussing the economic part of the decision process. We have not considered the moral or social parts of a person's behavior. There is something in all of us that wants to do the "right" thing. We have not considered issues like how the worker would feel after stealing the TV, or what it would be like to live in the fear that someday the TV would be discovered. These opportunity costs are too complicated to be analyzed here.

Realizing that crime is a costly problem to society, what does economics suggest as a solution? There are many options available to society. To reduce crime, society can (1) raise the opportunity cost of committing the crime, (2) increase the probability of apprehension, (3) increase the probability of conviction, and/or (4) increase the penalties for criminal acts.

REVIEWING THE CHAPTER

4–1, 4–2
1. The private sector is that part of the economy owned by and operated for the benefit of private individuals. It includes private business, institutions, and individual citizens. The owners of private property can exclude the public from the use and benefits of their property. The private sector engages in individual choice for private benefit. Efficiency, therefore, is the primary concern of the private sector.

4–4
2. Competition for profit in the private sector strongly encourages producers to be efficient. Each producer attempts to provide goods of a specific quality to the market at the lowest cost to them. This makes producers choose carefully and improves their efficiency. Competition among buyers for the available goods causes buyers to choose carefully.

4–5 3. Exchanges take place because both parties benefit from the exchange. Markets enable exchange to take place more efficiently by providing price information and substitutes from which to choose. In market situations, producers must take risks in trying to produce goods that they think consumers will buy. Profits are the incentives which encourage producers to take risks and to provide goods and services to consumers.

4–7 4. The market system does not solve all economic problems. In some cases, the competition that encourages efficiency in markets does not exist. Either buyers or sellers band together to swing the market in their favor. In some cases, price fixing by producers can force market prices up. In other cases, consumer actions can force market prices down. Either of these actions destroys much of the efficiency of the marketplace.

4–7 5. The private sector depends, in part, on public goods. Some productive parts of our society, therefore, cannot be provided by the private sector.

4–7 6. The production of goods and services often produces by-products such as air or water pollution. These are really costs passed on to consumers outside of the marketplace—not dollar costs, but reductions in satisfaction. The private sector sometimes passes on externalities to the consumer.

REVIEWING ECONOMIC TERMS

4–1 Supply definitions for the following terms:

private sector   market
private goods   entrepreneurs
exchange   private enterprise
efficiency   externalities
competition

REVIEWING ECONOMIC CONCEPTS

4–2 1. What guides individual choices in the private sector?

4–3 2. List the major differences between the private sector and the public sector.

4-4 3. What is the effect of competition on producers?

4-4 4. What is the effect of competition on consumers?

4-4 5. How do markets increase the efficiency of individual decisions?

4-5, 4-6 6. How do profits and entrepreneurs benefit consumers?

4-7 7. What are three major pitfalls associated with the private sector market system?

4-7 8. How can producers reduce competition?

4-7 9. How can consumers reduce competition?

4-7 10. Why does the private sector avoid producing public goods?

APPLYING ECONOMIC CONCEPTS

4-3, 4-4 1. Is it fair that our economy permits private property? Should individuals have the sole benefit of their property? If so, why? If not, why not?

4-5 2. What role do markets play in conducting exchanges between private parties?

4-7 3. What should be done about markets where producers or consumers band together to swing the market in their favor?

4-7 4. Are negative externalities fair to the consumer? Would you feel the same way if the externalities were positive?

4-7 5. Should all of our economy be privately owned? If so, why? If not, why not? Can the private sector meet all the needs of the citizens of our society?

4-7 6. Name at least three industries into which it might be difficult for new entrepreneurs to enter.

INFORMATION FOR INSURANCE DECISIONS

As indicated on pages 14, 15, and 62, consumers and businesses make decisions about insurance. In doing so you should get as much information as possible. One good source of information is *Your Insurance Dollar,* which is published by Money Management Institute, Household Financial Services, Prospect Heights, Illinois (1988).

CHAPTER 5

PUBLIC SECTOR DECISIONS: PUBLIC GOODS AND SERVICES

Learning Objectives

5–1 Define terms related to the public sector.

5–2 List the five major functions of the public sector.

5–3 Name the primary concern of the public sector.

5–4 Describe three problems with the public sector.

WHAT IS THE PUBLIC SECTOR?

5–1
public sector
The part of an economy which is owned by and operated for the benefit of the whole society.

5–1
public institutions
Publicly owned organizations established by government to serve the wants and needs of a whole society.

The **public sector** is the part of an economy which is owned by and operated for the benefit of the whole society. The public sector consists of government at all levels in our economy—federal, state, and local—and the public institutions. **Public institutions** are publicly owned organizations established by government to serve the wants and needs of a whole society. Our courts, state universities, and Federal Reserve Bank System are examples of public institutions. Government establishes public institutions to help our economy function efficiently.

The public sector forms a large part of our entire economy. By one measure, about 13 percent of our total national income stems from government.[1] While providing an environment in which the

Illustration 5–1
State universities are publicly owned and regulated institutions which provide higher education opportunities to many members of our society.

[1]U.S. Bureau of the Census, *Statistical Abstract of the United States: 1990*, 110th ed. (Washington, D.C., 1990), 429.

private sector can function, the public sector also provides the following:

1. Courts to define rights and settle disputes

2. Monetary institutions, such as the Federal Reserve System, to control our system of money

3. Regulatory agencies to promote competition among producers

GOVERNMENT'S ROLE IN THE PUBLIC SECTOR

No single force in our economy is more powerful than government. Government makes the laws of the land, thereby establishing rules that all producers and consumers must obey. Our government sets broad limits on what can and cannot be produced and how it can be produced. For example, our government permits and encourages the production of milk. It also sets safety standards and regulations as to how milk must be produced. Government also allows the mining of coal. However, it closely regulates the safety and health conditions under which coal is mined. Government creates and enforces the laws by which organizations such as the miners' unions and the coal companies must settle their differences.

Government also prohibits the unlicensed production of some goods and services such as nuclear power, radio and television broadcasts, and military weapons. The government's decisions to regulate or prohibit the production of such items are made by our whole society through our votes. It is government, however, that enforces these decisions.

Individual citizens acting together as a society create the public sector (government) to carry out certain functions. As citizens, we give this vast economic power to government. Therefore, you must understand the economic role of government.

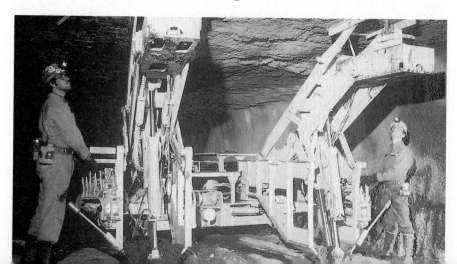

Illustration 5–2
Government allows the mining of coal, but it sets safety and health standards under which coal must be mined.

FIVE MAJOR FUNCTIONS OF THE PUBLIC SECTOR

5–2   The public sector often does what the private sector either cannot or is not willing to do. Let's take a closer look at the five major functions of the public sector. These are tasks that the public sector performs more effectively than the private sector.

Promoting Competition in the Private Sector

Illustration 5–3
When AT&T grew too large, government stepped in to make the telephone industry competitive. Now consumers may choose their telephones and telephone services from many competing companies.

The efficiency of the private sector is improved by competition. Producers compete for the consumers' dollar votes by producing the most wanted goods at the lowest possible prices at which producers can make a profit. If one company grows so strong in the market that it pushes out all other producers, there will be no competition. The remaining giant company will be the only producer. Then it may not work as hard to produce the goods consumers want most at the lowest possible prices. Once a single producer grows so powerful that it controls an entire market, other producers will not be able to grow strong enough to compete.

Many times in this country's history, several companies joined together to set higher prices or to refuse to compete with each other in certain geographical areas. By joining together, they eliminated competition. The cooperating producers were able to control market forces in their favor. They reduced the supply of goods or services, therefore driving up prices and often profits.

The only force in our economy powerful enough to change this situation is government. In our history, government often has intervened in such cases by passing laws prohibiting companies from working together to dominate a market. The *Clayton Antitrust Act* is one of many such laws against unfair competition. The government also has established the *Federal Trade Commission* which promotes competition in industry and prevents unfair competition. The Federal Trade Commission polices the nation's businesses to keep our markets competitive.

Most economists agree that there is a need for government to do this kind of work. However, they do not agree on how it should be done. Government regulation is not always able to do everything that we would like it to do. We can pass laws forbidding producers from cooperating in setting prices. It is difficult, however, to detect this kind of behavior. It is also very expensive to pass and enforce laws against unfair competition. To pass and enforce such laws requires many people such as legislators, investigators, judges, and office workers. Your tax dollars pay the salaries of all these people. Therefore, a small price increase may be less costly to you as a consumer than the cost of prosecuting businesses that are cooperating unlawfully.

Defining and Enforcing Property Rights

In our economy, the whole productive process depends on the concept of private property. All productive resources such as land, labor, capital, or management skills are owned by people. When you own property, you have certain rights. **Property rights** are the rights which define who owns what rights to property and how individuals or groups may use their property. As a worker, you own your own labor and sell that labor to an employer. The employer uses the labor you have sold to produce some product or service. The producer also buys raw materials such as steel, iron, electric power, lumber, plastic, and glass to use in producing the product or service. The producers own these goods and services until they sell them.

In most cases, once the goods or services are sold, they become the private property of the buyers. The buyers or owners have the private right to benefit from the ownership and use of these goods or services. They can enjoy the goods or services, or they have the right to sell them to others. The right to benefit from the use or sale of the items is a private right for the direct benefit of the owner. This system of private property rights strongly influences us to work hard to produce goods and services. We have this incentive because we can benefit directly from our hard work.

How is this system of private property rights established and enforced? Who is powerful enough to enforce these laws? The answer is *government*. Government defines what rights individuals and producers have. Government establishes and enforces the laws that give us the use and benefit of our private property. Without this system of rights and enforcement, our system of production would not be as efficient as it is.

When you sell your labor to an employer, you and your employer enter into a contract. A **contract** is a legally binding agreement between two or more competent persons. Suppose you decide to sell your labor to an employer and that employer cheats you or breaks the contract. The employer would be breaking the law, and you would have the power of the law behind you. You could force your employer to live up to the contract under the law.

The law also protects the employer's rights. Suppose your employer had paid you in advance for a week's work, and you only worked two days. The power of the law would be on the employer's side. The employer could force repayment from you through the legal system. The law establishes a system of property rights and

5–1

property rights
The rights which define who owns what rights to property and how individuals or groups may use their property.

5–1

contract
A legally binding agreement between two or more competent persons.

enforces contracts between individuals and businesses. In short, the law defines the rights of all parties and protects those parties equally.

If there were no laws to enforce contracts, individuals and businesses probably would break their agreements more often. Then all businesses would become less efficient because they could not be sure that agreements would be fulfilled. Employers could not depend on employees to fulfill their promise to work. Production would go up and down depending on how many workers decided to work on any given day. A producer could not promise buyers any specific delivery date. Also, workers would not be able to count on an employer to pay the agreed-upon wages. If producers could not deliver goods to buyers, they might not have enough revenues to pay the workers. Therefore, a system of contracts in which all parties must fulfill their legal obligations is extremely important to our business system.

The legal system also defines what you can and cannot do with your property. If you own a piece of residential land, you may legally occupy that land yourself or sell it. You own the private property rights to that land. The law also defines what you and your neighbors cannot do with your land. For example, you may not build a slaughterhouse on your land in a residential neighborhood. You cannot do anything that would injure your neighbors' property rights. And your neighbors cannot do anything that would injure your property rights. If you decide to build a house on property that you own, there are many legal restrictions. For example, you must follow electrical safety codes. You cannot build a firetrap that might burn down and spread fire to your neighbors' homes. In general, laws are designed to protect the property rights of all owners. You can do whatever you want with your property as long as it does not hurt the property rights of others.

The legal system is for your benefit. It protects your rights and also prevents you from injuring others. Government, by defining these rights, sets up a system in society that helps all of us to live and work together more efficiently. By defining what is fair or equitable, government contributes to the efficiency of an economy. It settles disputes between individuals and forces everyone to fulfill their legal agreements.

5-3

Providing Public Goods

As you learned in a previous chapter, many goods and services are produced more efficiently in the public sector. Roads, schools, national defense, and police and fire protection are some of these goods and services. Obviously it is more efficient for a country to maintain one army than for citizens to try to defend themselves individually. Roads are too expensive to build to be used efficiently by just one individual. The public goods rationale indicates that these goods are most efficiently produced by government.

Government also often undertakes activities that the private sector will not. The government, for example, has taken over much of our railway system and has partially paid for its operation through Amtrak. Several private railway companies once owned this system. But they failed financially. There were not enough profits for them to stay in business. The private sector, for several reasons, failed in its attempts to provide rail service to parts of the country. Believing that train service is important to our country, the public sector spends tax dollars to keep trains running. Some economists say this is a wasteful and inefficient use of tax dollars. This may be a fair criticism. However, keeping the trains running does provide train service in places where it is vital to our nation's interest. It also provides competition for the trucking industry and other kinds of businesses that transport freight and people. Every government action clearly has both benefits and costs. If train service is important and the private sector cannot provide that service profitably, the public sector must step in.

Dealing with Negative Externalities

Many kinds of costs and benefits are passed on to individuals outside the market system. It can be said that these costs or benefits "spill over" to people who are not involved in that market. Thus, these costs and benefits are often called *spillover effects*. In economic (and legal) discussions, the word that is used to describe these costs and benefits is *externalities*. They affect people who are "external" to (or outside of) the market that produces the costs or benefits. When discussing externalities, the term *cost* does not necessarily mean a dollar cost. Instead, cost can be a reduction in individual satisfaction or well-being.

For example, assume your neighbors are playing their radio at high volume while you are trying to sleep. Your neighbors are passing on a negative externality to you. They are reducing your satisfaction or well-being by passing on a cost to you outside the market system. There is no dollar price involved, just a reduction in your well-being. A business world equivalent of this is the pollution of a stream by a chemical plant. Air pollution by a coal-burning electric power plant is another example. Both activities pass on a cost to residents of the area outside the market system. Clean air and clean water clearly contribute to our health and well-being. Pollution of the environment reduces our satisfaction and quality of life.

Illustration 5–4
If one person causes pollution, that has an effect on the rest of us. Even though putting up with pollution may not cost us money, it does reduce our satisfaction or well-being.

Government is often called on to deal with negative externalities in the private sector. If a local chemical plant is polluting the river, you might complain directly to the plant. Many of your neighbors might do the same. It is not likely, however, that the plant would stop polluting if measures needed to stop the pollution were expensive. You and your neighbors would probably need the power of the law behind you. So far, only the public sector has been powerful enough to force companies to spend a large amount of money to stop pollution. It is not that most companies do not want to be good citizens. They are simply trying to produce the goods and services consumers desire at the lowest possible price. If a business must spend millions of dollars to clean up pollution, its costs of production must rise. Finally, the prices of the goods it produces must rise. You and your neighbors, with the help of government, may be successful in forcing a company to clean up its pollution. However, you will pay for it by paying higher prices for goods made by that company.

Pollution and other kinds of externalities are often hard to detect. It is also difficult to find a sole cause of an externality and apply the blame to the proper party. A chemical plant may be the main cause of pollution. On the other hand, every plant that uses the river probably contributes to the pollution in some way. (The city sewer system, run by government itself, might be dumping sewage.) The large research and monitoring effort needed to control externalities can be most efficiently provided by government.

In controlling externalities, the government defines and enforces property rights. The public sector can deal with this issue more effectively than the private sector. The public sector can protect you by passing laws that prohibit companies or individuals from injuring you by polluting air and water or by making your property less attractive. The public sector can also force companies to buy pollution control equipment. It can even force persons or companies to pay for damages due to externalities caused by them. All this effort, however, will be paid for by the individual in one way or another. The costs to pass and enforce the laws will be paid for through tax dollars. The costs to clean up the pollution or install better equipment will be paid for through higher market prices. The real choice as to how much externality will be tolerated and at what cost is up to the consumer.

The consumer's voice in these matters is heard in two places. First, the consumer's voice reaches producers in the marketplace. What consumers buy and do not buy tells producers how they feel about the goods and services offered at various prices. Second, the consumer's voice reaches government in the voting booth. How individuals vote determines the reactions of the public sector to externalities.

Redistributing Income

In our economy there are some individuals who are unable to earn enough income to live on. Often this is not their fault. There are members of our society who are handicapped, unskilled, or simply not able to work at a productive job. The public sector taxes the income of those who work and redistributes part of that income to those who cannot earn. This is more than just an attempt to be compassionate. In our system of private enterprise, the ability to earn income increases with wealth. The more private property you own, the more income you have, and the more chances you have of being able to produce. This tends to make the rich get richer. By redistributing income, our government attempts to provide equity. It tries to make the opportunity to earn income more equitable. This effort does not give everyone an equal income. However, it does keep all the income in our economy from going only to a few individuals. It keeps income distributed more equally across the population than would be the case without redistribution.

Data on how incomes are distributed in the United States indicate that some minorities are over-represented in the lower income brackets. This is particularly true of blacks and Hispanics. Income redistribution programs that provide public assistance to low-income households help make more opportunities available. This attempts to break the cycle of poverty.

America still has its share of poverty. The distribution of income in America, however, is more equitable than in many capitalistic countries of the world. Extremely uneven distribution of income in a country is often the cause of revolutions. Much of the political upheaval in Latin America has been due, in part, to an uneven distribution of income. In some Latin American countries, a very small part of the population controls most of the country's income.

We realize, then, that income redistribution may be an equitable and desirable act. To redistribute income on any large scale also takes the power of law. Americans give large sums to charity every year, but this is a very small amount compared to the income redistributed by government. Each year our government redistributes hundreds of billions of dollars to needy people. It is highly unlikely that any individuals or businesses would willingly turn over large parts of their incomes to be redistributed if it were not required by law. You might feel that everyone should do their share. You probably would say that if everyone else chipped in, you would, too. However, if everyone did not give their share, you might refuse to bear the redistribution burden alone. Redistribution without the power of law is not likely to be effective. Therefore, the public sector can redistribute income more efficiently than the private

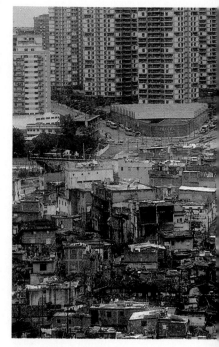

Illustration 5–5
In this Latin American city, the wealthy live side by side with the poor. Extreme uneven distribution of income is often the cause of political upheaval.

5-3 sector. The public sector's primary concern is to serve the wants and needs of our society in an equitable manner.

PROBLEMS WITH THE PUBLIC SECTOR

5-4 We have discussed the five major areas in which the public sector is engaged. These five areas seem to function best in the public sector. However, three major problems can occur in the public sector.

Abuse of Public Goods

Public goods such as schools, roads, public housing, parks, and recreational facilities are goods the whole community or society owns. For example, no individual owns the public roads or parks. These goods are provided through public ownership. This is an application of the concept of economies of scale (that some economic activities become more efficient when done on a large scale). Many people can enjoy a large public park at a lower cost per person than if individuals try to provide their own parks.

Public ownership, however, does not always encourage the pride and conscience of individual ownership. Often individuals do not take care of publicly owned goods as well as they do their own property. For example, graffiti often is seen on public goods such as school buildings or parks but rarely on privately owned property. Individuals who deface or destroy public property usually do not ruin their own property. Other examples of this disregard for public property are litter on highways and poor upkeep in public housing. These activities detract from the satisfaction we get from the use of public goods. To repair, clean up, and maintain public property is costly. This cost is passed on to all members of society, even though only a few citizens cause the problem.

Once started, the problem of public property abuse grows. It becomes a sport to add more graffiti to a wall already defaced. People throw even more garbage on a badly littered highway in the mistaken belief that "everyone does it." People who would never throw a soda can in their own front yard think nothing of throwing one out the car window. Many people do not see these acts as the costly activities that they really are. This simply increases the costs all citizens will pay for public goods in the future.

Abusive private behavior toward public goods has been a problem for many years in our country. Some societies, however, have been able to improve this kind of behavior. The Montreal subway system in Canada is a public good in which many citizens take great pride of ownership. There is almost no graffiti there. The public

Illustration 5–6
Only a few individuals are responsible for covering our public property with graffiti. But all members of society must share the cost of cleaning it up.

parks of Japan are a showplace of public pride. Citizens who foolishly litter or foul the area are quickly reminded by other citizens of their civic responsibility. These examples of changing private behavior show some hope for improving the problem of private abuse of public goods.

Special Interest Groups

Since government defines and enforces property rights and redistributes income, there are always those individuals who try to use the system to their own advantage. Laws are made through our system of representative government in Washington. A **special interest group** is an organized subgroup of a society bound together by a common concern. **Lobbying** is the act of communicating with government representatives to influence their votes on a specific issue.

5–1
special interest group
An organized subgroup of society bound together by a common cause.

5–1
lobbying
The act of communicating with government representatives to influence their votes on a specific issue.

Over the years, special interest groups have developed to lobby for laws that will benefit them. There are many such groups. The National Rifle Association lobbies against gun control. The Sierra Club lobbies in Congress against the use of wilderness lands for public parks and recreation. The National Dairy Association lobbies for higher subsidized, or legally set, minimum prices on dairy products. All these organizations devote large amounts of money and time to make sure that government representatives hear their points of view. If a particular senator or member of Congress votes against laws the organization favors, the organization tries to influence its members against reelecting that representative. These organizations are believed to influence tens of thousands of votes for each candidate.

Such special interest groups are very powerful politically. They strongly influence the passing of laws that will benefit the special interest groups at the cost of all citizens. If the National Dairy Association succeeds in getting laws passed that raise the minimum price of milk, everyone pays higher milk prices. The producer of

Illustration 5–7
Special interest groups work together toward a common concern. The Sierra Club, for example, lobbies against the use of wilderness lands for public parks and recreation.

dairy products receives the benefits of such laws. The cost is passed on to every member of the economy who buys milk. The outcome is the same anytime a law benefiting only one particular group in society is passed. The whole society pays for a benefit that is enjoyed by only a small group. This is not necessarily bad. You should be aware, however, that special interest groups number in the thousands. When you pay your taxes or buy the goods and services these groups represent, you are supporting their cause whether you like it or not.

Each of these special interest groups has organized an effective lobby in Congress to make sure that the group's particular circumstances were heard. Individuals, however, do not have the time and resources to lobby for their own interests. It would be difficult for you to write thousands of letters to Congress or to go to Washington to make your views known. So, like all other individual voters, you participate in the process of representative government by electing individuals who represent your views.

Unfortunately when political power is concentrated in any organization or group, individual interests of all citizens are sometimes not well represented. There will always be individuals and groups who try to use the public sector to their advantage. There will always be situations where smaller groups and individuals benefit at a cost passed on to everyone in the society. This is very much the nature of the social decision-making process we discussed earlier.

Problems of Size

Some goods and services are produced in the public sector because of economies of scale. On the other hand, some productive activities can be done more efficiently on a smaller scale. In the private sector, many companies realize this. Therefore, they break their companies down into several smaller subsidiaries or smaller companies. This structure helps keep more efficient control of a giant company's efforts. However, even with this structure, it is difficult to control any very large organization.

In the past, the public sector has had problems with size. Some of the programs of our federal government have grown so large that they cannot be controlled effectively. The Federal Youth Summer Employment program has been criticized in the past for being too spread out geographically and poorly controlled. Its efficiency is questionable.

MILTON FRIEDMAN

Milton Friedman is a strong supporter of laissez-faire. The concept of *laissez-faire* means that government involvement in economic matters should be highly limited. Friedman's main argument is that while trying to do good, government actions usually end up doing just the opposite. Most government efforts to protect consumers by regulating business create higher prices or lesser quality services. Many of the regulatory agencies are not very efficient in promoting competition in markets. They frequently end up representing the interests of the very businesses they regulate. Friedman has contended for more than three decades that minimal government ownership and control in the economy is in everyone's best interest.

Friedman won the Nobel Prize in Economics in 1976 for his work on monetary theory. He is professor emeritus at the University of Chicago and a fellow at Stanford University's Hoover Institute.

Friedman and his wife, Rose, have written three books together and are perhaps best known for their television series, *Free to Choose*.

JOHN KENNETH GALBRAITH

John Kenneth Galbraith urges an affirmative role for government. He argues that because of their size, corporations have too much influence in the modern society. This influence is so strong that it sometimes overpowers the classical market forces of supply and demand. Through advertising, these corporations tend to *create* wants and needs for consumers. Thus more private goods are produced, sometimes to the detriment of needed public goods. Galbraith's views are controversial; however, he has gained attention and respect in the field of economics.

John Kenneth Galbraith has been a professor of economics at Harvard University and a president of the American Economic Association. He has served as ambassador to India and provided economic advice to several presidents. His books, *The Affluent Society, The New Industrial State*, and *Economics and the Public Purpose*, have been widely read by the public and have contributed to economic thinking for more than two decades.

Some of our government bureaus are so large that parts of them lay off workers to reduce their size, while other parts of the same bureaus hire more employees. The efficiency of a bureau of such size might leave a great deal to be desired. For example, according to the *Statistical Abstract of the United States: 1985,* the Department of Agriculture employed 128,595 people in 1981. There were only about 2,434,000 farms in the United States in that year. This was nearly one federal employee for every 19 farms. It is difficult to understand why the Department of Agriculture needs so many employees.

There may be logical explanations for why the public sector has such problems. But the point is that the problems do exist. The Reagan administration began taking steps to reduce the size of government and to increase its efficiency. By 1988 employment in the Department of Agriculture had been reduced to 120,869. There were about 2,197,000 farms that year. This was nearly one federal employee for every 18 farms. The goals of many other government bureaus were redefined. Some bureaus of questionable value were eliminated altogether.

In the years ahead, we may see a more streamlined and perhaps a more efficient government. Even though there will always be problems in the public sector, new and innovative solutions are a primary goal of economists.

THE ECONOMICS OF POLITICS AND THE POLITICS OF ECONOMICS

Decision making in the public sector is a complex process. The national debt is an example of the conflict between good economics and good politics. Three reasons for this conflict are

1. *The Rational Ignorance of Voters:* People may make a rational decision not to be well informed. They may feel that their individual votes make little difference (little benefit). It is time consuming to gather information on which to base their votes (high cost).

2. *The Special Interest Effect:* Members of special interest groups may benefit a great deal from certain policies and so will spend money to influence the government. The cost of the policies is likely to be spread over the general public, so no one person has too high a cost. Thus, there is little opposition to special interest groups.

3. *The Shortsightedness Effect:* Politicians are likely to vote for government spending. Rational politicians would rather be in office explaining an increased deficit than defeated and explaining why they did not support spending programs.

REVIEWING THE CHAPTER

5-3   1. The private sector's primary goal is efficiency. The public sector includes all levels of government and its institutions that assist the functioning of the entire economy. The primary concern of the public sector is to provide equity in our system which, in turn, improves efficiency.

5-2   2. The public sector undertakes activities that the private sector cannot or is not willing to do. Some of the functions of the public sector (such as controlling negative externalities) come about because they require the power of law. Other activities of the public sector (such as providing private parks) are undertaken by the public sector because, although they are important, they are not profitable for private industry.

5-2   3. The government serves as a referee to encourage competition among firms. The government also sets up the legal system to define and enforce the property rights of individuals and the public. The public sector provides public goods, such as roads and police protection, which improve the efficiency of the private sector. The public sector deals with externalities that pass costs or benefits on to others outside of the market system. Finally, the public sector redistributes income as a charitable act and to improve equity within the economy.

5-4   4. The public sector encounters problems because public goods are frequently abused by individuals. Another problem in the public sector is the existence of special interest groups organized to manipulate the process of government to their advantage. These groups use political power to gain benefits for themselves at the cost of all members of the society. The third problem in the public sector is size—it has grown so large that portions of its efforts are not very efficient.

REVIEWING ECONOMIC TERMS

5-1   Supply definitions for the following terms:

public sector	contract
public institutions	special interest group
property rights	lobbying

REVIEWING ECONOMIC CONCEPTS

5-3 1. What is the primary concern of the public sector?

5-2 2. What are five major functions of the public sector?

5-2 3. How does the public sector promote competition?

5-2 4. How does the public sector enforce property rights?

5-2 5. What can the public sector do about negative externalities?

5-2 6. Give one major reason why the public sector redistributes income.

5-4 7. Discuss three major problems with the public sector.

5-4 8. Why does abuse of public goods affect all members of a society?

5-4 9. How can a special interest group affect those individuals who do not support the cause of the special interest group?

APPLYING ECONOMIC CONCEPTS

5-3 1. Do you think that equity or efficiency is a more important goal for our economy? Why? Do you feel that both are necessary? If so, why? If not, why not?

5-2 2. What do you feel is the single most important function of the public sector? Why is this function more important to you than the other major functions provided by the public sector?

5-2 3. Are property rights necessary for an advanced industrial society to function efficiently? If so, are *private* property rights necessary? What do you think is the difference between property rights in general and private property rights? Are there property rights involved with a public good like a park? If so, are they public or private property rights?

5-2 4. Are externalities sometimes efficient, but not equitable? If so, give an example of an efficient, but inequitable, externality.

5-4 5. Suggest a solution to each of the three problems of the public sector.

5-2 6. Do you feel that the public sector should keep businesses from cooperating to set prices or from competing with each other? If so, explain.

PART II

MICROECONOMICS

CHAPTER 6

DEMAND: ACHIEVING CONSUMER SATISFACTION

Learning Objectives

6–1 Define terms related to demand.

6–2 Construct a demand schedule and a demand curve.

6–3 Distinguish between a change in quantity demanded and a change in demand.

6–4 Describe how the determinants of demand affect demand.

6–5 Explain sensitivity of demand.

6–6 Calculate elasticity.

6–7 Calculate total revenue for a demand schedule.

WHAT IS MICROECONOMICS?

In this chapter you begin your study of the branch of economics called *microeconomics*. The term *micro* means small. So, microeconomics involves looking at *small* parts of the total economy. It includes the choices we all make as individual consumers. Should we spend our limited amount of money on clothes or on recreation? Or, should we spend some money on each? Microeconomics studies these and similar decisions made by individual consumers.

Production of goods and services is also a part of microeconomics. Businesses must make decisions about what kinds of goods or services to produce and how to produce them. Other decisions are made that determine what inputs will be used in the production process. For example, how much labor will be necessary and what part of the labor input will be skilled labor are results of the production decisions made by businesses.

The decisions consumers make about what goods to buy plus the decisions businesses make about what to produce determine the level of individual product prices. You will see why as you study about the forces of supply and demand in the economy. In this chapter, we will focus our attention on the role of demand in the economy.

WHY CONSUME?

Think about the last time you spent money. It could have been spent on a pizza, a sweater, a new tennis racquet, or a concert. No matter what you purchased, you decided to buy something because it would please you. We do not have to make purchases. We do so because we expect them to increase our personal satisfaction. Economists say that we buy goods and services to increase our utility. Recall that utility is the satisfaction one receives from the consumption, use, or ownership of a good or service.

We all get pleasure, or satisfaction, from consuming a variety of things. But how much pleasure do we get? How much satisfaction do you get from eating a pizza? from wearing a new sweater? from having your hair styled?

If someone asked you how much you like orange juice, you could not give a meaningful numerical answer. Suppose you said that you enjoy orange juice "100." What would that mean? If you answered "100" and another person answered "200," you still wouldn't know who likes orange juice more. The numbers have no common basis. Thus, it is more likely that you would answer the question by making comparisons. You might say, "I like orange juice better than tomato juice." Or, "I don't like orange juice as well as grapefruit juice." It is a lot easier for us to explain how much we like something by making comparisons than by assigning a number that would measure satisfaction.

Suppose you like grapefruit juice better than orange juice and orange juice better than tomato juice. As long as the three types of juice cost the same, one could make certain predictions about your consumption. Given a choice between orange juice and tomato juice, you would choose orange juice. It also would be safe to predict that you would prefer grapefruit juice to tomato juice. You would rather drink grapefruit juice than the other two juices because grapefruit juice gives you a greater satisfaction at the same cost.

VALUE AND PRICES

We say that things have value if they give us satisfaction. The word *value* really implies a *value in use*. Air has a value in use, because we benefit from breathing air. But air is free. If air has value to us, why is it free? We certainly would be willing to pay for air rather than do without it. However, air is available in such abundance that we treat it as a free good. You would not buy a quart of air, since you can get as much air as you can use for free.

Illustration 6–1
Before America was colonized, native Americans viewed the land in the same way as we view air — a free, abundant good with an important *value in use*.

We also get satisfaction from consuming gasoline. Gas has value in use. But unlike air, we must pay for the gas we consume. That is, gasoline has *value in exchange* as well as value in use. We are willing to exchange something—usually money—for the use of some gas. Why is air free, but gas costly? The most important reason is that gas is scarce while air is abundant.

The amount of money we must exchange to obtain a unit of some good is called the *price* of the good. For example, a cassette tape may have a price of $8.00. That price measures the economic value of the cassette tape.

We all have a limited amount of money that we can exchange for goods and services. For some of us, that limit is more severe than for others. A public school teacher typically has far less money to spend than a successful Wall Street banker. A family on welfare usually has less money to exchange for goods and services than the family of a skilled laborer. However, we all have a limited amount of money for buying things that can bring us satisfaction. As a result, we all make decisions about how we will spend, save, or borrow money. Exactly how we choose to allocate our money is an important factor in determining the demand for various goods and services in the economy.

DEMAND

Demand refers to the quantities of a good that consumers are willing and able to purchase at various prices during a given period of time. Let's take a closer look at the important elements of this definition.

First, you must be *able* to make a purchase; that is, you must have enough money to make the purchase. There are many items you may be willing to purchase. However, you may not have a demand for them, because you don't have the money to make the purchase. For example, you might want to buy a ski lodge in the Colorado Rockies and a private jet to get you there. But if you do not have the money to purchase these luxuries, you do not have a demand for them.

Second, you must be *willing* to make the purchase. There are products that you can afford but you may not be willing to spend your income on them. Examples might include a pet snake or prune-flavored yogurt. If you are not willing to purchase these items, you do not have a demand for them.

Third, when we discuss demand, we are referring to purchases made during a *given period of time*. For example, you might have a yearly demand for shoes and a weekly demand for candy bars.

6–1

demand

The quantities of a good that consumers are willing and able to purchase at various prices during a given period of time.

If you are willing and able to buy four candy bars at a price of 40¢ each, your demand is four candy bars a week.

Finally, demand represents the *quantities* consumers would purchase at *various prices*. If the price of candy bars drops to 25¢ each, you might increase the quantity you demand from four to six. If the price rises to 80¢, you might only be able to buy two candy bars a week.

The Law of Demand

For most goods, consumers are willing to purchase more units at a lower price than at a higher price. If someone came to your school selling quality aluminum tennis racquets for $180 each, the person might sell only a few. If, however, the price were lowered to $120 each, more racquets could be sold. If the price were reduced still further to $70 each, even more could be sold. This pattern is true with most products and services. The inverse relationship between price and the quantity consumers will buy is so widely observed that it is called the law of demand. The **law of demand** is the rule that people will buy more at lower prices than at higher prices, if all other factors are constant.

6-1

law of demand
The rule that people will buy more at lower prices than at higher prices, if all other factors are constant.

Diminishing Marginal Utility. One reason for observing the law of demand is that as a person consumes more units of a particular product, each additional unit provides less and less additional satisfaction. A person's total satisfaction may continue to increase, but at a slower rate.

Consider your consumption of your favorite sandwich. Suppose that you make one sandwich. You eat the sandwich and it gives you a certain amount of satisfaction. Now suppose that you eat a second sandwich. You might enjoy it, but you probably will not enjoy it as much as the first one. What if you eat a third, a fourth, or a fifth sandwich? Most people would lose their appetites by then! Each additional sandwich gives you less and less additional satisfaction. This principle is what economists call diminishing marginal utility. **Diminishing marginal utility** is the principle that as additional units of a product are consumed during a given time period, the additional satisfaction becomes less and less.

6-1

diminishing marginal utility
The principle that as additional units of a product are consumed during a given time period, the additional satisfaction becomes less and less.

Stop and think about the products that you consume. This principle applies to most of them. Shoes, sweaters, records or tapes, and posters all follow this principle. Buying additional units of each good during a given time period provides less and less additional satisfaction.

About 200 years ago, economists used this principle of diminishing marginal utility to support the idea that people would buy more of a product only at a lower price. Thus, the principle of

Illustration 6–2
The concept of diminishing marginal utility helps explain why, if you tried to eat fifteen peanut butter sandwiches, you would receive less and less additional satisfaction from each additional sandwich.

diminishing marginal utility provides a basis for the law of demand. But there are two other reasons for this relationship between price and the quantity demanded. As the price of a product falls, there are income and substitution effects that encourage increased consumption of the product.

The Income Effect. Let's first consider the income effect. The **income effect** is the effect of increasing or decreasing prices on the buying power of income. As the price of a product we buy declines, we feel that we can afford to buy more of that good and other things as well. That is, our income appears greater because we can buy more things with a given number of dollars.

6–1

income effect

The effect of increasing or decreasing prices on the buying power of income.

Suppose, for example, that Beth Smith has a part-time job that pays $30 a week. Beth collects cassette tapes of her favorite recording artists and usually buys two tapes each week. If the store where she shops has a sale reducing the price of each tape by $2, Beth may buy three tapes rather than two. She may also increase her consumption of other items in addition to or instead of buying another tape. This change in her buying habit results from the fact that her $30 income now goes further. This increase in buying power that resulted from the lower price of tapes is called an income effect. Beth's higher effective income makes it possible for her to buy more tapes (and/or more of other goods). Therefore, when prices decrease, the income effect causes people to buy more because their incomes have more buying power.

The income effect may work in the other direction, too. As the price of items we buy goes up, our income doesn't go as far. We must buy less with a given amount of money as prices rise. Our buying power goes down. In an economic sense, our income is reduced when prices rise. Therefore, the income effect when prices increase lowers the amount bought because income has less buying power.

The Substitution Effect. Let's return to our example of the lowered price of cassette tapes. The decrease in the price of tapes also causes a substitution effect that will increase the number of tapes people purchase. As cassette tapes become cheaper relative to records or compact discs, people like Beth are likely to change their buying habits. They may substitute the now lower priced cassette tapes for the other products. This is called the substitution effect of a price change. The **substitution effect** is the effect of increasing or decreasing relative prices on the mix of goods purchased.

6–1

substitution effect

The effect of increasing or decreasing relative prices on the mix of goods purchased.

This substitution effect is seen relatively often. As the prices of oil and gas go up, people may substitute wood-burning stoves and solar collectors for heating their homes. When the price of coffee goes up, people substitute tea or chicory for coffee. When the price of beef falls, consumers substitute beef for chicken and pork. So, the substitution effect works in two directions. If the price of a good falls, we may substitute it for other items. But if the price of a good rises, we may substitute other items for the now relatively more expensive good.

Both the income effect and the substitution effect support the law of demand. Both cause a greater quantity of an item to be purchased at a lower price than at a higher price.

Demand Schedules

6–2

6–1

demand schedule

A listing of the quantities that would be purchased at various prices.

It is often convenient to look at an individual's demand in the form of a listing of the quantities that would be purchased at various prices. A listing of the quantities that would be purchased at various prices is called a **demand schedule**. Look at Table 6–1. This demand schedule shows the number of hot fudge sundaes Mike Lin would buy per month at different prices. You see that at $2 a sundae, Mike would not be willing to buy any. However, if the price were lower, Mike would have a demand. For example, at a price of $1.80 a sundae, he would buy two sundaes each month. At a price of $1.20, the quantity he would demand increases to eight sundaes a month.

Note that Mike's demand for hot fudge sundaes follows the law of demand. More units would be purchased at lower prices than at higher prices. Other consumers in Mike's community also have a demand for hot fudge sundaes. It is reasonable to expect that their demand schedules would also follow the law of demand. That is, we would expect them to purchase a greater number of hot fudge sundaes at lower prices than at higher prices.

Let's say that there are 1,000 people in Mike's neighborhood who like hot fudge sundaes. For simplicity, we will also say that each consumer has a demand schedule exactly like Mike's. If the price is $1.40 a sundae, those 1,000 consumers would *each* be will-

TABLE 6–1

MIKE LIN'S DEMAND SCHEDULE FOR HOT
FUDGE SUNDAES

Price	Quantity Purchased per Month
$2.00	0
1.80	2
1.60	4
1.40	6
1.20	8
1.00	10
.80	12
.60	14

ing and able to buy six sundaes a month. In *total*, they would have a demand for 6,000 sundaes at a price of $1.40 a sundae. If the price went down to $1.20 a sundae, the quantity demanded would increase to 8,000. If the price increased to $1.60 a sundae, only 4,000 sundaes would be demanded. When we list the quantities bought at each price for all 1,000 people, we have a market demand schedule. This is shown in Table 6–2.

A market demand schedule shows the quantities of a product that all consumers are willing and able to purchase at various prices. Remember that each individual is likely to purchase a greater quantity of an item at a lower price than at a higher price. Thus, when we add up the individual demand schedules for all consumers, this law of demand is still true. As shown in the demand schedule for an entire market in Table 6–2, more hot fudge sundaes would be purchased as the price of the product decreases.

TABLE 6–2

MARKET DEMAND SCHEDULE FOR HOT
FUDGE SUNDAES IN MIKE LIN'S
NEIGHBORHOOD

Price	Quantity Purchased per Month
$2.00	0
1.80	2,000
1.60	4,000
1.40	6,000
1.20	8,000
1.00	10,000
.80	12,000
.60	14,000

Demand Curves

Any demand schedule shows only a small number of the possible price and quantity combinations. For example, Table 6–1 shows only eight such combinations. From that table, you can see how many sundaes Mike would buy at certain prices, such as $1.40 or $1.20. But what if the price of a hot fudge sundae fell between these two points? How many sundaes would Mike buy at $1.30 each? We cannot answer this question directly from the demand schedule.

6–2 However, we can construct a demand curve which helps us to find the quantity that Mike would demand at any price. A **demand curve** is a graphic illustration of the relationship between *price* and the *quantity purchased* at each price. Let's construct Mike's demand curve for hot fudge sundaes. Begin by drawing a vertical line along which we can represent prices. From the bottom of that vertical line, draw a horizontal line to the right along which we can represent the quantity of hot fudge sundaes Mike purchases at each price. These are illustrated by the two blue lines in Figure 6–1. Each line is called an axis.

Prices are measured from bottom to top along the vertical axis in 20-cent intervals. The horizontal axis measures the quantities which increase from left to right. Each of the eight price-quantity combinations in Table 6–1 can now be represented in the space bordered by these axes. The positioning of two such points will be used as examples.

6–1
demand curve
A graphic illustration of the relationship between price and the quantity purchased at each price.

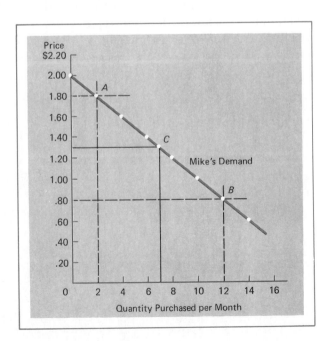

FIGURE 6–1 MIKE LIN'S DEMAND CURVE FOR HOT FUDGE SUNDAES
At lower prices, Mike will purchase more sundaes per month than at higher prices. His demand curve slopes downward to the right which illustrates the law of demand.

First, consider a price of $1.80. Table 6–1 shows that at $1.80, Mike would purchase two sundaes a month. We locate the point corresponding to two sundaes on the horizontal axis and draw a dashed line up from that point. Now locate $1.80 on the vertical axis and draw another dashed line to the right from that point. Where these two lines cross represents one point on Mike's demand curve for hot fudge sundaes. This point is labeled *A* in Figure 6–1.

The same process is repeated for a price of $.80. Table 6–1 shows that Mike would have a demand for 12 sundaes at that price. In Figure 6–1, we have drawn a dashed line up from the point representing 12 units along the horizontal axis. A dashed line drawn to the right from $.80 on the vertical axis crosses this line at Point *B*. Thus, *B* represents another point on Mike's demand curve for hot fudge sundaes.

If we did this for all the prices and quantities in Table 6–1, we would have eight points like *A* and *B*. Connecting all the points shows Mike's demand curve for hot fudge sundaes. This line represents the quantities Mike would buy at each possible price. Using this demand curve allows us to determine how many sundaes Mike would buy at prices that are not shown in Table 6–1. In doing this, we must be careful not to go too far outside the range of observed prices. Since Table 6–1 includes prices between $.60 and $2.00, we have a fairly wide range in which to work. However, a projection to a price like $.20 should not be done since it is well below the lowest price in our table of observations.

It is reasonable to expect that at a price of $1.30, Mike would buy seven sundaes each month. We can tell this from the demand curve in Figure 6–1, but not from the demand schedule in Table 6–1. In Figure 6–1, a solid line is drawn to the right from a price of $1.30 on the vertical axis. This line meets Mike's demand curve at the point labeled *C*. If we then draw a line down from *C* to the horizontal axis, it comes down at a quantity midway between six and eight. This is how we can conclude that if the price were $1.30, Mike would buy seven sundaes a month.

The demand curve in Figure 6–1 only shows Mike's demand for the product. Suppose you owned an ice cream shop in Mike's neighborhood. You would care how many sundaes Mike would purchase. But your real interest would be how many sundaes all 1,000 people in the neighborhood would buy. That is, you would be interested in the market demand.

We can construct a market demand curve based on the market demand schedule in Table 6–2. We see from that table that at a price of $1.80, 2,000 sundaes would be purchased each month. If the price were $.80, 12,000 sundaes would be purchased. These two price-quantity combinations are represented by the Points *A** and *B** in Figure 6–2.

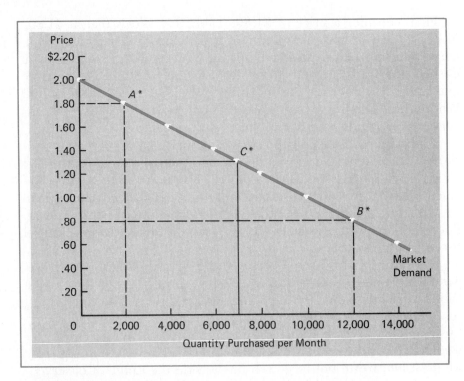

FIGURE 6–2 MARKET DEMAND CURVE FOR HOT FUDGE SUNDAES
Adding together all 1,000 consumers' demand curves gives the market demand
curve. The market demand curve also follows the law of demand and has a
negative slope.

If we plotted all the points in Table 6–2 and then connected
them with a line, we would have the market demand curve for sundaes. The market demand curve in Figure 6–2 shows the quantities
that all 1,000 people would be expected to purchase at each price.
Thus, at a price of $1.30, the market demand would be 7,000 hot
fudge sundaes. This is determined from the point marked *C**
along the market demand curve.

Both the market demand schedule and the market demand
curve show that the quantity purchased goes up from 2,000 to
12,000 units as price falls from $1.80 to $.80. This is called a
6–3 *change in quantity demanded.* As the price falls, a greater quantity is
demanded. As the price goes up, a smaller quantity is demanded.
A change in quantity demanded is caused by a change in the price
of the product for any given demand curve. This is true of individual consumers' demand as well as for the market demand.

From our discussion and from Figure 6–2, it is clear that the
market demand curve has a negative slope. A negative slope means
that the curve slopes downward to the right. Thus, the law of
demand is true for the market demand as well as for individual
demand. But what determines how much will be bought at each

price? Why are more wood-burning stoves bought now than ten years ago? Why are more books bought today, even though the price has gone up? These questions are answered by looking at the determinants of demand.

DETERMINANTS OF DEMAND

The overall level of demand is determined by consumers' incomes and attitudes and the prices of related goods. These are often referred to as the determinants of demand. **Determinants of demand** are the factors that determine how much will be purchased at each price. As these determinants change, the overall level of demand may change. People may buy more or less of a product because of changes in these factors — even though the product's price does not change.

Such changes can be shown by a shift of the entire demand curve. If the demand curve shifts to the right, we say that there has been an *increase in demand*. This is shown as a move from the demand curve D to the demand curve D_H in Figure 6–3. The initial demand curve D can be thought of as being the market demand curve for hot fudge sundaes first shown in Figure 6–2. As shown in Figure 6–3, at a price of $1.30, given the initial level of demand D, consumers would purchase 7,000 units. If demand increases to D_H, consumers would purchase 11,000 units at a price of $1.30 rather than the 7,000 units along the demand curve D.

6–4

6–1
determinants of demand
The factors that determine how much will be purchased at each price.

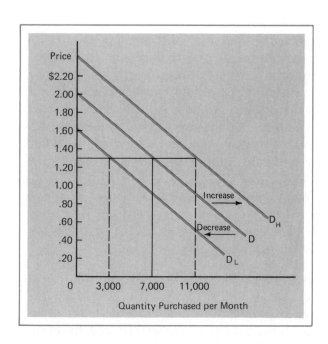

FIGURE 6–3   SHIFTS IN THE MARKET DEMAND FOR HOT FUDGE SUNDAES
An increase in demand can be represented by a shift to the right such as from D to D_H. A decrease in demand is shown by a shift to the left such as from D to D_L.

A *decrease in demand* can be illustrated by a shift of the whole demand curve to the left. In Figure 6–3 this is represented by a move from the original demand D to a lower demand D_L. Given the lower level of demand, just 3,000 hot fudge sundaes would be purchased at $1.30 each.

6–3 It is important to see that these changes in demand are different from the changes in quantity demanded. We discussed how changes in price cause a change in quantity demanded. As price changes, people buy more or less along a given demand curve. Movement from A* to B* or to C* in Figure 6–2 shows the change in quantity demanded as price changes. It is not a shift in the whole demand curve, such as that shown in Figure 6–3. When the whole demand curve changes, there is a change in demand. Some of the things that cause a change in demand are changing incomes, changing tastes of consumers, and changes in other prices.

Increases in Demand

Four factors can cause an increase in demand for a certain product:

1. Consumers' incomes may increase.

2. Consumers' attitudes may change.

3. The price of a complementary product may decrease.

4. The price of a substitute product may increase.

Let's look at each of these factors in more detail.

The Effect of Increasing Incomes. As our incomes go up, we are likely to consume more of almost all goods. Persons with higher incomes can be expected to buy more clothes, records, theater tickets, and hot fudge sundaes than persons with lower incomes. These goods, as well as most others, are what economists refer to as normal goods. **Normal goods** are goods for which demand goes up as income goes up. Goods which are not normal goods are called inferior goods. **Inferior goods** are goods for which demand goes down as income goes up. For example, some people think of ground meat as an inferior good. As a family's income goes up, they may buy less ground meat and more steak and other solid meat products. Most goods and services we see in the marketplace, however, can be thought of as normal goods.

The Effect of Changing Attitudes. A change in consumers' attitudes (tastes and preferences) can also cause demand to rise. Demand will go up if, for some reason, consumers develop a more favorable attitude about a product. Our attitudes are influenced by many

6–1
normal goods
Goods for which demand goes up as income goes up.

6–1
inferior goods
Goods for which demand goes down as income goes up.

factors. Family members often affect our attitudes about various goods and services. Other groups may also influence our attitudes about consumption. Think of the people you know at school, in clubs, at the gym, or at work. In some way, these groups probably influence your desire for certain products or your attitudes about them.

Our attitudes also are influenced by advertising. We see and hear many messages from producers and sellers of goods and services every day. These messages, or *advertisements*, attempt to influence our attitudes favorably toward a product. Almost all radio or television broadcasts include many advertisements. Magazines and newspapers also include much advertising.

(Music) Yessir, this drive started over a hundred years ago, back in California.

Just a few head of Levi's Blue Jeans, and a lot of hard miles.

Across country that would've killed ordinary pants.

But Levi's? They <u>thrived</u> on it! If anything, the herd got stronger —and bigger.

First there was <u>kid's</u> Levi's. Ornery little critters...seems like nothing stops 'em.

Then there was <u>gal's</u> pants, and tops, and skirts. Purtiest things you ever set eyes on.

And just to prove they could make it in the big city, the herd bred a new strain called Levi's Sportswear.

Jackets, shirts, slacks... a bit fancy for this job, I reckon, but I do admire the way they're made.

Fact is, pride is why we put our name on everything in this herd.

Tells folks, "This here's <u>ours</u>!" If you like what you got, then c'mon back!

We'll be here. You see, fashions may change...

...but quality <u>never</u> goes out of style!

Illustration 6–3
This advertising storyboard stirs up feelings of pride in old-fashioned quality and the Old West. Rather than showing specific styles or bargains, the ad tries to sway consumers' attitudes toward a feeling of loyalty for the Levi's name.

Exactly how much influence any of these factors has on our actual purchasing is hard to determine. However, they do affect our attitudes, and our attitudes influence how we view various forms of consumption.

The Effect of Changing Prices of Other Goods. Changes in the prices of other products can cause an increase in the demand for a good. Suppose, for example, that the price of margarine goes up. We then would expect that the amount of margarine demanded would decline. People might substitute butter for the now relatively more expensive margarine. A rise in the price of margarine, then, will cause an increase in the demand for butter. Thus, butter and margarine can be thought of as substitute products. **Substitute products** are products whose uses are similar enough that one can replace the other. The same might be true of cassette tapes and records. As the price of records goes up, the demand for tapes may rise.

Complementary products are products that are used together. If two goods are complementary products, a decrease in the price of one can increase the demand for the other. For example, suppose that the price of ski equipment would go down. More people could afford to buy skis. Thus, the demand for ski clothing and ski facilities, such as lodges and lifts, would go up.

Decreases in Demand

You have just learned the four factors which can cause demand to increase. Demand may be decreased when the opposite of these factors occurs. For example, if the price of a complementary product goes up, the demand for the original product would go down. Consider the effect of gasoline prices on the demand for automobile tires. As the price of gas goes up, people reduce the number of miles they drive. This results in less overall tire wear; therefore, tire demand goes down.

If incomes fall, people cut back on their consumption of most products (normal goods). Also, changes in attitudes can decrease as well as increase demand. Perhaps this is most noticeable with respect to clothing fashions. As our ideas about clothing change, so do our purchases of different clothing items.

Finally, consider some determinants of the demand for hot fudge sundaes. This helps explain the increase and the decrease in demand illustrated in Figure 6–3. If the price of strawberries decreased, thus making strawberry sundaes less expensive, the demand for hot fudge sundaes might fall from D to D_L. Hot fudge sundaes and strawberry sundaes are substitute goods. If the in-

6–1
substitute products
Products whose uses are similar enough that one can replace the other.

6–1
complementary products
Products that are used together.

comes of consumers in that market area went up, the demand for hot fudge sundaes might rise from D to D_H. Such a rise in demand also could result from advertising done by the ice cream shops in the area.

THE SENSITIVITY OF DEMAND

It is often useful to measure the sensitivity of changes in demand to changes in one of the determinants of demand. Elasticity is a general concept that economists, business people, and government officials rely on for such measurement. **Elasticity** may be defined as the ratio of the percentage change in quantity to the percentage change in some factor that stimulated the change in quantity.

6–5

6–1

elasticity
The ratio of the percentage change in quantity to the percentage change in some factor that stimulated the change in quantity.

Price Elasticity of Demand

The most commonly used type of elasticity is the price elasticity of demand. The **price elasticity of demand** is the ratio of the percentage change in quantity demanded to the percentage change in price that caused the quantity demanded to change. This ratio measures the relative responsiveness of quantity demanded to a change in the product's price. The formula for price elasticity of demand is shown below.

6–6

6–1

price elasticity of demand
The ratio of the percentage change in quantity demanded to the percentage change in price that caused the quantity demanded to change.

$$\frac{\text{Price}}{\text{Elasticity}} = \frac{\text{Percentage Change in Quantity Demanded}}{\text{Percentage Change in Price}}$$

Elastic Demand with Respect to Price. Suppose, for example, that a 5 percent decrease in price stimulated a 10 percent increase in the quantity demanded. The price elasticity of demand would be 2. This is found as shown below.

6–6

$$\begin{aligned}\frac{\text{Price}}{\text{Elasticity}} &= \frac{10\% \text{ Change in Quantity Demanded}}{5\% \text{ Change in Price}} \\[4pt] &= 10\% \div 5\% \\[4pt] &= 2\end{aligned}$$

If this were true for a product, we would say that the quantity demanded was quite responsive to changes in price. A 5 percent reduction in price resulted in a percentage increase in sales that is two times the percentage reduction in price.

Economists would say this demand was quite elastic with respect to price. The term *elastic* implies responsiveness. If something is elastic, it is responsive. If the calculated value of a price elasticity is greater than one, we classify demand as being *price elastic*. Thus, when economists say that a product is price elastic, they mean that the quantity demanded is quite responsive to a change in price. This is true when the percentage change in quantity is greater than the percentage change in price, as in the above example.

Cassette tape players may be a good example of products for which demand is elastic. Since there are many substitutes (radios, compact disc players, record players, and other forms of entertainment), consumers' demand for cassette players may be quite elastic. Think of some other products that you consider to be price elastic. That is, try to think of products for which you would expect the quantity demanded to be very responsive to a price change.

Inelastic Demand with Respect to Price. Now suppose that a 4 percent increase in price for a product causes the quantity demanded to fall by just 1 percent. The quantity demanded in this case is not very responsive to a price change. The numeric value of the price elasticity of demand would be 0.25. This is calculated as shown below.

6–6

$$
\begin{aligned}
\text{Price Elasticity of Demand} &= \frac{\text{1\% Change in Quantity Demanded}}{\text{4\% Change in Price}} \\
&= 1\% \div 4\% \\
&= 0.25
\end{aligned}
$$

The percentage change in quantity demanded is just one fourth as large as the percentage change in price.

When the quantity demanded is not very sensitive to a change in price, we say that demand is *price inelastic*. This is true in cases where the percentage change in quantity is less than the percentage change in price. When this happens, the calculated value of the price elasticity is less than one. Thus, in the present example, demand would be considered price inelastic since the calculated value is just 0.25. Table salt is a good example of a product which has an inelastic demand. There are few good substitutes and spending on salt is a small part of total household spending. Thus, people are not very sensitive to the price of salt.

Unitary Price Elasticity of Demand. It is possible that the percentage change in quantity demanded would exactly equal the percentage change in price. In such a case the calculated value of the price elasticity would equal one. For example, suppose that a 3 percent decrease in price caused a 3 percent increase in the quantity demanded. The price elasticity of demand would be figured as below.

$$\text{Price Elasticity of Demand} = \frac{3\% \text{ Change in Quantity Demanded}}{3\% \text{ Change in Price}}$$

$$= 3\% \div 3\%$$

$$= 1$$

This is a case of *unitary price elasticity* because the calculated value is equal to one (or unity).

What Determines the Price Elasticity of Demand?

It is possible to make some predictions about the price elasticity for a product. There are three factors which generally are considered important in determining the price elasticity of demand:

1. The number of substitute products
2. The importance of the product in the consumer's budget
3. The time period considered

The Number of Substitute Products. The most important factor in determining the elasticity of a product with respect to the price is the number of substitute products available. The more substitutes available, the more price elastic we can expect demand to be. If there are few substitute products available, we would expect demand to be inelastic.

Consider some specific examples to illustrate this point. The demand for gasoline in the United States has been estimated to have a price elasticity of about 0.30. Thus, we would classify gas as price inelastic. How does this fit with our explanation of the number of substitute products available? Given the current state of technology, there are virtually no substitutes for gasoline. Gasohol and even electric-powered cars *may* one day provide important substitutes. Until then, the only real substitute is to use other forms of transportation which use no gas or which conserve gas. Bicycles use no gas. Using buses, car pools, or more efficient cars conserves gas. Americans have shown that they are not willing to reduce gas consumption by very much as the price increases.

There are products that are much more sensitive to price changes. It has been found, for example, that the demand for haddock (an Atlantic fish) is quite price elastic. The price elasticity for haddock has been estimated to be 2.2. There are, of course, many substitutes for haddock such as codfish and other fish. Even meats such as beef, lamb, pork, chicken, and turkey are substitutes for haddock.

The Importance of the Product in the Consumer's Budget. A second factor which often influences the price elasticity of demand is the importance of the product in the consumer's budget. If expenditures on a product are a small fraction of a consumer's budget, demand will be more price inelastic. If the product represents a large fraction of consumer spending, demand will be more elastic. For example, we would expect table salt to have a very inelastic demand. Few consumers purchase enough salt to even remember if it is 20¢ per pound or 60¢ per pound. At either price, a pound of table salt would be a small fraction of a consumer's food budget. The fraction of the total budget would be even less. On the other hand, products which represent major purchases would be expected to have a more elastic demand. Examples include the purchase of an appliance such as a refrigerator, range, or microwave oven.

The Time Period Considered. Finally, price elasticity may depend on the length of the time period being considered. The shorter the time period, the more inelastic demand will be. As the time period considered increases, estimates of demand will usually be more elastic. Consumers will have more time to adjust to price changes and perhaps to find substitute products. If your home is heated with fuel oil and its price doubles, you may not be able to do much about it this winter. You can keep the house cooler and take shorter showers, but you cannot do much more. Over a longer period of time, you may be able to convert to other energy sources, such as wood or solar heating.

Income Elasticity of Demand

6–1

income elasticity of demand

The percentage change in quantity divided by the percentage change in income that caused the change in demand.

Economists are interested in how responsive demand is to changes in consumers' incomes. To measure this responsiveness, economists use the income elasticity of demand. **Income elasticity of demand** is the percentage change in quantity divided by the percentage change in income that caused the change in demand. This is calculated using the following formula:

$$\text{Income Elasticity of Demand} = \frac{\text{Percentage Change in Quantity}}{\text{Percentage Change in Income}}$$

Illustration 6–4
Buying a refrigerator would take up a large part of a household's budget. Therefore, the demand for refrigerators tends to be price elastic.

This ratio measures the relative responsiveness of demand to changes in consumers' incomes.

Income Elastic Demand. If demand is very responsive to changes in income, that demand is *income elastic*. When demand is income elastic, the percentage change in quantity is greater than the percentage change in income. Therefore, the calculated value of the income elasticity will be greater than one.

We might expect, for example, that the demand for eating out at restaurants would be fairly sensitive to people's incomes. The income elasticity in this case has been estimated at about 1.5. Thus, a 2 percent increase in income would be associated with about a 3 percent increase in restaurant consumption. We would calculate this income elasticity as shown below.

$$\text{Income Elasticity of Demand} = \frac{3\% \text{ Change in Quantity}}{2\% \text{ Change in Income}}$$

$$= 3\% \div 2\%$$

$$= 1.5$$

Income Inelastic Demand. When demand is not very responsive to a change in income, the income elasticity is less than one. In these cases, the product is *income inelastic*. This means that the percentage change in quantity is less than the percentage change in income that caused demand to change.

Haddock, an Atlantic fish, is a product that is income inelastic. A 4 percent increase in consumers' incomes could only be expected to increase haddock consumption by 2 percent. Thus, the income elasticity of demand for haddock can be calculated as below.

$$\text{Income Elasticity of Demand} = \frac{2\% \text{ Change in Quantity}}{4\% \text{ Change in Income}}$$

$$= 2\% \div 4\%$$

$$= 0.5$$

Since the calculated income elasticity is less than one, the product (haddock) is income inelastic.

Unitary Income Elasticity of Demand. If the calculated value of an income elasticity equals one, the good has a *unitary income elasticity*. This would be true if the percentage changes in quantity and in income were exactly the same. For example, if a 5 percent increase in income stimulated a 5 percent sales increase, income elasticity would equal one.

$$\text{Income Elasticity of Demand} = \frac{5\% \text{ Change in Quantity}}{5\% \text{ Change in Income}}$$

$$= 5\% \div 5\%$$

$$= 1$$

TOTAL REVENUE AND DEMAND

So far, we have looked at demand from a consumer's point of view. Let's shift our attention to the seller. After all, in every sale there is a buyer and a seller. Sellers of products have a strong interest in the demand for those products. In particular, the sellers of a product are interested in the amount of money they can obtain from various levels of sales.

6–7

6–1

total revenue

The amount of money a company receives from sales of a product.

The amount of money a company receives from sales of a product is called **total revenue**. A company's total revenue is the same dollar amount as the total spending of the consumers who purchase the company's product. Suppose, for example, that Mike Lin (the consumer of hot fudge sundaes) buys six sundaes a month at a price of $1.40 each. (See Mike's demand schedule for hot fudge sundaes in Table 6–1.) Mike's total spending for hot fudge sundaes is $8.40 a month. This total amount is found by multiplying $1.40 per sundae by the number of sundaes purchased each month.

Mike's Total Monthly Spending on
Hot Fudge Sundaes   = ($1.40 per sundae) × (6 sundaes)

= $8.40

Assume that Mike always goes to Sally's Sundae Shop for his hot fudge sundaes. If Sally sells hot fudge sundaes only to Mike, her total revenue will be $8.40 a month.

Sally's Total Monthly Revenue from
Mike's Purchases   = ($1.40 per sundae) × (6 sundaes)

= $8.40

Of course, Mike is not Sally's only customer. Assume that in this market Sally's shop is just one of five sundae shops. Furthermore, assume that the market demand (from Table 6–2) is equally divided among all five stores. Then the demand for hot fudge sundaes from Sally's Sundae Shop equals one fifth (or 20 percent) of the total market demand. The demand schedule for sundaes from her shop is shown in Table 6–3.

TABLE 6–3

DEMAND SCHEDULE FOR HOT FUDGE
SUNDAES FOR SALLY'S SUNDAE SHOP

Price	Quantity Purchased per Month
$2.00	0
1.80	400
1.60	800
1.40	1,200
1.20	1,600
1.00	2,000
.80	2,400
.60	2,800

At a price of $1.40 per sundae, Sally's total revenue from all sales would be equal to the price ($1.40) times the quantity sold (1,200). The formula for calculating total revenue is as follows: 6–7

Total Revenue = Price × Quantity Sold

Sally's Total

Revenue from All Sales = ($1.40 per sundae) × (1,200 sundaes)

= $1,680.00

You already know that the quantity sold is determined in part by the product's price. You might then expect that a company's total revenue will vary, depending on the price charged for the product. To illustrate this, let's again use the demand for Sally's hot fudge sundaes. In Table 6–4, we have calculated the total revenue from the sale of hot fudge sundaes for each of the prices used before. In each case, total revenue equals price times the quantity sold.

TABLE 6–4

DEMAND SCHEDULE FOR HOT FUDGE SUNDAES
FROM SALLY'S SUNDAE SHOP AND THE TOTAL
REVENUE DERIVED FROM SALES

Price (P)	Quantity Sold per Month (Q)	Total Revenue per Month $TR = P \times Q$
$2.00	0	$ 0.00
1.80	400	720.00
1.60	800	1,280.00
1.40	1,200	1,680.00
1.20	1,600	1,920.00
1.00	2,000	2,000.00
.80	2,400	1,920.00
.60	2,800	1,680.00

This table shows some interesting relationships. You see that, at first, price cuts stimulate enough new sales that total revenue goes up. But note that this is not always the case. Down to a price of $1, total revenue rises as price falls and quantity goes up. However, if price is reduced below $1, the additional sales do not compensate for the lower price per unit. This results in lower total revenue.

THINKING
ABOUT ECONOMIC ISSUES

Advertising plays an important role in our economy. Companies advertise to inform consumers about their products or services. Advertising is also used to change people's attitudes about a company's products or services. We all see many types of advertising every day.

Some advertising is meant to encourage us to take some immediate action. For example, the grocery store advertisement in the morning paper may urge us to buy turkey, or laundry detergent, or a tube of toothpaste. This type of advertising often gives us very specific information about sizes, prices, and other product characteristics.

Other advertising focuses on creating an overall product image. Consider television commercials. Some have little specific product information and instead project an image of what it's like to consume that product. Airline commercials are often like this. They show happy, smiling people in pleasant, popular vacation areas. They say little about specific schedules, prices, or types of planes.

The purpose of nearly all advertising is to increase the demand for some product. By changing consumers' attitudes, a producer can expect to increase the amount it can sell at each price. This can be shown by a rightward shift of the firm's demand curve. Look at the two demand curves below. The one to the left shows the quantities that consumers would buy at each price with no advertising. At the $20 price the firm would sell 100 units. However, if the firm advertises, the demand curve may shift to the right. Then, at the same price, 150 units could be sold. Product managers must evaluate whether the increase in sales is enough to justify the money spent on the advertising.

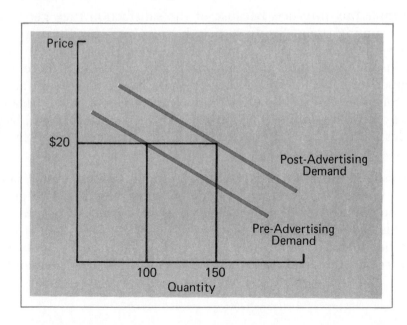

There is a great deal of evidence that managers believe advertising is a good way to increase sales. For example, in a recent year nearly $118 billion was spent on advertising. Some of the major advertising media and the amounts spent on each are shown below:

Medium	Amount Spent
Newspapers	$31,197,000,000
Television	25,686,000,000
Direct Mail	21,115,000,000
Radio	7,798,000,000
Magazines	6,072,000,000

The rest of the $118 billion was spread over such media as farm publications, business papers, and outdoor advertising.[1]

You might want to look in your school library for the most recent *Statistical Abstract of the United States* and see how these amounts have changed over recent years. Look for a table entitled "Advertising—Estimated Expenditures, by Medium."

---

[1]U.S. Bureau of the Census, *Statistical Abstract of the United States*, 110th ed. (Washington, D.C., 1990), 557.

REVIEWING THE CHAPTER

1. People buy products because of the satisfaction they get from consuming them. Products may have *value in use* but may not have an *economic value*. For example, we get satisfaction from consuming air, but we do not pay for its use because there is so much available for free. Other products have a *value in use* and a *value in exchange*. These goods have an economic value because we are willing to pay for their use. Products such as pizzas, bicycles, and clothes have an economic or exchange value that is expressed as a price.

6-1 2. Most goods that we consume give us diminishing marginal satisfaction. As we consume a greater number of units (in a given time period), each *additional unit* gives less *additional satisfaction*. This is one reason that people will buy a greater quantity of a good only at lower prices. The inverse relationship between price and the quantity demanded is called the law of demand.

6-2, 6-4   3. The relationship between price and quantity demanded can be shown in a table as a demand schedule or in a graph as a demand curve. The overall level of demand can be affected by four factors: (1) consumers' incomes, (2) consumers' tastes and preferences (attitudes), (3) the prices of substitute products, and (4) the prices of complementary products. Changes in any of these four factors can cause a change in demand. A change in demand can be represented on a graph as a shift of the demand curve. An increase in demand is shown as a shift of the demand curve to the right. A shift of the demand curve to the left indicates a decrease in demand.

6-5, 6-6   4. It is important to measure the sensitivity of demand to changes in various factors. The most important of these factors are the product's price and consumers' incomes. The measure of responsiveness or sensitivity most often used is called elasticity. Price elasticity measures the responsiveness of quantity demanded to price changes. Income elasticity measures the responsiveness of demand to changes in consumers' incomes.

6-7   5. A business usually is concerned with the total revenue received from selling a product. If a company changes its price, the quantity sold is likely to change. It is also likely that the total revenue received will change. It is useful to understand how total revenue will change as price changes. A company can always increase sales by lowering price, but total revenue may increase or decrease as a result.

REVIEWING ECONOMIC TERMS

6-1   Supply definitions for the following terms:

demand	normal goods
law of demand	inferior goods
diminishing marginal utility	substitute products
income effect	complementary products
substitution effect	elasticity
demand schedule	price elasticity of demand
demand curve	income elasticity of demand
determinants of demand	total revenue

REVIEWING ECONOMIC CONCEPTS

6–1 1. What happens to demand as a result of the income effect?

6–1 2. What happens to demand as a result of the substitution effect?

6–2 3. What is the advantage of a demand curve over a demand schedule?

6–4 4. How does changing income affect demand?

6–4 5. How do changing attitudes affect demand?

6–4 6. How does changing other prices affect demand?

6–5 7. What are three kinds of price elasticity of demand? What do they mean?

6–5 8. What factors influence the price elasticity of demand?

6–5 9. What are three kinds of income elasticity of demand? What do they mean?

6–7 10. How is total revenue determined from a demand schedule?

APPLYING ECONOMIC CONCEPTS

1. Why are people willing to pay a price for the right to consume any product or service? Why would you be willing to pay for a cassette tape?

6–1 2. Explain how the principle of diminishing marginal utility would influence your consumption of hot fudge sundaes. Give several other examples of goods you buy that have diminishing marginal utility.

6–2 3. Explain the difference between a demand schedule and a demand curve. Construct an example of each.

6–4 4. What factors have influenced the demand for bicycles in the last few years? Focus your attention on income, attitudes, and the prices of other products. Explain how changes in these factors would have either increased or decreased the demand for bicycles.

6–1 5. If the price of housing (rent or house payments) goes up, there may be an income effect on your family. What does this mean? What is the relationship between prices and income?

6–5 6. Since the early 1970s, much public attention has been focused on the demand for gasoline. Economists have found that the demand for gas is inelastic with respect to price. What does this mean? Why would the demand for gasoline be price inelastic?

6–7   7. A simple demand schedule for a company is given below.

Price	Quantity
$6	0
$5	1
$4	2
$3	3
$2	4
$1	5

Find the dollar value of total revenue at each of the six prices. At what price will total revenue be the greatest? How many units would sell at that price?

6–5   8. Choose two products and explain why you think their demand is price elastic or price inelastic. Be sure to consider the three things that determine price elasticity in preparing your answer.

6–3   9. Explain the difference between a change in quantity demanded and a change in demand. Draw a graph to show this difference.

DEMAND AND PERSONAL CREDIT

You have seen that consumers' demand is affected by their level of income. Current income can, however, be supplemented by the use of credit (borrowing). Often the availability of credit makes it easy for people to spend more than they can really afford. Credit cards from banks (such as a VISA or MasterCard), from retail stores (such as Sears or Penneys), or from gasoline retailers (such as Mobil or Texaco) are readily available. People may also borrow from banks, credit unions, or savings and loans for such things as appliances or cars.

You need to be careful about how much you borrow. How much credit can you afford? As a rule of thumb, the amount of credit payments you make each month should be less than 20 percent of your take-home pay. Thus, if you make $2,000 per month with take-home pay of $1,500, you should not have more than $300 a month in credit payments. This does not include housing. Many experts say that 20 percent is a maximum and that 15 percent is better. Thus, with take-home pay of $1,500 per month you would want credit payments of $225 or less.

For additional information on consumer credit see either of these two publications: *Your Guide to Consumer Credit*, American Bar Association, Public Education Division, 1988, and *Using Plastic: A Young Adult's Guide to Credit Cards*, Federal Trade Commission, January 1989.

CHAPTER 7

SUPPLY: PRODUCING GOODS AND SERVICES

Learning Objectives

7-1 Define terms related to supply.

7-2 Describe four factors of production.

7-3 Calculate average product and marginal product.

7-4 Describe three kinds of returns to scale.

7-5 Explain the difference between a change in quantity supplied and a change in supply.

7-6 Calculate price elasticity of supply.

7-7 Describe three kinds of price elasticity of supply.

7-8 Explain how costs and the principle of diminishing marginal productivity affect the level of production.

WHY PRODUCTION TAKES PLACE

In a society that depends on a market economy, most production decisions are made by people in the private sector. People produce goods and services to gain certain benefits. These benefits include money income as well as several kinds of psychic income or satisfaction.

Working involves opportunity costs. Most of us would rather play tennis, dance, hike, or enjoy some activity other than work. To make up for those opportunity costs, we must get some benefits from working. We work because of the compensation, particularly money, that we receive for our efforts. We then use this money to buy goods and services.

It is often said that the desire to make money fuels the great engine of a productive economy. Each of us uses our productive abilities in a way that satisfies us the most. Suppose you have the chance to clerk at a store or to work an equal number of hours in the public library. Furthermore, suppose that you would like both jobs equally well. The job as a clerk pays $4.25 an hour, but the library job pays just $3.75 an hour. Which job would you choose? Given these choices, almost everyone would choose the job as a clerk. Some people, however, might choose the library job if it provided greater psychic income. We are all free to follow our own best interests in using our productive abilities.

Illustration 7–1
Production does not take place just because people like to work. We work for the benefits we receive. Like the nurse shown here, we might work for the psychic income we receive as well as for the salary we get to pay for food and other items we need.

The Four Factors of Production

7–2

7–1

factor of production
Anything used to produce a good or service.

A **factor of production** is anything used to produce a good or service. Labor is not the only contributor to the production process. There are four broad categories of factors of production: (1) land, (2) labor, (3) capital, and (4) entrepreneurship. Each of these factors can be divided into many smaller parts.

Land. Land is a broad measure representing all the basic natural resources that contribute to production. A Midwestern farm, a coal field in Wyoming, a Florida orange orchard and a natural gas well in Oklahoma are all examples of the factor of production called land.

Labor. Labor represents the human factor of production. Truck drivers, nurses, dockworkers, baseball players, and authors are all part of the factor of production we call labor. The jobs and skills are very different, but they all fall into this broad category of labor.

Capital. Capital includes previously produced goods that aid in producing still other goods. Office buildings, schools, factories, automobiles, tractors, and computers are all forms of capital equipment. Look around and you will note other kinds of capital equipment.

Entrepreneurship. Entrepreneurship includes the managerial ability and risk taking that contribute so much to a productive economy. Few people can organize, direct, and control other people and resources efficiently and productively. Only an able person who is willing to accept risks will be a successful entrepreneur. We all benefit from the work of such people.

Ownership and Control of Factors of Production

In a free enterprise economy, all factors of production are owned or controlled by individuals. Therefore, we can use our labor and the other factors we control to produce goods and services in exchange for monetary and nonmonetary rewards. If you own a large truck, you can use it to haul any goods you wish. You probably will choose to haul those things for which you can receive the most money.

Production takes place as owners of the factors of production allocate their land, labor, capital, and entrepreneurship in a manner that maximizes their expected returns. Thus, the profit motive is of great importance in guiding the production of goods and services in the economy.

MEASURING PRODUCTION

Businesses measure how much is produced during different time periods. For example, a company may keep track of how much is produced on a yearly, monthly, weekly, or even an hourly basis. Without accurate measures of production, it is impossible to manage a business well.

Counting Units Versus Counting Dollars

Output is best measured in units sold rather than in the money value of sales. Using units sold makes it easier to compare sales from one time period to another. To see why this is so, let's look at a simple example. Table 7–1 shows the Lumin Company's production and sales of table lamps for six years. The first column indicates the year. The second column is sales in units, and the third column shows the total dollar value of sales per year.

TABLE 7–1

LUMIN COMPANY LAMP SALES (YEARS 1–6)

Year	Unit Sales	Dollar Sales
1	121,292	$5,882,662
2	128,570	6,360,358
3	124,998	6,492,834
4	121,747	6,576,924
5	126,253	6,956,750
6	124,727	7,078,885

A sales pattern such as this is fairly common and can be misleading. If the company's owners look only at the dollar amount of sales, they might think the company was doing quite well, because sales in Year 6 were up 20 percent over Year 1. One could even say that sales increased each year. But what has really happened? The number of units produced and sold has only increased about 3 percent between Year 1 and Year 6. Also, there have been ups and downs from year to year that can cause scheduling problems.

The dollar sales hide the fact that sales actually dropped in Years 3, 4, and 6. During times when prices are going up, this can happen easily. A company that looks only at the dollar level of sales may make bad business decisions. So, it is better to measure output in units.

Total Product

7–1

total product

All the units of a product produced in a given period of time, such as one year.

The production and sales listed in units for the Lumin Company represent a measure of output called total product. **Total product** is all the units of a product produced in a given period of time, such as one year. For the Lumin Company, 124,727 lamps represent the total product for Year 6.

Average Product

7–1

average product

The number of units of output produced per unit of input.

Two other measures of output are often used. One is average product. **Average product** is the number of units of output produced per unit of input. Suppose we want to calculate the average product of labor for the Lumin Company. Think of one day's work as one labor unit. During Year 6, 88 people worked for Lumin for five days each week for 50 weeks a year. Therefore, the number of labor units used in Year 6 would be figured as follows.

$$\text{Labor Units} = (88 \text{ workers}) \times (5 \text{ days/week}) \times (50 \text{ weeks/year})$$
$$= 22{,}000 \text{ workers/year}$$

7–3

The average product per labor unit then would be total output for Year 6 divided by the number of labor units. Since 124,727 lamps were produced in Year 6 by 22,000 labor units, average product is figured as below.

$$\text{Average Product} = \text{Units of Output} \div \text{Units of Input}$$

$$\text{Average Product} = 124{,}727 \text{ lamps} \div 22{,}000 \text{ workers}$$
$$= 5.67 \text{ lamps/worker}$$

Thus, each worker produced an average of almost six lamps per day.

Marginal Product

7–3

7–1

marginal product

The amount that total product increases or decreases if one more unit of an input is used.

The other measure of output that is often used is marginal product. **Marginal product** is the amount that total product increases or decreases if one more unit of an input is used. We can illustrate this concept using the Lumin Company again. Suppose that the company employed 90 workers each day last week and produced 504 lamps per day. Then yesterday the company hired

Illustration 7–2
We can measure production in many different ways. We could, for example, count the number of cookies produced here. Or we could count the dollar value of the cookies this man bakes. We could measure, in a larger sense, the total number of baked goods produced by the entire factory. Or we could calculate the average number of cookies the baker can make in a day's work.

one additional worker and the total product increased to 509 lamps. The additional output, or marginal product, would be five lamps.

Marginal product is very important in making production decisions. The dollar value of additional output should always be compared with the dollar cost of the additional input. If the dollar value of the added output is larger than the cost of the added input, then hiring that unit of input will raise the firm's profit.

The Short Run and the Long Run

Production has two time frames: the short run and the long run. The **short run** is any period during which the usable amount of at least one input is fixed, while the usable amount of at least one other input can change. The **long run** is a period during which the amounts of all inputs used can be changed.

Suppose you own a small bakery and have a 2,000 square-foot building in which you prepare and sell baked goods. Assume that your capital is limited to the existing ovens, building space, and other equipment. You would then be operating in the short run. The amount of labor you hire may be the only variable factor of production.

If sales are good, you might hire more bakers and salespeople to increase your production. But you may not be able to increase

7–1
short run
Any period during which the usable amount of at least one input is fixed, while the usable amount of at least one other input can change.

7–1
long run
A period during which the amounts of all inputs used can be changed.

output in this way for long. Eventually you will need extra space and more equipment. As you begin to change all factors of production, you move from the short run to the long run.

Short-run and long-run periods are not determined by the calendar. They are determined by the ability to change the rate of use of the factors of production. For the bakery example, the long run may not be long in terms of time. You probably could expand your building and get additional equipment in place in two or three months. For some firms it would take much longer. A power company, for example, may need ten years or more to increase plant capacity.

The average and marginal product measures defined earlier in this chapter are short-run measures. They are short-run measures because there is some base of fixed factors that the variable factor worked with in both cases. Calculating the average or marginal product of labor assumes other factors are constant. If the amount of capital for workers to use goes up, we would expect their average and marginal products to rise. For example, an accountant using just paper and pencil may be able to service only 2 accounts per day. The same person could handle perhaps 6 accounts per day using an electronic calculator and maybe 25 accounts per day using a small computer.

DIMINISHING MARGINAL PRODUCTIVITY

7–1

diminishing marginal productivity
The principle that as more of any variable input is added to a fixed amount of other inputs, the rate at which output goes up becomes less and less.

Diminishing marginal productivity is the principle that as more of any variable input is added to a fixed amount of other inputs, the rate at which output goes up becomes less and less. This does not mean that output necessarily declines as more of the input is used. It means that output increases less and less rapidly as additional units of the input are used.

Diminishing Marginal Productivity in Retail Sales

Suppose that K mart decides to open a new store in your city. If the store hires no labor (clerks, cashiers, etc.), no sales can be made. If only one person is hired, not many customers can be served. But as more people are hired, more customers can be served and more sales will result.

Will each extra employee increase K mart's sales by an equal amount per employee? Even if we assume that each worker is equally skilled, the answer is no. As more and more workers are added, the rate at which they add to higher production eventually becomes less. Indeed, K mart could hire so many workers that sales per worker would decrease. If the typical K mart had 2,000 workers in the store, there would be no room for customers. Sales would fall to zero, just as if the store had hired no workers.

With no workers, sales are zero. But as people are hired, sales increase up to some point. If the number of workers eventually becomes too large, sales can fall and go back to zero. The best level of employment is somewhere in between. However, the best level varies from case to case. The tools of economics can be very helpful in finding the best level of employment.

Diminishing Marginal Productivity in Farming

Suppose you have a small farm in Ohio with a fixed amount of land. You have a given amount of equipment and two people's labor to use. The input we will consider as variable in this example is fertilizer.

The first pound of fertilizer used on each acre of ground will increase your crop yield by some amount. Exactly what amount will depend on how badly the soil needs fertilizer. A second pound added to each acre of land will likely be a little less effective in helping you grow more per acre. As you add more and more fertilizer, each additional pound per acre has less effect on output.

What do you think would happen if you spread three inches of fertilizer over one acre of land in which you have planted corn? How much corn would you expect to grow? Probably nothing would grow on that acre of land. It would be burned out by too much fertilizer.

A small amount of fertilizer helps, but three inches is clearly too much. By using careful analysis, the best amount of fertilizer can be determined for each field. One branch of economics, *agricultural economics,* deals directly with problems like this. In almost every state, at least one major college has a large staff of agricultural economists who help farmers determine the best level of inputs to use.

More is not necessarily better when it comes to productive inputs. As in the two examples discussed, it is possible in all cases to have too much of any one input. This is so because of the principle of diminishing marginal productivity.

Diminishing Marginal Productivity: A Numerical Example

Table 7–2 illustrates this concept with a numerical example. When no labor is hired, output is zero. With 10 units of labor, output goes up to 100. With 20 units of labor, output increases to 160.

TABLE 7–2

NUMERICAL EXAMPLE OF HOW THE THREE MEASURES OF OUT-
PUT VARY AS THE AMOUNT OF THE LABOR INPUT CHANGES

Level	Labor Units Hired	Total Output Produced	Average Product	Marginal Product
A	0	0	*	*
B	10	100	10	10
C	20	160	8	6
D	30	180	6	2
E	40	160	4	−2
F	50	100	2	−6

*A value cannot be determined

Using 30 units of labor, 180 units of output result. However, using another 10 units of labor (40 units total) causes output to fall back to 160. Output falls still further if yet another 10 units of labor are hired.

7–3 **Calculating Average Product.** Remember that average product is found by dividing the amount of output produced by the number of units of input used. For example, at Level *C*, 20 units of labor produce 160 units of output. At that point, average product is figured as shown below.

Average Product at Level *C* = Total Output ÷ Number of Units of Labor

$$= 160 \div 20$$
$$= 8$$

Practice finding the average product at the other levels and compare your results with those in Table 7–2.

7–3 **Calculating Marginal Product.** Marginal product is the change in total output as a variable input is increased. Marginal product is found by dividing the change in output by the corresponding change in input. For example, marginal product between Levels *A* and *B* is calculated on page 123.

Marginal Product = Change in Total Output ÷ Change in Input

$$\text{Marginal Product Between } A \text{ and } B = \text{Change in Total Output} \div \text{Change in Labor Units}$$
$$= (\text{Output } B - \text{Output } A) \div (\text{Labor } B - \text{Labor } A)$$
$$= (100 - 0) \div (10 - 0)$$
$$= 100 \div 10$$
$$= 10$$

Notice in Table 7–2 that marginal product can be negative. This means that total output would decline as additional units of the input are used. This could happen if too many sales clerks were hired or if too much fertilizer were spread on a field. For the examples in Table 7–2 and Figure 7–1, this can be seen between Levels *D* and *E*, as well as between *E* and *F*.

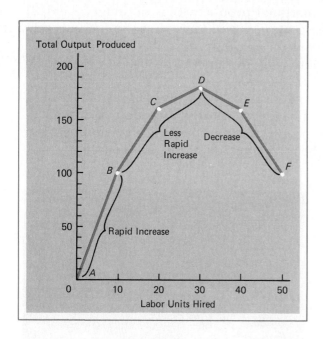

FIGURE 7–1   A GRAPHIC REPRESENTATION OF DIMINISHING MARGINAL PRODUCTIVITY

Total product increases rapidly at first when labor usage is increased. Then output increases less rapidly when labor goes from 10 units to 20 units, and from 20 units to 30 units. Beyond 30 units of labor, output actually declines.

$$\text{Marginal Product Between } D \text{ and } E = \text{Change in Total Output} \div \text{Change in Labor Units}$$
$$= (\text{Output } E - \text{Output } D) \div (\text{Labor } E - \text{Labor } D)$$
$$= (160 - 180) \div (40 - 30)$$
$$= (-20) \div (10)$$
$$= -2$$

Practice finding marginal product between other levels and check your answers against the values in Table 7–2.

Figure 7–1 is a graphic representation·of the total output shown in Table 7–2. Notice that total output increases rapidly at first when labor units are increased. Then output increases less rapidly and finally declines, as more labor units are added.

The concept of diminishing marginal productivity is very important. It is not possible to go on adding any one factor of production without getting less and less *additional* output. This is true in nearly all production situations, from farming to education to steel production.

CHANGING THE SCALE OF PRODUCTION

7–1

scale of production
The overall level of use of all factors of production.

7–1

returns to scale
The relationship between changes in scale of production and changes in output.

7–4

Remember that in the long run the level of use of all inputs can be changed. When all inputs are increased, we say that the scale of production increases. **Scale of production** is the overall level of use of all factors of production. If all inputs are increased, the principle of diminishing marginal productivity is no longer valid. If K mart kept enlarging a store, it could hire more employees without having the problem of crowding described earlier. Or if a farmer kept adding more land, the amount of fertilizer used could be increased as well.

Returns to scale is a term used to describe what happens when the scale of production changes. **Returns to scale** is the relationship between changes in scale of production and changes in output. Returns to scale may be increasing, decreasing, or constant.

Illustration 7–3
Scale of production is the overall level of use of all factors of production. For example, the level of use of labor, capital equipment, and everything else it takes to make a car would equal the scale of production.

Increasing Returns to Scale

Many products, such as cars, steel, and home appliances, are produced more efficiently on a large scale. In each case, production is characterized by *increasing returns to scale*, in which the level of output increases more rapidly than the rate of increase in the use of inputs. For example, if the use of all inputs is doubled and output more than doubles, there are increasing returns to scale.

Constant and Decreasing Returns to Scale

In some forms of production, doubling all inputs results in exactly twice as much output. That is, output increases at the same rate as all inputs are increased. Using 20 percent more inputs would cause 20 percent more output to be produced. When this is true, there are *constant returns to scale*.

In other situations, output may go up less rapidly than the rate at which input usage goes up. This is called *decreasing returns to scale*. For example, if the use of all inputs were increased by 50 percent but output increased by only 30 percent, there would be decreasing returns to scale.

PRODUCTION RESULTS IN COSTS

If you ask people in business about problems they face, their answers almost always include the problem of dealing with rising costs. Costs are incurred through the production process.

Costs Represent Payments to Factors of Production

The costs that a company incurs represent payments to factors of production or to the supplier of some intermediate good, such as steel used in making a car. Remember that the factors of production are land, labor, capital, and entrepreneurship. The payments to these factors are called rent, wages, interest, and profit, respectively. The four factors of production and their payments are shown in Table 7–3.

Dollars that are spent for intermediate goods are eventually used for these same factors of production. Thus, all costs are related to the factors of production at some stage in the production process.

TABLE 7–3

THE FOUR FACTORS OF PRODUCTION AND THEIR PAYMENTS

Payment		Factor of Production
Rent		Land
Wages	in	Labor
Interest	exchange	Capital
Profit	for	Entrepreneurship

Explicit Costs and Opportunity Costs

Some costs are easy for the firm to see and account for. Others can often be overlooked. For example, suppose that Mr. and Mrs. Tando have both been working for the past 20 years. Most recently, Mr. Tando has been a word processing specialist for a large firm, and Mrs. Tando has been a computer programmer for a bank. They have always wanted to own a business. Now that they are both about 40, they have decided to open their own business selling small computers for home use.

After looking into this type of business, they believe that they can get one started using $50,000 from savings accounts and stock. They could also borrow money based on the value of their house. The bank has said that the Tando's house could be the basis for a $60,000 bank loan. So, they can get $110,000 to start the business.

They can rent store space in a shopping center for $1,200 per month. They will have to spend $20,000 to get the space designed for their use. They will have to buy $90,000 worth of computer equipment to stock the store to begin business. Also, they will have to hire two employees and pay for a telephone, electricity, and advertising.

Mr. Tando has drawn up the estimate in Table 7–4 of a typical month's costs for the business. He has assumed that they will borrow $60,000 from the bank at 20 percent interest. They will make a $1,500 monthly payment on this loan.

The costs in Table 7–4 are all clear and easily recognizable. They represent explicit payments to other people. For this reason, they are called explicit costs. **Explicit costs** are payments made to others as a cost of running a business.

Mrs. Tando has made her own list of their monthly costs, which are much higher than Mr. Tando's. She thinks they should count on $8,475 a month in costs. Since the Tandos have been working together in planning this business, we might have thought they would be closer in their cost estimates. Why would they be so far apart? What costs might Mr. Tando have left out of his list? Let's

7–1
explicit costs

Payments made to others as a cost of running a business.

TABLE 7–4

MR. TANDO'S MONTHLY COST ESTIMATES

Item	Monthly Cost
1. Rent (to the mall)	$ 1,200.00
2. Loan Payment (to the bank)	1,500.00
3. Wages (to two employees)	1,800.00
4. Electricity (to electric company)	100.00
5. Telephone (to telephone company)	40.00
6. Advertising (to local papers)	160.00
Total Monthly Costs	$4,800.00

look at Mrs. Tando's costs in Table 7–5 to answer these questions. In Mrs. Tando's cost estimate, the first six items are the same as Mr. Tando's. The difference comes in the last two items.

TABLE 7–5

MRS. TANDO'S MONTHLY COST ESTIMATES

Item	Monthly Cost
1. Rent (to the mall)	$1,200.00
2. Loan Payment (to the bank)	1,500.00
3. Wages (to two employees)	1,800.00
4. Electricity (to electric company)	100.00
5. Telephone (to telephone company)	40.00
6. Advertising (to local papers)	160.00
7. Owners' Salaries (to themselves)	3,300.00
8. Interest (to themselves)	375.00
Total Monthly Costs	$8,475.00

Look at the last two items in Table 7–5 more closely. Mrs. Tando reasons that their present earnings are a cost of giving up their jobs and using their time to run the new business. Mr. Tando presently earns $1,500 per month, and Mrs. Tando earns $1,800 per month. They make a total of $3,300 each month at their present jobs. Mrs. Tando believes (and correctly so) that this income they would give up is a cost of the new business. It is an example of an *opportunity cost*.

What about the last item in Mrs. Tando's list—interest to Mr. and Mrs. Tando? Remember that they would be using $50,000 of their own money to start the business. Part of this money is currently in a savings account, and part is in the stocks they own. They earn an average of 9 percent interest per year on this money. That amounts to $4,500 per year, or $375 per month. By putting the $50,000 into their own business, they give up that $375. Interest on savings is also an opportunity cost that should be included as part of the cost of their new business.

You can see the importance of including both explicit costs that are easily recognized and opportunity costs. Assume the Tandos' business is expected to have net revenue from sales of $6,000 per month. Then the business would appear worthwhile, based on Mr. Tando's original estimate of their monthly costs. But using the total costs from Mrs. Tando's list, $6,000 in sales per month is less than the business's monthly costs. Therefore, the Tandos should keep their other jobs and leave their $50,000 in savings and stocks. Only if net sales will be greater than $8,475 per month will the Tandos be better off with the new business. (If the Tandos get a lot of psychic income from owning their business, however, they might still do so even if they earn less money.)

Costs and the Level of Production

7–8   As businesses change the level of output, the cost of producing each unit is likely to change. Remember that in the short run, production is subject to the principle of diminishing marginal productivity. That is, as added units of labor (or other variable inputs) are used, the rate at which output increases becomes less. Each new worker adds less to total output than the previous one.

This diminishing marginal productivity means that as output is increased, each added dollar's worth of labor input adds fewer units to output. So, the cost per unit of output goes up. Firms that want to increase production without increasing all inputs will find that the cost per unit of output becomes greater.

Over the long run, costs per unit of output may fall, rise, or stay the same. What happens depends on whether the type of production has increasing, decreasing, or constant returns to scale. If doubling all inputs would cause output to more than double, then the cost per unit of output would fall. This is a case of increasing returns to scale.

If doubling all inputs would produce less than twice as much output, then the unit cost of the output would rise. This represents decreasing returns to scale. In those cases in which there are constant returns to scale, the cost per unit of output would remain constant. In this case, doubling all inputs will exactly double output.

SUPPLY: THE INDIVIDUAL FIRM

Supply is defined as the quantities of a product or service that a firm is willing and able to make available for sale at different prices. Firms are not in business just to provide a good or service to customers. They also want to make money for the owners of the business. So, we should expect that firms will only supply goods at prices that at least cover the cost of making those goods available.

In the last section, we found that in the short run the cost per unit of output goes up as more is produced. We should then expect that firms must get higher prices for the products they sell if they are to increase the quantity they supply. In other words, firms will produce more when prices are higher.

> 7–1
> **supply**
> The quantities of a product or service that a firm is willing and able to make available for sale at different prices.

A Firm's Supply Schedule

This relationship between price and the quantity made available for sale can be shown in both table and graphic form. A table showing quantities that would be supplied at each price is called a **supply schedule**. A supply schedule for Zeno's Sandwich Shop is shown in Table 7–6.

> 7–1
> **supply schedule**
> A table showing quantities that would be supplied at each price.

TABLE 7–6

SUPPLY SCHEDULE FOR ZENO'S SANDWICH SHOP

	Price	Quantity Supplied per Day
(A)	$2	120
(B)	$3	140
(C)	$4	160
(D)	$5	180
(E)	$6	200
(F)	$7	220

At a price of $2 per sandwich, Zeno would be willing to make 120 sandwiches each day. But at higher prices, Zeno would be willing to make a greater quantity. For example, if the price went up to $4, he would supply 160 sandwiches each day. At a price of $7, Zeno would be willing to make 220 sandwiches per day. Because the quantity supplied goes up when price goes up, there is a positive relationship between price and quantity supplied. A higher price stimulates greater production.

A Firm's Supply Curve

7–1

supply curve

A graphic representation of the quantities that would be supplied at each price.

The information in Table 7–6 is illustrated by the graph in Figure 7–2. This is called a supply curve. A **supply curve** is a graphic representation of the quantities that would be supplied at each price. A supply curve shows price and the quantity supplied in a way that makes the positive relationship between them easy to see.

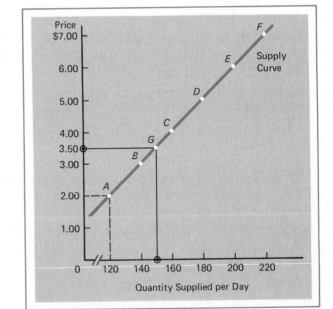

FIGURE 7–2 SUPPLY CURVE FOR ZENO'S SANDWICH SHOP

As price goes up, Zeno increases the number of sandwiches he is willing to supply. At a price of $2, he will supply 120 sandwiches. If price increases to $4, he will supply 160, and at a price of $7, he will supply 220 sandwiches per day. Note that the double slash (//) on the horizontal axis indicates the scale is broken at that point.

You can read any price/quantity combination from this supply curve. For example, if you want to know how many sandwiches would be supplied at a price of $2, you would do the following:

1. Find $2 on the price axis (the vertical axis).

2. Go from that point straight across to the supply curve at Point *A*.

3. Then from Point *A* read straight down to the quantity axis (the horizontal axis) and see that 120 sandwiches would be supplied.

This is illustrated by the dashed lines in Figure 7–2. You should be able to do the same thing for each of the other five points in the supply schedule of Table 7–6. Note that Points *A* through *F* in Table 7–6 correspond to Points *A* through *F* on the supply curve (Figure 7–2).

Now suppose you wanted to know how many sandwiches Zeno would supply at a price not shown in either Table 7–6 or Figure 7–2. For example, how many sandwiches would Zeno supply if the price were $3.50 each?

This price would be halfway between $3 and $4. A point halfway between $3 and $4 on the price axis has been circled. Go from that circled point straight over to the supply curve at Point *G*. From *G* go down to the quantity axis. This point on the quantity axis is circled. The circle on the horizontal axis is halfway between 140 and 160. Half of the way from 140 to 160 is 150. Therefore, at a price of $3.50, Zeno would supply 150 sandwiches per day.

Remember that the reason for this positive relationship between price and the quantity supplied lies in the principle of diminishing marginal productivity. The added output produced by more units of labor input becomes less as input goes up. Therefore, it becomes more costly to produce more units of output. In order to produce more, firms must get a higher price. So, the supply curve is determined by the level of cost. The level of cost is influenced by the principle of diminishing marginal productivity. Thus, the supply curve is positively sloped because production is subject to diminishing marginal productivity.

MARKET SUPPLY

Market supply is defined as the quantities of a product or service that the total of all firms will make available for sale at various prices. Thus, to get the market supply, simply add up all the quantities each firm would supply at each price.

Suppose that in the market served by Zeno's Sandwich Shop there are four other firms. We will use a small number of firms for illustration purposes, even though there would probably be many more in real life. We will call these Firm W, Firm X, Firm Y, and Firm Z.

7–1
market supply
The quantities of a product or service that the total of all firms will make available for sale at various prices.

The Market Supply Schedule

The supply schedule for these four firms is given in Table 7–7, along with Zeno's supply schedule. In the last column of Table 7–7, the market supply schedule is given. It is simply the sum of

TABLE 7–7

DETERMINATION OF THE MARKET SUPPLY OF SANDWICHES

	Individual Firms' Supply Schedules					Market Supply = Total of the Five Firms
	Quantity Supplied per Day by					
Price	Zeno's	Firm W	Firm X	Firm Y	Firm Z	
$2	120	90	115	140	135	600
$3	140	100	120	150	140	650
$4	160	110	125	160	145	700
$5	180	120	130	170	150	750
$6	200	130	135	180	155	800
$7	220	140	140	190	160	850

columns two through six. That is, the market supply is the sum of the amount supplied by all of the firms in the market at each price.

To check your understanding of how to figure the market supply, look at the calculations in general form and for one of the prices.

Market Supply = Sum of Quantity Supplied by Each Firm

$$\frac{\text{Market}}{\text{Supply}} = \frac{\text{Zeno's}}{\text{Quantity}} + \frac{\text{Firm W's}}{\text{Quantity}} + \frac{\text{Firm X's}}{\text{Quantity}} + \frac{\text{Firm Y's}}{\text{Quantity}} + \frac{\text{Firm Z's}}{\text{Quantity}}$$

The market supply at a price of $3 would be figured as follows.

$$\frac{\text{Market Supply}}{\text{at Price of \$3}} = 140 + 100 + 120 + 150 + 140$$
$$= 650$$

Check your understanding of market supply by finding the quantities supplied in the market at the other prices.

The Market Supply Curve

The market supply curve is a graph of the information contained in the market supply schedule. The market supply curve for sandwiches is illustrated in Figure 7–3. In Figure 7–3 (as in Table 7–7), at a price of $3, the five firms would supply a total of 650 sandwiches per day. If the price were to go up to $4, the firms would increase the quantity supplied to 700 sandwiches per day.

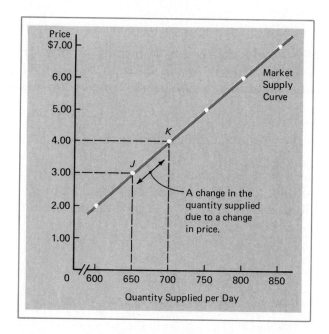

Price
$7.00

Market Supply Curve

A change in the quantity supplied due to a change in price.

Quantity Supplied per Day

FIGURE 7–3   MARKET SUPPLY CURVE FOR SANDWICHES
The market supply curve for sandwiches is the sum of the quantities supplied by all firms in the market at each price. At a price of $2, there would be 600 sandwiches supplied in the entire market. At a price of $6, the quantity supplied would increase to 800 sandwiches per day.

The market supply curve has a positive slope. A positive slope means that the curve slopes upward to the right. As price goes up, firms supply a greater quantity of the good.

A Change in Quantity Supplied

You have learned that a change in price will cause a change in the number of units supplied. This is true for the individual firm and for the whole market as well. If price goes up, more units will be made available for sale. If price goes down, fewer units will be made available.

This change in the number of units made available for sale due to a price change is called a *change in the quantity supplied.* For the market supply curve in Figure 7–3, movement from Point *J* to Point *K* is an example of a change in quantity supplied. When price goes from $3 to $4, the quantity supplied goes up from 650 to 700 sandwiches per day. If the price falls again from $4 to $3, there would be another change in quantity supplied as firms in the marketplace cut production from a total of 700 to 650 per day.

A change in the quantity supplied is always shown as a change along a given supply curve. The change in quantity supplied in response to a price rise will be upward along a supply curve. For a fall in price, the change in quantity supplied will be downward along the supply curve. This is illustrated by the double-headed arrow between Points *J* and *K* in Figure 7–3.

7–5

A Change in Supply

7–5   A *change in supply* means a shift of the whole supply schedule or curve. An increase in supply means more units would be supplied at each price. A decrease in supply means fewer units would be supplied at each price.

Representative changes in supply are illustrated in Figure 7–4. The curve labeled S_o is the original supply curve (it is the same as the market supply in Figure 7–3). The curve S_d represents a decrease in supply. Less would be supplied at each price along S_d than along S_o. For example, at a price of $4, the original supply was 700 units. After the decrease in supply, only 650 units would be supplied at that same price.

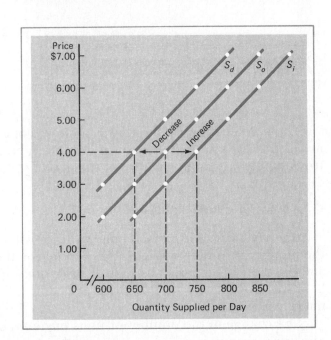

FIGURE 7–4   CHANGES IN SUPPLY REPRESENTED BY SHIFTS IN THE SUPPLY CURVE
An increase in supply is shown as movement from the original supply curve (S_o) to the supply curve S_i, which is to the right of it. A decrease in supply is shown in the shift from S_o to a lower level of supply illustrated by S_d.

An increase in supply is shown by the shift from S_o to S_i. More is supplied at each price along S_i than along S_o. For example, at a price of $4 there would be 700 units supplied. After an increase in supply to S_i, 750 units would be supplied at a price of $4.

What would cause a shift in the supply curve (a change in supply)? The two most common causes are technological change and a change in the cost of inputs.

A technological change would generally increase productivity. This in turn would lower the cost of production. (Remember the link between production and cost.) If the cost of production is lower, firms could sell any given level of output at a lower price. Thus, the supply curve would shift downward or to the right, such as from S_o to S_i in Figure 7–4. For example, a technological change that increases productivity and lowers cost may cause firms to sell 650 units at a price of $2 rather than at $3.

There is another way of looking at an increase in supply. If the technological change lowers cost, firms would be willing to supply more at any given price. For example, at a price of $4, firms may be willing to increase the amount they produce from 700 to 750 units. This is an outward shift of supply from S_o to S_i.

Technological changes generally cause costs to fall due to higher productivity. However, there are other changes that may cause costs to rise. Examples are higher labor costs, a rise in the cost of petroleum products used in production, and higher energy costs.

If production costs go up, firms may either charge a higher price for a given level of output or cut production back at the present price. These reactions to higher costs can be seen by the shift from S_o to S_d in Figure 7–4. If production costs go up, the firms that were producing 650 units at a price of $3 would charge $4 to cover the higher costs.

You can also think of the starting point as a price of $4 with firms producing 700 units along S_o. If costs go up, firms may hold the price at $4 but cut production back to 650 units. This is shown by the decrease in supply from S_o to S_d.

You can see, then, that a change in supply is a shift of the entire supply curve. A shift to the left represents a decrease in supply, such as from S_o to S_d. An increase in supply can be shown as a shift to the right from S_o to S_i.

PRICE ELASTICITY OF SUPPLY

The price elasticity of supply measures the responsiveness of the quantity supplied to changes in the product's price. This concept is very similar to the price elasticity of demand.

The **price elasticity of supply** is defined as the ratio of the percentage change in the quantity supplied to the percentage change in the product's price. If E_s represents the price elasticity of supply, the formula for price elasticity of supply is as follows:

7–6

7–1

price elasticity of supply

The ratio of the percentage change in the quantity supplied to the percentage change in the product's price.

$$E_s = \frac{\text{Percentage Change in Quantity Supplied}}{\text{Percentage Change in Price}}$$

7-7   When E_s is *greater than one*, supply is *price elastic*. That is, the quantity supplied is very responsive to price changes. If E_s is *less than one*, supply is *price inelastic*. This means that the quantity supplied does not respond very much to price changes. When E_s *equals one*, supply is said to be *unitarily price elastic*. In such a case, the percentage change in quantity supplied exactly equals the percentage change in price.

Let's calculate a couple of price elasticities of supply for the market supply schedule given in Table 7–7.

Price	Market Supply
$2	600
$3	650
$4	700
$5	750
$6	800
$7	850

If price increases from $2 to $3, the quantity supplied increases from 600 to 650. The percentage change in price is 50 percent, while the percentage change in quantity is 8.3 percent.

$$E_s = \frac{\text{Percentage Change in Quantity Supplied}}{\text{Percentage Change in Price}}$$

$$= \frac{8.3}{50}$$

$$= .17$$

In this interval (from $2 to $3), supply is very price inelastic. E_s is well below one.

For a price change from $5 to $6, the quantity supplied would increase from 750 to 800 units. The percentage change in price is 20 percent and the percentage change in quantity is 6.7 percent.

$$E_s = \frac{6.7}{20}$$

$$= .34$$

The price elasticity of supply would again be inelastic in this interval, since E_s is found to be less than one.

THINKING
ABOUT ECONOMIC ISSUES

The productivity of workers in the United States rose at a little more than 3 percent a year from just after World War II until the late 1960s. But from 1970 through 1990, the growth in productivity fell sharply to about 1 percent a year.

Because the United States economy had been very productive in the past, this downturn upset many Americans. It meant we might not be able to keep on making enough to satisfy our needs and desires. Why did our ability to supply goods and services decline? Who was to blame? How could the downward slide be changed?

Some people tried to blame such problems on one or two groups. But there are usually many factors that come together to cause such problems. Some of these are listed below:

1. *Higher costs for many resources.* Oil, coal, and other resources have risen in cost. This makes it more expensive to use methods of production that use many machines and other kinds of capital.

2. *Lower personal savings.* The fall in the savings rate makes less money available for businesses to borrow and invest in more productive equipment.

3. *Lack of cooperation between labor and managers.* Without a spirit of cooperation among all of the people working for a business, productivity cannot be at its best. Workers must feel pride in what they do and try to make high quality products. Managers must create a work situation that brings out the best efforts of everyone.

4. *More service-oriented economy.* It is harder to measure output in services. But it is generally thought that productivity in this part of the economy is below that of other parts of the economy. As more people work in service jobs, overall productivity appears lower.

5. *Lower educational levels.* By some measure, high school graduates may be less well educated than in the past. Achievement scores on the Scholastic Aptitude Test dropped for a while, and this can have a bad effect on productivity.

6. *Higher interest rates.* Businesses that have to pay high interest rates to borrow money are less likely to buy new capital equipment. Workers are most productive when they have the newest and best equipment to use. So, if businesses cannot afford new capital, worker productivity may fail to go up or may even fall.

7. *Increased concern for our environment.* Americans are concerned about keeping the environment free of pollution. Thus, there are government rules that require business to use more labor and capital on pollution control. This use of money and labor does not show up as

being productive in the normal output of the business. It may be good for society because it improves the environment. However, it can also cause productivity measures to fall.

These are some of the major factors that cause productivity to fall. We should watch for changes that may make the effect of these factors more (or less) severe.

Our ability to supply goods and services to meet society's needs depends on keeping our productivity up. As you have seen, our personal attitudes toward work, savings, and education can affect the country's productive ability.

REVIEWING THE CHAPTER

7–2   1. In a market economy, production decisions are made primarily by individuals acting in their own self-interest. We work in some form of production for the money and psychic income we get in exchange for our work effort.

7–2   2. Individuals own and/or control nearly all the factors of production in a market economy. These factors of production include land, labor, capital, and entrepreneurship.

7–2   3. The output that results from production can be measured in units or in dollars. It is better to use units because the dollar measure can be misleading if prices change over time.

7–3   4. Almost all production is subject to diminishing marginal productivity. This means that as the use of a variable input (such as labor) increases, output will increase at a decreasing rate. A point can even be reached where so much of the input is used that output will actually decline.

7–4   5. If all inputs can be increased at the same time, production may become more efficient due to increasing returns to scale. This is true in the production of cars, household appliances, steel, aluminum, and many other products. In some forms of production, there may be constant or even decreasing returns to scale. However, increasing returns to scale is the most common.

7–8   6. Costs are a natural result of the production process. Because of diminishing marginal productivity, the cost of production per unit of output increases as the rate of production goes up in the short run.

7–8   7. It is important to consider both explicit costs and the opportunity costs in making economic decisions. Failure to do so will often result in bad decisions with undesirable results.

7–6   8. The amount a firm supplies is related to the price for which the product can be sold. The higher the price, the more firms will supply. This relationship can be shown in either a supply schedule or a supply curve.

7–5   9. The market supply of any product is the sum of what all the individual firms will supply at each price. This can be shown in a market supply schedule or a market supply curve.

7–6   10. The responsiveness of the amount supplied to changes in the product's price can be measured by the price elasticity of supply. The price elasticity of supply is the percentage change in the quantity supplied divided by the percentage change in price. If this ratio is greater than one, supply is elastic. If it is less than one, supply is inelastic. When it equals one, supply is unitarily elastic.

REVIEWING ECONOMIC TERMS

7–1   Supply definitions for the following terms:

factor of production	scale of production
total product	returns to scale
average product	explicit costs
marginal product	supply
short run	supply schedule
long run	supply curve
diminishing marginal productivity	market supply
	price elasticity of supply

REVIEWING ECONOMIC CONCEPTS

7–2   1. What are the four basic factors of production?

7–2   2. Who controls the factors of production in a market economy?

7–3   3. If a company can produce 10,565 golf balls in one day with 50 workers, what is the average product? If the same company can produce 10,580 golf balls by adding one more worker, what is the marginal product of labor?

7–4   4. Name three kinds of returns to scale and describe each.

7–5   5. What is the difference between a change in quantity supplied and a change in supply? How would these look different on a graph?

7–6   6. Market supply at $8 is 1,000 units of a product and 1,200 units at $9. The percentage change in price is 12.5 percent, and the percentage change in quantity supplied is 20 percent. What is the price elasticity of the product at this interval?

7–8   7. What is the relationship of costs and level of production over the short run?

7–8   8. What is the relationship of costs and level of production over the long run?

7–7   9. What are the three kinds of price elasticity of supply and what do they mean?

APPLYING ECONOMIC CONCEPTS

1. Why do people work if it is not a pleasurable activity? Why would someone take a lower paying job rather than a higher paying one?

7–1, 7–8   2. Explain how the concept of diminishing marginal productivity would work in two situations other than the two examples used in this chapter.

7–4   3. Why would you expect increasing returns to scale to result in a lower cost per unit of output?

7–1   4. Suppose you decide to start a housecleaning business with some friends next summer. List the types of costs you would expect in this new business. Which of the costs would be explicit costs and which would be opportunity costs?

7–5   5. Why are supply curves generally positively sloped? What relevance do production and cost concepts have in this regard?

7–5   6. Home video recorder sales have been increasing. What factors do you think have contributed to the increase in supply of this product? Can you think of some other products for which supply has increased recently?

7–8   7. Why might an increase in gasoline and diesel fuel costs cause a decrease in the supply of wheat in the United States? What technological changes might offset this effect?

CHAPTER 8

DEMAND, SUPPLY, AND PRICES

Learning Objectives

8–1 Define terms related to the balance of supply and demand.

8–2 Explain the effects of a shortage or a surplus.

8–3 Describe the effects of a change in demand.

8–4 Describe the effects of a change in supply.

8–5 Identify two ways in which the balance between supply and demand is prevented.

8–6 List the effects of a price floor and a price ceiling.

THE MARKET SYSTEM

In a market system, people acting in their own self-interests make the decisions that guide the economy. Every time you make a purchase, you guide the direction of the economy. If you buy a new wool sweater, you signal to producers that people want wool sweaters. Of course, your signal alone won't mean a great deal. But if many thousands of buyers send the same signal, the message becomes clear. You do not buy a wool sweater with the idea of increasing employment in woolen mills or adding to the profits of mill owners. You buy a wool sweater because you know you will like owning and wearing it. That is, your decision to buy the sweater is based on your own self-interest. No one makes you buy it.

Meanwhile, producers of wool sweaters respond to consumers' signals by employing more factors of production to make more sweaters. Producers don't have to make more sweaters. No government agency tells them to do so. They make more because they expect to make money. The producers make more sweaters because it is in their own self-interest to do so.

A system of markets, such as the market for wool sweaters, is the heart of our economic system. We depend on free markets to communicate information between consumers and producers. We do have some government regulation and influence in the economy. But there is much less government involvement than in economies that lean toward the command type of economic systems.

Markets provide the mechanism for exchange. Consumers exchange money for goods and services from producers. Producers then exchange that money for factors of production used in making their products. The owners of these factors use that money in their own roles as consumers. So, the exchange process starts over again. At each stage, the exchange is made more efficient because of the existence of the market system.

Illustration 8–1
You don't buy a wool sweater with the intention of creating new jobs for people at woolen mills. Still, by purchasing wool sweaters, consumers send signals to the producer to increase production and make more sweaters.

The function of a market is to bring consumers and producers together. The interaction of demand and supply is also an essential part of a market system. Because demand and supply are so important, we will briefly review these concepts. Then we will look at how demand and supply interact in a market system.

Demand: A Review

Demand is defined as the quantities of a product that consumers are willing and able to buy at various prices. The law of demand is that consumers will buy a greater quantity at a lower price than at a higher price. The market demand for a product is the sum of all individual consumers' demands. So, the market demand represents the total amount that all consumers are willing and able to buy at each price.

The market demand can be shown by either a table or a graph. Table 8–1 is a hypothetical demand schedule for wheat. Note that this demand schedule follows the law of demand. The amount demanded becomes less as the price goes up.

TABLE 8–1

HYPOTHETICAL DEMAND SCHEDULE FOR WHEAT

Price (in Dollars per Bushel)	Quantity (in Millions of Bushels)
$2.80	2,400
3.00	2,300
3.20	2,200
3.40	2,100
3.60	2,000
3.80	1,900
4.00	1,800
4.20	1,700
4.40	1,600

The demand schedule in Table 8–1 is also shown as a demand curve in Figure 8–1. All nine price and quantity combinations from Table 8–1 are marked by small dots in Figure 8–1. Connecting these points gives the demand curve. Looking at the demand curve, you quickly see the inverse relationship between price and quantity. At high prices such as $4.40 per bushel, the amount demanded would be fairly low (1,600 million bushels). At lower prices, the amount demanded goes up.

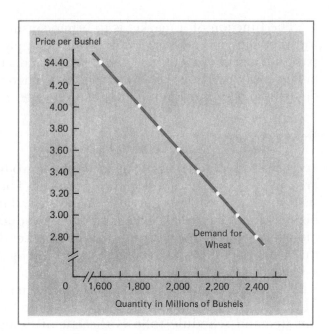

FIGURE 8-1 HYPOTHETICAL DEMAND
CURVE FOR WHEAT
Each of the nine price and quantity combinations
given in Table 8–1 is represented here by a dot.
Connecting these nine points gives the demand
curve.

Supply: A Review

Supply is the amount firms are willing and able to make available for sale at different prices. How much a firm will supply at any price depends on the firm's cost of production. Because of diminishing marginal productivity, the cost per unit of output rises as more is produced in the short run. The price a firm gets for a product must cover production costs. So, we can expect that firms will only increase the amount supplied if price goes up.

If each producer produces more at a higher price than at a lower price, the same will be true for all firms combined. Adding together the amounts supplied by all firms at each price gives the market supply of the product. Market supply can be shown by either a table or a graph.

A hypothetical market supply of wheat is given in Table 8–2. In that supply schedule you can see a positive relationship between price and the quantity supplied. As price goes up from $2.80 to $4.40 per bushel, the quantity supplied goes up from 1,600 to 2,400 million bushels.

The supply schedule given in Table 8–2 can also be shown as a supply curve. The nine price and quantity combinations from Table 8–2 are shown as small dots in Figure 8–2. The line connecting these points is the supply curve. The slope of the supply curve is positive because, in total, all firms supply a greater quantity the higher the price.

TABLE 8–2

HYPOTHETICAL SUPPLY SCHEDULE FOR WHEAT

Price (in Dollars per Bushel)	Quantity (in Millions of Bushels)
$2.80	1,600
3.00	1,700
3.20	1,800
3.40	1,900
3.60	2,000
3.80	2,100
4.00	2,200
4.20	2,300
4.40	2,400

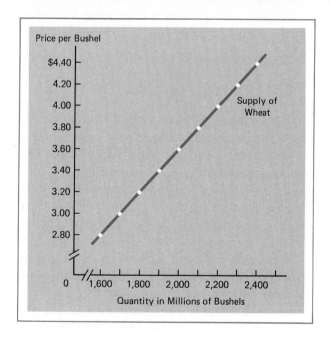

FIGURE 8–2   HYPOTHETICAL SUPPLY CURVE FOR WHEAT
Each of the nine price and quantity combinations given in Table 8–2 is represented here by a dot. Connecting these nine points gives the supply curve.

PRICE AS A RATIONING DEVICE

You have seen that price is important in both demand and supply. Consumers look at prices as they decide how to spend their money. Producers look at prices as they decide what goods or services to produce. So, prices act as signals for both consumers and producers. As such, prices help to ration both finished goods and raw materials among competing uses. You will see that when there

146

Illustration 8–2

Illustration 8–2
Prices act as signals for both consumers and producers. They give us information about how much in demand a product is or how much surplus exists for a product that few consumers are buying.

is a shortage of something, price tends to rise. When there is a surplus, price tends to fall. We will now examine how price changes help to eliminate either a shortage or a surplus.

Eliminating a Shortage

What does it mean to say there is a shortage of some product? What does it mean when a newscaster announces that there is likely to be a shortage of heating oil next winter? When cold weather hits the orange groves of Florida, people in New York find a shortage of orange juice in the grocery stores. What does that mean?

A shortage exists when people are willing to buy more than producers have for sale at a particular price. That is, there is a shortage when the amount demanded at a certain price is greater than the amount supplied. A shortage of heating oil means that consumers want to buy more at the present price than is available for sale. Therefore, a **shortage** can be defined as the condition in which demand is greater than supply at a certain price.

Figure 8–3 helps explain a shortage. The demand and supply curves shown in Figure 8–3 are the same as those first used in Figures 8–1 and 8–2. We will use these curves several times in the rest of this chapter. In using this set of demand and supply curves, we will call a million bushels of wheat one unit of output. Thus, rather than saying 1,600 million bushels, we will just say 1,600 units.

At a price of $3.20, the amount supplied is 1,800 units. This can be found by following the dashed line from the price of $3.20 to the supply curve at the point marked *A*. Then from *A*, follow the dashed line down to the horizontal axis at 1,800 units. You can see that 1,800 units would be supplied at a price of $3.20 by checking back to Table 8–2.

8–1

shortage

The condition in which demand is greater than supply at a certain price.

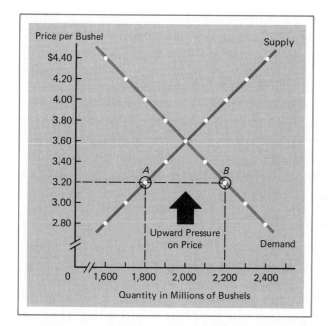

FIGURE 8–3   A SHORTAGE

A shortage results when demand is greater than supply at a certain price. In this case, at a price of $3.20, the quantity demanded is 2,200 units while only 1,800 units would be supplied. The distance between *A* and *B* (400 units) is a measure of the amount of the shortage.

But what about demand at that price? From the demand curve, 2,200 units would be demanded at a price of $3.20. This can be seen by extending the dashed line from the $3.20 price over to the demand curve at *B*. Then from *B*, follow the line down to the quantity axis at 2,200 units. Looking back to Table 8–1, you can also see that 2,200 units would be demanded at a price of $3.20.

At a price of $3.20, there would be a shortage of wheat. Consumers would have a demand for 2,200 units, but suppliers would only be willing to supply 1,800 units. Demand is greater than supply at that price. Not everyone who would like to buy wheat at that price will be able to do so. There is a shortage of 400 units. This is the distance between *A* and *B*.

Some people would be willing to pay more than $3.20 per bushel for their wheat. We know this because of the information given by the demand curve. For example, we know that enough consumers would be willing to pay $4.20 per bushel for 1,700 units to be sold at that price. So, there are consumers who stand ready to buy wheat at prices above $3.20. Some of them are likely to pay more than $3.20, rather than do without the wheat.

Suppliers are likely to know when demand is greater than supply and that some people would be willing to pay a higher price. The suppliers in such a situation will probably raise their prices.

Thus, a shortage causes upward pressure on the price. This is   8–2
shown by the arrow pointing up in Figure 8–3. This upward pressure is due to natural economic forces on both the demand and supply sides of the marketplace.

As price rises, the amount demanded becomes less. Some consumers may drop out of the market while others will cut back on their use of the product. At the same time, producers will increase the amount they supply as price rises. As the amount demanded decreases and the amount supplied increases, the shortage is reduced.

As long as demand is greater than supply, this process will continue. There will be upward pressure on price. This in turn will decrease the amount demanded and increase the amount supplied. Only when there is no shortage will there no longer be upward pressure on price.

Eliminating a Surplus

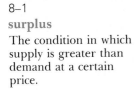

8-1
surplus
The condition in which supply is greater than demand at a certain price.

The opposite of a shortage is a surplus. A **surplus** is the condition in which supply is greater than demand at a certain price. There is a surplus of a product when people are not willing to buy as much as is produced at a given price. That is, if the amount demanded is less than the amount supplied at any price, there is a surplus.

At times, American car manufacturers have produced more cars than people have been willing to buy at existing prices. When weather and other conditions cooperate, the agricultural sector may produce more wheat or corn than consumers wish to purchase. In such cases, a surplus of the product results. Supply is greater than demand.

A surplus is illustrated in Figure 8–4. At a price of $4.20, the amount demanded is 1,700 units. This is determined from the

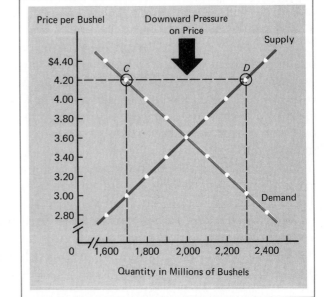

FIGURE 8–4 A SURPLUS

A surplus results when supply is greater than demand. In this case, at a price of $4.20, the quantity supplied is 2,300 units, but consumers would only purchase 1,700 units at that price. The distance between C and D (600 units) is a measure of the amount of the surplus.

point labeled *C* along the demand curve. As indicated by Point *D* along the supply curve, 2,300 units are supplied at that price. There is a surplus of 600 units. This surplus is shown by the distance between *C* and *D* in Figure 8–4.

Suppliers have more of the product than they can sell at this high price. They are likely to reduce price to try to increase sales. At the same time, consumers are likely to know about the surplus. They will recognize that they have greater bargaining power and may offer to buy the product, but only at a reduced price. Thus, when there is a surplus, there will be downward pressure on price. This is shown by the arrow pointing down in Figure 8–4.

8–2

When car companies produce too many cars, they frequently offer rebates to improve sales. A rebate is a lowering of price. If you get back a $500 check from the company after buying a car, that is like having the price reduced by $500. In fact, the rebate often can be deducted from the price at the time of purchase.

Forces on both the demand and supply sides of the market react with downward pressure on price when there is a surplus. As price comes down, the amount demanded increases. This helps reduce the surplus. Also, as price falls, the amount supplied falls as firms reduce production. This also acts to reduce the surplus.

As long as demand is less than supply, price will continue to fall. As price falls, the amount demanded increases and the amount supplied decreases. When there is no longer a surplus, the downward pressure on price is eliminated.

EQUILIBRIUM: DEMAND AND SUPPLY IN BALANCE

We have just established two important points:

1. If demand is greater than supply, there will be upward pressure on price.

2. If supply is greater than demand, there will be downward pressure on price.

8–1

equilibrium price

The price at which the quantity demanded equals the quantity supplied.

From these two points, we can reach an equally important conclusion: When the quantity demanded equals the quantity supplied, there will be no pressure for price to change.

The price at which the quantity demanded equals the quantity supplied is called the **equilibrium price**. The condition in which two forces exactly balance one another is called **equilibrium**. In the economy, those forces are demand and supply. If demand equals supply, the market is in equilibrium.

8–1

equilibrium

The condition in which two forces exactly balance one another.

In a market economy, natural economic forces lead to an equilibrium, or balance, between demand and supply. In Table 8–3, the demand and supply schedules we have been working with are shown in a single table. At prices higher than $3.60, supply is greater than demand. You have learned that at such prices there will be downward pressure on price. At every price less than $3.60, demand is greater than supply. When demand is greater than supply, there will be upward pressure on price. Only at a price of $3.60 will there be no pressure for a price change. In this case, then, the equilibrium price is $3.60.

TABLE 8–3

HYPOTHETICAL DEMAND AND SUPPLY SCHEDULES FOR WHEAT

Price	Quantity Demanded	Quantity Supplied
$2.80	2,400	1,600
3.00	2,300	1,700
3.20	2,200	1,800
3.40	2,100	1,900
3.60	2,000	2,000
3.80	1,900	2,100
4.00	1,800	2,200
4.20	1,700	2,300
4.40	1,600	2,400

8–1

equilibrium quantity
The quantity that is both demanded and supplied at the equilibrium price.

At the $3.60 price, the quantity demanded is 2,000 units, as is the quantity supplied. Thus, 2,000 units represent the equilibrium quantity. The **equilibrium quantity** is the quantity that is both demanded and supplied at the equilibrium price.

In Figure 8–5, the equilibrium price and quantity are shown in boxes. From this graph, you can see that equilibrium occurs at the point where the demand curve crosses the supply curve. That is, demand and supply are equal where the two lines cross. This is an important point that will be used often in our future discussions. At equilibrium, there is no shortage or surplus. Thus, there is also no incentive for price to change.

The equilibrium point, or the intersection of demand and supply, is labeled E in Figure 8–5. Only at this point does demand equal supply. At any price above $3.60, supply is greater than demand. At such prices, economic forces would push prices downward. The quantity demanded would then rise, and the quantity supplied would fall until Point E was reached.

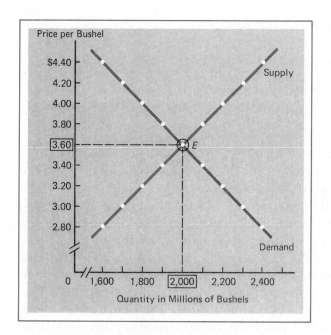

FIGURE 8–5   BALANCE BETWEEN DEMAND AND SUPPLY
When the price is at a level where the quantity demanded equals the quantity supplied, the market is in equilibrium. That is, there is a balance between demand and supply. In this graph, at a price of $3.60, both demand and supply would be 2,000 units. There would be neither a shortage nor a surplus. Thus, there is no incentive for the price to change.

For any price below $3.60, demand is greater than supply. When this is true, economic forces will put upward pressure on prices. The quantity supplied will rise, and the quantity demanded will fall until Point *E* is reached.

This is true in all markets. Any market is in equilibrium, or balance, when the quantity demanded equals the quantity supplied. In a graph, this is the point where the demand curve crosses the supply curve. To find the equilibrium price and quantity for a market, you first find the point where demand crosses supply. This is Point *E* in Figure 8–5. Then read over to the price axis to find the equilibrium price ($3.60 in this example). The equilibrium quantity is found from the quantity axis directly below where the two curves cross (2,000 units in this example).

CHANGES IN DEMAND

You have seen that, in a market economy, natural economic forces will lead to a balance between demand and supply. But in Chapter 6 you learned that demand may change. The demand curve may not stay in the same place. It may shift to the right as demand for the product increases. Or the demand curve may shift to the left as demand for the product falls.

Illustration 8–3
One factor that affects demand for a product is the price of the substitute product. For example, as the price of beef rises, products made with soybeans (shown above) increase in popularity.

To review, there are three things that can cause a change in demand:

1. Consumers' incomes may change

2. Consumers' attitudes or expectations may change

3. The prices of substitute or complementary products may change

As incomes rise, the demand for most products also goes up. But if income falls, demand will fall as well. Consumers' attitudes may change in a way that causes demand to either rise or fall. Advertising is aimed at increasing demand by changing our attitudes about products. But the advertising that makes us view Pepsi more favorably also may cause the demand for Coke to fall.

If the price of a substitute product goes up, demand for the other product will increase. For example, if the price of Pepsi goes up, the demand for Coke will rise. This also works in the other direction. If the price of Pepsi comes down, the demand for Coke will fall. Changes in the prices of complementary products will also affect demand. As the price of gas goes up, the demand for car tires will go down. Gas and tires are complementary because the use of one increases the use of the other. This works in reverse, too. If the price of gas falls, people will drive more and the demand for tires will go up.

Effects of an Increase in Demand

8–3

When the demand for a product goes up, the equilibrium price and quantity are affected. An *increase in demand* means that consumers are willing to buy more at each price than they would have before the rise in demand. If the amount supplied did not change, price would surely rise. That original supply would no longer satisfy demand at the original price. There would be a shortage at the original price. As you have seen, price will be pushed up when there is a shortage. But remember that if price goes up, the quantity supplied will go up also as producers respond to the higher price.

Figure 8–6 will be helpful in seeing exactly what would happen. The supply curve and original demand curve shown in Figure 8–6 are the same as the supply and demand curves used earlier in this chapter. They cross at Point *A* at a price of $3.60 and a quantity of 2,000 units. This is the original equilibrium.

Suppose that demand goes up so that consumers now are willing to buy 100 more units of wheat at each price. This is shown by the new higher demand curve in Figure 8–6. With this higher demand,

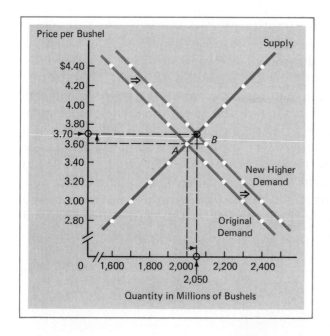

FIGURE 8–6   EFFECTS OF AN INCREASE IN DEMAND
When demand shifts to the right, the equilibrium price and quantity both go up.

consumers would want to buy 2,100 units rather than 2,000 units at a price of $3.60. There would be a shortage of 100 units if the amount supplied did not change. This shortage is represented by the distance between Points *A* and *B*.

Remember that when there is a shortage there will be upward pressure on price. As price rises, the quantity supplied goes up as well. A new equilibrium price is reached when the new higher demand crosses the supply curve. This is at the circle in the center of Figure 8–6. The price at that level is $3.70. This is found by following the dashed line to the left from the point where the new higher demand crosses the supply curve.

At a price of $3.70, consumers would want to purchase 2,050 units. This is the quantity directly below the intersection of the new higher demand and supply. This is exactly the same as the amount that would be supplied at a price of $3.70.

So, there are two important changes when there is an increase in demand. If demand goes up and the supply curve remains the same, the following will occur:

1. Price will rise.

2 Quantity exchanged will rise.

Effects of a Decrease in Demand

When the demand for a product falls, consumers are willing to buy fewer units at each price. This will also affect both equilibrium

8–3

price and equilibrium quantity. With a lower level of demand, there would be a surplus if the quantity supplied did not change. A surplus would put downward pressure on price. As price falls, the quantity supplied by producers would also fall. This process would go on until supply and demand were once more in balance.

Look at Figure 8–7 to see how this would happen. The original equilibrium is at a price of $3.60 and a quantity of 2,000. Demand and supply are in balance. But suppose that demand fell to the level given by the new lower demand curve. The first effect would be a surplus of 100 units at the $3.60 price. Consumers would now only be willing to buy 1,900 units, while producers are supplying 2,000 units. This surplus is shown by the distance between Points *A* and *B* in Figure 8–7.

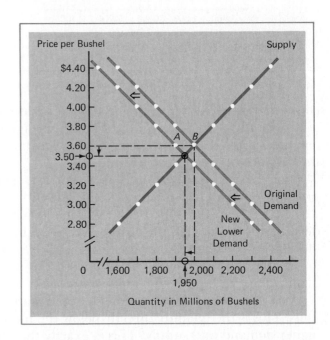

FIGURE 8–7   EFFECTS OF A DECREASE IN DEMAND
When demand shifts to the left, the equilibrium price and quantity both go down.

This surplus would result in downward pressure on price. As the price falls, producers will cut back on the amount supplied. Price will go on falling, and the amount supplied will fall until a new equilibrium is reached. This will be at the point where the new lower demand crosses the supply curve. In Figure 8–7, this point is circled.

The price at this new equilibrium is $3.50, and the quantity is 1,950 units. The 1,950 units will satisfy consumers at a price of $3.50. Also, suppliers only want to supply 1,950 units at a price of $3.50. Demand and supply are once more in balance.

Thus, if demand falls while the supply curve stays the same, the following will occur:

1. Price will fall.
2. Quantity exchanged will fall.

CHANGES IN SUPPLY

A shift of the supply curve can also upset the balance between demand and supply. Remember that the two main causes of a change in supply are a technological change and a change of input prices. For example, if input prices go up, the firm's cost goes up. Therefore, the quantity the firm would supply at each price would be less. Higher costs result in a decrease in supply. This is a leftward shift of the supply curve.

Technological changes usually result in a greater supply. Using a more advanced technology increases productivity. As productivity increases, the cost per unit of output goes down. When this happens, firms either supply more at each price or can sell any given amount at a lower price. In either case, supply would increase as shown by a rightward shift of the supply curve.

Illustration 8–4   A change in supply can result from a change in the technology involved in making a product. Shown here are the first computer and a present-day computer. Not only has the product itself grown more efficient and sophisticated, but the modes of producing it have also improved.

Effects of an Increase in Supply

An *increase in supply* means that producers are willing to supply more at each price. If there is an increase in the amount of wheat supplied, the supply curve would shift from the original supply to

8–4

the new greater supply, as shown in Figure 8–8. This shift shows that firms would supply 100 more units at each price. For example, at the original equilibrium price of $3.60, firms now would supply 2,100 units rather than 2,000 units.

At the $3.60 price, there would now be a surplus. Producers would supply 2,100 units, but consumers would only want to buy 2,000 units. This surplus of 100 units is shown by the distance from *A* to *B* in Figure 8–8. The existence of the surplus means that there would be downward pressure on price.

As the price begins to fall, the amount demanded would go up. This follows from the law of demand. Consumers will be willing and able to purchase more at lower prices than at higher prices. As the amount demanded goes up, the surplus is reduced.

At the same time, producers will be cutting back on the amount supplied, due to the fall in price. This further helps to lower the amount of the surplus. After all changes, the price will have fallen just enough that demand and supply are balanced again.

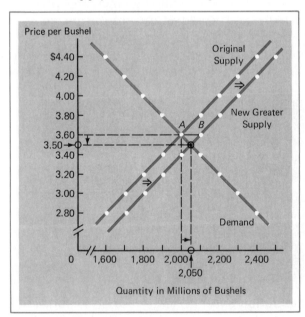

FIGURE 8–8   EFFECTS OF AN INCREASE IN SUPPLY

When supply shifts to the right, price will fall and the quantity exchanged rises.

In the example shown in Figure 8–8, the new equilibrium price would be $3.50. At this price, consumers would want to buy 2,050 units, as shown by their demand curve. Given the new greater supply, we see that producers would want to supply 2,050 units at a price of $3.50. Thus, demand and supply are once more in balance.

If supply increases while the demand curve remains the same, the following results can be expected:

1. Price will fall.

2. Quantity exchanged will rise.

Effects of a Decrease in Supply

Supply will shift to the left when the cost of production goes up. 8–4 This is most often caused by a rise in the costs of inputs to the firm. It could also be caused by lower labor productivity that increases the cost per unit of output produced. An increase in the cost per unit of output gives suppliers two choices: either offer fewer units for sale at each price or charge more for any given rate of output.

Higher costs for labor, fertilizer, fuel, and machines might combine to cause a reduction in the supply of wheat. This is shown in Figure 8–9 by the shift from the original supply to the new lower supply. The first effect of this drop in supply is a shortage of wheat. In Figure 8–9, the shortage is 100 units. At the original equilibrium price of $3.60, consumers would want to buy 2,000 units. But now with the reduced supply, producers only want to supply 1,900 units. This 100-unit shortage is shown by the distance from *A* to *B* in Figure 8–9.

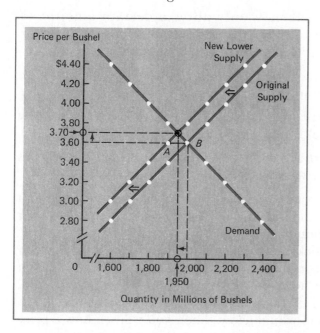

FIGURE 8–9 EFFECTS OF A DECREASE IN SUPPLY
When supply shifts to the left, price will rise and the quantity exchanged will fall.

We know that when there is a shortage there will be upward pressure on price. As the price rises, consumers will reduce the quantity they demand in keeping with the law of demand. This helps to reduce the shortage. As price goes up, producers expand production along the new lower supply curve. This process goes on until demand and supply balance again.

In the case we have shown, the new equilibrium is where the demand curve crosses the new lower supply curve. The price at this level is $3.70. At this new equilibrium price, consumers would want to buy 1,950 units. Producers would want to supply this same amount at that price. So, at a price of $3.70, demand and supply balance. The quantity demanded and the quantity supplied are both 1,950 units.

If demand stays the same and supply decreases, we can expect the following results:

1. Price will go up.

2. Quantity exchanged will be less.

GOVERNMENT MAY BLOCK THE MARKET SYSTEM

There are times when the government may act to block the market system, thus preventing a balance between demand and supply. Elected officials may give in to special interest groups who believe the market price is either too high or too low. This can take many forms:

1. The government may only allow a certain amount of imported steel to enter the economy. This cuts down on supply and, as you have seen, results in a higher steel price.

2. The government may buy grain products. This increases the demand and results in a higher price.

3. The government may set rent controls to keep rents below the market level.

4. The government may set a minimum wage because it believes the free market wage is too low.

These are just a few examples of how the government may prevent a balance between demand and supply. There are many other examples in our economy.

Programs that block the market often can be evaluated using demand and supply concepts. Looking at two types of government actions will illustrate how such programs can be analyzed. First, you will see how a price floor may be used to keep prices higher than the market system would allow. Then you will see how a price ceiling can keep price down.

Illustration 8–5
One way government may block the market system is by providing subsidized housing at lower-than-market rates.

8–5

Price Floor

8–1
price floor
A minimum price set by government that is above the market equilibrium price.

A **price floor** is a minimum price set by government that is above the market equilibrium price. A price floor is illustrated in Figure 8–10. If there were no interference with the wheat market, an equilibrium price of $3.60 would result. But what if wheat farmers convinced the government that $3.60 was too low a price? The

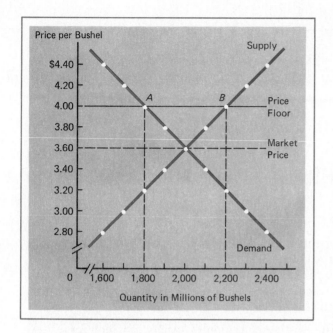

FIGURE 8–10 EFFECTS OF A PRICE FLOOR
A price floor at $4.00 prevents the market from working and balancing demand and supply at a price of $3.60. A surplus results and consumers pay a higher price, but they buy less.

farmers and government might agree that $4 per bushel is a better price (at least for wheat growers). The $4 would be a price floor if the government decided that no wheat would be sold below that price.

Why do we use the term *price floor*? If you were on the second floor of a building and dropped your pencil, where would it stop? On the floor. The floor would keep your pencil from falling farther. Similarly, a price floor keeps price from falling below a certain level.

To be effective, a price floor must be above the equilibrium price. If a price floor were lower than equilibrium price, it would not be useful. Such a price floor would already be below the natural market price.

If the government said that there would be a price floor of $4 per bushel of wheat, how would the amount supplied compare to the amount demanded? From Figure 8–10, you see that the amount supplied would be 2,200 units. But the amount demanded at $4 is 1,800 units. Supply would be greater than demand by 400 units. This 400-unit surplus is shown as the distance from *A* to *B* in Figure 8–10.

In a free market, you know that when there is a surplus, price will be pushed down. The amount demanded will increase, and the amount supplied will decrease. This would continue until price fell enough that demand and supply were balanced. But with a price floor, such a free market adjustment is blocked. The market is kept from working.

8–6

ALFRED MARSHALL

Alfred Marshall was born in London on July 26, 1842. His father wanted him to have a career in the church. But at the age of 19, he decided to study mathematics at St. John's college in Cambridge. Marshall graduated with honors and followed a teaching career for about nine years. His interests then slowly turned to ethics and economics.

Marshall was upset by the existing condition of society in which there were many poor people despite the general economic well-being. Throughout his life, he was concerned with finding ways to lessen the misery and suffering of the poor. The study of economics was a natural direction for a person with these concerns to take. He clearly thought that religious and economic forces were the most important influences on people's behavior.

In the 1870s, Alfred Marshall married Mary Paly, who was also an economics teacher. They worked together all through their 47 years of marriage. In fact, they worked together in preparing his first book, the *Economics of Industry*. Marshall also wrote a book called *Principles of Economics* which may have had more impact on the study of economics than any other single book. Much of what is found in economics texts today had its origins in Marshall's work.

Marshall was the first person to see the importance of putting together *supply and demand* to find the price of a product. Before Marshall, some economists had thought that only demand or supply forces were important. However, Marshall explained the importance of looking at demand and supply together by comparing it to how a pair of scissors works. One blade of a scissors is not very useful in cutting a piece of paper. Both blades must work together to have a good cutting tool. Likewise, neither supply nor demand alone can determine price. Both forces together, however, are very powerful in the economy.

Another of Marshall's contributions to the study of economics is in the application of elasticity concepts to demand. However, some people think that Marshall's greatest contribution was the use of diagrams to help explain economic ideas. This use of diagrams continues to help us in studying economic problems. Partly for this reason, Marshall is often called the father of modern economic science. Marshall's methods and insights will be seen in the study of economic problems for years to come.

We are left with an unbalanced market situation. Supply is greater than demand at the government's set price. Producers will produce more than consumers will buy. What happens to the extra production? The government must either buy up the surplus or keep producers from producing so much. To cut down on production, firms must be kept from producing more than the government wants them to by some type of penalty. When the government buys the surplus, it is really *we* who buy it since our tax dollars are used for the purchase. Also, we all (as taxpayers) pay to store the surplus, in many cases.

Look at the result of the price floor for consumers. At the free market equilibrium, price would be $3.60, and consumers would purchase 2,000 units. With the price floor at $4, consumers would purchase less (1,800 units), but pay a higher price ($4).

Price Ceiling

A **price ceiling** is a maximum price set by government that is below the market equilibrium price. A price ceiling is the opposite of a price floor. It keeps the price from going above some upper limit. If you threw your pencil up in the air as hard as you could, it would hit the ceiling. The pencil would not go any higher because the ceiling would limit how high it could go. A price ceiling keeps price down to the level the government thinks is right. To be effective, a price ceiling must be below the equilibrium price. If it were above the equilibrium price, the natural market price would already be below the ceiling.

Suppose the government thought that wheat producers were making too much money at the expense of consumers. The government might set a ceiling price of $3.20 per bushel. This is shown by the horizontal line at $3.20 in Figure 8–11.

At a price of $3.20, consumers would want to buy 2,200 units. Producers, on the other hand, would only be willing to supply 1,800 units. A 400-unit shortage would result. This is shown as the distance from *A* to *B* in Figure 8–11. You have seen that a shortage normally results in upward pressure on price. In a free market, price would rise. The amount supplied would increase, and the amount demanded would decrease. When the price had risen to $3.60, there would have been no shortage. Demand and supply would balance at that price.

But this cannot happen if there is a price ceiling. If the $3.20 price is enforced, supply would be less than demand. The government would have to find some artificial way of allocating the 1,800 units among consumers who would want 2,200 units at that

8–1

price ceiling
A maximum price set by government that is below the market equilibrium price.

8–6

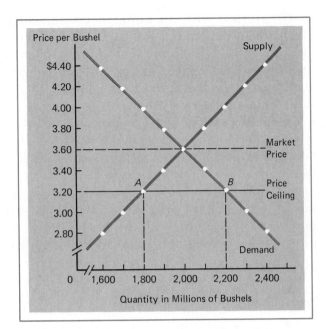

FIGURE 8–11 EFFECTS OF A PRICE
CEILING
A price ceiling at $3.20 blocks the market from
working and balancing demand and supply at a
price of $3.60. A shortage results. Consumers
pay less but cannot satisfy their demand.

price. Ration coupons are sometimes used in cases like this. However, a large system of people usually is needed to issue and keep track of the use of the coupons. This can be very costly. It is sometimes possible for the government to produce enough of the product to make up for the shortage. However, this also costs taxpayers money. Finally, the government can set the price ceiling and let the consumers and producers deal with the shortage problem. In this case, many illegal nonmarket transactions are likely to take place. Those consumers who can afford to pay more will offer secret payments to suppliers to get the product.

REVIEWING THE CHAPTER

1. In a free market economy, individuals make the decisions that guide the direction of the economy. Demand and supply are the key factors involved in the working of a market economy.

8–2   2. Price acts as a rationing mechanism in a market economy. If there is a surplus because supply is greater than demand, there will be natural downward pressure on price. This decreases the quantity supplied and increases the quantity demanded. The result is to eventually do away with the surplus.

8–2   3. This rationing role of price also acts to eliminate a shortage. A shortage exists when demand is greater than supply. When this is true, natural economic forces put upward pressure on price. This decreases the quantity demanded and increases the quantity supplied. The shortage is eventually eliminated.

8–1, 8–2   4. As price changes to eliminate either a surplus or a shortage, a balance between demand and supply is reached. This balance is called an equilibrium because there is no longer any pressure on price to change. The price at which this balance is reached is called the equilibrium price. At the equilibrium price, the quantity demanded equals the quantity supplied. This is then the equilibrium quantity. In a graph, the equilibrium is determined where the demand curve crosses the supply curve.

8–3   5. If demand increases while supply stays the same, price will rise as will the quantity bought and sold.

8–3   6. If demand decreases while supply stays the same, price will fall, as will the quantity bought and sold.

8–4   7. If supply increases while demand stays the same, price will fall, but the quantity bought and sold will increase.

8–4   8. If supply decreases while demand stays the same, price will rise and the quantity bought and sold will decrease.

8–5, 8–6   9. For various reasons, the government may block the functioning of the market system with a price floor or a price ceiling. A price floor is above the equilibrium price and keeps price from falling below the official price floor. A surplus will result from a price floor. This causes other problems for government to handle.

8–2, 8–6   10. A price ceiling is the opposite of a price floor. A price ceiling is set below the market price to keep price from rising. This results in a shortage of the product. Illegal nonmarket transactions are likely to result, and the government must find some nonprice mechanism for allocating the product. Rationing coupons are often used.

REVIEWING ECONOMIC TERMS

8–1   Supply definitions for the following terms:

shortage	equilibrium quantity
surplus	price floor
equilibrium price	price ceiling
equilibrium	

REVIEWING ECONOMIC CONCEPTS

8–2   1. What happens to price and the quantity supplied and demanded when there is a shortage?

8–2   2. What happens to price and the quantity supplied and demanded when there is a surplus?

8–1   3. When a market is in equilibrium, what is the relationship between the quantities supplied and demanded?

8–3   4. If demand increases, what is the effect on equilibrium price and quantity?

8–3   5. If demand decreases, what is the effect on equilibrium price and quantity?

8–4   6. If supply increases, what is the effect on equilibrium price and quantity?

8–4   7. If supply decreases, what is the effect on equilibrium price and quantity?

8–6   8. When government sets a price floor, what is the effect on the market? on consumers? on taxpayers?

8–6   9. When government sets a price ceiling, what is the effect on the market? on consumers? on taxpayers?

APPLYING ECONOMIC CONCEPTS

8–1   1. What is meant by the concept of a market system? What roles do demand and supply play in such a system?

8–2   2. Suppose that there is a news report of a shortage of gasoline. What does this mean? If the market system were left alone, how would this shortage be eliminated?

8–2   3. If growing conditions were ideal in the next crop season, a surplus of wheat might be produced. What does the phrase *surplus of wheat* mean in this context? How would a market system reduce or eliminate this surplus?

8–1   4. "When demand and supply are in balance, the market is in equilibrium." Explain what this statement means.

8–3   5. Some years ago, there was a "cranberry scare" in the United States. In the fall of the year, there were widespread stories that cranberries had been contaminated by a cancer-causing chemical. This affected consumers' attitudes and reduced the demand for cranberries. Use your knowledge of supply and demand to analyze this situation. What would happen to price? What would happen to the quantity sold that holiday season? Use a graph to help explain your answer. (You may assume that supply did not change.)

8–6 6. The wage rate is the price that is paid per labor hour for the use of a person's labor skills. A minimum wage enacted by government is then a type of price floor. Explain how the minimum wage affects the labor market. Begin by drawing a graph of the demand and supply of labor. Assume that demand will have a negative slope and supply will have a positive slope.

8–6 7. Rent controls are often suggested as a method for keeping housing costs down. Explain how this type of price ceiling affects the rental housing market.

8–3, 8–4 8. Pick some product or service that you buy on a regular basis and explain how the concepts of demand and supply relate to that product. Can you identify any changes in demand and/or supply that have influenced the price and the quantity people consume?

BUYING A CAR: SOME ECONOMIC ISSUES

At some time nearly everyone considers buying a car. Buying a car is a major economic decision. Economic reasoning can help you make a good decision when buying a car. First, you need to shop carefully for both the car and the car loan (unless you can pay cash). Leasing is also an option that you might explore.

When shopping for financing, consider the interest rate, the down payment, the length of the payoff period, the size of the monthly payments, and how long you expect to keep the car. It is often tempting to spread the financing over a long period, such as 60 months (five years). This may be all right, but if you only intend to keep the car a short time, perhaps two years, you may not be able to sell or trade the car for as much as you still owe on it.

The purchase price of a car is only part of the cost. You also need to consider such things as gas and oil, license fees, insurance, maintenance, tires, and the fact that the value of the car declines over time. The annual operating cost for a car that is driven 15,000 miles a year and kept for four years is about $5,700 for a typical new car and about $3,900 for a typical used car. That amounts to $325 to $475 per month. This is a big financial burden, so use careful economic reasoning when you make such a substantial purchase.

CHAPTER 9

BUSINESS
FIRMS
IN
THE
ECONOMY

Learning Objectives

9–1 Define terms related to the forms of business organization.

9–2 Identify the advantages and disadvantages of the three kinds of business organization.

9–3 Understand how the three kinds of business organizations obtain financing.

9–4 Explain the relative importance of the three kinds of business organizations in the economy of the United States.

9–5 List three kinds of mergers and tell how they are viewed by government.

9–6 Describe the test of the market.

PRIVATE BUSINESSES IN THE MARKET ECONOMY

In our market economy we depend a great deal on the private sector to produce goods and services. More than 80 percent of our total production comes from private businesses. These businesses are guided by supply and demand in deciding what to produce and how to produce it.

All firms, large or small, must satisfy the *test of the market*. That is, they must provide goods that satisfy consumers' needs and desires at prices consumers are willing to pay. And they must be able to pay all the necessary factors of production in doing so. Small firms are more likely than large firms to fail this market test. Small, and especially new, firms have little money to spend on a product that may fail in the marketplace. A large firm can afford to try some risky products, because one failure out of many products may not ruin the company.

9–6

Each year, thousands of firms fail and go out of business. At the same time, other new firms start up. You probably notice this in your community with retail stores and local services such as clothing stores, restaurants, bakeries, bicycle shops, automotive repair shops, and sporting goods stores. You probably also know of some businesses that have recently closed. The market economy is ever-changing. Some businesses fail, while others succeed.

As long as we rely on the market system and the private sector, these changes will continue. The market system tends to respond fairly to consumers' wishes. It may not always respond perfectly. But it certainly provides goods and services more in line with what consumers want than command-oriented economies do.

Suppose you wanted to open a bicycle repair shop. You would do so only if you thought you could provide a service for which customers were willing to pay. You might find out how many people own bicycles in your area of the city and how often they

Illustration 9–1
Private businesses, like these small shops and service organizations, provide more than 80 percent of our total production.

repair them. Once you assure yourself of a demand for repair services, you would want to know if you could provide the service needed. You would check on the cost of tools and supplies. You would find out what space is available for your shop and how much it would cost. Don't forget that you should also include the opportunity cost of your time. When you have determined that the business could be successful, you would be ready to start.

But what form of organization should your business take? Should it be a proprietorship, a partnership, or a corporation? Before you can answer this question, you must understand each form. You also need to know the advantages and disadvantages of each of these three forms of business organization.

FORMS OF BUSINESS ORGANIZATION

Our economy often appears to be dominated by very large businesses. Names such as General Motors, Mobil, Citicorp, and Sears are familiar to everyone. These big companies and others like them account for most of the total sales in our economy. Yet, there exist many more small firms than large ones. Small firms remain unknown outside of a relatively small geographic area. However, they are an important part of our economy. New firms almost always start out small. If successful, they may grow to become large firms with national reputations. But, like the bicycle repair shop you may start, the beginnings are small.

Each form of business organization (proprietorship, partnership, and corporation) has certain advantages. If not, all three would not exist. Each form also has very important disadvantages of which you should be aware.

Proprietorships

9–1

proprietorship
A form of business in which one individual owns the entire business.

A **proprietorship** is a form of business in which one individual owns the entire business. If you want to open a bicycle repair shop as a proprietorship, the process is simple. You just open the shop. You should check to be sure that you satisfy any state or local laws, but few regulations govern proprietorships. You can borrow the money you need, buy tools and supplies, and hire any necessary labor.

The money that the shop makes is your money. But you also suffer any losses. In a proprietorship, the owner and the business are one and the same. If business is bad and you can't pay your bills, the bank (and others) can collect from any other source of money you may have. You can feel the pride of ownership and success. But you must also bear the burden of failure.

Illustration 9–2   New firms usually start out small, known only to their own immediate geographic area. The Kroger Company began as a family-owned proprietorship and grew to become a major national corporation.

Advantages of a Proprietorship. Setting up a proprietorship has many advantages. Check this list and compare a proprietorship with other forms of organization: 9–2

1. A proprietorship is *easy to start.* There is usually little governmental red tape involved. Almost anyone with a good idea and the willingness to accept some risk can start a business as a proprietorship.

2. There is *relatively little government regulation.* Once started, the operating proprietorship does not face much regulation. Accurate tax records must be kept, and employment must meet certain guidelines. But there are not many regulations in most cases.

3. *All of the profit goes to the owner.* The owner does not have to share money from the business with anyone else.

4. Usually much *pride of ownership* comes with having a proprietorship. The owner can see the progress of the business and have a sense of pride from running it.

5. The owner has *complete control* over what the business does. The owner decides which product or service to sell, the hours the firm should be open, and all other aspects of the business. The owner is boss.

6. In many cases, *taxes are lower* than if the business were a corporation, particularly if the small business has a low profit. The taxes for a proprietorship are the same as for personal income. Remember that the business and the owner are the same.

9–1

unlimited liability

The concept that an owner's personal assets can be used to pay bills of the business.

Illustration 9–3

If you opened a bicycle shop by yourself, it would be a proprietorship. You would earn all the profits from the business but would also be responsible for all losses.

9–1

partnership

A type of business organization in which two or more people form a business.

9–2
Disadvantages of a Proprietorship. A proprietorship may sound very attractive as a form of business organization. But there are some important disadvantages that sometimes outweigh the advantages:

1. The owner of a proprietorship has *unlimited liability for the debts* of the firm. **Unlimited liability** is the concept that an owner's personal assets can be used to pay bills of the business. These personal assets may include the owner's home, car, or savings account. This means that the owner risks all the money put into the business, plus all other savings or assets.

2. The *business stops when the owner dies* or becomes unable to run the business. Once more, the business and the owner are one. If the owner dies, the business ceases to exist. The assets can be sold or assigned to someone else who may start the business again. But then it would become a new firm with different ownership.

3. It is *difficult and expensive to raise money* for a proprietorship. This is particularly true when the business is just getting started and has no record of success. But even a successful proprietorship may be seen as risky to most lenders. Often the owner of a proprietorship has difficulty borrowing money. When the owner is able to get a loan, it is often at a high rate of interest and is thus expensive for the business.

4. In a proprietorship, *the owner bears the entire risk of loss.* In other forms of business organization, the risk of loss is shared among more than one owner. But the owner of the proprietorship takes all the risks alone.

Partnerships

A **partnership** is a type of business organization in which two or more people form a business. Each person involved agrees to provide some portion of the work and start-up money and then to share the profits or losses. For example, you alone might not have enough money to open your bicycle repair shop. In this case, you could form a partnership with someone else who could bring more money into the business. Often a partnership is formed by one person who has the skill to run the business and another who has the money to get it started.

You also might have started the repair shop alone, but needed to expand to keep up with customer demand. Taking on one or more partners is often how a proprietorship grows. Each new partner brings something to the business and shares in the good or bad fortune of the firm. New partners may contribute their personal skills, money, or even ideas to the business.

Suppose that two of your friends come into your repair shop with a new idea. They have figured a way to change old one-speed bikes into ten-speed bikes at a much lower cost than a new ten-speed bike. You might offer them partnerships in the firm in exchange for their idea. They would then share in the profits and operations of the firm. They would also share responsibility for the losses. You would no longer have complete control. The three of you together would make decisions about the partnership.

Advantages of a Partnership. A business organized as a partner- 9–2 ship has many of the same advantages as a proprietorship. The following are the main advantages of organizing a business as a partnership:

1. Partnerships are *easy to start*. As in a proprietorship, there is little governmental red tape. The partners need only agree to the terms of the partnership.

2. There are *few governmental regulations*. Like a proprietorship, most partnerships do not face many regulations. But they must keep good records for tax purposes and meet guidelines related to employment practices.

3. It is *easier to raise money* for the operation of the business. All partners' financial assets are considered by a bank or other lender. This makes it possible for the partners to borrow more together than any one of them could alone. Also, each partner may have some money available to put into the business directly.

4. Partnerships are often *more efficient*. Using the different skills of each partner may increase the efficiency of the firm. One partner may be good at selling and the other better at record keeping. The first, then, should have sales responsibilities and the second should handle accounting and taxes. In a proprietorship, the owner is not likely to have as many skills as in a partnership of two or more people.

Disadvantages of a Partnership. There are also disadvantages to 9–2 forming a partnership. While some resemble the disadvantages of proprietorships, others result from the partnership itself. There are four major disadvantages of a partnership:

1. The members of the partnership have *unlimited liability* for the debts of the business. Just as with a proprietorship, the owners' personal assets can be used to pay debts of the firm. Even a partner who has not put any money into the business is subject to unlimited liability.

2. The partners must *share the profits* according to their original agreement. Even if one of the members of the partnership puts in more work than originally agreed on, the split of profits will follow the original agreement. This also works in reverse. A partner who doesn't work as much as is expected still gets the share of profits specified in the agreement.

3. The *business stops when any one of the partners dies* or is unable to participate. Thus, a successful business may have to be ended even though other partners may want to continue it. A new partnership often can be formed to continue the business, but sometimes this is not easy. Part of the firm's assets may have to be sold to pay off the deceased partner's share.

4. There is always *the potential for disagreement* among the partners. Unlike a proprietorship in which one owner makes all decisions, partners must reach an agreement. While they all may have the same plan, their choices of how to carry it out may differ. These disagreements can lead to inefficient operations and even to the end of the partnership.

Corporations

9–1

corporation
An organization of people legally bound together by a charter to conduct some type of business.

9–1

articles of incorporation
A written application requesting permission to form a corporation.

charter
The legal authorization to organize a business as a corporation.

9–1

stock
Shares of ownership in a corporation.

A **corporation** is an organization of people legally bound together by a charter to conduct some type of business. It is a legal entity separate from its owners. The types of business a corporation can participate in are determined by the articles of incorporation. **Articles of incorporation** are a written application requesting permission to form a corporation. The articles of incorporation give the name, address, and type of business for the corporation; the names of the initial directors of the firm; and the amount of money being put into the business.

If the articles of incorporation satisfy state and federal laws, a charter will be issued and the corporation becomes a legal entity. A **charter**, then, is the legal authorization to organize a business as a corporation. A lawyer familiar with the laws concerning corporations should be hired to write the articles of incorporation.

Suppose that your bicycle repair and conversion business continues to grow. You find that if you had the money to buy some new equipment, you could increase production. You may even consider making your own brand of bikes. You might consider forming a corporation. Doing so would allow you to sell stock to raise more money. (Shares of ownership in a corporation are called **stock**. The sale of stock is one way a corporation can raise money. More will be said about stock later in this chapter.)

You could trade your share of the business for some of the stock. Your partners could do the same. And other people could buy some of your company's stock. Then all the stockholders would elect a board of directors. The board of directors supervises the operation of the business but usually does not take an active part in running it. The board of directors also selects the people who run the company. In your case, you would be the most likely choice for president. Your original partners would be wise choices for other corporate offices such as vice-president and treasurer. You would continue to run the business, but now you would be responsible to all the stockholders.

Some of the advantages and disadvantages to forming a corporation are clear from the discussion above. Compare the advantages and disadvantages of corporations with the other kinds of business organization.

Illustration 9–4
If your bike business grew and grew, you might sell shares of stock to raise money and market your own line of bicycles. Your company would then be considered a corporation.

Advantages of a Corporation. There are more than 2 million corporations in the United States. You should expect, then, that there are some real advantages to this form of business organization. The most important advantages are listed below:

9–2

1. The corporate form is the most effective for *raising money*. This is particularly true if large amounts of money are needed to run the business. Corporations have more alternative methods of getting money than either a proprietorship or a partnership.

2. Owners of a corporation have *limited liability*. **Limited liability** is the concept that owners of a business are only responsible for its debts up to the amount they invest in the business. This means that the stockholders (owners) only risk the money they paid for their stock. If the corporation goes bankrupt or is sued, the owners' other assets cannot be used to pay the debts of the business.

9–1

limited liability
The concept that owners of a business are only responsible for its debts up to the amount they invest in the business.

3. A corporation has an *unlimited life*. The corporation does not cease to exist if a major stockholder dies. Even if all the owners of stock died, the corporation would continue. For example, USX (formerly U.S. Steel) has outlived Andrew Carnegie, its founder, and J. P. Morgan, its second owner. It almost certainly will still exist long after all the present stockholders have died.

4. Corporations can use *more specialized management*. Most corporations are big businesses. They can afford to have specialized managers in all parts of the business. They can hire people who are experts in marketing, accounting, forecasting, etc. Smaller businesses just cannot afford such specialization.

LEADERS
IN
ECONOMIC
THOUGHT

ANDREW CARNEGIE

Andrew Carnegie, known for his wealth, thought that "to die rich is to die disgraced." He was born to a poor, working-class family in Scotland in 1835. But at his death in 1919, he was worth about $23 million! And this was only a small part of his total wealth, since he gave away some 90 percent of it during his lifetime.

When Carnegie was 13, his family moved from Scotland to Pennsylvania. He and his father found jobs working 12-hour days in a cotton factory for $1.20 a week. At 15, Carnegie became a messenger for the Pittsburgh telegraph office. He memorized the names and locations of all the local businesses and learned Morse code. His hard work paid off, and he became a telegraph operator.

Thomas Scott, the Pittsburgh superintendent of the Pennsylvania Railroad, hired Carnegie in 1853 as his personal clerk and telegraph operator. When Scott was made vice-president of the company, the 24-year-old Carnegie became superintendent of the Pittsburgh division of the Pennsylvania Railroad. Carnegie bought $500 worth of stock in the Adams Express Company. A few years later, his investment was paying a yearly dividend of $1,400! Carnegie continued to obtain stock in many different companies.

He left the railroad in 1865 at age 30 to concentrate his efforts on the growing iron and steel industry. By 1900 Carnegie Steel had more output than the entire steel industry in Great Britain, which had led world production just 14 years before. Carnegie saw the benefits of vertical mergers, so he diversified into mining coal and iron ore. In 1901 Carnegie sold his company to J. P. Morgan for $429 million. In 53 years he had gone from earning $1.20 a week to selling part of his holdings for hundreds of millions of dollars. Carnegie shared his wealth, however. He endowed nearly 3,000 public libraries and his money helped start Carnegie-Mellon University in Pittsburgh.

Carnegie's story shows how the corporate kind of business can develop successful companies. Because he saw the advantages of horizontal and vertical mergers, he was more successful in business than he could have been otherwise.

5. There are usually some *tax advantages* to the corporate form of organization.

6. In a corporation, the *risks of the business are spread* among many owners. Each stockholder takes some risk. But no one person has to accept all the risk.

Disadvantages of a Corporation. Our economy depends heavily on corporations, but there are some disadvantages to this form of business organization:

1. A corporation is *more difficult to begin.* It is easier to start a proprietorship or partnership than a corporation. Government approval must be obtained to form a corporation. However, the other forms of business can be started by individuals without any such approval.

2. In a corporation, the *owners have less direct control* over the business. This is more common in large corporations than in small ones. In large corporations, the owners are usually far from the day-to-day operation of the business. Professional managers actually run the business and are in charge of the firm's operations.

3. To some extent, corporations are subject to *double taxation.* The corporation's profits are taxed by corporate income taxes. The corporation pays dividends to stockholders out of the firm's after-tax income. **Dividends** are a part of corporate income paid to owners of a corporation's stock. The stockholders then pay personal income taxes on the dividends. So, each dollar of a corporation's earnings gets taxed twice.

4. Corporations are *limited to activities stated in their articles of incorporation.* The articles of incorporation state the purpose of the business. Unless these are written carefully and in broad terms, the corporation's activities can be limited. This is not a problem for proprietorships or partnerships.

9–2

9–1
dividends
A part of corporate income paid to owners of the corporation's stock.

DISTRIBUTION OF THE THREE BUSINESS FORMS

Think about the last time you went shopping. As you walked down the street or through the shopping center, what kinds of stores did you see? Most were probably small proprietorships or partnerships: shoe stores, hardware stores, and record stores.

Some of the larger stores were part of a corporation such as Sears, J.C. Penney, Wal-Mart, or K mart. Many retail stores are fairly small and are proprietorships or partnerships. But what about the products they sell? Arrow shirts, Levi's jeans, Head tennis racquets, Pioneer stereos, and almost all other products come from corporations. In manufacturing, corporations are the dominant form of business organization.

9-4   As Table 9–1 shows, the majority of companies in the United States are proprietorships. In 1987, there were more than 13 million proprietorships. At the same time, there were over 3.6 million corporations and roughly 1.6 million partnerships. Proprietorships represent about 71 percent of all companies; corporations, 20 percent; and partnerships, 9 percent. These proportions have been about the same since 1960.

TABLE 9–1

NUMBER OF FIRMS AND DOLLAR VALUE OF SALES FOR PROPRIETORSHIPS, PARTNERSHIPS, AND CORPORATIONS

	Proprietorships	Partnerships	Corporations
Number of Firms	13,091,000	1,648,000	3,612,000
Percentage of All Firms	71%	9%	20%
Dollar Value of Sales	$610,800,000,000	$411,400,000,000	$9,185,500,000,000
Percentage of All Sales	6%	4%	90%

Source: U.S. Bureau of the Census, *Statistical Abstract of the United States: 1991*, 111th ed. (Washington, D.C., 1991), 525.

If you look at sales rather than the number of firms, you get a different picture. Proprietorships and partnerships appear much less important. Corporations clearly produce a greater dollar value of sales than the other two combined. The sales of corporations are measured in trillions of dollars. Such numbers are too high to be meaningful to most of us. Perhaps it would mean more to note that this represents over $37,000 of sales for each person in the United States.

Figure 9–1 uses pie charts to show the percentage distributions of the number of firms and the dollar value of sales. In the pie chart on the left, the number of proprietorships is far larger than the other two types of organizations. But the right-hand chart tells a different story. There, corporations account for most of the sales. You can see that the proprietorships are fairly small businesses, and the real giants of business are the corporations.

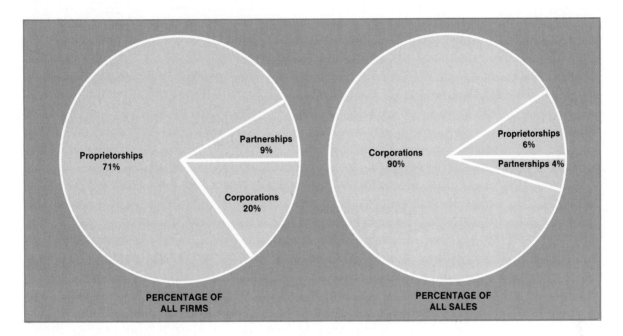

FIGURE 9–1 PERCENTAGE OF FIRMS AND SALES FOR EACH TYPE OF BUSINESS ORGANIZATION
Proprietorships represent the greatest percentage of all firms. Corporations represent a smaller percentage of firms, but the largest percentage of sales.

To see how big corporations are, let's look at the 20 largest United States corporations. Table 9–2 lists these firms along with their sales, employment, and headquarter cities. The firms are listed in order of size as measured by their 1990 sales.

The dollar value of sales for these firms is huge. In total, these 20 firms had sales of over one trillion dollars. For just these 20 corporations, sales represent more than $4,000 per person in the United States. These firms employed a total of 4,424,100 people in 1990. That represents over 4 percent of the total labor force. The employment of just those 20 firms was about the same as the entire population of the Detroit metropolitan area.

TABLE 9–2

SALES AND EMPLOYMENT FOR 20 LARGEST U.S. CORPORATIONS
(Rank Based on 1990 Sales)

Company	Sales	Employment	Corporate Headquarters
1. General Motors	$124,705,000,000	761,400	Detroit, MI
2. Exxon	105,519,000,000	104,000	Irving, TX
3. Ford Motor	97,650,000,000	381,400	Dearborn, MI
4. IBM	69,018,000,000	378,500	Armonk, NY
5. General Electric	59,414,000,000	295,000	Fairfield, CT
6. Mobil	57,819,000,000	67,600	Fairfax, VA
7. Sears, Roebuck	55,972,000,000	480,000	Chicago, IL
8. Philip Morris Cos.	44,323,000,000	161,600	New York, NY
9. Texaco	40,899,000,000	38,100	White Plains, NY
10. El duPont	39,709,000,000	144,900	Wilmington, DE
11. Chevron	38,607,000,000	54,500	San Francisco, CA
12. Citicorp	38,385,000,000	93,500	New York, NY
13. AT&T	37,285,000,000	278,600	New York, NY
14. Wal-Mart Stores	32,742,000,000	299,000	Bentonville, AR
15. K mart	32,339,000,000	369,000	Troy, MI
16. Chrysler	30,620,000,000	109,900	Highland Park, MI
17. Amoco	28,010,000,000	54,100	Chicago, IL
18. Boeing	27,595,000,000	161,700	Seattle, WA
19. Procter & Gamble	25,848,000,000	84,100	Cincinnati, OH
20. American Express	24,332,000,000	107,200	New York, NY

Source: *Forbes: The Forbes 500's Annual Directory,* 147, no. 9 (April 29, 1991), 164, 238–282.

The largest United States corporation, as measured by sales, was General Motors. GM had sales of $124,705,000,000 in 1990. That represented about $500 per person in the United States.

Comparing the sizes of corporations with the sizes of selected countries also helps you to understand how large some corporations are. For example, in Table 9–3 you can see that Ford's sales were greater than the total production of Portugal, or Colombia, or Morocco as well as other countries, many of which are not listed.

FINANCING A BUSINESS

Every business needs money to get started and run day-to-day operations. Start-up money for most proprietorships and partnerships comes from the savings of the people involved and some borrowed funds from banks or friends. Borrowing from a bank usually requires some form of collateral as security to back up the loan. The people starting the company may pledge their homes and/or other assets as security. If business is bad and they are unable to repay the loan, they risk having to sell their property to pay the loan.

TABLE 9-3

COMPARATIVE ECONOMIC SIZES OF SELECTED
COUNTRIES AND U.S. CORPORATIONS

Country or Corporation	Total Production (Countries) or Sales (Corporations)*
United States	$4,881,000,000,000
Japan	2,856,000,000,000
United Kingdom	801,600,000,000
Switzerland	188,900,000,000
Austria	123,700,000,000
General Motors	121,817,000,000
Ford	92,446,000,000
Exxon	80,868,000,000
IBM	59,681,000,000
Sears, Roebuck	50,251,000,000
General Electric	49,773,000,000
Mobil	48,198,000,000
Portugal	40,600,000,000
Colombia	36,600,000,000
K mart	27,550,000,000
Morocco	18,800,000,000

*Data are 1988 sales for U.S. corporations and 1988 GNP for countries.

Source: For corporations: "The Forbes Sales 500," *Forbes,* 143, no. 9 (May 1, 1989), 178–183.
For countries: U.S. Bureau of the Census, *Statistical Abstract of the United States: 1991*, 111th ed. (Washington, D.C., 1991), 841.

Once the business has been established, partnerships and proprietorships will try to establish a line of credit with a local bank. Having a line of credit makes getting short-term loans easier. The business owners will not have to go through a lot of paperwork each time a loan is needed. Short-term loans based on a line of credit usually are not secured. That is, they are not backed by other assets of the owners.

Corporations can use other types of financing, too. Issuing bonds and selling stock are the two most common methods corporations use to get money. A **bond** is a certificate stating the amount the corporation has borrowed from the holder of the bond and the terms of repayment. Bonds can be issued at any amount, but bonds of $1,000, $5,000, and $10,000 are very common. If a firm wanted to raise $1 million by selling bonds, it might offer to sell a thousand $1,000 bonds.

People who buy bonds get a yearly payment in exchange for the corporation's use of their money. A $1,000 bond paying 6 percent would give the lender $60 per year in interest. In financial dealings, interest is the payment for using someone else's money.

bond

A certificate stating the amount the corporation has borrowed from the holder of the bond and the terms of repayment.

Each bond has a maturity date. That is, each bond has a date when the amount of the bond must be paid back to the buyer. Suppose you bought a $1,000 bond that paid 9 percent and had a 10-year maturity. You would get $90 each year in interest and, at the end of 10 years, you would get your $1,000 back.

Corporations can also sell stock. There are several types of stock, but the most important is called common stock. **Common stock** gives the holder a partial ownership of the corporation. If a corporation issued 10,000 shares of common stock and you bought 1,000 of them, you would own one tenth of the business. In turn, the corporation would have use of your money to run the business.

Owners of common stock are not guaranteed any payment. They may receive dividends if the company is successful. If the company does well, the market value of the stock may go up. For example, shares that were purchased for $15 may go up to $20, $25, or more. If the company is not successful, the owners of common stock lose money. If a corporation goes out of business, bondholders' interest will be paid and bonds repaid before common stockholders receive anything.

Stockholders are the owners of the business. The stockholders elect people to the board of directors. So stockholders have a lot of power in a corporation.

MERGERS: ONE WAY BUSINESSES GET BIGGER

In addition to growing by selling more, many firms grow by buying other businesses. A corporation buys another corporation by buying its stock. This may be all of a corporation's stock, or just enough to control the company. When two firms combine in this way, they have merged. A **merger** is the combining of one company with another company it buys. A corporate merger results when one corporation buys another. There are three kinds of mergers: horizontal, vertical, and conglomerate mergers. Let's look at each of these.

Horizontal Mergers

A **horizontal merger** is a merger of two companies in the same business. An example would be a merger between two large retailing corporations such as K mart and Sears (see Table 9–2). The term *horizontal merger* indicates that the two firms operate at the same level, or stage, in the production process. Sears and K mart are both at the retail sales level. There are other examples of horizontal mergers. Two coal mining companies, or two airlines, or two companies that make bicycles might merge.

9–1

common stock

Stock that gives the holder a partial ownership of the corporation.

9–1

merger

The combining of one company with another company it buys.

9–1

horizontal merger

A merger of two companies in the same business.

Horizontal mergers are watched carefully by the Antitrust Division of the Federal Justice Department. If horizontal mergers reduce competition in an industry, they may not be in the public interest. The merging of two small companies would probably cause little harm. There even may be benefits to the public if products can be produced at a lower cost because of the merger. However, if the companies already have a large share of the market, the government would probably block the merger. For example, if General Motors and Ford wanted to merge, the government probably would not allow them to do so. Such a merger would give the new firm too much control over the automobile industry.

9–5

Vertical Mergers

A **vertical merger** is a merger of two companies which are at different stages in the same production process. For example, a merger between a steel company and a car manufacturer would be a vertical merger. The steel would be an input to making cars. A merger between a department store chain and an appliance manufacturer would be a vertical merger, because the appliances could be sold through the department stores. The appliance manufacturer and the department store chain operate at different levels, or stages, in the process that gets appliances from the manufacturer to individual buyers.

9–1

vertical merger
A merger of two companies which are at different stages in the same production process.

The Antitrust Division of the Justice Department also keeps a close eye on vertical mergers. If such a merger might reduce competition, the government may block the merger. Suppose there were many firms that made steel but only a few that mined iron ore. Now suppose that one of the steel producers merged with one or more of the ore companies. The steel company could restrict the flow of ore to the other steel companies. This, then, could reduce competition in steel production. Therefore, the government might not permit this merger.

9–5

Conglomerate Mergers

A **conglomerate merger** is a merger of two companies which are in different businesses. One of the most widely publicized conglomerate mergers was the purchase of Montgomery Ward (a large retail sales firm) by Mobil (an oil firm). The two businesses have little in common. The public was alarmed by this conglomerate merger because people thought Mobil should use its money to expand oil production. But remember that horizontal and vertical mergers are often discouraged by the government. Had Mobil used its money to expand in the energy field, the merger may well have been blocked.

9–1

conglomerate merger
A merger of two companies which are in different businesses.

9–1

conglomerates

Firms made up of many divisions and/or subsidiaries that may not have much in common in their lines of business.

This type of merger results in the formation of large conglomerates. **Conglomerates** are firms made up of many divisions and/or subsidiaries that may not have much in common in their lines of business. What they have in common is that they are owned by one firm. An example of a conglomerate that almost everyone knows is PepsiCo, Inc. PepsiCo owns divisions and subsidiaries such as

> Pepsi-Cola Company
> PepsiCo Wines and Spirits
> Frito-Lay, Inc.
> Kentucky Fried Chicken Corporation
> Pizza Hut, Inc.
> Taco Bell
> Redux Realty, Inc.

9–5   The government has less actively opposed conglomerate mergers because it is not certain that they reduce competition. For example, Redux Realty would not be in competition with Frito-Lay or other parts of PepsiCo, Inc. Kentucky Fried Chicken, Pizza Hut, and Taco Bell are all in the same fast food sector of the economy. However, each of these has a small enough market share that their joint ownership probably does little to reduce competition.

REVIEWING THE CHAPTER

9–6   1. All businesses must meet the *test of the market* if they are to survive. This means they must provide goods or services for which consumers are willing to pay. Therefore, the goods must give consumers satisfaction, and they must be affordable. Firms that are not able to do this will eventually go out of business.

9–2   2. A proprietorship is a form of business in which one person owns the entire business. There are more proprietorships in the United States than any other form of business. In part, this is because they are easy to start. The major disadvantage of a proprietorship is that the owner faces unlimited liability. This means that the owner's personal assets can be used to pay debts of the firm should the business fail.

9–2   3. A partnership is very similar to a proprietorship. In a partnership, two or more people own the business together. They agree to share in the work and in the profits of the business. Each partner's share of the work or profits need not be equal. Partnerships are also easy to start. And with more than one owner, it is usually easier to raise money for the firm's operations. The major disadvantage of a partnership is that the partners are subject to unlimited liability.

9–2   4. A corporation is a form of business which is itself a legal entity. The owners are people who have purchased common stock in the business. In a corporation, these owners are usually separate from the managers who run the daily affairs of the business. A corporation becomes a legal entity when its articles of incorporation have been approved and it receives a charter. The articles of incorporation specify the corporation's purpose, how it is financed, and other details about its formation. Two major advantages of a corporation are limited liability for the owners and the availability of more ways to raise money.

9–4   5. While proprietorships represent over 70 percent of all U.S. firms, they make less than 10 percent of all sales. This means that most proprietorships are fairly small firms. There are far fewer corporations—20 percent of all firms. But corporations account for about 90 percent of all sales. Therefore, corporations must be fairly large firms.

9–4   6. The 20 largest firms in the United States sold over one trillion dollars in 1990. This equals about $4,000 for every man, woman, and child in the country. Those same 20 firms employed over 4 million people in 1990. That is about the same as the population of the Detroit metropolitan area.

9–3   7. Money to start or run a business can be obtained from several sources. Proprietorships and partnerships use money mostly from the owner(s) and from bank loans. Corporations can also raise money by issuing bonds or selling stock.

9–5   8. Mergers are one way in which firms can grow and expand. A merger takes place when one firm buys all the stock in another firm (or enough to control the company being bought). When one firm buys another that is in the same line of business, it is a horizontal merger. When the two firms are at different stages in one production process, it is a vertical merger. If the firms are in unrelated types of businesses, it is a conglomerate merger.

REVIEWING ECONOMIC TERMS

9–1   Supply definitions for the following terms:

proprietorship   partnership
unlimited liability   corporation

articles of incorporation   common stock
charter   merger
stock   horizontal merger
limited liability   vertical merger
dividends   conglomerate merger
bond   conglomerates

REVIEWING ECONOMIC CONCEPTS

9–6   1. What is meant by "the test of the market"?

9–4   2. What are the three kinds of business organization?

9–2   3. What are the advantages and disadvantages of organizing a business as a proprietorship?

9–2   4. What are the advantages and disadvantages of organizing a business as a partnership?

9–2   5. What are the advantages and disadvantages of organizing a business as a corporation?

9–4   6. Describe the size of the three kinds of business organizations in relation to each other. Use both the number of businesses in each category and the sales volume of each.

9–3   7. How do the three kinds of business organizations raise money?

9–5   8. Why does government watch horizontal mergers closely?

9–5   9. Why might government prevent a vertical merger?

9–5   10. Why does government usually not oppose conglomerate mergers?

APPLYING ECONOMIC CONCEPTS

9–2   1. List three businesses in your city that you think are proprietorships. Then talk to the owner or manager of one of these to see if you are correct. Ask why the business is operated as a proprietorship and write a paragraph summarizing the owner's answer.

9–2   2. Why would some businesses use the partnership form of organization rather than operate as a proprietorship? Are there any disadvantages to doing so? If so, what are they?

9–2   3. Why do you think most very big businesses are corporations?

9–2 4. Choose two corporations that you are familiar with, either because you buy a product each makes or because you know someone who works for the company. Then go to the library and find the following information about those two corporations. Use *Forbes* magazine's latest list of the "Forbes 500's" which is always in a late spring issue of the magazine. Try to find the following: (a) the firm's sales, (b) the firm's employment, (c) where the firm's home office is located (city and state), and (d) the firm's rank by sales volume. From the *Directory of Corporate Affiliations (Who Owns Whom)*, find other companies those firms may own. Or find who owns the firms you chose to research.

9–6 5. Do corporations, partnerships, and proprietorships all have to meet the "test of the market"? What happens if they fail the test?

9–5 6. Think of an example of each of the three kinds of mergers. Explain why you classify them as you do.

9–4 7. Compare the three types of business organizations in terms of the volume of sales each has and how many of each there are in the United States. Why do you think the number of firms and sales are distributed in the way they are?

9–3 8. What is the difference between getting money for a corporation by issuing bonds or by selling stock? Which would you rather own: $10,000 worth of General Motors stock or a bond issued by General Motors with a value of $10,000? What would you think is important in making this decision?

IS A NEW BUSINESS IN YOUR FUTURE?

You may be one of many people who decide to start your own business rather than work for someone else. Over a half-million new firms are started each year. Both the risks and rewards of opening your own business can be quite high. As many as 50 percent fail to meet the test of the market; many fail within the first five years. There are high risks; however, the rewards may be more than worth the risks. You might have considerable financial success, but what is equally important, you may gain a great deal of personal satisfaction. Often this part of the benefit is called "psychic income."

In starting a new business, you should be sure to obtain professional help. You should consult a lawyer for advice on legal details, an accountant to set up needed accounting procedures, and a marketing expert to help you develop a marketing plan. You can also obtain free information and advice from the Small Business Administration.

CHAPTER 10

PERFECT COMPETITION AND MONOPOLY

Learning Objectives

10–1   Define terms related to the organization of markets.

10–2   List five characteristics of market organization.

10–3   Name four kinds of market organization.

10–4   Explain perfect competition in terms of the five characteristics of market organization.

10–5   Explain monopoly in terms of the five characteristics of market organization.

10–6   Describe the demand curve and level of output and price for the perfectly competitive firm.

10–7   Describe the demand curve and level of output and price for the monopolistic firm.

HOW MARKETS DIFFER

Firms can be organized as proprietorships, partnerships, or corporations. These three kinds of business organization refer to ownership and internal control of the business. But it is also important to know how firms are organized with respect to each other. In this chapter, you will study the overall, external organization of firms that sell products that are substitutes for each other.

Every firm is part of some market. General Motors, Ford, and Chrysler are three of the firms that make up the seller's side of the automobile market. Wheat farmers from Montana, Iowa, Ohio, and Nebraska are part of the wheat market. Schwinn, Huffy, and Peugeot are active in the bicycle market. Kroger, Safeway, and IGA all sell products in the retail grocery market. When the term *market* is used this way, it means the industry or activity that represents the firm's most important line of business. **Market organization** refers to the way participants in markets are organized and how many participants there are. The word *industry* often means the same as *market*.

10–1

market organization
The way participants in markets are organized and how many participants there are.

10–2

The five characteristics listed below can be used to differentiate between forms of market organization. We will explore each of these five market characteristics in the following sections:

1. Number of firms

2. Type of product sold

3. Ease and freedom to enter or leave the industry

4. Amount of information about the market

5. Amount of price control

Number of Firms

From the seller's side, markets differ in five major ways. First, the number of firms that are active in the market differs. Compare the number of firms selling electric power in your hometown with the number of firms selling groceries. In some markets, there are many firms trying to get your business. In others, there may be just a few firms or even just one firm. The number of firms in active competition with each other influences how each one behaves. This is especially true with respect to how each firm prices its product, what services each firm offers, and how much each produces.

188

Illustration 10–1
Many firms belong to the seller's side of the market for business equipment. Large markets like this one often hold trade shows, which bring many buyers and sellers together under one roof.

Type of Product Sold

In some markets, the products offered by every firm are very similar. Wheat from one farm is very much like wheat from another farm. Gasoline from Exxon is nearly identical to gasoline from Mobil. However, in other markets, the product of one firm may be quite different from that of another firm. A Bic pen is very different from a Cross pen. A Cadillac is very different from a Ford. The extent to which products differ between sellers also influences the seller's behavior.

Ease and Freedom to Enter or Leave the Industry

It is relatively easy to enter some industries, but very hard to get started in others. If you wanted to open an ice cream shop, it would not be too difficult. You would need just a small amount of space. And you would not need a great deal of highly technical equipment. So, it would be fairly easy to get into the ice cream shop business. The same is true for growing corn, wheat, tomatoes, or most other agricultural products. Agriculture is becoming a more complex industry and uses more sophisticated capital equipment every year. But it is still easier to enter this industry than most others. Businesses that are easy to enter are also usually easy to leave. You can quit and sell your buildings, machines, and/or land without too much loss of value.

On the other hand, some businesses are very hard to enter. To successfully enter the automobile industry, for example, you would probably have to spend hundreds of millions of dollars. The amount of technical knowledge and sophisticated equipment necessary would be huge. The same is true for industries such as steel and telephone communications. In the phone industry, entry is further restricted by government controls. Industries that use a lot of sophisticated equipment—like metal engraving or newspaper printing—are also difficult to leave. The equipment is usually highly specialized; so it has few, if any, other uses. This makes it hard to sell the equipment without a substantial financial loss. So, once a firm is in business, there is much pressure not to leave.

Amount of Information About the Market

In some industries, firms know a great deal about their markets. They know how much rival firms pay for inputs, how other firms operate, and how much others sell their products for. Wheat farmers, for example, know how much other wheat farmers pay for seed, fertilizer, tractors, and fuel. They also know the selling price for the wheat produced, because television stations in agricultural areas generally report prices for wheat and other products on regular newscasts.

The flow of information among firms is not always this complete. In the production of computers, cars, tents, radios, and most other products, there is not a perfect flow of information among firms. Each firm has some trade secrets it tries to protect. When one firm finds a new and better method of production, it is kept a secret as long as possible. The list price for a product often does not represent the actual sales price. Other buyers and sellers may find it difficult to determine what price you actually paid for a stereo system with a list price of $800. You might have paid $700 while another buyer paid $750 and yet another buyer paid the full list price.

Amount of Price Control

Some firms have a good deal of control over the prices they charge, while others have very little control. The amount of control a firm has over price is determined in part by the market characteristics just described. You will see this as you study the major forms of market organization in this chapter.

If a firm has no control over price, we say the firm is a price taker. A **price taker** is a firm that takes a price determined by forces outside of the firm's control. On the other hand, a **price setter** is a firm that has some control over the price at which its product sells. There are different degrees to which a firm that is a price setter can set price. In some situations, the firm may have a great deal of control over price. In other cases, there is only a very small amount of control in the hands of a single firm.

10–1
price taker
A firm that takes a price determined by forces outside of the firm's control.

10–1
price setter
A firm that has some control over the price at which its product sells.

FORMS OF MARKET ORGANIZATION: AN OVERVIEW

10-3

Using the five market characteristics we have just described, firms can be placed in four major types of market organization. You will see that firms behave differently depending on the kind of market organization. The four major kinds of market organization are listed below:

1. Perfect competition

2. Monopolistic competition

3. Oligopoly

4. Monopoly

The most important characteristic is the number of firms selling in the market. In perfect competition there are a great many firms, while in a monopoly there is just one firm. Monopolistic competition and oligopoly lie between these two extremes. Most business in the United States takes place in these two market structures. However, it is important to understand perfect competition and monopoly because they are used in many public policy debates. But in terms of total sales in the economy, they are not as important as the other two.

Let's look at the characteristics and the good and bad aspects of these four types of market organization. Perfect competition and monopoly are discussed in this chapter. In Chapter 11 you will learn about monopolistic competition and oligopoly.

PERFECT COMPETITION

10-4

10-1

perfect competition
A form of market organization in which a great many small firms produce a homogeneous product.

Perfect competition is a form of market organization in which a great many small firms produce a homogeneous product. Let's examine perfect competition by using the five characteristics of market organization.

Number of Firms

In a perfectly competitive market, there are *a great many sellers of a product*. An industry that comes close to satisfying the characteristics of perfect competition is agriculture. There are certainly many farms in the United States. Although the number varies from year to year, there are about 2.2 million firms involved in agriculture. Most of these firms are proprietorships and are small farms. Each firm is very small in relation to the entire market.

For example, the percentage of wheat grown by any one farmer would equal less than even one tenth of a percent. There are about 2.7 billion bushels of wheat grown each year in the United States. If a farmer grew 40 bushels of wheat per acre of land, that would be above-average production. A 50,000-acre wheat farm certainly would be considered very large. A farmer with 50,000 acres, with each acre yielding 40 bushels of wheat, would produce the following:

50,000 acres × 40 bushels per acre = 2,000,000 bushels of wheat

This is about 0.07 percent of total wheat production. So, even a very large farm is not likely to produce a meaningful percentage of total output.

Type of Product Sold

Each firm in a perfectly competitive market produces *a product which is just like the output of other firms* in that market. A bushel of wheat from one farm is very much like a bushel of wheat from any other farm. A buyer of the wheat, such as General Mills, would not care whether the wheat was grown on the Myers farm in North Dakota or on the Durkin farm in Montana. General Mills not only wouldn't care, but it would have almost no way of knowing which farm produced which bushel of wheat.

When the output of one firm so closely resembles that of other firms, we say the product is homogeneous. **Homogeneous products** vary little from producer to producer. That is, the products of all producers are exactly the same. There is no way to tell them apart. There are no brands or trademarks. In such a case, buyers do not care from which firm they buy.

10–1
homogeneous products
Products that vary little from producer to producer.

Illustration 10–2
Perfect competition involves many small firms producing a homogeneous, or identical, product. Egg production is a good example of perfect competition, since all eggs are about the same.

Ease and Freedom to Enter or Leave the Industry

In perfect competition, there must be *complete freedom for new firms to enter the industry as well as for existing firms to leave.* This must also be fairly easy to do. Each year some farmers leave farming while others start farming. In recent years, more people have been leaving than entering agriculture, so the number of farms has been declining.

No one forces a person to start or to quit farming. This decision is made by individuals. Farmers do not try to block others from starting or from leaving the industry. The amount of money necessary to get started in agriculture on a small scale is not great. At least, the amount is not large when compared with the cost of entering many other industries.

Amount of Information About the Market

In perfect competition, information flows freely and completely among participants in the market. All *buyers and sellers have perfect information.* Each seller knows the prices others charge for products as well as the prices paid for inputs. Each producer can have the same information regarding production methods.

In agriculture, for example, firms have nearly perfect information about the market. There is a wide network of sources that provides information to farmers. Farm cooperatives, university agriculture extension programs, seed and fertilizer companies, equipment dealers, and many government agencies help to spread information throughout the industry.

A great deal of information also is available to farmers through the news media. Radio, television, and newspapers give daily information about prices, sales, and factors expected to influence the market in the future. The daily papers in cities such as Minneapolis, Chicago, Bismarck, Great Falls, and hundreds of others list such information. Newspapers often list prices, price changes from the previous day, and volume for such products as wheat, oats, barley, and soybeans, as well as hogs, cattle and calves, and sheep. For many of these products, information will be given for several subgroups, too. Different types of wheat and different weight classes of cattle, for example, will be included.

Illustration 10–3
In a perfectly competitive industry like farming, producers have complete information available. A farmer can check daily prices, price changes, and other factors which influence the agricultural market.

Degree of Price Control

You have now seen that in perfect competition there are a great many firms selling products that are perfect substitutes for each other. There is free entry into, or exit from, the industry. And all firms have complete knowledge about the market. From these characteristics of perfect competition, you should expect that *no one firm would have any control over the market price for its output.*

Once more, think about the example of agriculture. Suppose the market price for No. 1 hard winter wheat is $4 per bushel. No buyer will pay more and no seller will sell for less. Suppose you went to the grain market with 5,000 bushels and said you wanted $4.10 per bushel. Buyers would likely tell you to move your trucks aside so the next seller could unload. They would not pay more than the $4 market price because they could buy as much as they wished at $4. Keeping your 5,000 bushels from the market would have no effect since they are such a small part of total wheat production.

On the other hand, the seller has no reason to offer to sell below the market price. If you were willing to sell the 5,000 bushels of wheat at $3.90, buyers would gladly buy it from you at that price. They would save $.10 per bushel. But you would lose $.10 per bushel, or $500. We are assuming that you are raising wheat to earn money. Therefore, it is most unlikely that you would sell it for less than buyers would be willing to pay. This is true, especially since you would know exactly what buyers were willing to pay.

Demand Curve

Producers in a perfectly competitive industry sell at the market price. The sellers take that price as given. They cannot sell anything at a higher price and have no reason to accept selling at a lower price. For this reason, perfectly competitive firms are price takers. They must accept a price that is determined outside of their control and sell whatever amount they wish at that price.

What determines the price in such cases? Price is determined by the interaction of market demand and market supply, as you saw in Chapter 8. The right-hand side of Figure 10–1 shows a diagram of the market demand and supply for wheat. The equilibrium price of $4 per bushel is determined at the point where the demand curve crosses the supply curve.

The demand for the output of any one firm is shown on the left-hand side of Figure 10–1. At the $4 market price, buyers are willing to purchase all that each producer wishes to sell. *In perfect competition, the demand for any firm's output is therefore a horizontal line at the market price.* Every seller takes the market price and sells all that is produced at that price.

10–6

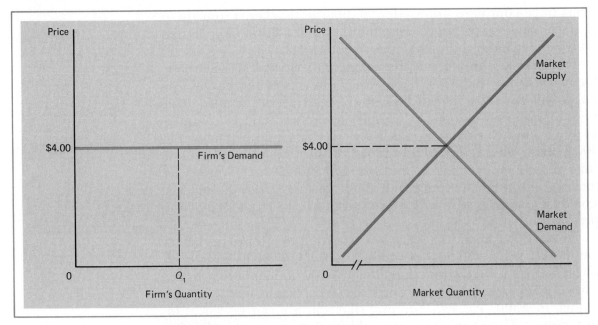

FIGURE 10–1 SUPPLY AND DEMAND IN PERFECT COMPETITION
The demand curve for the output of a perfectly competitive firm is a horizontal line at
the level of the market price. This is shown in the left-hand graph. The market price
is where market demand equals market supply, as pictured in the right-hand graph.

Output and Price Levels

10–6   Because of the characteristics of perfect competition, firms will
be led to produce an amount of output at which economic profit is
zero. This does not mean that the owner (a farmer, for example)
would not make a good living. The farmer's income is a part of
the cost of running the business and so should be included in the
firm's total cost. **Profit** is defined as total revenue minus total
costs. A perfectly competitive firm will be led by natural economic
forces to produce where total revenue equals total cost. So, profit
would be zero. There is no excess return to people in that form
of production.

10–1
profit
Total revenue minus
total costs.

If profit were above zero, new firms would enter the industry.
This would increase supply — thus, price would fall, which would
reduce profits. If profit were less than zero (negative profit, or a
loss), firms would leave the industry. This would decrease supply.
Price would rise and profits would rise (losses would become less).
These natural economic forces would direct each firm to produce
at a level such as Q_1 in Figure 10–1. At Q_1, the firm would have a
zero economic profit. Remember, though, that each firm would
still have enough revenue to pay for all inputs including the
owner's salary. But there would be no excess returns.

This rate of output has several important results. First, price is equal to the average cost of producing each unit of output. This again means that profit must be zero and that there is no excess return to the owners or workers in the industry. Second, at this level of production, the average cost of production is as low as possible. This is often taken as a measure of economic efficiency. Since perfectly competitive firms produce at the lowest possible unit cost, they are said to be economically efficient.

Third, at this level of output, price is just equal to the additional cost of producing that unit of output. If one more unit were produced, the added cost would be greater than the price. But if one less unit were produced, price would be greater than the added cost. The equality of price and the additional cost of producing one more unit of output is considered a measure of the ideal (optimum) allocation of resources in production. So, in perfect competition, just the right level of resources is used to produce each good.

MONOPOLY

A **monopoly** is a form of market organization in which there is only one seller of a product. Electric, water, natural gas, and local telephone companies are examples of monopolies in most communities. Let's again use the five characteristics of market organization to examine monopolies.

10–5

10–1

monopoly
A form of market organization in which there is only one seller of a product.

Number of Firms

Monopoly refers to a situation in which there is *a single seller of a good or service.* For most households, there is a single source of electric power. You buy electricity from the local power company, or you don't buy it at all. Just one seller is available to you. True, there are many firms from coast to coast that sell electricity. Montana Power, Ohio Edison, and Consolidated Edison are examples of such firms. But the consumer cannot shop around. In almost any geographic area, there is just one seller of electricity. The same is true of local phone services, natural gas for home heating, and water piped to your home. In each case, there is a single seller.

There are still other cases in which a local monopoly exists. In many smaller cities and towns there is just one taxi company, one movie theater, one hospital, or one grocery store. As long as the buyer cannot obtain the good or service (or a close substitute) elsewhere, the owner of such a business has a local monopoly.

Illustration 10–4
In your town, probably only one power company is available to provide electrical power. You buy electricity from the local power company, or you don't buy it at all.

Type of Product Sold

The product of a monopolist is usually unique. This means that there are no products which are directly comparable. There are no good substitutes. In perfect competition, the product of one firm is a perfect substitute for the product of any other firm. But for monopoly this is not true. There is no close substitute for electrical power or local telephone access. If you want the kind of satisfaction that comes from consuming such a product, you must buy it from the monopolist who sells it.

Ease and Freedom to Enter or Leave the Industry

In monopoly, the *entry of new firms or the ability of firms to leave is very difficult, if not impossible.* There are several reasons for this, and they are at the heart of why monopolies develop in the first place.

First, there are usually very high costs in getting machines and other equipment necessary for production. For example, producing electrical power requires a generating plant and a transmission system, plus office and related equipment. These necessary factors of production add up to hundreds of millions of dollars for even a small electric company. This much cost in equipment can prohibit entry into an industry.

A related aspect helps to keep such an industry a monopoly. Once one firm gets started, it can sell its product at a lower price because costs are spread over a large number of units of output and customers. A new firm entering such an industry starts out with fewer customers and has a higher cost of production per unit of output. The new firm's price would have to be higher than the existing firm's price to cover those higher costs.

In many monopolistic industries, the unit costs of production decrease with every additional unit produced. When this is true, it is more efficient (less costly) to have one firm than several or many firms. It may be impractical to have more than one firm. An example would be having more than one electric power company in a community. Competition in such an industry is not practical and is not in the public interest. These cases are called natural monopolies. A **natural monopoly** exists in an industry in which it is not practical to have competition.

A monopolistic industry may prevent competition through use of a patent. A **patent** is a legal protection for the inventor of a product or process which gives that person or company the sole right to produce the product or use the process for up to 17 years. This can keep other firms from entering a new industry.

In some cases, one firm may control access to critical raw material for producing a product. For some years, ALCOA controlled access to bauxite to limit entry into the aluminum industry. Until after World War II, ALCOA had a near monopoly in producing aluminum, mostly because it controlled this raw material.

In addition to these factors that can restrict entry, a monopoly may also be maintained by government regulations. Suppose that you could raise enough money to start an electric power company or a telephone company. To start your business, you would have to get approval from one or more regulatory agencies. It is very doubtful that you could get such approval. In most regulated monopoly cases, it is believed that the public interest is best served by having just one firm. If we had two electric companies, there would be twice as many lines running along our highways and through our cities. Each company would have separate electricity-generating plants. And each would have to operate at a smaller rate of output, if the market were shared. This almost certainly would mean higher electricity prices to consumers. So, the government often restricts entry and maintains a monopoly.

Leaving an industry in which a firm has a monopoly may be equally difficult. The equipment is usually highly specialized. Therefore, it may not be possible to sell it except at a very large loss. If the product is considered necessary for consumers, the government may not allow the firm to leave or go out of business. It is hard to imagine an entire city without electricity. Therefore, government would not allow a major electric power company to go out of business.

10–1

natural monopoly

A monopoly which exists in an industry in which it is not practical to have competition.

10–1

patent

A legal protection for the inventor of a product or process which gives that person or company the sole right to produce the product or use the process for up to 17 years.

Illustration 10–5
Sometimes a firm can control the amount of raw materials available to an industry. Until after World War II, ALCOA controlled access to bauxite and thus created a near-monopoly in the aluminum industry.

Amount of Information About the Market

The monopolist is the only firm in the market. So, you should expect that *the monopolist knows as much as can be known about the market.* The firm knows how much it pays for inputs, how it produces the product, the selling price, and the number of customers. Local monopolies that are part of a larger industry get a good deal of additional information through trade publications and corporate associations. A lot of information about regulated monopolies becomes a matter of public record and is available to all other firms. We can say, then, that monopolists generally have very good information about the market in which they sell.

Amount of Price Control

In a monopoly *the firm has a good deal of control over price,* since the monopolist is the only available seller of the product. With no other firms to supply a substitute product, consumers must either pay the price set by the monopolist or do without the product.

This leads to an important point. The monopolist can set the price but cannot force consumers to buy any particular amount at that price. The firm cannot raise price *and* make us buy more of the product. We, as consumers, may well decide to buy less at a higher price. Even for a product such as electricity, consumers have a choice in how much they buy. Most households could be far more careful about unnecessary use of electricity. Leaving lights on in an empty room and doing laundry in small loads are common wastes of electricity. There are many ways consumers can reduce the amount of electricity they use. Consumers could also switch, in part at least, to other forms of energy if electricity prices become too high.

Most monopolies are subject to government regulation, so prices are not set just by the firm. Some regulatory agency, such as the Public Service Commission, must approve all prices. Open public hearings usually allow consumers to have some voice in this process along with the company, stockholders, and other interested parties. Therefore, you can see that both consumers and the government have some power to limit the control a monopolist has over price.

Demand Curve

10–7   You now know that a monopolist is the only firm selling the product in a given market. So, it stands to reason that *the demand curve for the output of a monopolist equals the market demand curve for the product.* This is illustrated in Figure 10–2. The market demand

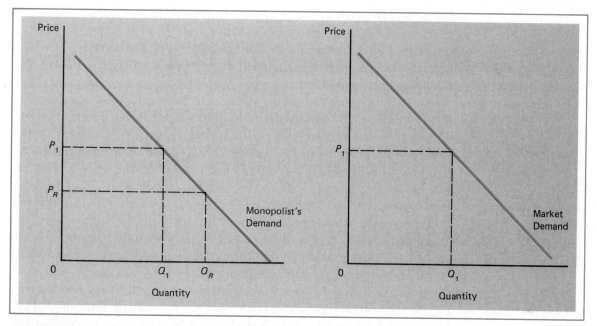

FIGURE 10–2 DEMAND IN MONOPOLY

The monopolist's demand curve and the market demand curve are exactly the same. This is because the monopolist is the only firm in the industry. Without regulation, the monopolist would produce Q_1 units and charge a price of P_1. With regulation, price would be lower, at P_R, and production would be higher, at Q_R.

curve is on the right-hand side, and the monopolist's demand curve is on the left-hand side.

At the price shown as P_1, the monopolist would sell Q_1 units. At that price, the market demand curve also shows that consumers would buy Q_1 units. This would be true of any price chosen. The monopolist's demand, then, must be the same as the market demand.

Output and Price Levels

Managers of a monopoly, like those of other firms, will try to make as much money as possible. They try to select the level of output with the greatest difference between total revenue from sales and total cost of production. This level of output occurs when 10-7 added revenue from selling one more unit equals the added cost of producing that unit.

At low levels of production and sales, the added revenue from increasing sales is normally greater than the added cost of producing the extra output. For example, $20 of added revenue might be obtained by spending $8 in added cost to produce one more unit of output. If so, the firm's profit would increase by $12. As long as the added revenue from new sales is greater than the added cost to produce the output, expansion is favorable. But as a firm expands, the added revenue tends to fall and the added cost tends to rise. Once added revenue and added cost are equal, it is not profitable to expand any more.

So, the monopolist determines the best and most profitable level of output by finding where the added revenue from sales equals the added cost of producing that output. This would be some level such as Q_1 in Figure 10–2. The price that corresponds to Q_1 along the demand curve becomes the best price to set. This is the price P_1. At P_1, consumers will purchase the Q_1 units the monopolist wishes to sell.

Often a regulatory agency will not permit the monopolist to charge this price. Rather, the agency may force the monopolist to set a price that equals the per-unit cost of production. This would result in a zero economic profit to the monopolist. Even so, production costs would be covered and stockholders would earn dividends since dividends are considered part of the cost of doing business. However, there would not be any excess return to the monopoly. Such a regulated price would be lower than P_1. In Figure 10–2, P_R might be such a regulated price. The corresponding quantity produced and sold would be Q_R.

COMPARISON OF MONOPOLY AND PERFECT COMPETITION

In a monopolistic market, prices will usually be higher than if the same industry were perfectly competitive. This is generally true because monopolies afford greater economies of scale in production. Again, electric power is a good example. If there were a great many firms supplying electric power to any area, the cost (and price) of electricity would be much higher.

If the monopolist's price is higher, you should expect that the total quantity purchased by consumers would be less than if the industry were perfectly competitive and price were lower. So, with monopoly we can expect price to be higher, but the quantity produced to be lower than in perfect competition.

In studying perfect competition, you learned that market forces work to assure the following conditions:

(a) Price would equal the per-unit cost of production, so there would be no excess profit.

(b) Price would equal the added cost of increasing output by one unit, so there would be a desirable allocation of resources in production.

(c) The per-unit cost of production would be as low as possible, so there would be efficiency in production.

How does a monopoly compare on these counts?

(a) In a monopoly, price will generally be greater than the per-unit cost of production, so some excess profit results. An exception is when the monopoly is regulated and forced to set price equal to the per-unit production cost.

(b) In a monopoly, price will almost always be greater than the added cost of producing one more unit of output. From society's view, this means that too few resources are allocated to this type of production. More should be produced and sold at a lower price.

(c) If there are not significant economies of scale, a monopolist normally produces where per-unit costs are higher than the lowest possible level. When this is true, some economic efficiency is lost. However, if there are economies of scale, per-unit costs will be lower with a monopoly than with perfect competition.

There are other benefits that society gets from monopolies besides the products the firms produce. Many monopolistic firms advertise on radio and television, as well as in newspapers and magazines. The money spent on such advertising helps cover the cost of making radio and television shows available. It also reduces the subscription price for magazines and newspapers. Monopolies are usually big firms and can afford to spend a good deal of money for research and development. All of us stand to benefit from the discoveries of such research. Perfectly competitive firms, on the other hand, are usually small and do virtually no advertising. They also spend almost nothing on research and development.

REVIEWING THE CHAPTER

10–1   1. Market organization refers to the way in which participants in a market are organized and how many participants there are.

10–2   2. From the seller's side, the kind of market organization is determined by five characteristics: (1) number of firms, (2) type of product sold, (3) ease and freedom to enter or leave the industry, (4) amount of information about the market, and (5) amount of price control.

10–4   3. Perfect competition is a form of market organization in which there are a great many firms producing products which are exactly the same. There is a very good flow of information among firms, and it is easy to enter or leave the industry. No one has any control over price.

10–6   4. These characteristics of perfect competition combine to give three important results: Price equals the per-unit cost of production, so there is no excess return to firms in that industry. Output is produced at the lowest possible unit cost, so there is economic efficiency. And price equals the added cost of producing the last unit of output. This is a measure of a desirable allocation of society's resources.

10–5   5. Monopoly is a form of market organization in which there is just one firm from which a consumer can buy the product. The monopolist has considerable control over price. But monopolies are usually regulated by the government to prevent misuse of their power.

10–7   6. A monopolist can be expected to produce at a level where price is greater than the per-unit cost. This means that excess economic returns result. The monopolist is not likely to produce at the lowest possible cost per unit of output. So, production is not as efficient as it could be. Also, since price is above the added cost of producing one more unit of output, the monopolist allocates too few resources to production.

10–7   7. In some ways, monopoly can benefit a market society. Due to economies of scale, many products are produced at a lower cost than could be done otherwise. Monopolists also do a good deal of research and development. And monopolists' support of the media through advertising helps make radio and television shows available and lowers subscription prices for newspapers and magazines.

REVIEWING ECONOMIC TERMS

10–1   Supply definitions for the following terms:

market organization   profit

price taker   monopoly

price setter   natural monopoly

perfect competition   patent

homogeneous products

REVIEWING ECONOMIC CONCEPTS

10–2   1. Identify five characteristics by which market organizations can be described.

10–3   2. List four kinds of market organization.

10–4   3. Describe perfect competition by using the five characteristics of market organization.

10–6   4. Describe the demand curve for the perfectly competitive firm. How does it compare with the market demand curve?

10–6   5. What is the level of output and price for the perfectly competitive firm?

10–5   6. Describe monopoly by using the five characteristics of market organization.

10–7   7. Describe the demand curve for the monopolistic firm. How does it compare with the market demand curve?

10–7   8. What is the level of output and price for the monopolistic firm?

APPLYING ECONOMIC CONCEPTS

10–4   1. Consider the characteristics of a perfectly competitive market. Why do you think governmental policy generally tries to promote competition?

10–5, 10–7   2. What are the good and bad features of a monopoly? Give examples of two items your household buys from firms that have a monopoly. Why do you think those firms have a monopoly?

10–6, 10–7   3. Explain why the demand curve for a perfectly competitive firm is a horizontal line at the market price. Why does the demand curve in the case of a monopoly have a negative slope?

10–4, 10–5   4. Make a chart like the one below, and then fill it in with one or two words per square to show how the market structures compare.

Form of Market Organization	Number of Firms	Type of Product	Market Knowledge	Ease of Entry	Degree of Price Control	Example of Each
Perfect Competition						
Monopoly						

CHAPTER 11

MONOPOLISTIC COMPETITION AND OLIGOPOLY

Learning Objectives

11-1 Define terms related to market organization.

11-2 Explain monopolistic competition in terms of the five characteristics of market organization.

11-3 Explain oligopoly in terms of the five characteristics of market organization.

11-4 Describe the demand curve and level of output and price for the monopolistically competitive firm.

11-5 Describe the demand curve and level of output and price for the oligopolistic firm.

MARKET ORGANIZATION: A REVIEW

You have learned that five characteristics can be used to classify market organization: (1) number of firms in the market, (2) type of product sold, (3) ease and freedom to enter or leave the industry, (4) amount of information about the market, and (5) amount of price control. After looking at perfect competition and monopoly, we will now explore the five characteristics within monopolistic competition and oligopoly.

MONOPOLISTIC COMPETITION

Monopolistic competition is a market organization in which many firms produce goods that are different, but similar enough to be substitutes. As the name implies, this form of market organization has some characteristics of monopoly and some of perfect competition. Overall, it is closer to perfect competition than to monopoly. In the next five sections, we explain monopolistic competition in terms of the characteristics of market organization.

11–1

monopolistic competition
A market organization in which many firms produce goods that are different, but similar enough to be substitutes.

11–2

Number of Firms

In monopolistic competition, there are *many firms from which a given type of product can be bought.* Although there are more firms in an industry classified as perfectly competitive, monopolistic competition does provide many different suppliers from which to choose.

Suppose, for example, that you wanted a haircut. You would have many choices as to where you bought that service. If you look at the Yellow Pages of your local phone book, you will find many listings under the headings *Barbers* and *Beauty Salons.* Even in fairly small cities, the combined listings can run more than ten pages. In almost any city, there are many places where you could get a haircut.

Type of Product Sold

In monopolistic competition there is product differentiation. **Product differentiation** is the concept that the product of one firm can be distinguished from the products of other firms. There may be actual physical differences between products, or the differences may be superficial. This can be illustrated by looking at the market for breakfast cereals. There are very clear taste and physical differences between corn flakes, raisin bran, and puffed rice, for example. Almost anyone would be able to taste the difference between

11–1

product differentiation
The concept that the product of one firm can be distinguished from the products of other firms.

these cereals. And anyone with reasonably good eyesight could tell them apart on the store shelf. The containers' colors and brand names also make them clearly different.

Product differences may not always be so clear. Consider, for example, two different brands of the same kind of breakfast cereal: Post Raisin Bran and Kellogg's Raisin Bran. Many people have a strong preference for one brand over the other. One person may eat only Kellogg's Raisin Bran, while someone else may eat only Post Raisin Bran. Still others may claim to have no preference at all. There is not as much physical and chemical difference between these cereals as between raisin bran, corn flakes, and puffed rice. Why, then, do some people form such strong brand preferences? The answer is based on psychological reasons. To some people, the ads for Kellogg's Raisin Bran may be more appealing. Other consumers may like the color and design of the Post Raisin Bran box better than the other box. The reason for brand preferences is not as important as the simple fact that preferences do exist and are sometimes very strong.

For products to be considered differentiated, consumers must be able to tell one product from another. The differences may be in physical characteristics, function, quality, or just in the brand, trademark, or package. Consider the example of a haircut. In a sense, one haircut is just like any other haircut. It makes little difference where you go. On the other hand, we know that people develop very strong preferences and loyalties to particular businesses and even to specific hair stylists. This appears to be true for both men and women.

Illustration 11–1
A haircut is a haircut, but people form strong loyalties for particular salons.

Below are ten representative names from the phone book of places where you could get a haircut:

1. Bell Hair Designs
2. Campus Barber Shop
3. Mirror's Image Barber Salon
4. Razor's Edge
5. The Squire Barber Salon
6. Creative Hair Designers
7. Lulu's Salon of Beauty
8. Star Barber Shop
9. Sande's Hair Shoppe
10. Guy's and Gal's Hair Styling

Knowing only that each place takes both female and male customers, which would you choose? If you ask 100 people this question, probably each of the ten choices would be selected. The firm's name alone would create some kind of preference. Lulu's Salon of Beauty gives a different image than Star Barber Shop. Some of these names may appeal more to women than to men, and vice versa. Some will appeal more to young people, while others will appeal more to an older group.

The important point is that the product (or service in this example) becomes differentiated in our minds as soon as we know the name. This service may also be differentiated by the shop's location, its cleanliness and design, and the quality of the haircuts.

The fact that products are differentiated in monopolistic competition is the most important characteristic separating this form of market organization from perfect competition. As you have seen, product differentiation can take many forms.

Ease and Freedom to Enter or Leave the Industry

With respect to the ability of firms to enter or leave the industry, monopolistic competition is much closer to perfect competition than to monopoly. *Entry into and exit from monopolistically competitive industries is relatively easy.* Usually there are few, if any, regulations imposed by the government. Getting started in business requires less money than, say, steel production or the production of electric power.

For example, think about the restaurant industry. Look in the Yellow Pages for your area under the heading *Restaurants.* You will probably find many firms listed. They all have at least one thing in common. They are all places where prepared meals can be bought. But they may also be very different from each other. At some restaurants, the meals may be eaten in the restaurant; while at others the meals may be taken out. In some cases, either choice is possible. The types of food available may differ quite a lot: from

salads and sandwiches to lobster and prime rib. Many of the restaurants in your area may be fairly new. Perhaps they opened within the past five years. At the same time, other restaurants may have gone out of business in the past five years. Businesses in monopolistic competition enter and leave the industry with relative ease and freedom.

Amount of Information About the Market

Firms in a monopolistically competitive industry have *reasonably complete information about conditions that may affect the business*. Each firm knows approximately how much other firms pay for labor, raw materials, and other inputs. All firms can find out the prices that the others charge. They all have the same access to existing technology. Through trade associations, government publications, and private sources, all firms can learn a great deal about the demand for the product or service produced.

Think about restaurants again. If you opened a sandwich shop, you would know how much other similar firms paid for bread, meats, cheeses, labor, rent, and other inputs. You could find out what prices they charged for similar products by watching their ads or visiting them. You could get information about how much money local residents spend at restaurants from government publications. And you could get a more personal feel for demand by observing business at other restaurants.

Amount of Price Control

Firms in monopolistic competition have *some control over price, but not very much*. This is mainly because there are many firms producing products that are good substitutes for each other. If the price of Coke were much higher than the price of Pepsi, few cola drinkers would buy Coke. The amount of price control any firm has depends on how different consumers think their product is. If buyers view two products as very different, the price difference between them will be greater. For example, economic reasoning would suggest that the price difference between Kellogg's Raisin Bran and Post Raisin Bran would be less than the price difference between Kellogg's Raisin Bran and a box of generic raisin bran cereal. Kellogg's and Post Raisin Bran cereals are generally seen as more alike than Kellogg's and a generic box of the same type of cereal.

The same situation can be observed with restaurants. Those that serve similar meals have prices that are usually close. A spaghetti dinner will not differ much in price from one family restaurant to another. A breakfast of two eggs, bacon, hash browns, and juice costs about the same regardless of where you buy it as long as the restaurants are of a similar type. As the type of meal or the type of restaurant becomes more different, price difference also increases. A steak dinner at an elegant restaurant will cost more than the same dinner at a cafeteria-style steak restaurant. But as long as the products and services are close substitutes, individual firms cannot exert much price control.

Demand Curve

As Figure 11–1 shows, the demand curve for a firm in monopo-   11–4 listic competition will have a negative slope. More can be sold at

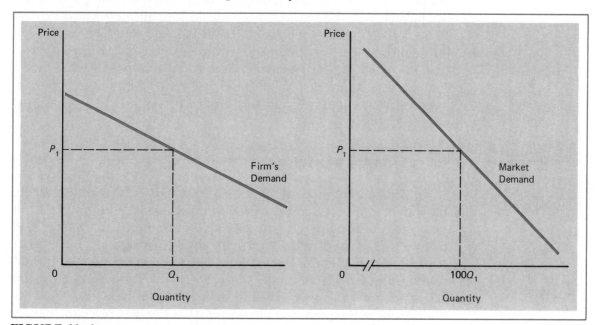

FIGURE 11–1   DEMAND IN MONOPOLISTIC COMPETITION
The left-hand diagram shows the demand curve for a monopolistically competitive firm. The market demand curve is shown in the right-hand diagram. The firm's demand curve is shown to be less steep than the market demand curve. This indicates that the firm's sales are more sensitive to price changes because there are many substitute products.

Illustration 11–3
Other pens may appear similar, but Bic has a monopoly over pens produced with the Bic name.

lower prices than at higher prices. The demand curve for the firm looks flatter than the market demand curve. This is because for the individual firm, the quantity demanded is likely to be fairly responsive to changes in price. Of course, this is because there are many close substitutes that buyers can get.

Remember, though, that even the closest substitute products are not exactly the same. There is some product differentiation. In fact, if we defined products narrowly, each firm would have a monopoly. You could not produce jeans and sell them under the Levi's name. If you wanted to open a fast-food restaurant, you could not construct a building with golden arches and call it McDonald's. These two firms have a legal monopoly over the use of those names. Bic has a monopoly in the production of Bic pens. There are other pens that are very similar, but they do not carry the Bic name. So, all such firms have some monopoly power. They are the only ones that can make and sell those exact products.

This small amount of monopoly power resulting from product originality is what gives the firm some slight control over price. This control over price is reflected by the negative slope of the demand curve. If Mobil raised the price of a gallon of regular gas to 25¢ above what others are charging, it would lose some sales but not all of its sales. In comparison, wheat farmers asking 25¢ more per bushel than the market price would lose all their sales. People with a strong brand preference for Mobil gas would probably pay the higher price. But people don't form a brand preference for wheat. What if Mobil raised its price to $3 more than what other gas stations charge per gallon? Do you think many people would have a strong enough brand preference for Mobil gas to continue buying Mobil?

Output and Price Levels

11–4   In determining how much to produce and what price to charge, firms in monopolistic competition act much like a monopolist. If the sale of an added amount increases revenue more than costs, the firm is well-advised to do so. If the added costs go up more than the added revenue, the firm should not sell more. By making such comparisons, the firm might settle on Q_1 (in Figure 11–1) as the best amount. And from the demand curve you know that Q_1 units can be sold at the price P_1. Therefore, P_1 is the best price to charge.

Suppose that the firm represented by the demand curve in the left-hand side of Figure 11–1 sells 1 percent of the total industry sales. That is, that firm has 1/100 of the total market. If the average price for the industry is also at P_1, all firms in total would sell

100 times Q_1. This is the amount labeled $100Q_1$ on the right-hand side of Figure 11–1, which represents the market demand.

Comparison with Monopoly and Perfect Competition

A firm in monopolistic competition has some monopoly power. But that power is not very strong since there are many substitute products available. Because there are so many other firms in the same market, they also have some characteristics of perfect competition. While they have some control over price, they don't have nearly as much control as a monopolist. In fact, they often have so little control over price that they are fairly close to perfectly competitive firms.

Suppose prices became very high in such an industry and there were large profits. Since entry is fairly easy, new firms would start up. In the restaurant industry, for example, new restaurants would open. Then, the total market demand would be shared by more firms. Therefore, demand for each firm's product would fall some. This would cause price to drop. As price dropped, so would profits. When profits had fallen to an equilibrium level, there would no longer be incentive for new firms to enter the business.

In the long run, this price will equal (or be very close to) the per–unit cost of production. Remember that this means no excess returns go to people in this industry. The cost of the quantity produced and sold will also tend to be fairly close to the lowest possible per–unit cost. Therefore, reasonable economic efficiency is approached. However, as with monopoly, price will be greater than the added cost of producing an added unit of output. This means that too few resources may be allocated to that industry.

OLIGOPOLY

Oligopoly is a form of market organization in which there are relatively few firms. There is no absolute number of firms that separates oligopoly from monopolistic competition. In some industries that are oligopolies, there may be quite a few more firms.

Like monopolistic competition, oligopoly has some characteristics of both perfect competition and monopoly. Overall, the industries that would be classified as oligopolies are closer to monopoly in terms of how the firms behave. Most economic activity in the United States takes place in industries that are classified either as oligopolies or as monopolistically competitive. We explain oligopoly in terms of the characteristics of market organization in the next five sections.

11–1

oligopoly
A form of market organization in which there are relatively few firms.

11–3

Number of Firms

We usually think of an oligopoly as *an industry in which there are few firms.* But it is hard to assign an absolute number to the meaning of the term *few.* The degree to which firms act independently of one another is more important than the exact number of firms. If there are a great many firms, such as wheat production, we would expect each to act on its own. That is, each firm would act independently of the others. But think about the car industry where a small number of firms dominate the industry. Each firm takes the actions and reactions of the other firms into account when making economic decisions. This interdependence that influences economic behavior is a key element of oligopoly.

Type of Product Sold

In oligopoly, the *products produced by different firms can be either nearly identical or differentiated.* Consider the case of steel beams used in building bridges. The product is very much the same whether it is produced by Bethlehem Steel or by USX (formerly U.S. Steel). In such cases, we say the products are the same for all firms, and we call the industry a pure oligopoly. A **pure oligopoly**, then, is an oligopoly in which the products are the same for all firms. The aluminum industry is a pure oligopoly. So, too, is the metal container industry. A can made by National Can is essentially identical to the same size can made by Continental Can.

In other oligopolistic industries, there is considerable product differentiation. As with the product differentiation discussed for monopolistic competition, this differentiation can be actual physical differences. Or it may be differences perceived by the consumer due to brands, trademarks, packages, or other factors. Consider, for example, the car industry. The products are clearly differentiated. A Jeep is very different from a Cadillac. A Buick is different from a Toyota. Even products that are very similar in a strict physical sense may be viewed as very different by consumers. The Mercury Sable and Ford Taurus are virtually the same, yet some people would buy one and not the other. Thus, the two cars are considered differentiated. An industry such as this is called a differentiated oligopoly. A **differentiated oligopoly**, then, is an oligopoly in which the product is differentiated.

11–1

pure oligopoly
An oligopoly in which the products are the same for all firms.

11–1

differentiated oligopoly
An oligopoly in which the product is differentiated.

Ease and Freedom to Enter or Leave the Industry

It is *fairly difficult to enter an industry that is oligopolistic.* There are a couple of reasons for this. First, most oligopolistic industries use very expensive and sophisticated equipment. It would cost a great deal of money to enter the car or steel industries at a scale that would be economically efficient. Hundreds of millions of dollars would be necessary to make even a serious attempt.

Illustration 11–4
It is fairly difficult to enter an oligopolistic industry. Entry into the steel industry, for example, would require the purchase of costly, complicated equipment.

Second, because the products have a brand, buyers develop brand preferences that can be quite strong. Some people have always bought the same brand of car. This is true of many other products including televisions, stereo equipment, and other home appliances. The buyer for a large construction firm may prefer one company's steel beams because of the product's past performance. This might happen even though other companies produce very similar steel beams. A new firm would have a hard time overcoming people's existing brand preferences. Therefore, it would be difficult to get those important first-time sales.

Leaving oligopolistic industries can also be pretty difficult. Because of highly specialized machines, it is often very hard for a firm to leave the industry and sell the equipment without great loss. When firms do leave the industry, they commonly do so by selling out to another firm. If the firm is in the same line of business, this is a horizontal merger.

Amount of Information About the Market

In oligopolistic industries, firms have *less complete information about the market* than in other forms of industry organization. Firms usually know how much other firms pay for labor, but there is much less reliable information for other inputs. One car company may pay more for steel than another car company. This can be true even though the published list price for the steel is the same for all car companies. Because of their size, some oligopolistic firms can get a price reduction that other firms cannot get. This is even true in the money markets. When two firms go to a major bank, they may find that the interest rate to borrow money is not the same for both of them.

More trade secrets exist in oligopolistic industries than in any other. Each car company will try to keep new designs, new advertising programs, and even major personnel changes a secret as long as possible. Chemical companies such as Dow or Monsanto closely guard new product development, sales, and cost information. However, it is very difficult for these firms to prevent information

JOAN VIOLET MAURICE ROBINSON

Joan Robinson (1903–1983), a leader of the British school of Keynesian economics, is given credit for developing the theory of monopolistic competition. To Robinson, each firm acts as a monopolist, facing a demand curve which slopes downward because of the product differentiation by "monopolist" firms in the industry. She believed that product differentiation *between* firms, not *within* one firm, leads to this monopolistic effect.

According to Robinson, capitalism is by nature an unstable economic system. A capitalist economy, she contended, forces business and labor to battle constantly over each other's share of the income.

Robinson contended that labor earnings should depend on union influence and bargaining power rather than on fickle market conditions. She believed government policy could more fairly determine the distribution of income between business and labor.

Born in London to a progressive academic family, Robinson had lifelong ties with Cambridge University and carried out its tradition of dissent from orthodox economic theory. She won a scholarship to Girton College of Cambridge and took a degree in economics at age 22. The following year she married economist Austin Robinson, and they lived for a short time in India. On their return to England, Joan began her work at Cambridge, where she taught until her retirement. Past that time she served as professor emerita until her death in 1983.

In the early years of her career (late 1920s and early 1930s) Robinson belonged to a group of Cambridge economists and was influenced especially by Richard Kahn and John Maynard Keynes. Her first book, *The Economics of Imperfect Competition* (1933), uses Alfred Marshall's measure of differences among products to define an industry. She established that interdependence exists among firms and then redefined the market demand curve to allow for this fact. Her second book, *Introduction to the Theory of Employment* (1937), directly responds to Keynes' own book, *General Theory*, which had been published the previous year. Robinson has gained credit for not only supporting but expanding Keynes' revolutionary doctrines of economic policy, adapting them for long-term growth and technological change. In her later years Robinson became interested in linking Keynesian theory with Marxist principles.

Several later books include *Freedom and Necessity* (1970), which pleads for progressive social science teaching as the best for students, and *Introduction to Modern Economics* (1973), a fairly difficult textbook written with John Eatwell.

In addition, Professor Robinson wrote about capital theory, international trade and comparative systems, Marxian economics, and economic growth. Her tough, witty personality left a radical influence on twentieth century economic theory.

from leaking out. People change jobs and move from one company to another. The firms are likely to buy things from the same suppliers and sell to the same buyers. So, information that either a supplier or a buyer may obtain can leak out (even accidentally) to other firms in the industry.

Amount of Price Control

Firms in a differentiated oligopoly have a great deal of control over price. These large firms spend a lot of money on advertising to create and maintain consumer brand preferences. The car buyer who has bought a new Buick every three years since 1960 is not likely to change now. Therefore, that buyer is probably not very sensitive to price. And surely the difference in price between a Buick and a Chevrolet will not be important.

Firms in a pure oligopoly have some control over price, but they usually have less control than firms in a differentiated oligopoly. A manufacturer of steel beams cannot price them much higher than other manufacturers do. Any firm's steel beams are likely to be satisfactory. In many cases, such products are bought solely on the basis of price. So, even favorable company preferences based on past performance may not give any one firm the ability to charge a higher price without hurting sales.

11–1
collusion

The situation of firms acting together rather than separately.

11–1
cartel

A formal organization of firms in the same industry acting together to make decisions.

Collusion and Cartels. Because there are relatively few separate firms in an oligopoly, there is often incentive for them to make joint decisions. This is especially true of pricing decisions. **Collusion** is the situation of firms acting together rather than separately. So, if two or more firms make joint decisions, we say there is collusion between the firms. If this collusive behavior becomes formal and well-organized, the firms become what is called a cartel. A **cartel** is a formal organization of firms in the same industry acting together to make decisions.

The objective of having collusion and/or forming a cartel is to give the group of firms power of monopoly. All the firms can act as one and earn greater profits than if they act separately. To consumers this usually means a higher price and a lower level of output to buy.

The most famous cartel is probably the international cartel known as OPEC (Organization of Petroleum Exporting Countries). This cartel has controlled oil prices and output throughout the world. In the United States, cartels are illegal. This does not mean firms do not practice collusion. However, it is often done secretly and is very hard to prove.

Illustration 11–5
Because of the small number of firms involved in an oligopoly, *cartels* sometimes result, in which firms make joint decisions to control prices. The most famous example of a cartel is OPEC, which controls oil prices and output throughout the world.

Price Leadership. In some oligopolistic industries, cooperation between firms exists but falls short of being a full cartel. Price leadership, for example, happens when one firm in an industry sets a price and other firms follow. The other firms then sell their product at the price set by the leader rather than setting their own price. The firm that acts as the price leader may vary from year to year. Often the largest firm in the industry will be the price leader, but this is not necessary. As long as all the other firms will follow, any firm could act as the leader.

Demand Curve

The demand curve for an oligopolist is negatively sloped. As with monopolistically competitive firms, this is due mainly to the *product differentiation that exists between firms.* Unlike the other forms of industry organization, there is not one type of demand curve that is good for all oligopoly cases. Probably the most famous type is a *kinked demand curve* such as the one shown in the left-hand graph of Figure 11–2.

The demand curve is kinked because the responsiveness of demand to price changes differs depending on whether the firm raises or lowers price. Suppose the current price is at the level marked P_1 in Figure 11–2. At P_1, the firm shown in the graph has 20 percent, or one fifth of the total market. The firm's sales are Q_1 units. In the right-hand graph, you can see that sales by all of the firms in the market would be five times Q_1 ($5Q_1$).

11–5

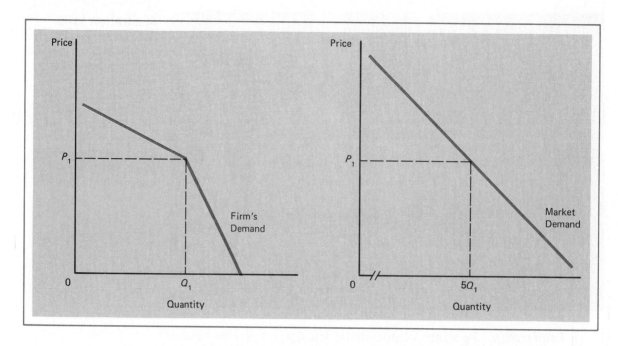

FIGURE 11–2 DEMAND IN OLIGOPOLY
The demand curve for an oligopolistic firm is shown to the left of the market demand curve. The firm's demand is often drawn as a kinked demand curve. This shows that sales may be more responsive to a price rise than to a drop in the firm's price.

Suppose the firm were to lower price to try to get a greater share of the market. The kinked demand curve shows that other firms would also cut price to prevent this firm from getting part of their sales. Therefore, the firm in the left-hand graph would not have much of a rise in sales by lowering price. So, its demand curve is very steep below the existing price (P_1).

Now suppose this firm were to raise price. Other firms would not necessarily follow. If the others did not increase price, the firm that did would likely see quite a drop in sales. For this reason, the demand curve for the firm is very flat above the existing price (P_1).

The kinked demand curve approach to an oligopolist's demand and pricing behavior does not explain all cases of oligopoly. It does, however, help to explain why some oligopoly prices do not change as frequently as prices in other industries. Many other approaches to oligopoly explain demand for the firm when the kinked demand curve is not appropriate.

Output and Price Levels

In deciding the levels of output and price, oligopolistic firms   11–5
behave very much like other cases discussed earlier. If selling an
added unit of output makes revenue go up more than costs go up,
it would be profitable to sell that added output. On the other hand,
if the added costs go up more than the added revenue, it would be
better not to sell more.

In cases where a cartel is formed or where price leadership is
followed, these principles may be altered by individual firms. Some
firms may produce and sell less while others produce and sell
more. By doing so, some firms may sacrifice profit for the overall
good of the industry.

Comparison with Other Market Structures

Firms in oligopolistic markets have some amount of monopoly
power. Generally they have more monopoly power than firms in
monopolistic competition. This is due largely to the smaller number
of substitute products available in oligopolies. There are fewer
firms to provide competition.

This monopoly power, along with relatively difficult entry of
new firms, means that high profits may result. There is no guarantee of high profits, of course. In the automotive sector, we sometimes see that even with few firms in a large market it is possible to
lose money. However, in an oligopoly, prices will stay high enough
to be profitable for most, if not all, firms involved.

In oligopoly, production is likely to occur at a level where the
per-unit cost of output is not as low as possible. This means that
the product is not produced as efficiently as is technically possible.
In this regard, oligopoly is very similar to monopoly. The similarity
continues if we compare price to the extra cost of producing an
added unit of the product. As in monopoly, price is higher than
this added cost, so we can conclude that too few resources are used
in producing that product. For society to be best served, more
should be produced and it should be sold at a lower price.

Firms in oligopolistic industries do benefit society, however.
Pharmaceutical companies, car companies, petroleum companies,
chemical companies, and others spend a great deal of money on
research and development. Some of that money does not pay off
since the research does not always produce a usable product. But
much of the spending supports successful research that may benefit the whole society in the long run. In this respect, oligopolies are
like monopolies.

Firms in oligopolistic industries, like those in monopolistic and monopolistically competitive industries, also spend a lot of money for advertising. Most of the television specials and sports broadcasts are paid for by oligopolistic firms through advertising. Magazines with a national distribution are full of ads by these companies. These firms also support broadcasts on public radio and television through donations.

REVIEWING THE CHAPTER

11–2   1. Monopolistic competition is a form of market organization in which firms create products that, while different in some ways, are good substitutes for one another. Firms have good information about the market, and it is fairly easy to enter or leave the industry.

11–4   2. In monopolistic competition, price is usually very close to the unit cost of producing the product—so there is little, if any, excess return. The degree of economic inefficiency is small since output is produced close to the lowest possible cost. There is some misallocation of resources since price is greater than the cost of producing one additional unit.

11–3   3. Oligopoly is a form of market organization in which there are just a few firms. In some cases, the output is very much the same no matter which firm it comes from. In other cases, products are very different between firms. It is usually quite difficult to enter or leave an industry that is oligopolistic.

11–5   4. In oligopoly, price is likely to be greater than the cost per unit of output, so excess profits result in the industry. At the level of output that is best for the firm, price is greater than the added cost of producing one more unit of the product. So, too few resources are allocated to production. Also, oligopolistic firms are not likely to produce at the lowest unit cost and therefore some economic efficiency can be lost.

11–5   5. Firms in oligopolistic industries tend to advertise heavily and thus help support newspapers, magazines, radio, and television. Oligopolists also spend a great deal of money on research and development, which is often of great benefit to society in the long run.

REVIEWING
ECONOMIC
TERMS

11–1   Supply definitions for the following terms:

monopolistic competition   differentiated oligopoly
product differentiation   collusion
oligopoly   cartel
pure oligopoly

REVIEWING
ECONOMIC
CONCEPTS

11–2   1. Describe monopolistic competition using the five characteristics of market organization.

11–4   2. Describe the demand curve for the monopolistically competitive firm. How does it compare with the market demand curve?

11–4   3. What is the level of output and price for the monopolistically competitive firm?

11–3   4. Describe oligopoly using the five characteristics of market organization.

11–5   5. Describe the demand curve for the oligopolistic firm. How does it compare with the market demand curve?

11–5   6. What is the level of output and price for the oligopolistic firm?

11–1   7. What is the difference between a pure oligopoly and a differentiated oligopoly?

APPLYING
ECONOMIC
CONCEPTS

11–1
11–2   1. Review what is meant by the term *monopolistic competition*. How does this form of market organization resemble a monopoly? How does it resemble perfect competition?

11–3   2. In a recent issue of *Time* magazine (or any other news magazine) pick out ads for industries you consider oligopolies. Explain your choices, using the characteristics of oligopoly as a guide.

11–5   3. Using news magazines in your school library for reference, write a brief history of the OPEC oil cartel.

11–4, 11–5 4. Explain why the demand curve for a perfectly competitive firm is a horizontal line at the market price, while demand curves for firms in the other market structures all have a negative slope.

11–2, 11–3 5. Make a chart like the one below and fill it in with one or two words per square to show how the market structures compare.

Form of Market Organization	Number of Firms	Type of Products	Market Knowledge	Ease of Entry	Degree of Price Control	Example of Each
Monopolistic Competition						
Pure Oligopoly						
Differentiated Oligopoly						
Pure Competition						
Monopoly						

DO MONOPOLISTICALLY COMPETITIVE AND OLIGOPOLISTIC FIRMS CARE WHAT YOU THINK ABOUT THEIR PRODUCTS?

You bet they do! These businesses spend billions of dollars every year on market research to learn more about your needs and desires. You or someone in your family may have participated in a market research project through phone, mail, or personal interviews, by filling out an information card for a product you have purchased, or by participating in a focus group.

Marketing research can focus on a variety of issues. Some common types of research include

Demand Analysis
Who buys?
Where do they buy?
When do they buy?
How do they buy?

Analysis of Competitors
Who are they?
What do people like or dislike about them?
What are their marketing programs?

Price Research
How important is price in people's purchasing decisions?
What is the price elasticity of demand?

All in all, firms believe that your opinion counts.

IMPROVING
THE
MARKET
ECONOMY

Learning Objectives

12-1 Define terms related to failures of the market system.

12-2 Analyze negative externalities in terms of marginal costs and benefits.

12-3 Describe how the effects of negative externalities on the market system can be controlled.

12-4 Analyze positive externalities in terms of marginal costs and benefits.

12-5 Describe how the effects of positive externalities on the market system can be controlled.

12-6 Explain why public goods are provided.

12-7 Explain why natural monopolies occur and how and why they are controlled.

THE MARKET CAN BE SUCCESSFUL

When a market is perfectly competitive, the economy benefits in several ways. First, economic efficiency results. Products are produced at the lowest possible cost per unit. Second, firms in the industry do not make excessive profits. This is because price equals the cost per unit of producing the product. Finally, there is the best possible allocation of resources to production in the industry. For the good of society, neither too much nor too little is produced because price equals the added cost of producing an added unit.

A graph of supply and demand helps explain why just the right amount of goods is produced when markets are competitive. Look at Figure 12–1. The graphs in this figure show demand and supply curves for bicycles. Let's quickly review what demand and supply curves show.

> *Demand*: A demand curve shows the quantities that people are willing and able to purchase at various prices.
>
> *Supply*: A supply curve shows the quantities that producers are willing and able to make available for sale at various prices.

12–1

marginal private benefit (*MPB*)

The added benefit that individuals directly involved in an activity get from increasing the activity by one unit.

12–1

marginal private cost (*MPC*)

The added cost individuals directly involved in an activity pay to increase the activity by one unit.

The demand curve reflects our willingness to buy. So, think of it as showing the added benefit we get from each unit. This is called marginal private benefit. **Marginal private benefit (*MPB*)** is the added benefit that individuals directly involved in an activity get from increasing the activity by one unit. It is *marginal* because it shows the benefit from each added unit. It is *private* because we only consider our own personal satisfaction, or benefit, in deciding whether or not to buy. You can see that marginal private benefits become less as more units are consumed.

The supply curve shows the firm's cost of producing each added unit. This is called the marginal private cost. **Marginal private cost (*MPC*)** is the added cost individuals directly involved in an activity pay to increase the activity by one unit. It is *marginal* because it is the cost of producing one more unit. It is *private* because the only costs included are those that the individual producer must pay. You can see that marginal private costs increase as more units are produced because of the effect of diminishing marginal productivity.

Look at Graph A in Figure 12–1. Suppose the number of bicycles produced is represented by Q_1. At that level, consumers would be willing to pay a fairly high price for the product. That is, consumers get a high marginal private benefit (MPB_1). But you also see that the marginal private cost (MPC_1) to produce that output is lower. Should the added unit of output given by Q_1 be produced?

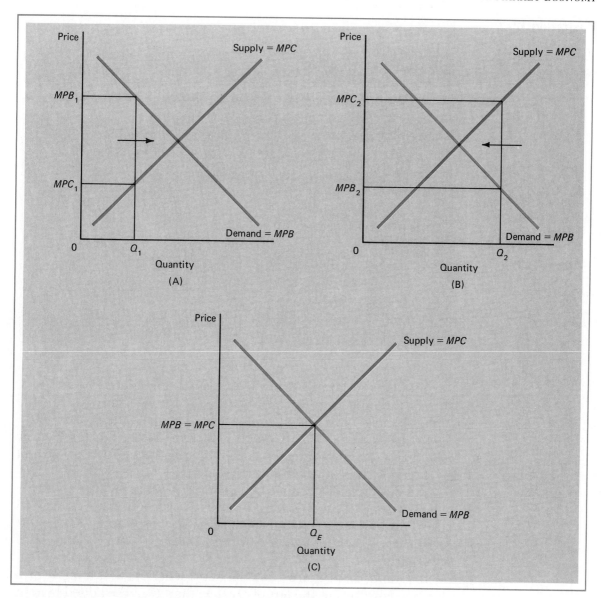

FIGURE 12–1 DEMAND AND SUPPLY CURVES FOR BICYCLES

Above are three possibilities in a competitive market with only private costs and benefits. (A) If marginal private benefits are greater than marginal private costs, output should be increased. (B) If marginal private costs are greater than marginal private benefits, less should be produced. (C) The best level of production and the best allocation of resources occur when marginal private costs equal marginal private benefits.

The answer is yes. The benefit from consuming the product is greater than the cost of making it available. So, it is desirable to produce that bicycle.

Illustration 12–1
A successful market offers consumers a variety of products.

Now look at Graph B in Figure 12–1. The added cost of producing the unit given by Q_2 is MPC_2. This is a high cost. But the added benefit consumers would get from that unit is just MPB_2. You can see that MPB_2 is much less than MPC_2. So, for Q_2, the added cost would be greater than the added benefit. It would not be desirable to produce that many bicycles.

It is desirable to produce Q_1 but not Q_2. Think again about why this is true. For Q_1, the added benefit is greater than the added cost. This leads to a general conclusion. *It is only desirable to produce an additional unit if the added benefit that results is greater than or equal to the added cost.*

In Graph C of Figure 12–1, Q_E represents the best level of production. For units to the left of Q_E (less than Q_E), the added benefit is greater than the added cost. Those units would be worth producing. For units to the right of Q_E (greater than Q_E), the added cost is higher than the added benefit. So, it would not be desirable to produce those units. At Q_E, which is the best level of production, the added costs are exactly equal to the added benefit. That is, at Q_E, $MPC = MPB$.

The economy's scarce resources are allocated in the best possible way when $MPB = MPC$. This happens when price equals the added cost of producing the last unit. In perfectly competitive markets, this is a natural result. The market system is successful in providing the best possible allocation of resources.

SOMETIMES THE MARKET CAN FAIL

We have been assuming that all costs and benefits are private. The benefits all go to the people who buy the product. The costs are all paid for by the producers. When this is true, all the costs and benefits go only to people involved in market transactions. In such cases, we say that all costs and benefits are *internalized.* None of the benefits or costs spill over to people who are not involved in the market transaction.

In some cases, however, this assumption is not correct. It is possible that some of the benefits or costs could go to third parties. Third parties are people not directly involved in the production or purchase of the product. When all the benefits or costs are not internalized, externalities exist. As you recall, an externality is a cost or benefit passed on to people not directly involved in the transaction. Three terms are used to describe these cases and any of the three is correct: spillovers, third-party effects, or externalities. Each of these terms refers to cases in which all the costs or benefits of production or consumption do not go to the people directly involved in producing or using the product.

The market system does not work well when there are spillovers. Resources will not be allocated to different types of production in the best possible way. In the following sections, we will look more closely at the effects of such externalities. We will also look at some examples of spillover benefits and costs. In addition, we will consider some ways to correct this failure of the market system to allocate resources in the best possible way.

NEGATIVE EXTERNALITIES

A **negative externality** is the result when *costs* are shifted to people who are not directly involved with the production or consumption of a good. When costs shift to third parties, producers and consumers of the good do not pay the full cost to society of providing the good. In other words, the social costs of providing the good are higher than the private costs.

12–1
negative externality
The result when *costs* are shifted to people who are not directly involved with the production or consumption of a good.

Examples of Negative Externalities

Suppose the Sulfa Chemical Company builds a new plant on the banks of the Green River. The company uses pure water from the river in the production of chemicals. Waste water containing various chemical impurities is dumped back into the river. As a result, fish die. The town of Greenville, which is downstream from Sulfa

Illustration 12–2
Some people consider billboards to be eyesores, and almost everyone's senses are affected by litter. These are examples of negative externalities, passed on to society as a whole.

Chemical, has to add new equipment for water treatment because the Green River is the town's main source of water. People for the next 50 miles downstream find that the Green River is no longer safe for recreation. The river can no longer be used for boating, fishing, swimming, or water skiing.

To whom does the Sulfa Chemical Company shift part of the production costs? Who are the third parties in this case? People who used to enjoy fishing in the river have to go elsewhere. This creates a cost to all of them. Every resident of Greenville has to pay more for water because of the added water treatment. Some people are affected by both these added costs.

Society as a whole bears some of the cost of producing the chemicals. The private costs of making the chemicals, as shown by the company's records, are less than the true costs. Some of the costs are shifted to third parties. So, the social cost is greater than the private cost. The cost to society is higher than the cost to the company. If the water returned to the river had been as clean as the water the company took out, there would have been no spill-over to other people. The company would have internalized all the costs. The private costs would then have equaled the cost to society of making the products. There would be no negative externality.

Examples of such water pollution are very common. Indeed, it is hard to find a major river or lake that has not been polluted in some way. Almost all major industries have dumped wastes into our water. Producers of steel, coal, cars, chemicals, wood products, paper, and food are only a few. And the problem is not found just in the industrial Northeast and Midwest. Lake Erie and the Ohio River are highly polluted. But so is the Yellowstone River at some locations.

Another common type of negative externality is air pollution. Industries all too often treat air as a free dump for waste products without cost to the firms involved. Each year hundreds of millions of tons of air pollutants are dumped into the air. You almost certainly share in the cause of this problem. One of the biggest sources of air pollution is the exhaust of cars and trucks. Industrial plants, many electric power plants, agricultural burning, and solid waste disposal also contribute to air pollution.

Air pollution causes an increase in health costs for many people. In some cities, air pollution sometimes gets so bad that people are warned to stay indoors and refrain from heavy physical activity. Air pollution also damages vegetation and personal property. People living near a source of air pollution also may have to paint their homes more often. In all these cases, as with water pollution, the firms or people involved shift part of the cost of activities to other members of society. Once more, the social cost is greater than the private cost.

Negative externalities also take less obvious forms. Consider, for example, the family next door. Their horse trailer sits in the street in front of the house and makes an otherwise very pretty street less attractive. They often have a disassembled car in their driveway. Their six-year-old son leaves his bike and other toys in their side yard and often in neighbors' yards. Their house needs painting, and the yard is overgrown with weeds. Their two dogs bark throughout the night. Even people living several houses away are kept awake. This family allows part of the cost of enjoying their lifestyle to spill over to others in the neighborhood. You can plant a nice hedge to separate your yard from theirs and to give you a more pleasant view. But this is a cost you have that is due to someone else's activities.

When people in an apartment play their stereo and television loudly, other people who live in the same building are affected. There is a negative externality. The other people incur some cost in the form of psychological discomfort, loss of sleep, or even the cost of moving to a quieter place.

Analysis of Negative Externalities

Negative externalities result when the social costs of some activity are greater than the private costs. So far in our analysis we have assumed that private and social costs were equal. No costs were shifted to third parties. Even in Figure 12–1, we assumed that this was true and that the competitive market system would yield the best allocation of resources.

Let's analyze the economic impact of negative externalities by modifying Graph C of Figure 12–1. The demand curve in Figure 12–2 shows the diminishing marginal private benefits (MPB) from consumption. For now, we will assume that all the benefits are private. The only benefits to society are internalized to private individuals. So, we can say that society's benefits are the same as private benefits. In Figure 12–2, we can then label the demand curve MPB and MSB as well. MSB stands for marginal social benefit. Marginal social benefit is the same as marginal private benefit, which was defined on page 224, except that it applies to society instead of individuals. **Marginal social benefit (MSB)**, then, is the added benefit that society gets from increasing an activity by one unit.

The curve labeled *Supply = MPC* shows the quantities that producers are willing and able to make available for sale, considering

12–2

12–1
marginal social
benefit (MSB)

The added benefit that society gets from increasing an activity by one unit.

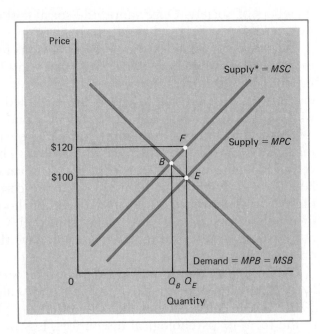

FIGURE 12-2 NEGATIVE EXTERNALI-
TIES AND MARGINAL COSTS
Negative externalities cause marginal social costs
(*MSC*) to be greater than marginal private costs
(*MPC*). The market system would lead to more
production than is socially desirable. Production
at the level Q_B would be best for society, but
market forces would lead to the production of Q_E
units.

12-1

**marginal social cost
(*MSC*)**

The added cost that
society pays to increase
an activity by one unit.

only private costs. This is the supply (or marginal private cost)
curve that firms use to determine the level of production.

In Figure 12–2, another supply curve is drawn above the firm's
own supply. This new blue supply curve, labeled *Supply* = MSC*,
reflects the full cost of producing the good. Since all costs are
included in this new supply curve, it is also the marginal social
cost (*MSC*) curve. Again, you should be able to define marginal social
cost. **Marginal social cost (*MSC*)** is the added cost that society pays
to increase an acitivity by one unit. The vertical distance between
the two supply curves is the amount of the full cost that is shifted
to third parties for each unit produced. This is the distance labeled
FE in Figure 12–2.

Left to competitive market forces, Q_E units would be produced
and sold. Each unit would cost the firm that produced it $100. But
the full cost of each unit would be $120. The difference, or $20 per
unit, would be shifted to third parties in the form of pollution
costs. In this case, the distance *FE* equals $20 per unit. Suppose
1 million units are produced (Q_E = 1 million). Then the total pollution cost to society would be $20 million. That is, the cost of this
negative externality would be $20 million.

Most people would agree that such a spillover of costs is not in
the public interest. Let's compare the full cost of producing Q_E
units with the price people are willing to pay for those Q_E units.
The full cost is $120 per unit. According to consumer demand,
people would only be willing to pay $100 per unit for Q_E units. The
cost to society of producing the last unit is greater than the benefit

received from the last unit. Therefore, society would be better served if fewer than Q_E units were produced.

How many units should be made? What is the best level of output? The best level is where the full marginal cost is just equal to the full marginal benefit. In Figure 12–2 this is where *MSC* crosses *MSB* (*MPB*). At this point (*B*), the marginal social cost of supplying the last unit is exactly the same as the marginal social (and private) benefit obtained from that unit. This best level of output is labeled Q_B on the horizontal axis.

Suppose firms did pay the full cost of making the product. If that were true, the *MPC* curve would be the same as the *MSC* curve. No costs would be shifted to third parties. The competitive market would naturally lead to the production of the best level of output, Q_B. Knowing this best level of output is helpful in deciding what should be done to control negative externalities.

Public Policy for Negative Externalities

When negative externalities are present, *MSC* is greater than *MPC*. (We are still assuming that all the benefits are private, or *MSB* = *MPB*.) You now know that the best level of output (Q_B) is where marginal social cost is the same as marginal social benefit. That is, the best level of output is where *MSC* = *MSB* (Point *B* in either Figure 12–2 or 12–3). The question is: How can we get firms to produce just Q_B units? If we could do this, the best possible allocation of our scarce resources would result.

We will now look at two types of public policy for controlling negative externalities. One way is for government to pass laws making pollution illegal. Of course, there would have to be some penalty for people who break the law. To avoid this penalty, owners and managers of businesses would have to buy machines to clean the air and water they use before discharging either back into the environment. More labor and other inputs would probably be necessary, too. So, the firms' costs would go up. As costs go up, the price the firms would have to charge for each unit produced would go up as well. That is, the firms' supply curves would shift upward. If no externalities were left, marginal social cost and marginal private cost would be the same.

This is shown in Figure 12–3. The original supply curve shows the quantities that firms would produce at each price before the passage of laws against pollution. This curve also represents the marginal private cost of production if firms do contribute to pollution problems. If firms did obey the antipollution laws, the supply curve would shift up to the blue curve labeled *New Supply*. With this new supply curve, firms would charge a higher price for each unit because of the higher production costs.

12–2

12–3

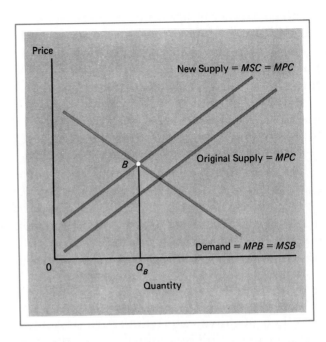

FIGURE 12–3 THE EFFECT OF ANTI-
POLLUTION LAWS

If the government passed a law prohibiting pollution, firms would have to clean up waste products. This would raise production costs so that
marginal private costs (*MPC*) would be the same
as marginal social costs (*MSC*). The new supply
curve would be to the left of the original supply
curve, and the best level of output (*Q_B*) would be
produced.

All the costs would be internalized. Marginal private costs (*MPC*)
and marginal social costs (*MSC*) would be the same. There would
be no negative externalities. Having decided to obey the laws
against pollution, firms would be led naturally to produce the best
amount of output (*Q_B*).

A second common way to deal with the problem of negative
spillovers is to use taxes. Any tax that is in some way tied to the
level of output can be used. The tax could be on the output itself
or on an input. The tax could even be on the actual pollution. The
easiest tax to use, however, is usually a tax on output.

To help explain how such a tax would work, look at Figure
12–4. To start, suppose that firms only consider the private costs of
production. We will also continue to assume that all of the benefits
are the same as marginal social benefits. That is, $MPB = MSB$.

The free, competitive market system would ignore any possible
negative externalities. Production would take place where marginal
private costs were equal to marginal private benefits. This is at the
point labeled *E* in Figure 12–4. The number of units produced
would be Q_E units.

But suppose there are negative externalities that equal $25 per
unit of output. The marginal social costs would then be $25 above
the marginal private costs. This is shown by the distance *FE* in
Figure 12–4, as well as on the vertical axis by the difference
between $85 and $60. If firms had to internalize that pollution cost
of $25 per unit of output, less would be produced.

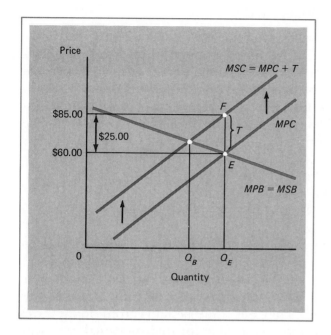

FIGURE 12–4 THE EFFECT OF A TAX ON OUTPUT
When there are negative externalities, a tax of *T* dollars per unit of output causes production to decrease from Q_E to Q_B. Q_B units is the best level of production.

Government could put a tax (*T*) on each unit of output equal to the pollution cost per unit ($25). Firms would have to pay the tax plus the cost of producing each unit. The cost for each additional unit of output would then be equal to *MPC* + *T*. Since the tax (*T*) equals the pollution cost ($25), the sum *MPC* + *T* would equal *MSC*. Firms would then base output decisions on the *MPC* + *T* curve, which is exactly the same as the *MSC* curve.

The result is that firms would find Q_B to be the best output level. This is where *MPC* + *T* crosses *MSB*. And as you have seen before, Q_B is the best amount from the viewpoint of the entire society. That is, at Q_B the *MSC* curve crosses the *MSB* curve. Marginal social costs are equal to marginal social benefits. Resources are then allocated in the best possible way.

POSITIVE EXTERNALITIES

A **positive externality** is the result when *benefits* are shifted to people who are not directly involved with the production or consumption of a good. There are situations when third parties benefit from an economic activity, even though they are not directly involved in it. This means that the social benefits of the activity are higher than the private benefits.

12–1

positive externality
The result when *benefits* are shifted to people who are not directly involved with the production or consumption of a good.

Examples of Positive Externalities

It may be hard to believe that we ever get something for nothing, but it is possible. Unfortunately, though, there are fewer cases of positive externalities than of negative ones. Let us look at some examples of positive spillovers.

People who live in big cities that have mass transportation systems may get a positive spillover from this. When people use the mass transit system rather than driving private cars, there is less air pollution. Other people in the city benefit because of the cleaner air, even though they may not use the mass transportation system. The benefit from the system is greater than just the benefit to direct users. That is, the social benefits are greater than the private benefits.

Consider again the family next door. Suppose they decide to spend some of their time and money fixing up their house and yard. They build a garage big enough for their trailer and their son's bicycle and other toys. They paint the outside of the house and improve their yard. They get some benefits from doing these things. The property is more enjoyable for their personal use. And the value of their property goes up. But there is a spillover of benefits to others as well. Your family and other neighbors will get some benefits. You will enjoy the use of your own yard more if there is a more pleasant view next door. If the people next door improve their house and property, the neighborhood is improved and your house becomes more valuable. So, the social benefits of the improvements made by one household are greater than just the private benefits.

Education also provides some external benefits. You will get many private benefits from your education. You are more likely to enjoy a wider variety of activities as you get more education. You will have a better understanding of the world around you. And you probably will earn more money. But other people will also get some benefits. As more people are educated, the number of crimes tends to decrease. There is a likelihood that welfare payments will be less. And the democratic process works better when people are better educated because they are more able to understand issues. While you get private benefits from your education, the rest of society gets some benefits, too. So, the social benefits are higher than the private benefits.

There are also positive externalities from many types of medical care. When one person is inoculated against an illness, that person clearly gets a private benefit. But other members of society benefit, too, because there will be less chance of their getting that illness. Again, the social benefits are higher than the private benefits that go just to the person who is inoculated.

Illustration 12–3
Your education will provide benefits not only to you but also to those around you. The contributions you can make to society, as a result of your education, have the effect of a positive externality.

Analysis of Positive Externalities

In this section on positive externalities, we will assume that the only costs involved are private costs. That is, we will assume that marginal social costs and marginal private costs are exactly the same ($MSC = MPC$). When there are positive spillovers, the social benefits are greater than the private benefits. So, the marginal social benefits curve is above the marginal private benefits curve. This is shown in Figure 12–5.

12–4

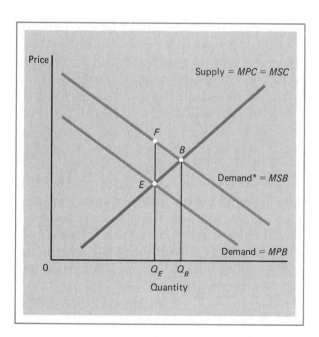

FIGURE 12–5   POSITIVE EXTERNALITIES AND MARGINAL BENEFITS
Positive externalities cause marginal social benefits (*MSB*) to be greater than marginal private benefits (*MPB*). The market system would allocate too few resources to production of this product. Only Q_E units would be produced when the best level of output is Q_B.

The competitive market economy will fail to take the social benefits into account. Only private benefits would be considered. The result is that firms will produce, and people will buy, the amount shown as Q_E in Figure 12–5. This is where marginal private benefits and costs are equal.

But from the view of the whole society, Q_E is too little of the good. The marginal benefits to society are greater than the marginal costs of producing the amount represented by Q_E. As you saw in Figure 12–1, this means that more resources should be allocated to this type of production. In Figure 12–5, the amount by which the marginal social benefit is greater than the marginal social cost is the distance *FE*.

The best level of output can be found only by comparing the marginal social cost with the marginal social benefit. The red demand curve labeled *Demand* = MSB* shows the demand that would result if all of society were included, including third parties. Since there are benefits to third parties in cases of positive spillovers, *Demand** is higher than the demand curve that includes only private benefits.

When you compare the marginal social cost with the marginal social benefit, you see that the best level of production is Q_B units. This is the level where *Demand** crosses the supply curve at Point *B*. Society's resources are allocated in the best way when Q_B units are produced.

Public Policy for Positive Externalities

12–5

12–1
subsidy
A payment made by government to encourage some activity.

Activities that have positive externalities should be encouraged by society. Government encourages such activities by subsidizing them. A **subsidy** is a payment made by government to encourage some activity. A subsidy is the opposite of a tax. For example, participants in a market transaction could be given money to get them to make or buy more of the goods that yield the positive externalities.

Subsidies are given for a number of activities. Think about the examples used for positive spillovers. Education gets very big subsidies. Education in public schools from kindergarten through high school is nearly free for most people. Even post-secondary education such as in technical schools, nursing schools, and colleges is subsidized. Tuition fees do not usually cover the full costs of education in such schools. Sometimes the subsidy goes directly to the supplier, such as a public school system. But it could also go to the consumer through student loan programs, for example. The government also provides large subsidies for medical programs and mass transit. In many areas, government programs have been used to help families or businesses pay for the costs of improving property.

In Figure 12–6, you can see how subsidies can work on either the supply side or the demand side. Graph A shows a subsidy of *BB'* dollars per unit for consumers. This would shift the demand curve up to *Demand**, and the best level of output (Q_B) would result.

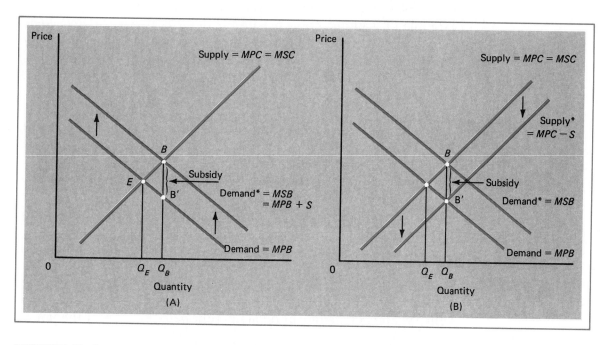

FIGURE 12–6   THE EFFECT OF A SUBSIDY ON OUTPUT
A government subsidy to consumers (A) or to producers (B) can correct the misallocation of resources due to a positive externality. In either case, output would be increased from Q_E units to the best level of output, Q_B.

If the subsidy were given to suppliers instead, Graph B of Figure 12–6 shows what would happen. The subsidy to suppliers would lower the cost of production so that the supply curve would shift to *Supply**. *Supply** crosses the original demand at Point *B'*. So, with the subsidy to suppliers, market forces would make sure Q_B units would be produced. And as you have seen several times now, Q_B is the best level of output. At that level, resources are allocated in the best way.

PUBLIC GOODS

12–6   The market system does not always give good signals about how much should be produced. Either too much or too little may be produced if the market is left alone. There is a special class of goods that the market would fail to provide at all, even though society wants them. These are public goods. You will recall that public goods and services are used by the whole society. To expand on this definition a little, public goods are goods that cannot be sold one unit at a time to individuals. And once the good is available for one person to consume, it is available for everyone to consume. An example of a public good is national defense. Everyone gets some benefit from national defense. Some people get more and some get less but the same amount of benefit is available for everyone.

If we tried to sell national defense through the market system, we would fail. Why should you or I voluntarily pay for something we know we can get for free once others pay for it? Of course, everyone would reason this way. So, if left to the market, we would have no national defense. This doesn't mean that we don't get any benefit from it. It just means that people will not express their demand through the market system. Therefore, national defense must be provided through the public sector. In this case, our demand is expressed through the political system rather than through the market system.

A lighthouse is another example of a public good. Once the lighthouse is built along a rocky coastline, all boaters can benefit from it without any direct payment. The owner of a small sailboat and the captain of a huge oil tanker both benefit from the warning light. Neither of them can be kept from benefiting from the light.

Illustration 12–4   National defense and city parks are examples of public goods. It would not make sense to produce these goods within the private sector and then try to exclude some people from using them.

This is called the exclusion principle. The **exclusion principle** is the principle that one person can keep others from benefiting from a private good. With public goods, people cannot be excluded from consumption. If you buy a new tennis racquet, you can exclude others from using it. This is true of all private goods. But for public goods, one person cannot exclude others from benefiting from the good. If you hike through Glacier National Park, that does not prevent others from also doing so. If you get some benefit from national defense, you cannot exclude others from benefiting, too. Since our demand for these goods cannot be expressed well through the market system, the public sector provides them. Of course, they are paid for by taxes.

There are some goods that could be provided through the market system but are not provided because they have large positive externalities. Examples include education, preventive medicine, highways, police and fire protection, and sewage disposal. It might be possible to charge a price for these services rather than provide them through the public sector. But we usually decide to make them available through the public sector at no charge (or at only a small charge). Goods such as these are sometimes called quasi-public goods.

Consider fire protection. If it were sold through the market system, some people would choose not to buy it. If their homes or businesses caught fire, no one would show up to put out the fire. But they would not be the only ones to lose. Nearby homes or other buildings might also catch fire. Because fire protection provides large positive spillovers, we usually provide it through the public sector and pay for it through taxes.

12–1

exclusion principle
The principle that one person can keep others from benefiting from a private good.

NATURAL MONOPOLIES

You have learned that natural monopolies exist in industries in which competition is not practical. Because competition does not exist in these markets, prices are not controlled by the laws of supply and demand. Thus, the market system fails to function in the control of prices, output, and profits.

Natural monopolies usually occur in industries in which average cost falls as output increases through the range of potential sales. To see why this is so, look at Figure 12–7.

The average cost curve shows that average cost decreases as output increases. If a monopolist produced so as not to make excess profits, production would be Q units. The average cost would be relatively low as shown on the vertical axis. But if two firms tried to share the market equally, the average cost per unit (and price)

12–7

JAMES M. BUCHANAN

Jim Buchanan's family wanted him to grow up to be a lawyer. Buchanan says it was for economic reasons that he, instead, got into economics: His poor, rural family in Tennessee could not pay his way through law school at Vanderbilt. Born in 1919, Buchanan grew up in a family that was poor but respected. His grandfather had been the county's only Tennessee governor, and the elementary school he attended bore his family's name.

Economic scarcity led Buchanan away from a legal career when he entered Middle Tennessee State Teachers' College during the Depression. Then it led him toward the field of economics when, in 1940, he accepted a fellowship of $50 per month to a master's program at the University of Tennessee. After serving in the Navy for four years, Buchanan entered the University of Chicago, where he earned a doctoral degree in 1945.

Considering himself a "libertarian socialist" in his youth, at Chicago Buchanan became an advocate of the market system. Influenced by Frank Knight and Knut Wicksell, Buchanan began to develop questions about taxation and public policy. About 40 cents of every dollar gets spent by the public sector, and Buchanan thought people should know more about how that money is spent.

Buchanan won the 1986 Nobel prize for his work in economics and public choice theory. To Buchanan, the theory of macroeconomic management assumes too easily that the political agents who make public choices will act in consideration of the "public interest." He insists on viewing the government as an outgrowth of people acting like individuals.

Buchanan has written widely on elementary public choice theory, tax theory, externalities, public goods, and public finance. His books include *Public Principles of Public Debt* (1958), *Cost and Choice* (1969), *The Calculus of Consent* (1962, coauthored with Gordon Tullock), and *The Power to Tax* (1980, coauthored with Geoffrey Brennan). Having directed two other Washington-area economic research centers at the University of Virginia and the Virginia Polytechnic Institute, Buchanan now serves as Distinguished Professor of Economics and director of the Center for Study of Public Choice at George Mason University.

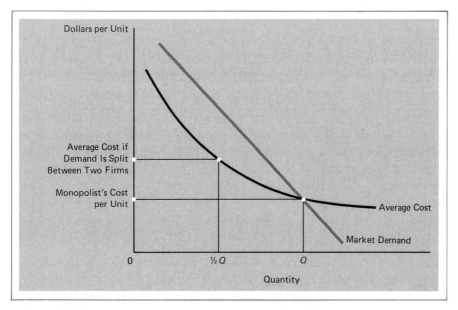

FIGURE 12–7   AVERAGE COST FOR A NATURAL MONOPOLY

A natural monopoly may result when average cost falls over the entire range of possible production. A monopolist could produce Q units at a lower cost per unit than if two firms split the market, each of which produced $\frac{1}{2}Q$ units.

would go up. Each firm would produce $\frac{1}{2}Q$, and as shown in Figure 12–7, the average cost would be higher. Neither firm can capture enough of the demand to produce at the lowest possible average cost.

The two firms would likely have price-cutting wars until one of them is forced out of business. The firm that survives would then have a low average cost and almost surely would reduce output and increase price. The natural monopolist would then make excessive profits. To prevent such profits, the government usually regulates natural monopolies so that price just equals average cost and Q units are produced.

Examples of natural monopolies include electric power production, natural gas distribution, and local telephone service. As you know, these are commonly called public utilities. They are not necessarily owned by the public sector, however. Public utilities are usually owned by stockholders just like other corporations. But they are closely regulated by public sector officials. Another example of a natural monopoly that is becoming very common is the cable television industry. Most cities permit only one cable television company to serve the city. The cities understand that, in this case, a natural monopoly can provide service at the lowest average cost possible. The cable companies, however, may also make excess profits if their prices are not regulated.

Illustration 12–5

Most cities and towns permit only one cable television company to operate. They understand that the resulting natural monopoly can provide service at the lowest possible cost.

REVIEWING

THE

CHAPTER

1. Normally we can expect competitive market forces to work fairly well. Goods will be produced efficiently. Firms will not be able to make excessive profits. And resources will be allocated efficiently. But the market can fail when benefits or costs go to third parties who do not directly make or consume a product.

12–2   2. The relation of the marginal social costs (*MSC*) of production to the marginal social benefits (*MSB*) from consumption is important. If the marginal social costs are greater than the marginal social benefits, too much of the good is produced. If the marginal social benefits are greater than the marginal social costs, too little of the good is produced. So, resources are allocated in the best possible way when *MSC* equals *MSB*.

12–2   3. Negative externalities result when the marginal social cost of some activity is greater than the marginal private cost, that is, when some of the cost is shifted to third parties. Pollution is a negative externality. Negative spillovers or negative third-party effects are other terms used for negative externalities.

12–3   4. Negative externalities can be reduced or eliminated by laws that prohibit pollution. They can also be reduced or eliminated by the use of a tax on the input or output of the firm causing the pollution. The tax per unit of output should equal the difference between the marginal private cost and the marginal social cost.

12–4   5. Positive externalities result when the marginal social benefit from an activity is greater than the marginal private benefit. That is, when some of the benefit from the activity is shifted to third parties. Positive spillovers or positive third-party effects are other terms used to describe positive externalities.

12–5   6. Activities involving positive externalities should be encouraged. This can be done by the use of government subsidies on either the supply side or the demand side. On the supply side, a subsidy reduces the firm's costs and encourages more production. On the demand side, a subsidy lowers the effective price consumers pay and causes demand to increase. The subsidy per unit should be equal to the difference between the marginal social benefit and the marginal private benefit.

12–5   7. Some goods have such big positive spillovers that they are provided entirely or nearly so by the government. When such a good cannot be provided by the private sector, it is called a public good. National defense is an example of a public good.

12–1   8. The exclusion principle is useful in distinguishing between public and private goods. If one person can exclude others from enjoying the benefits of some good, the good is considered a private good. But if one person cannot exclude another, such as with the benefits from national defense, the good is a public good.

12–7   9. A natural monopoly can result when the average cost of producing a product falls over the entire *range* of potential sales and when a firm cannot capture enough demand to produce at the lowest average cost. If more than one firm tried to operate in such a market, a price war would be likely. All but one firm would be forced out of business, and the remaining firm could then charge high prices and make big profits. We usually regulate such natural monopolies closely. Public utilities, such as phone companies, are examples of natural monopolies.

REVIEWING ECONOMIC TERMS

12–1   Supply definitions for the following terms:

marginal private benefit (*MPB*)	marginal social cost (*MSC*)
marginal private cost (*MPC*)	positive externality
negative externality	subsidy
marginal social benefit (*MSB*)	exclusion principle

REVIEWING ECONOMIC CONCEPTS

1. In a competitive market with no externalities, describe the relationship of marginal private costs and benefits which produces the best level of production and allocation of resources.

2. In a competitive market with no externalities, if marginal private benefits are greater than marginal private costs, what is the level of output?

3. In a competitive market with no externalities, if marginal private costs are greater than marginal private benefits, what is the level of output?

12–2   4. What is the relationship between marginal private and social costs when there are negative externalities?

12–3   5. What level of output would an unregulated industry produce when there are negative externalities? What can be done to cause the best level of output to be produced?

12–4   6. What is the relationship between marginal private benefits and marginal social benefits when there are positive externalities?

12–5   7. What level of output would an unregulated industry produce when there are positive externalities? What can be done to cause the best level of output?

12–6   8. How does the exclusion principle apply to public goods?

12–7   9. Under what circumstances is a natural monopoly likely to occur? What would happen if two firms tried to share such a market equally instead?

APPLYING ECONOMIC CONCEPTS

12–3   1. It is generally recognized that many positive externalities result from education. But there may be some negative externalities, too. Look at your own school carefully and see if you can find any negative spillovers. For example, consider the noise that spills over to people who live near the school. Suggest a way of correcting each of the negative externalities you find.

12–6   2. Why is police protection treated as a public good? Explain what would happen if communities tried to offer police services as a private good through the market system.

12–2, 12–3   3. Explain the type of negative externalities you might find for each of the following activities:

a. Driving a car   c. A professional football game

b. Producing electric power   d. Car production

Suggest ways of correcting each of the negative externalities you have identified.

12–2   4. Use a graph of marginal private costs, marginal social costs, and marginal private benefits to explain the concept of negative externalities. You can assume there are no positive externalities.

12–6   5. How does the exclusion principle relate to the following?

a. A city park   d. National defense

b. A banana split   e. A car

c. A highway   f. A school

12–2   6. The ABCO Manufacturing Company is located along the Pheasant River. In the production of children's toys, ABCO dumps several waste products into the river. What third parties are likely to be affected by ABCO's use of the river? How might you measure the dollar amount of the negative externalities created? What corrective measures would you suggest?

CHAPTER 13

THE LABOR MARKET AND PERSONAL INCOME

Learning Objectives

13–1 Define terms related to labor and individual income.

13–2 Describe the supply and demand for labor.

13–3 Analyze minimum wage laws.

13–4 Explain the history of labor unions.

13–5 Identify two ways of viewing interest.

13–6 Describe the factors that influence interest rates.

13–7 Tell why it is important to shop for interest rates.

THE LABOR MARKET

Just as there is a market for cars or stereos, so is there a labor market. People are not bought and sold, but their time and skills are. Suppose a restaurant hires you to wait on customers. The manager doesn't buy *you* but does buy (pay for) some of your time and ability to take and process orders correctly. So it is with all jobs. A school buys someone's time and skill to act as a teacher. A steel mill buys an engineer's time and skill to watch over a production process.

Labor is one of the four factors of production in the economy. Each company has some *demand* for labor to use in the production of the products or services to be sold. There is also a *supply* of labor. Each of us has an equal amount of time to use (24 hours a day). We must decide how much of that time to use for work and how much to use for other activities. You will see how the forces of demand and supply determine how much labor is hired and how much labor is paid.

The Demand for Labor

13–2

13–1

demand for labor

The amount of labor that firms would want to hire at each wage rate.

13–1

wage rate

The price paid for each unit of labor.

13–1

derived demand

A demand for factors of production which is dependent on the demand for the product.

Demand for labor is the amount of labor that firms would want to hire at each wage rate. The **wage rate** is the price paid for each unit of labor. The demand for labor is called derived demand. **Derived demand** is a demand for factors of production which is dependent on the demand for the product. The amount of labor demanded depends on the demand for the good or service produced. One hundred years ago, when the country used horses instead of cars, blacksmiths were in high demand. As cars came into use, fewer services of blacksmiths were needed. Thus, the demand for blacksmiths declined. But at the same time, the need for skilled workers in the automobile factories rose. Due to our higher demand for cars, there was a higher derived demand for workers to make those cars.

Demand for the company's product clearly determines a company's demand for labor. If consumers do not want to buy the product, the company will not need to hire any labor. The firm needs labor to produce what it wants to sell.

The level of productivity of the workers themselves also helps determine the demand for labor. *Labor productivity* is measured by the amount of output produced per hour of labor input. Productive labor will be more in demand than unproductive labor. Keep this important point in mind. Anything you can do that will increase your productivity will help you in the labor market. Education and training programs are two means of increasing your productivity.

Illustration 13–1 Demand for blacksmiths has fallen almost completely since the turn of the century. Horses have been replaced with cars, and now robots help produce the necessary parts.

An inverse relationship exists between the quantity of labor a business will hire and the wage rate it will offer. If the wage rate is high, businesses will hire little labor. Perhaps you can already guess why this is true. First, at a high wage it is cheaper to use methods of production that employ less labor. More equipment, more machines, and even robots will be used. Second, as the wage level goes up, the cost of production goes up and prices are likely to rise. As the product's price goes up, fewer units will be demanded. This means there will be less demand for labor to produce the product. The inverse relationship between the wage rate and the quantity of labor demanded is illustrated in Figure 13–1.

Think of the demand for labor in Figure 13–1 as the total demand for labor each day in a local labor market. Two thousand labor hours is the same as 250 people working an eight-hour day. The wage rate of $9 means $9 an hour of labor hired. At this high wage, only 2,000 hours of labor would be hired in that market each day. But if the wage rate fell to $5 an hour, 8,000 hours of labor would be demanded.

There are two factors that may cause the demand for labor to increase:

1. Demand for the output may increase.

2. The productivity of labor may increase.

An increase in the demand for labor is shown by a shift of the demand curve to the right. This is shown as the move from the original demand for labor (red curve) to the higher demand for labor (yellow curve).

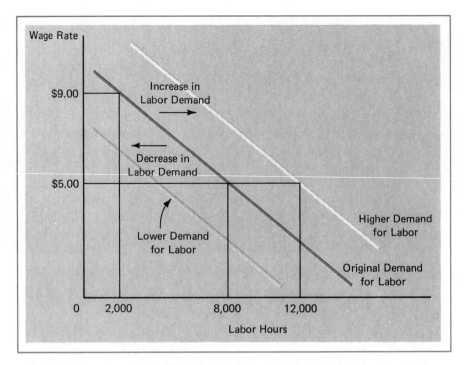

FIGURE 13–1 DEMAND CURVE FOR LABOR

The demand curve for labor slopes down to the right. A greater quantity of labor will be demanded at a lower wage than at a higher wage. If the demand for labor increases, the demand curve shifts to the right (the yellow line). If the demand for labor decreases, the demand curve shifts to the left (the orange line).

A decrease in the demand for labor would have opposite causes. Demand for output might fall and/or the productivity of labor might decrease. If the demand for labor did go down, its demand curve would shift to the left (orange curve).

A rise in the demand for labor means that more labor will be hired at each wage rate. The entire demand for labor curve moves to the right. In Figure 13–1, after the increase in demand for labor, 12,000 labor hours would be demanded at a wage of $5 an hour. This is 4,000 labor hours more than were demanded with the original demand for labor.

Before going to the next section about the supply of labor, think about what kind of work you want to do. What will determine the demand for people in that line of work? Do you wish to work in a field where demand for the product or service will be high? Do you have, or can you develop, the necessary skills to be productive in the kind of work you want to do? Thinking about these questions can help you make better career decisions. Your answers may influence how you will participate in the labor market.

The Supply of Labor

How many hours would you work next Saturday if an employer   13–2
offered to pay you $.50 an hour? Probably not very many. Why?
You probably feel that your time is worth more to you when doing
other things. You may be able to work for someone else at a higher
wage. Or you may figure that your relaxation and recreation are
worth more to you than $.50 an hour.

What do you think would happen if the same offer were made
to the entire class? Would anyone work for $.50 an hour? What if
the wage offer were slowly raised to $1, then to $2, $3, $4, $5, and
so on up to $10 an hour? At some wage you would surely offer to
work some hours. At $10 an hour, nearly everyone would be will-
ing to work a full eight-hour day. You might even be willing to
work ten hours, twelve hours, or more.

What else would determine your willingness to work? Perhaps
the hours would be important. What if workers were needed from
3 a.m. to 7 a.m.? Fewer people probably would be interested than
if the hours were from 8 a.m. to noon. Wouldn't the type of work
also be important? What if people were needed to demonstrate the
use of swimming pools? More people would want this job rather
than a job digging post holes three feet deep in rocky ground. In
addition to the wage, the hours, and the type of work, people consider other factors. You might consider the possibilities for job
advancement, the work effort required, and the physical conditions
in which the work is to be done.

Even with all these nonwage aspects of a job, you can still expect
that more labor hours will be offered at higher wages than at lower   13–1
wages. The **supply of labor** is the amount of labor that would be
available at each wage rate. The supply curve for labor increases   **supply of labor**
from left to right. It has a positive slope. For example, in   The amount of labor
Figure 13–2, at a wage of $2 an hour only 2,000 hours of labor   that would be available
would be offered. As the wage rate goes up, so does the number of   at each wage rate.
labor hours people are willing to work. As shown in Figure 13–2,
when the wage in this labor market reaches $10 an hour, 12,000
labor hours would be offered.

The supply of labor may rise or fall over time. A rise in the
labor supply would shift the supply of labor curve to the right.
More hours would be available at each wage. An example is given
by the green line in Figure 13–2. After the increase in the labor
supply, 5,000 hours would be offered at the $2 an hour wage
rather than 2,000 hours. Anything that makes work more enjoyable (or less objectionable) can cause an increase in the supply of
labor. Better and safer working conditions or more opportunities
for job advancement are examples.

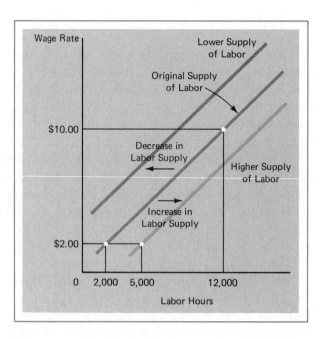

FIGURE 13–2   SUPPLY CURVE FOR LABOR
The supply curve for labor slopes up to the right. A greater quantity of labor will be supplied at a higher wage than at a lower wage. An increase in the supply of labor can be shown as a shift to the right of the supply curve (from the blue line to the green line). When the labor supply declines, the supply curve shifts to the left (from the blue line to the gray line).

The increasing number of women in the labor force has caused a dramatic rise in the U.S. labor supply. The percentage of women in the labor force has steadily risen. In 1960, 37.7 percent of all women over 16 years of age were in the labor force. By 1980, 51.5 percent of adult women were in the labor force; and in 1990, 57.5 percent of women over 16 were in the labor force. During the same period, the percentage of men over 16 years of age who were in the labor force dropped from 83.3 percent to 76.1 percent. This decrease is less than the rise for women. So, on balance, a greater percentage of the population is active in the labor force.

Illustration 13–2   The supply of labor has been greatly affected by increasing numbers of working women. From 1960 to 1990, the number of women employed outside the home rose by over 200 percent.

These changes in the labor force can be seen in Figure 13–3. The heights of the bars in this figure indicate the percentages of men and women currently active in the labor force. You can see that the height of the bars for women has been rising. For men the height of the bars has been falling.

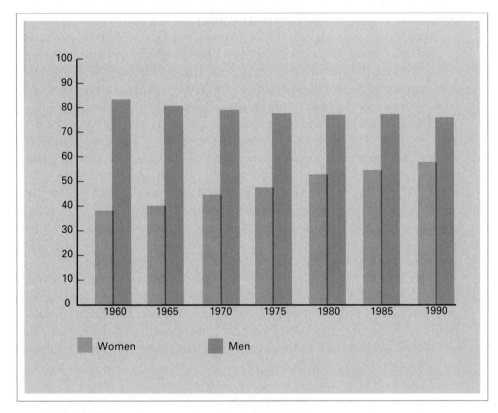

FIGURE 13–3   LABOR FORCE PARTICIPATION RATES FOR MEN AND WOMEN OVER 16 YEARS OLD, 1960 TO 1990
The percentage of women in the labor force rose from 37.7 percent in 1960 to 57.5 percent in 1990. This is shown by the height of the bars representing women. During the same period, the percentage of men in the labor force fell from 83.3 percent to 76.1 percent.
Source: *Economic Report of the President 1991* (Washington, D.C.: U.S. Government Printing Office, 1991), 327.

There are also forces that can cause the supply of labor to fall (or to increase less rapidly). Unpleasant labor conditions, artificial labor supply restrictions, or unnecessarily long training or apprenticeship programs could all cut down on supply. Discrimination by race, sex, age, or other characteristics also limits supply. Even though such discrimination is illegal, it still exists.

A decline in the supply of labor is shown by the gray line in Figure 13–2. You can see that a shift of the labor supply curve to the left shows a decrease in supply. Less labor is offered at each wage.

Balancing Labor Demand and Supply

You have learned that product markets are in balance, or equilibrium, when demand and supply are equal. The same is true in the labor market. When the demand for labor equals the supply of labor, the labor market is in balance. That is, the labor market is in equilibrium when demand equals supply.

Remember that the demand curve for labor slopes downward to the right. Companies will demand more labor hours at a lower wage than at a higher wage. For supply, the relationship is reversed. The supply curve for labor slopes upward from left to right. More labor will be offered at a higher wage than at a lower wage.

Look at Figure 13–4. Suppose that the wage rate is $8 an hour. You see that the distance between the points marked *A* and *B* shows the excess of supply over demand. In other words, the amount of labor demanded is less than the amount of labor supplied. When this happens there will be downward pressure on the wage, as indicated by the large arrow pointing down. As wage falls, the quantity of labor demanded will go up (movement to the right along the demand curve). At the same time, the quantity of labor supplied will fall (movement to the left along the supply curve).

Now suppose the wage is $3 an hour. Can you explain what would happen at this relatively low wage? Think about it step by step just as you did for the high $8 wage. At $3 an hour, companies would want to hire more labor hours than people would be willing to offer. The distance between the points marked *C* and *D* shows

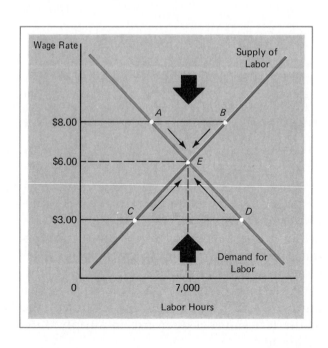

FIGURE 13–4   MARKET EQUILIBRIUM FOR LABOR

The market equilibrium wage is found where the supply of labor curve crosses the demand for labor curve. This is at Point *E*. The equilibrium wage is $6, and the amount of labor employed is 7,000 labor hours. At a wage above equilibrium ($8), labor supply is greater than demand for labor. There will be downward pressure on the wage rate. At a wage below equilibrium ($3), demand for labor is greater than supply. There will be upward pressure on the wage rate.

how much greater demand is than supply at the $3 wage. Businesses would not be able to hire all the labor they wanted. Some companies would start to offer a higher wage to attract workers. So, this would cause upward pressure on the wage rate, as indicated by the large arrow pointing up. As wage goes up, more hours of labor will be offered (movement to the right along the supply curve). At the same time, less labor will be demanded (movement to the left along the demand curve).

At the high wage, there is downward pressure on the wage rate. At the low wage, there is upward pressure on the wage rate. You should then expect that somewhere in between these two wage rates there would be a balance between demand and supply. Look at the wage rate of $6 an hour. At that wage, the amount of labor demanded is 7,000 hours. And at the $6 wage, the amount of labor supplied is also 7,000 hours. Demand and supply are in balance. The labor market is in equilibrium at the wage where the amount of labor demanded is equal to the amount of labor supplied. So, the labor market equilibrium is found where the supply and demand curves cross. This is the point marked *E* in Figure 13–4. The **equilibrium wage**, then, is the wage rate at which the demand for labor equals the supply of labor.

13–1

equilibrium wage
The wage rate at which the demand for labor equals the supply of labor.

Wages Can Stay Above or Below Equilibrium

Wages *can stay* above or below equilibrium. We have been assuming that the labor market functions in a free and competitive way. But this may not always be true. A variety of noncompetitive forces may cause wages to be higher or lower than this equilibrium. Two of these forces—unions and minimum wage laws—are important enough to be discussed in separate sections later in this chapter.

A third noncompetitive force results when a given labor market is dominated by one employer. That single employer may have enough influence over the market to keep wages low. After all, you may either work for that employer or not work at all. This is sometimes called a *monopsonistic influence*. The term **monopsony** means a market in which there is only one buyer. (It is similar to the word *monopoly* which means one seller.) If there is only one buyer of labor (one employer) in a labor market, that employer can influence wage rates considerably.

13–1

monopsony
A market in which there is only one buyer.

This often happens in university towns where the community is small relative to the size of the university. It is not uncommon for a university to employ as much as 60 or 70 percent of the labor force of a town. When this is true, an abundant supply of people want sales, clerical, and other such jobs. Students, spouses of students and faculty, and other people from the town compete for jobs. Most jobs in such an area are with the university. As a result of the abundant labor supply, jobs with universities tend to be low paying, especially in university-dominated towns. In large cities where a university represents a small part of the total population, wages for university workers are likely to be more competitive.

You know that different jobs offer different rates of pay. You also know that the same jobs pay a different amount in different parts of the country. The reasons for such differences can be explained by looking at the forces of supply and demand. On page 264, we explore the reasons for the high salaries of some professional baseball players.

MINIMUM WAGE LAWS

13–1

minimum wage law
A law which sets the lowest wage that can be paid for certain kinds of work.

A **minimum wage law** is a law which sets the lowest wage that can be paid for certain kinds of work. In 1950, the minimum wage was just $.75 an hour. In 1956, it was increased to $1 an hour. By the late 1960s, the minimum wage was $1.60 an hour. Starting in 1974, there were increases nearly every year that resulted in a minimum wage of $4.25 an hour beginning April 1, 1991.

Why would Congress want to set up a minimum wage? The reason usually given is to help provide low-income families with more money to spend. The reasoning Congress seems to use is as follows. If the market wage is $4 an hour and a person works 40 hours per week, the income earned will be $160 (40 hours × $4/hour). But if the government forces employers to pay $4.25 an hour, the person would earn $170 (40 hours × $4.25/hour).

At this point in your study of economics, perhaps you can already see the problem with this reasoning. You now know that the demand curve for labor slopes down to the right. This means that if the wage increases, the amount of labor that companies will demand decreases. Fewer labor hours will be employed at a higher wage than at a lower wage. So, when Congress forces the minimum wage up, you should expect that some low-wage workers will be laid off. Those who keep their jobs with no cut in their work hours will earn more. But some workers will earn less, or even nothing at all.

13–3

To help you analyze this problem, draw a graph on a piece of paper. Label the vertical axis *wage rate* and the horizontal axis *labor hours*. Draw a downward sloping line for the demand for labor and an upward sloping line for the supply of labor. Make a small circle where these two lines cross and label it *E*. This is the equilibrium point where the labor demand and supply are in balance. Draw a line to the left from Point *E* to the vertical axis. This shows the equilibrium wage, or the market wage. Drawing a line down from E to the horizontal axis shows the amount of labor hired at that wage.

Now draw a horizontal line across the graph above the equilibrium wage (that is, above where demand crosses supply). This line represents the government's minimum wage. How much labor would firms want to hire at this wage? You can tell from your demand curve. It is less than the number hired at the equilibrium wage, isn't it? Thus, fewer labor hours would be employed with the minimum wage than without it.

Compare your graph with the one in Figure 13–5. The size and exact shape of the curves may differ, but your graph should look very much like Figure 13–5.

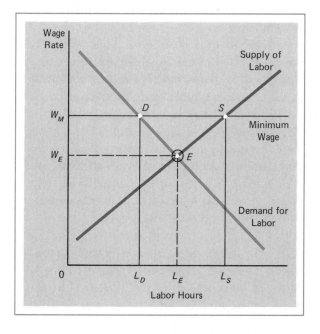

FIGURE 13–5   MINIMUM WAGE AND SUPPLY AND DEMAND FOR LABOR
The minimum wage (W_M) is set by government above the market equilibrium wage (W_E). At the minimum wage, fewer units of labor will be employed, but those who still have jobs get a higher wage per hour. Young workers and relatively unskilled workers are hurt the most by a minimum wage.

In Figure 13–5 you see that at the minimum wage (W_M) the demand for labor would be at the point marked D. This is L_D labor hours on the horizontal axis. But at that wage, the supply would be at the point marked S (or L_S labor hours on the horizontal axis). The supply of labor would be greater than the demand for labor, so there would be unemployment. Some people who might have had jobs at the market wage (W_E) are pushed out of those jobs.

What groups of people would be hurt the most? Those who are not skilled. That is, the less productive workers. Young people make up a large part of this group. They have yet to learn productive and marketable skills. This is why unemployment is particularly high among teenagers. And the minimum wage makes this problem worse than it would be otherwise.

Illustration 13–3
Minimum wage laws can work against teenagers.

LABOR UNIONS

13-4 The labor movement came about because workers wanted more control over working conditions and other job-related matters. Many workers felt that the market system gave too much power to management and not enough to labor. Employees had only their own labor with which to bargain. Laborers worked for whatever management would pay or else the laborers could quit. Each employee acting alone had very little bargaining power. If management decided fewer workers were needed, some were fired. Workers had the choice of either accepting the working conditions and hours set by management or not working at all. But often the choices were not good ones for the workers. Because they had to support themselves and their families, they were forced to work despite the conditions or wages.

How did workers try to solve their problem? They started to band together in groups called labor unions. A **labor union** is an organization of workers formed to give workers greater bargaining power in their dealings with management. The first labor union was a group of tailors in Philadelphia. They called themselves the Noble and Holy Order of the Knights of Labor. In 1869 the union was founded in secret. But the union gradually came into the open, and by 1886 it had nearly 1 million members. Also in 1886, Samuel Gompers founded the American Federation of Labor (AFL). The AFL was formed as a voluntary association of craft unions such as carpenters' and bricklayers' unions. Even though the Knights of Labor died out by 1917, the AFL has survived to this day. In 1955, the AFL merged with the Congress of Industrial Organizations (CIO). The CIO had been formed 20 years earlier during the Great Depression under the leadership of John L. Lewis. The CIO was made up of industrial unions such as the steelworkers' and the rubber workers' unions.

The formation of unions helped to balance out the bargaining power between labor and management. While management didn't need any one worker, it did need workers as a group. While a single worker had little power, workers as a group did have economic power. If management did not listen to workers' demands, there was always the threat of a strike—the ultimate union weapon.

Management, of course, did not like this. It struck back by asking the courts to say that unions were conspiracies and should be outlawed. The courts, however, ruled that unions were not illegal. Employers then turned to other weapons of their own, such as injunctions, yellow-dog contracts, and the use of antitrust laws.

An **injunction** is a court order to stop doing something (or *to* do something). If unions acted in ways that management did not like,

13-1

labor union

An organization of workers formed to give workers greater bargaining power in their dealings with management.

13-1

injunction

A court order to stop doing something (or *to* do something).

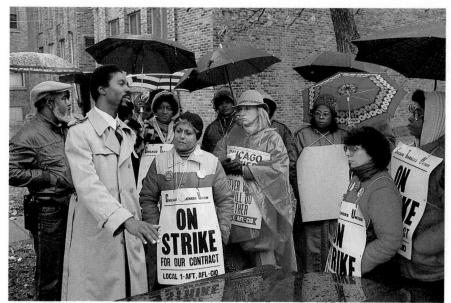

Illustration 13–4
Labor unions organize in an attempt to give workers greater bargaining power with management. If management ignores the union's demands, workers may use their ultimate union weapon—the labor strike.

management would try to have an injunction issued against the union. And management usually succeeded. The penalties for violating an injunction included fines and jail sentences.

A **yellow-dog contract** was a contract workers had to sign before they were hired saying that they would not join a union. Anyone who wouldn't sign did not get hired.

The Sherman Antitrust Act was passed partially to make combinations that were in restraint of trade illegal. The law was aimed at big corporate businesses. But much of its early use was against unions that used strikes to fight management. Management claimed that the unions' strike activities were in restraint of trade, because the strikes limited the flow of goods across state lines.

By the early 1930s, public opinion began to favor labor unions. Public opinion was against business, because many people blamed business for the Depression. As a result, the Norris LaGuardia Act was passed in 1932. The act held that labor activity was not in violation of antitrust laws and that yellow-dog contracts were illegal. The act also greatly limited businesses' use of injunctions against unions. This opened the door for the development of labor unions. But near economic warfare developed. Armed conflicts between labor and the people hired by management to keep unions in check were common.

Partly as a result of such conflicts, the National Labor Relations Act, also called the Wagner Act, was passed in 1935. One of the most important pieces of labor legislation, the bill defines management practices that are considered to be unfair to labor. Management could no longer interfere with or restrain union activities. It

13–1

yellow-dog contract

A contract workers had to sign before they were hired saying that they would not join a union.

could not discriminate against workers who wanted to join unions and could not act against workers who filed charges against the business. The employer had to recognize and bargain with unions that were properly formed. The law also established the National Labor Relations Board that set up procedures for conducting union elections.

As a result of the National Labor Relations Act, union activity grew. There were restraints on management but almost none on unions. After World War II, unions began a flurry of strike activity. Public opinion started to turn against union activity. In 1947, the Taft-Hartley Act was passed. This act specified which union actions were considered unfair labor practices. For example, the closed shop was made illegal. A **closed shop** is a business which agrees to hire only those who are members of a union. A union shop is still legal, however. A **union shop** is a business that requires workers to join a union shortly after taking a job. The Taft-Hartley Act also set up emergency procedures to allow government to interfere with union activity if labor problems threaten the national security.

Today there is a better balance between the power of unions and the power of management. People still join unions, and union growth is greatest in white-collar jobs such as teaching. Overall, however, the percentage of all nonagricultural workers who belong to unions has been declining.

When workers belong to a union, individual workers no longer negotiate working conditions with management. Benefits such as wages, hours, vacation time, and insurance coverage are determined through collective bargaining. **Collective bargaining** is the process of having the union negotiate with management to determine the terms of employment for all workers rather than having each worker negotiate separately.

13–1

closed shop

A business which agrees to hire only those who are members of a union.

13–1

union shop

A business that requires workers to join a union shortly after taking a job.

13–1

collective bargaining

The process of having the union negotiate with management to determine the terms of employment for all workers rather than having each worker negotiate separately.

SOURCES OF INCOME

The income that individuals get depends on the quality and quantity of the factors of production over which they have control. We can work to earn income. In fact, most of the income earned in the United States is labor income. We may also own stocks in corporations. This allows us to share in the profits earned by those firms. We may own land or the right to natural resources which gives us rental income. Finally, we can get interest income from lending money to people who invest it in productive machinery. Or we might even invest the money ourselves. Interest income is the second most important source of income in the United States.

INTEREST

Interest is the price paid for the use of money. The concept of interest dates back at least to biblical times when all payments for the use of money were considered evil. Money was thought of as useless and nonproductive. The collection of money for the use of money was called *usury*, and it was considered sinful and illegal. Not until the development of modern business did people accept interest as a justifiable charge for the use of money. Modern businesses often must borrow large sums of money to buy the productive equipment they need. The money firms borrow has productive use because it buys productive equipment. So, a charge for its use is fair and reasonable. Today the term *usury* is used only to refer to the act of charging interest rates above the maximum rates allowed by law.

13–1

interest
The price paid for the use of money.

Two Views of Interest

There are two ways of looking at the concept of interest. One is to think of interest as the price that is paid for the use of money or credit. For example, if you borrow money to buy a car, you must pay interest on the amount you borrow. Another aspect of interest is the rate of return that a productive piece of machinery earns. Machines, buildings, and computers are examples of capital equipment that can be productive. Capital contributes to production just as labor does. And the payment to capital is interest, just as the payment to labor is a wage.

13–5

Suppose you borrow $1,000 today and agree to repay that $1,000 plus $50 one year from today. You are willing to repay the extra $50 for the right to use someone else's money for the year. The $50 is the interest you pay. That $50 is the cost of borrowing the $1,000. But interest is almost never stated in terms of the number of dollars paid. Instead, interest is stated as a percentage, or a rate of interest. The rate is the amount of interest paid per year divided by the amount that is borrowed. In this example the interest rate is 5 percent (50/1000 = .05 = 5%).

Banks, savings and loan associations, and credit unions all pay interest when people save and charge interest when people borrow. In either case, the interest paid or charged is stated as a percentage. Interest paid on savings is always less than the interest charged on new loans. For example, a bank may pay 7 percent on your savings, but charge you 12 percent on a loan. The 7 percent paid on your savings means that each year you would get an added $7 for each $100 in your savings account. The 12 percent loan rate means that for every $100 borrowed for a year you would be charged $12 in interest.

Now let's look at interest as a return to capital. Suppose a business bought a $20,000 machine to use in producing some product. To simplify this example, we will assume that the machine is useful for only one year. To find the earnings related to the machine, you would subtract all other payments, such as wages, from the revenue obtained by selling the product. If the revenue from sales were $100,000 and all other costs amounted to $97,000, the earnings due to the machine would be $3,000. The rate of return on the machine would be $3,000 divided by $20,000 which is .15 or 15 percent. This is the interest earned by that piece of capital equipment. If the company could borrow the money to buy the machine for less than 15 percent, it would be profitable to do so. But if the market rate of interest were higher than 15 percent, the company should not invest in the machine.

Factors Which Influence the Interest Rate

13–6   On television and radio, as well as in newspapers and magazines, we get many reports and articles about the rate of interest. Actually there are many different interest rates in the economy. You may have heard of the prime rate, the corporate bond rate, or the federal funds rate. Every lending market has its own interest rate. The rate in each market depends upon many factors. Among these are time involved, risk, rate of inflation, costs of making the loan, and tax treatment of interest.

In general, the shorter the time period of the loan, the lower the interest rate. Lenders prefer a shorter time period because there is less chance of changes that would affect the profitability of the loan. Loans that extend over long periods of time reduce the lender's ability to change and to adjust to changing economic events.

Risk is another factor that influences interest rates. For example, suppose you had the choice of lending your money to IBM or to the Wickey Wackey Widget Corporation. It seems more likely that IBM could repay your money in full and on time. You might then lend money to a company such as IBM at a relatively low interest rate. But you would charge the Wickey Wackey Widget Corporation more since you wouldn't be as sure of repayment in full and on time. There is a general rule in lending money: The higher the risk, the higher the interest.

The rate of inflation also influences interest rates. We will discuss inflation in more detail later, but for now we will define it in broad terms. Inflation is a rise in the average level of prices. You can quickly see why inflation would influence interest rates. Suppose the average level of prices was increasing at 10 percent a year. Next year it would take $110 to buy what $100 would buy today. If

Illustration 13–5
Many factors, such as inflation rates and tax laws, cause interest rates to rise and fall.

you were loaned $100 today at 5 percent interest, you would owe $105 a year from now. But that $105 a year from now wouldn't even be enough to buy what the $100 would buy today. It would take $110 to do so. So, the lender would not earn any real interest and, in fact, would lose buying power. It follows, then, that lenders will not want to lend money unless the interest rate is greater than the inflation rate. This means that in times of high inflation we should expect high interest rates.

The costs a lender has in making a loan will also influence the interest rate. There are costs involved in checking the borrower's credit and in administering the loan.

Finally, the ways in which tax laws treat different forms of interest can influence the interest rate. If a lender can get tax benefits by loaning money in some market, that market's interest rate is likely to be lower. Most of the time, a lender must pay taxes on interest that is collected. For example, if you lend IBM money by buying its bonds, you pay taxes on that interest income. But if you lend money to the city of Tulsa by buying a bond the city issues, the interest income is tax free. So, you might be willing to lend money to Tulsa at a lower interest rate than you would to IBM. People will be more likely to lend money if the interest income is not taxed.

As you study more about macroeconomics in Part III, you will see some ways that national economic policy can influence interest rates. You will also see how interest rates influence investment, productivity, and economic growth.

Particular Interest Rates

What do people in the news media mean when they refer to rising or falling interest rates? Usually they are referring to the prime rate. The **prime rate** is the interest rate that banks charge their best corporate customers. Companies such as General Motors, IBM, and AT&T may be charged the prime rate. The risk involved in lending money to those firms is very small. Therefore, the prime rate is usually lower than most other interest rates. It is also often used as a standard indicator of changes in interest rates in general.

Another interest rate that is commonly talked about is the corporate bond rate. As the name implies, the **corporate bond rate** is the interest rate paid on corporate bonds. A corporate bond is a certificate issued by a corporation promising to pay bondholders a specific amount of money by a specific date.

A third interest rate that is often reported in the news is the federal funds rate. The **federal funds rate** is the interest rate banks pay to borrow from each other on a short-term basis. The time

13–1

prime rate
The interest rate that banks charge their best corporate customers.

13–1

corporate bond rate
The interest rate paid on corporate bonds.

13–1

federal funds rate
The interest rate banks pay to borrow from each other on a short-term basis.

may be as short as overnight. Such loans have little risk and last for a very short time. Therefore, the federal funds rate usually stays low, even lower than the prime rate.

Another rate we hear about often is the discount rate. The **discount rate** is the interest rate that banks must pay to borrow from the Federal Reserve System. (The Federal Reserve System and the discount rate will be discussed more fully in Part III of this text.) The discount rate is lower than the prime rate and the other rates mentioned, but it is not available to private individuals and businesses except banks.

Consumer Credit and Interest Rates

13–7   The rates charged for consumer credit are usually higher than other rates. There are three reasons for these higher rates:

1. Consumer loans have higher risk.

2. They are costly to set up.

3. They often run over a long period of time.

Most consumer loans involve much more risk than loans to corporations that qualify for the prime rate. The costs of checking credit and handling the loan account are also higher for individuals. This is particularly true in comparison to the dollar amount of a loan. There may be high costs in trying to collect the balance due if the person fails to keep up with the payments. Also, many consumer loans are made for three or more years. It is not uncommon for people to have car loans that run four or even five years.

Consumer credit comes from credit unions, life insurance companies, commercial banks, savings and loan associations, finance companies, charge accounts, and credit cards. The interest charged by these lenders varies, so consumers should shop around when looking to borrow money. It will always cost you money to borrow money. But by shopping around, a person can often save. Let's look at two common examples where it pays to shop for interest rates: buying a car and buying a house.

Suppose that you have saved enough money for a down payment on a new car, but you need to borrow $5,000 to make the purchase. You check on borrowing the money from two places. A credit union will lend you the money at a 12 percent interest rate. A local finance company will lend you the same amount but at a 15 percent interest rate. (A difference of 3 percent or more on a car loan would not be uncommon.) Both loans would be for four years. Your monthly payments and total payments are shown at the top of page 263 for the $5,000 loan.

13–1

discount rate

The interest rate that banks must pay to borrow from the Federal Reserve System.

	Credit Union (12% Interest)	Finance Company (15% Interest)
Monthly Payment	$ 131.67	$ 139.15
Total Payments	$6,320.16	$6,679.20
Difference in Total Payments	$359.04	

As we see, there is a $359.04 savings over the four years at the lower interest rate. But if you don't shop around, you might not borrow at the lowest rate.

At some point you may want to buy a house, and finding the lowest interest rate will be even more important. Assume that you want to borrow $70,000 to buy a house. A home loan may be for as long as 30 years, so we will use that time period. You might go to a bank and to a savings and loan to see about borrowing the money. Perhaps the bank will lend you the money at 14.5 percent, and the savings and loan will lend you the money at 14 percent. This does not seem like much of a difference. But is it? Your payments on the $70,000 are summarized below.

	Bank (14.5% Interest)	Savings and Loan (14% Interest)
Monthly Payment	$ 857.19	$ 829.41
Total Payment	$308,588.40	$298,587.60
Difference in Total Payments	$10,000.80	

A one half of one percent difference in the interest rate means a difference in total payments of $10,000 over the 30-year loan. It may also surprise you to see that even at the lower rate, you would have paid $298,587.60 for the $70,000 home loan. The interest payments would total $228,587.60, which is more than three times the amount you borrowed. Interest can add up to a large amount of money. So, it is as important to shop around when you borrow money as it is when you make purchases.

THINKING
ABOUT ECONOMIC ISSUES

Why do you think some professional baseball players can ask for, and get, $4 million a year? Not many are able to command such a large salary. But even the average professional baseball player is very well paid. Let's first look at the supply side of the market.

It takes a high level of skill to be a professional athlete. Only a very small percentage of the population has such great skill. So, the *supply* of highly skilled, well-trained athletes is very small. Not only is it small, it is also very inelastic. This means that even at higher and higher wages, few, if any, additional people with the necessary skills will be available. If the Pittsburgh Pirates want to hire a new left fielder, the team will have to choose from a limited pool of people. A supply curve with these characteristics is shown on the graph below. Notice that it is a very steep, almost vertical, line.

Now let's look at the demand side of the market. Remember that the demand for labor is derived demand. In this case, it is derived from the demand for baseball games. People express their demand for baseball by going to baseball games and by watching baseball on television. Our demand for baseball, as with other sporting events, is high. As a result, the demand for the skilled athletes who play the game is also high. This high demand for baseball players is also shown in the graph below.

Remember that the market is in equilibrium, or supply and demand are balanced, where the demand curve crosses the supply curve. This is marked by Point *E*. You can see that the equilibrium is at a high wage.

SUPPLY AND DE-
MAND FOR BASE-
BALL PLAYERS
The high payments made to the most highly skilled professional athletes result from high demand combined with low and inelastic supply.

Baseball Players'
Wage or Salary

Supply of Highly
Skilled Baseball
Players

Wage or
Salary
Paid

E

Demand for Highly
Skilled Baseball
Players

Number Employed
Number of Highly Skilled Baseball Players

REVIEWING THE CHAPTER

1. Labor is bought and sold in a market, very much as goods and sevices are bought and sold. People are not bought or sold, but their labor time is.

13–2 2. The demand for labor can be represented by a negatively sloped labor demand curve. This means that firms will hire more units of labor at a lower wage than at a higher wage.

13–2 3. The supply of labor can be represented by a positively sloped labor supply curve. This means that more units of labor will be made available for work at a higher wage than at a lower wage.

13–2 4. When the labor demand equals the labor supply, the labor market is in balance. This is called an equilibrium in the labor market. If the wage is above the market equilibrium, labor supply will be greater than demand. If the wage is below the market equilibrium, labor demand will be greater than supply. In either case, economic forces will push the wage toward the equilibrium.

13–3 5. The government sets a minimum wage to prevent firms from paying a wage that is considered too low. Congress periodically votes to increase the minimum wage. This puts some people out of work and reduces the hours that others work. This is particularly hard on teenagers and people with less well-developed labor skills. If minimum wage earners are not laid off or do not have their hours cut back, they do earn more after increases in the minimum wage.

13–4 6. Labor unions developed because management seemed to have too much control over labor. Since the late 1800s, much conflict has occurred between business managers and unions. Laws favoring both sides have been passed by Congress. Power between unions and management appears better balanced now than 100 years ago when the labor movement was gaining recognition and strength.

7. People's incomes depend on the quantity and quality of the factors of production that they control. We all have our own labor to use in whatever form of production we wish. Some people own much land and capital, while others have none of these resources within their control.

13–5 8. Interest is also used to describe the payment made for the use of someone else's money. You get interest when you put money into savings for someone else to use until you want it. You pay interest when you borrow money to buy things before you have enough of your own money to do so. When borrowing money, you should always shop around for the lowest interest rate.

13–5   9. Another way of looking at interest is as a return to productive machines and other forms of capital equipment. Just as labor and land are productive, so is capital. The return to capital is called interest and is usually stated as a percentage. For example, suppose a $10,000 machine with a one-year useful life has $2,000 worth of productivity in that year. The return expressed as a rate of interest would be 20 percent (2,000/10,000 = .20 = 20%).

REVIEWING ECONOMIC TERMS

13–1   Supply definitions for the following terms:

demand for labor	yellow-dog contract
wage rate	closed shop
derived demand	union shop
supply of labor	collective bargaining
equilibrium wage	interest
monopsony	prime rate
minimum wage law	corporate bond rate
labor union	federal funds rate
injunction	discount rate

REVIEWING ECONOMIC CONCEPTS

13–2   1. What factors determine the demand for labor?

13–2   2. What factors may cause the demand for labor to increase?

13–2   3. What has been the major cause of the increase in the supply of labor in the last 20 years?

13–2   4. Name three forces that can prevent labor market equilibrium.

13–3   5. Which groups do minimum wage laws help and hurt?

13–4   6. Why did labor unions develop?

13–4   7. Describe three labor unions mentioned in this chapter.

13–4   8. Describe the effect of four laws (mentioned in this chapter) on labor.

13–5   9. What are two ways of looking at the concept of interest?

13–6   10. What five factors influence interest rates?

13–7   11. List three reasons why interest rates on consumer loans are higher than other rates.

APPLYING ECONOMIC CONCEPTS

13–3   1. What is a *minimum wage*? In what types of jobs are people paid the minimum wage? Why do you think this is so?

13–2   2. Explain how the market system would determine an equilibrium wage rate and the level of employment. Use a supply and demand graph for labor to help with your explanation.

13–7   3. Why is it important for consumers to shop around when they need to borrow money? Where might people go if they want to borrow money to buy a car? Call two different places and ask what their current interest rates are on a new car loan. Why might the results be different at each place?

13–1   4. What determines the demand for bank tellers? Why is the demand for bank tellers called a *derived demand*?

13–6   5. Suppose you were in business and bought a new machine for $40,000. After paying all other expenses, $7,000 is left that can be attributed to the productivity of the machine, which only has a one-year useful life. What is the rate of interest earned by this machine? If you had to pay 20 percent to borrow the money to buy such a machine, would you do so? Would you borrow the money at 10 percent?

13–2   6. Teachers' salaries have not been increasing as fast as the pay in many other types of work. Explain why you think this might be true. Use a graph of the supply and demand for teachers' labor to help answer this question. (Hint: Think about how the supply and demand curves may be shifting over time.)

BIG BUCKS FOR BALLPLAYERS

Demand and supply forces can result in high salaries for some ballplayers. The following 1993 contract amounts were reported in *USA Today* (June 28, 1990, p. 3C). These amounts do not include payments the players may receive for product endorsements.

José Canseco	$4,800,000	Mark Langston	$3,500,000
Will Clark	$4,750,000	Don Mattingly	$3,820,000
Mark Davis	$3,625,000	Robin Yount	$3,575,000
Rickey Henderson	$3,250,000		

CHAPTER 14

AGRICULTURE IN THE ECONOMY

Learning Objectives

IMPORTANCE OF AGRICULTURE

Agriculture is important in any economy. As agricultural methods and technology raise the productivity of each farm worker, fewer workers are needed to make the farm goods we need. Yet, for many years farmers have felt that they have not received their fair share of the wealth in the United States. It is important to know the economic causes of the low and changing level of farm incomes. With this background, you can better understand our federal farm policies.

The farmer has always been a respected figure in American life. We think of farmers as hardworking, self-reliant, and rugged. Farmers work long, hard hours to supply the nation with food and other crops such as cotton. Farmers must live through nature's trials: floods, hailstorms, droughts, and insect plagues. Nature controls the lives of farmers and causes wide variations in their annual incomes. There are good years and bad years. But what most concerns farmers is that farm incomes have historically been lower than nonfarm incomes.

Today there are about 2 million farms in the United States. Later in this chapter, you will see that the farm population has fallen fairly steadily. U.S. agriculture makes up less than 3 percent

Illustration 14–1
The farmer in America has always been a respected figure, representing hard work and rugged ideals.

Source: Grant Wood, *American Gothic*, 1930, oil on beaverboard, 79.5 × 63.5 cm., Friends of American Art Collection, 1930.934 © The Art Institute of Chicago. All rights reserved.

of our GNP in both current and constant dollars. This may seem like a small part of the economy. But it is an important part since we all need many farm products for food and clothing. This part of the economy must stay healthy.

UPS AND DOWNS OF FARM INCOME

Good years and bad years are a part of life for farm families. The incomes of farm families go up and down much more often than the incomes of nonfarm families. Two main reasons explain these changes in farm incomes from year to year. First, farmers must cope with natural disasters more than most other workers. A drought, flood, or hailstorm can destroy a farmer's whole crop. Often nothing can be done to stop the damage. Such natural disasters can reduce farmers' incomes to almost nothing. At one time, there was nothing farmers could do about income losses. But today they can buy crop insurance to help protect against such losses. Second, economic reasons such as the forces of supply and demand can cause farm incomes to change greatly from one year to the next.

Demand for Farm Goods Is Inelastic

14-3   The demand for goods that farmers produce is not very sensitive to price changes. In a rich country such as the United States, people eat what they think they want or need. When food prices go up, we may spend less on other things, but we probably will buy about the same amount of food. We may cut back a little, but not much. On the other hand, if food prices go down, we are not likely to buy much more food.

It has generally been shown that prices for farm products would have to fall 40 to 50 percent in order to get people to buy 10 percent more. That is, to get a 10 percent change in sales, prices would have to change by 40 to 50 percent. This kind of demand is called *inelastic* because sales are not very responsive to changes in price. Most of the things that farmers produce have an inelastic demand. As you will now see, this can cause farm incomes to go up and down quite a bit.

A Good Year Can Be a Bad Year

14-2   In 1981 farmers enjoyed good weather. There were no late spring frosts and no early fall freezes. There was plenty of rain, but not too much rain. No major hailstorms or insect infestations destroyed large areas of crops. It was a good year for farming. Near-record and record-setting crops of wheat, corn, soybeans, cotton, and other products were produced.

But *U.S. News & World Report* ran a headline that stated, "For Farmers, Big Crops Bring Big Troubles."[1] How can big crops bring trouble? The reason relates to the inelastic demand for the goods farmers produce. When the amount of goods brought to market goes up more than expected, the price falls. As one farmer from Nebraska said in that article, "The more we raise, the less we get." Farm income (in real terms) fell that year to less than 60 percent of what it had been just two years before. A good year had indeed turned out to be a bad year.

To illustrate what can happen, let's look at the graph in Figure 14–1. Assume that the expected supply of wheat is 2.0 billion bushels. This is shown as a line straight up from 2.0 billion bushels. This happens because once the seed is in the ground, the amount of wheat produced is outside the farmers' control. More or less wheat cannot be produced, no matter the price level. But due to good weather, the actual amount produced is higher than expected. This is shown by the line going up from 2.4 billion bushels of wheat.

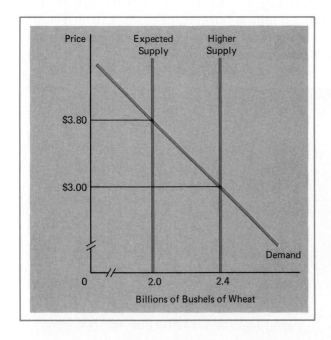

FIGURE 14–1   A HIGHER SUPPLY OF WHEAT LOWERS PRICE
A good year in terms of the amount produced can lower price so much that farm income falls.

---

[1]Joanne Davidson et al., "For Farmers, Big Crops Bring Big Troubles," *U.S. News & World Report* (2 November 1981), 55–57.

The demand curve in Figure 14–1 along with the two supply curves show what happens to price. In order to sell all the wheat, the price has to drop. An expected price of $3.80 dropped to an actual price of $3.00. If the expected 2.0 billion bushels were produced and sold at $3.80 per bushel, wheat farmers would receive $7.6 billion for their wheat. ($3.80 per bushel × 2.0 billion bushels = $7.6 billion.) But due to good weather, 2.4 billion bushels are produced. As a result, price falls to $3.00. After the fall in price, farmers get $7.2 billion for their wheat. ($3.00 per bushel × 2.4 billion bushels = $7.2 billion.) So, a good farming year could cost wheat farmers $0.4 billion. (This is the same as $400 million.) This means their incomes fall.

A Bad Year May Not Be All Bad

Think about what might happen in a bad year. Drought, hailstorms, and other bad weather may cause the amount farmers produce to fall. This would cause prices to rise. For most farm goods, the rise in price would be greater than the fall in the amount produced. This is because of the inelastic demand for farm products. The result would be an increase in farm income.

You can see this by reversing the change shown in Figure 14–1. If output falls from 2.4 to 2.0 billion bushels, price rises from $3.00 to $3.80. Wheat farmers' sales would then go up from $7.2 billion to $7.6 billion, and their incomes would go up, too.

Illustration 14–2
Surprisingly, a year of bad weather and scarce crops may result in increased farm incomes. The higher prices we pay for food products in a bad year often more than make up for the fall in the amount produced.

These examples show that farm income is very sensitive to changes in supply. It takes big price changes to get rid of extra supply or to ration a smaller supply. Any large price changes cause wide fluctuations in farm income.

Demand Changes Also Affect Income

Changes in demand for farm goods also cause changes in farm incomes. Again, assume that supply for the current year is fixed based on the amount of planting done at the start of the season. Then suppose demand goes up, perhaps due to higher exports. This is shown in the left-hand graph of Figure 14–2. As demand goes up, price will also rise. This will bring about higher farm incomes as well. It is no wonder that farmers support programs to increase exports of farm goods to other countries.

A fall in demand works in the opposite way. This is shown in the right-hand graph of Figure 14–2. As demand goes down, so will price. This also causes farm incomes to fall. Sometimes the government cuts food exports to China or to other countries to show that we do not agree with those countries' political actions.

14–3

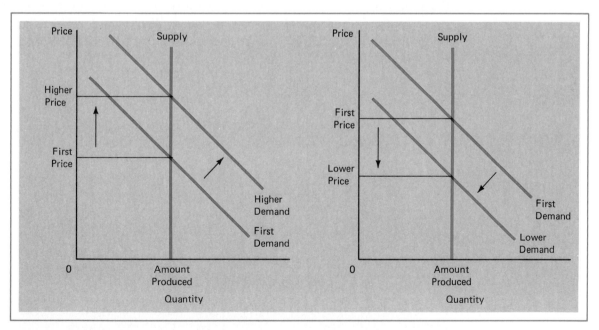

FIGURE 14–2   CHANGES IN DEMAND AFFECT PRICE AND INCOME
The left graph shows demand and price going up. The right graph shows demand and price falling. As price rises, so will income. But as price falls, income also falls.

You should not be surprised to learn that stopping food exports upsets American farmers. It decreases demand, prices, and farmers' incomes.

The problem of rising and falling farm incomes has been hard to deal with. Many different government programs, which will be discussed later in the chapter, have helped but not solved the problem. Some of these programs cost a lot, and that cost falls on the nonfarm taxpayers. The most successful programs that have prevented farm income from falling due to natural disasters are crop insurance and research on farm production. Researchers have found stronger, disease-resistant hybrid crops, better ways to stop insect damage, and better ways to irrigate fields in dry growing seasons. Because of these advances, farmers today are less at the mercy of natural disasters.

FARM INCOME COMPARED TO NONFARM INCOME

14–4   For most of this century, farm incomes have been lower than the average for the entire economy. It has been estimated that for some years during the middle part of this century, farm incomes have been close to half of those for nonfarm families. Most recently there appear to be meaningful increases in the average level of income for farm households. The statistics in Table 14–1 reflect the relationship between the average income for farm households and the average income for all households.

TABLE 14–1

COMPARISON OF AVERAGE HOUSEHOLD FARM AND NONFARM INCOMES

Year	Average Household Income		Ratio of Farm to all Households
	Farm Households	All Households	
1980	$18,434	$21,063	0.88
1981	17,411	22,787	0.76
1982	20,422	24,309	0.84
1983	20,623	25,609	0.81
1984	22,347	27,464	0.81
1985	29,436	29,066	1.01
1986	34,246	30,759	1.11

Source: U.S. Bureau of the Census, *Statistical Abstract of the United States: 1990*, 110th ed. (Washington, D.C., 1990), 648.

As you might expect, farm income is not evenly divided among farmers. Slightly more than 14 percent of the largest farms get 76 percent of the farm income. The smallest 23.5 percent of farms get .4 percent of farm income. Table 14–2 shows this unequal distribution of farm incomes. The table shows that the largest 1.5 percent of the farms get 38.1 percent of the income.

TABLE 14–2

DISTRIBUTION OF FARMS AND NET FARM INCOME
BY FARM SIZE AS MEASURED USING SALES
(For a Typical Year)

Sales	Percentage of All Farms	Percentage of Gross Farm Income
less than $ 2,500	23.5%	0.4%
$ 2,500 to $ 4,999	12.6%	0.7%
$ 5,000 to $ 9,999	13.2%	1.4%
$ 10,000 to $ 24,999	15.6%	3.9%
$ 25,000 to $ 49,999	10.5%	5.8%
$ 50,000 to $ 99,999	10.4%	11.5%
$ 100,000 to $249,999	9.7%	22.9%
$ 250,000 to $499,999	2.9%	15.2%
$ 500,000 to $999,999	1.0%	10.3%
$1,000,000 and over	0.5%	27.8%

Source: U.S. Bureau of the Census, *Statistical Abstract of the United States: 1991* (Washington, D.C., 1991), 648.

DEMAND AND SUPPLY FORCES IN FARMING

Several forces keep farm incomes low in relation to incomes in other parts of the economy. You already know about the *price* inelasticity of farm goods. Farm products are also *income* inelastic. This means that the demand for these goods is not very responsive to changes in people's income. It has been found that a 10 percent rise in real per capita disposable income brings only a 2 percent rise in the sales of farm goods. Again, this is true because people are generally well fed in the United States. The extra money from a 10 percent rise in income is much more likely to be spent on goods such as dishwashers, video recorders, and ten-speed bicycles. This income inelasticity has made the demand for farm goods in the United States fall behind the demand for other goods and services.

The demand for farm products has fallen behind demand for products in other parts of the economy. But the supply of farm goods has gone up rapidly. In fact, agricultural productivity has

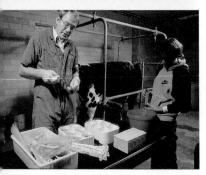

Illustration 14–3
Better fertilizers, new methods of irrigation, and research for improved care and breeding of farm animals all help increase farm productivity.

gone up much faster than productivity in the rest of the economy. In 1820, one farmer could support four people. Now one farmer can support about 80 people. This rise in productivity is the result of technological advances. Research programs at land-grant agricultural colleges have contributed greatly to these technological advances. So have the research and development programs of the makers of farm equipment and other supplies. The following are some technological changes that have increased farm productivity:

1. introduction of electricity into rural areas
2. greater use of machinery
3. improved land use
4. soil conservation
5. new methods of irrigation
6. miracle seeds
7. better fertilizers
8. more efficient insecticides
9. improved care and breeding of farm animals

Table 14–3 shows increases in farm productivity. Read carefully across each row of this table. In row after row, you can see that farm labor has become more and more productive. Look at the production of corn as shown in the first row. During the period from 1950 to 1954, it took 34 hours of labor to get 100 bushels of corn. By the period from 1982–1986 it took just three hours of labor to get the same amount of corn. This kind of higher productivity is found throughout the farming sector. This shows what happens to labor's productivity as more machinery is used and as there are improved ways of producing things. The higher productivity has greatly contributed to the big rise in the supply of farm goods.

You have just learned that there have been relatively small increases in demand for farm products but rapidly rising supplies. In the long run, these two trends have led to a drop in farm prices and a resulting drop in farm incomes. These continuing lags in farm incomes have made many farmers leave farming for more profitable work. The farm population has fallen steadily, as shown in Table 14–4.

Many have incomes below the poverty level. Why haven't these farmers left farming? One reason may be that federal farm programs have helped keep them in business. Another reason is that farm resources—land, tractors and equipment, barns, silos,

TABLE 14-3

INCREASES IN AGRICULTURAL PRODUCTIVITY
(Labor Hours Per Unit of Output)

Selected Products	1950 to 1954	1960 to 1964	1970 to 1974	1982 to 1986
Corn (labor hrs/100 bushels)	34.0	11.0	5.0	3.0
Wheat (labor hrs/100 bushels)	27.0	12.0	9.0	7.0
Hay (labor hrs/short ton)	4.4	2.8	1.8	1.2
Cotton (labor hrs/bale)	107.0	47.0	18.0	5.0
Tobacco (labor hrs/100 lbs)	36.0	26.0	14.0	10.0
Milk (labor hrs/100 lbs)	2.2	1.2	0.6	0.2
Cattle (labor hrs/100 lbs)	3.6	2.6	1.7	0.9
Hogs (labor hrs/100 lbs)	2.7	1.9	1.0	0.3
Eggs (labor hrs/100 eggs)	1.3	0.6	0.3	0.2
Turkeys (labor hrs/100 lbs)	6.8	2.4	0.8	0.2

Source: U.S. Bureau of the Census, *Statistical Abstract of the United States: 1987* (Washington, D.C., 1987), 641.

TABLE 14-4

FARM POPULATION

Year	Farm Population* (in millions)	Farm Population As a Percentage of the Total Population
1920	31.9	30.1%
1925	31.2	27.0%
1930	30.5	24.9%
1935	32.2	25.3%
1940	30.5	23.2%
1945	24.4	17.5%
1950	23.0	15.3%
1955	19.1	11.6%
1960	15.6	8.7%
1965	12.4	6.4%
1970	9.7	4.8%
1975	8.9	4.2%
1980	7.2	3.3%
1983	7.0	3.0%

*There was a change in the way the farm population was identified starting in 1969. Therefore, numbers after 1969 do not represent exactly the same situation as before 1969. The downward trend of the farm population has not changed, however.
Source: U.S. Bureau of the Census, *Statistical Abstract of the United States: 1970* (p. 582), *1981* (p. 657), and *1991* (p. 643), (Washington, D.C.: U.S. Government Printing Office).

fences—have few other uses. Farmers have a lot of money tied up in these resources. Even though they find that farming isn't very profitable, they may not be able to sell the land, equipment, and buildings except at a loss. Because this investment cost is high, it is hard to leave farming. Thus, about 65 percent of all farmers end up splitting only about 6.4 percent of the total farm income. You can see why many of them have very low incomes.

Figure 14–3 shows what can happen when a dramatic rise in supply accompanies a small rise in demand. In any market, if supply goes up more than demand, there will be downward pressure on price. This is shown by the move from the First Price down to the New Price. In the case of farming, this has been one of the reasons why farm incomes have remained low for many years. As you will see in the next part of this chapter, some government programs have helped farmers get around the economic laws of supply and demand.

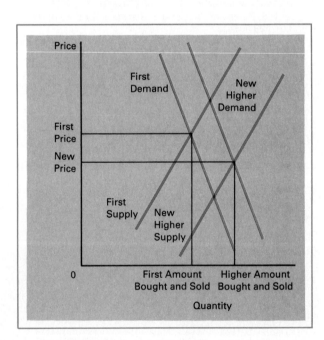

FIGURE 14–3 CHANGES IN FARM SUPPLY AND DEMAND
Over time, supply has gone up more than demand. This has resulted in downward pressure on price and lower farm incomes.

AGRICULTURAL POLICY

The federal government has been active in setting up programs to help keep farm income from falling. These programs have included price supports, low interest loans, crop insurance, farm research, and soil conservation programs. Most government farm programs have centered on keeping farm prices up. This has been the result of strong political pressure from farmers who have usually seen falling prices as their main problem.

Price Support Programs

A **price support program** is a government program designed to keep prices from falling below some level the government decides is fair. Many price support programs are based on parity prices. A **parity price** is a price that changes as prices of other goods change so that the income of producers can purchase the same amount of these goods as in some base year. In agriculture, the period from 1910–1914 is often used as the base year in figuring parity prices. This period is considered to be the time when farmers' incomes were best in comparison to the rest of society.

Price support programs began with the Agricultural Marketing Act of 1929. This act helped farmers to set up farmers' cooperatives. A **cooperative** is a business owned and run by a group with a common interest. Cooperatives are often called *co-ops*. This Act gave the co-ops more than $500 million for buying surplus grain. This helped to keep prices higher because of added demand for grain from co-ops. The co-ops set a price that they felt was fair. This price was above the market price based on supply and demand. At the higher price, there were not enough buyers for the whole supply, so the co-ops bought the extra output. In the early 1930s, the Federal Farm Board took over the price support program. Even though the Farm Board spent $676 million, farm prices still fell.

The Agricultural Adjustment Act of 1938 established the Commodity Credit Corporation. The **Commodity Credit Corporation (CCC)** is the part of the Department of Agriculture that makes loans to farmers using their crops as security. This meant that if the farmers could not or did not repay their loans in money, the CCC would take the crops as payment instead. This had the effect of setting a lower limit on farm prices.

Suppose that the CCC set a loan value of $3.00 for a bushel of wheat. As a farmer, you could borrow $12,000 from the CCC using 4,000 bushels of wheat as security. As long as the market price was above $3.00, you would sell your wheat and pay off the loan. But what if the price fell below $3.00, say to $2.50 per bushel. You would simply turn the 4,000 bushels of wheat over to the CCC and consider the loan paid. So, the lowest price any farmer would get was the loan price, $3.00 in this case. In effect, the CCC had the power to set price support levels by determining the loan value of a

14–6
14–1
price support program
A government program designed to keep prices from falling below some level the government decides is fair.

14–1
parity price
A price that changes as prices of other goods change so that the income of producers can purchase the same amount of these goods as in some base year.

14–1
cooperative
A business owned and run by a group with a common interest.

14–1
Commodity Credit Corporation (CCC)
The part of the Department of Agriculture that makes loans to farmers using crops as security.

Illustration 14–4
During the 1950s, the U.S. government spent as much as $1.1 million a day to store wheat.

certain crop. These price support programs left the government owning large amounts of surplus farm crops.

During the 1950s, big farm surpluses built up. In 1952 the government held $1.3 billion in surplus farm products. By 1955 this was up to $6.7 billion, and by 1959 it reached $8 billion. During this time, the government had to spend as much as *$1.1 million a day* to store wheat. The dollar value of commodities owned by the Commodity Credit Corporation varies from year to year. In the 1980s the CCC owned over $10 billion worth of farm products at various times. You can check the most recent amounts by looking in the most recent issue of *Statistical Abstract of the United States* (see "Commodity Credit Corporation" in the index).

Set Aside Programs

14–6   The government has thought of other ways to keep prices up besides price support programs. In 1933 the Agricultural Adjustment Act was passed. That act set up the Agricultural Adjustment Administration (AAA), whose job was to keep farm prices up by lowering supply. The AAA accomplished this by limiting the amount of land farmers could use. This is an example of a set aside program. A **set aside program** is a government program that reduces the supply of farm products by keeping land out of production. The AAA would figure out the demand for farm goods. Then it could tell how much land would be needed to grow just the amount to meet this demand. The total amount of land to be used was split up among the states and then among farms. This act was later found to be unconstitutional because it forced farmers to remove land from production. But the government found other ways, such as the Soil Bank program, to limit land use.

14–1

set aside program
A government program that reduces the supply of farm products by keeping land out of production.

To try to lower the amount of products held by the government, the Soil Bank Act of 1956 was passed. Under the Soil Bank program, the Department of Agriculture rented land from farmers so the land would not be used to grow things. That means that the government paid farmers not to grow corn, wheat, cotton, and other crops. But this program did not work well. Farm production did not fall because farmers rented their worst land and farmed their best land.

Programs to Increase Demand

14–6   The programs discussed so far were supposed to help farmers keep prices up by either directly supporting prices or lowering supply. The government has also tried to raise the demand for farm products. Several food distribution programs were started, such as the school lunch program and the food stamp program. The government also supported research programs to find new uses for farm products, but these did not work very well. There were also export subsidy programs. Since worldwide prices for farm products were generally lower than United States prices, the government paid exporters the difference between U.S. and world prices.

ECONOMIC ANALYSIS OF FARM PROGRAMS

Some of our economic tools can be used to evaluate the programs we have discussed. The simple tools of supply and demand show what we should expect from farm programs. We will look at three kinds of programs: price supports, set asides, and programs to push up demand.

Analysis of Price Support Programs

As you have seen, the government has run programs to keep farm prices up for some time. Figure 14–4 shows the effects of these price supports. Any kind of price support program sets a price higher than the market price. You see in Figure 14–4 that supply and demand are equal at Point E, which is at the level of the market price. At the support price, the amount demanded is found

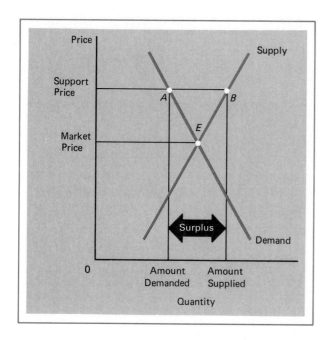

Illustration 14–5
One way the government can increase demand for farm products is to sponsor school lunch programs.

FIGURE 14–4   THE EFFECT OF A PRICE SUPPORT PROGRAM
A support price is above the market price. At the support price, supply is greater than demand, so a surplus exists. The government must buy and store this surplus in order to keep price at the higher level.

where the demand curve meets Point *A*. This is less than the amount farmers would supply at that price, which is Point *B*. Since people buy less than is made available, there is a surplus, which is shown by the arrow.

The government has to buy this surplus in order to keep the price from falling below the support price. The government has to pay for the crops and then pay to store the amount that it buys. This can be very expensive. From Figure 14–4, you can also see that consumers pay a higher price for a good under a price support program. And we get less of it than we would under a free market system.

Analysis of Set Aside Programs

You have seen that the government has tried to lower supply by limiting amounts of land farmers could use. Government has even paid farmers not to grow crops on some of their land. The effect of such set aside programs can be seen in Figure 14–5.

You see again that market supply and demand would cross at Point *E*. The price would be at the level labeled *Market Price*. At this price the amount of the good produced and consumed would be directly below Point *E*. This amount is labeled *Market Quantity*. But by cutting back on supply with a set aside program, the government can force price up. The actual supply is now lower, as shown by the line marked *Supply Less Set Asides*. This forces price

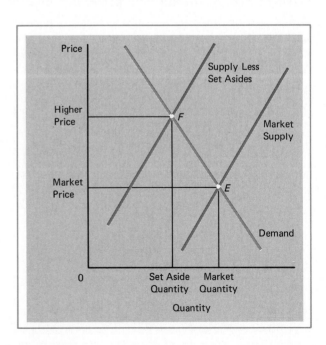

FIGURE 14–5   THE EFFECT OF A SET ASIDE PROGRAM

A set aside program lowers supply, makes price higher, and results in a lower amount of the crop being bought and sold.

up to the Higher Price and reduces the amount produced and bought to the Set Aside Quantity. Consumers again pay more, but get less.

Remember that the demand for farm goods is inelastic. This means that consumers do not cut back much on the amount they buy as price goes up. This also means that more dollars will go to farmers at the higher prices shown in both Figures 14–4 and 14–5.

There would always be some farmers who would try to cheat on the set aside program. If all other farmers reduce output, price will rise. So, for any farmers who use all their land, the possible gain is even greater. To prevent this, government often ties loan programs and other benefits to cooperation with the set aside program. This means that farmers who do not set aside the right amount of land cannot get price supports such as CCC loans.

Analysis of Programs to Increase Demand

If the government can cause demand to rise, farmers' incomes will likely rise. The school lunch program, food stamp programs, and finding more uses for farm products can increase demand. Demand can also be increased by encouraging more exports to other countries. The results of such actions can be seen in Figure 14–6.

Figure 14–6 shows that if demand goes up, the price of farm products will rise. Not only does price rise, but the amount sold

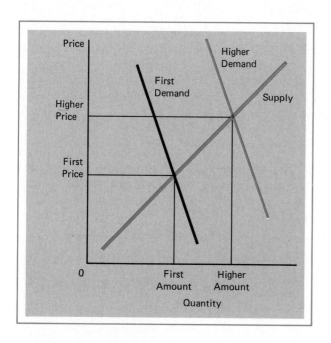

FIGURE 14–6   THE EFFECT OF A HIGHER DEMAND FOR FARM GOODS
Programs that increase the demand for farm products will result in a higher price, more production, and more sales of the good.

CESAR CHAVEZ

Cesar Chavez, president of the United Farm Workers of America (UFW), founded and leads the first successful farm workers' union in U.S. history. Through the UFW, tens of thousands of California farm workers have won better lives.

Chavez was born in 1927 near Yuma, Arizona, on his grandfather's small farm. At age 10, life began as a migrant farm worker when his father lost his land during the Depression. Together with thousands of other displaced families, the Chavezes migrated to farms throughout the Southwest.

After serving the U.S. Navy, Chavez married his wife, Helen, in 1948. The Chavez family settled in the San Jose, California, barrio of "Sal Si Puedes" (which means "get out if you can").

While working in orchards outside San Jose, Chavez became involved in the Community Service Organization (CSO), a self-help group for California Mexican-Americans. He soon became a full-time organizer with CSO, coordinating voter registration, battling racial discrimination, and forming new CSO chapters.

Chavez served as CSO national director in the late '50s and early '60s. But his dream was to create an organization to help the farm workers whose suffering he had shared. In 1962 he quit his paid CSO job, moved his wife and eight small children to Delano, California, and founded the National Farm Workers Association (NFWA).

In 1956, with 1,200 member families, Chavez's NFWA joined the AFL-CIO's Agricultural Workers Organizing Committee (AWOC) in a strike against Delano-area grape growers. Against great odds, Chavez led a successful five-year strike/boycott. The NFWA and AWOC merged in 1966 to form the UFW and the union affiliated with the AFL-CIO.

By 1970, the boycott convinced most table grape growers to sign contracts with the UFW. But to limit the UFW's success to the vineyards, growers in the vegetable industry signed "sweetheart" pacts with the Teamsters Union. To protest the grower-Teamster agreements, ten thousand farm workers in California's coastal valleys walked out of the fields. In 1973, when the farm workers' table grape contracts came up for renewal, most growers signed with the Teamsters, sparking the largest and most successful boycott of grapes, head lettuce, and wines.

About 20 percent of California farm workers currently earn decent pay, have medical benefits and pension plans, and are protected from dangerous pesticides. But for the rest, poverty and abuse are still daily facts of life. As president of the UFWA, Chavez is still very active in the struggle against the poverty and abuse of migrant farm workers.

"Farm workers will never again be treated like agricultural implements to be used and discarded," Chavez says. "We have tasted freedom and dignity, and we will fight to the end before we give it up. We have come too far and we have too much further to go to give up now!"

also rises. This means that farmers benefit on two counts. They sell more and sell at a higher price. Programs to get a higher demand for farm products are probably the best way to increase farm incomes. There is less interference with the market system and less cost to government and taxpayers.

HOW WELL DO FARM PROGRAMS WORK?

14-7   Sometimes these federal programs have led to confusion and inefficient results. First, the government supports agricultural prices and research on the production of agricultural products. This helps to create a surplus. To get rid of the surplus, the government may subsidize exporters so that the U.S. price is in line with world prices. The government may spend tax dollars to pay farmers higher-than-market prices and to store goods the government buys. With one hand, government programs help to develop a surplus. With the other hand, government has to buy that surplus production in one way or another.

Have federal farm policies solved the farm income problem? Since many farm incomes have remained at low levels, it is difficult to say that the farm income problem has been solved. This is understandable, since the income from price supports and other programs ties directly to production. These subsidies go mainly to large farms, as you see in Table 14–5.

TABLE 14–5

AVERAGE GOVERNMENT PAYMENT PER FARM
(Size of Farm Measured by Acres)

Size	Average Payment Per Farm
Under 50 acres	$ 1,788
50 to 179 acres	$ 3,351
180 to 499 acres	$ 8,852
500 to 999 acres	$19,459
1,000 acres or more	$36,028

Source: U.S. Bureau of the Census, *Statistical Abstract of the United States: 1991* (Washington, D.C., 1991), 654.

REVIEWING
THE
CHAPTER

1. The agricultural part of the economy is important to us. There are about 2 million farms in the United States. We all need farm goods for food and clothing.

14–3   2. Farm incomes rise and fall more often than the incomes people earn in other parts of the economy. This is partly because the demand for farm products is inelastic with respect to price.

14–2   3. A year that may be called a good year because weather conditions result in large crops may really be a bad year for farm income. The higher supply of farm goods may cause prices to fall so much that farmers end up with lower incomes.

14–3   4. Anything that causes the demand for farm products to change can also affect farm prices and farm income. As long as supply does not change, a rise in demand will cause price to go up as well. This, in turn, makes farm incomes rise.

14–4   5. In comparison, farm incomes have stayed historically below the incomes of the nonfarm population.

14–5   6. Over the years, the supply of farm products has increased much more than demand. Much of the rise in supply has resulted from higher productivity of farm workers. In almost all kinds of farm production the amount of labor used for each unit of output has dropped a great deal just since 1950.

14–7   7. The government has used many different programs to help keep farm incomes from falling. Price support programs have been used to keep prices above the level that would be found in a free market economy. The government has also cut supply to keep prices up and has taken steps to increase the demand for farm products.

REVIEWING
ECONOMIC
TERMS

14–1   Supply definitions for the following terms:

price support program
parity price
cooperative

Commodity Credit Corporation
  (CCC)
set aside program

REVIEWING ECONOMIC CONCEPTS

14–2   1. Name two natural causes that can make farm incomes rise and fall more than nonfarm incomes.

14–3   2. What does it mean to say that the demand for farm products is price inelastic?

14–3   3. How does an increase in demand for farm goods affect prices and farm incomes?

14–4   4. What is the relationship between farm incomes and nonfarm incomes?

14–3   5. What does it mean to say that the demand for farm products is income inelastic?

14–5   6. What is the trend in agricultural productivity? What is the major reason for this trend?

14–3   7. Identify two trends in supply and demand that have led to a drop in farm prices and farm incomes.

14–6   8. Name the three main government agricultural programs.

14–7   9. Explain the effects of price support programs on market supply, on taxpayers, and on consumers.

14–7   10. Explain the effects of set aside programs on market supply, on taxpayers, and on consumers.

14–6   11. In what four ways can government increase demand for farm goods?

APPLYING ECONOMIC CONCEPTS

14–3   1. How does the price inelasticity of farm products contribute to the ups and downs of farm income? What other factors cause farm incomes to change so often?

14–4   2. What is meant by the farm income problem? How is the information in Table 14–2 related to this question? Direct government payments are meant to help solve this problem. Explain whether or not these payments helped the low farm income problem.

14–2   3. *U.S. News & World Report* ran a story entitled "For Farmers, Big Crops Bring Big Troubles." What did this headline mean? Why aren't big crops good for farmers?

14-4   4. Why has the gap between the average income of people on farms and the nonfarm population narrowed over the years?

14-3, 14-5   5. Use a graph of supply and demand to show why there has been downward pressure on farm prices over the years. What has caused supply to rise? What has caused demand to rise?

14-7   6. What is a price support program? Use a graph of supply and demand to show the effects of such a program. Explain why these programs increase farm incomes and why they are costly for consumers and taxpayers.

14-7   7. Explain set aside programs. What kinds of set aside programs have we used in the United States?

14-7   8. What happens to the surplus products the government buys in order to keep farm prices up? How would a program to give surplus cheese to poor families across the country affect the normal market for cheese?

14-3   9. What does it mean to say that the demand for farm products is both price and income inelastic?

14-7   10. Assume that you raise soybeans and expect a crop this year of 4,000 bushels of soybeans. You take out a CCC loan for $20,080, using your crop as security. At harvest time, if the market price of soybeans is $5.25 per bushel, would you sell the soybeans and pay off the loan? Or would you default on the loan and let the CCC claim your 4,000 bushels of soybeans? What will you do if the market price is $4.90 per bushel? (You can assume that the expected crop of 4,000 bushels is actually obtained and the loan rate for soybeans is at $5.02 per bushel.)

U.S. AGRICULTURE IN THE 1990s

Several major issues will be important to the agricultural sector of the economy in the 1990s. First, the market for agricultural products increasingly will be worldwide. Since the agricultural recovery that began about 1987, the United States is in a strong position to compete in world markets.

Second, environmental concerns will affect the agricultural sector more than ever before. The use of fertilizers, herbicides, and pesticides has led to groundwater contamination in almost half of all U.S. counties and increasing concerns about food safety.

Third, we can expect to see more advanced technologies in agricultural production. It is likely that biotechnology will have impacts on animal and crop production. Genetic changes might make plants and animals more resistant to disease and pests.

PART III

MACROECONOMICS

CHAPTER 15

MEASURING ECONOMIC ACTIVITY

Learning Objectives

15–1   Define terms related to macroeconomics and GNP.

15–2   List seven problems when using GNP as a measure of economic well-being.

15–3   Analyze production possibilities curves.

15–4   Describe the makeup of GNP.

15–5   Discuss the uses of income.

15–6   Explain a circular flow diagram of the economy.

15–7   Analyze macroeconomic equilibrium.

WHAT IS MACROECONOMICS?

In this chapter you begin your study of the branch of economics called *macroeconomics*. The term *macro* means large or big. Thus, macroeconomics means the big view of economic activity. Recall that macroeconomics is defined as that part of economics that examines the behavior of the whole economy at once. You will now look at the total level of economic activity as well as ways of measuring and evaluating that activity.

In Part II (microeconomics) you looked at consumers' demands for certain kinds of goods. You learned how much of those goods firms would supply, and how individual firms were organized. You studied how a person's wage was determined and how much labor would be hired. In all of these you were looking at individual people and firms, both small economic units.

Part III focuses on the big picture. Macroeconomics includes the following topics: (1) total level of employment, (2) general level of prices, (3) level of national income, and (4) total amount of consumption and production. Explaining ups and downs (often called *business cycles*) in levels of employment, prices, income, consumption, and production is a major concern of economists.

Think of the national economy as a circular flow, as shown in Figure 15–1. The box on the right represents households like yours. The box on the left represents the business sector of the economy. Households spend money to buy goods and services from businesses. For example, you buy records and tapes, ice cream, cars, radios, jeans, haircuts, and many other products. In each case, an exchange of money for the good or service takes place.

15–6

Look at the two flows in the upper loop of the circular flow diagram. Goods and services flow from businesses to households. In exchange, money flows in the form of consumer spending that goes from households to businesses. This upper loop shows the total dollar value of all the goods and services produced and sold.

What would happen if these two were the only flows in the economy? Soon households would run out of money! Businesses would have all the money, and we would have many goods and services. But as soon as we spent all the money we had, there could be no more flow in either direction. The economy would quickly grind to a stop. And everyone would soon be unemployed. There would be no production and, of course, no consumption. But this is not what really happens. Year after year these two flows continue, and they usually get bigger each year.

The reason the flows do not stop is shown by the lower loop. You can see in Figure 15–1 that the lower loop also has two flows.

FIGURE 15–1 A CIRCULAR FLOW DIAGRAM OF THE ECONOMY
Money flows from households to businesses in exchange for goods and services.
Money flows from businesses to households in exchange for labor and other productive inputs.

One is a money flow from businesses to households. Every company has an outflow of money to individuals who provide companies with productive resources. The most obvious resource is the labor individuals provide. When people work for a business, they expect to be paid. That pay is almost always in the form of money income.

The bottom loop of the circular flow represents all the money income that is earned in the economy. It is the income earned by the people who produce the goods and services in the upper loop. This circular flow view of the national economy is a simple yet fairly accurate model of how the entire economy works. This simple model shows the kinds of exchanges that keep the economy going.

As we progress through this chapter, we will add to this simple model of the economy. You will see that consumers do not spend all their income. They save some of it, and you will see what happens to those savings. You will discover that businesses not only produce goods but also buy goods. You will also see that there is a very active government sector in our economy. Taxes and government spending are important parts of our economy. Near the end of this chapter, you will see a more complete circular flow model of the economy that includes these ideas.

HOW BIG IS THE TOTAL ECONOMY?

People all over the country worry about the well-being of the economy. Some say that political leaders should make solving economic problems their top priority. But economists, business leaders, and politicians cannot analyze or evaluate the health of the economy without measuring that health. Gross National Product, or GNP, is the measure most often used for this purpose.

Gross National Product Defined

Gross national product (GNP) is the total dollar value of all final goods and services produced in the economy during one year's time. We use the dollar value as a measure because lists of goods and services become meaningless. Long lists of the numbers of clocks, bookshelves, lamps, radios, bicycles, and food products produced would be hard to comprehend or add together. After all, one lamp plus four oranges plus one roast is not meaningful to any of us. However, the amount of money paid for each of these items can be added. And a product's dollar value shows, at least to some degree, the amount of economic well-being we get from such a good.

Only final goods, such as cars, are counted when we measure GNP. If intermediate goods were counted as well, such as the steel in a car, the value of the intermediate goods would be counted twice. It would be included when the maker of the car bought the steel and included again in the price of the car. To count the steel twice would overstate the value of our total national output.

15–4

15–1

gross national product (GNP)
The total dollar value of all final goods and services produced in the economy during one year's time.

Why Should We Know About GNP?

In order to keep track of economic changes and policies, economists and political leaders often use GNP as their measure. Not only is GNP important to domestic economic policy, but it is also important in international affairs. For example, GNP provides a measurement when looking at the economic status of foreign countries to determine foreign aid budgets.

When you read a daily paper or weekly news magazine, you often see GNP used in articles about the economy. On the evening news, you hear about recent changes in the level of GNP. In every national election, the level of GNP is discussed again and again. To be an informed member of society, you need to be able to understand the concept of GNP.

GNP AS A MEASURE OF WELL-BEING

The more goods and services we produce, the healthier our economy gets. A society producing many goods, such as food, televisions, cars, and houses, has a higher GNP than a country producing very few goods. The country with the higher GNP usually is thought to have the higher standard of living.

The size of GNP for any country depends on many factors. The amount of natural resources available greatly contributes to the GNP level. A country is limited in the amount of goods it can produce due to its limited natural resources. Water, fertile soil, ore, wood, and oil are examples of natural resources. People are also an important natural resource. Usually the more natural resources a country has, the more goods it can produce—and the higher its GNP can be.

For example, the United States has fairly large amounts of natural resources. Iron ore, coal, water, good farm land, and a productive labor force are just a few examples. We have used these resources to become one of the most productive countries in the world, as measured by GNP. Many other countries, such as Pakistan, have fewer natural resources and produce much smaller levels of output.

Even countries with the same number of people and the same amount of natural resources can have very different levels of GNP. One reason is that the countries may have different amounts and qualities of machines and equipment available. The country with more and better machines and equipment will be able to produce a higher GNP. Also, the skill of labor forces in various countries may differ. The country with a better skilled and educated labor force will be able to produce more. Over the years, the United States has had very good equipment and a well-educated, highly skilled labor force. This, along with large supplies of natural resources, has made the United States a world leader in terms of GNP produced.

Illustration 15–1
One factor that determines the level of GNP is the amount of natural resources a country has. In the United States, we have many natural resources, such as forests full of timber and a highly skilled labor force, to produce lumber.

PROBLEMS IN USING GNP

While GNP is often cited, there are some problems with its use as a measure of well-being. In using it, or in evaluating other people's use of it, you should know about these problems. Then you can make better economic judgments than you could have made otherwise.

GNP Doesn't Consider Kinds of Items Produced

The composition of GNP makes a big difference to a country's well-being. Consider two countries that are the same size. We'll call them *A* and *B*. In our example, Country *A* and Country *B* have the same number of people who like the same kinds of goods. However, the two countries differ in the size of their GNP. Country *A* has a GNP of $250 billion, and Country *B* has a GNP of $150 billion. At first glance, Country *A* appears to be economically better off.

15–2

However, suppose that in Country *A* all of the GNP is made up of military goods. Tanks, planes, bombs, etc., are all that Country *A* makes. Also, suppose that Country *A* cannot trade these products for the food and clothing needed to support the people.

On the other hand, Country *B*'s GNP includes tractors, corn, clothes, houses, milk, etc. Country *B*'s mix of goods and services produced balances the economic well-being of its society. The mix of products that makes up the GNP may be more important to individual well-being than the dollar volume of output.

In our society, consider the government's decision to produce a number of new military fighter planes. The dollar cost of the planes will count in GNP, even if it does not show the true value we place on having such planes. In fact, if we do not want the planes, then we are economically worse off when they are produced. However, GNP increases when the planes are made; and this indicates that we are economically better off. Therefore, one of the major weaknesses of GNP is that it does not take into account the *kinds* of goods produced.

This matters more when economic decisions are made in the public sector. When the market system allocates resources, our purchases determine which products survive the test of the market. When governments decide what to produce, we have some influence through voting. But it is not always clear that politicians act in the best interest of the entire country.

GNP Doesn't Measure Amount Produced Per Person

15–2   Another problem in using just the dollar value of GNP as a measure of well-being is that it doesn't tell us how much is available per person. To show this, think of two countries that have the same GNP, say $150 billion. Country *A* has a population of 10 million people, and Country *B* has a population of 20 million people. This means that the people in Country *A* will have twice as many goods per person. In Country *A*, the $150 billion of GNP must be divided among only half as many people as in Country *B*. In Country *A* there would be $15,000 worth of GNP per person. But in Country *B* there would be just $7,500 worth of GNP per person. The people in Country *A* would be better off than the people in Country *B*, even though the total value of GNP is the same for both countries.

To show the importance of comparing GNP on a per-person basis, let's look at two countries, India and Austria. In one recent year, the GNP of India was about $246 billion. Austria's GNP was just under $117 billion. So, India's GNP was about two times (actually 211 percent) as large as Austria's. However, India has a much larger population than Austria. It is so much larger that GNP per person in Austria was over 50 times as much as in India. GNP per person in Austria was $15,440, but in India, it was only $307. In the same year, GNP per person in the United States was $18,543.[1]

Illustration 15–2   Using GNP as a measure of a country's well-being can be misleading. The GNP of India was more than double the GNP of Austria in a recent year. But because India's population is so much larger than Austria's, GNP *per person* in Austria was over 50 times as much as in India!

---

[1]U.S. Bureau of the Census, *Statistical Abstract of the United States: 1990*, 110th ed. (Washington, D.C., 1990), 428, 840.

GNP Doesn't Measure How Goods Are Distributed

An additional problem in using GNP as a measure of well-being   15–2
involves the distribution of goods among different people in a
country. Suppose that most of a country's GNP is consumed by a
small fraction of the people. In this case, there would be a few very
rich people and many poor people. On the other hand, suppose
that the GNP of a country is more evenly distributed. Then a
smaller number of people will be poor. But there will also be fewer
very rich people.

A more equal distribution of income means there will be a large
middle class, and few people will be very rich or very poor. Severe
economic problems could result if the distribution of GNP was
exactly equal among all people in a country.

GNP Doesn't Allow for Changing Price Levels

We often want to compare GNP figures from year to year. And   15–2
many people think that we are economically better off if GNP goes
up from one year to another. But we need to be very careful about
making this kind of comparison. GNP figures usually express the
current dollar values of the goods and services produced. If prices
change, then this unit of measure (current dollar values) can
change, even if the actual number produced does not change.

Since about 1940 the average level of prices has gone up
steadily. An increase in the average level of prices is known as   15–1
inflation. **Inflation** is the economic condition in which the average   **inflation**
level of prices goes up. If the average level of prices goes up,   The economic condition
the reported value of GNP would go up even if there were no   in which the average
added production.   level of prices goes up.

Suppose, for example, that in 1991 a pair of jeans cost $22. The
same jeans in 1992 cost $26. When the jeans were counted in GNP
in 1992, each pair would add $4 more to GNP than in 1991. So,
even if the same number of jeans were sold, GNP would go up in
1992. The actual amount of goods available in the economy would
not go up. But the dollar measure would increase. The GNP would
not show a growth in goods available but a rise in prices. When we
use GNP to judge growth, we must be sure to understand that part
of the growth may be due to inflation.

Economists use price indexes to adjust GNP figures so that the
figures only show changes in actual output. Suppose that GNP in
one year was $1,000 billion in current dollars. Then suppose that
the next year's GNP was reported to be $1,188 billion in current
dollars. Did the rise in GNP really increase the well-being of society

by $188 billion? No, not if some of the increase was due to inflation. If the rate of inflation was 8 percent (.08), then we could convert the second year's GNP to constant dollar terms (comparable to the first year) by dividing by 1.08. (The 1.08 is a price index using the first year as a benchmark.) This means that prices in the second year were 1.08 times the prices in the first year. Or prices in the second year were 1.08 percent of the first year prices due to the 8 percent rate of inflation.

15–1

constant dollar GNP

The value of gross national product after taking out the effect of price changes.

Dividing the second year's GNP by this 1.08 price index gives us the constant dollar GNP for the second year. **Constant dollar GNP** is the value of gross national product after taking out the effect of price changes.

> Constant Dollar GNP = Current Dollar GNP ÷ Price Index

$$= \$1,188 \text{ billion} \div 1.08$$

$$= \$1,100 \text{ billion}$$

So, using a comparable price measure, GNP in the second year was only $1,100 billion. The goods and services available increased by $100 billion rather than by $188 billion. When we convert any dollar measure to constant dollar terms, we take out the effect of price changes. Only actual, or real, changes remain. For this reason we often use the term *real GNP* or *GNP in real terms.*

When GNP is adjusted in this way, any changes that remain represent actual changes in the volume of goods and services produced. Unadjusted or *current dollar GNP* is not nearly as meaningful. Unfortunately, however, current dollar GNP is often reported in the media.

The graph in Figure 15–2 on page 301 shows what happened to GNP from 1955 to 1990 in the United States. The yellow line shows GNP in current dollars (the actual dollars in a particular year). The orange line shows GNP in constant dollars, or in real terms. GNP, measured either way, has increased steadily during this period. Notice that the two lines in Figure 15–2 cross in 1982. This is because 1982 is the base year for the price index used to adjust current dollar GNP to real GNP.

Other Problems with GNP

15–2

There are several other weaknesses in GNP as a measure of economic well-being. For example, people who maintain homes for

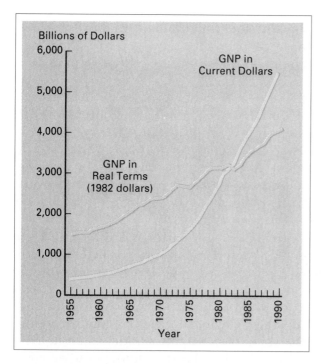

FIGURE 15–2 GROSS NATIONAL PRODUCT IN CURRENT DOLLARS AND IN REAL TERMS FROM 1955 TO 1990
Due to inflation, current dollar GNP goes up more rapidly than real GNP.

their families produce many goods and services. They prepare meals, drive children to school and to other activities, clean house, paint, cut the lawn, wash clothes, and provide many other valuable services. Yet the value of this work is not counted in GNP. As long as such jobs as housecleaning, lawn care, and painting are done by household members, these jobs don't add to GNP. But if Service-Master is hired to clean the house, Lawn-Green to care for the

Illustration 15–3
GNP does not measure the value of jobs performed within the home.

lawn, and Wilcott Co. to paint, then the value of the work is added to GNP. Either way, the total production in society is the same. However, in order for these jobs to count in GNP, there must be a market exchange.

There is growing interest in a similar problem with reported GNP figures. To avoid taxes, some people are finding ways to exchange goods without going through the normal market. For example, a dentist might provide dental services for a car mechanic in exchange for car repairs. An accountant might do the accounting free of charge for a law firm in exchange for legal services. In such cases, no one declares any income from the services, and so the income tax owed for the year is reduced.

15–1

barter
A direct trade of goods or services.

15–1

irregular economy
The economy consisting of economic activity that purposely avoids the market system in order to avoid reporting income for tax purposes.

Such activities are called barters. A **barter** is a direct trade of goods or services. Barters are part of what is often called the *underground economy* or the *irregular economy*. The **irregular economy** is the economy consisting of economic activity that purposely avoids the market system in order to avoid reporting income for tax purposes. Since barters and other activities in the irregular economy do not show in GNP, the value of GNP must understate our true economic well-being. Of course, it is hard to know how much is involved in the irregular economy. But estimates run in the hundreds of billions of dollars each year.

15–2 The quality of items produced is also not measured in GNP. An electronic calculator that cost $400 in 1975 can be bought today for less than $40. Due to product improvements, the $40 calculator today is better than the $400 1975 model. But using GNP measures, it adds less to our economic well-being. The price of color televisions today does not greatly differ from the price 20 years ago. The quality today is far better, however. But again, there is no way for such increases in quality to show up in GNP.

15–2 Another problem with GNP as a measure of well-being is that leisure time has no value in GNP. The GNP of a country could be increased if every member of the society worked longer hours. For example, in the United States, we could return to 60- and 80-hour workweeks. (The current, average workweek is about 35 hours.) If we did increase the number of hours we all worked, GNP would increase. But our well-being probably would not go up. Leisure time is highly valued, and we would suffer if it were cut. Yet the value of leisure time is not included in GNP.

PRODUCT TRADE-OFFS WITHIN GNP

Many types of goods and services make up our gross national product. You have already seen that the makeup of GNP can determine how much benefit we get from it. Society has many choices about how to allocate resources. We can make many different goods and services. Or we can concentrate production on just a few kinds of goods.

There are always trade-offs to be made. In the United States we use many resources to produce cars and items used by car owners. These include highways, parking lots, garages, gasoline, and other products or services that are used along with a car. The trade-off is, at least in part, that we have spent less on other forms of passenger transportation. It has been said that if railroads had as much government support for railroad tracks as the car industry has for road construction, railroads would be more useful today. You have seen several times now that resources used in one type of production have an opportunity cost in terms of other products that could have been made.

Resources that are used by governments are not available for production in the private sector. Resources used to make goods for consumers cannot be used to make machines for business use. Such trade-offs can be represented using the concept of a production possibilities curve.

A **production possibilities curve** is a graphic illustration of the combinations of output an economy can produce if all of its resources are utilized and utilized efficiently, given the state of technology. Resources include natural resources, labor, and capital. In Figure 15–3, the gray curve represents the production possibilities curve. We have assumed that all of the production in an economy functions as either a private good or a public good. All of the country's resources could be used to produce either private goods only or public goods only. These two extremes are represented by Points A and B.

15–1

production possibilities curve

A graphic illustration of the combinations of output an economy can produce if all of its resources are utilized and utilized efficiently, given the state of technology.

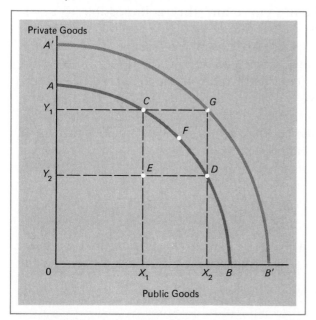

FIGURE 15–3   TWO PRODUCTION POSSIBILITIES CURVES

The curve AB shows possible amounts of private and public goods a society can produce at a given time. With some economic growth, the production possibilities curve would shift to curve A'B'.

15-3   No economy would produce only one type of good and nothing else. Some combination will be produced. For example, Y_1 amount of private goods and X_1 amount of public goods are represented by Point C on the production possibilities curve. Point D also represents full use of the country's resources but with greater production of public goods (X_2) and less production of private goods (Y_2). This is an important point. If an economy is using all of its resources efficiently, to increase production of one good the production of another good must be decreased. The cost of adding more production of public goods (from X_1 to X_2) means a decrease in the production of private goods (from Y_1 to Y_2). This is an example of an opportunity cost.

Suppose that the economy shown in Figure 15–3 produced Y_2 amount of private goods and X_1 amount of public goods. This combination of production would be represented by Point E in the figure. Point E could represent two cases: (1) The economy might not be using all of its resources. There are *unemployed* resources. Or (2), the economy is using its resources inefficiently. Economists refer to this as *underemployment of resources*. If the economy is at Point E, a gap exists between what is being produced and what could be produced. With the same resources and technology, such an economy could produce more private goods by moving to Point C or more public goods by moving to Point D. It could also produce more of both goods by moving from E to any point on the production possibilities curve between C and D. An example would be movement to Point F.

Suppose that the people of the economy wanted to have Y_1 of private goods and X_2 of public goods produced. That combination of output would be represented at Point G. But Point G lies outside the production possibilities curve and thus is impossible to reach, given the resources and technology available. Points beyond the production possibilities curve are called *unattainable levels of production*. However, with new resources or advanced technology, the production possibilities curve will shift outward. Such a case is represented by the purple curve in Figure 15–3. With this new production possibilities curve, Y_1 amount of private goods and X_2 amount of public goods can be produced. So, Point G becomes an attainable level of production.

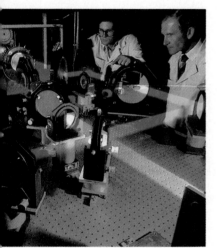

Illustration 15–4
The introduction of new resources and advanced technology shifts the production possibilities curve outward. This allows more public and private goods to be produced.

MAKEUP OF GNP

15-4   The trade-offs we have to deal with as a society involve more than just public versus private goods. The total production in the economy can be divided into several classes of goods. The most important are consumer goods, investment goods, and the government sector. Each of these can be further divided into more specific kinds of goods. The following list shows some important categories:

I. Consumer Goods
   A. Durable Goods
   B. Nondurable Goods
   C. Services
II. Investment Goods
   A. New Plants and Equipment
   B. Private Housing
   C. Inventories
III. The Government Sector
   A. Federal Government
   B. State Government
   C. Local Government

All production in the economy can be put into one of these categories. We will briefly look at each of these in the following sections.

Consumer Goods

Consumer goods are items that are made for final consumption. Most of the goods and services you use are consumer goods. To list all of them would be an almost endless job. A few examples are given below:

15–4
15–1
consumer goods
Items that are made for final consumption.

Sweaters	Oranges
Bicycles	Footballs
Calculators	Cars
Radios	Eyeglasses
Steaks	Pencils
Haircuts	Magazines
Chairs	Dishes

You can see that there is a good deal of variety just in this list. Look around, and you will likely see many other things to add to the list. About 65 percent of our gross national product is allocated to consumer goods.

15–1
durable goods

Goods that can be used over and over again and that last for a relatively long time.

15–1
nondurable goods

Goods that do not last a long time.

Some consumer goods last for a fairly long time. These are called durable goods. **Durable goods** can be used over and over again and last for a relatively long time. We benefit from them for a number of years. Bicycles, cars, washing machines, refrigerators, and furniture are some examples of consumer durable goods. Because these products last for some time, consumers often delay buying them during periods of economic hard times. This means that industries such as the car industry are more sensitive to national economic problems than many other industries.

Other products are entirely consumed almost as soon as they are purchased. These are called nondurable goods. **Nondurable goods** are goods that do not last a long time. Food products clearly are nondurable goods. We usually eat food items within a few days or weeks after we buy them. The clothes we buy wear out more quickly than a freezer would. A magazine becomes old within a few days or weeks, but a bicycle does not.

Still other forms of production result in services that have value to us. We get some satisfaction from consuming services just as we do from physical products. A haircut is a service for which many of us pay. Other services include those of a doctor, a dentist, a travel agent, and a lawyer. The service sector of the economy is a growing part of GNP. In 1980 the services part of personal consumption spending was about 30 percent of GNP. As shown in Figure 15–4, the percentage of total consumer spending on services increased from about 33 percent in 1950 to about 54 percent in 1990.

Illustration 15–5
Nondurable goods, like shoes and clothing, generally do not last very long because of wear and tear and changes in fashion.

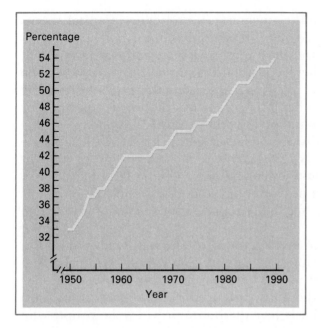

FIGURE 15–4   PERCENTAGE OF CON-SUMER SPENDING FOR SERVICES
Since 1950 there has been growth in the service part of the economy. We not only spend more money on services, but we also spend a greater percentage of our money for services.

Investment Goods

Investment goods make up the second category of GNP. But before we learn about the different kinds of investment goods, we need to know the difference between two uses of the word *investment*: there is physical investment and financial investment. If you buy stock in a company such as IBM, you have invested in IBM. This is a form of financial investment. Normally when people discuss their investments, they are referring to financial investments.

When economists use the term *investment*, they are referring to physical investment. If the investment part of GNP goes up, physical investment has increased. Physical investment refers to an increase in the amount of productive capital in the economy. Therefore, in economic terms, **investment** is an increase in the amount of productive capital in an economy. It is an increase in the number of factories, office buildings, stores, and machines or equipment used in producing goods and services.

We also need to know the difference between the two uses of the word *capital*. There is financial capital and physical capital. To someone in business, the word capital means money to pay bills and make purchases. The owner of a small business often worries about having enough working capital. This means the owner worries about having enough money to pay employees, to pay bank loans, and to buy supplies. In the late 1970s, Lee Iacocca, president of Chrysler Corporation, was worried about getting enough financial capital (money) to keep the company running.

15–4

15–1

investment
An increase in the amount of productive capital in an economy.

15–1

capital
Goods that are produced and can be used as inputs for further production.

But capital has another meaning in economics. **Capital** means goods that are produced and can be used as inputs for further production. It refers to the machines, factories, and computers that help in producing other goods. This is physical capital. When the amount of physical capital has increased, there has been some physical investment. When economists use the words *investment* or *capital*, they mean physical investment or physical capital.

Just as we could divide consumer goods into several parts, we could study three kinds of investment. New plants and equipment use the majority of investment money. When a firm buys a new computer or puts in a new assembly line, this is one type of investment. Building a new steel mill or a new office building is the same type of investment.

The second type of investment is in housing. A new house is a type of physical investment. (Buying a new house is a financial investment, too.) Why is the building of a new house a physical investment? Because the house will produce housing benefits for a long period of time. Each year the house provides the people who live in it a new amount of housing satisfaction. A house continues to be productive in this sense until no one uses it any more.

Finally, an increase in business inventory is considered an investment. A company's inventory is the amount of goods it has on hand. Suppose a business makes 100,000 washing machines during the year, but only sells 90,000. The 90,000 that are sold show up in GNP as consumer durable goods. The 10,000 that are not sold do not count as consumption. But they were made. They should be part of that year's GNP. To solve this problem, the 10,000 machines that are not sold to consumers are thought of as being sold to the company itself. Therefore, when a company adds to its inventory, that inventory is counted in GNP as its own investment. This way, all production gets counted.

The Government Sector

15–4

The third major part of our GNP measures the government sector of the economy. The government sector includes all government purchases of goods and services. Federal, state, and local governments belong to this sector. The total of government purchases has increased almost every year since the late 1940s. In 1990, total government purchases were about $1,100 billion. This was about 20 percent of that year's GNP.

The percentage of GNP accounted for by the government sector has fluctuated over the years. During World War II the percentage was more than 46 percent. By 1950 it had dropped to 13.5 percent.

After 1950 the percentage of GNP in the government sector increased steadily and reached more than 22 percent during the Vietnam War period.

State and local government spending has also increased. In 1950 state and local governments represented about 51 percent of total government purchases. By 1970 this figure was 54.7 percent, and by 1990 it was about 62 percent.

Makeup of GNP: A Quick Review

Three major sectors make up our gross national product: personal consumption, investment, and government purchases. The process of producing goods for each sector results in people earning some income. If you worked in a factory making radios, you would earn money from making a consumer good. If you worked on the construction of a new steel mill, your income would come from making an investment good. And if you were a public school teacher, your income would come from the government sector.

GNP

=

Personal Consumption

+

Investments

+

Government Purchases

USES OF INCOME

By working and being productive we earn an income. In this section, we will answer the question: Where does that income go? That is, we will see how we (as a nation) use our income. In the next chapter we will look at how the total income in our economy is distributed among different individuals.

Consumption

Most of our income is used for consumption. That is, we *spend* most of our money. Think about how your family spends its money. A large part of the total income probably pays for housing. For most families, the rent or mortgage payment is the biggest single part of the family budget. Food also takes a big part of our income. Spending on housing and food along with clothing are often thought of as necessary spending. We also spend money on things that are unnecessary. Examples include candy, movies, tennis, and records. We often spend a good deal of money on these luxuries because we get a lot of satisfaction from them. What do you spend money for? Try making a list of items you and your family have purchased in the last few weeks. It will probably be a long list and include many different kinds of goods and services.

15–5

Taxes

15–5   We cannot spend all our earnings on consumer goods. Part of our income must pay different kinds of taxes. We all pay income taxes to the federal government. Most states and many cities and counties have income taxes, too. State and local governments also use sales taxes to pay for their programs. In addition to paying income and sales taxes, property owners pay property taxes to local governments.

15–1

disposable income
The income that is left after deducting tax payments.

Only disposable income is available to spend on consumer goods. **Disposable income** is the income that is left after deducting tax payments. Taxes will be discussed in more detail in a later chapter.

Savings

15–5   Even after paying taxes, we do not spend all of our income for consumer goods. Part of our income is put aside as savings to be used for consumption at a later time. Some families or individuals do spend all of their income. But for the total of all people in the society, some fraction of income is saved. Figure 15–5 shows the percentage of disposable personal income that has gone into savings since 1950.

These same data are given in Table 15–1. Look at what happened to savings in the late 1970s and into the 1990s. The percentage of disposable personal income that we saved was fairly low. This meant that less money was available for business firms to invest in new capital than if savings had been higher. The low rate

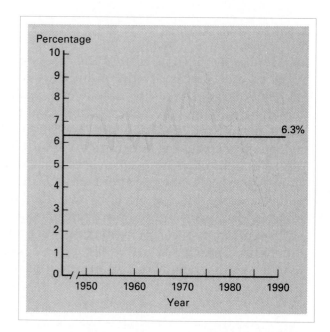

FIGURE 15–5   SAVINGS AS A PERCENTAGE OF DISPOSABLE PERSONAL INCOME, 1950 TO 1985
For the period shown, the average percent saved was 6.3 percent. Notice that recently we have had savings below this long-run average.

Source: Table 15–1, p. 311.

of savings in the United States has been a matter of concern to economists, as well as to business and political leaders.

How do we save our money? Much goes into some kind of savings account. We put our savings in banks, savings and loan associations, and credit unions. We may use passbook accounts or other forms of savings that pay us a higher rate of interest on our money. We also save money when we invest in stocks and bonds. (Remember, these are financial investments.) Various types of life insurance include some savings, too.

In all these forms of savings, the money we save does not sit in a bank vault but returns to the spending flow of the economy. This spending may be some kind of investment, government spending, or spending by other consumers. If you buy a corporate bond with your savings, the money is likely to be used by the company to invest in new capital (physical capital). If you buy government bonds, the money will be spent for government programs. It might help build a school or highway. If you put savings in a savings and

TABLE 15-1

SAVINGS AS A PERCENTAGE OF DISPOSABLE PERSONAL INCOME, 1950 TO 1990

Year	Percentage	Year	Percentage
1950	6.1	1970	8.1
1951	7.3	1971	8.5
1952	7.3	1972	7.3
1953	7.2	1973	9.4
1954	6.3	1974	9.3
1955	5.8	1975	9.2
1956	7.2	1976	7.6
1957	7.2	1977	6.6
1958	7.5	1978	7.1
1959	6.3	1979	6.8
1960	5.8	1980	7.1
1961	6.6	1981	7.5
1962	6.5	1982	6.8
1963	5.9	1983	5.4
1964	7.0	1984	6.3
1965	7.0	1985	4.5
1966	6.8	1986	4.0
1967	8.0	1987	3.2
1968	7.0	1988	4.2
1969	6.4	1989	4.6
		1990	4.7

Sources: *Survey of Current Business* (Washington, D.C.: U.S. Government Printing Office), November issues of successive years, S-2; *Business Statistics 1986* (Washington, D.C.: U.S. Government Printing Office, 1986), S-2; and *Economic Report of the President 1990* (Washington, D.C.: U.S. Government Printing Office, 1990), 324.

Illustration 15–6
Much of the money we save is in the form of savings accounts.

loan association, it will likely be lent to someone to build or buy a house. Money saved in a credit union will probably be loaned to someone else to buy a consumer good. Savings put into a bank may be loaned for almost any of these uses.

Occasionally you hear of someone who has saved hundreds of thousands of dollars in an attic or basement. But only a very small part of our savings is in the form of cash hidden in the home. What little money is saved in such a way leaks out of the spending flows in the economy. If this were a large amount of money, it would be a drain on the economy and would eventually cause GNP to fall. But most of our savings gets right back into the spending flows in the economy.

SOCIETY AND THE CIRCULAR FLOW

15–6   Figure 15–6 shows another circular flow diagram of the economy. This figure is very much like Figure 15–1 on page 294; but it is more detailed. It is more realistic because government is added and both savings and investment are included.

We have just discussed savings, which is a leakage out of the flow of consumer spending. It is a part of income that does not get back immediately into the flow of the economy as we buy goods and services. But money we save does get back into the economy when banks, savings and loans, or other such institutions lend money to others. In Figure 15–6 this process is shown by the flow labeled *Savings* that comes out of the household sector. As this money flows into the business sector, it is used for investment. Investment functions as an injection back into the economy. For the total economy, this investment is only as much as individuals are willing to save.

The government sector is added to the circular flow in the middle of Figure 15–6. What kinds of flows run between governments and households or between governments and businesses? A full description could fill an entire chapter or even a whole book. But the eight most important flows can be summarized as follows:

A. Government and Households

Flow 1. The flow of money from governments to households. Examples include a teacher's paycheck, a senator's paycheck, or a welfare payment.

Flow 2. The flow of labor and other inputs to governments from households. In exchange for the paycheck, a teacher provides

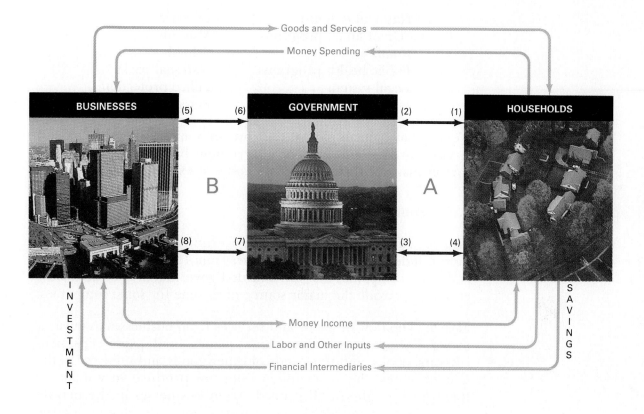

FIGURE 15–6   A MORE COMPLETE CIRCULAR FLOW DIAGRAM OF
THE ECONOMY
In addition to the flows between business and households, the government sector
and savings and investment are shown in this diagram.

labor skills for educational services. A senator works in exchange
for the money payment. In general, Flows *1* and *2* work like the
loop that connects households and businesses in which money is
exchanged for labor and other inputs. The government makes
some payments to people, however, for which there is nothing
given in exchange. Welfare payments are an example.

Flow 3. The flow of money from households to governments. This
flow mainly includes the taxes we pay. We pay income taxes, property taxes, sales taxes, and other taxes which give governments the
money they need to function.

Flow 4. Do we get anything in exchange for those tax dollars? We
sure do. The government provides us with a flow of goods and services. A sample includes the following:

National defense	Libraries
School lunch programs	Museums
Roads	Schools
Public health programs	National parks
Legal system	Police protection
Fire protection	Mass transit

We may pay a small part of the cost for some of these goods and services directly. But without government backing, we would not have as many of them as we have come to expect.

B. Government and Business

Flow 5. The flow of money from governments to businesses. This flow includes payments for purchases from IBM, Boeing, Rockwell, and other companies that are awarded government contracts. Governments provide the major source of income for some companies.

Flow 6. The flow of goods and services from businesses to governments. The government buys tanks, planes, food, paper clips, pencils, cars, books, and thousands of other goods and services. In the United States, the government does not produce very many of these. It buys almost all it needs from businesses in the private sector. So, these goods flow to governments in exchange for the dollar flow in *Flow 5.*

Flow 7. The flow of money from businesses to governments. This flow is made up mainly of taxes, particularly corporate income taxes and property taxes.

Flow 8. What does the business sector get in exchange for those tax dollars? Basically it gets the same services that we listed in *Flow 4.* Just think how much the car industry benefits from having the system of roads provided by governments. Companies benefit from national defense, police and fire protection, and from having an educated labor force. Also, the legal system makes it possible to enforce contracts. This helps business to run smoothly.

MACROECONOMIC BALANCE

What would happen to our economy if some savings leaked out of the spending flow and never got back into it? Each year perhaps $100 billion would be stuffed into our pillows or hidden in attics. This money would not be spent; therefore fewer goods would be bought. Fewer workers would need to be hired. Less income would be earned. With less income, there would be even less spending, less production, and still fewer jobs. The economy would slowly become drained and weakened. The same thing could happen if tax dollars did not get back into the flow of spending.

But as you saw in Figure 15–6, savings does work its way back into the spending stream as a financial investment. Banks and other financial intermediaries help our savings get to others who need that money for current spending. Our tax dollars get back into the spending stream as the government provides goods and services. Because investment and government spending put this money back into the economic system, we call such spending an *injection*. Money is injected back into the circular flow of the economy by investment and government spending.

So, money leaks out of the circular flow in the form of savings and taxes. But these leakages are also injections back into the system in the form of investment and government spending. There is a macroeconomic balance (or equilibrium) when the leakages equal the injections. That is, macroeconomic equilibrium results when the sum of savings and taxes equals the sum of investment and government spending.

15–7

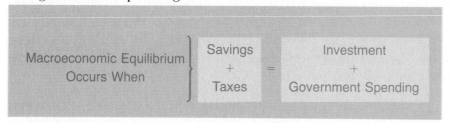

| Macroeconomic Equilibrium Occurs When | Savings + Taxes | = | Investment + Government Spending |

A macroeconomic balance or equilibrium is very much like keeping the water level the same in a tank that has both a leak and a source of water. Look at Figure 15–7 on page 317. Think of the water tank as our economic system. As long as the flow of water into the top of the tank (investment and government spending) equals the leak out of the bottom (savings and taxes), there will be equilibrium. That is, the water level will stay the same.

If the leakage is greater than the injection, the tank will run dry. In the economy, if leakages are greater than injections, the economy will slowly run down. Too few goods will be purchased and businesses will cut back on production. As cutbacks in production occur, fewer people will be employed. Less employment will result in less spending and still more cutbacks in production.

If the injection is more than the leakage, the tank will overflow. Water will spill over beyond the ability of the tank to contain it. In the economy, if the injections are greater than the leakages, the economy can't handle the additional demand for goods and services. This will cause inflation (a rise in the overall level of prices).

JOHN MAYNARD KEYNES

John Maynard Keynes ranks as one of the most important economists of all time. His writings and theories have had wide-ranging impact on economies throughout the world.

Keynes was born in Cambridge, England, on June 5, 1883. His parents, John Neville and Florence Ada Keynes, were both professionals. His father was a lecturer in logic and political economy at Cambridge University. His mother was involved in social work and served as mayor of Cambridge. A younger sister, Margaret, and brother, Geoffrey, completed the middle-class household in which John Maynard Keynes grew up.

Keynes, an avid reader who also enjoyed sports, attended a private high school and eventually enrolled in Cambridge University. In 1918 he first met Lydia Lopokova, a member of a Russian Ballet Company, at a party at a friend's house. He began seeing her and became her business advisor of sorts. He negotiated terms for her performances and advised her not to keep her savings in the safe at the Waldorf Hotel where she lived. Keynes, of course, recognized the importance of using her money to earn interest. They were married on August 4, 1925.

The General Theory of Employment, Interest, and Money, published on February 4, 1936, was probably Keynes's most famous work. In that book he developed the theory that a country's level of national income and employment was determined by demand forces. He showed that the theory that economies would self-adjust to full employment sometimes proved wrong. Indeed, as evidenced by the Great Depression, economies could reach equilibrium at less than full employment. Keynes advocated governmental intervention to stimulate an economy that had stabilized below a full employment level. Most Western economies today follow fiscal policies based to a large extent on Keynesian theories.

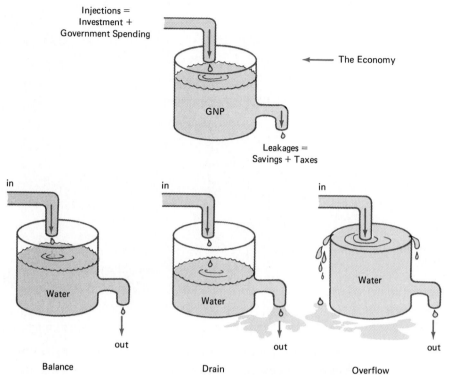

FIGURE 15–7   MACROECONOMIC EQUILIBRIUM COMPARED TO A TANK OF WATER
Injections must be equal to leakages for the economy to be in balance (equilibrium). This can be compared to water flowing into and out of a tank. If the amount going in equals the amount going out, the water level does not change. If more water leaks out than is put in, the tank drains down. If more water is put in than leaks out, the tank overflows and can't handle all the water.

AGGREGATE DEMAND AND SUPPLY

Each person has a demand for many different goods and services. When everyone's demand for all products is added together, the result is aggregate demand. **Aggregate demand** is the total demand of all people for all goods and services produced in an economy. This is the total demand in the whole economy. This total, or aggregate demand, is graphed in Figure 15–8. Since we are adding together many different kinds of products, their dollar value is used to represent quantity in Figure 15–8. To keep out the effect of inflation, this quantity is in *real* terms, or in *constant* dollars. As you should expect from your study of demand, the lower the price the more real output will be demanded. So, the aggregate demand curve slopes down to the right.

15–1

aggregate demand
The total demand of all people for all goods and services produced in an economy.

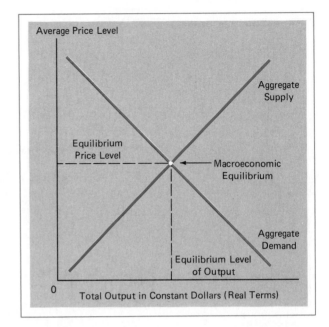

FIGURE 15–8 AGGREGATE DEMAND
AND SUPPLY
The economy is in equilibrium when aggregate
demand equals aggregate supply. This is where
the aggregate demand curve crosses the aggregate supply curve. This intersection determines
the equilibrium price level and output for the
economy.

15–1

aggregate supply
The total supply of all
goods and services in an
economy.

Many firms produce a wide variety of goods and services in
our economy. **Aggregate supply** is the total supply of all goods and
services in an economy. Aggregate supply is also graphed in Figure 15–8. You know that individual company and market supply
curves slope up to the right. More will be supplied at higher prices
than at lower prices. This is also true of the aggregate supply for
the whole economy, as shown in Figure 15–8.

We have said that the economy is in equilibrium when leakages
out of the spending flow equal injections into the spending flow.
We can also think of macroeconomic equilibrium using aggregate
demand and aggregate supply. The economy is in equilibrium
when aggregate demand equals aggregate supply. This is where
the two lines cross in Figure 15–8.

15–7

REVIEWING
THE
CHAPTER

15–1

1. Macroeconomics involves the study of the entire economy. In
   microeconomics you looked at the output of individual firms
   and workers, but macroeconomics looks at the total output for
   the whole economy. Macroeconomics also studies the total level
   of income in the economy, the overall level of employment, the
   average level of prices, and total levels of consumption and
   production.

15–1, 15–4   2. One measure of economic well-being is Gross National Product (GNP). GNP is the total current dollar value of all final goods and services produced in the economy during a year.

15–3, 15–4   3. The size of GNP for any country depends on many factors. These include the amount of natural resources the country has, the amount of capital (machines and equipment) it has, and the skills of the labor force.

15–2   4. There are some problems with using GNP as a measure of well-being: (a) It does not describe what kinds of goods are produced. (b) It does not describe how much is produced per person. (c) It does not tell how GNP per person is distributed. Are there many poor people and a few rich people? Or is the GNP well distributed among all of the people? (d) Only GNP in real terms, after taking out the effects of price changes, should be used for comparisons. (e) Official GNP figures do not include production that does not go through a formal market. (f) GNP does not count leisure time as having any value. (g) The quality of what is produced is not included in GNP.

15–3   5. Every society decides which goods should be produced. A production possibilities curve can help show and evaluate the trade-offs that must be made. Producing one item involves some opportunity cost in terms of other items that cannot be made with these same resources.

15–4   6. Consumer goods are goods that are made for final consumption. Consumer durable goods are goods that last a fairly long time in normal use, such as cars, refrigerators, and furniture. Consumer nondurable goods are those that are consumed more quickly, such as food, clothing, and magazines. Services, such as a haircut or radio repair, are intangible forms of production. The percentage of consumer spending that goes for services has been increasing.

15–4   7. When economists use the term *investment* they mean physical investment. This is an increase in the amount of capital that can be used in making goods and services. Capital, in this context, means machines and equipment that are made for use in further production.

15–4   8. The government sector of the economy includes the federal government as well as state and local governments. The total dollar value of this sector has increased almost every year for the past 40 years.

15–4   9. GNP is equal to the sum of spending for consumer goods, plus spending on investment goods, plus the value of production in the government sector.

15–5   10. In the process of producing GNP, an equal amount of income is earned in the economy. We use that income to buy goods and services, to pay taxes, and for savings.

15–6, 15–7   11. Savings and taxes can be thought of as leakages out of the flow of spending in the economy. Only if those leakages of money get back into the economy will the economy continue to run. The injections of investment and government spending get this money back into the flow of the economy. When savings plus taxes equal investment plus government spending, the economy is in equilibrium.

15–7   12. Another way of identifying macroeconomic equilibrium is when aggregate demand and aggregate supply are equal.

REVIEWING ECONOMIC TERMS

15–1   Supply definitions for the following terms:

gross national product (GNP)	durable goods
inflation	nondurable goods
constant dollar GNP	investment
barter	capital
irregular economy	disposable income
production possibilities curve	aggregate demand
consumer goods	aggregate supply

REVIEWING ECONOMIC CONCEPTS

15–2   1. List seven problems with using GNP as a measure of economic well-being.

15–3   2. How does the amount of natural resources a country has affect its GNP?

15–2   3. If current dollar GNP is $5 billion and inflation has been 5 percent since the base year, what is constant dollar GNP?

15–3   4. In an economy that is using all its resources efficiently, what happens if production of one good is increased?

15–5   5. List three kinds of consumer goods.

15–4   6. What three sectors make up GNP?

15–6   7. What are the three flows of money between households and businesses?

15–6   8. Explain the flows of money and goods and services between households and governments.

15–6   9. Explain the flows of money and goods and services between businesses and governments.

15–7   10. Describe two ways of looking at macroeconomic equilibrium.

APPLYING ECONOMIC CONCEPTS

15–1   1. Explain how macroeconomics is different from microeconomics.

15–4   2. Make a list of ten consumer goods and explain why you think they are consumer goods. Mark the durable goods with a *D* and the nondurable goods with *ND*. Briefly explain why some are durable and others are nondurable.

15–4   3. Why is gross national product measured in dollars rather than in units? Why are only final goods counted in GNP?

15–3   4. Draw a production possibilities curve to show the trade-off between producing consumer goods and capital goods (use Figure 15–3 as a model). Explain what happens when society chooses to produce more of either type of good.

15–4   5. What are investment goods (or capital goods)? List six examples of such goods and explain why you think they are capital goods.

15–4   6. Explain the difference between the following pairs of terms:
         physical investment versus financial investment
         physical capital versus financial capital
In your explanation include an example of each type of good.

15–5   7. Write a short explanation of the three ways that people spend their incomes. How would you classify the use of money for a charitable contribution, such as giving money to United Appeal?

15–4   8. What is the difference between *real GNP* and *GNP in current dollars*? Which is the better measure to use in comparing activity in the economy from one year to another? Explain your answer.

15–7   9. What do economists mean when they talk about leakages and injections in the economy? What are the major leakages? What are the major injections? Why is it important for leakages to equal injections?

CHAPTER 16

THE DISTRIBUTION OF INCOME

Learning Objectives

16–1 Define terms related to income distribution.

16–2 Discuss how income is distributed by industry.

16–3 Describe the functional and personal distribution of income.

16–4 Analyze a Lorenz curve of income distribution.

16–5 Explain important factors in choosing a career.

16–6 List seven characteristics of the poor.

16–7 Discuss the causes of poverty.

16–8 Discuss solutions to poverty.

A RICH NATION

The United States is a rich nation. Our level of economic well-being is very high. More than 80 percent of the families in the United States own at least one car. Of homes with electric service, 99.8 percent have refrigerators, 99.9 percent have at least one television, and more than 75 percent have washing machines. More than half of all families have room air conditioners, and many others have central air conditioning. In such a society, it is sometimes hard to believe that poverty exists.

In the early 1990s, the per capita income in the United States was about $19,000 a year. **Per capita income** is the average income per person. It is calculated by dividing total personal income by total population. If our national income was divided evenly among all the people in the United States, each person would get about $19,000. This includes the old and the young, people with jobs, and people without jobs. So, if there are three people in your family and if national income were shared equally, your family would have about $57,000 in annual income ($19,000 × 3 = $57,000). Many families have incomes much higher than this. And many have far less income.

On the average, we are rich. But the average includes the very rich and the very poor. As a country, we have concern for the poor. We spend a lot of time and money working to assist the poor. But it is hard to think of ways to help that are fair to rich and poor alike. Probably the best way to help the poor is to have a healthy, growing economy. Then there would be enough well-paying jobs for everyone. Furthermore, we need to make sure that everyone has an equal chance for those jobs. Equality of opportunity is even more important than equality of income.

16–1
per capita income
The average income per person.

Illustration 16–1
Overall, the level of economic well-being in the United States is very high.

INCOME COMES FROM PRODUCTION

You know that people earn income by working. The act of being productive makes it possible for us to earn money. Some people make physical objects such as bicycles, cars, or watches. Others, such as teachers, barbers, or senators, provide valuable services. People can earn an income in any of these occupations.

Distribution of Income by Industry

Our economy has been manufacturing-oriented for years. Therefore, a high percentage of income has been earned in the

16–2

manufacturing sector of the economy. In 1960, about 30 percent of the national income was from manufacturing industries. By 1990, this had fallen to less than 20 percent of the national income. The percentage of earnings coming from the agricultural sector also went down.

If earnings from the manufacturing and agricultural sectors have declined in importance, what has taken their place? Table 16–1 helps answer this question. This table shows the percentage distribution of income earned by industry for certain years starting with 1950. You can see that the greatest growth has been in finance, insurance, and real estate; services; and government. Earnings in the service sector grew from 9.5 percent in 1950 to 21.8 percent in 1990. The percentage of income earned in the government sector rose from 9.7 percent in 1950 to 15.9 percent in 1975, then fell to 14.5 percent in 1990.

Looking at trends such as these helps to predict future trends. From these data we might project slow growth in communications and utilities. More substantial growth may continue in the service sector. The government sector may have reached a high in the mid-1970s, so we might not look for much change there.

TABLE 16–1

THE PERCENTAGE DISTRIBUTION OF NATIONAL INCOME BY
INDUSTRY SECTORS

Industry	1950	1955	1960	1965	1970	1975	1980	1985	1990
1. Agriculture, Forestry, and Fisheries	7.4	4.9	4.2	3.6	3.1	3.5	2.8	2.8	2.1
2. Mining and Construction	6.9	7.0	6.4	6.4	6.5	6.4	6.7	6.8	5.9
3. Manufacturing	30.8	31.6	29.7	30.0	26.4	25.1	24.2	21.7	18.2
4. Transportation	5.5	4.8	4.3	4.0	3.8	3.6	3.7	3.5	3.3
5. Communications and Utilities	3.0	3.5	4.1	4.0	4.0	4.1	4.2	4.6	4.2
6. Wholesale and Retail Trade	17.7	16.7	15.4	14.9	15.2	15.4	14.6	14.8	14.3
7. Finance, Insurance, and Real Estate	9.0	9.4	11.9	11.6	11.7	11.5	13.4	12.6	14.7
8. Services	9.5	10.2	10.6	11.3	12.8	13.3	14.3	16.3	21.8
9. Government	9.7	11.4	12.5	13.2	15.8	15.9	14.1	14.9	14.5
10. Other	0.5	0.5	0.9	1.0	0.9	1.4	2.1	2.0	1.0

Sources: U.S. Bureau of the Census, *Historical Statistics of the United States, Colonial Times to 1957* (Washington, D.C.: U.S. Government Printing Office, 1960), 140. *See also* U.S. Bureau of the Census, *Statistical Abstract of the United States: 1985,* 105th ed. (Washington, D.C.: U.S. Government Printing Office, 1985), 437; and Bureau of Economic Analysis, *Survey of Current Business* (Washington, D.C.: U.S. Department of Commerce, July, 1986, and December, 1990) 64, 12.

Income and the Factors of Production

You already know that economists classify inputs into four *factors of production*. They are land, labor, capital, and entrepreneurship. The earnings related to each of these factors are rent, wages, interest, and profit, respectively.

Factors of Production		Earnings of Each Factor of Production
Land	earns	Rent
Labor	earns	Wages
Capital	earns	Interest
Entrepreneurship	earns	Profit

According to the broad categories used by the U.S. Bureau of Economic Analysis, the percentage distribution of income in 1990 was as follows:[1]

Compensation of employees and proprietors' income ...	82.5%
Rental income of persons	0.2%
Corporate profits	6.8%
Net interest	10.5%
Total	100.0%

This distribution is called the functional distribution of income. The **functional distribution of income** is the way in which income is divided by economic functions.

Because of some definition and data collection problems, this is not a perfect match to the economic meaning of wages, rent, profits, and interest. For example, there is no reliable information available on economic profit. The profit included here is accounting profit, which is greater than profit in economic terms. Accounting profit includes dividends, which should be counted as a return to capital and perhaps included in net interest. Despite these problems, this distribution of national income sheds some light on how the total income of the economy is divided among the functional areas. Clearly most of our national income is earned by the labor output. How much of our national income certain people get is determined by their work effort, inheritances, and other factors.

16–3
16–1
functional distribution of income
The way in which income is divided by economic functions.

---

[1]*Survey of Current Business* (Washington, D.C.: U.S. Government Printing Office, December, 1990), 5.

PERSONAL DISTRIBUTION OF INCOME

16–3

16–1
personal distribution
of income
How income is shared
among people in our
society.

Illustration 16–2
The more education you
receive beyond high
school, the higher your
income is likely to be.
Education beyond high
school includes learning
a skill, such as
electronics, at a trade
school.

How income is shared among people in our society is called the **personal distribution of income**. We all know some families who appear to have a lot of money to spend. We also know others that have little income. How much economic inequality exists? At the beginning of the 1990s, over 10 percent of the families in the United States had less than $10,000 in total annual family income. That is less than $835 a month. This is not much to live on when you note that there was an average of three people in each of these families. For this low income group, the level of education of the head of the household is typically low. Often the head of such a household has never completed high school.

About 37 percent of the families in the United States had incomes between $15,000 and $35,000 during that time. The typical head of the household in this income bracket had finished high school plus some further education. Education after high school can include college, trade school, nursing school, and secretarial school. About 21 percent of the families in the United States at that time had incomes in the $35,000 to $50,000 range. The heads of the families in this group had even more education. At the upper end of the income ladder, over 20 percent of families had incomes of more than $50,000. It shouldn't surprise you that the heads of these households had the most education.

You often see news stories about the very poor or the very rich. And as you have seen, some families do fall into one or the other of these classes. But we also have a very large and fairly wealthy middle class. For example, about 58 percent of U.S. families have a total family income between $15,000 and $50,000. This is a wide income range. This large middle income class is considered a very good feature of our economic system.

Two opinions about income distribution are generally shared. First, it is not good to force an equal income distribution on the economy. In order to keep people's work efforts high, they should have the chance to earn more income. If all people were guaranteed an equal share of national income, there would be less incentive for them to work hard. They might not even work at all. This would cause production and incomes to fall so we would have less to share.

Second, there should not be too much inequality in the distribution of income. A lot of inequality can create social problems. This is especially true if people at the lower end think they have little chance to improve their economic standing. But how much is too much inequality? There is no clear answer to this question. People have different feelings about what the best distribution is. Public policy has favored making the income distribution more equal, but not completely equal. Our tax and welfare programs are a result of this thinking.

Income Inequality: A Graphic Representation

In order to know how income is distributed, you need some way to measure the amount of inequality that exists. There are a number of ways to do this. One popular way is to use a graphic measure called a Lorenz curve of income distribution. A **Lorenz curve of income distribution** is a graphic method showing the amount of income inequality that exists in society at any point in time. By comparing Lorenz curves for different time periods, you can tell whether income inequality is becoming less or greater. In the United States there is a slight trend toward greater income equality. But the changes from year to year, or even from decade to decade, are small. This is because for years our income distribution has included the large middle class mentioned earlier.

In order to graph the Lorenz curve we need some information about the distribution of income. In recent years, distribution in the United States has been fairly stable and can be shown by the following numbers. If you ranked all families from the poorest to the richest, you would find the following:

1. The poorest 20 percent of all U.S. families has only about 5 percent of the income.

2. The next 20 percent of all U.S. families has about 11 percent of the income.

3. The next (and middle) 20 percent of all U.S. families has about 17 percent of the income.

4. The next 20 percent of all U.S. families has about 24 percent of the income.

5. The richest 20 percent of all U.S. families has about 43 percent of the income.

You can see that the richest 20 percent of the families has more than twice as large a fraction of the nation's income—over 40 percent. But the poorest 20 percent of the families shares a much smaller fraction of national income—only 5 percent. The middle 60 percent of families has about 52 percent of the income.

These basic data about income distribution form the Lorenz curve. In a Lorenz curve, the cumulative percentage of income is measured along the vertical axis. The cumulative percentage of families is measured on the horizontal axis. So, you need to find

16–4
16–1
Lorenz curve of income distribution
A graphic method showing the amount of income inequality that exists in society at any point in time.

cumulative percentages. This means that you must add the percentages for each step (1 to 5 above) in the distribution of income. The cumulative percentages, then, are as follows:

A. The lowest 20 percent of all U.S. families has 5 percent of the income.

B. The lowest 40 percent of all U.S. families has 16 percent of the income (5% + 11%).

C. The lowest 60 percent of all U.S. families has 33 percent of the income (16% + 17%).

D. The lowest 80 percent of all U.S. families has 57 percent of the income (33% + 24%).

E. The entire 100 percent of all U.S. families has 100 percent of the income (57% + 43%).

This gives five points to graph, one for *A*, *B*, *C*, *D*, and *E*.

These five points are graphed in Figure 16–1. The vertical axis measures the cumulative percentage of income, and the horizontal axis measures the cumulative percentage of families. Each of the five points above (*A*, *B*, *C*, *D*, and *E*) is labeled with the same letters in Figure 16–1. To be sure you understand what each point in the graph represents, let's look at two of them in detail. The point marked *A* is directly above 20 percent on the horizontal axis, so it represents 20 percent of the families. Reading directly from *A* over to the vertical axis, you find that *A* represents 5 percent of the

FIGURE 16–1   THE LORENZ CURVE OF INCOME DISTRIBUTION IN THE UNITED STATES

The line through Points *A*, *B*, *C*, *D*, and *E* shows how income is distributed in the United States. For example, Point *A* shows that the lowest 20 percent of families has only 5 percent of the nation's personal income. The other points can be interpreted in the same way. At Point *C* you see the lowest 60 percent of families has 33 percent of the income.

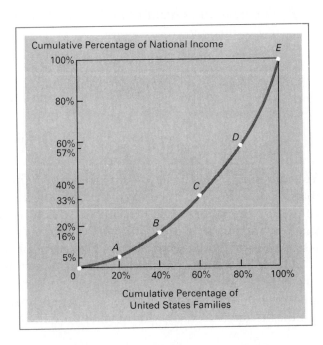

national income. Therefore, Point *A* shows that the poorest 20 percent of all U.S. families shares just 5 percent of our national income. Now look at Point *C* in Figure 16–1. Would you agree that Point *C* is directly above 60 percent on the horizontal axis? If not, look at the figure again. Find 60 percent of the families along the horizontal and go straight up. You come to Point *C*. Put your finger on *C* and move it directly left to the vertical axis. You find that this point on the vertical axis represents 33 percent of national income. So, Point *C* shows that the lowest 60 percent of all U.S. families shares 33 percent of the national income.

If all five of these points are connected, they represent the Lorenz curve for income distribution. The curve starts at the origin (Point 0) since 0 percent of the families would have 0 percent of the income.

The Line of Equality

What would the Lorenz curve look like if there were perfect equality in the distribution of income? To find out, first look at the percentage distribution of income if there were complete equality.

1. The lowest 20 percent of all U.S. families would have 20 percent of the income.

2. The lowest 40 percent of all U.S. families would have 40 percent of the income.

3. The lowest 60 percent of all U.S. families would have 60 percent of the income.

4. The lowest 80 percent of all U.S. families would have 80 percent of the income.

5. The entire 100 percent of all U.S. families would have 100 percent of the income.

If these points are graphed, they will be the straight line from 0 to *E*. This is the straight line from the lower left corner of Figure 16–2 to the upper right corner.

The straight line from 0 to *E* would be the Lorenz curve if there were a perfectly equal distribution of income. So, we call the line from 0 to *E* the *line of equality*. When income is not shared equally, the Lorenz curve is below this line. Our line joining Points *A*, *B*, *C*, *D*, and *E*, the actual Lorenz curve for the distribution of income in the United States, is below this line. The further the actual Lorenz curve is below the line of equality, the greater the inequality of the distribution of income.

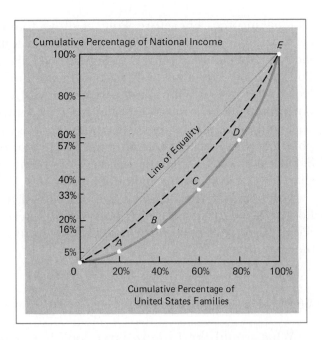

FIGURE 16–2 A LORENZ CURVE OF INCOME DISTRIBUTION IN THE UNITED STATES
The straight line from 0 to *E* shows a perfectly equal distribution of income. The curved line through *A, B, C, D,* and *E* shows the actual distribution of income in the United States. A move to the dashed line would show a change to a more equal distribution of income.

Suppose the government starts a new program to make the distribution of income more equal. It would be nice to be able to measure the success or failure of the program. This could be done by drawing Lorenz curves for income distribution before and after the program. If the *after* curve is closer to the line of equality, the program successfully made the distribution of income more equal. For example, suppose the Lorenz curve moves from the line drawn for the United States to the dashed line. This would show more equality in the distribution of income.

Your Career Choice

At some time in your life, you have to choose a career. Do you want to be a plumber? a dentist? a homemaker? a sales clerk? a teacher? an artist? The list of choices is almost endless. You have a great deal of freedom to choose a career. You probably have more freedom to choose now than at any time in our country's history.

16–5 The income you can earn is one major consideration in choosing a career. Most people would rather have more money than less money! People do not want to be poor. But there is more to a job than money. You need to do work that you like. And you need to consider the work environment and chances for advancement. In choosing a career, use the five-step personal decision-making process you learned earlier to help you decide which career would be best for you.

In making your career choice, consider the sectors of the economy that are growing. You know that people's earnings are at least partly determined by the demand for the things they produce. Look at the growth areas, such as services, to see which kinds of jobs are available. Next, consider the education or training you need in order to get those jobs. Can you qualify for, and do you have interest in, such education and training? You have seen that the heads of households in higher income classes have higher levels of education. So, if you want a well-paying job, you should probably think about getting more education and/or training. The next chapter on unemployment will discuss this further.

Despite your freedom to choose a career, job discrimination still exists. **Job discrimination** is the refusal to hire certain people because of their gender, race, or other characteristics that have nothing to do with their ability to do a job. For example, at one time women rarely became doctors or business executives. Today, women can enter these fields much more easily. Although there is still discrimination, minority groups and women have far more freedom to choose careers that they want than they ever had before.

16–1

job discrimination

The refusal to hire certain people because of their gender, race, or other characteristics that have nothing to do with their ability to do a job.

POVERTY: AN OVERVIEW

Poverty goes hand-in-hand with helplessness and hopelessness. It brings to mind images of starving children in Africa, Asia, and Latin America. It makes us think of the bloated bellies and skinny limbs of some American children in Appalachia or in crowded city tenements. Some people think that the poor are lazy and worthless people who live off of the government. Or they picture the poor living in broken-down dwellings with huge television antennae rising above them or expensive cars parked outside. The ideas and feelings about poverty are many and varied.

When we speak of **poverty**, we are usually referring to the condition in which people do not have enough income to provide for their basic needs such as food, clothing, and shelter. But it is difficult to settle on a universal definition of poverty. According to Barbara Ward in *The Lopsided World*, approximately 80 percent of the world's population lives in countries where the per capita income is less than $600 a year. However, poverty is not found only in countries with low per capita incomes. As already mentioned, even the United States, with an average income of about $19,000 per capita, has poor people. It is difficult to understand that poverty exists in a country where the overall standard of living is as high as it is in the United States.

16–1

poverty

The condition in which people do not have enough income to provide for their basic needs, such as food, clothing, and shelter.

Poverty in the United States

Poverty in the United States is unnecessary. We produce enough food, clothing, and shelter for all of our people to live well. But some Americans are very poor and do not share in the national prosperity. In the United States we have plenty of income, but that income is distributed unevenly. Our poverty problem is thus partly a problem of income distribution.

You have seen that if the population of the United States is divided into fifths, the bottom fifth receives only 5 percent of the total income of the country. The second fifth receives only 11 percent; the third fifth, 17 percent; the fourth fifth, 24 percent; and the top fifth, 43 percent of the money. These figures only represent income. If actual wealth were used, including property and assets plus income, the distribution would be even more lopsided.

The United States government did very little about poverty until the Great Depression of the 1930s. Before that time, poverty was considered a private affair. Many people thought that the poor were lazy and so deserved to be poor. However, the high rates of unemployment in the 1930s added millions to the ranks of the poor. Not all of these people were poor because they were lazy. Many were poor because the economic system did not provide enough jobs. Therefore, the government took some responsibility for the care of the poor during this period. Government programs included public works projects, bank reform, and encouragement of labor unions. Perhaps the most important legislation was the Social Security Act, which provided income for older citizens past employment age.

During the 1940s and 1950s, the United States prospered, and the issue of poverty dropped into the background. However, it was brought back to public attention in the 1960s and 1970s. The civil rights movement, the War on Poverty, and President Johnson's Great Society Program all helped refocus our attention on poverty.

Some people think about poverty in terms of a fixed income level, such as $5,000 per year. But this is not a good measure of poverty because as prices change, the buying power of $5,000 also changes. For example, after adjusting for price changes, it would have taken $9,088 in 1975 to buy as much as you could buy for $5,000 in 1960. By 1990, an income of $21,960 was needed to buy the same things that $5,000 bought 30 years before. So, using a fixed income level is not a good way to define the poverty level.

The Poverty Line

The United States government defines poverty in terms of a *poverty line*. To determine the poverty line, the United States

Department of Agriculture first figures the cost of a year's nutritious, low-cost diet. This figure is multiplied by three to arrive at the poverty line. The number three is used because statistics indicate that the poor spend about one third of their income on food. Different poverty lines are determined for different areas based on varying food prices. Also, family size affects the poverty line. For example, the poverty line for a family of four in 1983 was $10,178.

There are some problems with this definition of the poverty line. First, the low-budget diet that forms the basis of the definition is not necessarily the least expensive nutritious diet. The government's standard diet allows for variety and choice. But people could provide a basic diet for less money by having less variety. Second, the definition considers only current income. The savings and assets of the family are not evaluated by the official definition of poverty. Therefore, some people who do not seem poor may sometimes qualify for poverty assistance programs such as the food stamp program. Despite their low incomes these people may own homes and have money in the bank.

To help remedy the problems caused by changing prices, the poverty level is changed every year. As prices go up, so does the official definition of the poverty level. For a family of four, the increase in the poverty level since 1960 is shown in Table 16–2.

TABLE 16–2

INCREASE IN POVERTY LEVEL
FOR FAMILIES OF FOUR

Year	Poverty Income Level
1960	$ 3,022
1965	3,223
1970	3,968
1975	5,500
1980	8,414
1983	10,178
1985	10,989
1988	12,092

Characteristics of the Poor

At the start of the 1990s, 31.9 million people in the United States were judged to be poor by the government. Those 31.9 million represented more than 13 percent of the population. That is, more than one in every eight people in the United States lived in poverty conditions. Poverty can be found all over the United States. About 65 percent of the nation's poor are white and about 30 percent are black. About 12 percent of the country's population is black. If black and white people were equally likely to be poor, we would expect only 12 percent of the poor to be black. But since about 30 percent of the poor are black, there are more than twice the number of black poor than is expected.

Comparing the percentage of a certain group of poor to their percentage of the total population highlights the characteristics of the poor. When you look at the poor as a percentage of an area's population, the greatest concentrations of the poor live in southern rural areas and in Appalachia. Small cities and towns have the next highest percentage of poor. Many people are surprised that, in terms of percentages, large cities have fewer poor people than rural areas or small cities and towns. It is not surprising, however, that the lowest percentage of poverty is in the suburbs.

16–6   Families with one or more of the following characteristics are most likely to be poor:

1. The family is a member of a minority group.

2. The head of the family is female.

Illustration 16–3
Surprisingly, large cities have relatively fewer poor people than rural areas or small cities and towns.

3. The head of the family has eight years or less of formal education.

4. The head of the family is handicapped by illness or physical or mental problems.

5. The family lives in a rural area.

6. The head of the family is over 65.

7. The family has seven or more members.

The data in Table 16–3 illustrate some of these characteristics. You can see that although only 10.1 percent of whites were living in poverty, the percent for blacks was 31.6, and for Hispanics (persons of Spanish origin) it was 26.8. You can also see that the percentage of the young and old who are living in poverty is higher than for people between 22 and 64 years of age.

TABLE 16–3

PERCENTAGE OF PERSONS BELOW POVERTY
LEVEL BY AGE, RACE, AND REGION

Age	Percent
Under 16 years	20.4
16 to 21 years	15.7
22 to 44 years	10.5
45 to 54 years	7.7
55 to 59 years	9.6
60 to 64 years	10.4
65 years and over	12.0
Race	
White	10.1
Black	31.6
Hispanic	26.8
Region	
Northeast	11.2
Midwest	10.5
South	15.4
West	11.3

Source: U.S Bureau of the Census, *Statistical Abstract of the United States: 1990,* 110th ed. (Washington, D.C.: U.S. Government Printing Office, 1990), 458, 460.

CAUSES OF POVERTY

16–7   Most causes of poverty can be classified into one of the following categories:

1. unemployment

2. low productivity

3. restrictions on job entry

During the Depression of the 1930s, the largest cause of poverty was *unemployment*. The economic system failed, and there was not enough total demand to provide jobs for all those who were willing to work. Poverty caused by decreases in total demand, such as the poverty of the 1930s, is a direct result of unemployment. This can be fought by applying the necessary tools of monetary and fiscal policy to reach a full-employment economy. Monetary and fiscal policies represent government actions designed to influence the level of national economic activity. These policies are discussed in detail later in Part III.

However, because of the way we define a full-employment economy, poverty will not be eliminated by these policies. We say the economy is *fully employed* when about 95 percent of the labor force is employed. Even when there is full employment, there may still be unemployed persons and poverty. At times the economy fails to grow as much as would be necessary to keep up with the growing work force. The unemployment rate then rises. Those people who are unable to find work may then fall below the poverty line.

A second cause of poverty is *low productivity*. Many people have characteristics which contribute to low productivity. These characteristics include low educational levels, physical and mental handicaps, and old age. Those who have jobs but do not make enough money to go over the poverty line also are considered to have low productivity. These people are called the "working poor." In one sense, low productivity is the major cause of poverty among these groups.

In our economy, labor, capital (machinery), and land are productive. All three are used to produce goods. The more of these three factors that people own, the more income they are likely to have. Usually the poor own neither capital nor land. All they have is their own labor, and their labor often is not very skilled. Thus, a low skill level leads to low productivity, which often results in poverty.

Restrictions on job entry also contribute to poverty by reducing the number of people who have access to skilled jobs. Many of the

Illustration 16–4
Old age tends to lower productivity, therefore contributing to poverty.

poor work in unskilled jobs, such as janitorial and assembly line work. In fact, the way out of poverty for many is to learn a skill and enter the skilled labor market. The skilled labor market includes such positions as electricians, plumbers, and millwrights. However, to get training in a skilled trade may be difficult. Many trade unions have very restrictive apprenticeship programs. Some unions allow only a few new workers to learn the trade, and they make the apprenticeship period very long. These trade unions may limit the number of skilled workers and thereby keep their wages high. Thus, the trade unions protect their members. However, this prevents others from getting jobs. Figure 16–3 shows the effects of restrictive apprenticeship programs and restricted entry into the skilled trades.

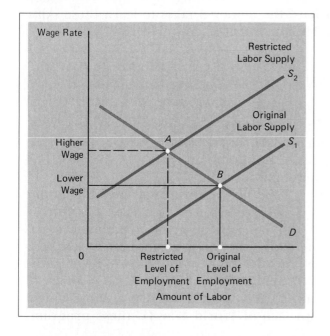

FIGURE 16–3   THE EFFECT OF JOB RESTRICTIONS
Restrictions on the labor force reduce employment. This factor can cause poverty because some people are prevented from getting jobs.

Curve *D* in the figure represents the demand for skilled labor. Curve S_1 represents the supply if there were unlimited entry to the skilled labor market. However, entry into the skilled trades is limited, and the actual supply of skilled labor shows at curve S_2. Notice on curve S_2 that for each price or wage rate there is less skilled labor supplied. Point *A* represents the wage for skilled labor when entry is restricted, and Point *B* represents the wage when entry is unrestricted. By restricting entry of workers into the skilled trades, workers can raise their wages. However, fewer workers are hired. Trade unions are not the only ones that make skilled jobs hard to get. Government often restricts entry to a trade by issuing only a certain number of licenses for such jobs as electricians, plumbers, and taxi drivers.

Another way some people are restricted from entering some jobs is discrimination on the basis of gender, race, or other factors. The largest percentages of poor are nonwhite or have a woman as the family head. This is the result of past and present discrimination against women and racial minorities. The economic forces at work here resemble those shown in Figure 16–3. However, the supply of workers in this case is not limited by apprenticeship programs and union policies. The supply is limited because employers refuse to consider a whole segment of the supply — blacks, women, Hispanics, or other minorities — from the market.

The poor are caught in a vicious circle of poverty. They do not have the skills to earn a living in today's society, and many have handicaps that prevent them from learning such skills. Since they lack skills, they don't have the money it takes to learn these skills even if they are able. They are trapped, and they stay poor.

POVERTY PROGRAMS

16–8   Since the 1930s, the government's attempts to help the poor have taken three major directions: (1) creating jobs for the poor, (2) setting up education and retraining programs for the poor, and (3) providing income support programs.

The Works Progress Administration (WPA) and the Public Works Administration (PWA) were set up to create jobs for the poor during the 1930s. Both programs involved public projects such as the building of roads, sidewalks, schools, and parks. Despite their many useful and desirable results, the WPA and the PWA received criticism as make-work projects. That is, much of the work was created only to keep people busy. As unemployment decreased with the approach of World War II, these programs phased out.

The Economic Opportunity Act of 1964 also provided jobs for the poor through the Job Corps, the Neighborhood Youth Corps Work Training Program, and the Work-Study Program. Many people thought of the Job Corps as a failure. Only one out of nine people who joined stayed in the program for a full year, and one third quit within three months. The Neighborhood Youth Corps subsidized 500,000 jobs for young people. The Work-Study Program provided part-time work for college students from poor families. In 1971, the Emergency Employment Act provided $2.25 billion for creating public service jobs for the unemployed and the underemployed. Job creation programs have helped our unemployment problems. However, the kinds of jobs created generally have provided little training or opportunity to improve skills. Often these jobs do not lead to permanent employment.

The second way to help the poor is to provide for their education and retraining. Instead of creating jobs to fit the skills of the poor, the poor learn skills that will fit the available jobs. The Manpower Development Training Act and the CETA program used this approach in their attempts to reduce poverty. In general, the training given under these programs succeeded. More than 90 percent of those who received aid in the Manpower programs stayed with the jobs they were trained for.

The third way to help the poor is through income supplement programs. Income supplements are crucial to stopping poverty. Many people are poor because they cannot work (and therefore cannot be trained for productive jobs) for reasons of handicaps or age. In addition, regardless of our success in educating and retraining the poor, poverty will continue because of the lack of jobs. In the United States, our current programs of income supplements have developed in a piecemeal pattern. These programs include Old Age and Survivors Insurance (OASI), Medicaid, Medicare, Aid to Families with Dependent Children (AFDC), and food stamps. These programs are not aimed specifically at the poor. They are aimed at people in certain categories, such as low-income families with dependent children, the blind, the aged, and the disabled. Many people suffer poverty as a result of such conditions.

Illustration 16–5
The food stamp program is one of the many ways in which the government supplements incomes of poor families.

There are problems with the poverty programs in the United States. Even when a lot of money supports these programs, the results often are not good. Some people argue that these programs discourage the poor from working and being productive. And it is true that some people get more money from welfare programs than they can earn by working. This is usually only true for people with low skill levels. They cannot qualify for jobs that pay very much, and so they are better off getting welfare benefits.

A great many people are employed in government agencies that run our welfare programs. Of course, these jobs cost taxpayers money. Many people think that it takes far too much money to run these programs. But many employees are needed to keep track of all the rules that determine who should have different benefits. There is a trade-off between our desire to make sure only the eligible poor get aid and our desire to keep welfare costs down.

A NEGATIVE INCOME TAX FOR THE POOR

Criticism of our public assistance or welfare programs has led to discussions of other ways of helping the poor. Most alternative

16–1

negative income tax
Poverty programs in which a person or family below some income level receives a payment from the government rather than paying some amount of tax to the government.

plans include some form of a guaranteed income program or a negative income tax program. They have been proposed by well-known economists such as Milton Friedman and James Tobin. The term **negative income tax** describes poverty programs in which a person or family below some income level receives a payment from the government rather than paying some amount of tax to the government. The payment, or subsidy, is the opposite of a tax and is called a negative tax.

Negative income tax proposals have three important characteristics: (1) a minimum income, (2) a tax rate, and (3) a cut-off income. The minimum income is the amount of income that every family is guaranteed. This is usually determined by finding out the amount of money necessary to support the basic necessities of life (food, clothing, shelter). That amount establishes the minimum income. Each family would be guaranteed that much income by the federal government. The minimum income level would be adjusted for family size and local cost of living. Traditionally we have used many different welfare programs such as food stamp programs and housing programs. These have been used to guarantee minimum levels of the necessities of life rather than give outright income subsidies. Many people believe that there would be less waste with a negative income tax plan than with our current welfare programs.

The income at which the individual must begin to pay positive taxes and thus lose benefits (negative taxes) is called the cut-off or break-even level of income. Under most negative income tax plans each family gets the basic minimum income grant from the government. But if they work and earn other income, their subsidy is lowered by some percentage of their earnings. This percentage is the tax rate. At the cut-off point, the reduction in the subsidy due to earnings equals the initial subsidy. Therefore, no government payment is forthcoming. Above that level, the family owes tax to the government.

An important result of negative income tax programs is providing incentive to earn more income. Only some percentage of income earned goes to the government as a positive tax or a subsidy reduction. Under many older welfare programs this incentive is not present. A dollar of earned income means a dollar of reduced benefits. Thus, there is little incentive to work because earning income only reduces benefits by the amount earned. With a negative income tax, however, some of the extra income is kept.

THINKING

ABOUT ECONOMIC ISSUES

For many years, a college education has been an important goal for young people. In the United States there was a real push to get more people into colleges at the end of the 1950s. This was, in part, a result of Soviet advances in space programs. We felt that we were falling behind in the ability to compete in high technology areas. The result was an even greater emphasis on more education. In addition, most people thought of a college education as the way to the American dream of prosperity.

How valuable is a college education? In order to answer this difficult question, many factors need to be considered. If you only count the dollar value of a degree, it may not be as good an investment as it used to be. However, there are many other benefits to a college education. Some students want to learn a skill, and some will attend college just because they enjoy learning. They can develop political and social awareness and a more positive self-image as a result of their education.

The figure below shows how educational level affects income. You can see that households with lower levels of education are likely to also have lower incomes. Having a college degree does not assure you of a high income, but it certainly improves your chances.

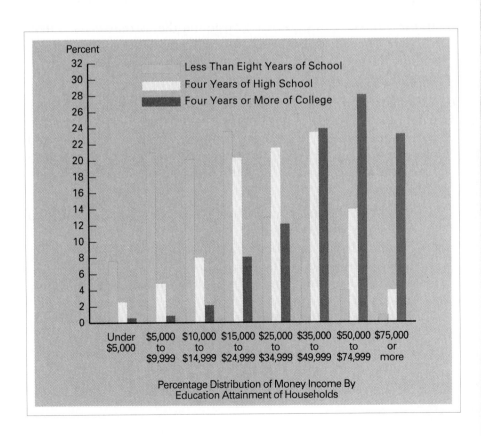

Percentage Distribution of Money Income By
Education Attainment of Households

REVIEWING THE CHAPTER

1. The United States is a rich nation. Our national income is so high that more than 80 percent of all families have cars. Almost every household has at least one television and many other expensive goods.

16-2   2. We earn our incomes by producing goods and services. Historically, manufacturing has been, and still is, the biggest income-earning sector of the economy. But this sector has been shrinking in relative terms. The government and service sectors have been growing.

16-3   3. The functional distribution of income is the way in which income is divided by economic functions. Most of our income is earned by our personal labor effort (about 82.5 percent). Other income comes from rent (about 0.2 percent), profits (about 6.8 percent) and interest (about 10.5 percent).

16-3   4. The average level of education goes up as income level increases. In the lowest income bracket, the typical head of the household did not complete high school. At the upper end of the income distribution, the average years of education include a college degree.

16-3   5. In the United States there is a large middle income class. There also are the very poor and the very rich. But our economic system has enough economic opportunity that the majority of people belong to a large middle class.

16-4   6. A Lorenz curve can show the amount of inequality in the distribution of income. The Lorenz curve bows down away from the line of equality. The more it bows, the greater the amount of inequality shown. The Lorenz curve is often used as a measure of the success of programs to make income distribution more equal.

16-6   7. The very poor in this country are likely to have one or more of the following characteristics:
(a) The family is a member of a minority group.
(b) The head of the family is female.
(c) The head of the family has eight years or less of formal education.
(d) The head of the family is handicapped by illness or by physical or mental problems.
(e) The family lives in a rural area.
(f) The head of the family is over 65.
(g) The family has seven or more members.

16–7   8. Some people are poor because there are not enough good jobs for everyone who wants one. Some are poor because they lack skills and training. And some people are poor because of restrictions, due to unionization or prejudice, on entry to high-skill and high-pay jobs.

16–8   9. Our country has used many programs over the years to help the poor. Some programs create jobs for the poor. Some help the poor get better job skills. Other programs transfer money or goods to the poor from the rest of the society.

16–8   10. A negative income tax is one kind of program that many people think could fight poverty. It is given this name because below some income level people receive money from the government rather than paying a tax to the government. This money from the government is thought of as a negative tax.

REVIEWING ECONOMIC TERMS

16–1   Supply definitions for the following terms:

per capita income	job discrimination
functional distribution of income	poverty
personal distribution of income	negative income tax
Lorenz curve of income distribution	

REVIEWING ECONOMIC CONCEPTS

16–2   1. What three industry sectors have increased the most in the distribution of income since 1950?

16–2   2. What two industry sectors have decreased the most in the distribution of income since 1950?

16–3   3. Explain the difference between personal and functional distribution of income.

16–4   4. What does the space between the Lorenz curve and the line of equality represent?

16–5   5. How does the demand for things produced affect career choice?

16–6   6. List seven characteristics that increase the chances of being poor.

16–7   7. Identify three factors that are considered to be causes of poverty.

16–8   8. Describe three approaches to helping the poor.

16–8   9. Explain the difference in incentives to work in traditional welfare programs and negative income tax programs.

APPLYING ECONOMIC CONCEPTS

1. You have read the following statement: "Equality of opportunity is even more important than equality of income." Do you agree or disagree with this statement? Why? What do you think a poor person would say about it? What would a rich person say about it?

16–4   2. Study the following two Lorenz curves that show the distribution of income in Countries A and B. Which country has the most inequality in the distribution of income? How can you tell? In which country would you rather live? Why?

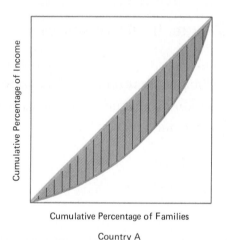

Country A

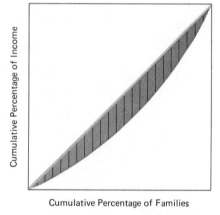

Country B

16–5   3. What type of career do you want to have? Have you considered the current and future demand for people in that career? What are some economic and noneconomic factors to look at in thinking about your career?

16–7, 16–8   4. Write a paragraph describing what poverty in the United States means to you. Why does a rich country like ours have a poverty problem?

16–7, 16–8   5. Do you agree with the way our government defines poverty? Why or why not? Would it be better or worse to use a fixed income level, such as $5,000, to define poverty? Why?

16–5, 16–7 6. How is low productivity related to poverty? What does this suggest about a person getting as much training and education as possible? Should you be selective in the skills you develop, or should you develop as many as you can? Why?

16–7 7. What are some of the causes of poverty in the United States? Which do you think are the most important?

16–7 8. Use a graph of the supply and demand for labor to help explain how restrictions in the labor supply may contribute to the poverty problem. Explain how both labor unions and discrimination can affect the supply of labor for certain jobs.

16–8 9. What kinds of programs have been used to fight poverty in the United States? Which kind do you think is best? Why?

SHOULD POVERTY BE MEASURED ON AN ABSOLUTE OR A RELATIVE BASIS?

In the 1960s, Mollie Orshansky, an economist, developed the current approach for establishing the poverty level of income. She found that a typical family spent one-third of its income on food. From this she reasoned that the minimum cost of living could be calculated by multiplying a minimally adequate food budget by three. This market basket of food products is now called the "Thrifty Food Plan." Each year the poverty level determined in this way is increased by the amount of the increase in the Consumer Price Index for urban consumers (CPI-U).

This type of determination of the poverty level is an *absolute* measure. It is absolute because it defines poverty using a subsistence level of income; that is, it determines the income level on which it is possible for a family to survive. For an economy with a rising living standard and a rising average income, this kind of absolute measure causes the poverty level to fall further and further behind the average household.

A relative measure of poverty is often suggested to get around this problem of the growing gap in living standards. Over 200 years ago, Adam Smith suggested that "the custom of the country" should be used as the standard. A recent study by the Joint Economic Committee of Congress supported this type of relative measure. It recommended raising the poverty level in line with the growth in median family income.

(This discussion is based on "Counting the Poor," Federal Reserve Bank of San Francisco Weekly Letter, April 6, 1990. More details are available in this publication, which can be obtained from the Federal Reserve Bank of San Francisco.)

CHAPTER 17

UNEMPLOYMENT

Learning Objectives

17–1	Define terms related to unemployment.
17–2	Analyze the economic, social, and personal costs of unemployment.
17–3	Identify ways the government can help soften the effects of unemployment.
17–4	Explain how the unemployment rate is determined.
17–5	Describe four kinds of unemployment.

UNEMPLOYMENT: AN OVERVIEW

The Employment Act of 1946 stated that the federal government takes responsibility for full employment, price stability, and economic growth. The Act also established the President's Council of Economic Advisors. In the 1950s and 1960s, economic policy appeared to work fairly well. Inflation of less than 3 percent a year on the average was the norm, and unemployment averaged less than 5 percent. The 1970s brought quite another situation. Inflation averaged about 7.2 percent throughout the decade (it hit 11.3 percent in 1979). During the same time, unemployment averaged roughly 6.2 percent. New terms were made up to describe the economy. *Sloom* was a mix of *slump* and *boom*. *Excession* was an expansionary recession. *Stagflation* described stagnation accompanied by inflation. These terms all describe an economy that has too much unemployment and prices that are going up too fast at the same time.

Unemployment and inflation represent the most difficult economic problems our country has to face. Not long ago, economists and politicians thought that we could completely control unemployment and inflation. There was much talk of *fine tuning* the economy during the mid-1960s. But as we moved into the early 1970s, it became clear that we could not do so. At that time, inflation and unemployment rates were nearly at double-digit levels. In 1975, for example, the inflation rate was 9.1 percent, down from the 11 percent rate of the year before. And the unemployment rate climbed to a post–World War II high of 8.5 percent. By autumn 1982, national unemployment reached 10 percent. As we entered the 1990s, the unemployment rate was under 6 percent.

This chapter discusses unemployment—its causes, effects, and ways to control it. Chapter 18 covers inflation. These topics, unemployment and inflation, strongly affect the health of an economy.

Unemployment hurts the economy, the family, and society. In economic terms, unemployed persons do not add to our gross national product. The difference between GNP when everyone works and GNP when many are unemployed is the major economic cost of unemployment to the economy. This reduction in GNP means fewer goods and services available for people to consume as a result of unemployment.

17–2

But unemployment hits hardest in the home. The family suffers most when the head of the household is unemployed. When paychecks stop coming in, families must worry about how to pay the rent and the bills and how to buy food. Unhappiness and tension result. Visits to psychiatrists increase because unemployment often destroys self-respect and self-confidence. Bill collection agencies

Illustration 17–1
Unemployment hits hardest at home. Families must worry about how to pay the rent and bills and even how to buy food.

try to collect payments, which adds to the unemployed person's stress. Even after a job is found, the struggle to pay old bills goes on. Unemployment causes much personal damage that usually lasts a long time.

In addition to these economic and personal costs, there are serious social costs. Unemployment leads some people to crime in order to support themselves and their families. Others turn to crime because they have too much free time. Unemployment also causes people to do without certain medical treatments, which in turn causes a higher rate of disease.

The article on pages 350–351 appeared in daily newspapers around the country during a recent period of high unemployment. It relates many of the costs of unemployment to the American people. Because it appeared as a major news story, it also shows that people feel intensely concerned about this economic problem.

THE FEDERAL GOVERNMENT AND UNEMPLOYMENT

The damaging personal, social, and economic effects of unemployment brought about the passage of the Employment Act of 1946. This act said the following:

> The Congress hereby declares that it is the continuing policy and responsibility of the Federal Government to use all practicable means ... for the purpose of creating and maintaining ... conditions under which there will be afforded useful employment opportunities ... for those able, willing and seeking to work and to promote maximum employment, production and purchasing power.

This act required government to try to keep the economy strong enough to provide jobs for all who want them and are able to work.

The government tries to soften the unemployment effects of recession when they happen. **Recession** is the condition in which unemployment is high and GNP falls for two or more quarters. Unemployment compensation (payments to the unemployed) gives unemployed persons a minimal level of income for a certain period of time. In most states unemployment benefits last 26 weeks.

During the 1974–1975 recession, one of the worst since the 1930s, more than 6 million unemployed workers collected unemployment benefits. Unemployment compensation payments lasted up to 65 weeks because of temporary extensions. The states paid the first 26 weeks, using money from employer contributions. The states and the federal government shared the cost for the next 13 weeks. The federal government financed the final 26 weeks of payments.

Eligibility requirements and the amount of payments received differed from one state to another. However, most people who had worked for 26 weeks out of the past year could receive benefits. The Labor Department estimated that the average payment to workers was about 40 percent of those workers' previous pay. Living on 40 percent of their previous income was not easy, but it kept starvation from the door.

THE UNEMPLOYMENT RATE

Not all people without jobs rank among the unemployed. It is foolish to consider a 5-year-old or a 95-year-old unemployed. Both are probably unable to work. Usually unemployment measures the percentage of the civilian labor force that is unemployed at any given time.

The Department of Labor defines the **civilian labor force** as the total number of people in the working age group (16 years and over) who are either employed or actively seeking work. This excludes people in the armed services or in institutions such as prisons or mental hospitals. The unemployed are part of the civilian labor force. However, unemployment has a special meaning that is not the same as simply not working. The Department of Labor defines **unemployment** as the condition of those who are willing and able to work and are actively seeking work, but who do not currently work.

A 25-year-old who has enough money to live without working and is not looking for work is not unemployed. That person does not want to work and chooses not to have a job. In a sense, some

17–3
17–1
recession
The condition in which unemployment is high and GNP falls for two or more quarters.

17–1
civilian labor force
The total number of people in the working age group (16 years and over) who are either employed or actively seeking work.

17–1
unemployment
The condition of those who are willing and able to work and are actively seeking work, but who do not currently work.

THE RECESSION TAKES ITS TOLL

Americans are beginning to show the strain of the recession —emotionally as well as economically.

If past economic downturns are an indicator, mental health experts say, the stress will mean more marital and drinking problems, child abuse and even suicide attempts.

In Michigan, where unemployment is high due to auto industry layoffs and people are beginning to use up financial cushions like unemployment benefits, there already are signs of serious problems: more suicide calls, "more calls from the general public that reflect general anxiety, abuse of family members, alcohol, suicide, et cetera," agencies report.

"We've noticed a considerable increase in 'cry for help' calls," said James Kipfer, executive director of the Mental Health Association in Michigan.

These are hard times for many Americans. The unemployment rate is 7.7 percent and rising. The annual rate of inflation is running at about 11 percent—and that's an improvement.

"Historically, when financial conditions from a national perspective are tighter, we will witness an increased incidence of emotional breakdowns," said David Turkot, a clinical psychologist with Atlanta Psychological Associates.

"We can't actually blame the breakdowns on the economy, but it increases stress on people already predisposed to breakdowns."

Paul Reed, executive director of Family and Children's Service of Greater St. Louis, agreed. "Problems are surfacing...," said the head of the private counseling agency with a caseload of 15,000.

"There is more violence because of this frustration," he said. "You would like to smack the boss or the foreman, but he's not there. Then you've got the crying baby or the wife nagging the breadwinner. The natural tendency is to strike out at them."

Many psychologists and mental health counselors see evidence that the recession has undermined people's sense of well-being, an Associated Press spot survey found.

"Our professional literature and the news media are both saying that the economy is pushing thousands of people over the brink, and I believe it," said Dr. William S. Hall, head of the South Carolina Department of Mental Health.

Some people have asked to be admitted to the state's mental hospitals. "Some patients are telling us now that they have nowhere to go, no money, no jobs, and they are very depressed about the economic situation," said Dr. Karl V. Doskocil,

people who are unemployed are unemployed by choice. They could find some work, perhaps as a janitor or gas station attendant. But they remain unemployed so that they can search for work that suits their interests or qualifications. However, the Department of Labor counts them as unemployed as long as they are looking for work.

The Labor Department determines the number of unemployed from figures gathered in a monthly survey. About 50,000 households located in each of the 50 states are included. The survey determines exactly how many members of these households are working and how many are not working. People 16 years or older who did any work for pay or profit in the week before the survey count as employed. Anyone 16 years or older who looked for work in the 30 days before the survey and who is in the job market but not working counts as unemployed.

superintendent of the State Hospital in Columbia.

Turkot said patients in therapy sessions speak of more family arguments over credit cards, how vacation money should be spent and whether children should be sent to public or private colleges.

"We've seen that people are becoming obsessed with matters relating to finances," he said.

Other findings of the survey:
- In Connecticut, there has been a "marked rise" in admissions to state mental hospitals, in part because people can't afford to care for elderly relatives at home.
- At the Northeast Jackson County Mental Health Center in Kansas City, Mo., admissions are up 20 percent over last year. Executive Director Jim McKee says money problems are "creating some cracks in the family structure."
- Catholic Charities of Chicago says family counseling contacts have risen 33 percent, and while it isn't all due to the economy "there is a financial component."
- United Way funding for the Dade County Consumer Credit Counseling Program in Miami was increased to meet a 39 percent increase in demand, largely from middle- and upper-middle income families, said United Way of America spokesman Steve Delfin.
- The United Way-supported Information and Referral Service of Toledo, Ohio, is getting 1,400 calls a month—up from 400-500 a year ago—and most of the calls are related to economics, said Delfin.
- In states where there has been little or no increase in mental problems, experts say problems may show up when people are no longer distracted by vacations and are faced with big fuel bills.

Especially hard hit are the poor and almost-poor.

"These people operate marginally to begin with, not only emotionally, but financially," said Brian Heath, president of the Mental Health Association of Connecticut.

"They're barely keeping their nose above water, and when something else comes along, like a recession, these are the people who feel it first.... They don't have the resources to cushion the blow."

To help people deal with the recession, counselors at the Northeast Jackson Center in Kansas City encourage them to look for activities "they can get involved in at no cost..."

United Way agencies nationwide have increased support for family preservation and strengthening services by 27 percent — to $86.2 million. Support for crisis centers and hotlines is also up, according to Delfin.

The Bureau of Labor Statistics determines the number of employed and unemployed people using the survey data. By adding these two figures, it arrives at the total labor force. The Bureau then finds the percentage of the total labor force that is unemployed. This percentage is the unemployment rate. The **unemployment rate**, then, is the percentage of the civilian labor force that is considered unemployed.

17–4

17–1

unemployment rate
The percentage of the civilian labor force that is considered unemployed.

$$\text{Unemployment Rate} = \frac{\text{Number Unemployed}}{\text{Number in Civilian Force}}$$

351

For example, in November 1990, the civilian labor force included 124,821,000 people; 7,211,000 of them were unemployed.

$$\frac{\text{November 1990}}{\text{Unemployment Rate}} = \frac{7,211,000}{124,821,000}$$

$$= .058$$

$$= 5.8\%$$

So, the unemployment rate in November 1990 was 5.8 percent.

Some fault may be found with this method of measuring unemployment. It does not count those people who have given up looking for a job even though they might still want a job. Economists call this kind of unemployment *hidden unemployment*. The procedure also gives temporary and part-time jobs the same weight as full-time jobs. However, both government and news reports use this definition of unemployment.

Unemployment during the Great Depression rose to as high as 25 percent. However, the unemployment rate since 1950 has generally been between 3 percent and 8 percent. Most of the periods when unemployment was near 8 percent were during recessions and usually lasted for only a short time. In the 1974–75 recession, unemployment reached a high of 9.2 percent in May, 1975. In 1982, again during a recession, unemployment was more than 10 percent by the end of the year.

Illustration 17–2
Unemployment measurements do not count people who are unemployed by choice. A person must be actively seeking work in order to be considered unemployed.

Geographic Differences in Unemployment

Unemployment figures gathered by the Department of Labor include a wide geographic spread. They show that different regions of the country have different unemployment rates. The map in Figure 17–1 shows how the unemployment rate differs from one state to another. Official unemployment rates are even given for some 150 smaller but important labor areas. In the smaller area data, some labor markets are nearly always well below the national rate of unemployment. Other areas are usually above the national rate.

FIGURE 17–1   UNEMPLOYMENT FIGURES IN THE UNITED STATES FOR 1989

The average unemployment rate for the entire country in 1989 was 5.3 percent. However, note the different percentages in each state. What economic and social factors would make unemployment higher or lower in one area of the country over another?

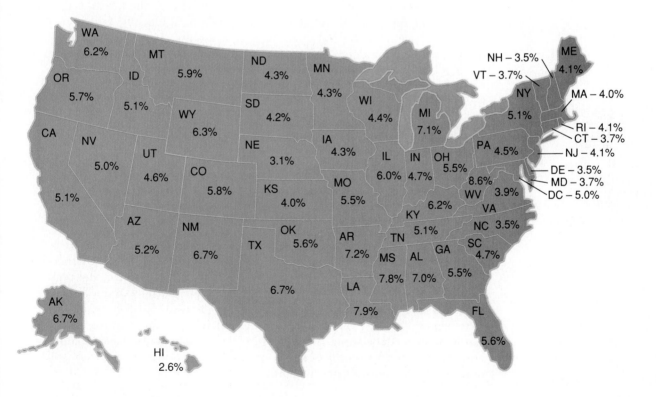

Source: U.S. Bureau of the Census, *Statistical Abstract of the United States: 1991*, 111th ed. (Washington, D.C., 1991), 387.

JUANITA KREPS

Juanita Kreps was born in Kentucky in 1921. She studied economics at Berea College and earned her doctoral degree at Duke University. She taught economics at Denison University, Hofstra University, Queens College (New York), and Duke University. In 1973 she was appointed James B. Duke Professor of Economics at Duke University. She also became a vice-president of that university.

Kreps has been active in many fields outside of teaching. She has served on the board of directors of the National Council on Aging, the Educational Testing Service, and the National Merit Scholarship Corporation. In 1972 she became the first female director of the New York Stock Exchange. She has also served on the boards of several large corporations such as Eastman Kodak, J.C. Penney, American Telephone & Telegraph Co., and United Airlines.

Kreps has written extensively on major economic issues. She coauthored *Contemporary Labor Economics* and *Principles of Economics*, textbooks used by many colleges. She has researched many topics in the fields of demography and labor force change, economics of aging and discrimination issues. Kreps published a book on women in the labor force entitled *Sex in the Marketplace: American Women at Work*. Her book, *Sex, Age, and Work*, which she wrote in 1975 with Robert Clark, expanded on this subject.

Kreps is probably best known as Secretary of Commerce during the Carter administration. As a member of the President's Cabinet, she influenced international trade policy, economic development and environmental regulations. She now serves as a Trustee of the Duke Endowment and a director of several major corporations. She continues to write and lecture on current economic issues. In 1982 she was elected vice-president of the American Economic Association. A member of the Council on Foreign Relations and the Trilateral Commission, she is also the recipient of a dozen honorary degrees from colleges and universities.

Unemployment Differences by Age, Race, and Gender

Look at Table 17–1 before reading further. You can see that unemployment rates are different for different groups of people. Young people between the ages of 16 and 19 are hit hardest by unemployment. Their unemployment rate often runs three times greater than the general unemployment rate. The unemployment rate among nonwhite workers is the next highest—about twice as high as the general unemployment rate.

There are many explanations for the differences in unemployment rates by gender, age, and race. The relative skill and educational levels of the groups cause differences in unemployment rates among different age groups. Skill and education may contribute to higher rates for gender and racial differences as well. But much of the problem in these cases stems from discriminatory patterns with deep historical roots. Fortunately these discriminatory patterns are changing even if slowly.

By closely examining statistical data, such as the data presented in Table 17–1, we can learn a lot about who is unemployed. We can also learn about long-term employment trends when we examine the employment rates for different groups of workers over time.

TABLE 17–1

UNITED STATES UNEMPLOYMENT RATES FOR
SELECTED YEARS BY GENDER, AGE, AND RACE
1960 TO 1990
(Civilian Workers)

Years	All Workers	Workers 16–19	Male Workers 20 or Older	Female Workers 20 or Older	White Workers	Nonwhite Workers
1960	5.5%	14.7%	4.7%	5.1%	4.9%	10.2%
1965	4.5%	14.8%	3.2%	4.5%	4.1%	8.1%
1970	4.9%	15.3%	3.5%	4.8%	4.5%	8.2%
1975	8.5%	19.9%	6.8%	8.0%	7.8%	13.8%
1980	7.1%	17.8%	5.9%	6.4%	6.3%	13.1%
1985	7.2%	18.6%	6.2%	6.6%	6.2%	13.7%
1990	5.5%	15.5%	4.9%	4.8%	4.7%	10.1%

Source: *Economic Report of the President 1991* (Washington, D.C.: U.S. Government Printing Office, 1991), 330.

KINDS OF UNEMPLOYMENT

All unemployment is not the same. Unemployment can be divided into four kinds. These divisions can help us better understand the causes of unemployment. Then programs can be planned to help ease the burden caused by unemployment. As you will see, some kinds of unemployment are not as important as others.

Structural Unemployment

17–5

17–1

structural unemployment
Unemployment resulting from skills that do not match what employers require or from being geographically separated from job opportunities.

Structural unemployment is unemployment resulting from skills that do not match what employers require or from being geographically separated from job opportunities. One form of structural unemployment results when people remain unemployed because they are not qualified for the available jobs. In our complex society, very few jobs exist for those who cannot read or do simple arithmetic, or who are badly handicapped. However, not only the uneducated or handicapped find that their qualifications do not match the jobs available. For example, a NASA engineer has highly specialized skills in rocket building. Such a person may find that no jobs call for those skills, either because of less demand for rockets or a change in the skills needed in rocket production. Economists consider this kind of unemployment to be structural unemployment. It represents a mismatch between workers' skills and the skills needed in the economy.

Illustration 17–3
People who have highly specialized skills may experience structural unemployment.

Another kind of structural unemployment occurs when there are jobs in one part of the country but the people with the skills for those jobs live somewhere else. In general, people do not like to move. The costs of moving, fear of the unknown, and family ties make moving very difficult. If labor moved more easily from place to place, the unemployment rate would even out throughout the United States. However, as the map in Figure 17–1 shows, the rate of unemployment differs from state to state. There are even greater differences between cities. Since both skill and location problems are generally long-term, structural unemployment is perhaps the most serious form of unemployment.

Cyclical Unemployment

Cyclical unemployment is unemployment resulting from too low a level of aggregate demand. Another name for cyclical unemployment is *demand deficiency unemployment*. The unemployment of the 1974–75 recession and the early 1980s arose partly from demand deficiency unemployment. Demand deficiency unemployment results from too little demand for goods and services in the economy. As you know, the demand for goods and services means low demand for labor. Remember that the demand for labor is a *derived demand*. It is derived from the demand for goods and services. There was a time after the 1930s until about 1970 when economists believed it was possible to eliminate this kind of unemployment. More recently this idea has become less accepted.

17–5
17–1
cyclical unemployment
Unemployment resulting from too low a level of aggregate demand.

Frictional Unemployment

Some people are unemployed because they cannot, at present, find work that matches their qualifications. For example, think of a class of vocational-technical students. When they finish school, they will look for jobs that use their skills, but finding such jobs may take time.

17–5

However, since the skills are useful, the students are likely to find jobs fairly soon. Their unemployment is temporary. Economists refer to this kind of unemployment as frictional unemployment. **Frictional unemployment** is unemployment of people who are temporarily between jobs. Between 3 and 5 percent of all unemployment is probably frictional. Another example of frictional unemployment is in the case of an employee who has an argument with the boss and quits. Until another job is found, the person is unemployed. Because such unemployment is temporary, it is not of much concern when dealing with the national unemployment problem.

17–1
frictional unemployment
Unemployment of people who are temporarily between jobs.

Seasonal Unemployment

17–5

Seasonal unemployment is unemployment of people who are out of work because of factors that vary with the time of year. People are often unemployed because their jobs depend on seasonal factors. For example, many people in ski resort areas will be unemployed when there is no snow. Farm workers also suffer seasonal unemployment because few crops need to be harvested or planted in the winter. Work in the food processing industry is also seasonal. Many workers join forces to can tomatoes, peaches, pickles, and other foods during the summer months. But during the rest of the year, food-processing plants hire only a few workers. Thus, many of them lose their jobs until the next season. This kind of unemployment is usually short-term and so it, too, is not the subject of much government unemployment policy.

**17–1
seasonal
unemployment**
Unemployment of
people who are out of
work because of factors
that vary with the time
of year.

REDUCING UNEMPLOYMENT

17–3

There are several ways to reduce unemployment. In general, economists and politicians do not worry about frictional and seasonal unemployment. In fact, they usually define **full employment** as the employment of about 95 percent of the labor force (allowing about 5 percent for frictional and seasonal unemployment).

Structural unemployment, which results from lack of needed skills or from problems in geographical location, is a more serious and difficult problem. One way to counteract this problem involves education and training (or re-education and retraining) of these workers. Programs organized by the Office of Economic Opportunity or programs sponsored by agencies such as Goodwill are examples of this kind of approach. Colleges and universities even help faculty members retrain in order to keep their jobs.

Another way to reduce unemployment is to lower the skill requirements for specific jobs. For example, many employers will not hire an applicant who has no high school diploma. But often the actual skills needed for a job may not include a passing grade in Senior English or World History. However, the applicants are barred from the jobs because they do not have the qualifications, even though those qualifications may not be needed to do the work. Labor unions share part of the blame for this problem. Restricted entry into union jobs, unnecessarily long apprenticeships, and pressure for higher wages without increased productivity are examples of ways unions may contribute to unemployment.

A third way to reduce structural unemployment would be to lower the minimum wage. Minimum wage rates add to structural unemployment because they block many workers from the labor

**17–1
full employment**
The employment of
about 95 percent of the
labor force.

Illustration 17–4
A person who works at
a ski resort may be
unemployed during the
months that there is no
snow on the ground.

market. They also discourage on-the-job training programs. Even unskilled and unproductive workers must be paid the minimum wage if they are hired. If employers could pay such workers lower rates during their training (when they are unproductive), they might soon become more productive workers and deserve a pay increase. A reduction in racial and gender discrimination can also reduce structural unemployment.

Demand deficiency or cyclical unemployment is usually to blame when the unemployment rate rises. Several methods which increase total level of aggregate demand can deal with this type of unemployment. We will look at these in detail when we discuss monetary policy and fiscal policy.

On the brighter side, today's economy employs more people than ever before, as shown in Table 17–2. The first column shows the number of people age 16 years and over employed in the economy. You can see that more and more people have jobs in each year shown. At some times the number of people employed has dropped from one year to the next. (For example, between 1981 and 1982, the number dropped from 100,397,000 to 99,526,000.) However, the overall trend has been upward.

The second column of Table 17–2 shows the percent of people 16 years and over who are employed. This number has fluctuated over the years but has generally risen. The first year that over 60 percent of this age group was employed was 1985.

Not only are more people employed today, but people also have greater total buying power. Their standard of living has improved greatly. Despite unemployment, the economy as a whole has provided a comfortable and even luxurious standard of living for most Americans.

TABLE 17–2

CIVILIAN EMPLOYMENT AND EMPLOYMENT RATES
IN THE UNITED STATES
(For Ages 16 and Over)

	Number Employed	Percent Employed
1960	65,778,000	56.1%
1965	71,088,000	56.2%
1970	78,678,000	57.4%
1975	85,846,000	56.1%
1980	99,303,000	59.2%
1985	107,150,000	60.1%
1990	117,914,000	62.7%

Source: *Economic Report of the President 1991* (Washington, D.C.: U.S. Government Printing Office, 1991), 332.

Illustration 17–5
One way to reduce structural unemployment is to train people to work in fields where the most jobs exist.

Historically, we have been greatly influenced by the work ethic. Americans believe that worthwhile people work and pull their own weight. Because of technological advances, the productivity of each worker has greatly increased. In fact, in the future we may be able to maintain our standard of living with increasingly smaller numbers of workers. Also, it may become increasingly difficult for our economy to supply enough jobs for all potential workers.

Economist Arthur M. Okun estimated that the United States economy must grow at least 4 percent a year in real terms just to keep the unemployment rate from rising. One percent of this growth is necessary because the labor force has been increasing by about 1 percent a year. The other 3 percent is needed because American workers have increased their productivity by about 3 percent a year. Okun also found that for each percentage point that real GNP increases above 4 percent, the unemployment rate falls roughly one third of a percent. For the high unemployment rate of 10.8 percent in late 1982, it would have taken a 21.4 percent increase in GNP to bring unemployment down to 5 percent. This high rate of growth is difficult, if not impossible, to maintain. You can see why it takes a long time to get the unemployment rate down once it rises.

The future may bring three- and four-day workweeks, split shifts, and job sharing. There may even be an increase in voluntary unemployment. It may be necessary for Americans to change their values. We may have to stop thinking of people as less worthy because they do not work a 40-hour week at a traditional job. There may be more public service jobs, such as cleaning up a public park, for people not employed in traditional jobs.

REVIEWING THE CHAPTER

17–2   1. Unemployment has several costs. There is a loss of output when people are unemployed. This costs society because there are fewer goods and services for consumption. There are also social and personal costs due to unemployment. These social and personal costs can be long lasting and very damaging.

17–3   2. The Employment Act of 1946 made it a responsibility of the government to try to keep the economy operating at full employment. In addition, this act gave the government responsibility for keeping the purchasing power of our money stable. That is, inflation should be avoided.

17–4   3. The number of unemployed people 16 years of age and over is determined by a monthly survey of about 50,000 households. The unemployment rate is found by dividing the number of unemployed persons by the civilian labor force. The unemployment rate is reported frequently in the news and is the focal point of much public attention.

17–4   4. Unemployment does not spread evenly among different groups of people. There is considerable variation in unemployment rates among states and among smaller labor markets. Also, young people, nonwhite workers, and women are hard hit by unemployment.

17–5   5. There are four major types of unemployment: structural, cyclical, frictional, and seasonal. The first two are of more social concern because they usually last longer. Most public attention is focused on the structural and cyclical types of unemployment.

17–3   6. Programs to help soften the hurt of unemployment are conducted by state, local, and federal government agencies. Some programs give financial aid to the unemployed, and some help people learn skills that are in greater demand in the economy.

REVIEWING ECONOMIC TERMS

17–1   Supply definitions for the following terms:

recession

civilian labor force

unemployment

unemployment rate

structural unemployment

cyclical unemployment

frictional unemployment

seasonal unemployment

full employment

REVIEWING ECONOMIC CONCEPTS

17–3   1. What did the Employment Act of 1946 require government to do?

17–2   2. What is the major economic cost of unemployment?

17–2   3. What are the major social costs of unemployment?

17–2   4. What are the major personal costs of unemployment?

17–4   5. How is the unemployment rate determined?

17–4   6. Which groups of people are most likely to be unemployed?

17–5   7. Of the four kinds of unemployment, which two usually receive the most public attention? Why?

17–3   8. Identify four ways of reducing unemployment.

APPLYING ECONOMIC CONCEPTS

17–4   1. List several characteristics that you think would increase a person's chances of being unemployed. Explain your choice of each characteristic. Can you suggest some ways to change these factors or to reduce their effect?

17–5   2. Explain each of the four types of unemployment presented in the text. Give at least one example of each type.

17–2   3. "We must change our attitudes toward unemployment. Since the economy may not be able to provide jobs for everyone who wants one, we must stop measuring people's worth by their work." Do you agree or disagree with this statement? Explain your answer.

17–4   4. Determine what the current unemployment rate is and whether it has gone up or down in recent months. (For this task, you will need to find current statistics on population and employment from an economic or government publication.)

17–3   5. How does the government help to soften the effects of unemployment? What kind of unemployment program do you think is best? Why?

17–2   6. Write an essay in which you summarize the economic, social, and personal costs of unemployment. Which of these do you consider the most severe? Why?

CHAPTER 18

INFLATION

Learning Objectives

WHAT IS INFLATION?

18–1   A sustained rise in the general level of prices is called *inflation*. During an inflationary period, the average level of prices rises. However, some prices may fall. For example, during recent inflationary periods, the price of small calculators fell while most other prices rose rapidly. In an inflationary period, however, rising prices outweigh falling prices. An upward movement of the general, or average, price level results. We often call this a *rise in the cost of living*.

Inflation causes uncertainty in the marketplace for both consumers and businesses. Shortly after World War I, Germany fell victim to runaway inflation. Prices were so uncertain that people in restaurants paid the bill as they ordered rather than paying when they finished eating. If they had waited, prices might have gone up. People wanted to be paid at the end of each day's work so they could spend their money before prices rose. Money lost its value so quickly that people would no longer use it as a medium of exchange. During this period, Germany suffered from extreme inflation. The uncertainty it produced was devastating to the German economy.

Less extreme inflation of perhaps 2 percent to 3 percent can actually stimulate an economy. During a mildly inflationary period, wages often rise more slowly than the prices of the products. This means that the price for products sold is high in relation to the cost of labor. The producer makes higher real profits and tends to expand production and hire more people. The newly employed workers increase spending, and the total demand in the economy goes up. This results in increased economic growth and prosperity.

If inflation rises to higher levels, however, it may contribute to unemployment. Slowly rising wages mean that workers' incomes are less in real terms, and so they buy fewer goods. As workers make fewer purchases, the total demand in the economy will fall. This falling demand, then, may result in unemployment. If wages go up faster than prices, businesses tend to hire less labor and so unemployment worsens.

Economists also argue that inflation distorts the economic system. It causes prices to increase, and they do not often increase evenly. All goods do not have the same rate of inflation. Consumers and producers react to price changes by buying and producing different amounts of goods. Thus, the distribution pattern of goods and the allocation of resources changes. It is hard to say for sure whether these changes lead to a less or more efficient economy. But the pattern of allocation clearly can be changed by inflation and many economists believe that this lowers economic efficiency.

Inflation may also lead to speculation, especially when prices increase rapidly for particular commodities. Speculation occurs when some people buy large amounts of a good and hope to resell it at a much higher price. For example, during one period the price of antifreeze rose rapidly. Many people stocked their garages with antifreeze, intending to sell it later at a high profit. This type of speculation is generally nonproductive and causes distortions in the market distribution of goods. In the case of antifreeze, the price did not go up much more, and people were stuck with large amounts of antifreeze. In the meantime, they lost the use of the money that went for the speculation.

INFLATION: WHO BENEFITS? WHO IS HURT?

Let's consider how inflation affects different groups of people. Inflation helps people whose incomes rise faster than the rate of inflation. For example, if a union can negotiate a pay increase that exceeds the rate of inflation, the union's members will benefit. However, this gain may be short-lived. The higher wages will result in higher prices. Then other workers will get higher wages, which will result in more price increases. This cycle continues on and on.

Debtors also benefit from inflation. The money they pay back at a later date actually has a lower value than the money they borrowed. Consider mortgage payments. A fixed mortgage payment starting in 1967 may have been only $140 a month. One hundred forty dollars a month is quite a bargain in today's housing market! The mortgage payments on the same home bought today might be about $800 a month.

People who own property or assets that gain value at a faster rate than the rate of inflation also benefit. For example, suppose you own real estate that increases 10 percent a year in value, while the rate of inflation is 5 percent a year. You are better off and less harmed by inflation than those who do not hold similar assets. Homeowners gain in at least two ways by inflation. Homes generally appreciate more rapidly than the general level of price increases. Also, homeowners often pay a constant dollar amount for the mortgage payment. Therefore, in real terms (or in buying power), the homeowner pays less each year. In recent years there has been a move to make mortgage payments change over time. In times of inflation this helps lenders but discourages borrowers.

People on a **fixed income** (income that is set and does not change from year to year) are hurt the most by inflation. For example, if your retirement pension check is fixed at $9,600 per year, inflation could greatly damage your spending power. If the rate of

Illustration 18–1
Inflation may lead to speculation.

18–2

18–1
fixed income
Income that is set and does not change from year to year.

18–3

365

Illustration 18–2   Inflation may actually benefit a family who purchased a home many years ago, because the mortgage payments they make at today's prices seem low. But inflation greatly harms people on fixed incomes (such as pension or retirement benefits), who must struggle to purchase the same needed goods with money that is worth less and less.

inflation is 5 percent per year, what you could purchase for $9,600 one year would cost $10,080 a year later. (The $10,080 is obtained by multiplying $9,600 by 1.05.) Each year you would be able to buy fewer goods on that $9,600 income.

Many workers retiring today face this problem. Their retirement programs began 30 or more years ago when a given income could buy much more. What was a good income at one time provides only limited buying power in retirement years. Many retirement and insurance programs as well as Social Security benefits now have cost-of-living adjustments. That is, they have automatic increases that protect against inflation to help reduce this problem of inadequate retirement income. People on semi-fixed incomes, or whose incomes are not adjusted often, can also be hurt by inflation.

Inflation also hurts people who have money in the bank or people who are creditors. Suppose you have money in a savings account that pays a 5 percent rate of interest and there is a 4 percent rate of inflation. All but 1 percent of your earnings are eaten away by inflation. If inflation is greater than the interest rate you receive, you actually lose buying power by having your money in that savings account. Creditors (people who have loaned money to others) such as savings and loans, banks, and credit unions can also be hurt by inflation. The money that debtors (people who have borrowed) pay back in the future is worth less than the money that was originally lent.

Perhaps most importantly, many economists think that high inflation can lead to a high rate of unemployment. Businesses do not run as well in an unstable economy as in a stable one. With high inflation, businesses find it hard to plan their production. Business growth is slower, fewer goods are produced, and fewer workers are hired. This means that the unemployment rate will likely go up. People could lose their jobs due to inflation. Or those already unemployed would have less chance of finding a job. In this way, inflation hurts nearly everyone. This is why so many people speak of the need to control inflation both in our country and in other countries.

MEASURING INFLATION: THE CPI

Inflation is usually measured by using price indexes. A **price index** is a number that compares prices in one year with some earlier base year. There are many different kinds of price indexes. These include specific price indexes for particular industries, as well as the Producer Price Index (PPI) and the Consumer Price Index (CPI). These are calculated by the United States Labor Department's Bureau of Labor Statistics. The **Consumer Price Index (CPI)** is a number used to compare the average level of prices for a number of typical items bought by urban families. For example, using 1982–1984 as the base period, the Consumer Price Index in 1990 was 130.7. This means that prices in 1990 were 130.7 percent of prices in the base period. Take the cost of a consumer good worth $50 in the base period and multiply it by 130.7 percent (1.307). You would then have a rough idea of the cost of the same good in 1990. This would be:

$$\$50 \times 1.307 = \$65.35$$

The Consumer Price Index does not include every good and service produced in the economy. Instead, the Bureau of Labor Statistics chooses about 400 items that seem most crucial to families' spending. These represent the goods and services that would be bought by typical city households. (Urban residents comprise about 80 percent of the population.) The Bureau sends people to several thousand retail stores and service establishments to find out the prices for each of these 400 items. The price for each item is averaged. The influence that each item has on the Consumer Price Index is found by a weighting process. This process is based on the importance of each item to families as determined by the fraction of their total spending that goes for that item. For example, families spend about 18 percent of their income on food. So, food prices make up about 18 percent of the final Consumer Price Index. The way in which different items are weighted in the CPI is shown in Table 18–1. You can see from the table that housing makes up 42 percent, and medical care makes up 6.2 percent of total expenditures.

18–1

price index
A number that compares prices in one year with some earlier base year.

18–1

Consumer Price Index (CPI)
A number used to compare the average level of prices for a number of typical items bought by urban families.

18–4

TABLE 18–1

THE MAKE-UP OF THE CONSUMER PRICE INDEX:
RELATIVE IMPORTANCE BY CATEGORY
(Breakdown for the "All Urban Consumers" CPI)

All Items 100.0

Food and Beverage
    Food at home 10.1
    Food away from home 6.1
    Alcoholic beverages 1.5
        Total Food and Beverages 17.7

Housing
    Renter's cost... 7.9
    Homeowner's cost.. 19.5
    Maintenance and repairs 0.2
    Fuel oil, coal, bottled gas 0.5
    Gas, electricity 3.6
    Other utilities... 3.2
    Furnishings and operation 6.4
        Total Housing.. 41.3

Apparel and Upkeep
    Commodities... 5.5
    Services... 0.6
        Total Apparel and Upkeep 6.1

Transportation
    Private 16.2
        New vehicles 5.0
        Used cars.................................. 1.1
        Motor fuel.................................. 4.1
        Maintenance and repairs............ 1.5
        Other... 4.5
    Public 1.6
        Total Transportation.............................. 17.8

Medical Care
    Commodities... 1.2
    Services... 5.2
        Total Medical Care 6.4

Entertainment... 4.3

Other Items... 6.4

Total of Primary Categories.. 100.0

Source: U.S. Department of Labor, *CPI Detailed Report: May 1991* (Washington, D.C., 1991), 7–8.

Note: These percentages change slowly over time as our pattern of consumption changes. If your library has the most recent *CPI Detailed Report,* you might want to look at it to see what changes have occurred. Parts may not sum to totals owing to rounding.

Once the price of the set of 400 items is determined each year, it is compared to prices in the base period. The other years are given as a percentage of the base period. For example, in Table 18–2, 1982–1984 is the base period. You can see in Table 18–2 that the CPI for 1946 was 19.5. This means that in 1946, prices were only 19.5 percent of prices in the base period. In 1985, prices were 107.6 percent of 1982–1984 prices and, as you saw earlier, prices in 1990 were 130.7 percent of 1982–1984 prices. The numbers in Table 18–2 show how the CPI has increased over the years.

TABLE 18–2

CONSUMER PRICE INDEX FOR SELECTED YEARS
WITH 1982–1984 AS THE BASE YEAR
(1982–1984 = 100)

Year	CPI	Year	CPI
1946	19.5	1978	65.2
1950	24.1	1979	72.6
1955	26.8	1980	82.4
1960	29.6	1981	90.9
1965	31.5	1982	96.5
1970	38.8	1983	99.6
1971	40.5	1984	103.9
1972	41.8	1985	107.6
1973	44.4	1986	109.6
1974	49.3	1987	113.6
1975	53.8	1988	118.3
1976	56.9	1989	124.0
1977	60.6	1990	130.7

Source: *Economic Report of the President 1991* (Washington, D.C.: U.S. Government Printing Office, 1991), 351.

Using the CPI to Find the Rate of Inflation

The Consumer Price Index can be used to find the rate of infla-   18–5
tion. To figure the rate of inflation between two years, take the CPI for the earlier year and subtract it from the CPI for the more recent year. This gives the percentage of inflation for that time period in terms of the base year. However, you will more likely want to know the rate of increase in prices between the two years. That is, you usually want to know the rate of inflation over just those years. To do this, you must divide the difference between the price indexes by the first year's price index. For example, look at Table 18–2 for the price indexes in 1989 and 1990. You see that it

was 124.0 in 1989 and 130.7 in 1990. To find the rate of inflation between 1989 and 1990, subtract 124.0 from 130.7 and divide the difference by 124.0.

$$\text{Rate of Inflation} = \frac{\text{More Recent Year's Price Index} - \text{Earlier Year's Price Index}}{\text{Earlier Year's Price Index}}$$

$$\text{1990 Rate of Inflation} = \frac{\text{1990 Price Index} - \text{1989 Price Index}}{\text{1989 Price Index}}$$

$$= \frac{130.7 - 124.0}{124.0}$$

$$= \frac{6.7}{124.0}$$

$$= .054$$

$$= 5.4\%$$

In this calculation, 130.7 is the 1990 CPI, 124.0 is the 1989 CPI, and 5.4 percent is the rate of inflation between the two years.

The inflation rate in the United States has varied considerably from year to year. The graph in Figure 18–1 will help you to see this. Note that in the early 1960s, inflation was less than 2 percent per year. Since that time there have been ups and downs but we have not been able to get the inflation rate back under 2 percent.

Limitations of the CPI

18–6   The Consumer Price Index must be used carefully for several reasons. First, even though the CPI is often called the *cost-of-living index,* it doesn't measure the *cost of living* for any one person. It is unlikely that your market basket of goods exactly matches the one chosen by the Bureau of Labor Statistics. Therefore, the Bureau's figures on the rate of inflation will not apply exactly to you. This is especially true of farm workers and people with a fixed housing payment.

Second, the CPI includes only those items that can be bought and sold in the market. It does not include such factors as taxes or government services. And third, price indexes do not account for changes in the *quality* of goods. For example, compare a television set made in 1960 with a new television. The new set may have cost

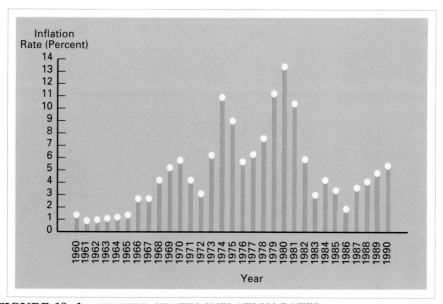

FIGURE 18–1   UNITED STATES INFLATION RATES
In the early 1960s inflation was less than 2 percent per year. Since that time there
have been wide variations in the inflation rate.

Source: Calculated from data in the *Economic Report of the President 1991* (Washington, D.C.:
U.S. Government Printing Office, 1991), 355.

more, but are the two sets the same? Part of the increase in price
reflects better quality. As you might think, it is difficult to measure
what percentage of a price increase results from improved quality
and what percentage is due to inflation.

Inflation for Particular Goods

The rate of inflation varies among certain kinds of goods. If
you spend most of your money on items with lower price increases,
you will not be affected as much by inflation. However, if you
spend a higher percentage of your income on food, housing, or
medical services, you may suffer more than the urban family that
the CPI represents. To help see the different effects of inflation,
look at the price indexes in Table 18–3 on page 372 for different
types of expenditures.

These price indexes are based on 1982–1984 prices. (They all
equaled 100.00 in 1982–1984.) You see that since 1980 shelter and
medical care have contributed most to inflation. Prices for transportation and apparel have increased less rapidly than the general
level of prices as measured by the Consumer Price Index since 1980.

TABLE 18–3

PRICE INDEXES FOR SELECTED GOODS AND SERVICES
1950–1990
(1982–1984 = 100)

Year	Overall	Food	Shelter	Transportation	Medical Care	Apparel
1950	24.1	25.4	NA	22.7	15.1	40.3
1955	26.8	27.8	22.7	25.8	18.2	42.9
1960	29.6	30.0	25.2	29.8	29.8	45.7
1965	31.5	32.2	27.0	31.9	31.9	47.8
1970	38.8	39.2	35.5	37.5	37.5	59.2
1975	53.8	59.8	48.8	50.1	50.1	72.5
1980	82.4	86.8	81.0	83.1	83.1	90.9
1982–1984	100.0	100.0	100.0	100.0	100.0	100.0
1985	107.6	105.6	109.8	106.4	113.5	105.0
1990	130.7	132.4	140.0	120.5	162.8	124.1

Source: *Economic Report of the President 1991* (Washington, D.C.: U.S. Government Printing Office, 1991), 351.

Inflation Is a Problem in Other Countries, Too

Figure 18–2 shows the rate of inflation for several countries. The inflation shown is the average rate in each country for a recent year. These averages hide some of the big differences over the period as well as between different classes of goods. You can see from the numbers in Figure 18–2 that inflation varies a good deal among countries and that it is a world-wide problem. For some countries, inflation is so high that the values would be off the scale of the graph in Figure 18–2. For example, in the same year, inflation was 114.2 percent in Mexico and 682.3 in Brazil.

DEMAND-PULL INFLATION

18–1
demand-pull inflation

A rise in the general level of prices caused by too high a level of aggregate demand in relation to aggregate supply.

Inflationary pressures in the economy are often separated into two kinds based on their causes. First we will look at demand-pull inflation. **Demand-pull inflation** is a rise in the general level of prices caused by too high a level of aggregate demand in relation to aggregate supply. The phrase *too many dollars chasing too few goods* is often used to describe this kind of inflation. *Too many dollars*

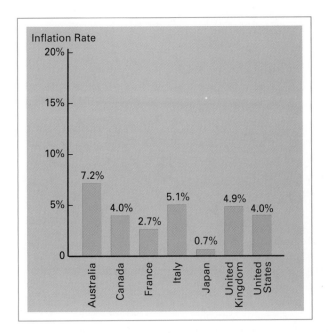

FIGURE 18–2   INFLATION RATES IN THE UNITED STATES AND SELECTED OTHER COUNTRIES FOR A RECENT YEAR
Inflation is a worldwide problem.

Source: U.S. Bureau of the Census, *Statistical Abstract of the United States: 1990*, 110th ed. (Washington, D.C.: U.S. Government Printing Office, 1990), 846.

means that the total demand in the economy is too high. *Too few goods* means that the total supply in the economy is too low in relation to that demand. Figure 18–3 illustrates demand-pull inflation.

The original aggregate demand and supply curves represent the level of demand and supply at some beginning point in time. The new demand curve shows the increase in demand that occurs during some period. The new supply curve shows a small increase in the total supply of goods during the same time. Notice that the increase in demand exceeds the increase in supply. You can see the amount of increase by comparing the distance between the original and new curves.

The equilibrium average price level of goods at the beginning of the period is at CPI_1. This is at the level where the original demand and original supply curves cross. CPI_2 represents the equilibrium average price level after the inflationary pressures of rising demand have been felt. The price level goes up from CPI_1 to CPI_2. In other words, inflation occurs.

Typically, demand-pull inflation has accompanied the ends of wars and military conflicts. The large amounts of resources tied up in fighting wars can cause large increases in demand when resources return to the civilian economy. The inflation in 1947–48 following World War II, the inflation in 1950 following the Korean conflict, and the inflation from 1965 through the early 1970s are all examples of demand-pull inflation.

The inflation from 1965 to 1970, however, differed from the other two examples. During World War II and the Korean conflict,

Illustration 18–3
When cabbage patch dolls became very popular in the mid-1980s, demand was high enough to pull the price up.

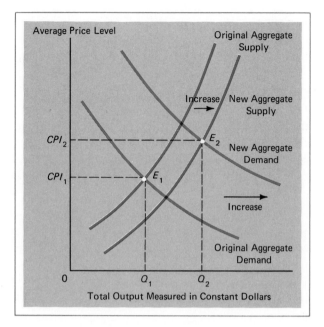

FIGURE 18–3   DEMAND-PULL INFLA-
TION
When aggregate demand increases more rapidly
than aggregate supply, the equilibrium moves
from E_1 to E_2. The average price level goes up
from CPI_1 to CPI_2.

total demand in the economy was kept low. Funds for the war
effort were taken out of the domestic economy. The ration books
and product shortages of World War II were signs of unsatisfied
consumer demand. However, during the Vietnam conflict high
defense spending was accompanied by continued high consumer
demand. There was also increased government spending on President Johnson's Great Society social programs. Much of this spending was financed by increasing the National Debt. The result: a
steady increase in inflation during the years of the Vietnam War.

Between 1966 and 1967, consumer prices rose an average of
only 2.9 percent. But between 1967 and 1968, the increase was
4.2 percent. By 1970, the economy had edged into a recession. In
December of that year unemployment reached a level of 6.2 percent. Unemployment typically results in decreasing demand, since
unemployed persons don't have as much money to spend as when
they were employed. The decreasing demand usually eases the
pressure of demand-pull inflation, and the inflation rate falls. But
inflation did not go down in 1970—it was 5.9 percent. We faced
instead the twin problems of inflation and recession. Of course,
later in the 1970s and in the early 1980s, a 4.2 percent rate of inflation would seem low.

18–1

cost-push inflation

A rise in the general
level of prices that is
caused by increased
costs of making and
selling goods.

COST-PUSH INFLATION

Economists explained that this continuing inflation was partially
made up of a second kind—cost-push inflation. **Cost-push inflation**

is a rise in the general level of prices that is caused by increased costs of making and selling goods. Cost-push inflation does not result from pressures on demand. Instead, the pressures are on the supply side. The inflation of the late 1960s put pressures on many of the costs of making industrial products. Workers and unions demanded pay increases to make up for real income they had lost to inflation during that period. Unions and laborers had come to expect inflation, so they negotiated cost-of-living increases in their contracts. As a result, the costs of labor continued to rise. Other business costs also rose during this period, and these rising costs contributed to price increases paid by consumers.

There is another factor that may have contributed to the cost-push inflation, but it is hard to prove. This factor is the increased concentration of economic power in the hands of a few companies and labor unions. Large, strong companies and unions can increase prices and wages if they have little competition. The costs of these higher prices and wages are paid by consumers and add to inflationary pressures.

Cost-push inflation can be explained by a graph such as the one in Figure 18–4. The demand curve in that figure represents the total demand in the economy. The original supply curve represents the total supply of goods in the economy at one point in time. The equilibrium price is at the level CPI_1. Suppose that something happens to cause production costs to rise. For example, perhaps raw material, energy, or labor costs go up. As costs go up, companies can afford to produce less at each price level. Therefore,

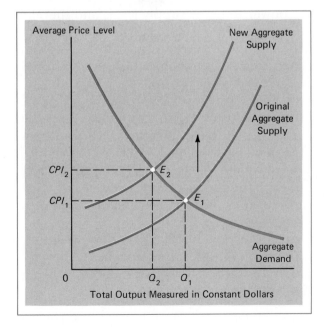

FIGURE 18–4   COST-PUSH INFLATION
An increase in production costs will shift the aggregate supply curve up. The equilibrium moves from E_1 to E_2 and the average price level goes up from CPI_1 to CPI_2.

the supply curve shifts to the left or upward to the position of the new supply curve in the diagram. This results in the increase of the equilibrium price to the level CPI_2.

Not all economists agree on the role cost-push inflation plays in the economy. High rates of inflation during periods of unemployment does point to its possible existence. Some economists think that cost-push inflation may cause a continuing type of inflation. When higher costs cause prices to rise, the level of output may decrease. Look at Figure 18–4. At the equilibrium level E_2, the amount produced (Q_2) is less than the amount produced at the equilibrium level E_1 (Q_1). This happens because at the higher price, people are willing and able to buy fewer of the goods. The reduction in output may cause unemployment. Government economists often interpret the unemployment as a sign that total demand is too low. They then might take steps to increase demand and thus cause demand-pull inflation. The demand-pull inflation might start another round of cost-push inflation, and the cycle would go on and on.

CAN INFLATION BE CONTROLLED?

18–7   We try to control demand-pull inflation largely through monetary and fiscal policy. These will be discussed in detail in Chapters 20 and 22. The battle against cost-push inflation is a hard one. To control this type of inflation, the supplies of all resources must be free from any artificial limits. Big companies and big unions must not have the power to lower supply levels and thereby artificially increase input costs. Supplies must be free to change in response to changes in demand. However, to free supplies from artificial controls is a hard, if not impossible, task. The United States cannot control the OPEC suppliers of oil, for instance. The concentration of economic power in a few large companies may be hard to correct using the present antitrust legislation. And the power of large unions often proves hard to control. To stop cost-push inflation, the government must support policies that reduce the control over important raw materials by special interest groups. Such policies might include strongly enforcing present antitrust laws and passing stronger antitrust laws. Government might also pass laws to limit the power of unions.

Inflation is a real problem in our modern economy. Whether cost-push or demand-pull inflation, it must be controlled. The consequences of rapid inflation are dire. It lowers standards of living for many and distorts the functioning of the entire economy.

Illustration 18–4
To control cost-push inflation, supplies of all resources (such as iron and steel) must be free to change in response to changes in demand.

DEFLATION

Deflation is the opposite of inflation. **Deflation** is a decline in the average level of prices. During a period of deflation, some prices may rise but the general or overall level of prices falls. Deflation has not often been a problem in the United States. The most important deflationary period in the United States was during the depression of the 1930s.

18–1

deflation
A decline in the average level of prices.

REVIEWING THE CHAPTER

18–1   1. Inflation, or a rise in the average level of prices, is as much of an economic problem as unemployment. Inflation can cause the allocation of resources in the economy to be inefficient. It can also cause labor to be less productive because people may use more time finding ways to reduce the impact of inflation on their lives. Perhaps most important, inflation makes it difficult for businesses and households to plan for the future. This can reduce economic activity and slow down economic growth.

18–4   2. Inflation is usually measured by using the Consumer Price Index (CPI). The Consumer Price Index is based on a typical market basket of goods and services consumed by urban families. It compares average prices for these goods to average prices of those goods in some base period, such as 1982–1984. The CPI shows what percentage the prices in any other year are of the base year prices.

18–6   3. All prices do not go up at the same rate. Table 18–3 shows food, shelter, and medical care prices rising faster than the overall average price level, as measured by the CPI. Some prices may go down even in periods of high inflation. But overall, in inflationary periods, rising prices will outweigh falling prices.

18–6   4. Inflation can be divided into two kinds: demand-pull inflation and cost-push inflation. These can be explained using the concepts of aggregate demand and aggregate supply (see Figures 18–3 and 18–4 and the accompanying discussions). Demand-pull inflation results from pressures on the demand side of the marketplace. The phrase *too many dollars chasing too few goods* is sometimes used to describe this type of inflation. Cost-push inflation comes from the supply side of the market. Factors that push up production costs can result in higher prices and inflation.

REVIEWING ECONOMIC TERMS

18–1   Supply definitions for the following terms:

fixed income	demand-pull inflation
price index	cost-push inflation
Consumer Price Index (CPI)	deflation

REVIEWING ECONOMIC CONCEPTS

18–2   1. What groups are hurt the least by (or benefit from) inflation?

18–3   2. What groups are hurt the most by inflation?

3. How does inflation distort the economic system?

18–4   4. How does the Bureau of Labor Statistics determine the Consumer Price Index?

18–5   5. How is the rate of inflation between two years figured?

18–6   6. List three limitations of the CPI.

18–6   7. In terms of aggregate demand and aggregate supply, what is the difference between demand-pull inflation and cost-push inflation?

18–6   8. How does government try to control demand-pull inflation?

18–6   9. How might government try to control cost-push inflation?

APPLYING ECONOMIC CONCEPTS

18–1   1. What does the term *inflation* mean? If meat prices go up, does this automatically mean that we have inflation? Explain your answer.

18–2, 18–3   2. Give an example of who is hurt and who is helped by inflation. Briefly explain how inflation affects each group you have named.

18–5   3. How is the Consumer Price Index used to measure the rate of inflation?

18–5   4. The Consumer Price Index was 118.3 in 1988. In 1989 it was 124.0. What was the rate of inflation between 1988 and 1989? Show your calculations.

18–6   5. Review the meaning of demand-pull inflation and cost-push inflation. Can one of these lead to the other? Explain your reasoning.

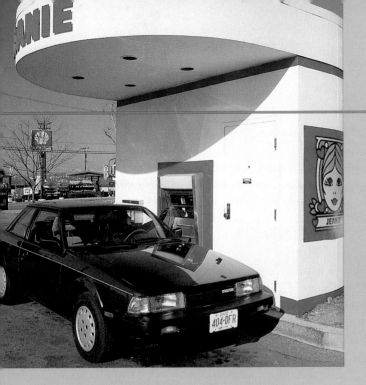

CHAPTER 19

MONEY
AND
BANKING

Learning Objectives

19–1 Define terms related to money and the banking system.

19–2 Describe the three main functions of money.

19–3 Analyze the demand for and supply of money.

19–4 Explain the organization and functions of the Federal Reserve System.

19–5 Identify three or more kinds of nonbank financial intermediaries.

WHAT IS MONEY?

So far in your study of economics, you have discovered many things that are measured in money. You have used money to measure price, the size of a business, total output in the economy, and income. But we have not yet discussed money itself. What is money?

At first this question may seem ridiculous. After all, we know what money is. Or do we? The United States has at least four official definitions of the money supply.

19–1

currency

Coins and paper money.

Every day we use coins and paper money, such as dimes, quarters, dollar bills, $20 bills, etc. Coins and paper are called **currency**. Currency makes up less than 30 percent of the money that is actually used in the United States. People use currency daily. When you go to a movie, you probably buy a ticket with this kind of money. If you buy snacks or soft drinks from machines, you use coins. If you borrow money from a friend, it is likely to be some kind of currency. Currency is sometimes referred to as *cash*.

Coins and paper currency work well for small purchases and when payment is made directly from one person to another. But for large purchases or when the payment travels through the mail, coins and paper currency are not practical. Very few people go to a car dealer with five hundred $20 bills to pay for a $10,000 car. Most people do not pay the rent or house payment with coins or paper currency. If you want to buy a $5 pocket calculator from a mail order store in Atlanta, you should not send a $5 bill with your order. If your order is lost in the mail, there is no way to get your money back. It is even possible that the clerk who opens your envelope in Atlanta will keep the $5 and never report the order. There would be no way to trace the money.

19–1

check

A written order to pay money from amounts deposited.

What kind of money is used for these types of purchases? For large purchases or purchases for which money must be sent through the mail, checks are the most common kind of payment. A **check** is a written order to pay money from amounts deposited. Therefore, deposits in checking accounts, credit union share draft accounts, and other similar accounts are considered money. Many stores and businesses accept checks as money as long as the person writing the check shows proper identification.

For most purposes we think of currency and checking accounts as money. Some of the four definitions of money mentioned above use what is called *near money*. These items do not take the form of currency or checking accounts but could easily be changed into one or more of these. A savings account at a bank is an example of near money. If you have $500 in a savings account, you cannot use that money directly to buy a stereo. But you can withdraw the $500 in either currency or a check from the bank and use that money to buy the stereo.

The question *What is money?* becomes more complex every year. As the line between money and different kinds of near monies becomes less clear, to define what should count as money becomes more challenging. Should CDs (certificates of deposit), money market funds, or insurance policies from which money can be borrowed be considered money? What about credit cards? It is often just as easy or easier to use credit cards to buy products as it is to use conventional money. Credit cards are often called *plastic money* because we can actually buy things with them. Some people think that we will one day have a cashless society in which there are no coins or paper money. Our paychecks would be sent directly to a bank account. Then the amount of all the products we buy would be deducted from our account and credited to the account of each seller. It is difficult to tell how far or how fast we may move in this direction. But one fact seems clear. The answer to the question *What is money?* is likely to keep changing.

THE FUNCTIONS OF MONEY

Without money we would have to barter for the mix of goods and services we want. For example, suppose you worked for a bakery in an economy that used no money. At the end of a week's work, you might be paid in cakes or pies. Or you might be paid 80 loaves of bread. You surely could not eat that much bread during the next week. So, you would have to trade it for other items, such as jeans, movie tickets, or gasoline. What if the person who sold jeans wanted milk instead of bread? You would have to trade your bread to someone else who had milk but wanted bread. Then you could trade the milk for jeans.

What a mess that would be. The use of barter in a modern society would eliminate the variety of goods we have come to expect. Money makes the economics of exchange much easier. Your economic life would be much less complicated if the bakery paid you in money rather than in bread.

One important function of money comes through in the above discussion. Money works as a medium of exchange. Money also serves as a measure of value and as a store of value. Let's look at each of these functions more closely.

Money As a Medium of Exchange

In order for something to function as money, it must be widely accepted in exchange for goods and services. What if you tried to buy a can of tennis balls with a $5 bill, but the tennis shop wouldn't

19–2

Illustration 19-2
Money must be accepted as a medium of exchange in order to function as money. If you tried to use bread as payment for auto parts, you wouldn't get very far.

accept it in exchange? Then you tried to buy a cake, but the baker wouldn't take the $5 bill, either. If no one will take that $5, it is worthless as money. But what if you had a cow's ear that the baker, the tennis shop owner, and others would take in exchange for their goods? The cow's ear, then, would be a valuable form of money. The point is that anything readily accepted as a medium of exchange can work as money. Cows' ears are not money in our society because we do not accept them in exchange for goods or services. You certainly would not consider it a good pay day if you got 500 cows' ears in return for your work!

Just because the government defines an item as money does not mean that it will function as money. For example, the government made one dollar coins called Susan B. Anthony dollars in the 1970s. But they did not become readily accepted for exchange. People often confused them with quarters and paid $1 for a $.25 candy bar or for other $.25 items. The Susan B. Anthony dollar had just as much value as a dollar bill. But because they did not function well as a medium of exchange, Susan B. Anthony dollars never became a widely accepted form of money.

Money As a Measure of Value

19-2   Money functions in a second way by measuring the value of things. We count our income in monetary terms: $10,000, $25,000, etc. We measure the value of what we make or buy with a price expressed in monetary terms. The price of a tire is $60. The price of a can of tennis balls is $5. The price of a sweater is $30. The price of a house is $90,000. We express all prices in dollar amounts. This makes it easy to compare different prices since the measure used—dollars—is the same for everything.

Think about how confusing buying would be otherwise. What if we had a barter economy? Prices would have to be stated in terms of goods. The price of a tire might be 15 cans of tennis balls, or 2 sweaters, or 1/1,500 of a house. There would have to be a cookie price for books, a book price for cars, and a fish price for steak. We would need a paper clip price for computers, a computer price for fish, etc. Such a system would make a modern economy impossible. The use of money as a measure of value is essential to our society. Yet we have come to take this for granted. You would never ask a salesclerk the *dollar* price of a necklace. You would just ask the price and would expect the answer to be in dollars. You would certainly be surprised if the clerk told you that the price of the necklace was 251 pounds of butter!

Money As a Store of Value

Money also functions as a store of value. This means that if we choose not to buy with our money today, we can save it to buy in the future. If money were a perfect store of value, we could buy the same items next year as we could today with the same amount of money.

19–2

But money does function poorly as a store of value when there is inflation in the economy. If inflation occurs, next year $100 will not buy as much as $100 will buy today. For this reason, people often keep their savings in other assets, such as stock, gold, or land. These may be a better store of value, but there is some risk involved. Their value could fall even faster than the value of money.

THE DEMAND FOR AND SUPPLY OF MONEY

The functions of money just discussed should tell you why there is a demand for money and what might change that demand. First, remember that the most important function of money is as a medium of exchange. Therefore, one reason we demand money is to make exchanges.

19–3

We can trade our labor for money and then trade the money for what we want to buy. This means that we have a transaction demand for money. **Transaction demand for money** is the demand for money to make exchanges. We need money to make economic transactions. We want to be paid in money, and we want to use money to buy goods and services. The main factor that affects the transaction demand for money is the level of income in the economy. The higher the level of income, the greater the demand for money and buying power.

19–1

transaction demand for money
The demand for money to make exchanges.

You can see from the third function of money as a store of value that there is also a demand for money as an asset. **Asset demand for money** is the demand for money in order to hold wealth in the form of money. Some people will always want to hold some part of their wealth in the form of money. Many factors, including the rate of inflation, will affect the asset demand for money. One of the most important and most interesting of these is the rate of interest.

19–1

asset demand for money
The demand for money in order to hold wealth in the form of money.

If we use money to buy an asset that pays interest, such as a government or corporate bond, we earn more money. But if we keep our money in $50 bills, we earn no interest on that asset. When the interest rate is very low, we don't give up much by *not* buying an asset that pays interest. Thus, when interest rates are low, we may hold money as an asset. But when interest rates are high, we give up more by holding money. So, we would want to hold less money as an asset. Therefore, the asset demand for money inversely relates to the interest rate. When interest rates rise, asset demand for money falls. And when interest rates fall, asset demand for money rises.

Look at Figure 19–1. If everything except the interest rate stays constant, including income, the demand for money looks like the black line that slopes down to the right. At high interest rates, there is less demand for money than at low interest rates. You should be able to use this relationship to show your understanding of opportunity cost. When we hold money, we have an opportunity cost equal to the interest we could have earned with that money. If the interest rate is high, our opportunity cost of holding money is high. Therefore, we will have little demand to hold money. But if the interest rate is low, our opportunity cost of holding money is low, so we might hold more.

In the United States, the Federal Reserve System controls the supply of money. The **Federal Reserve System** is the central banking system in the United States. It is frequently called *the Fed*. We will talk about the structure and functions of the Federal Reserve System in the next section of this chapter. You will learn how the Fed controls the money supply. For now we will simply state that the Fed determines the supply of money in the economy. Therefore, at any given time some fixed amount of money circulates through the economy. This is shown by the vertical blue line in Figure 19–1.

19–1

Federal Reserve System

The central banking system in the United States.

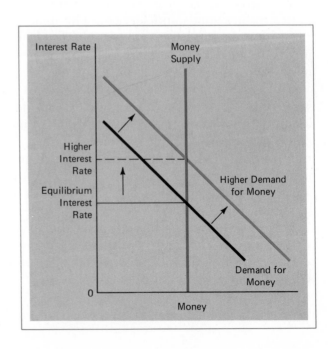

FIGURE 19–1 DEMAND FOR AND SUP-PLY OF MONEY
The money supply is fixed and is determined by the Federal Reserve. The demand for money depends, in part, on the interest rate. We will want to hold more money the lower the interest rate. The equilibrium interest rate is at the level where supply and demand cross.

The market or equilibrium interest rate is at the level where the demand for money crosses the supply of money. This is a general level of interest. There are many different interest rates and all tend to move up or down at about the same time. If this general rate changes, all specific rates will also change.

What causes this interest rate to change? Anything that causes the money demand or the money supply to change also causes this general interest rate to change. In the next chapter we will discuss changes in the supply of money. Using Figure 19–1, see what happens if the demand for money goes up, such as a move to the red demand curve. The interest rate could be expected to rise. The opposite also occurs. A fall in the demand for money will cause interest rates to fall.

THE FEDERAL RESERVE SYSTEM

The United States was slow to adopt a central banking sys-   19–4
tem. Not until 1913 did Congress, under pressure from President Woodrow Wilson, pass the Federal Reserve Act of 1913. Many other countries had central banking systems long before this. The Bank of England was founded in 1694, the Bank of France in 1800, and the Bank of Japan in 1882. Americans, however, felt skeptical about having too much centralized authority in banking. So, the Federal Reserve System was set up with 12 separate banks. Each of them was to act as the central bank for a given part of the country. Since 1913, the 12 banks have become much less independent. They now act, for the most part, as one central bank.

The Federal Reserve System (the Fed) began as an independent agency. It was not controlled by the executive branch of the government, nor was it controlled by Congress. The Fed had to report to Congress each year, but for years this was just a formality. A weak relationship existed between the Federal Reserve and the government. More recently the government has tightened its control on the Fed. Since 1975 the Fed has reported to Congress on a more regular and formal basis.

In the next chapter you will discover that the Fed is a powerful force in the United States economy. To get a better idea of what the Federal Reserve System is and does, let's explore its structure and functions.

Structure of the Federal Reserve System

The structure of the Federal Reserve System is shown in Figure 19–2. Each section of this chart will be discussed in some detail.

FIGURE 19–2   ORGANIZATION OF THE FEDERAL RESERVE SYSTEM
The Board of Governors supervises the Federal Reserve System. The Federal Open Market Committee buys and sells U.S. government securities. The Federal Advisory Council has no real power, but meets with the Board of Governors to discuss policy. The 12 Federal Reserve Banks are the central banks of their geographic areas and issue Federal Reserve notes (currency).

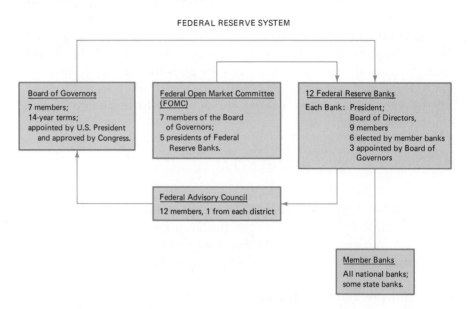

FEDERAL RESERVE SYSTEM

Try to keep the various parts of the chart in mind as you read the following discussion.

Federal Reserve Banks. The Federal Reserve Act of 1913 divided the United States into 12 districts, each with a Federal Reserve Bank. These districts are shown in Figure 19–3. The Federal Reserve Banks for each district are located in the cities listed below.

District	Federal Reserve Bank Location
1	Boston, MA
2	New York, NY
3	Philadelphia, PA
4	Cleveland, OH
5	Richmond, VA
6	Atlanta, GA
7	Chicago, IL
8	St. Louis, MO
9	Minneapolis, MN
10	Kansas City, MO
11	Dallas, TX
12	San Francisco, CA

Look at the map in Figure 19–3 to find your Federal Reserve district.

FIGURE 19–3 THE FEDERAL RESERVE SYSTEM

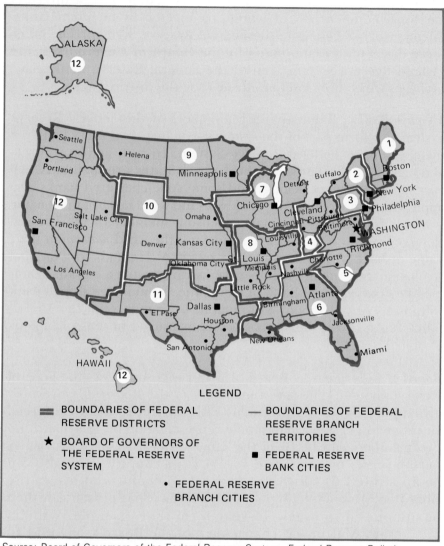

Source: Board of Governors of the Federal Reserve System, *Federal Reserve Bulletin*.

The Federal Reserve Banks in each district issue Federal Reserve notes (paper money) with the number of the district on each note. Look at a dollar bill or any larger bill. On the same side as the president's picture, you will see the number of a Federal Reserve district about one inch in from each corner. If that number is 10, the money came from the tenth Federal Reserve district headquartered in Kansas City, Missouri. Most of the paper money you see in your area probably comes from the Federal Reserve district in that area. People in Pittsburgh, for example, see more money with a 4 on it than any other number.

Illustration 19–3
Federal Reserve Banks are found in 12 cities across the United States. The Federal Reserve System helps keep the flow of money in our economy stable.

Each Federal Reserve Bank operates as a private business with its own president and board of directors. The board of directors has nine members, six of whom are elected by member banks. (Member banks belong to the Federal Reserve System.) The other three directors are appointed by the Board of Governors of the Federal Reserve System. Ten of the Federal Reserve Banks have branches which are closely controlled by the district banks.

Member Banks. Banks that are members of the Federal Reserve System also form part of the system's structure. Not every bank is a member of the Federal Reserve System. In fact, as you will see, about half of the banks in the United States are members. All national banks must belong, and some state-chartered banks also apply for membership. Any bank with the word *national* in its name is a national bank. That makes it also a member of the Federal Reserve System. National banks must use the word *national* in their name or have *N.A.* following their name. *N.A.* stands for National Affiliation. Size among member banks varies quite a bit. For example, the First National Bank of Geraldine, Montana, is a small bank with assets of only about $10 million. By comparison, the Mellon Bank, N.A., of Pittsburgh has assets measured in tens of billions of dollars.

Board of Governors. A Board of Governors supervises the Federal Reserve System. The seven members of the Board of Governors are appointed by the president with the approval of Congress. In order to get good geographic representation on the Board, no two members can be from the same Federal Reserve district. A person serves on the Board for 14 years. But a person also can be appointed to finish the term of someone who leaves the Board before completing a 14-year term. That person can then be appointed to a new 14-year term. For example, William McChesney Martin was chairperson of the Board from 1951 to 1970. He replaced a retiring member and then served a 14-year period of his own. Martin was chosen as chairperson of the Board of Governors by Presidents Truman, Eisenhower, Kennedy, and Johnson.

Because the seven 14-year terms are staggered, each president should appoint two people to the Board of Governors during the president's four-year term of office. But because some governors quit early because of old age or for financial reasons, some presidents select more members. Even though the term of office lasts 14 years, the average term runs between 5 and 6 years because people leave before their terms expire. Board members can be removed from office if there is cause, but this has never been done.

The president chooses the chairperson and the vice-chairperson of the Board of Governors, with the approval of Congress. Each serves a four-year term in these positions, and then can be replaced with other Board members by the president. For example, President Reagan initially retained Paul Volcker as the chairperson. In 1987 President Reagan appointed Alan Greenspan as chairperson of the Board of Governors. Alan Greenspan was kept on by President Bush. Who is the current chairperson?

Members of the Board of Governors have their offices in Washington, D.C. They have a large staff of economists, lawyers, and other professionals who research the economy and the role of money and banking in the economy. The Board must rule on bank mergers and on many nonbanking activities with which banks may want to become involved. The Board also administers truth-in-lending laws and laws that relate to eliminating discrimination in lending. In addition, members of the Board of Governors have a great deal to say about the direction of monetary policy. You can see, then, that membership on the Board of Governors is an important and powerful position.

Federal Open Market Committee. The Federal Open Market Committee (FOMC) is a powerful part of the Federal Reserve System. This group acts on the most important part of monetary policy — the buying and selling of United States government securities by the Federal Reserve Banks. (You will read more about this in Chapter 20.) There are 12 members on the FOMC, 7 of whom are members of the Board of Governors. The chairperson of the Board of Governors also chairs the FOMC. The other five members of the FOMC are the presidents of five of the Federal Reserve Banks. The president of the New York Federal Reserve Bank is a permanent member of the FOMC. The other four slots are rotated among the remaining 11 Federal Reserve Districts. The monthly meetings of the FOMC take place in Washington, D.C., and usually all 12 Federal Reserve Bank presidents attend. All of them can participate in the meeting, but only the five official members can vote.

Federal Advisory Council. The Federal Advisory Council has 12 members, one from each Federal Reserve district. The members are usually bankers who are selected by the Federal Reserve Banks. The Council meets four times each year with the Board of Governors to discuss the economic situation and policies of the Board. This gives the Board of Governors a chance to hear the concerns of the banks in each district. It also gives the bankers some direct contact with the Board. The Federal Advisory Council has no real power. However, it links bankers with the Board of Governors, which has much control over bankers' activities.

Functions of the Federal Reserve System

The Federal Reserve System functions as a *banker's bank* and as the bank for the government. The Fed acts as a banker's bank because banks use the Federal Reserve Banks much like you use your local bank. A bank can have an account with the Fed and keep money on deposit in a Federal Reserve Bank. In addition, banks can borrow from the Fed. In fact, the Federal Reserve is sometimes called a *lender of last resort*. This means that banks can always borrow from the Fed if they need money to satisfy withdrawals by bank customers. This function reduces the threat of panics and runs on banks. Thus, if everyone with a deposit at your local bank tried to withdraw their money, your bank could borrow from the Fed to meet this abnormal demand.

There have been no major runs on *national banks* in the United States since the Depression of the 1930s. Today people can have great faith in national banks. One of the major reasons we can always get our money is because the bank can borrow from the Fed if necessary. For example, in 1974 the Franklin National Bank in Philadelphia borrowed $1.75 billion from the Fed to help prevent a complete collapse of the bank.

As you have seen, each Federal Reserve Bank issues currency to meet our demand to hold money in the form of currency. If we want a greater fraction of our money in $20 bills, the Fed will make more $20 bills available. If we want to hold most of our money in currency rather than in checking accounts, the Fed makes the necessary amount of currency available.

Another function of the Federal Reserve System is to provide a way for checks to flow from one part of the country to another. This is called the *check-clearing* process. Suppose you send a check

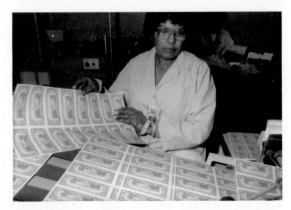

Illustration 19–4   Each Federal Reserve Bank issues currency to meet our demand to hold money. The number of the Federal Reserve district is printed on the same side of the bill as the president's picture.

drawn on your account at a bank in Great Falls, Montana, to a company in Freeport, Maine. There must be some way for that check to get back to your bank. Look at the upper right-hand corner of the check in Figure 19–4. You will see some numbers (other than the check number) called *routing numbers*. These are codes for Federal Reserve districts and individual banks which help to send checks easily back to the bank from which they originated.

The Federal Reserve System also acts as the bank for the government. The government has accounts with the Fed and can write checks on these accounts. Also, the government can borrow from the Fed if necessary. These functions, along with control on the banking system, give the Fed control over the supply of money. Controlling the supply of money is the most important job of the Federal Reserve System and is the very heart of monetary policy. Because this function is so important, we will discuss it exclusively in Chapter 20.

FIGURE 19–4   A PERSONAL CHECK SHOWING ROUTING NUMBERS
The routing numbers on this check help in sending it through the banking system.

Illustration 19–5
Today, many commercial banks advertise themselves as *full service banks*, because they offer not only checking and savings accounts but also loans, credit cards, and other financial services.

COMMERCIAL BANKS

Commercial banks are one kind of financial institution. Commercial banks were originally formed to make loans to businesses (commercial customers). Today, commercial banks provide a number of services to both individuals and commercial customers. They offer a much broader set of services than just making loans. They have checking accounts and savings accounts. They rent safe-deposit boxes. They make business, consumer, and residential loans, and they issue credit cards. They sell travelers checks and exchange foreign currency for American currency. The term *full service bank* is used in some bank advertisements. This accurately describes most banks because they provide a broad range of financial services.

19–1

demand deposit
Money that must be paid upon demand by the holder of a check.

19–1

NOW account
An account that earns interest on deposits and from which amounts can be withdrawn easily using a negotiable order of withdrawal.

19–1

share draft account
An account with a credit union from which withdrawals can easily be made using a draft.

19–1

Federal Deposit Insurance Corporation (FDIC)
The agency that insures deposits of individuals and businesses for up to $100,000 in the event of bank failure.

Not so long ago, having a checking account separated banks from other financial institutions. Economists usually call checking accounts demand deposits. A **demand deposit** is money that must be paid upon demand by the holder of a check. But today, savings and loan associations, credit unions, and other financial institutions can have accounts that do the same thing as checking accounts. There are NOW accounts (NOW stands for *negotiable order of withdrawal*) and share draft accounts. A **NOW account** is an account that earns interest on deposits and from which amounts can be withdrawn easily using a negotiable order of withdrawal. A **share draft account** is an account with a credit union from which withdrawals can easily be made using a draft. Often a share draft account will earn interest on deposits, as do NOW accounts. Today little difference exists between banks and the other financial institutions.

Some banks are chartered by the federal government, and some are chartered by a state government. The federally chartered banks are called national banks, and the others are called state banks. About 30 percent of the insured banks in the United States are national banks. As stated earlier, national banks must be members of the Federal Reserve System. State banks may apply for membership if they meet certain qualifications. Only about 10 percent of state banks are member banks.

An important feature of the United States banking system is the role played by the Federal Deposit Insurance Corporation (FDIC). The **Federal Deposit Insurance Corporation (FDIC)** is the agency that insures deposits of individuals and businesses for up to $100,000 in the event of bank failure. This, along with the ability of banks to borrow from the Fed, has been responsible for much of the stability of banks since the 1930s. More than 98 percent of all banks belong to the FDIC, even though only national banks are required to belong. Since the founding of the FDIC in 1934, 99 percent of all depositors have been paid in full when banks have had to close. This means that there is almost no risk of losing the money you have deposited at an insured bank.

If you had more than $100,000 in an account at a bank that failed, you would get at least $100,000 from the FDIC. But you probably would get back your full deposit. This is because the FDIC tries to merge a failing bank with a healthy bank so that no one loses money. You can also protect your deposits above $100,000 by putting the money in two separate accounts in the same bank. (By law, one must be a joint account with someone else in order to be protected.) Then both accounts will be insured for the full $100,000. You can also protect yourself by having separate accounts in as many different banks as you choose. So, there is no reason to risk losing any money at all.

NONBANK FINANCIAL INTERMEDIARIES

At one time banks were not interested in providing financial services to individuals and households. Their main interest was in businesses. Therefore, other financial intermediaries formed to serve the needs of special groups of people. A **financial intermediary** is an organization that helps the flow of money from people with money to save to people who need to borrow money.

Savings and Loan Associations

Savings and loan associations are probably the best-known of the nonbank financial intermediaries. A **savings and loan association** is a financial intermediary that mainly provides a place for people to save money and then lends that money to people to buy houses or other things.

These were first formed by groups of people who needed a way to put together enough money to buy a house. A group of people pooled their savings until enough was collected to buy one house. A member of the group was selected to receive the money by using some method that gave each member an equal chance of being selected. That member then used the money to buy a house and began paying back into the savings and loan association. Those payments, along with continued savings from the other members, built the pool of money up again until another member could buy a house. The savings and loan association did what no one person could do. It collected money from many different members and made that money available to one borrower.

Today, savings and loan associations operate much more formally and make many more services available to their customers. But the principle is the same: Many people put money into savings accounts while others borrow it to buy homes or other things. Before 1980, savings and loans were very limited in how they could lend their money. More than 80 percent of their assets were in loans for housing. Now they can lend some money to businesses and have more flexibility to lend money to people for other (non-housing) purposes. Since 1981 all savings and loans have been able to issue NOW (negotiable order of withdrawal) accounts. These days, very little differentiates banks from savings and loan associations. Both provide a full range of financial services.

Savings and loans, like banks, can be started by getting a state or federal charter. There are more state-chartered savings and loans, but the biggest ones have federal charters. All federally chartered savings and loans must belong to the Federal Savings and Loan

19–1
financial intermediary
An organization that helps the flow of money from people with money to save to people who need to borrow money.

19–5
19–1
savings and loan association
A financial intermediary that mainly provides a place for people to save money and then lends that money to people to buy houses or other things.

Illustration 19–6
Savings and loan associations loan the savings of some people to others who want to build or purchase houses.

Insurance Corporation (FSLIC). The FSLIC insures deposits up to $100,000. State savings and loans can also belong to the FSLIC. In total, about 85 percent of all savings and loan associations are insured by the FSLIC. An important and further safeguard for savings and loans is a recent change which allows them to borrow from the Fed much like banks can.

Mutual Savings Banks

19-5

19-1

mutual savings banks
Banks that were first formed for the same reasons as savings and loan associations and which promote thrift by their members.

Mutual savings banks are banks that were first formed for the same reasons as savings and loan associations and which promote thrift by their members. Their loans are used mainly for housing, and they have usually appealed to the depositor with a small savings account. In fact, the names of many mutual savings banks give the idea that the banks began with small accounts. For example, one of the oldest mutual savings banks is the Boston Five Cent Savings Bank. Today it is large enough to be listed in Dun & Bradstreet's *Million Dollar Directory*. Mutual savings banks are found mainly in the northeastern United States.

Credit Unions

19-5

19-1

credit union
A financial intermediary formed around something that its members have in common.

A **credit union** is a financial intermediary formed around something that its members have in common. Credit unions often originate from an occupational group, a labor union, or a religious group. They may be based on anything that a group has in common, including where the members live. The names of credit unions give an idea of the bases on which a credit union can be founded: The Tulsa Teachers Credit Union, the Isabella County Employees Credit Union, The Great Falls Telephone Employees Federal Credit Union, or the Westside Federal Credit Union.

For years credit unions have made most of their loans for consumer purchases such as appliances, cars, furniture, and other items. Since about 1980 they have changed their financial services to the extent that they now resemble banks. Credit unions have share draft accounts which work almost exactly like a bank checking account. Some credit unions will even finance the purchase of a house. To borrow from a credit union you must be a member of it. This usually means that you must have at least $5 in a share account. (A share account is like a savings account.) Accounts in credit unions may also be insured up to $100,000 by the National Credit Union Association (NCUA).

Other Financial Intermediaries

Many other kinds of organizations act as intermediaries between   19–5
savers and borrowers. Life insurance companies, finance companies, pension funds, and investment companies are some examples
in the private sector of the economy.

The Farm Credit Administration supervises a number of federal
government financial intermediaries. These include 12 Banks for
Cooperatives, 12 Federal Intermediate Credit Banks, and 12 Federal Land Banks which make loans through 800 Federal Land
Bank Associations. All these are aimed mainly at providing credit
to the agriculture sector for equipment, marketing or storing crops,
and housing.

REVIEWING
THE
CHAPTER

19–1   1. Money can be anything that is generally accepted as a medium
        of exchange. In the United States, coins, paper currency, and
        checking accounts of various kinds are all forms of money. Small
        purchases are usually made with currency, while larger pur-
        chases are usually paid for by check. Currency is made up of
        coins and paper money. Checks include bank checks, credit
        union share drafts, and checks written on NOW (negotiable
        order of withdrawal) accounts.

19–2   2. Without money we would have to barter to buy products we
        want. That is, we would have to trade what we have for what we
        would like to get from others. Without money we would be paid
        for our work by getting some of the products that we made. A
        bakery worker's salary might be in bread or cookies. If you were
        paid in cookies and wanted to buy a bicycle, you would have to
        find someone with a bicycle who would trade it for cookies. Life
        in a barter economy would be complex. A modern society such
        as ours simply would not work without money as a medium of
        exchange.

19–2   3. Money has three functions. First and most important, money
        acts as a medium of exchange. For something to act as money, it
        must be readily accepted as payment for goods and services any-
        where in the economy. Second, money is a measure of value. We

measure such things as prices, income, and GNP in terms of money. Finally, money is a store of value. We can save money and use it to buy something at a later time. Inflation makes it difficult for money to work well as a store of value. Therefore, people sometimes trade their money for other things, such as gold, stocks, or land, to use as a store of value.

19-3   4. The supply of money is determined within the banking system. The Federal Reserve has the power to change the nation's amount of money, but at any time there is some given amount of money available. There are two kinds of demand for money. We demand money to make transactions; that is, to buy things. We need more money for this as incomes rise. Second, we may want to hold money as an asset. This kind of demand for money is related to interest rates. The higher the interest rate, the less money we would want to hold.

19-4   5. The Federal Reserve acts as the central bank in the United States. It was set up by the Federal Reserve Act of 1913. There are 12 Federal Reserve districts, each of which has a Federal Reserve Bank. All national banks must belong to the Fed, and state-chartered banks may apply for membership.

19-4   6. The Board of Governors is the group of people who manage the Federal Reserve. These seven people have a great deal of power over economic events in the United States. Each member of the Board is appointed by the president for a term of 14 years. In addition to their other duties, the members of the Board of Governors also serve on the Federal Open Market Committee (FOMC). The FOMC controls the most important part of monetary policy — the buying and selling of United States government securities by the Federal Reserve Banks.

19-4   7. The Federal Reserve functions as a *banker's bank* and a *lender of last resort*. National banks can borrow money from the Fed. In general, banks use the Federal Reserve Banks much as we use our local banks. The Federal Reserve Banks also issue paper currency and help clear checks from one part of the country to another. Finally, the Federal Reserve acts as the bank for the government.

19-5   8. There are many financial intermediaries between people who want to save and those who want to borrow. These include commercial banks, savings and loan associations, credit unions, and mutual savings banks. All of these take in savings from some people and then loan that money to others. In recent years, these institutions have become increasingly similar. All of them can now offer a broad range of financial services to their customers.

REVIEWING

ECONOMIC

TERMS

19–1   Supply definitions for the following terms:

currency

check

transaction demand for money

asset demand for money

Federal Reserve System

demand deposit

NOW account

share draft account

Federal Deposit Insurance
   Corporation (FDIC)

financial intermediary

savings and loan association

mutual savings bank

credit union

REVIEWING

ECONOMIC

CONCEPTS

19–2   1. What is money?

19–2   2. Why do we have money?

19–2   3. What three functions does money perform?

19–3   4. What determines the supply of money and the demand for money in the economy?

19–3   5. What happens to interest rates if the demand for money increases and the supply of money remains the same?

19–4   6. What are the functions of the Fed?

19–5   7. List the three main nonbank financial intermediaries. What has been the trend in recent years in the services they offer?

APPLYING

ECONOMIC

CONCEPTS

19–2   1. Could we use paper clips as money? Why or why not? What problems might develop if people started using paper clips as money?

19–2   2. Review the three functions that money should perform. Which of these functions does American money do best? Which of these functions does American money do worst? Explain your answer.

19–2   3. What does the term *barter* mean? Think of a recent purchase you made. How might that purchase have been made by using barter rather than by using money?

19–3   4. How do interest rates affect the demand for money?

19–4   5. Give the number of the Federal Reserve district in which you live. In what city is your district's Federal Reserve Bank located?

19–4   6. Write an essay in which you explain what the Board of Governors of the Federal Reserve is, what the Board does, and how the members are appointed. Who currently chairs the Board of Governors?

19–5   7. Explain the differences between commercial banks, savings and loan associations, and credit unions. Look in the Yellow Pages of your phone book and count the number of each in your area. Which ones are more numerous?

19–4   8. What is the difference between the following: (a) national banks and state banks and (b) member banks and nonmember banks. Are there state banks and national banks where you live? List an example of each type of bank in your area.

19–4   9. What are the FDIC and FSLIC? Why are these an important part of the financial system in the United States?

ALL CHECKING ACCOUNTS ARE NOT EQUAL: WHICH IS BEST FOR YOU?

Most people prefer to use a checking account or a share draft account rather than relying solely on cash for making purchases. When thinking about opening a checking account, there are several things you should consider.

You should ask questions about the fees that are used. Is there a monthly service charge? What is the charge per check, if any? What is the overdraft fee? What is the charge for a returned check? How much do checks cost?

You should also ask about restrictions that affect the account. Is there a minimum balance required? How long is the holding period for checks you deposit in your account? Sometimes you cannot use funds until the check you deposit clears back to its origin. Since 1990, the maximum holding period is two business days for local checks and five business days for out-of-town checks.

Ask about special services that come with the account. Is there overdraft protection? Can you use an automatic teller machine (ATM) to access your account 24 hours a day? Is such access part of a network so you can get money from your account when you travel to other locations?

CHAPTER 20

MONETARY POLICY

Learning Objectives

20-1 Define terms related to monetary policy.

20-2 Explain the relationship between interest rates and money demand and supply.

20-3 Describe the effects of tight and loose monetary policies.

20-4 Describe the effects of the reserve requirement on the supply of money.

20-5 Identify three ways the Fed can cause the money supply to change.

20-6 Discuss the effects of monetary policy on:

(a) investment in factories and equipment

(b) investment in inventories

(c) the housing market

(d) personal spending

MONEY AND ECONOMIC GOALS

How important is money in our economy? Surprisingly, there is much debate about this question. But there is no doubt that the amount of money available for use affects our economy in several important ways. Remember that the Employment Act of 1946 gave three goals for the national economy: full employment, price stability, and economic growth. Each of these is affected by the amount of money in the economy.

In this chapter you will learn how money affects these economic goals. You will also see how the Fed (the Federal Reserve) changes the amount of money in the economy. If you follow the national news, you probably have seen or heard stories that cover these topics. As you study this chapter, you will see how the Fed can inject reserves of money into the banking system. You will also find out how such actions can affect employment, inflation, and economic growth.

20–3

20–1

loose monetary policy

A policy of the Fed that causes the money supply to rise.

20–1

tight monetary policy

A policy of the Fed that causes the money supply to decrease.

In discussing monetary policy, the terms *loose monetary policy* and *tight monetary policy* are often used. You should know what these terms mean. A **loose monetary policy** is a policy of the Fed that causes the money supply to rise. Such a policy tends to favor economic growth and more employment, but it may also cause inflation. A *tight* monetary policy is just the opposite. A **tight monetary policy** is a policy of the Fed that causes the money supply to decrease. This may help lower inflation but at the same time may cause higher unemployment. A tight monetary policy may also lower the rate of economic growth.

MONEY DEMAND AND SUPPLY: A CLOSER LOOK

The amount of money in the economy, or the *money supply*, has important effects on the functioning of our economy. Many highly respected economists, such as Anna Schwartz and Nobel prize-winner Milton Friedman, have spent much time studying how money affects the economy. But no one agrees about the exact role of money or how money affects employment, the growth rate, and prices. One major discovery has been made, however. The balance between the demand for money and the supply of money is crucial.

Demand for Money

20–2

You may think that there is no limit to our demand for money. After all, do you know anyone who would *not* like to have more money? However, this line of thinking confuses money with income. We all would like to have more income and be able to buy more things. But income and money are *not* the same. Income gives us the ability to buy things. Money is something we invented to help make buying and selling easier. The main function of money is as a medium of exchange. Although we get our income in the form of money, most people do not want to hold or keep all their income as money. If you earned $500, would you keep it all as money? Or would you use some of it to buy other things? History shows that most people hold only a part of their income as money. They use the rest to buy food, clothing, housing, or cars, or to add to their savings.

In Chapter 19, you saw that more money will be demanded in the economy at lower interest rates. Why is this? First, consider how people may change the amount of money they want to hold when interest rates change. When the interest rate is high, such as 15 percent in Figure 20–1, people will not want to hold much money. This is because of the high opportunity cost in doing so. People would rather invest that money in an interest-earning asset. Holding on to money would have a high opportunity cost. At a lower rate, such as 3 percent, the cost of holding money is not high. We would then be more willing to hold money. Generally, the lower the interest rate, the greater the demand for money.

How does the interest rate affect the demand for money by businesses? Businesses demand money mainly to invest in more capital, such as a larger plant or a new machine. Such capital investments earn a return for the firm that is usually expressed as a

Illustration 20–1
If we all had more money, we would be able to buy more of the things we like. But what is at issue here is *income*, not money. Money is just a device we invented for buying and selling.

20–2

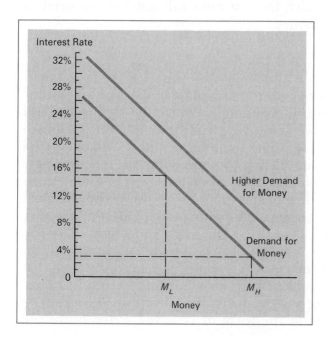

FIGURE 20–1   THE DEMAND FOR MONEY
People and businesses will have a demand for more money at lower interest rates than at higher interest rates. At an interest rate of 15 percent, a low amount of money would be demanded (M_L), but at 3 percent, a higher amount (M_H) would be demanded.

percentage. For example, an oil company might expect the investment in a new refinery to earn a return of 12 percent. Suppose the oil company had to pay 15 percent interest to borrow the money to build the refinery. The company would not build the new refinery because it would lose money. But if it could borrow at 3 percent interest, the investment would be profitable. Therefore, at the lower interest rate, the oil company would borrow the money and build the refinery. Many business projects would be more profitable at low interest rates than at high interest rates. So, businesses' demand for money also slopes down to the right. This means that for the whole economy the demand for money looks like Figure 20–1. Both households and businesses will demand a greater quantity of money at lower interest rates than at higher ones.

The demand for money may shift to the right or left, depending on economic conditions. Shifts to the right are the more likely, since as our economy grows there are more people and businesses to demand money. Also, the wealthier we become, the greater our demand for money becomes. As you have seen in earlier chapters, our country has been getting richer over the years. An increase in the demand for money is shown in Figure 20–1 by the line labeled "Higher Demand for Money."

You now know that interest rates affect the quantity of money demanded. But what determines the rate of interest? The public always wants to know about the level of interest rates. Changes in interest rates are often featured in the news. But before we can explore the level at which interest rates will stabilize, we need to look at the supply of money.

Supply of Money

20–2   You will remember from the last chapter that the amount of money that exists in the economy is controlled by the Federal Reserve. This is why the money supply is drawn as a vertical line in Figure 20–2. At any given time some fixed supply of money stays within our economy. But this does not mean that the money supply never changes. The Fed may cause more money to be available. In fact, over the years, our money supply has grown greatly. It must grow in order for us to have enough money to allow a growing economy to function.

20–1

fractional reserve banking system

A system in which banks must keep some fraction or part of their deposits in the form of reserves.

The money supply grows as banks "create" more money. In order to understand the *creation of money*, you need to know that banks operate within a fractional reserve banking system. In a **fractional reserve banking system**, banks must keep some fraction or part of their deposits in the form of reserves. *Reserves* are the

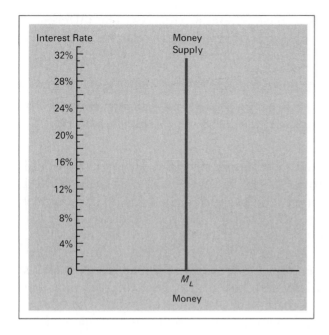

FIGURE 20–2   THE SUPPLY OF MONEY
The money supply is determined by the Federal Reserve. It is a vertical line because at any given time there is some fixed supply of money in our economy.

money a bank has in its vaults and on deposit at the Federal Reserve Bank. The **reserve ratio** is the fraction of deposits that the Fed determines banks must keep on reserve. The **reserve requirement** is the dollar amount banks must keep on reserve.

Suppose that the Fed sets a 20 percent reserve ratio. This means that for each dollar a bank has in deposits, it must keep $.20 in reserve. A bank with $100,000 of deposits would have to keep $20,000 in reserves. A bank with $800,000 of deposits would need $160,000 in reserves. The reserve requirement equals .2 times the amount of deposits, as long as the reserve ratio is 20 percent. (Twenty percent is the same as .2 or one fifth.)

Now suppose you start a new bank that is the only bank around. Suppose also that Ms. Juanita Sanchez finds $10,000 hidden in her closet. If Ms. Sanchez puts that $10,000 in a checking account at your bank, she still has $10,000 to spend. She has simply substituted one kind of money for another. She has traded currency for a checking account deposit. She can now buy a $50 pair of shoes with a check rather than with a $50 bill.

Your bank would now have a $10,000 deposit. The Fed requires you to keep 20 percent of that amount, or $2,000, on reserve. What would you do with the rest of the money? As a banker you wish to make money, so you might lend as much as possible to someone else. In this case, you have money that you could lend. This money is called excess reserves. Your bank has $10,000 in

20–1
reserve ratio

The fraction of deposits that the Fed determines banks must keep on reserve.

20–1
reserve requirement

The dollar amount banks must keep on reserve.

20–1

excess reserves

The difference between actual reserves and required reserves.

reserves but only needs to have $2,000 in reserves. The difference ($8,000 in this case) is excess reserves. **Excess reserves** is the difference between actual reserves and required reserves.

> Excess Reserves = Actual Reserves − Required Reserves

By lending more money to other customers, your bank would earn money in the form of the interest paid on the borrowed money. So, bankers usually lend as much as possible, to earn money for the owners. Suppose Miss Osami Eto comes in and asks you for an $8,000 loan to buy a new car. If you lend her the money, you could give it to her by opening an $8,000 checking account for her. Now you would have checking deposits of $18,000 (Ms. Sanchez's $10,000 plus Miss Eto's $8,000). How much do you have to have in reserves? At a reserve requirement of 20 percent, you need $3,600 to meet the reserve requirement. (The $3,600 equals 20 percent of the $18,000 of deposits; that is, .2 × $18,000 = $3,600.)

Since you have $10,000 of reserves from Ms. Sanchez's deposit and only need $3,600, you can still make more loans. By doing so, you would create more checking account deposits, which is one kind of money. How many dollars' worth of deposits could you legally have with $10,000 of reserves? The answer is $50,000. If you had $50,000 in deposits, you would need 20 percent of that amount in reserve. Twenty percent of $50,000 is $10,000 (.2 × $50,000 = $10,000). So, you could continue to loan out money by creating new checking account deposits until you had $50,000 of deposits. Then you would be *loaned up*. A bank is loaned up when it has loaned all it can and still meets the required reserve.

Illustration 20–2
Every bank is required to keep a certain percentage of its deposits as *reserves* in its vaults or at the Federal Reserve Bank.

The total amount of deposits that could be supported by any given amount of reserves can be found as follows.

> Total Deposits = Reserves ÷ Percentage Reserve Requirement

In this example:

$$\$50,000 = \$10,000 \div .2$$

As banks lend money by issuing new checking account deposits, the money supply becomes larger. People have more money (in the form of checking accounts) to spend. Remember that most of our money takes the form of checking accounts. So, as the volume of checking deposits changes, so does the biggest part of the money supply.   20–4

Figure 20–3 shows that the interest rate does not affect money supply. Once the Fed decides that the money supply should be at the lower level, M_L, it does not matter what the interest rate is. If the interest rate is low, such as 3 percent, the money supply is M_L. If the interest rate rises to 15 percent, the money supply would still be M_L dollars. The money supply would change only if the Fed takes action to change the money supply. If some Fed action caused the money supply to rise, the money supply line would shift to the right. Such a larger money supply is shown by the vertical line at M_H.   20–2

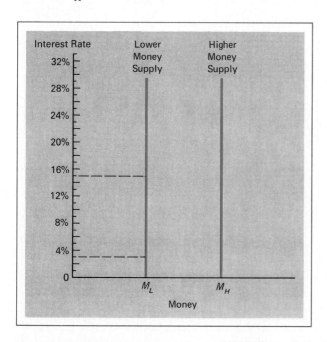

FIGURE 20–3 THE SUPPLY OF MONEY
The money supply is determined by the Federal Reserve. It stays the same until the Fed does something to make it rise or fall.

You have seen that the Fed can affect the amount of total deposits banks can have. You will soon see how the Federal Reserve can use several kinds of policy to change the money supply. But first, let's look at how money supply and demand interact to affect the rate of interest in the economy.

Balance Between Money Supply and Demand

20–2   You have learned that interest serves as a price for using money. You should then expect that supply and demand forces may affect interest much as they affect other prices.

Suppose the amount of money demanded exceeds the supply of money at the current interest rate. You would expect upward pressure on the interest rate. This is true at the 3 percent interest rate in Figure 20–4. The amount of money demanded is at M_3 but only M_2 dollars are being supplied by the Fed. Excess demand forces up the price of money (the interest rate).

But at high interest rates, such as at the 15 percent rate in Figure 20–4, there is a lower amount of money demanded. Demand (M_1) is less than supply (M_2); therefore, you can expect the interest rate to fall. Market forces tend to push the interest rate toward a level where demand and supply are in balance. This would be so at Point A in Figure 20–4. If the money supply is at the level represented by M_2 dollars, a 10 percent interest rate would bring demand into balance with supply. At an interest rate of 10 percent, people and businesses would want M_2 dollars' worth of money. M_2 dollars is the amount currently supplied by the Fed-

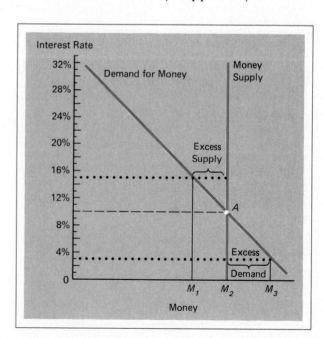

FIGURE 20–4   BALANCING MONEY DEMAND AND SUPPLY
At high interest rates, money demand is less than the supply, so the interest rate is likely to fall. At low interest rates, money demand is greater than the supply, so the rate of interest is likely to rise.

eral Reserve. So, at 10 percent the demand and supply of money are in balance.

Now you know how the demand and supply of money determine the rate of interest. You have also learned that the Fed controls the supply of money. This is done through monetary policy. **Monetary policy** is the changing of the amount of money in the economy in order to reduce unemployment, keep prices stable, and promote economic growth. The Federal Reserve watches over monetary policy with these objectives in mind.

20–1

monetary policy
The changing of the amount of money in the economy in order to reduce unemployment, keep prices stable, and promote economic growth.

MONETARY POLICY

As discussed at the beginning of this chapter, the Fed can follow either a *tight* monetary policy or a *loose* monetary policy. A tight policy involves reducing the money supply or holding down its rate of growth. The left side of Figure 20–5 shows that a smaller money supply causes the interest rate to go up. In the example shown, the interest rate goes up from 8 percent to 12 percent.

A loose monetary policy means that the Fed causes the amount of money in the economy to rise. A loose monetary policy is shown in the right-hand graph in Figure 20–5. An increase in the money

20–3

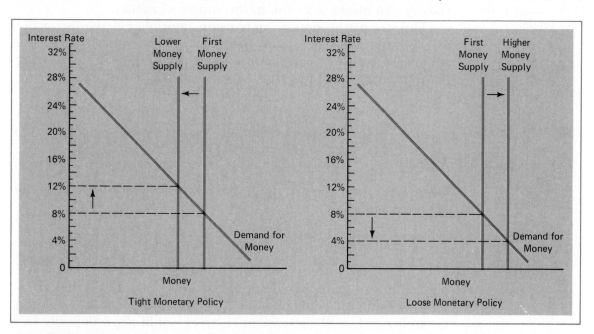

FIGURE 20–5   TIGHT AND LOOSE MONETARY POLICIES
The left-hand graph shows that interest rates go up when the Fed follows a tight monetary policy. The graph on the right shows that a loose monetary policy can cause interest rates to fall.

supply causes a movement of the money supply curve to the right. As the money supply increases, the interest rate falls. In the example shown, the interest rate goes down from 8 percent to 4 percent.

20-5   How does the Fed cause the money supply to fall or rise? What can the Fed do to cause the money supply line to move to the left or to the right? The following paragraphs discuss the three main tools the Fed can use to change the supply of money.

Changing the Reserve Requirement

20-4   The Fed requires banks to keep part of their deposits on reserve, either in the bank or with the Federal Reserve. Earlier in this chapter we used an example of a bank that was required to keep 20 percent of its deposits in reserves. In that example the reserve ratio was 20 percent (or one fifth).

With a reserve ratio of 20 percent you saw that reserves of $10,000 would support $50,000 in deposits. The amount of deposits supported equals five times the amount of reserves. The five is called the deposit expansion multiplier. The **deposit expansion multiplier** is the number that expresses the relationship between a change in bank reserves and the change in the money supply. A deposit expansion multiplier of 5 means that a $1 increase in reserves could lead to a $5 increase in deposits. This, of course, also means a $5 rise in the supply of money.

The size of the deposit expansion multiplier depends on the reserve ratio. Once you know the reserve ratio, you can figure the size of the deposit expansion multiplier. This can be done by using the following equation:

20-1

deposit expansion
multiplier
The number that
expresses the
relationship between a
change in bank reserves
and the change in the
money supply.

$$\text{Deposit Expansion Multiplier} = 1 \div \text{Reserve Ratio}$$

For a 20 percent reserve ratio, the deposit expansion multiplier is calculated as below.

$$\text{Deposit Expansion Multiplier} = 1 \div .20 = 5$$

Suppose the reserve ratio went up to 25 percent. What would happen to this multiplier? It would go down to 4. Check this yourself by solving the equation ($1 \div .25 = 4$). If the deposit expansion multiplier is 4, a $1 increase in reserves would allow deposits and the money supply to rise by $4. With reserves of $10,000, only $40,000 of deposits could now be supported.

This relationship gives the Federal Reserve a great deal of power over the money supply. If the Fed raises the reserve ratio, banks will have to reduce the level of their deposits. In doing so, the money supply is reduced. Banks can cut the level of their deposits by not making new loans when old loans are paid off.

What would happen if the Fed lowered the reserved requirement? First, banks would have lower required reserves and more excess reserves. They would then make loans until they were loaned up. This would create new deposits and would therefore increase the money supply.

So, you see that changing the reserve requirement can cause a change in the money supply. However, the Fed does not often use this tool of monetary policy. One reason is that even small changes in the reserve ratio can cause large changes in the money supply because of the multiplier effect. Also, it is hard to predict exactly how long it will take for the entire change in the money supply to be completed.

Changing the Discount Rate

The discount rate is the interest rate banks must pay when they borrow money from the Federal Reserve. Why would a bank borrow money from the Fed? Remember that banks must keep enough reserves to meet the reserve requirement. Sometimes bankers simply cannot know exactly when loans will be paid off. Therefore, they may need to borrow money in order to meet the reserve requirement. Often they will borrow from other banks, but sometimes they have to borrow from the Fed. When they do, they must pay interest on the money they borrow, and the interest rate is called the *discount rate*.

In theory, a bank could borrow from the Fed to increase its reserves. It could then make new loans based on these added reserves. This would cause the bank's deposits to rise and would increase the money supply. Banks would be more likely to borrow at a low discount rate than at a high discount rate. In this respect, banks work like other businesses. So, by lowering the discount rate, the Fed may encourage banks to borrow more money. This would tend to increase the money supply.

In practice, banks try not to borrow from the Federal Reserve. Therefore, changes in the discount rate are not as useful a tool of monetary policy as you might think. But such changes do tell us about the type of monetary policy the Fed intends to follow. When it raises the discount rate, you know that it intends to follow a tight monetary policy. You could then expect other moves that would reduce the money supply. On the other hand, if the Fed lowers the discount rate, it can be expected to follow other loose monetary policies, too. The money supply is then likely to rise.

Open Market Operations

20–1

open market operations
The buying and selling of United States government securities by the Federal Reserve.

Open market operations comprise the most important kind of monetary policy. **Open market operations** are the buying and selling of United States government securities by the Federal Reserve. These securities resemble the savings bonds you or your parents might buy. They are the IOUs issued by the government when it borrows money to provide the goods and services we expect.

When the Fed buys or sells such government bonds, it has a direct effect on the country's money supply. Let us see why this is true. Suppose that the Fed buys a $1,000 government bond from you. You would trade the $1,000 bond to the Fed for a $1,000 check. When you cash the check or deposit it in the bank, the money supply goes up by $1,000. In this process you have traded a nonmoney asset (the bond) for money. You could not have used the $1,000 bond to purchase anything. But you can do so with the money you got in exchange for the bond.

Is that $1,000 all the money that would be created when the Fed bought your bond? The answer is no. Remember the deposit expansion multiplier. If the required reserve ratio is 20 percent, the deposit expansion multiplier would be 5 (1 ÷ .20 = 5). When the added $1,000 is deposited in the banking system, it represents new reserves. Those $1,000 of new reserves could then support $5,000 of new deposits (5 × $1,000 = $5,000). So, the money supply would go up by $5,000 when the Fed buys a $1,000 government bond.

What happens when the Federal Reserve sells bonds? The whole process is reversed. If the Fed sells you a $1,000 bond, you pay for it by check. Your bank checking deposit account would fall by $1,000. In exchange, you would get a $1,000 government bond—a nonmoney asset. The Fed would take that check to your bank for payment. This would make the bank's reserves fall by $1,000. The bank would then have to reduce its deposits by $5,000 due to the deposit multiplier. In this case, when the Fed sells a $1,000 bond, the money supply goes down by $5,000.

The Federal Open Market Committee (FOMC) that you learned about in Chapter 19 decides the amount of government securities to buy or sell. Since this is the most widely used method of changing the money supply, the FOMC has a great deal of power over the whole United States economy. Its decisions about buying and selling securities are carried out by the Federal Reserve Bank of New York.

MONETARY POLICY AND INTEREST RATES

One way to see how monetary policy affects the economy is by examining its influence on interest rates. Let's look at this with the help of Figure 20–6. A loose or easy monetary policy is shown by a rise in the money supply from M_1 to M_2. This is a shift of the money supply line to the right. Such a rise in the money supply causes interest rates to fall. On the other hand, a tight monetary policy is shown as a move from M_2 to M_1. The movement of the money supply line to the left shows a move to a lower money supply. This decline in the money supply causes interest rates to rise.

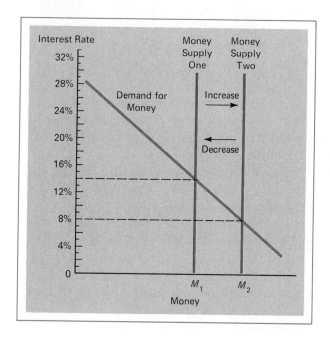

FIGURE 20–6   THE EFFECT OF MONETARY POLICY ON INTEREST RATES
A loose monetary policy is a shift of the money supply from M_1 to M_2. The interest rate decreases with a loose monetary policy. A tight monetary policy results in a shift of the money supply from M_2 to M_1. The interest rate increases with a tight money supply.

The level of interest rates is very important in determining the level of economic activity. Interest rates affect nearly every part of our economy. Let's look at the effect of interest rates on four major parts of the economy.

Interest and Investment in Factories and Equipment

Businesses will only invest in new factories and new equipment   20–6
if they can expect to profit from doing so. An investment schedule like the one in Figure 20–7 is common for most firms. It shows that new factories and new equipment would be more profitable at lower interest rates than at higher interest rates. If the market rate of interest were 8 percent, businesses would invest an amount equal to $I*$ dollars per year.

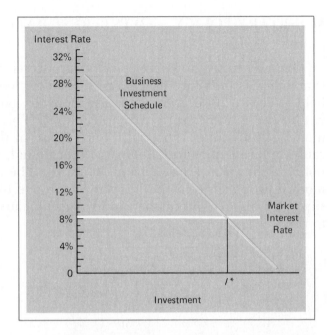

FIGURE 20–7 A TYPICAL BUSINESS INVESTMENT SCHEDULE
The lower the interest rate, the greater the demand of business for money to invest. At 8 percent interest, business invests I* dollars.

This means that a loose monetary policy that lowers interest rates leads businesses to invest more than they would otherwise. This investment leads to more economic activity, greater employment, and a higher rate of economic growth. But increasing investment by a loose monetary policy has a disadvantage: The added aggregate demand could also cause inflation.

The opposite is also true. A tight monetary policy causes interest rates to rise. This leads businesses to cut back on investment spending. A positive result of this action is that inflation might be reduced. But at the same time, the level of economic activity will be reduced. This can increase unemployment and slow the rate of economic growth.

Exactly how much investment spending changes when the interest rate changes remains debatable. Some economists think that the investment line is steep. This means that even fairly large changes in the interest rate will have only a slight effect on investment spending. Others think the investment line is fairly flat so that small changes in the interest rate greatly affect the level of investment. The debate concerns only a matter of degree. Nearly everyone agrees that, other factors being equal, investment spending will be greater at lower interest rates than at higher rates.

Interest and Inventory Investment

20–6   Businesses would like to have enough products on hand to meet the demands of all possible customers. Suppose you want to buy a pink four-door car with a green interior. Your car dealer would like to have one for you to buy. But you would not likely find that car on the dealer's lot. Your dealer would need an inventory large enough to have nearly every combination of colors. For several reasons, a business would not keep such large inventories. First, large inventories cause high storage costs. Second, there is the risk of costs incurred if products spoil, are damaged, or go out of date. A third and very important cost involves the interest rate.

Many firms have to borrow money to pay for their inventory. A high interest rate makes the firm's cost high, so it will carry less inventory. This means that the firm orders fewer products to sell, and so producers make less. Fewer people are hired, and unemployment rises. At the same time, though, the rate of inflation may be reduced since aggregate demand is lower. During periods of high interest rates, many stores cut back on the number of alternate styles and colors that they carry.

On the other hand, when interest rates are lower, it costs businesses less to keep a large inventory. This results in more goods being ordered and in more production and employment. While this is good for businesses, the added aggregate demand may cause inflation.

Illustration 20–3
When interest rates rise, businesses cut back on inventory levels.

Interest and the Housing Market

The market for houses is especially sensitive to interest rates. When interest rates rise, the cost of housing also rises. This affects both home buyers and renters. Suppose you wanted to borrow $60,000 to buy a house. If the interest rate increased from 12 percent to 15 percent, your monthly payment would go up by about $140. Over 30 years, you would pay over $50,000 more for the house at the higher interest rate than at the lower interest rate.

20–6

When the housing market falls off, construction also falls. So does the employment of construction workers, plumbers, electricians, and other skilled laborers. If fewer homes are built, other industries are also affected. People need fewer new appliances, less new carpeting, and less new furniture. You can see the ripple effects through other parts of the economy. The entire economy can shift because of the housing industry. Higher interest rates due to a tight monetary policy can then greatly affect the whole economy through its effects on housing. Again, this would cause unemployment to rise, but it could reduce inflation.

When interest rates fall due to a loose monetary policy, the housing market usually picks up. The ripple effects work through the economy as activity in other parts of the economy rises as well. Employment goes up, but there is a danger of creating more inflation.

Illustration 20–4
High interest rates also cause a decline in the number of new homes that are built. This affects many other markets, such as plumbing and electrical installers.

ALICE M. RIVLIN

An insider in government policy making, Alice Rivlin (1931–) has directed the Congressional Budget Office to evaluate spending and taxes and propose budget cuts and program controls.

After 22 years' experience as Assistant Secretary of Health, Education, and Welfare and as Senior Fellow of the Brookings Institute in Washington, D.C., Rivlin became the first director of the Congressional Budget Office (CBO), which formed in 1975.

This new office was set up to function independently of the executive branch of the U.S. government, providing Congress with information about and evaluation of the budget. Each house of Congress, though, held a different notion of the new CBO's function: The House of Representatives desired straight technical analyses of the budget, while the Senate wanted dynamic suggestions and alternatives to current budget strategy.

The appointment of Rivlin to direct the CBO's 200-member staff stirred some controversy at first, because of her liberal economic stance. But her nonpartisan office proved itself to be more concerned with economics than politics. Rivlin, said a *Time* article during that period, "has proved that sex does not count in political economics, and her balanced judgments have made her popular even with conservatives."[1]

Committed to reducing government spending, Rivlin sees long-term planning as the way to keep budgets under control. That's why she proposed five-year goals to replace the usual one-year spending budgets Congress usually establishes. This allows spending cuts to happen in a gradual, orderly fashion.

Her targets for reduced spending have been in subsidies and transfer payments to retired civil servants, veterans, and farmers; hospital costs; increases in supply; and some deregulation. Budget deficits cannot continue, she insists, and careful future planning and cutting corners—even by a small percentage—are her solutions for budget deficits. As for inflation, Rivlin has said, "Do everything that you can think of because there is no simple answer."[2]

Born in Indiana, Rivlin attended Bryn Mawr and then earned a Ph.D. in economics from Radcliffe College. Through her Congressional work, she evaluated and formulated projections for unemployment, taxes, interest rates, the deficit, and economic growth. In 1983 Rivlin returned as director of the Economic Studies Program at Brookings Institute, continuing her study of government policy. In 1985, Dr. Rivlin was elected first woman president of the American Economic Association.

---

[1]Marshall Loeb, "Her Hand Is on the Future," *Time*, 113 (June 18, 1979), 58.

[2]*Ibid*.

Interest and Personal Spending

20–6   Individuals tend to change their personal spending as interest rates change. With a tight monetary policy and higher interest rates, we are likely to cut back on those purchases we have to finance. This includes cars, appliances, stereo equipment, furniture, some types of clothing, vacations, and some costly recreational items. Once more, this reduces employment, but it also eases inflationary pressures. A loose monetary policy would have the opposite effects. Employment would tend to rise, as would inflation.

EVALUATION OF MONETARY POLICY

The above discussion may make you think that there is complete agreement about the role and effectiveness of monetary policy. This is far from true. Some of our best economists believe that changing the money supply will have no lasting effect on output or employment. This group, which includes Milton Friedman, thinks that monetary policy has its main effect on price levels. These economists argue that we should only increase the money supply to match the rate of real growth in the economy. If average real economic growth is 3 percent a year, they say that we should increase the money supply at a steady 3 percent rate.

Other economists think that we should use monetary policy as the main tool to control the level and direction of our economy. They point to the great flexibility in monetary policy to make large or small changes. Such changes can also be made very quickly. The **inside time lag** is the time it takes to decide on a policy. Since relatively few people determine monetary policy, they can usually reach agreement quickly and make the changes almost at once. Therefore, the inside time lag for monetary policy is usually short. As you will see in a later chapter, other policies to change economic activity cannot be brought about nearly as quickly.

Finally, some economists think we should always follow a loose monetary policy to keep employment growing and to keep a high rate of economic growth. These people believe that nearly all our inflation is the cost-push type. Therefore, they believe that increasing aggregate demand will not cause further inflation. But it does appear that a loose monetary policy leads to higher inflation.

We should consider such views since the true effect money has on the economy is not yet known for certain. Partly, this uncertainty stems from the fact that changes in the money supply take a long time to work their way through the economy. How long is not known exactly, but it takes at least 6 months and it may take as long

20–1

inside time lag

The time it takes to decide on a policy.

as 18 to 24 months. This is called the outside time lag for monetary policy. The **outside time lag** is the time it takes for the effects of a policy change to be completely felt in the economy. The outside time lag for changes in monetary policy is usually long. There is a short inside time lag, but a long outside time lag. In other words, even though monetary policy can be changed rather quickly, the effects of such changes may take a long time to be felt.

In recent years some people have become confused about monetary policy. This is because its effect on interest rates has seemed different from what we would normally expect. For example, sometimes a loose monetary policy has been followed by rising interest rates. And at times, a tight monetary policy has been accompanied by falling interest rates. One reason for this seeming inconsistency is that the money demand may be changing at the same time the money supply is changed. For example, if the Fed sets up a loose monetary policy, people in businesses may expect greater inflation. This may lead them to think that they can charge higher prices. They may then want to increase production which could in turn cause them to have a higher demand for money. The rise in demand for money could cause interest rates to rise, even though the Fed follows a loose monetary policy. But remember that there is a demand and a supply side to every market, and both should be considered.

We have learned something about money from the history of monetary events. That is, *too much* of an increase in the money supply causes inflation. It may be that a moderate rise in the money supply will stimulate aggregate demand. In turn, this helps the economy toward higher employment and more economic growth. But just increasing the money supply cannot solve all of our economic problems. Besides, doing so raises the risk of great damage due to excessive inflation.

20–1

outside time lag
The time it takes for the effects of a policy change to be completely felt in the economy.

REVIEWING THE CHAPTER

20–1   1. Monetary policy is the changing of the amount of money in the economy with the objectives of reducing unemployment, keeping prices stable, and promoting economic growth. Monetary policy is under the control of the Federal Reserve.

20–5   2. There are three ways the Fed can change the money supply:

1. The reserve ratio can be changed.

2. The discount rate can be changed.

3. Open market operations can be used.

20–3   3. The Fed follows a loose monetary policy when it allows the money supply to grow larger. This can be done by lowering the reserve ratio, lowering the discount rate, and/or buying government securities. All these actions will likely cause interest rates to fall and aggregate demand to rise. This helps reduce unemployment and stimulate economic growth. These results are desirable, but the same actions also worsen inflation, which is undesirable.

20–3   4. A tight monetary policy is the opposite of a loose monetary policy. If the Fed holds back on the growth of the money supply or decreases it, it is following a tight monetary policy. This can be done by raising the reserve ratio, raising the discount rate, and/or selling government securities. All these actions are likely to cause interest rates to rise and aggregate demand to fall. This reduces inflation but could also cause higher unemployment and slow the rate of economic growth.

REVIEWING ECONOMIC TERMS

20–1   Supply definitions for the following terms:

loose monetary policy	excess reserves
tight monetary policy	monetary policy
fractional reserve banking system	deposit expansion multiplier
	open market operations
reserve ratio	inside time lag
reserve requirement	outside time lag

REVIEWING ECONOMIC CONCEPTS

20–3   1. What effect does a loose monetary policy have on the money supply, economic growth, employment, and inflation?

20–3   2. What effect does a tight monetary policy have on the money supply, economic growth, employment, and inflation?

20–2   3. What is the relationship between interest rates and the demand for money?

20–5   4. What determines the supply of money?

20–2   5. How do money supply and demand affect the interest rate?

20–5   6. List three ways the Fed can control the money supply.

20–4   7. How does changing the reserve ratio affect the money supply?

20–5   8. List two reasons why the Fed does not often change the reserve ratio.

20–5   9. How does changing the discount rate affect the money supply?

20–5   10. How does changing open market operations affect the money supply?

20–6   11. How do interest rates affect investment in factories and equipment?

20–6   12. How do interest rates affect investment in inventories?

20–6   13. How do interest rates affect the housing market?

20–6   14. How do interest rates affect personal spending?

20–1   15. Why do we say that the inside time lag for monetary policy is short?

20–1   16. Why do we say that the outside time lag for monetary policy is long?

APPLYING ECONOMIC CONCEPTS

20–3   1. Explain the difference between a loose monetary policy and a tight monetary policy.

20–5   2. Of the three methods the Fed uses to change the money supply, which is used more often? Why?

20–1, 20–6   3. What is monetary policy? What are the objectives of monetary policy? Is there any conflict between these objectives? Explain your answer.

4. Why does aggregate demand go up when the money supply is increased? Include in your answer business investment in factories and equipment, business investment in inventories, the housing sector of the economy, and personal spending.

5. What is a fractional reserve banking system? Write an essay in which you explain how the terms *required reserves*, *excess reserves*, and *reserve ratio* are related to each other.

20–5   6. If the Fed sells bonds, how will the money supply change? How will it change if the Fed buys bonds? Which of these actions is most likely to cut down on inflation? Why?

20–5   7. Assume that the reserve ratio is 20 percent and that the total amount of deposits in the banking system is $8 million. How many dollars of reserves would be required in the banking system?

20–4   8. Suppose that the reserve ratio is 25 percent and there are total deposits of $5 million. Required reserves would then be $1.25 million. Assume that there are no excess reserves so that the banking system is loaned up. Based on this information, answer the following questions:

   a. If the Fed lowered the reserve ratio to 20 percent, what amount of reserves would be required?
   b. How many dollars of excess reserves would there be?
   c. What volume of deposits could be supported with the $1.25 million of total reserves with the 20 percent reserve ratio?
   d. How much could the money supply increase due to the Federal Reserve action of lowering the reserve ratio from 25 percent to 20 percent?

20–6   9. A business has a project that is expected to earn a 10 percent rate of return each year. How will interest rates affect the business's decision about going ahead with the project?

20–3   10. Draw a chart like the one below. Decide whether a tight monetary policy and a loose monetary policy would increase or decrease each item at the left of the chart. Use a + to indicate an increase and a − to indicate a decrease.

	Tight Monetary Policy	Loose Monetary Policy
a. supply of money		
b. interest rate.....................		
c. employment		
d. rate of economic growth.........		
e. inflation		
f. investment in factories and equipment.....................		
g. investment in inventories		
h. housing market		
i. personal spending..............		

CHAPTER 21

TAXES

Learning Objectives

21-1 Define terms related to taxes and tax policy.

21-2 Describe several reasons why we have taxes.

21-3 List major sources and uses of revenue for the federal government.

21-4 List major sources and uses of revenue for state and local government.

21-5 Discuss four ways in which the tax burden is distributed.

21-6 Distinguish between direct and indirect taxes.

21-7 Describe the seven major types of taxes in the United States.

WHY DO WE HAVE TAXES?

21-2   Everyone complains about taxes. Nobody likes taxes. A politician who promises to cut taxes generally wins votes. Politicians do not like to vote for new taxes because people may not reelect them to office. If taxes are such an awful and unpopular burden, then why have them? The following sections discuss several reasons why taxes are necessary in our economy.

Taxes Pay for Public Goods

It would be difficult to have a society like ours without a government. We must have a government to provide defense, law enforcement, transportation, and other services. All of these government services are public goods.

A public good is one that a person can consume without reducing the consumption of the good for another person. Unlike the consumption of private goods, it is difficult to keep anyone from consuming a public good. As you saw earlier, one of the best examples of a public good is national defense. One person can benefit from our national defense without reducing another person's benefits. In fact, it is difficult to keep any person in our society from enjoying the benefits of national defense.

The market system does not work well in producing public goods. This is because a person who refuses to pay for a public good cannot be kept from using it. Suppose that the neighbors in a high crime area decide to hire a police force. Each neighbor, except Mrs. Smith, agrees to pay $100 a year to finance the force. Mrs. Smith refuses to pay because she knows that if all the others pay the $100, the police will patrol the area anyway. Burglars and other criminals will be discouraged from committing crimes in the area. And Mrs. Smith can enjoy the services of the police force without paying $100.

The market system has no way to deal with this type of problem. For this reason, we cannot ask each person to make a direct payment in the form of a product price. Therefore, we finance public goods by using taxes. No one likes taxes, but they do serve a real need in our society by providing many important goods and services. Figure 21–1 shows some public goods which are paid for with tax dollars.

Taxes Correct Problems Caused by Negative Externalities

In a market system such as ours, due to negative externalities, the market does not always work as well as we might hope. Two examples of negative externalities in our economy are water and air pollution. Pollution problems arise because producers have to pay only part of the real costs of making their products. Producers must pay for their raw materials. They must also pay for labor, the machines they use in production, and energy. However, producers may put tons of waste into the air, or into rivers, lakes, or oceans at little cost to themselves. In doing so they pollute our water and air, making both less valuable to society.

In these cases, taxes can correct this market failure. The government can collect taxes on the pollutants a business puts into the air and water. The money from that tax can be used to clean up the pollution. The tax may also make production more expensive; thus, the firm's cost will more closely represent the true cost of making the good. This is just one way that a tax helps to correct a market failure.

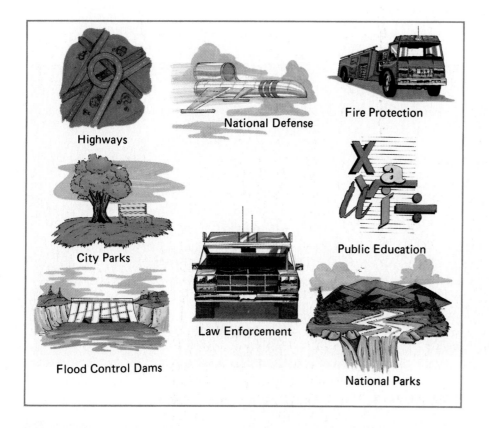

FIGURE 21–1   PUBLIC GOODS FINANCED USING TAX DOLLARS
The market system does not work well in producing public goods. Therefore, we usually pay for public goods, such as these shown here, with tax dollars. You can see that taxes pay for many of the important goods and services we enjoy every day.

Taxes Can Help Stabilize the Economy

The implementation of fiscal policy depends on the government's ability to change the level of aggregate demand in the economy. (You will learn more about this in Chapter 22.) This is done partly by changing the amount of taxes paid by consumers and corporations. So, another reason for having taxes is that they make it possible for our government to redistribute income and to influence the amount of income generated.

FEDERAL TAX REVENUES AND SPENDING

Our federal government collects taxes from many sources. The left side of Figure 21–2 shows the percentage of federal dollars that came from each tax in a recent year. The right side shows how that revenue was spent.

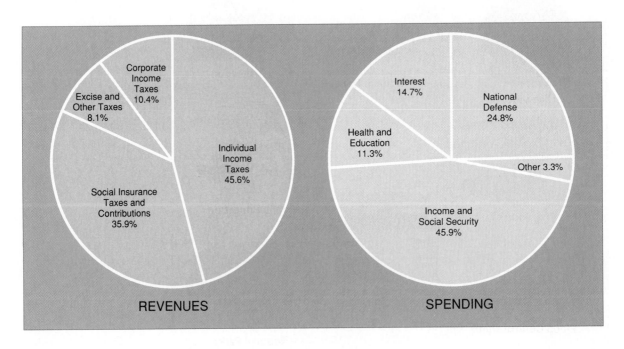

FIGURE 21–2   FEDERAL TAX REVENUES AND GOVERNMENT SPENDING FOR A REPRESENTATIVE YEAR
Individual income taxes produce the largest part of government revenues. The largest part of government spending is for income security.

Source: U.S. Bureau of the Census, *Statistical Abstract of the United States: 1991*, 111th ed. (Washington, D.C., 1991), 316–317.

Sources of Revenue

From Figure 21–2 you can see that most of the tax revenues   21–3
collected by the federal government come from private citizens.
Personal income taxes and social security taxes comprise about
81 percent of all tax dollars collected. Taxes on corporate income
make up about 10 percent of federal tax dollars. Later in this chapter we will discuss these and other kinds of taxes.

Spending for National Defense

A large amount of money is spent on national defense. There   21–3
are many social arguments against the military and against over-
spending for defense. It is hard to see the benefits received from
defense spending. On the other hand, it is easy to add up the costs
of defense spending. The evaluation of national defense necessarily takes on a political nature. The defense budget, whether
too large or too small or wasteful or efficient, protects our freedom
and gives us national security. Most Americans would consider this
freedom and protection a great benefit.

Spending for Health and Income Security

The largest portion of federal government spending goes to   21–3
health and income security, including social security. This includes
expenditures for social insurance, public aid, health and medical
programs, and some other social welfare programs, as well as medical research. It is hard to evaluate this spending because so many
benefits reach the public indirectly. Payments for social security
benefits have direct and measurable benefits. But what about medical research? How much benefit would result from finding a cure
for cancer? Think of the large sums of money that now support
cancer treatment. But also think of the value of the lives saved.

Another indirect benefit of these programs is that the cost of
caring for dependent children, the aged, and the disabled spreads
across all taxpayers. Thus, needy people do not have to rely on private charity for survival. The social costs of riots and disease that
can result when the poor do not get care may also be less. Many
people believe that there is much waste in our welfare system.
There may indeed be many ways to improve our welfare programs. Even as they now stand, though, they probably result in a
net benefit to our society.

Illustration 21–1
Tax dollars spent on the space program provide benefits such as improvements in technology and increased national pride.

Spending for Other Government Programs

Many other government programs give us different kinds of benefits. For example, all Americans felt national pride as Neil Armstrong took his first step on the moon. In addition, the technology of the space program brought us improvements in transistors, computers, and calculators. Even Tang and Teflon were first developed for use in the space program. Farm programs pay for research that makes crops better. Other government spending gives aid to people for job training, school lunches, and other benefits. Some veterans may receive health and educational benefits as well as housing loans on relatively favorable terms.

STATE AND LOCAL TAX REVENUES AND SPENDING

Individuals and businesses pay taxes to state and local governments to raise revenue for other kinds of public goods. These state and local government revenue sources and spending programs are discussed below.

Sources of Revenue

21–4   Most states depend heavily on sales taxes as a revenue source. Some states rely on income taxes as well. Local governments get most of their money from property taxes. Local governments in many parts of the country also use income taxes. The percentage distribution of state and local revenues by source is shown in Table 21–1 below. These percentages represent a composite for all

TABLE 21–1

PERCENTAGE DISTRIBUTION OF STATE AND LOCAL
REVENUES BY SOURCE

Source	Percentage of Total Revenue
Revenue from Federal Government	13.3%
Sales Taxes	17.7%
Property Taxes	15.0%
Insurance Trust Revenue	11.9%
Personal Income Taxes	10.0%
Utility Revenue	5.5%
Corporate Income Taxes	2.7%
All Other Sources	23.9%

Source: U.S. Bureau of the Census, *Statistical Abstract of the United States: 1991*, 111th ed. (Washington, D.C., 1991), 284.

states. The map in Figure 21–3 shows how the state and local tax burden differs among states. Such differences sometimes affect a person's decision about where to live.

Spending Programs

State and local revenues are spent differently from federal revenues in several important ways. First, the federal government spends only a small part of its budget on education. On the other hand, state and local governments together spend about 30 percent of their money for education. State and local revenues also provide police and fire protection, sanitation services, parks and recreation, health programs, and highways. The list of benefits we get from the spending of all tax dollars runs long. Some people believe that our tax dollars are wasted, or spent unwisely, or stolen by corrupt politicians. There may be some waste, dishonesty, and inefficiency. But the public does receive many benefits from the

21–4

FIGURE 21–3   STATE AND LOCAL TAXES PER PERSON
See how your state compares to others in terms of state and local taxes paid per person.
Source: U.S. Bureau of the Census, *Statistical Abstract of the United States: 1991*, 111th ed. (Washington, D.C., 1991), 286.

spending of its tax dollars. Without taxes we could not have most of these benefits. The private sector would not be likely to provide national defense, highways, public education, or many of the other programs mentioned above. Taxes are needed to provide these beneficial public programs.

PRINCIPLES OF TAXATION

You have seen that taxes are necessary and that we receive many benefits from the spending of our tax dollars. Because public goods are used by all citizens of a society, people must pay their share of taxes. This raises an important question in taxation. How can we be sure that each person pays a fair share of the tax burden?

Benefit Principle

21-5

21-1
benefit principle of taxation
The concept that those who benefit from the spending of tax dollars should pay the taxes to provide the benefits.

One argument that answers the above question is called the benefit principle of taxation. The **benefit principle of taxation** is the concept that those who benefit from the spending of tax dollars should pay the taxes to provide the benefits. This means that the people who benefit should pay. Our gasoline taxes follow the benefit principle. The amount of gasoline bought is a good measure of the amount of highway services used. So, a tax on gasoline makes users of the highways pay for their use. The money collected from gasoline taxes is used to repair and improve highways.

But often the benefit principle of taxation does not apply. Most public goods such as national defense and social welfare programs cannot use this principle. All people benefit from national defense spending, but all people cannot be charged directly for the benefit. People who benefit from social welfare payments cannot afford to pay for those benefits. If they could afford to pay for them, they would not need them.

The very nature of public goods often makes it hard to apply the benefit principle of taxation. It is often impossible to separate those who benefit from those who don't. Even when this is possible, it is difficult to find ways of charging only those who benefit. So, two conditions are necessary to use the benefit principle of taxation: (1) Those who benefit from a particular good must be easily identified; (2) ways to charge only those who benefit must be found. However, when these conditions exist, it is usually more efficient to have the private sector produce that particular good.

Illustration 21–2
Money collected from gasoline taxes pays for highway maintenance and improvement. This follows the benefit principle of taxation.

Ability-to-Pay Principle

The second principle of taxation is the ability-to-pay principle of taxation. The **ability-to-pay principle of taxation** is the concept that those who can best afford to pay taxes should pay most of the taxes. Generally the rich or the economically better off can best afford to pay. Most economists believe that every extra dollar earned has value. For a person earning only $1,000 a year, extra dollars of income mean more food, or badly needed clothing, or medical care. On the other hand, a person earning $100,000 a year does not need the extra dollars to meet basic needs. This person would hardly notice an extra dollar of income. Therefore, the extra dollars may not have nearly the value to that person as to the person earning $1,000 a year. The ability-to-pay principle of taxation would tax the person earning $100,000 a year more heavily than the person earning $1,000 a year.

21–5
21–1
ability-to-pay principle of taxation
The concept that those who can best afford to pay taxes should pay most of the taxes.

Progressive Taxes

Closely connected to the ability-to-pay principle is the concept of how the tax burden is distributed among people in relation to their level of income. A **progressive tax** is a tax that takes a larger percentage of higher incomes and a smaller percentage of lower incomes. For example, if a person earning $100,000 a year paid $25,000 for a particular tax, the tax is 25 percent of the person's income. If a person earning $1,000 a year paid $100 for that same tax, the tax is 10 percent of that person's income. This tax is a progressive tax because it takes a larger *percentage* of the richer person's income and a smaller *percentage* of the poorer person's income.

21–5
21–1
progressive tax
A tax that takes a larger percentage of higher incomes and a smaller percentage of lower incomes.

Regressive Taxes

Taxes can also be regressive. A **regressive tax** is a tax that takes a larger percentage of lower incomes and a smaller percentage of higher incomes. Assume that a tax took $10,000 from a person earning $100,000 per year and $2,500 from a person earning $10,000 a year. The tax rate is 10 percent for the richer person and 25 percent for the poorer person. This tax is regressive since the richer person pays a smaller *percentage* of income than the poorer person. Regressive taxes go against the ability-to-pay principle of taxation. They take greater percentages of the incomes of those who can least afford to pay.

21–5
21–1
regressive tax
A tax that takes a larger percentage of lower incomes and a smaller percentage of higher incomes.

Proportional Taxes

21–1

proportional tax

A tax that takes the same percentage of income from all taxpayers.

Taxes also can be proportional. A **proportional tax** is a tax that takes the same percentage of income from all taxpayers. For example, consider a tax that takes $10,000 from a person earning $100,000 a year and $100 from a person earning $1,000 a year. Both taxpayers must give up 10 percent of their incomes for that tax. The tax is proportional because it taxes all taxpayers at the same percentage rate.

Proportional taxes are based less on the ability-to-pay principle than progressive taxes. They take proportional amounts of income at all levels. The proportional amounts taken at lower income levels may have much more value to the individual than the proportional amounts taken from those with higher incomes. So, a proportional tax may take more dollars necessary for survival from lower income families than it takes from higher income families.

DIRECT AND INDIRECT TAXES

To evaluate whether each taxpayer pays a fair share of taxes, we must find out who really pays a certain tax. *Tax incidence* refers to the group on which the tax burden actually falls. Often the person on whom a tax is levied passes the tax on to someone else.

21–6

21–1

direct tax

A tax paid by the person against whom the tax is levied.

21–1

indirect tax

A tax that can be shifted, at least in part, to a party other than the one on whom the tax is levied.

There are two kinds of taxes—direct taxes and indirect taxes. A **direct tax** is a tax paid by the person against whom the tax is levied. The tax is levied against the individual taxpayer, and that taxpayer must pay the tax.

Sometimes the person against whom a tax is levied can shift the tax so that someone else must pay it. This is a case of an indirect tax. An **indirect tax** is a tax that can be shifted, at least in part, to a party other than the one on whom the tax is levied. For example, property owners must pay property taxes. However, property owners who rent their property can make renters pay some of that tax by including it in the rent payment. Thus property owners may shift the incidence of some of the property tax to the renter.

Taxes on businesses can often be shifted to the person who uses the company's products. For example, businesses must pay taxes on the sale of certain items, such as cigarettes, liquor, and gasoline. Excise taxes function this way. These taxes are indirect taxes because although they are levied on the business, the consumer actually pays part of the tax. Other taxes on business, including property taxes, can be shifted in part to consumers. Many times companies raise prices in order to cover the cost of new taxes.

The amount of the tax that can be shifted to the consumer depends on how much importance the consumer places on the product. If people must have a certain product (or think they must), almost all of the tax can be shifted to the consumer. This might hold true for certain medicines. If a patient must have a certain medicine no matter what the price, any tax on that medicine can be shifted entirely to the patient. In the same way, some people feel that they must smoke cigarettes at any price. Therefore, a tax on cigarettes can be passed on to smokers. The company can simply raise the price of the medicine or the price of the cigarettes to pay for the tax.

If a tax is placed on a good not essential to a consumer, the producer cannot shift the tax as easily. Suppose a new tax is levied on the producers of chewing gum. If the producers of chewing gum raise the price of gum to cover the tax, many people will buy less chewing gum. Some may switch to eating candy or mints. Chewing gum producers cannot afford to have too many people stop chewing gum. Therefore, they will want to keep the price of gum low and pay at least part of the tax from their profits. If the good is not essential to a consumer, it is harder for the producer to shift the incidence of the tax (to add the tax to the price of the product). It is easier to shift the incidence of a tax to consumers when the good is needed by consumers.

Illustration 21–3
Taxes levied on medicines can often be shifted to the consumer.

PERSONAL INCOME TAXES

A **personal income tax** is a tax on the income of individuals. The federal government gets more than 45 percent of its revenues from the personal income tax. State and local governments get 10 percent of their revenues from taxes on personal income. The Internal Revenue Service (IRS) defines the tax base, or taxable income, as total income minus (1) some excluded income, (2) certain adjustments, (3) deductible expenses (or a standard deduction), and (4) personal allowances. The income tax owed is then figured from this tax base.

21–7

21–1

personal income tax
A tax on the income of individuals.

Personal Income Tax Is a Progressive Tax

Persons with higher incomes pay a higher percentage of their income for federal personal income tax than persons with lower incomes. Therefore, our federal personal income tax is a progressive tax. At the low end of the income structure, the tax rate is the lowest. As income increases, added income is taxed at higher rates. A progressive tax rate structure is shown in Table 21–2.

TABLE 21–2

A PROGRESSIVE INCOME TAX STRUCTURE

Taxable Income Bracket		Average Percentage Rate on Base Amount	Tax on Base Amount	Percentage Rate on Income Above the Base and Below the Upper Limit*
Base	Upper Limit			
$ 5,000	$18,000	0%	0	15%
$18,001	$43,000	10.83%	$ 1,950	28%
$43,001	and above	23.72%	$10,200	33%

An example:

1. Jack Kettes has a taxable income of $25,000.

2. Jack pays 10.83 percent of the first $18,000 (which is $1,950) plus 28 percent of the $7,000 of taxable income over the $18,000 base for his bracket. The 28 percent of $7,000 adds $1,960 to Jack's tax bill.

3. His total tax bill is $1,950 + $1,960, or $3,910. Thus, his average tax rate is 15.64 percent ($3,910 ÷ $25,000 = .1564), even though he is in the 28 percent tax bracket.

*This is sometimes called the marginal tax rate.

You can see in the table that each bracket has a base amount and an upper limit. The upper limit of the lower bracket becomes the base amount of the next higher bracket. The taxpayer pays a percentage of the base amount in the bracket plus another percentage (the *marginal rate*) of all income over the base amount but under the upper limit. From zero to the base of the first bracket is called the *zero bracket* since income in that range is not taxed.

Assume that Ms. Reiko Kimura's taxable income as a fire fighter is $17,000. She will be in the $5,000 to $18,000 bracket. This means she must pay 15 percent of her income over $5,000. Thus, $12,000 of her income will be taxed at 15 percent. Multiplying $12,000 by .15 (15%), we get $1,800. Ms. Kimura must pay $1,800 in federal income tax. So, on the average, she pays 10.6 percent of her taxable income to the federal government as her personal income tax. The 10.6 percent is found by dividing her tax payment of $1,800 by her income of $17,000. That is, $1,800 ÷ $17,000 = .106, or 10.6 percent.

Many people think that the progressive tax rate system penalizes them. They think that if they earn extra money they end up with less take-home pay because the extra money raises them to a higher tax bracket. This is absolutely wrong. If people earn more money in a year, they will take home more money during that year. The tax table shows that there is no bracket for which the marginal tax rate (the tax rate on added income) is greater than 100 percent.

Personal Income Tax Is a Direct Tax

A personal income tax is levied against the individual taxpayer who, in turn, pays the tax. Thus, the personal income tax is a direct tax. The individual who earns the income must pay tax on that income. Shifting the incidence of a personal income tax to another individual is difficult, if not impossible.

Personal Income Tax Follows Ability-to-Pay Principle

Our progressive federal personal income tax requires that a larger percentage of income be paid in taxes as incomes increase. A progressive tax follows the ability-to-pay principle. Therefore, our federal personal income tax follows the ability-to-pay principle.

Many state and local governments also collect a personal income tax. These taxes resemble the federal income tax in most ways, including their incidence. They differ mostly in the tax rate structure. State and local income taxes are at a much lower rate. For example, a city might have a 1/2 percent income tax. A state income tax is often about 4 or 5 percent.

When flat rates such as these are used, the income tax is proportional. A proportional income tax is the most common when such a tax is used at the local level. At the state level, both proportional and progressive income taxes can be found. In those states such as Montana, which use a progressive income tax, the rates fall well below those used for the federal income tax.

Illustration 21–4
Because the federal personal income tax charges higher tax rates to people with higher incomes, this tax follows the ability-to-pay principle.

Depending on their tax rates, then, some state and local personal income taxes do follow the ability-to-pay principle. Like the federal personal income tax, these taxes are progressive. However, state and local personal income taxes that are proportional tax all people at the same rate. Therefore, they are not based as much on the ability-to-pay principle.

CORPORATE INCOME TAXES

21-7

21-1

corporate income tax
A tax on the earnings of corporations.

A **corporate income tax** is a tax on the earnings of corporations. The federal corporate income tax works like the personal income tax. The tax base (the amount of income to be taxed) is figured in much the same way as the tax base for personal income taxes. First, the company must add all of its income to determine its gross income. The company's tax base is then determined by subtracting certain business expenses and depreciation. Depreciation measures the cost of equipment as it wears out.

For example, suppose a bakery has a delivery truck that costs $8,000. The bakery could deduct part of that $8,000 each year from its gross income as depreciation. Most business expenses are deductible. A bakery might deduct rent, employee wages and salaries, utilities, the cost of ingredients, advertising, and other costs of running the business.

There is a great deal of controversy as to who actually pays the corporate income tax. Some economists argue that the burden of corporate taxes shifts almost completely to consumers in the form of higher product prices. Others argue that the stockholders in corporations pay the tax. Since taxes reduce the amount of money available for dividends, stockholders receive less dividend income. Thus, they pay part of the corporate income tax.

Illustration 21-5
To determine its tax base, a bakery organized as a corporation subtracts equipment depreciation and certain business expenses from its gross income.

Some people believe that corporations shift the burden of corporate income taxes to their employees by paying lower wage rates. The reasoning behind this argument is rather complex. But economists generally agree that the combination of stockholders, employees, consumers, and the corporation itself all appear to bear some part of the corporate tax burden.

SALES AND EXCISE TAXES

21-1

sales tax
A tax on goods that are bought.

Corporate and personal income taxes provide more than 55 percent of federal tax revenues, but only about 13 percent of state and local tax revenues. At the state level, the most important source of tax revenue is the sales tax. A **sales tax** is a tax on goods that are bought. Sales taxes apply to most products we buy. State and local sales taxes are usually this kind. Sometimes taxes are levied only on certain items such as cigarettes, liquor, or gasoline. Sales taxes levied only on specific items are called **excise taxes**.

21–1

excise tax

A sales tax levied only on specific items.

Sales Taxes

Sales taxes are most often levied by state governments, but some local governments also levy sales taxes. In general, sales taxes apply to all goods bought or sold in the state. However, certain states exempt food, clothing, and medical purchases because these items are thought to be necessities. The sales tax may act as a regressive tax. At first glance, it appears proportional, since it takes an equal percentage from each purchase. However, it is the total *percentage* of a person's income paid for the tax that counts.

21–7

The poor spend a very high percentage of their incomes on taxable items. They have little or no money to save, invest, or use for other expenditures immune to sales tax. Those who are better off spend a smaller part of their incomes. (They can afford to save or invest more of their incomes.) The poor spend a larger percentage of their income than do the rich. Since the poor spend a higher percentage of their income on commodities, they must also pay a higher percentage of their income in sales taxes.

Consider a general sales tax of 4 percent with no exempted items. Suppose a poor family has $8,000 of income after paying income taxes and must spend all of it to live. They pay $320 in sales tax, or 4 percent of their income. Suppose a wealthier family has $40,000 of income after paying income taxes. They may save or invest $15,000 per year and spend the remaining $25,000. They would pay $1,000 in sales taxes on that $25,000 of spending. This $1,000 represents only 2.5 percent of their total income. Thus, the sales tax takes 4 percent of the poor family's income and 2.5 percent of the rich family's income. This sales tax is regressive because it takes a larger percentage of the poorer family's income. Sales taxes with exemptions for necessities may be less regressive.

Excise Taxes

Excise taxes function as a sales tax, but they are levied on certain goods. Excise tax rates are usually higher than general sales tax rates. Taxes on gasoline, alcoholic beverages, and cigarettes are examples of excise taxes. In general, excise taxes have the same advantages and disadvantages as the sales tax. Like sales taxes, many excise taxes are regressive and discriminate against the poor. However, excise taxes on luxury items, such as furs and jewelry, are not regressive because the poor do not usually buy such goods.

21–7

ARTHUR LAFFER

Arthur Laffer was born in 1941. He earned a doctoral degree at Stanford University and first gained national attention as an economist for the Office of Management and Budget (OMB) during the Nixon administration in 1971.

While working for the OMB, Laffer developed a model of the economy that was different from those widely used at the time. His model ignored many factors that most economists considered important, but it emphasized the level of federal spending, interest rates, stock prices, and the rate at which the Fed expands the money supply. Laffer believed that an increase in the money supply was felt instantly throughout the economy. But most economists felt that the time lag was much longer. Laffer's model predicted that growth in GNP would be much larger than others predicted. But his model did not prove to be totally accurate.

Laffer is probably best known as an advocate of the Laffer curve, which is an attempt to show the relationship between tax rates and revenue. The Laffer curve shows that there is no revenue at a tax rate of zero. At a tax rate of 100 percent there is also no revenue because there is no incentive to work. Going up from a zero tax rate, the curve shows that tax revenues increase as the tax rate increases. But then the curve reaches a point where revenues begin to fall.

According to Laffer, the economy in the early 1980s was above the point on the curve where tax rates where so high that revenues were decreasing. Not everyone agreed with this. In fact, a major criticism of the Laffer curve is that it is difficult to determine where the economy is on the curve at any given time. But the Laffer curve did influence many people in the Reagan administration who favored tax cuts.

Laffer was an economic advisor to Ronald Reagan during Reagan's presidential campaign. After Reagan's election, however, Laffer declined any government jobs. He continued to give economic advice to the government, however, while teaching at the University of Southern California.

Some excise taxes illustrate the benefit principle of taxation. A good example is the excise tax on gasoline. The revenues from this tax help to support highway construction and repair. Those people who buy the most gasoline pay most of the gasoline excise taxes. They also make the greatest use of our highway system. So, those people who receive greater benefits pay most of the cost as well. When the revenue from a tax is specifically designated for a specific use such as this, we say the tax revenue is *earmarked*. This means that the revenue is set aside for a particular use rather than being put into the general fund.

Effects of Sales and Excise Taxes

The concepts of demand, supply, and market equilibrium can help evaluate the incidence of sales or excise taxes. The diagram on the left side of Figure 21–4 shows the supply and demand for a product when no sales tax exists. The equilibrium price is $1.50, and the equilibrium quantity is 10. These values are determined by the intersection of the supply and demand curves at Point *E*.

Now suppose that a sales tax of $.20 per unit is placed on this product. Such a tax would shift the supply curve up by $.20 to the

Illustration 21–6
Excise taxes levied on luxury items, such as furs and jewelry, are not regressive because the poor cannot afford to purchase these expensive goods.

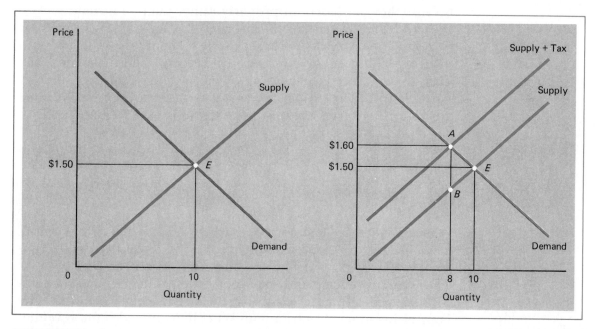

FIGURE 21–4   THE EFFECT OF A $.20 SALES TAX ON PRICE AND QUANTITY
The supply curve shifts up to the *Supply + Tax* curve. The new equilibrium point (*A*) shows a drop in quantity demanded from 10 to 8 and a rise in price from $1.50 to $1.60.

line labeled *Supply + Tax*. This is shown on the right side of Figure 21–4. The distance between Point *A* and Point *B* represents the $.20 tax. You see that a new equilibrium results at Point *A*. On the vertical axis you see that the equilibrium price rose to $1.60 while the equilibrium quantity fell from 10 to 8.

The sales tax of $.20 has lowered the amount people buy and has raised the price. But note an important point about this example. Price went up by just $.10 (from $1.50 to $1.60), even though the tax was $.20. So, part of the tax is paid by the buyers and part is paid by the sellers. The sales tax is actually levied on the seller. It is the seller, such as a gas station owner, who really pays the tax money to the government. But *part* of the burden of the tax shifts to consumers in the form of a higher price.

PROPERTY TAXES

21–7

21–1
property tax
A tax levied on real estate, such as a home, land, and buildings.

Property taxes are most often used by local governments. A **property tax** is a tax levied on real estate, such as a home, land, and buildings. In general, the value of property is assessed, and then a certain percentage of the assessed value of the property must be paid in taxes. Property taxes are generally regressive because they are based on property rather than on income.

The regressiveness of the property tax shows most for senior citizens. They may have worked hard for many years in order to pay for their homes. However, after age 65 their incomes may drop sharply. Despite this drop in income, they must continue to pay taxes on their property which generates no income. In some areas, property taxes are lowered for people over 65 or some other age used as a cut-off point.

SOCIAL SECURITY TAX

21–7

21–1
social security tax
A tax that provides disability and retirement benefits for most working people.

Social security tax is a tax that provides disability and retirement benefits for most working people. Social security taxes contribute a large part of tax revenues, as you saw in Figure 21–2. They pay for old-age and survivors' benefits, unemployment compensation, health care for the aged, and disability benefits. The Federal Insurance Contribution Act (FICA) provides the revenues for social security retirement payments. It taxes the yearly wages and salaries of employees. The amounts of wages and salaries subject to tax and the rates of taxation go up over time in order to allow for inflation.

For employees, the social security tax rate and the highest tax base have been rising. Back in 1977, the most you could have paid in social security tax was $965 for the year, or about $80 each month. By 1991, this had risen to $5,179 for the year, or nearly $432 each month. In addition to what employees pay, employers also pay a social security tax for each person they employ. There is so much ongoing discussion about the social security system that you will likely see continuing changes.

Arguments For and Against Social Security Taxes

A common argument against the social security system is that it offers fewer benefits than could be attained by investing the same amount of money in a private insurance program. This may be true. However, social security payments have, on the average, amounted to more than four times the amount paid in by each taxpayer (including the employer's contributions).

There are benefits to social security. Since almost everyone must pay social security taxes, benefits for everyone are more certain. If no one paid social security taxes, some people might invest in private retirement insurance programs, but many would not. Sooner or later, the country would be faced with caring for these individuals without their having made any contribution to the system. Those people who did not buy insurance or start a retirement plan might starve or die from lack of good medical care. Society prefers not to let that happen, so other people must pay for their aid. The social security system began in part for this reason. Even though social security taxes may not provide a generous retirement benefit, they at least provide some benefit for most retired workers.

Illustration 21–7
Almost everyone will receive social security benefits upon retirement. But those who save additional money for the future will enjoy a more secure and comfortable retirement.

Principles of Taxation Applied to Social Security Taxes

In applying the principles of taxation to social security taxes, we must consider the employees' share separately from the employers' share. For employees, the social security tax is a direct tax. For employers, social security tax is probably best described as an indirect tax. Just as the burden of corporate income tax appears to be partly shifted to stockholders, employees, and consumers, the employer's share of the social security tax can be shifted the same way.

For employees, the social security tax is regressive. Those earning more than the highest income taxed pay a smaller percentage of their incomes than those earning less than the highest income taxed. Therefore, social security tax is a regressive tax on some employees. For employers, it is difficult to say whether social security tax is proportional, progressive, or regressive.

For employees, social security taxes follow the benefit principle of taxation to a large extent. Those who pay the taxes will draw social security benefits at some time in the future. The employer, however, gets no direct benefit from paying social security taxes. Also, because the tax is not based on the employer's income, social security tax does not follow the ability-to-pay principle, either. Therefore, neither of these principles applies to the employer's share of social security tax.

ESTATE AND GIFT TAXES

21–7

21–1

estate and gift taxes
Taxes levied on wealth (money and property) passed from one person to another either at death or as a gift.

Estate and gift taxes are taxes levied on the wealth (money and property) passed from one person to another either at death or as a gift. These taxes are designed to stop the passing of great fortunes from one generation to the next. Estate taxes would not be very effective without also having a gift tax. A gift tax prevents people from giving their wealth to their children before death in order to avoid the tax. People may receive a gift of up to $10,000 per year, however, without paying either tax.

Many people, mostly in lower income groups, say that estate and gift taxes should be higher, since they tax money for which the receiving person has not worked. Others, mostly in higher income groups, say that if people have worked hard to gather a lot of wealth, they should be able to pass all of it on to their heirs. They would prefer to do away with or reduce these taxes. Doing so, they argue, would provide more reason to work and gather wealth, and greater productivity would result.

Estate and gift taxes tend to be progressive. The tax rates range from a low of 18 percent to a high of 65 percent. In practice, most small estates pay no tax at all. Therefore, these taxes also follow the ability-to-pay principle. In addition, they are direct taxes on the estates and gifts. It is very difficult to shift such taxes to other parties.

REVIEWING THE CHAPTER

21–2

1. Taxes are necessary to raise the money needed for government activities. Tax money pays the people who work at each level of government. We receive many goods and services from the public sector in exchange for the taxes we pay.

21–3

2. The federal government gets most of its money from income taxes. These include personal income tax, corporate income

tax, and social security tax. Most state governments rely most heavily on sales taxes with some income taxes. Local governments rely most heavily on property taxes.

21–5   3. In the United States, we tend to favor the use of taxes that follow the ability-to-pay principle. Our income taxes reflect this preference.

21–5   4. Taxes can be classified as progressive, regressive, or proportional. A tax is progressive if the percentage of income paid for that tax goes up as income goes up. A tax is regressive if the percentage of income paid for that tax goes down as income goes up. A tax is proportional if the percentage of income paid for the tax is the same at all levels of income.

21–6   5. The incidence of a tax refers to who actually pays a tax. Sometimes it is possible to shift a tax from one person to another. For example, an excise tax is levied on the seller of a product, but part of the tax is shifted to the buyer of the product.

21–6   6. Our federal personal income tax is a progressive tax that follows the ability-to-pay principle.

21–7   7. A corporate income tax is collected from corporations. It is based on the firm's income after expenses and depreciation have been deducted.

21–7   8. The amount of sales and excise taxes we pay is based on our purchase of certain goods and services. A sales tax is a broad-based tax on many kinds of purchases. Sales taxes are an important part of state tax revenues. An excise tax applies only to a specific good such as tires or gasoline. Both sales and excise taxes tend to be regressive.

21–7   9. A property tax is one which is levied on real estate such as property, a home, or some other building. It tends to be regressive, especially for older people. Property taxes are important sources of revenue for local governments.

21–7   10. The social security tax provides disability and retirement benefits for most working people. It is a proportional tax up to the highest income taxed, but it is regressive beyond that level. Changes in the tax rate and in the amount of income taxed have made social security taxes a growing burden on working families.

21–7   11. Estate and gift taxes are levied on wealth passed from one person to another. Estate taxes cover wealth that changes hands at the death of the wealth holder. Gift taxes cover transfers of wealth from one living person to another.

REVIEWING ECONOMIC TERMS

21–1   Supply definitions for the following terms:

benefit principle of taxation

ability-to-pay principle of taxation

progressive tax

regressive tax

proportional tax

direct tax

indirect tax

personal income tax

corporate income tax

sales tax

excise tax

property tax

social security tax

estate and gift taxes

REVIEWING ECONOMIC CONCEPTS

21–2   1. Give several reasons why we have taxes.

21–3   2. List the four major sources of federal tax revenue.

21–3   3. List the two major uses of federal tax revenue.

21–4   4. What is the major source of state revenue for most states?

21–4   5. What is the major source of local government revenue for most local governments?

21–3, 21–4   6. In terms of percentage of total revenue, compare the spending of federal, state, and local governments on education.

21–4   7. Besides education, list five other benefits we receive through state and local government spending.

21–7   8. Tell whether each of the following taxes is progressive, regressive, or proportional.
   a. personal income tax
   b. corporate income tax
   c. sales tax
   d. excise tax
   e. property tax
   f. social security tax
   g. estate and gift taxes

21–5, 21–7   9. List whether each of the seven taxes in Question 8 follows the benefit principle of taxation or the ability-to-pay principle of taxation.

21–6   10. List whether each of the taxes in Question 8 is a direct tax or an indirect tax.

APPLYING
ECONOMIC
CONCEPTS

21–3 1. Refer to the most recent issue of the *Statistical Abstract of the United States*. Look up the current data on the pattern of federal tax revenues and federal government spending. Compare this pattern to the one in Figure 21–2, and write an explanation of the differences that appear. Refer to an issue of the *Statistical Abstract of the United States* from the early 1960s and make a similar comparison. Explain the differences between the patterns that appear now and the patterns of the early 1960s.

21–3 2. Obtain a copy of the current federal income tax form and the instructions for completing it from the local Internal Revenue Office or from a local accounting firm. Calculate the amount of tax paid by a single individual who earned $25,000 last year. Assume the person claims the standard deduction.

21–3 3. If two single persons living in the same household each earned $25,000, they would each owe the tax you calculated in Question 2. Now suppose those two people are married. How much tax would they owe on the total $50,000 income? Again assume they take the standard deduction. Use the same tax forms as you did in Question 2.

21–4 4. Identify the major sources of revenue for your local government. Which of these correspond most closely to the ability-to-pay principle, and which follow most closely the benefits-received principle? What are the major uses of these revenues? List at least ten services supported by your local government. Compare your list with those of other members of your class and compile a composite list.

21–4 5. Would it be better for your state government to rely more heavily on a state income tax or on a sales tax as a revenue source? List good points and bad points about each type of tax. For whichever type of tax you favor, write a paragraph explaining the tax base and any exemptions you would allow. Also explain why you think that the tax you prefer is fair.

USING EXCISE TAXES TO REDUCE THE DEFICIT

Excise taxes (special sales taxes) were part of the 1990 program to increase government tax revenues. Cigarettes, gasoline, and expensive cars were some of the products targeted for higher taxes. These products all have one thing in common. Their demand is relatively price inelastic. The government knew that consumers would not reduce their consumption of these items by much.

CHAPTER 22

FISCAL POLICY

Learning Objectives

WHAT IS FISCAL POLICY?

Fiscal policy is the changing of government spending and taxes in order to control the level of economic activity. The government can raise or lower taxes to try to change the levels of aggregate demand and supply in the private sector. Also, changes in government spending can cause changes in aggregate demand. Such actions aim to achieve the goals stated in the Employment Act of 1946. Remember that these goals are full employment, stable prices (no inflation), and a good rate of economic growth.

Inflation and unemployment can be caused by an imbalance between the level of spending (aggregate demand) and the amount of production (aggregate supply). You have also learned that monetary policy can fight these problems by changing the money supply. In this chapter you will see that the government uses other tools in this supply and demand battle—fiscal policy and wage and price controls.

22–1

fiscal policy
The changing of government spending and taxes in order to control the level of economic activity.

FISCAL POLICY CHANGES AGGREGATE DEMAND AND SUPPLY

Changing aggregate demand and supply through fiscal policy is an important economic concept. In this section you will study it in a general way. Then the next three parts of the chapter will explore how fiscal policy can be used for specific purposes. But first, a word of caution. As you know from your study of economics so far, economics offers few simple answers. The economy changes constantly. Also, a change in any part of the economy is likely to affect many other parts. As society changes, so does the economy. The policies that work today may not work tomorrow. This makes the study of our economy frustrating but also very interesting.

Expansionary Policies

Expansionary fiscal policies cause the economy to run more rapidly by increasing aggregate demand. As you will see, the emphasis of fiscal policy is on the demand side of the marketplace. The diagram in Figure 22–1 shows the effect of an increase in aggregate demand. The point of balance between the forces of demand and supply moves from *A* to *B* as demand goes up. This change means that both the price level and the amount of goods produced will go up.

22–2, 22–4

22–1

expansionary fiscal policies
Fiscal policies that cause the economy to run more rapidly by increasing aggregate demand.

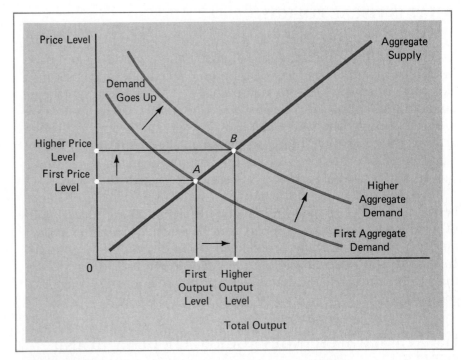

FIGURE 22–1 AN EXPANSIONARY FISCAL POLICY

A rise in aggregate demand causes a higher level of output. But it will also put upward pressure on price.

22–3

The question that probably comes to mind is: What government actions will cause aggregate demand to rise? Remember that government spending is one part of aggregate demand. If the government spends more money, the total demand in the economy will go up. In fact, total demand will rise by more than just the added government spending.

To see why this is true, let's look at an example. Suppose the government adds $10,000 to its spending by buying a new car for the FBI. Part of that $10,000 becomes income to the person who sold the car. Other parts become income to an auto worker, income to the trucker who hauled the car from Detroit to Washington, etc. These people will spend at least part of their added income on products such as food, clothing, appliances, and gasoline. The people who make and sell these products, then, have more income. And they spend some part of their income. Each round of added spending increases aggregate demand a little more. This is called the multiplier effect. A **multiplier effect** is the concept that any change in policy affects total demand and total income by an amount larger than the amount of the change in policy.

22–3

Other than increasing spending, can you think of any other way the government could cause aggregate demand to rise? What about cutting taxes? The Reagan administration tried to do this with the

22–1

multiplier effect

The concept that any change in policy affects total demand and total income by an amount larger than the amount of the change in policy.

Economic Recovery Act of 1981. Lowering taxes on personal income increases the amount of spendable income people have. If take-home pay goes up, we can expect that people will save and spend more than they did before the tax cut. The added spending helps increase aggregate demand directly. The added savings makes more money available for business investment and so may indirectly increase demand.

A tax cut for corporations can also cause demand to rise. After a tax cut, businesses have more money left to buy new equipment. They may also distribute more money to shareholders who, in turn, would spend at least part of it. Tax cuts also have a multiplier effect, but it is less than for government spending.

You see, then, that tax cuts and spending increases are *expansionary* fiscal policies. Both actions cause aggregate demand to rise. This results in more activity in the economy.

Restrictive Policies

Restrictive fiscal policies cause the economy to run more slowly by reducing aggregate demand. Some restrictive fiscal policies may also slow the growth of aggregate supply. But again, we will focus our attention on aggregate demand. In Figure 22–2 you

22–2, 22–4

22–1

restrictive fiscal policies
Fiscal policies that cause the economy to run more slowly by reducing aggregate demand.

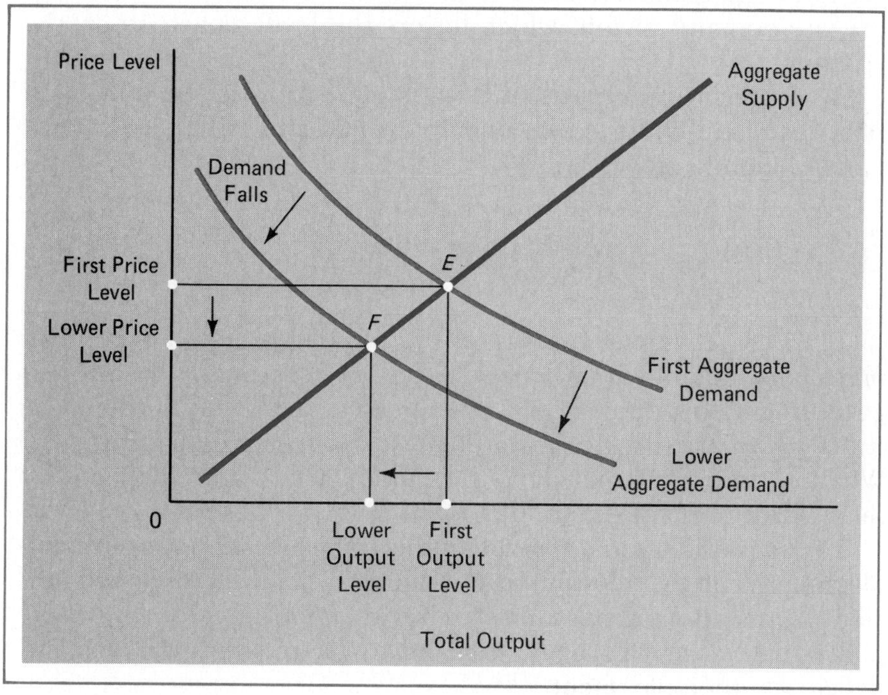

FIGURE 22–2   A RESTRICTIVE FISCAL POLICY
A fall in aggregate demand can cause a lower level of prices. But it also lowers the level of output.

see the effect of a fall in demand. The point of balance between demand and supply moves from *E* to *F*. This change causes both the price level and the amount of goods produced to be lower.

22–5   Two kinds of government actions will cause aggregate demand to fall. As you might have guessed, these are the opposites of the actions that cause demand to rise. One is that the government can reduce the level of its own spending. This reduces aggregate demand directly. It also has an indirect multiplier effect on government spending cuts. If the government buys fewer cars, fewer auto workers will be employed, so income in that part of the economy is less. If income decreases, demand for the goods and services those workers would have bought also decreases. This means less income in other parts of the economy, and demand decreases even more.

22–5   Raising taxes also causes aggregate demand to fall. If people have to pay higher taxes, they will have less money to spend for goods and services. This causes them to cut back on the amount of goods and services they buy. As a result, businesses hire fewer people and total income in the economy falls. This further reduces demand. You can see the multiplier effect at work here also. Raising the corporate income tax would have the same general effect on the economy.

You see that both cuts in government spending and increases in tax rates represent restrictive fiscal policies. Both actions cause aggregate demand to fall, which lowers the level of activity in the economy.

In the next three parts of this chapter, you will see how fiscal policy can be used to reduce unemployment and inflation and promote economic growth.

Illustration 22–1
To combat demand deficiency unemployment, government could use a fiscal policy that will cause aggregate demand to increase.

FISCAL POLICY AND UNEMPLOYMENT

22–4   If the government wants to use fiscal policy to lower the unemployment rate, an expansionary policy is needed. This means that government spending should be increased and/or taxes should be cut. Both of these actions would cause aggregate demand to rise. Whether this will actually help the employment picture depends on the kind of unemployment that exists.

In Chapter 17, you learned that there are several kinds of unemployment. The two most important kinds are cyclical (demand deficiency unemployment) and structural unemployment. A fiscal policy that causes aggregate demand to go up will lower demand deficiency unemployment.

But what about structural unemployment? Will an expansionary fiscal policy help alleviate this problem? Answers to these questions are not clear-cut. To some degree, we can expect a rising demand to help a little. Remember that one reason for structural unemployment is that many workers are unskilled. Businesses that have a strong demand for their products are more likely to help train new workers. This can help those workers get into the mainstream of economic life. Businesses may also offer to help people move from one area of the country to another. This may help to solve the geographic mismatch between workers and jobs, another problem associated with structural unemployment. So, a rise in demand may help to reduce structural unemployment.

The kind of fiscal policy used can make a difference in how well the program works to lower unemployment. The source of the increased demand (government spending, consumer spending, or business spending) can also affect the outcome of fiscal policy. Government spending is not evenly spread throughout the country. So, how much a program of higher government spending helps depends on where the spending takes place and where the unemployment is. A personal income tax cut will have a fairly even effect across the country and will do less to change the mix of employment opportunities. If a corporate tax cut is part of the expansionary fiscal policy, the industrial regions of the country will be affected most.

We can be fairly sure that programs that cause demand to rise will also cause employment to rise. As long as this does not attract too many more people into the labor market, the unemployment rate will fall. Why, then, don't we just increase government spending until the desired level of unemployment is reached? (Remember that due to frictional unemployment we probably would not want to shoot for a zero rate of unemployment.) The reason is that the expansionary programs may also cause inflation. You will learn more about this trade-off as you go through the rest of the chapter.

FISCAL POLICY AND INFLATION

Fighting inflation calls for restrictive fiscal policies. As you saw in Figure 22–2, the price level can be reduced by cutting back aggregate demand. But we really don't want to cause prices to fall. We want stable prices. That is the real aim of a restrictive policy. Population growth and general economic growth push aggregate demand up every year. By following a restrictive fiscal policy, the government may be able at least to slow the rise in price levels.

22–4

The kinds of actions that would lower inflation are cutting government spending and raising the level of taxes. As mentioned earlier, the Reagan administration pushed a tax cut through Congress in 1981 to help lower the unemployment rate. But faced with high unemployment and high inflation, President Reagan needed to try something to lower inflation, too. Cuts in government spending were used to help reduce aggregate demand. Reagan blamed inflation largely on too much government spending in our economy. To really attack inflation, he might have pushed for higher taxes as well as for less government spending. The cost of doing this, of course, would have been an even higher rate of unemployment.

Once more, think back to the discussion of unemployment and inflation in Chapters 17 and 18. You will remember that some inflation may result from demand-pull forces. But part of our inflation may come from the cost-push side as well. The restrictive fiscal policies that we've looked at will only affect the demand side of the market. If demand is the cause of inflation, the policies will work. But if inflation is cost-push, we cannot look for help from fiscal policy. For cost-push inflation, we need some other kind of program. Perhaps better antitrust laws and enforcement would help. Some economists also suggest using wage and price controls of some kind. Wage and price controls will be discussed later in this chapter.

THE UNEMPLOYMENT/INFLATION TRADE-OFF

22-4   At one time people believed that there was a clear trade-off between unemployment and inflation. There was much talk about *fine-tuning* the economy by using monetary and fiscal policies to get exactly the unemployment rate and inflation rate we wanted. Today we realize that we cannot reach such exactness. It is no longer true that when inflation gets worse, unemployment gets better, and vice versa. The 1970s and 1980s taught us that both inflation and unemployment can rise to high levels at the same time. Our society faces the problem of finding policies that can lower unemployment and inflation at the same time.

From your understanding of how fiscal policy affects each problem, you know that what helps one hurts the other. An expansionary policy may reduce unemployment but increase inflation. A restrictive policy that reduces inflation can cause unemployment to rise. The same kind of trade-off results from monetary policies. A loose monetary policy may help unemployment but will raise prices. A tight monetary policy may keep inflation in line but will make unemployment worse.

So, from a monetary and fiscal policy point of view, the problem of the trade-off between inflation and unemployment remains unsolved. This problem will likely be the focus of much attention for a long time to come.

FISCAL POLICY AND ECONOMIC GROWTH

Only a stable and healthy economy can encourage economic growth. This means that inflation and unemployment must be kept down. This is clearly hard to do. But the better we deal with those economic problems, the better economic growth will be.

An expansionary fiscal policy generally promotes economic growth better than a restrictive policy. However, this is true only if inflation does not get out of hand due to the high level of economic activity. Businesses find it hard to plan for the future in an inflationary economy and are likely to cut the spending that might lead to economic growth.

22–6

Other than controlling unemployment and inflation, the government can use certain policies to promote economic growth. One is to follow tax policies that make it desirable for businesses to invest in new plants and machines. Investment tax credits have often been used for this purpose. A business that spends money for investment is given a tax reduction under such a plan. This lowers the cost of investment to the business, which results in greater investment spending. You have seen that investment plays an important part in increasing the growth rate in the economy. Government spending on research and development (R&D) can also promote growth. Tax cuts for businesses that spend more for R&D could also be used.

When the savings rate in the economy falls, the government could use tax policies to try to increase savings. This makes more money available for business investment which can be expected to help increase the rate of economic growth.

Economic growth will be spurred on by expansionary fiscal policies. This is particularly true of policies that encourage more savings, more investment, and more spending for research and development.

Illustration 22–2
One way government can promote economic growth is through tax policies that enable businesses to invest in the latest technology.

PUTTING FISCAL POLICY TO WORK

22–7

Congress and the president should work together in forming fiscal policies. Failure to do so greatly reduces the chances of having timely and effective policies. But the way Congress works makes it difficult to get quick action on fiscal policy. A lot of debate always occurs before fiscal policy can change. Therefore, the inside time lag for fiscal policy is long. This means that, at best, it takes months, and often years, for the president, the House of Representatives, and the Senate to agree on fiscal policy measures.

There are several reasons for this long debate. First, it is often hard to decide what the best fiscal policy should be. What mix of tax changes do we want? Should the changes affect consumer spending, business spending, or both? What changes in government spending will work best? Which programs should change and by how much? Politicians, economists, and the president hold strong opinions about the answers to such questions. Thus, reaching agreement can take a long time.

Problems arise partly because the economy often sends unclear and sometimes contradictory signals. People who are more worried about the negative effects of inflation may interpret the economic signals one way. People who are more worried about unemployment may interpret the same signals differently. This is further complicated by the fact that many politicians do not understand economics very well. Therefore, they do not understand the signals coming from the economy. Try to imagine answering a question asked by someone speaking in a foreign language that you do not know. Any answer you give is more likely to be wrong than right. The same is true for economic policy made by people who do not understand economic reasoning.

Also, remember that we elect politicians to office. If they vote for unpopular economic policies, they risk losing their jobs. It is always easier to get Congress to agree to tax cuts and more government spending than the reverse. Voters rarely object to a cut in their taxes or to getting federal funds for some local project. This gives rise to an inflationary bias in fiscal policy. An **inflationary bias in fiscal policy** is the natural tendency for Congress to favor expansionary policies over restrictive policies. What might serve the economy best may give way to what will win votes in the next election. This results in long debates as our representatives and senators try to please the voters who elected them.

An important message should surface from this discussion. If we, the voting public, want to have responsible fiscal policy, we must understand economic issues ourselves. And we must let our representatives and senators know that we understand that higher

Illustration 22–3
Politicians want to please their voters, so they tend to favor tax cuts and spending increases.

22–1

inflationary bias in fiscal policy
The natural tendency for Congress to favor expansionary policies over restrictive policies.

taxes or lower government spending may be necessary to control inflation. They must know that we will continue to vote for them only if they vote for responsible, economically sound fiscal policy measures.

Consider the length of the outside time lag for fiscal policy. Once agreement is reached on the kind of fiscal policy needed, the policy can become effective in the economy very quickly. Changes in taxes can be effected almost immediately by changing the amount withheld from paychecks. Many government spending programs can also be changed quickly. For these reasons we say that fiscal policy has a short outside time lag.

22-7

MONETARY OR FISCAL POLICY: WHICH IS BETTER?

There is a good deal of disagreement between people who favor monetary policy and those who favor fiscal policy. Those who argue for fiscal policy point out that it has a more direct effect than monetary policy. Government spending can increase demand directly. Tax changes can be made that are sure to increase or reduce demand in a fairly predictable way. Fiscal policy is probably more effective than monetary policy in getting the economy out of a recession. More government spending and/or tax cuts will increase total spending. But a loose monetary policy can only make money available. Businesses may not increase borrowing because their leaders may feel pessimistic about the future due to their experiences during the recession.

People who favor monetary policy will quickly point out that monetary policy can effectively control inflation. If there is less money available, people have less to spend. Monetary policy certainly combats the kind of demand-pull inflation we speak of as *too many dollars chasing too few goods*. Some economists believe that monetary policy has greater flexibility than fiscal policy. They say using fiscal policy to control inflation is like a jeweler using a sledge hammer to cut a diamond. The wrong fiscal policy can damage the economy as surely as the hammer would ruin the diamond.

Some who favor monetary policy think that fiscal policy should be used only in times of complete economic breakdown, such as during the 1930s. Some also think that monetary policy should not be used to try to fine-tune our economy. They believe that the best monetary policy increases the money supply at a steady rate equal to the rate of growth in real GNP. This makes a good deal of sense to many people. Suppose real GNP expanded to the extent that production doubled. It is likely that twice as much money would be needed to support transactions in the expanded economy.

Part of the debate about monetary policy versus fiscal policy concerns the time lags involved. Both the Board of Governors and the Federal Open Market Committee of the Federal Reserve System can act quickly on a policy change. Therefore, the inside time lag for monetary policy is short. But once a change is made, it can take a long time for the entire impact to be felt in the economy. Some experts say that the effects of monetary policy may take two years to filter through the economy—quite a long outside time lag.

With fiscal policy you have seen that, once a policy is determined, changes can be put into effect quickly. If Congress and the president agreed on a tax change today, the results would show up in paychecks within the next couple of weeks. But it takes a long time to achieve agreement on fiscal policy. In the House of Representatives, it takes time for the Ways and Means Committee to agree. Then the whole House has to be convinced to pass the measure. Once this is done the Senate must act, and then the president must approve. Any program may be recycled several times in this process for changes and revisions. This often results in long delays between the time when the need for a new policy is recognized and when changes are made.

As you can see, there is no clear winner in this debate. The choice depends on the state of the economy at any particular time as well as on personal preferences. Many intelligent people may not agree on what is best for the economy at any moment. We have to weigh the advantages and disadvantages of each kind of policy and decide for ourselves. Very good economists, even Nobel prize-winners, argue on both sides of the debate.

THE NATIONAL DEBT

22–8

22–1
national debt
The amount of money that the federal government owes.

The **national debt** is the amount of money that the federal government owes. To whom does the government owe money? In part, the government owes money to people like you. Do you own a government savings bond? If so, part of the national debt is owed to you. The Federal Reserve Banks also own part of the debt, as do other domestic investors such as insurance companies. Also, some of the national debt is owned by people or governments outside of the United States.

The national debt began in 1790 and has fluctuated up and down over the years. But mostly, the debt has gone up. By 1929 it was $16.9 billion. In the next ten years it grew to $48.2 billion. During World War II the debt rose so rapidly that in 1945 it was more than $260 billion. In 1975 the debt was at $544.1 billion. During 1981 the national debt crossed the $1 trillion mark. One trillion dollars was about $4,700 for every man, woman, and child in this country. Despite considerable comment by politicians that the debt was growing too rapidly, the government continued to spend more than it collected in taxes. During 1990 the national debt rose to over $3 trillion, or over $13,000 per person.

You may have heard people say that the government should not borrow money. The government should learn to live within a budget just as private citizens and businesses must do. Actually, borrowing money is often a wise thing to do. A family will probably have to borrow money to buy things such as a home or a car. Businesses also need to borrow money to build new factories and to buy new machinery. Borrowing money, and the debt that results, make up an important part of a modern economy.

It may often make sense for the government to borrow, too. We have seen that in periods of high unemployment, the economy may be healthier if government spending is increased without increasing taxes. This means the government would have to increase its debt. What matters is whether the government can afford to pay the interest on the debt. Since the government has unlimited power to tax, it can always raise taxes enough to meet its interest payments on the debt.

People worry most about the effect the national debt has on business investment. When the government borrows large amounts of money, it may reduce the flow of money to businesses. In order for the government to sell bonds, it must pay an attractive interest rate on them. This may cause people to shift their money to government bonds and away from the kinds of savings that provide money to businesses. This shift is called crowding out. **Crowding out** is the effect on private businesses when increased government borrowing raises interest rates and reduces private borrowing. Private businesses may get pushed out of the money markets by the high interest rates caused by high government borrowing. This can reduce the amount of capital in the private sector, which can lower our productive ability.

Another concern about the national debt is the portion that is external debt. **External debt** is the part of the national debt that is owed to people or governments outside the United States. Interest paid on the external debt does not become income to people in the United States and therefore drains our economy. In the mid-1980s, over 10 percent of the national debt was owned by foreign countries.

The national debt is not really an *economic* problem, however. It is a *political* problem. Politicians have not accepted the responsibility of carefully balancing the costs and benefits of the spending programs they consider. As we discussed earlier, fiscal policy

22–1

crowding out
The effect on private businesses when increased government borrowing raises interest rates and reduces private borrowing.

22–1

external debt
The part of the national debt that is owed to people or governments outside the United States.

inspires an inflationary bias because politicians do not like to increase taxes enough to pay for increased spending. The result has been yearly deficits that continue to add to the national debt.

In December 1985, Congress and the president agreed to take dramatic action to balance the budget. They passed the *Gramm-Rudman Balanced Budget and Emergency Deficit Reduction Control Act of 1985*. The intent of the Gramm-Rudman bill was to force politicians to spend only as much money as the government gets in tax revenues each year. There was considerable debate about this act at that time, and the real impact of the act may not be known for many years.

WAGE AND PRICE CONTROLS

22–1
wage and price controls
Government controls on the levels of wages and prices.

Wage and price controls are government controls on the levels of wages and prices. Such controls are also called an *incomes policy* because they try to keep control over people's income and buying power. There are many kinds of wage and price controls. These include wage-price freezes, wage-price guideposts or voluntary controls, and mandatory wage-price guidelines with penalties for violators.

Why Use Wage and Price Controls?

22–9   We do not like to see unemployment rise when we try to slow inflation. As you have seen, monetary and fiscal policies result in a trade-off between inflation and unemployment. Policies that slow inflation tend to make the unemployment problem worse. The voting public is sensitive to unemployment, so the use of monetary and fiscal policies to lower inflation is politically unpopular. Therefore, the government sometimes turns to wage and price controls to guide the economy.

22–9   Another reason for using wage and price controls is that our economy also faces unemployment and inflation that are not caused by too much or too little demand. This cost-push inflation is not easily corrected with the usual methods, and so controls are often suggested. Further, many people believe that big businesses and big labor unions have too much power. They can raise prices and wages more than is necessary or desirable because there is little competition in many markets. This again may necessitate specific government controls.

Wage and Price Controls in the United States

We used controls a lot during World War II. With the heavy demand caused by the production of war goods, inflation rose rapidly. President Roosevelt ordered the control of prices to keep inflation down. This meant that prices no longer provided good signals to business, and the economy had many shortages. Many goods had to be rationed. Consumer goods such as gasoline, meat, sugar, and cigarettes grew scarce. To make them available to rich and poor alike, a rationing system was set up. In 1944 the banking system was handling 5 billion ration coupons each month. As you

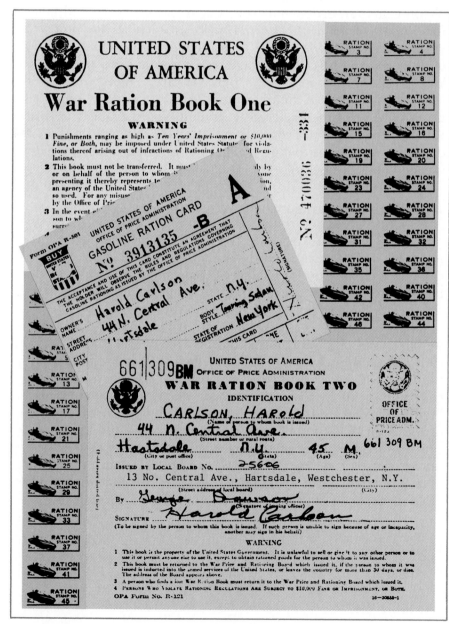

Illustration 22–3
During World War II price controls and production cutbacks caused shortages of many consumer goods such as gasoline, meat, and sugar. To make these scarce goods available to all consumers, ration coupons were issued. Shown here are the cover of the ration coupon booklet, coupons for general goods, and a special coupon for gasoline rations.

might guess, the rationing program needed many workers. The government had about 50,000 paid employees and more than 200,000 volunteers to manage the controls.

Overall, the controls worked well during the years of World War II. People were willing to cooperate with the program. The war gave people a sense of purpose, and they were willing to make sacrifices for the war effort. It is doubtful that in peacetime people would willingly go along with such controls.

Our most famous peacetime attempt at wage and price controls came during the Nixon presidency. On August 15, 1971, President Nixon issued an order that froze wages, prices, rents, and salaries for 90 days. During this period, prices rose relatively little. This 90-day period was followed by a second phase which lasted 14 months. During this phase, wages could rise at a 5.5 percent rate, and prices could rise at a 2.5 percent rate. Then January 1973 launched a period of voluntary guidelines. Prices and wages shot up rapidly. On June 13, 1973, President Nixon again froze prices for 60 days to try to "cool off inflationary expectations" in the economy. As soon as that 60-day period was over, prices once more started rising.

What Have We Learned About Wage and Price Controls?

Clearly, wage and price controls of the kinds we have tried do not work well. Controls cause price signals to fail, and supply and demand get badly out of balance. People and businesses spend too much time trying to get around the controls and seeking special treatment. Time spent in this way is not productive.

Some economists believe that controls have not worked because we have used only short-term controls. They think that if the controls operated on a long-term basis, the controls could keep inflation down. Others think that our mistake has been in trying to control too much. They say that we need only use controls for highly concentrated kinds of businesses and for a small number of the large labor unions. If we can keep wages and prices under control in these parts of the economy, maybe the rest will come under control, too. There is no way to know for sure unless these ideas are tried. Most economists, however, do not favor the use of controls.

THINKING
ABOUT ECONOMIC ISSUES

Wage and price controls are upper limits the government may set on wages and prices. Sometimes this is done to help keep prices from going up too fast. We often hear about the problem of *inflation*, which is a rise in the average level of prices in the economy. Some people think that using government controls to keep prices low can solve the problem of inflation. The tools of supply and demand can help show some of the effects of using such controls.

For all of recorded history, there have been some times when prices rose rapidly. As early as 1800 B.C. wage and price controls were used by the Babylonians to keep prices from rising too fast. The Roman Emperor Diocletian controlled prices on many goods and controlled wages for many kinds of work.

In the United States, wage and price controls were common during World War II to help keep prices from getting too high. Our most famous use of price controls in peacetime came in the early 1970s. President Richard Nixon was worried about the effect that rapidly rising prices had on the economy. So, in August of 1971, he issued an order that made it illegal for wages, prices, rents, and salaries to go up for 90 days. After that there were less rigid controls until the summer of 1973.

Overall, the use of price controls has not been as successful as it was hoped. Part of the reason is that price controls cause the price signals from supply and demand to be blocked. When this happens, supply and demand can get badly out of balance. To see why, look carefully at the graphs below.

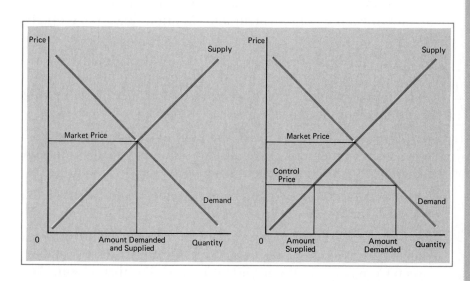

459

The left-hand graph shows what would happen if the market were left to work by itself. At the market price, the amount people would want to buy would be exactly the same as the amount businesses would make. That is, the amount demanded would equal the amount supplied at the market price.

Now suppose a control price were set below the market price. This is shown in the right-hand graph. At the lower control price, a greater amount would be demanded than the amount supplied. Demand would then be greater than supply. In the free economy, price would rise until a balance was obtained. But with the control price, a shortage will result.

When there is a shortage, people try to find ways around the system. A network of illegal markets usually develops. In such cases, it is often the rich and powerful people who end up with the limited amount of the good. In order to try to make the allocation of goods more fair, the government might use ration coupons. Of course, it is not easy to decide who gets how many coupons. During World War II when ration coupons were common, there were about 250,000 people working to manage the controls. The expense of running such a program must be paid in some way—perhaps through higher taxes.

Keeping prices below the market level is not easy. Doing so creates many new problems that may be as bad as or worse than the problem of high prices.

REVIEWING THE CHAPTER

22–1   1. Fiscal policy is the changing of government spending and/or taxes in order to control the level of economic activity. It aims mainly to keep unemployment and inflation down to acceptable levels.

22–4   2. Expansionary fiscal policies raise the level of demand in the economy. By doing this more people are likely to be hired to work, and economic growth will increase. While this will reduce unemployment, it may also increase inflation.

22–4   3. Restrictive fiscal policies lower the level of demand in the economy. This will help lower the inflation rate but at the same time may make the unemployment problem worse.

22–4   4. There is a trade-off between unemployment and inflation that results from the use of fiscal policy.

22–7   5. Congress and the president are responsible for putting fiscal policies to work. Getting agreement within Congress and between Congress and the president is hard. For this reason, there is a long inside time lag in forming fiscal policy. But once there is agreement, fiscal policy can be put into effect very quickly and can be felt in the economy almost at once. This means that there is a short outside time lag for fiscal policy.

22–1, 22–8   6. The national debt is the amount of money the federal government owes. The government borrows money when its spending projects cost more than the amount of money it gets from taxes.

22–9   7. Wage and price controls are government controls over the level of wages and prices. These controls are sometimes suggested as a way to get around the inflation/unemployment trade-off by using another way of controlling prices.

REVIEWING ECONOMIC TERMS

22–1   Supply definitions for the following terms:

fiscal policy	national debt
expansionary fiscal policies	crowding out
multiplier effect	external debt
restrictive fiscal policies	wage and price controls
inflationary bias in fiscal policy	

REVIEWING ECONOMIC CONCEPTS

22–3   1. What two actions can government take for an expansionary fiscal policy?

22–4   2. What is the effect of an expansionary fiscal policy on aggregate demand? on the level of prices? on the amount of goods produced?

22–5   3. What two actions can government take for a restrictive fiscal policy?

22–4   4. What is the effect of a restrictive fiscal policy on aggregate demand? on the level of prices? on the amount of goods produced?

22–4   5. Will an expansionary fiscal policy increase or decrease unemployment? Which kind of unemployment will it affect the most?

22–4   6. Will a restrictive fiscal policy increase or decrease inflation? Which kind of inflation will it affect the most?

22–6   7. Which kind of fiscal policy is better for economic growth? When might this not be true?

22–9   8. Besides changing the level of spending or taxes, what other actions can government take to promote economic growth?

22–7   9. Why is there a long inside time lag for fiscal policy?

22–7   10. Is the outside time lag for fiscal policy long or short? Why?

22–8   11. What are two major concerns about increasing the national debt?

22–9   12. Give two reasons why wage and price controls might be used. Have they usually been effective in controlling inflation?

APPLYING ECONOMIC CONCEPTS

22–4   1. Use a graph of aggregate demand and aggregate supply to show how a fiscal policy of cutting income taxes might increase output and therefore increase employment. Are there any harmful effects of such a policy on the level of inflation? If so, explain why by using your graph. Write a paragraph that carefully explains your graph.

22–4   2. For each of the following parts of the economy, give an example of a fiscal policy that would reduce inflation by influencing that part of the economy: (a) consumer spending, (b) business investment, and (c) government spending. Draw a graph like the one in Figure 22–2 to represent such fiscal policies and explain how each of your examples relates to the graph.

22–4   3. For each of the following parts of the economy, give an example of a fiscal policy that would reduce unemployment by influencing that part of the economy: (a) consumer spending, (b) business investment, and (c) government spending. Draw a graph like the one in Figure 22–1 to represent such fiscal policies and explain how each of your examples relates to the graph.

22–3   4. Explain the multiplier effect. In your explanation, describe how this effect comes about when the government uses a fiscal policy of increasing government spending.

22–4   5. "It is impossible to control both unemployment and inflation. The trade-off between the two is so strong that solving one problem *always* makes the other problem worse." In what ways do you agree with this statement? In what ways do you disagree?

22–4   6. The overall economy is always changing. Go to a library and read recent issues of *Time, Newsweek, U.S. News & World Report,* and *The Wall Street Journal* to find out whether inflation or unemployment is the most important current problem. Based on what you find out, what type of fiscal policy would you suggest the government use? What evidence can you find that the government is following a path similar to the one you suggest? If there are differences, explain them.

CHAPTER 23

ECONOMIC GROWTH

Learning Objectives

23–1	Define terms related to economic growth.
23–2	Explain why real GNP instead of current dollar GNP is used as a measure of economic growth.
23–3	Identify the record of growth in GNP in the United States.
23–4	List four factors that contribute most to economic growth.
23–5	Describe the trade-offs involved in economic growth.
23–6	Explain how the government encourages economic growth.

MEASURING ECONOMIC GROWTH

23–1
economic growth
The change in the level of economic activity from one year to another.

23–1
real GNP
The value of gross national product after taking out the effect of price changes.

23–2

Economic growth is simply the change in the level of economic activity from one year to another. Some people say that our economy is growing while others say it is not. The most likely reason for these different opinions is that the people are probably using different measures of economic growth. One person may look at whether or not the current dollar value of gross national product (GNP) is going up. If it is going up, that person might say that the economy is growing. Another person may look at real GNP, removing the effects of price changes, to measure economic growth. **Real GNP** is the value of gross national product after taking out the effect of price changes. This is also the definition for *constant dollar GNP*. The two terms have the same meaning.

Is it better to use real GNP or current dollar GNP to measure economic growth? To answer this question, consider three cases.

CASE 1

Assume that in 1980 the economy of Country A produced a GNP of $1,000 million. The price index in 1980 was 1.00 (or 100). In 1990 Country A had a GNP of $1,600 million, and the price index was 1.80 (or 180). How much did Country A's economy grow during those ten years? The dollar value of GNP grew by $600 million ($1,600 − $1,000 million). That represents a 60 percent increase in GNP ($600 million ÷ $1,000 million = .60 = 60%). But notice that prices went up at the same time. In fact, prices went up by 80 percent [(1.80 − 1.00) ÷ 1.00 = .80 = 80%]. Let's see what happens if we compare GNP in *real terms* —after taking out the effect of inflation.

Real GNP in 1980 = $1,000 million ÷ 1.00 = $1,000 million

Real GNP in 1990 = $1,600 million ÷ 1.80 = $888.9 million

So, you see that in real terms GNP fell during this period. Real GNP in 1990 was less than real GNP in 1980. In real terms, the people of Country A had fewer goods and services to consume in 1990 than in 1980.

CASE 2

Now assume that in 1980 Country B had a GNP of $800 million. Its price index for 1980 was 1.10 (or 110). In 1990 Country B's GNP was $1,360 million, and the price index was

1.87 (or 187). How much did the economy in Country B grow during this period? The dollar value of GNP went up by $560 million. That is an increase of 70 percent [($1,360 million − $800 million) ÷ $800 million = .70 = 70%]. Prices also increased by 70 percent, as shown by the increase in the price index [(1.87 − 1.10) ÷ 1.10 = .70 = 70%]. Let's see what has happened to real GNP, since GNP and the level of prices both increased at the same 70 percent rate.

Real GNP in 1980 = $800 million ÷ 1.10 = $727.3 million

Real GNP in 1990 = $1,360 million ÷ 1.87 = $727.3 million

You see in this case that real GNP has stayed the same. In terms of the amount of goods and services available for people to consume, there has been no change in Country B's economy.

CASE 3

Assume that Country C in 1980 had a GNP of $900 million and a price index for 1980 of 1.20 (or 120). In 1990, Country C's GNP grew to $1,350 million, and the price index was 1.68 (or 168). How much did Country C's GNP grow during this period? The dollar value of GNP went up by $450 million. That is a 50 percent increase in GNP [($1,350 million − $900 million) ÷ $900 million = .50 = 50%]. But during this period prices also increased, since the price index went from 1.20 to 1.68. This is a 40 percent increase in prices [(1.68 − 1.20) ÷ 1.20 = .40 = 40%]. Let's see what happened to real GNP in Country C.

Real GNP in 1980 = $900 million ÷ 1.20 = $750.0 million

Real GNP in 1990 = $1,350 million ÷ 1.68 = $803.6 million

In Country C, real GNP increased during this period. In real terms, the people had more goods and services to use in 1990 than in 1980.

Think for a moment about these results. In all three countries, GNP grew during the decade between 1980 and 1990. And there was inflation in all three countries during this period. See the results of the three cases in Table 23–1. You can see that when the percentage increase in prices was greater than the percentage increase in GNP, real GNP went down (Country A). What appeared to be an increase in GNP was really an illusion caused by rapidly rising prices. In Country B, the percentage increase in GNP was

TABLE 23–1

PERCENTAGE CHANGE IN GNP
IN COUNTRIES A, B, AND C

	Country A	Country B	Country C
Percentage Increase in GNP	60%	70%	50%
Percentage Increase in Prices	80%	70%	40%
Change in Real GNP	Down	No Change	Up

exactly the same as the percentage change in prices. So, all of the increase in Country B's GNP was caused simply by higher prices. No more goods and services were produced in 1990 than in 1980. But in Country C, GNP went up more rapidly than prices (50 percent rather than 40 percent). Only part of this increase in GNP was due to inflation. The rest was actually a rise in the amount of goods and services produced.

You can see in these three examples that only Country C was better off in 1990 than in 1980. Without looking at changes in real GNP, you might have reached a different conclusion. So, you can see that real GNP is a better measure of economic growth than current dollar GNP.

As you have learned, even using real GNP presents problems as a measure of economic growth. An increase in real GNP does not tell us about distribution of income among people. It says nothing about the quality of goods produced. And it does not show the average amount produced per person. In the three cases, suppose all three countries started with the same number of people. Suppose the populations of Countries A and B increased 10 percent over the period, but the population of Country C doubled. Would you still say that Country C was better off? Probably not. So, even using real GNP as a measure of economic growth can lead to mistaken conclusions if we are not careful.

23–1
rate of growth
The percentage change in the level of economic activity from one year to the next.

Rate of Growth in an Economy

Another way of looking at economic growth is to look at the rate of growth in an economy. The **rate of growth** is the percentage change in the level of economic activity from one year to the next. If in Year 1 real GNP is 200 and in Year 2 real GNP is 210, the rate of growth would be as follows.

$$\text{Rate of Growth} = \frac{(\text{Year 2 GNP} - \text{Year 1 GNP})}{\text{Year 1 GNP}}$$

$$= \frac{(210 - 200)}{200}$$

$$= \frac{10}{200}$$

$$= .05$$

$$= 5\%$$

So, the rate of growth for this economy between Years 1 and 2 would be 5 percent. In the news you often hear reports about changing GNP in terms of a rate of growth. You now have seen how that rate of growth is determined.

Slight Changes in GNP Have Great Impact

Have you ever wondered why so much fuss is sometimes made over a few percentage points of difference in the rate of economic growth? Why is it a news story if the rate of growth in real GNP goes up from 2.6 percent to 3.0 percent? Why is the difference important if the Soviet Union's growth rate is 5 percent while the United States' growth rate is 4.2 percent during the same time? The answer is because over a number of years even small differences in the rate of growth can have magnified results.

To see this, let's look at some examples. Let's see what would have happened to real GNP in the United States from 1960 to 1990 using five different growth rates. Real GNP figures are given in billions of dollars in Table 23–2.

A 2 percent difference in the growth rate (from 2.5 percent to 4.5 percent) during that time makes a $1,214.7 billion difference in real GNP for 1990: a difference of about $4,860 per person. If we project these growth rates into the future, even greater differences occur. The figures in Table 23–3

TABLE 23–2

EFFECTS OF DIFFERENT GROWTH RATES ON GNP,
1960–1990

1960 Real GNP	Average Annual Growth Rate	1990 Real GNP
$737.2	2.5%	$1,546.3
737.2	3.0%	1,789.4
737.2	3.5%	2,069.2
737.2	4.0%	2,391.0
737.2	4.5%	2,761.0

use the same starting point and the same growth rates as those in Table 23–2, but they extend the period to the years 2000 and 2010. By the year 2010, real GNP would more than double if our growth rate were 4.5 percent rather than 2.5 percent. Which of these five growth rates for real GNP comes closest to the actual value for the United States economy? The next part of this chapter will answer that question.

TABLE 23–3

EFFECTS OF DIFFERENT GROWTH RATES ON GNP,
1960–2010

1960 Real GNP	Average Annual Growth Rate	2000 Real GNP	2010 Real GNP
$737.2	2.5%	$1,979.4	$2,533.8
737.2	3.0%	2,404.8	3,231.8
737.2	3.5%	2,918.8	4,117.2
737.2	4.0%	3,539.3	5,239.0
737.2	4.5%	4,287.8	6,658.9

But first, let's look at the effect of small changes in growth rates on a more personal level. Suppose you were offered two jobs with the same starting pay of $15,000 a year. In Job A you can expect an average increase of 8 percent a year for the next ten years. In Job B you can expect an average yearly increase of 10 percent in each of the next ten years. How would your yearly earnings differ after the ten years? You might be surprised by the numbers in Table 23–4. After ten years, your yearly income would be more than $6,500 higher in Job B. And during the ten years you would earn well over $20,000 more in Job B than in Job A. Even though the difference in the growth rates for income in the two jobs is not large, it results in big differences in income.

TABLE 23–4

EFFECT OF GROWTH RATES
ON YEARLY INCOME

	Job A 8% Income Growth	Job B 10% Income Growth
Yearly Income Now	$15,000	$15,000
Yearly Income in Ten Years	$32,384	$38,906
Total Income Earned During the Ten Years	$217,304	$239,063

RECORD OF U.S. ECONOMIC GROWTH

There is a great deal of interest in economic growth in the United States. People in the business sector want a growing economy because that usually means more sales and higher profits. Government officials like a growing economy because it makes their jobs easier. There is less need for social welfare programs, and more tax dollars are spent on public sector services. We like a growing economy because growth provides more jobs and more chances for better jobs, newer products, and higher incomes. The growth of the economy directly affects you.

23–3

To evaluate our record of economic growth, we will look at two measures: real GNP and real GNP per person. Note that both measures use real terms so that the effect of inflation is taken out. We will look as far back as 1929 but will look more closely at the record in recent years.

Growth in Real GNP

Table 23–5 shows how much real GNP has increased in the United States since 1929. The table also shows the drop in real GNP during the Great Depression of the 1930s. A **depression** is a severe and prolonged decline in the level of economic activity. Except for the early and middle 1930s, the U.S. economy has grown rather than declined. During those hard years, real GNP fell from $709.6 billion in 1929 to only $498.5 billion in 1933. This negative economic growth made life unhappy for most people. From 1929 to 1939, real GNP only increased by about $7 billion. This was a yearly average growth rate of only about 0.1 percent.

23–1

depression

A severe and prolonged decline in the level of economic activity.

TABLE 23–5

REAL GROSS NATIONAL PRODUCT IN THE UNITED STATES
FOR SELECTED YEARS, 1929–1990
(Figures are in Billions of Dollars in 1982 Prices)

Year	Real GNP	Year	Real GNP
1929	$ 709.6	1980	$3,187.1
1933	498.5	1981	3,248.8
1939	716.6	1982	3,166.0
1940	772.9	1983	3,279.1
1945	1,354.8	1984	3,501.4
1950	1,203.7	1985	3,618.7
1955	1,494.9	1986	3,717.9
1960	1,665.3	1987	3,845.3
1965	2,087.6	1988	4,016.9
1970	2,416.2	1989	4,117.7
1975	2,695.0	1990	4,155.8

Source: *Economic Report of the President 1991* (Washington, D.C.: U.S. Government Printing Office, 1991), 288.

The great rise in production during World War II is shown by the jump in real GNP between 1940 and 1945. After World War II there was a bit of a drop in real GNP. But people may have been better off then, since more consumer goods than war goods were produced. In economic terms, the period from 1940 to 1950 was generally good. As shown in Figure 23–1, the average yearly growth rate during the 1940s was very high (4.5 percent).

During the 1950s our economy grew, although more slowly in the last half of that period. Real GNP increased from $1,203.7 billion in 1950 to $1,665.3 billion in 1960. This gave us an average yearly growth rate of 3.3 percent for the decade. The 1960s were good years for economic growth. This was not due to just the Vietnam conflict, as many people thought. The average annual growth rate from 1960 to 1965 was 4.6 percent (before the peak of the Vietnam War). The second half of the decade was not as strong as the first half. But the average yearly growth rate for the 1960s was still fairly high (3.8 percent) as shown in Figure 23–1.

The 1970s and 1980s showed a slowing in the rate of economic growth. The average rate of growth for both of these decades was close to 2.7 percent. As shown in Figure 23–1, the long-term growth rate in real GNP averaged 2.6 percent a year from 1929 to 1990. Keep this number in mind. When you hear a politician say we should aim for a 5 percent rate of real growth, you will know that such a rate is well above our long-term

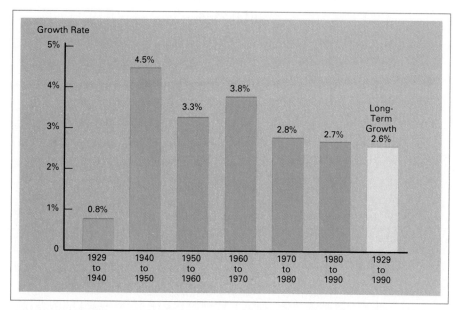

FIGURE 23–1   AVERAGE YEARLY PERCENTAGE INCREASES IN REAL
GROSS NATIONAL PRODUCT IN THE UNITED STATES, 1929–1990
The above percentages are based on the GNP figures in Table 23–5.

average. Could we reach this high a rate? Use the history shown in
Table 23–5 and Figure 23–1 to judge which growth rates seem
likely for the United States.

Growth in Real GNP per Person

The population of the United States has been increasing. This
means that production and income must be shared among more
and more people each year. In countries where population grows
faster than the economy, this means falling incomes per person.
Fortunately economic growth in the United States has risen faster
than population growth, and average income has gone up.

To consider the effects of population growth on economic
growth, the measure called real GNP per person is frequently
used. **Real GNP per person** is simply the real value of the total
output of goods and services divided by the number of people
in the economy. That is, real GNP per person is real GNP divided
by the population. Real GNP per person is often called *real GNP
per capita.*

Let's look at the record of growth in real GNP per person in the
United States. Table 23–6 shows that in 1929 real GNP per person
was $5,828, when measured in 1982 dollars. This fell to $3,970 in
1933 but has generally gone up since then. By 1985 real GNP per
person was $14,963, and by 1990 it was $16,531.

23–1

real GNP per person
The real value of the
total output of goods
and services divided by
the number of people in
the economy.

TABLE 23–6

REAL GROSS NATIONAL PRODUCT IN THE UNITED STATES
PER PERSON FOR SELECTED YEARS, 1929–1990
(Figures in Constant 1982 Dollars)

Year	Real GNP Per Person
1929	$ 5,828
1940	5,850
1945	9,682
1950	7,905
1955	9,009
1960	9,217
1965	10,744
1970	11,783
1980	13,995
1985	14,963
1990	16,531

Source: Calculated from real GNP and population data in *Economic Report of the President 1991* (Washington, D.C.: U.S. Government Printing Office, 1991).

In Figure 23–2 the growth rate of real GNP per person is shown in percentage terms for seven time periods. Note that from 1929 to 1940 there was almost no growth on a per-person basis.

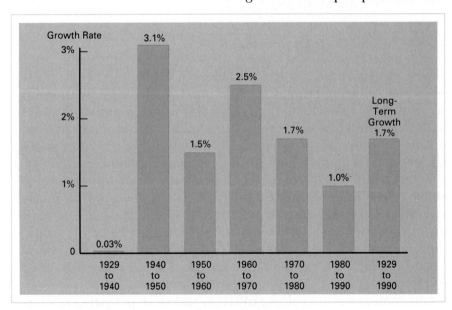

FIGURE 23–2 AVERAGE YEARLY PERCENTAGE INCREASES IN REAL GROSS NATIONAL PRODUCT PER PERSON IN THE UNITED STATES, 1929–1990
The above percentages are based on the GNP figures in Table 23–6.

This period, during which the Great Depression occurred, saw an average yearly increase in real GNP per person of just 0.03 percent. The next ten years brought more rapid increases in real GNP per person because World War II greatly stimulated the economy. After a drop during the 1950s, the growth rate for real GNP per person jumped back up during the 1960s. However, it fell again in the 1970s and 1980s. Over the whole period from 1929 to 1990, real GNP per person grew at an average yearly rate of 1.7 percent.

SOURCES OF ECONOMIC GROWTH

Four factors usually can be shown to affect economic growth: natural resources, human resources, capital, and technology. Let's look at each of these closely. How much each contributes toward economic growth can differ from one economy to another. For example, a country with poor natural resources still can have good economic growth if other factors are strong.

23-4

Natural Resources

Natural resources are the total raw materials supplied by nature. Natural resources include land, minerals, water, timber, and wildlife. The base of natural resources that an economy has plays a significant part in the economy's growth. The United States has a rich supply of natural resources. But even though the United States has rich resources compared to many other countries, those resources are limited. Early in the history of our country it seemed that our natural resources would last forever. There were few people and great amounts of fertile land, clean water, green forests, and minerals. Much of our early economic growth stemmed from these resources.

Not only are our resources numerous, but they are also of very high quality. Land that cannot be used to grow crops or raise livestock will not contribute as much to economic growth as fertile land. Coal deposits with soil and many unusable minerals mixed in have less value than pure coal. The same can be said of all other natural resources. Our economy has had a base of high quality natural resources as well as fairly large amounts of them. Both the quantity and the quality of natural resources have impact on economic growth.

As we use natural resources, we need to find new ones to replace depleted supplies. New supplies of natural resources almost always cost more than the old ones. We have to drill deeper to find oil. We have to dig deeper or in more remote areas to find coal. And water must be piped greater distances. This means that

23-1

natural resources
The total raw materials supplied by nature.

Illustration 23-1
Economic growth is encouraged when we find new supplies of natural resources. When drilling for oil, we need to drill deeper and find new areas for exploration.

the use of such natural resources will cost more, which can then reduce economic growth. Many people feel that natural resource shortages may lead to zero, or even negative, economic growth. It is yet to be seen if this will prove true.

Human Resources

23–1

human resources

The people who work or may be able to work.

Human resources are the people who work or may be able to work. You are part of the human resources of this country. You can personally contribute to the economic growth of the country. So, you and others like you offer a potentially productive resource. People make up the stock of human resources without which production would be impossible. Human labor is needed to drive trucks, wait on tables in restaurants, teach classes, sell stereos, build houses, and do thousands of other jobs.

At one time the physical ability of labor made up the most important part of the labor resources' productivity. The physical strength of the laborer was most important. Skill and mental abilities have received greater emphasis in recent years. Today, a person needs a good deal of skill and/or education to be a productive member of society.

Let's now look at the quantity and quality of our human resources. The quantity has been increasing because of population growth of about 1 percent a year. In 1940 there were about 132 million people in the United States. The population had grown to nearly 181 million by 1960, to 228 million by 1980, and to about 250 million in 1990.

Higher educational levels are an important change in the value of our human resources. These are shown in Figure 23–3. In 1940 almost 28 percent of the population over 25 years of age had only an eighth grade education. Also in 1940, less than 5 percent of people 25 or older had finished college. Since that time the number of high school and college graduates has risen steadily. During the same time, the percentage of people 25 years old and older with only an eighth grade education had fallen to well under 10 percent.

The trends in Figure 23–3 show that the quality of our human resources has been rising steadily. As people get more training and more education they become better able to add to production. People who cannot read or write have less chance of becoming productive members of society. Unskilled workers also find few opportunities. The uneducated and/or unskilled members of our society are not high quality resources in terms of economic productivity and growth. People with well developed skills and more education have more ability to add to the country's economic growth. The

Illustration 23–2
Only highly skilled human resources can change raw natural resources, such as oil, into products useful to society.

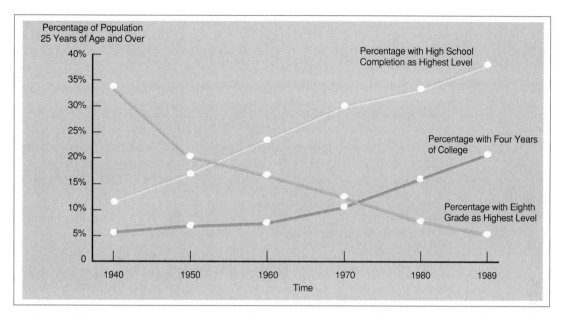

FIGURE 23–3 TRENDS IN EDUCATIONAL LEVEL, 1940–1989
The quality of our human resources has risen steadily. Since 1940, the percentage of the population with four years of college has increased as has the percentage that has completed high school.

Sources: U.S. Bureau of the Census, *Statistical Abstract of the United States: 1991,* 111th ed. (Washington, D.C., 1991), 138; U.S. Bureau of the Census, *Historical Statistics of the United States, Colonial Times to 1970* (Washington, D.C., 1970), 380.

trends graphed in Figure 23–3 show that the quality of our human resources is getting steadily better. This should help us to have continued economic growth.

Capital

In economic terms, *capital* means goods that are produced and can be used as inputs for further production. Each year hundreds of billions of dollars are spent on capital in the United States. New machines, tractors, computers, factories, schools, and other forms of capital are put into use every year. As we have more capital to work with, we become more productive. A good stock of capital contributes to the mix of factors that add to a country's economic growth.

Table 23–7 shows the average amounts of capital used per employee hour worked in selected industries. The amounts have been adjusted to remove the effects of inflation. If you read across the table for these industries, you will see some important changes. The amount of capital used per worker has generally been going up since 1950. This shows we are becoming more capital intensive in these representative industries. People have more and better

Illustration 23–3
The oil industry needs capital like this sophisticated rig to reach oil under the sea.

TABLE 23–7

AMOUNT OF CAPITAL PER EMPLOYEE HOUR WORKED
FOR SELECTED INDUSTRIES
(Data in Real Terms Using 1972 Dollars)

	Dollars of Capital Per Employee				
	1950	1960	1970	1980	1982
Public Utilities	$69.5	$110.0	$134.4	$161.0	$165.6
Petroleum	34.2	46.3	63.2	94.6	96.7
Transportation	34.6	44.1	43.3	30.0	33.3
Chemicals	15.1	20.2	22.4	32.3	36.9
Food	9.0	9.7	10.7	14.2	15.8
Lumber and Wood	5.9	4.2	6.2	10.2	12.8
Textiles	3.6	7.3	8.5	11.4	13.8
Construction	2.0	3.0	4.6	3.9	4.3

Source: U.S. Bureau of the Census, *Statistical Abstract of the United States: 1981,* 102nd ed. (Washington, D.C., 1980), 546; and *Statistical Abstract of the United States: 1986,* 106th ed., 528.

machines to help them with their work. And industrial robots perform more and more of our physical labor. Human workers direct and control the robots—often through the use of computers.

Table 23–7 also shows that some industries use much more capital per hour worked than others. For example, in construction there is much less use of capital per worker than in other industries such as transportation and public utilities. Think for a minute about the building of a house or school and the process of generating electricity. When you pass by a construction site, you see many workers carrying wood, pounding nails, pouring cement, and performing other similar jobs. But in a large electricity-generating plant, there may be very few workers. Most of the work in making electricity is done by machine.

Investment in new capital equipment is important in order to keep a strong rate of economic growth. So, we should continue to invest in new capital if we are to have a growing economy. One measure of our rate of investment is the percentage of GNP invested in net private domestic goods each year. Table 23–8 shows that this investment has been between 4 percent and 9 percent most of the time. A drop in the rate of investment can mean that lower productivity and lower economic growth may follow.

The data from Table 23–8 for 1950 through 1990 are plotted for five-year increments in Figure 23–4. Looking at this figure will help you see that the rate of net private domestic investment decreased in some recent years. This could mean that growth in productivity may not be as high as we might hope it would be in coming years.

TABLE 23–8

NET PRIVATE DOMESTIC INVESTMENT AS A
PERCENTAGE OF GNP
(Percentages Based on Data in Real Terms)

Year	Percentage
1950	8.7
1955	7.4
1960	5.8
1965	7.6
1970	5.9
1975	4.0
1980	5.0
1985	5.6
1990	4.1

Source: Calculated from data in *Economic Report of the President   1991* (Washington, D.C.: U.S. Government Printing Office, 1991), 297, 305.

To maintain a steady rate of investment, interest rates must be kept fairly low. But interest rates seem to rise in periods of high inflation. So, it is crucial to control inflation in the economy. If inflation is low, we can expect interest rates to be fairly low and the rate of investment to be fairly high. And a high rate of investment helps us to have continued strong economic growth.

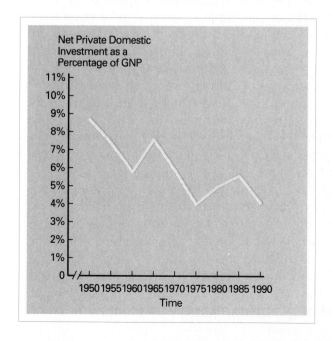

FIGURE 23–4   NET PRIVATE DOMESTIC INVESTMENT AS A PERCENTAGE OF GNP, 1950–1990
The percentages are based on percentages in Table 23–8 above.

Technology

23–1
technology
The body of knowledge that is used for the production of goods and services.

Technology is the body of knowledge that is used for the production of goods and services. People in the United States have become used to rapid technological change. At first, we felt excited by space travel and landing on the moon. But we now think those amazing feats are commonplace. We play complex computer games on high quality televisions. We fly from place to place without thinking about what a wonder air travel really is. In the late 1960s electronic calculators that could multiply, divide, add, subtract, and find a square root sold for more than $1,000. They weighed well over 50 pounds and were larger than a typewriter. Now a calculator with greater capabilities costs less than $20. It weighs but a few ounces and fits in a pocket or wallet. Technological advancement has greatly influenced our economy.

It is difficult to measure exactly how much of the rise in our standard of living is due to technological advances. But technology probably has contributed a great deal. We owe many new and improved products to technological advance. These advances grow out of research and development which takes place in many fields all over the country. **Research and development** refers to the activities undertaken to find new and more efficient methods of production. Research and development often is simply called *R&D*.

23–1
research and development
The activities undertaken to find new and more efficient methods of production.

Chemists, biologists, home economists, geologists, agricultural economists, and researchers in many other areas add to our technological base. Researchers contribute as much to our economy as workers in other fields. Their contribution is not obvious, however, because not all research results in technological application. Even for successful research, the actual applications may take years to be put to use in products we buy. Also, much research aims to improve present ways of making a product. The goal is to keep costs from rising as fast as they might otherwise. Consumers of the products usually are not aware of valuable research such as this.

Research and development spending results in most of the technological advances that are important in our daily lives. This spending leads to better products and methods of production. So, research and development greatly adds to the economic growth of the country. Much of our research and development spending is supported by the federal government. In recent years, about one half of all *R&D* spending has been government supported.

Illustration 23–4
Research leads to new technology and better means of production. Here, engineers design a new oil rig electronically.

Figure 23–5 shows the level of *R&D* spending as a percentage of gross national product. You can see that after reaching a peak of 3 percent in 1964 this percentage fell through 1974. However, it held steady at about 2.3 percent through 1980 and has since increased to about 2.7 percent. Research and development spending today is likely to lead to higher productivity and growth in the future.

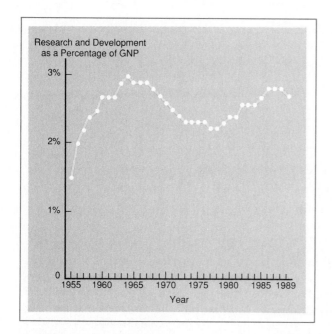

FIGURE 23–5 RESEARCH AND DEVEL-
OPMENT EXPENDITURES AS A PERCENT-
AGE OF GROSS NATIONAL PRODUCT,
1955–1989

Source: U.S. Bureau of the Census, *Statistical Abstract of the United States: 1991*, 111th ed. (Washington, D.C., 1991), 588.

Summary of the Sources of Economic Growth

You have seen that economic growth is influenced by natural resources, human resources, capital, and technological advances. Edward F. Denison, a noted economist, has studied the sources of economic growth. He has found a way to measure what part of our total growth comes from different sources.

Table 23–9 shows how Denison has classified economic growth for the United States economy. Increases in the amount of inputs

TABLE 23–9

SOURCES OF ECONOMIC GROWTH
IN THE UNITED STATES

Sources of Growth	Percentage of Total Growth
Increases in Inputs	
More Work Done	23.9%
More Capital	21.6%
Increases in Productivity	
Advances in Knowledge	34.1%
More Education Per Worker	11.9%
Better Resource Allocation	9 %
Irregular Factors	−0.5%
Total	100%

Source: Edward F. Denison, *Accounting for United States Economic Growth 1929–1969*, (Washington, D.C.: The Brookings Institution, 1974), 130.

ARTHUR OKUN

Arthur Okun was born in New Jersey in 1928. He completed his doctoral degree at Columbia University and taught economics at Yale from 1952 to 1964. He left Yale and served on the president's Council of Economic Advisers from 1964 to 1969. He also chaired the Council during 1968 and 1969.

Okun's publications include *The Battle Against Unemployment, The Measurement and Significance of Potential GNP*, and *The Political Economy of Prosperity.* He may be best known for the relationship he expressed between changes in unemployment and economic growth as measured by real GNP. Okun theorized that it takes considerable improvement in economic growth to produce even a small reduction in unemployment. This theory is known today as *Okun's Law.*

Okun studied and wrote about the effect of government policies on people. For example, he saw that some government attempts to stimulate the economy sometimes led to higher inflation. Okun was concerned about the costs of such programs to people who are especially hurt by inflation, such as those on fixed incomes. It became clear in the 1970s that there was a trade-off in programs designed to lower inflation because such programs often increased unemployment. Okun pointed out that minorities and young people, who comprised the largest percentage of the unemployed, bore heavy burdens in the fight against inflation. Rather, he argued for programs that would help control wages through tax incentive plans.

When Okun addressed a group of government employees who were responsible for figuring GNP, he admitted that GNP did not really show how well off the country is. He agreed that GNP did not measure such things as the value of leisure time or the contributions of homemakers. He argued, however, that GNP provided a valuable measure of output resulting from market-oriented activity. He also argued that GNP was objective because it was based on price tags and that adding in less objective concepts would make GNP less useful.

Okun left the Council of Economic Advisers in 1969 and joined The Brookings Institution where he worked until his death in 1980.

have accounted for 45.5 percent of the total economic growth. That is, just under one half of our growth has been due to having more labor and capital. This supports the earlier statement that to promote more economic growth we need to continue to have a good deal of investment.

Qualitative changes or increases in productivity account for more than half of the economic growth in the United States. The largest part of this qualitative portion is the use of better technologies (advances in knowledge). A more highly trained and educated labor force has also been very important and accounts for 11.9 percent of our economic growth.

TRADE-OFFS BETWEEN THE PRESENT AND FUTURE

In some ways, the goal of having continued economic growth   23-5
conflicts with our desire for present consumption. Looking at a production possibilities curve helps to explain this relationship. The production possibilities curves in Figure 23–6 show the trade-off between making products for current consumption and making capital goods. Making more capital goods would help to make the economy more productive in future years. But making more consumer goods gives us more products for current consumption.

Suppose that the lower curve, labeled Curve *1*, shows the immediate trade-off between consumer and capital goods. If we decided to make the combination of goods represented by Point *A*, we

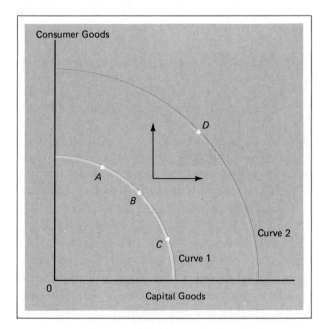

FIGURE 23–6   PRODUCTION POSSIBILI-
TIES CURVES SHOWING THE TRADE-OFF
BETWEEN CONSUMER GOODS AND CAPI-
TAL GOODS
As we produce more capital goods, fewer goods can be made for present consumption and vice versa. Economic growth, represented by the shift from Curve *1* to Curve *2*, relies on having a good stock of capital goods.

would have many products for present consumption. But by choosing this bundle of goods, we would make relatively few capital goods. This might mean that we would have fairly slow, or even zero, economic growth.

We could use more of our productive resources to make capital goods by moving from *A* to either *B* or *C*. This means we would give up some consumer goods now. But it also means we would be likely to have more economic growth and more goods to consume in the future.

The production possibilities curve labeled Curve *2* in Figure 23–6 shows economic growth compared to Curve *1*. An outward shift of the production possibilities curve means that the economy has a greater ability to produce goods and services. The point marked *D* shows a bundle of items that could not be produced given the production possibilities shown by Curve *1*. There is no point on Curve *1* that represents as many consumer goods *and* capital goods as Point *D*. But with economic growth, this bundle could be produced.

The amount of economic growth the economy has is shown by the distance between the two curves. If we made all consumer goods now but made no capital goods, the economy would not grow very much; output might even fall. Only by making some capital goods can we have continued growth. Of the points labeled *A*, *B*, and *C* in Figure 23–6, *C* would lead to the most growth. But we would not want to make so many capital goods that we wouldn't have enough consumer goods to consume right now. This trade-off must be balanced in order to have the best allocation of resources for a prosperous present and a bright future.

SOCIAL ATTITUDES AND ECONOMIC GROWTH

Social attitudes in the United States generally favor economic growth. First, and perhaps most important, we have a strong work ethic. The term *work ethic* means that people generally believe in hard work and in pulling their own weight in economic life. If people expected a *free ride* or *to get something for nothing*, our economy would be much weaker. We would also have a lower rate of growth.

Also, people in the United States seem to think highly of successful business executives, inventors, and innovators. Their successes lead to a better standard of living for all of us. Young people often hope to have careers in business management, which is one sign that we have a positive attitude toward business.

Illustration 23–5
Young people can learn about careers in business from experienced business executives through classroom programs such as Project Business. Sponsored by Junior Achievement, Project Business helps students develop positive attitudes toward business.

Not everyone thinks we should seek economic growth. Some people think that economic growth will cause us to run out of natural resources more quickly than we would otherwise. Some also think that blind acceptance of the goal of economic growth has caused us to pollute our environment unnecessarily. It is difficult to either totally reject or support these arguments. The logic of economic thinking should help you reach your own decisions.

GOVERNMENT ENCOURAGEMENT OF ECONOMIC GROWTH

Economic growth is one of the goals that was mentioned in the Employment Act of 1946. The government tries to form policies which stimulate activities that promote economic growth. Such activities include federal spending on research and development, spending for capital equipment, educating more people, and using natural resources more efficiently.

23–6

But since our economy is mainly a free enterprise system, most of the decision making that influences the rate of economic growth happens within the private sector. Many of your personal decisions will influence growth. You, and others like you, decide how much education or training to get, how much money to save, and how you spend your money. In these cases and in many others, you make decisions that affect the rate of growth of the economy.

Government encourages economic growth in three specific ways. The first is through the tax system. Historically, the government has provided special tax benefits to encourage investment. These have included tax credits for investment in capital equipment, tax credits for homeowners who install energy conservation equipment, liberal depreciation schedules for businesses, and mortgage interest deductions for homeowners. Such tax benefits change as the tax laws change.

Second, the rate of investment can be influenced through the use of monetary policy. Policies that act to control inflation while still providing a sufficient supply of money to keep interest rates down will encourage investment. If too little money is available or if inflation is high, the interest rate will rise. This in turn will tend to lower the level of investment.

Finally, the government can encourage investment through expenditures on social capital which help the economy function. Expenditures on schools and highways are good examples of such social capital spending by the government.

REVIEWING THE CHAPTER

23–2   1. The rate of change in real GNP is usually used as the measure of the rate of economic growth. Real GNP is used so that price changes do not cloud the view of what is really happening in the economy. Growth in real GNP per person gives an even better feel for our current economic well-being.

23–3   2. A small change in the rate of growth can be important. Over a number of years, a minor difference in the growth rate can become magnified into a big difference in our economic well-being.

23–3   3. Real GNP grew at an average yearly rate of about 2.6 percent between 1929 and 1990. Real GNP per person has grown a bit more slowly, averaging about 1.7 percent during the 1929 to 1990 period.

23–4   4. The natural resources that a country has help determine the rate of economic growth. A country rich in natural resources can be expected to have better growth than a country with few natural resources. This is one reason that the United States has such a strong economy.

23–4   5. The amount and quality of labor have a good deal of influence on economic growth. Together these have accounted for about 36 percent of the economic growth in the United States. (See

Table 23–9.) A well-educated and well-trained labor force is one of the real strengths of our economy.

23–4   6. Capital equipment has been an important factor in economic growth in the United States. It is estimated that about 22 percent of our economic growth has been due to the use of more capital. (See Table 23–9.)

23–4   7. Technological improvements have been responsible for about 34 percent of the economic growth in the United States. (See Table 23–9.) Money spent for research and development programs helps to strengthen our technological base.

23–5   8. There is a trade-off between economic growth and current consumption. If we do not save, we have the ability to buy more today, but that may mean having less in the future. Investment in capital increases future economic growth; but to invest in capital, we must give up some current consumption.

REVIEWING ECONOMIC TERMS

23–1   Supply definitions for the following terms:

economic growth	natural resources
real GNP	human resources
rate of growth	technology
depression	research and development
real GNP per person	

REVIEWING ECONOMIC CONCEPTS

23–2   1. Why is real GNP a better measure of economic growth than current dollar GNP?

23–2   2. If a country's GNP has increased 70 percent and its prices have increased 80 percent, how has real GNP changed?

23–2   3. If a country's GNP and prices have both increased 25 percent, how has real GNP changed?

23–2   4. If a country's GNP has increased 40 percent and prices have increased 20 percent, how has real GNP changed?

23–3   5. What was the average increase in our country's real GNP during the period from 1929–1990?

23–3 6. During what period since 1929 did our country's real GNP suffer a large decrease?

23–4 7. Name four factors that contribute the most to economic growth.

23–4 8. A large amount of natural resources can promote economic growth if the resources are of good quality. How does this statement apply to human resources?

23–5 9. If more capital goods are produced than consumer goods, what is the likely effect on economic growth? What is the effect on consumers?

23–6 10. Name three ways in which the government encourages economic growth.

APPLYING ECONOMIC CONCEPTS

23–2 1. Would using real GNP per person instead of total real GNP make any difference in our rate of economic growth? Why or why not?

23–3 2. A United States senator once said: "To get rid of unemployment and poverty we need government policies that will guide the economy to a yearly growth rate of 5.5 percent." Based on our economic history, do you think we can achieve this rate of economic growth? Explain your answer.

23–4 3. Write a paragraph in which you explain how the educational level of the adult population of the United States has been changing. How will these trends affect our economic growth?

23–4 4. Is there any relationship between technological advance and the educational level of a country? Is a higher average educational level likely to lead to more technological advances? As technology becomes more advanced, are laborers likely to need more or less education and training?

23–4 5. Choose some type of production, such as farming, steel manufacturing, education, etc. Determine how the use of capital has changed in that field during this century. You will need to do research in your school library to answer this question. You might also talk with someone who works in the kind of production you chose.

23–4 6. Write a short essay in which you explain what the major sources of economic growth in the United States have been. Give an example of something that would represent each source of growth. (Use the information in Table 23–9 as the basis for your essay.)

23–5   7. Explain what is meant by the trade-off between current consumption and economic growth. How does the level of savings in the economy relate to your answer?

23–6   8. Is economic growth a good objective for the United States economy? Why or why not? List some reasons why growth is desirable. List some reasons why we might want to limit the rate of economic growth.

23–3   9. Using the information in the table below, analyze the economic growth in Countries A, B, and C.

	Country A		Country B		Country C	
	1992	1982	1992	1982	1992	1982
GNP (in millions of dollars)	$1,350	$1,000	$1,600	$1,000	$1,800	$1,000
Price index	1.70	1.00	1.60	1.00	1.50	1.00

How would your opinion change if you knew that Countries A and B had no increase in population from 1982 to 1992 but that Country C's population increased by 40 percent?

NEW TECHNOLOGIES HELP MAINTAIN ECONOMIC GROWTH

New technology can often offset other factors that can slow economic growth. Reduced availability of oil can slow economic growth dramatically. However, new technologies can diminish that effect. Electric cars now appear likely to emerge as one important way to decrease our dependence on oil. Employment in industries related to the development, production, and maintenance of electric cars will increase as other jobs are lost.

It is hard for each generation to imagine what new technologies will exist in future years. One thing you can be sure of is that the way most things are produced today will change dramatically during your lifetime.

PART IV

THE
UNITED STATES
AND THE
WORLD
ECONOMY

ALTERNATIVE ECONOMIC SYSTEMS

Learning Objectives

24–1   Define terms related to types of economic systems.

24–2   Analyze market, command, and mixed economic systems by how they answer the three basic economic questions.

24–3   Describe the effects of scarcity, economic choice, and incentives on efficiency and equity.

24–4   Analyze market, command, and mixed economic systems by ownership of resources.

ECONOMIC SYSTEMS AND ECONOMIC CHOICES

You have learned that all economies must decide three basic economic questions: what to produce, how to produce, and for whom to produce. The way a society answers these questions determines the kind of economic system it will have. Every society uses a different combination of individual and social choices to answer the economic questions. Therefore, a society's **economic system** is the combination of social and individual decision making it uses to answer the three economic questions.

There are four basic types of economic systems: traditional economies, market economies, command economies, and mixed economies.

1. Traditional economies. A **traditional economy** is one in which the three economic questions are decided mainly by social customs.

2. Market economies. A **market economy** has been defined as an economy in which the three economic questions are decided mostly by individuals in the marketplace.

3. Command economies. A **command economy** is an economy in which the three economic questions are decided by government. *Social economy* and *planned economy* are other terms for a command economy.

4. Mixed economies. A **mixed economy** is an economy in which the three economic questions are decided by a combination of market decision making and government decree.

Many different combinations of these kinds of economic systems are operating today and with different degrees of success. A comparison of the decision-making structures of market, command, and mixed economies will help you understand how each operates. You will see how the choices of what, how, and for whom to produce are made under each system.

Because traditional economies are not very efficient, they have tended to evolve into market, command, or mixed economies. Therefore, in the following discussion we will focus attention on these three most important kinds of economic systems.

24–1

economic system
The combination of social and individual decision making a society uses to answer the three economic questions.

24–1

traditional economy
An economy in which the three economic questions are decided mainly by social customs.

24–1

market economy
An economy in which the three economic questions are decided mostly by individuals in the marketplace. (U.S. system)

24–1

command economy
An economy in which the three economic questions are decided by government.

24–1

mixed economy
An economy in which the three economic questions are decided by a combination of market decision making and government decree.

24–2

492

Illustration 24–1
Because traditional economies are not very efficient, they have tended to evolve into market, command, or mixed economies.

What to Produce

Alternative economic systems answer the question of what to produce in different ways. As a result, the goods and services from which consumers can choose vary in the three different systems.

How Market Economies Decide What to Produce. In market economies, the question of what to produce is decided by individual consumers and producers in the marketplace. Consumers, in effect, cast dollar votes (spend money) in the marketplace. Thus, producers of the products consumers want most are rewarded with profits. Consumers do not buy goods and services that they do not want. Those goods and services do not get as many dollar votes. This tells producers that there are other goods of better quality or lower price which consumers want more. Producers then must respond quickly to consumer desires or lose money and perhaps go out of business. In market economies, the question of what to produce is answered by the millions of individual choices that producers and consumers make in the marketplace.

Consumers try to maximize their satisfaction (utility) at a minimum cost. Producers try to produce the goods consumers want most and will buy. Producers take risks to bring new and better products to the market. Consumers either accept or reject these new products. In effect, consumers decide which products will continue to be produced and which will not. Also, because entrepreneurs risk producing new products, a market economy generally has a wide variety of products available from which consumers may choose to buy.

How Command Economies Decide What to Produce. In command economies, a central planning agency decides what goods will be produced and offered in the marketplace. There is no system of dollar votes in effect. Consumers must either accept the products the planning agency has decided to produce or do without.

This system produces the goods that a relatively small group of individuals (the planning agency) thinks are important to produce. It takes away from individual consumers the power to choose what will be produced. This system also tends to overproduce some goods and underproduce others. This occurs because sometimes consumers simply choose to do without rather than accept goods they do not want. Then some of the undesired goods simply sit in the marketplace unused. Eventually they will be disposed of by some means other than consumer purchase.

Sometimes consumers desire much more of a good than has been produced. Since there is no system of profits in a command economy to encourage producers to produce more of these desirable goods, a shortage occurs. Unlike the market economy, the system of central planning does not have an effective system to balance what is produced with what is desired by consumers. There also is generally not a wide variety of kinds of products from which consumers may choose.

How Mixed Economies Decide What to Produce. Mixed economies answer the question of what to produce by a combination of market forces and central planning. Usually some of the most basic industries, such as electric power generation, coal and steel production, transportation, and communication, are centrally planned. The government owns and operates these basic industries, which sell their goods and services to independent producers and consumers. The remainder of industry is private and works through the market mechanism. This means that most consumer products come from industries that respond to consumer desires. The system of dollar votes in the marketplace encourages production of highly desired goods and discourages production of less desired goods.

How to Produce

The decision of how to produce goods and services has the same overall goal under all economic systems. All economies hope to produce the maximum amount of goods and services at the lowest cost. Some economies, however, have greater efficiency and success at this than others. Private decision making is generally more concerned with efficiency. On the other hand, public decisions are frequently concerned with providing equity or equality of opportunity. Some economies use much more social decision making than others. Systems that rely heavily on social decision making might not run as efficiently as those which operate mainly through private choice. However, they may be more equitable.

Illustration 24–2
In a market economy, the more efficiently goods are produced, the more profitable they will be for the producer.

How Market Economies Decide How to Produce. Market economies allocate resources to be used in the production of goods and services by the price of the resources. Individual producers decide what resources they need and in what amounts. Producers try to use less of the most costly resources and more of the cheapest resources. Individual producers closely monitor their own production processes and constantly try to produce the same quality of goods at the least cost. This occurs because producers' profits are the difference between the costs to produce a product and what consumers will pay for it in the market. Each producer has a strong incentive to economize, use resources wisely, and buy the right amounts of each resource. If a producer does buy too much of a resource, it can be resold in the market to another producer.

How Command Economies Decide How to Produce. In command economies, planning agencies allocate resources to specific producers. For example, steel mills are provided a certain amount of iron ore, coal, and other needed resources. The same process applies in allocating all resources to all producers. Deciding how much of each resource every producer in an entire economy will receive is a very big job. Mistakes sometimes occur. Many producers receive too much of some resources and not enough of others.

In command economies, no formal system exists for the resale of resources between producers. When producers have excess amounts of one resource and shortages of others, it is a very long and slow process to trade with other producers. In some command economies, government discourages these trades. Managers do not have strong incentives to produce efficiently, because no profit system will reward them. In a market system, on the other hand, producers benefit directly from their efficiency. The more efficient producers are, the greater their profits. Because there are no profits in command economies, managers who do not produce efficiently have no strong and direct incentive to improve. If a company produces poorly, it may not meet its quota. However, it will not go bankrupt or be forced out of business. Even if managers produce very efficiently, they cannot receive profits. Their rewards are basically the same as those who produce with average efficiency.

How Mixed Economies Decide How to Produce. Mixed economies use a combination of planning and market forces to decide how to produce. Some incentives exist for producers to operate efficiently. Generally profits are earned by private producers; and basic industries, such as transportation and communications, are nonprofit. The efficiency of private firms is sometimes greater than government-owned enterprises.

For Whom to Produce

The question of how goods and services are distributed also is answered differently under different economic systems.

How Market Economies Decide for Whom to Produce. In market economies, who gets what goods is generally decided by who can pay for them. This system has two positive effects. First, it rations goods by price. This means that individuals buy goods based on the price of the goods and the benefit they will get from them. The higher the price a person is willing to pay, the greater the benefit the good must offer them. This means that goods will be sold to those individuals willing to pay the price and therefore put the goods to the most beneficial use.

Suppose you have a severe headache. You might consider three alternative solutions: (1) You can take two aspirins and try to forget about the headache. (2) You can go to a doctor (a general practitioner) for treatment. (3) You can go to a neurosurgeon (a specialist) for treatment. Each of these efforts to cure your headache has a cost. Taking aspirin is cheaper than a doctor's visit. A general practitioner's examination will be cheaper than being examined by a neurosurgeon. You will make this choice based on how bad your headache is and what you can afford. If the headache is minor, the aspirin will probably be your choice. If you have been having trouble with headaches, a visit to the general practitioner might be your next choice. Finally, if you are desperate and fear a brain tumor might be the cause of your headache, you might go to the neurosurgeon. In any case you, alone, choose what goods or services you will use to fulfill your need. Your choice is guided by price and the strength of your need, and you choose carefully. You receive the benefit, and you pay the price. You individually ration the scarce goods such as aspirin, doctor's visits, or time with the neurosurgeon.

How Command Economies Decide for Whom to Produce. Let's look at the case of socialized medicine in a command economy like the Soviet Union's. Consider the headache example again. You would have access to free doctors' services. If you pay no market price for these services, which would you choose? Obviously you would choose the very best. You would go directly to the neurosurgeon for your minor headache. Others in need of the surgeon would not be able to use the same time period in which you were examined. The scarce resource of the surgeon's time would not have been used efficiently.

In a system which provides goods or services without a price to ration their use, these goods and services are generally overused and sometimes wasted. The consumer does not ration the available good as carefully as if there were a market price attached. It is also important to note that no resources are free. The neurosurgeon is paid somehow. In the Soviet Union, for example, the surgeon is paid by the government. The government pays for these services through taxes that all citizens must pay. So, people indirectly pay for the surgeon's time with taxes. Everyone has an incentive to overuse the so-called free good (medical services). These resources, therefore, are partially wasted. In the long run, everyone must pay more for medical service than they would if they rationed the surgeon's services by a price system. If you extend the example of the surgeon's time to all goods and services produced in a planned economy, you can see just how inefficient such a system can become. A command economy tries to provide equal goods and services for all citizens. Therefore, a command economy may indeed by very equitable. Everyone has somewhat equal access to goods and services. On the other hand, a command economy may not be as efficient as its market economy counterparts.

How Mixed Economies Decide for Whom to Produce. Mixed economies frequently have two or more systems of providing goods and services to consumers. Different types of consumers use different systems.

For example, every modern economy provides some type of education for its citizens. The United States operates like a mixed economy in the way education is provided. In the United States, education is provided in several different systems. A public school system is paid for by taxes and is free to all citizens. In a public school system, government decides the minimum quality and quantity of education you can get. There is also a private school system which is supported by tuition fees rather than by public tax dollars. Parents of students who attend private schools pay two costs. They pay tuition for the private school as well as taxes for public education. Other school systems in the United States are supported by churches. These usually require some student tuition. Parents of students in these nonpublic systems also must pay the taxes for public education.

With these three parallel school systems, many choices exist for students in the United States. It is important to note that, in this case, the government determines the minimum availability of education in the economy. But it does not limit educational choice only to that which government provides. This is the case of a public good supplemented by a private good. How goods and services are distributed here is determined by government decree and the price system.

Illustration 24–3
School systems in the United States are supported in three ways: Public schools are funded by taxes; private schools are funded by student tuition and/or supported by churches.

EQUITY AND EFFICIENCY IN ECONOMIC SYSTEMS

Regardless of the kind of economic systems, all economies face several economic realities. All economies must make choices because there are not enough resources available to do everything. If these choices encourage efficiency, the society will have more economic goods to share than would be true otherwise. This issue of equity involves how the goods are shared among people in the society.

Scarcity and Choice Exist in All Economies

Scarcity exists in market, command, and mixed economies. There are just not enough resources available in any economic system to fulfill all the wants and needs of its citizens. All economies must satisfy their unlimited wants and needs as best they can with the limited resources they have.   24–3

Since scarcity exists, economies must choose how to allocate their resources in order to maximize satisfaction. You already know that to allocate resources, we choose among alternative uses of the resources. Whenever we choose, there is a benefit and a cost involved. Every choice has an opportunity cost. Therefore, all economies face opportunity costs no matter what process they use to make choices.

Incentives Guide Choices

All economies are made up of people. Regardless of their eco-   24–3
nomic system, people choose in order to maximize their benefits or minimize their costs. They respond to the incentives placed before them.

Individual Choices, Individual Benefits, and Efficiency. Two different examples show that incentives do matter in all economic systems. Let's look first at an example in a command economy.

The Soviet Union once stressed a quota system of production that required managers to reach a certain level of output. The quotas were usually expressed either in pounds of output or units of output. Managers were rewarded with bonuses or promotions for meeting or exceeding their quotas. When quotas were expressed in pounds, a furniture plant might produce very large, heavy furniture. Clothing plants might produce mostly very heavy clothing in large sizes. The heavy furniture would not be useful to most Soviets because of their limited living space. Of course, the clothing produced would also have limited usefulness.

If quotas were changed to units of output, plants might produce small, flimsy furniture and lightweight clothing in small sizes. In all these cases, plant managers had incentives to meet their quotas and did so as efficiently as they could. But markets were full of goods that nobody wanted. These examples illustrate the concept that human beings respond to the incentives placed before them, regardless of the kind of economy in which they live.

A second example involving a market economy illustrates this concept of incentive in contrast. Assume you are a travel agent. You sell vacations to Florida and Europe. Your commission rate is 10 percent of the total cost. Florida vacations cost $1,000, and European vacations cost $2,000. Therefore, if you sell one vacation to Florida, you earn a $100 commission. Selling a European vacation nets you a $200 commission. Which of these two vacations would you most emphasize to your customers? It is reasonable to expect that you might describe Europe as *the* place to go this year. However, if the Florida tourism service increased your commission to 25 percent your selling focus might change. Is this behavior a reality? Of course it is! There is much statistical evidence to support this claim. As commission rates to travel agents for a particular vacation spot go up, the emphasis the agents place on this opportunity to their customers also goes up. This is the way most business behavior is guided in a market economy.

Scarcity, opportunity cost, and human response to incentives exist in all economies. What, then, does this have to do with *equity* and *efficiency* in different economic systems? These three concepts form the key to efficiency. Human beings make choices based on the costs and benefits of each choice. They try to maximize their benefits and minimize their costs. The structure of costs and benefits determines the incentives faced by individuals. No economic system is more efficient today than one in which individuals have strong incentives to choose carefully in their own best interest. This insures that resources are generally allocated to their most beneficial use. This kind of system frequently produces the greatest output from a given amount of resources.

A system of individual choice such as in market economies is not, however, always the most equitable system. Consider the case of income distribution. In our economy, sports stars such as Michael Jordan or entertainers such as Julia Roberts earn very large salaries. Other members of our economy earn much less, and some citizens earn nothing at all. Some people live very well, whereas others bear hardships. Is this *equitable*? The answer is yes and no. From the point of absolute equity, it may not be. Everyone is not exactly the same in our economy. What our economy offers is equality of opportunity. We are all equal under the law. We all have the right to undertake any legal economic activity. Whether your family is rich or poor, or well educated or ignorant, makes no difference under the law. Examples of this equality under the law abound in our economy. Colonel Harlan Sanders, the founder of Kentucky Fried Chicken, did not have much formal education, but he did have equality of opportunity. He built one of the largest and most profitable businesses in the world.

Market economies, in general, provide equality under the law. The legal system gives everyone the same equality of opportunity. Everyone has about the same chance to try to achieve. The market system rewards success very well. However, it does not make everyone completely equal in income, wealth, or success.

Social Choices, Social Benefits, and Equity. Command economies provide more absolute equity than market economies. At least in theory, everyone is equal in almost every way. This type of system has very little private property, and fewer individual decisions are made. While these economies may not be as efficient, they do strive to provide more equality. Absolute equality is indeed a noble goal; however, even in the distribution of income, command economies are not completely equitable. On the subject of income distribution, Marx can be summarized as saying, "From each according to ability, to each according to need." However, in practice this is not the case in the Soviet Union. Skilled workers in crafts earn much more than unskilled farm workers. Professionals such as scientists, doctors, engineers, and computer programmers earn more than the average Soviet citizen. Some athletes, ballet dancers, and opera singers also generally have above-average incomes. Part of the reason for this is that higher salaries are needed to attract the best people to difficult and demanding professions.

There appears to be at least a partial trade-off between equity and efficiency in economic systems. All types of systems satisfy

Illustration 24–4
Even though command economies strive for equity among all workers, some people, like ballet dancers and athletes, have above-average incomes.

some wants and needs. Some degree of equity and efficiency exist in all economic systems. The specific mix, however, varies from system to system. Some societies desire more efficiency and may give up some degree of equity to achieve that efficiency. Others may desire more equity and will sacrifice some efficiency to have a more equitable economy.

COMPARATIVE ECONOMIC SYSTEMS

In this chapter, we have discussed the major types of economic systems: market, command, and mixed. It is important to note, however, that no economy makes all its decisions either in the marketplace or through central planning. All economies use some mix of individual and social decisions to carry out their economic affairs. In that sense, all economies could be considered mixed economies.

Spectrum of Economic Systems

To understand this concept, visualize all economic systems as a *spectrum* or continuous sequence. At one end of the spectrum are economies that make most of their choices through central planning and command situations. At the opposite end of the spectrum are economies that conduct the majority of their economic affairs through individual decisions in markets. A wide range of economies exists between these two extremes which use combinations of the two decision processes. Figure 24–1 illustrates this concept.

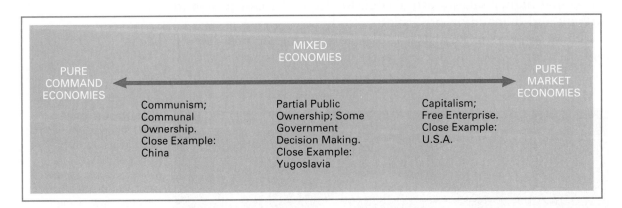

FIGURE 24–1   SPECTRUM OF ECONOMIC SYSTEMS
At the left end of the spectrum, most economic decisions are dictated by central planning committees. At the right end, economic decisions are made through individual decisions in the marketplace. Between the two extremes, economic decisions are made through combinations of central planning and individual marketplace decisions.

Ownership of Resources

Ownership of the means of production is important in comparing economic systems. Some economies permit more private ownership of property than others. In our economy, individuals are permitted to own the means of production, such as factories, machines, and raw materials. That is, most of the capital used in production is owned by private individuals. For this reason, the American economy is frequently referred to as a system of capitalism. **Capitalism** is an economic system in which most of the means of production are owned by private individuals. *Capitalists* are individuals who own the means of production.

24–4

24–1

capitalism
An economic system in which most of the means of production are owned by private individuals.

In economies such as China's, almost all factors of production are owned by the state. In effect, all the factories, machines, and resources become public goods. This obviously makes ownership more equitable, but it also subjects the means of production to all the problems involved with public goods.

For example, under private ownership there is a strong incentive for individuals to take care of their property. Individuals benefit from using their property efficiently. This helps to explain why, as you move across the spectrum in Figure 24–1 from left to right, equity declines but economic efficiency increases. Economies that fall between the two extremes have varying degrees of private ownership. Figure 24–2 explains some of these differences in ownership as well as other characteristics of economies in the spectrum.

In this chapter you have seen the different roles played by government in both command and market economies. The appropriate role of government in our market economy has been debated by economists for many decades. Some market economists feel that the government should play a very small role in our economy. Others argue that the government should play a significant role in regulating our country's economy. These are the two very different economic views held by well-known American economists John Kenneth Galbraith and Milton Friedman. Their views are contrasted in the vignette on page 80.

Socialism and Government-Assisted Capitalism

In the center of the spectrum of economies are mixed economies. These economies use elements of both command and market systems to carry out their economic decisions. Two subcategories of mixed economies, socialism and government-assisted capitalism, are discussed in the next two sections.

	Command Economy	Mixed Economy		Market Economy
		Socialism	Government-assisted Capitalism	
Government Involvement in the Market	Most market supplies and prices are government regulated.	Many prices and supplies are government regulated.	Few prices or supplies are government regulated.	Some particular market prices are regulated—most are determined by market forces. Limited government intervention.
How Resources Are Allocated	Planning agency allocates quality and quantity of resources to state-owned producers. No profit incentive.	Many government controls over distribution of resources.	Most resources allocated by price. Some government assistance in basic industry.	Individual producers allocate resources and choose with regard to price. Profits are the final incentive.
Ownership of Resources (Private Property)	Government owns all productive resources and directs their use for the public benefit.	Much public ownership. All basic industries are government owned.	Primarily private property.	Most productive resources are privately owned and operated for private benefit. Almost no government-owned firms.
Income Distribution	Determined by governments.	Determined by government and market forces.	Determined by market forces.	Determined by market forces.
Close Example	China	Yugoslavia	Japan	United States

FIGURE 24–2 COMPARATIVE ECONOMIC SYSTEMS
Four kinds of economic systems are compared in terms of government involvement, allocation of resources, ownership of resources, and income distribution.

24–1
socialism
An economic system in which most of the basic industries are government owned and operated.

Socialism. An economic system in which most of the basic industries are government owned and operated is called **socialism**. Yugoslavia's economic system is an example of socialism. In socialist economies like Yugoslavia, all the basic industries are owned and operated by government. Small-scale private businesses and shops can be owned privately, but the majority of goods and services are produced through government-owned firms. Workers in the government firms, however, make many of the management decisions in their own interest. There is a modified profit system where revenues that are greater than costs are returned to the workers. This creates stronger incentives for efficiency than a pure command system. In a socialist economy, therefore, income distribution is determined by a mixture of government direction and market profit.

Many human social services including health and education are also provided by government.

Government-Assisted Capitalism. In **government–assisted capitalism**, most economic decisions are made in the marketplace, and government enacts policies to assist individual decision making. This other major kind of mixed economy involves indirect government support for the market process. In Japan, for example, the government does not own any of the producing firms. However, it does work with businesses to improve efficiency. Many government policies are directly aimed at encouraging savings and investment in industry. This type of economic system differs very little from the United States in ownership and control of resources. But there are two major differences.

In Japan, the government takes a more active role in matters such as limiting imports of foreign goods. Government quotas have kept many foreign producers from supplying large amounts of goods to the Japanese economy. Such goods would compete with Japanese industries. This competition would take away profits. Japanese firms needed profits to modernize and improve their plants and equipment. This proved especially true in the formative years of Japanese industry.

The Japanese government also has developed tax policies that strongly encourage savings. Unlike the United States, the Japanese

24–1

government-assisted capitalism

An economic system in which most economic decisions are made in the marketplace, and government enacts policies to assist individual decision making.

government does not tax personal savings very heavily. Such government policies explain why the Japanese save about three times as much of their income as Americans. These savings accumulate in banks. Banks then loan these savings to industry to build new plants and buy new equipment. This program of modernization has placed Japan in the forefront of modern industrial growth. Through the last half of the twentieth century, Japan has had more consistent positive economic growth than most other countries, including the United States.

It appears that there can be advantages when government actively supports the economy but does not interfere in its operation. In many ways, Japan could even be considered more market-oriented than the United States. Perhaps in the years to come, governments in other market-oriented economies will actively encourage savings, investment, and industrial growth.

Over the past three decades, several command and market economies have enjoyed rapid growth rates. The more rapid growth has occurred in countries such as Japan and Germany. This growth, however, cannot be attributed only to the fact that these countries had market economies. Even though market economies create strong incentives for efficiency, many other factors contributed to the growth rates of these countries.

Market economies are not perfect models of efficiency. Neither are command economies perfect models of equity. The type of economic system each of us prefers involves personal choice. The personal choices of individual citizens acting together determine the type of economy that society will have. The choices involve consideration of both equity and efficiency. Most societies now have systems with some elements of both market and command economies. Perhaps some new form of economic system will evolve in the future to deal even more effectively with people's material and emotional needs.

EASTERN EUROPEAN ECONOMIC REFORM

Eastern European countries, such as Czechoslovakia, Hungary, and Poland, are moving toward more market-directed economies. After years of having a tightly controlled centralized economy, this transition will not be easy. To be successful, they must have internal consensus and political commitment to reform. They must develop new laws regarding contracts, ownership of property, and other areas essential to the functioning of a market economy. It is not clear how fast a country can go from controlled prices to market-determined prices. To avoid great social disruption, this process must be managed carefully. We cannot expect these countries to move from command economies to market economies overnight.

THINKING
ABOUT ECONOMIC ISSUES

In March 1960, W. W. Rostow published a short book titled *The Stages of Economic Growth*. In this book Rostow put forth the idea that "It is possible to identify all societies in their economic dimensions, as lying within one of five categories:

1. the traditional society,
2. the preconditions for take-off,
3. the take-off,
4. the drive to maturity, and
5. the age of high mass-consumption."[1]

The characteristics that define each of these stages can be summarized as follows:

The Traditional Society has limited types of production based on pre-Newtonian scientific principles. Production is so limited that these societies must devote most of their resources to agriculture. Society's structure leaves little chance of moving away from the life situation into which one is born.

The Preconditions for Take-off include the adoption of some forms of modern technology along with a change in social and political attitudes to those that favor economic advancement. The stimulus to change may come from outside the society itself.

The Take-Off is a stage in which investment rises to 10 percent or more of national income and attitudes turn toward economic progress. Economic growth becomes the normal condition. New natural resources and new forms of production develop.

The Drive to Maturity sees investment increase to perhaps 20 percent of national income. The economy grows to a much broader base, the country begins to participate more in international trade, and society demonstrates its ability to apply technological and entrepreneurial skills to a wide range of activities.

The Age of High Mass Consumption is one in which real income per person rises to a level where most members of society have considerable discretionary income. Societies in this stage become more urbanized and can allocate increased resources to social welfare and security.

Are There Stages of Economic Development?

---

[1]W. W. Rostow, *The Stages of Economic Growth* (Cambridge: Cambridge University Press, 1960), 4. (Numbers added.)

This theory of development has some descriptive appeal and has gained considerable initial acceptance. However, as economists tried to actually identify movement through these stages for specific economies, it became clear that the stages were ill defined. Some economies have skipped various stages while others have failed to leave the traditional stage despite possessing some of the characteristics of latter stages. As a result, most economists today question whether it is possible to define clear stages of economic development. It may well be that there is no universal pattern of development. Rather, societies probably have so many unique features that economic development follows many diverse paths.

REVIEWING THE CHAPTER

24–2 1. All economies must decide the economic questions of what, how, and for whom to produce. Different economies use different combinations of individual and social choice to answer these questions. The mix of social and individual decision making an economy uses determines the type of economic system it has.

24–2 2. All economies can be classified into one of four broad categories. Traditional economies answer the three basic economic questions through reliance on social customs. Command economies answer the three basic economic questions mainly through central planning, government decree, and social decision making. Market economies answer the three basic questions mostly through individual choice in the marketplace. Mixed economies use elements of both systems in making economic decisions. In reality, almost all economic systems contain some elements of both command and market systems.

24–3 3. Since scarcity and choice exist in all economies, the incentives individuals face are important. Economic systems that provide incentives with individual benefits are, in general, more efficient systems. Efficiency is frequently a by-product of self-interest. However, the most efficient economic systems are not always the most equitable economic systems. There may be some sacrifice in efficiency for a more equitable economic system and vice versa. Some inefficiencies and some inequities exist in all economic systems.

24–4 4. Ownership of productive resources is another means of classifying economic systems. In market economies, most productive resources are owned by individuals who receive the benefits (profits) of these resources. In command economies, all productive resources are owned by government. Socialist economies have government ownership of the basic industries and private

ownership of many other industries. Ownership of private property affects the distribution of income in an economy.

24–3   5. Some market economies enjoy the direct benefit of government
policies aimed at improving efficiency in industry. In Japan,
government tax policy strongly encourages savings and investment in industry. Government policy also assisted Japanese
industry in its formative years by regulating foreign competition. These forms of government-assisted capitalism may
explain at least part of Japan's impressive industrial growth during the past 50 years.

REVIEWING ECONOMIC TERMS

24–1   Supply definitions for the following terms:

economic system   mixed economy
traditional economy   capitalism
command economy   socialism
market economy   government-assisted capitalism

REVIEWING ECONOMIC CONCEPTS

24–2   1. What are the four basic types of economic systems? How are
economic systems classified?

24–2   2. How do market, command, and mixed economies determine
what goods and services will be produced?

24–2   3. How do market, command, and mixed economies decide what
resources and methods will be used to produce goods and
services?

24–2   4. Who decides how goods and services will be distributed among
the population in market, command, and mixed economies?

24–3   5. What roles do scarcity, economic choice, and incentives play in
the efficiency of an economy?

24–3   6. What roles do scarcity, economic choice, and incentives play in
the equity of an economy?

24–4   7. Name four kinds of economies classified by ownership of
resources. How are resources owned in each of these ec_____
systems?

24–3, 24–4   8. How do economies such as those of Japan or Yugoslav____
from command economies or market economies?

APPLYING
ECONOMIC
CONCEPTS

24–2,
24–3

1. Which type of economic system do you feel is best? Which type of system would you choose to live in and why?

24–2,
24–3

2. Do you think that individuals or governments should decide what goods will be produced in an economy? Why?

24–3

3. Is equity or efficiency the most important concern in an economic system? Should an economy try to achieve both goals? If so, at what cost? Would you give up part of your wealth or income so that the economy could be more equitable to those who make less than you? If so, how much would you give up?

24–3, 24–4

4. "Ownership of capital such as factories or machines is unfair. It just makes the rich get richer and the poor get poorer!" Do you agree or disagree with this statement? Why? What does ownership have to do with efficiency?

24–3

5. Do you think that government should assist industry and still leave the benefits of production to individuals such as in Japan? When the entire economy grows, does everyone benefit? If so, how? If not, why not?

24–3

6. What role do you think incentives play in the efficiency of an industry? Do you take better care of and use more carefully public property or your own private property? Does this idea have a parallel in managing private industry as opposed to managing government-owned firms?

PERESTROIKA: RESTRUCTURING THE SOVIET ECONOMY

In the post-Stalin era, the Soviet Union had reasonable success with rapid industrialization based on a centralized command economy. But this system began to show its deep-seated weaknesses as partial attempts at reform continued to fail in the 1960s and 1970s. It was not until Mikhail Gorbachev came to power in 1985 that the Soviet Union became committed to real economic reform.

This economic reform process will involve consideration of the wishes of consumers. Reform will be opposed by bureaucrats with vested interests in old ways, as was the case in the attempted coup in 1991. The system will have to slowly give way to prices that are determined by the market.

Given the initial shortage of consumer goods and the rapidly increasing prices, it will be a real challenge to find ways to increase wages so that people can afford to purchase the goods they desire. New entrepreneurial freedoms will promote additional production of consumer goods in response to higher prices.

CHAPTER 25

INTERNATIONAL TRADE

Learning Objectives

25-1 Define terms related to international trade.

25-2 Explain why countries trade with each other.

25-3 List the major imports and exports of the United States.

25-4 Name and describe three different systems for valuing one country's money in relation to another country's money.

25-5 Give four reasons for restricting world trade.

25-6 Give four reasons for not restricting world trade.

25-7 Describe the major events that have led to better world trade since 1947.

REASONS FOR INTERNATIONAL TRADE

25–2   Nations trade with each other because they can make some goods more efficiently than others. They use the money from the goods they can make efficiently to buy those goods they cannot make efficiently or that they make less efficiently.

Trade makes nations economically better off. David Ricardo, an English economist, explained the reasons for international trade in 1817 by using the law of comparative advantage. The law of **comparative advantage** is the principle that a country benefits from specializing in the production at which it is relatively most efficient. This law holds true, even if one country is more efficient than other countries in all kinds of production. The law of comparative advantage explains why a country that can make everything at a lower cost than any other country still benefits from trade. This law shows that such a country should concentrate on making the goods for which its cost advantage is highest.

To illustrate Ricardo's law of comparative advantage, assume there are only two countries in the world—Germany and England. Also, assume that there are only two products—steel and cloth. Suppose that Germany can make both steel and cloth more cheaply than England. Germany can make one unit of steel using 80 labor hours, while England can make one unit of steel using 120 labor hours. Germany can make one unit of cloth using 90 labor hours, while England can make one unit of cloth using 100 labor hours. Table 25–1 shows this relationship.

25–1

comparative advantage
The principle that a country benefits from specializing in the production at which it is relatively most efficient.

Illustration 25–1
The law of comparative advantage shows that a country should concentrate on making goods for which its cost advantage is highest.

TABLE 25-1

PRODUCTION COSTS OF STEEL AND CLOTH
IN TERMS OF LABOR HOURS

	Germany	England
One unit of steel (1 ton)	80 hours	120 hours
One unit of cloth (50 yards)	90 hours	100 hours

You can see from Table 25–1 that Germany has an absolute cost advantage in making both goods. An **absolute advantage** exists in the production of a good when one country can produce that good more efficiently than another country. In our present example, Germany can make both goods using fewer labor hours than England. So, Germany would have lower costs for a unit of steel or for a unit of cloth. Think of a unit of steel as one ton of steel and a unit of cloth as 50 yards of cloth.

Now let's look at the opportunity cost of making cloth. That is, what amount of steel must be given up when labor is used to make cloth rather than steel. As you read the next four paragraphs, refer to Table 25–1 often. Make sure that you see how the numbers in this table relate to the numbers used in these paragraphs.

If you decide to make one added unit of cloth in Germany, you will have to take 90 labor hours away from making steel. Those 90 labor hours could have made 9/8 units of steel (90 ÷ 80). So, Germany would have to give up 9/8 (or 1.125) units of steel to make one added unit of cloth. If you decided to make one more unit of cloth in England, you would have to take 100 labor hours away from making steel. These 100 labor hours could have made only 5/6 (or 0.83) of a unit of steel (100 ÷ 120).

So, you see that to make an added unit of cloth, Germany would have to give up 1.125 units of steel. But England would give up only 5/6 (or 0.83) of a unit of steel. England would have to give up less steel to produce an additional unit of cloth. Therefore, England would have a comparative advantage in making cloth. This is true even though Germany has an absolute advantage in making cloth.

Now think about the opportunity cost of making steel. This is the cost of a unit of steel in terms of the amount of cloth that must be given up. Suppose you decide to make one more unit of steel. In Germany, you must give up 80 labor hours of cloth production to make one more unit of steel. Those 80 hours could produce 8/9 (or 0.89) of a unit of cloth (80 ÷ 90). So, to make one more unit of

25–1

absolute advantage
Economic advantage which exists in the production of a good when one country can produce that good more efficiently than another country.

steel in Germany, you must give up 8/9 unit of cloth. In England, you must take 120 labor hours away from cloth production in order to make one more unit of steel. Those 120 hours could make 1 1/5 (or 1.2) units of cloth (120 ÷ 100). So, in England you would have to give up 1.2 units of cloth to make one unit of steel. But in Germany you would only have to give up .89 of a unit of cloth. Germany would have to give up less cloth to produce an added unit of steel. Therefore, Germany would have a comparative advantage in steel production. The costs of these alternatives are shown in Table 25–2.

TABLE 25–2

PRODUCTION COSTS OF PRODUCING AN ADDED
UNIT OF CLOTH AND STEEL

	Cost of producing an added unit of:	
	Cloth	Steel
England	0.83 units of steel	1.2 units of cloth
Germany	1.125 units of steel	0.89 units of cloth

The law of comparative advantage shows that both countries could gain if they specialized in making the good for which they have the comparative advantage. England would be willing to trade cloth for steel if it could get more than .83 unit of steel for each of its units of cloth. Germany would be willing to trade steel for cloth if it could get more than .89 unit of cloth for a unit of steel. If Germany and England agree to trade one unit of steel for one unit of cloth, both countries will be ahead. The one unit of cloth traded gains a whole unit of steel. If England had tried to produce the steel itself, it would have had to give up 1.2 units of cloth. By trading, it had to give up only one unit of cloth. If Germany had tried to produce the one unit of cloth itself, it would have had to give up 1.125 units of steel. By trading, it lost only one unit of the steel. Both countries gain by trading. Nations trade because of this mutual benefit.

UNITED STATES EXPORTS AND IMPORTS

25–1

exports

Goods and services that one country sells to another country.

International trade consists of exports and imports. **Exports** are goods and services that one country sells to another country.

Imports are goods and services that one country buys from another country. Imports come in to a country; exports go out of a country.

For the United States, exports account for about 10 percent of our GNP. For some countries, exports are an even larger percent of GNP. So, many people's jobs and incomes depend on world trade.

To see which jobs may be most sensitive to world trade, let's first look at what we export to other countries. In Figure 25–1, you can see that the automotive and chemical industries export heavily. For chemicals, this is probably not surprising. Making chemical products is a high technology area in which the United States has always been a world leader. It is probably more of a surprise to see the high percentage of automobiles and parts we export. However, most of our exports in this category are auto parts rather than new cars. You can also see that grains—particularly corn and wheat—are exported at high levels. Many American workers are employed making these products, which are sold to other countries.

About half of our exports go to Canada, Japan, and to countries in the European Economic Community. The **European Economic Community (EEC)** is a group of European countries that have joined together and agreed on ways to improve trade among

25–1

imports

Goods and services that one country buys from another country.

25–3

25–1

European Economic Community (EEC)

A group of European countries that have joined together and agreed on ways to improve trade among themselves.

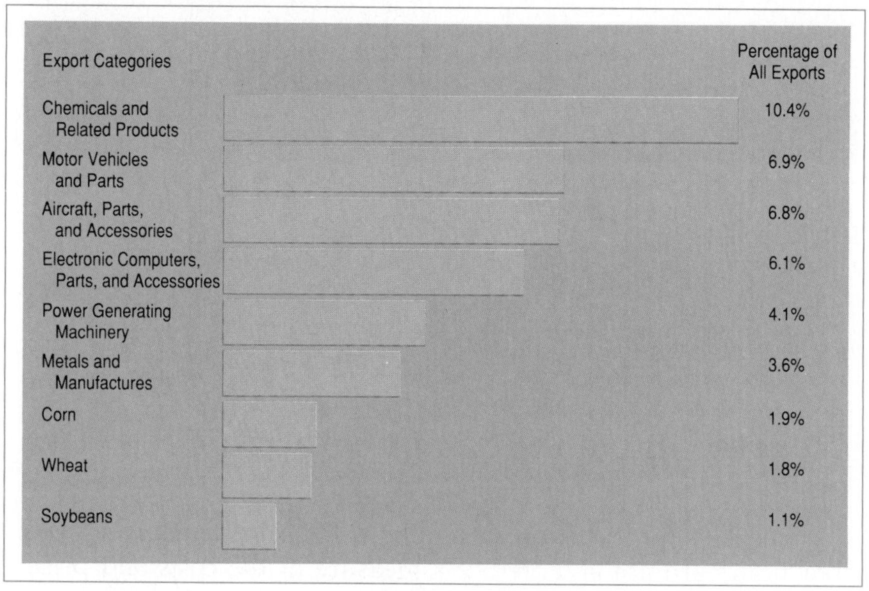

Export Categories	Percentage of All Exports
Chemicals and Related Products	10.4%
Motor Vehicles and Parts	6.9%
Aircraft, Parts, and Accessories	6.8%
Electronic Computers, Parts, and Accessories	6.1%
Power Generating Machinery	4.1%
Metals and Manufactures	3.6%
Corn	1.9%
Wheat	1.8%
Soybeans	1.1%

FIGURE 25–1   SOME MAJOR EXPORTS OF THE UNITED STATES
Chemicals, aircraft, and motor vehicles are some of our most important exports.

Source: U.S. Bureau of the Census, *Statistical Abstract of the United States: 1991*, 111th ed. (Washington, D.C., 1991), 811–812.

themselves. The EEC includes Belgium, Denmark, France, Germany, Greece, Ireland, Italy, Luxembourg, the Netherlands, and the United Kingdom.

Imports can also affect jobs for American workers. In recent years the effect of this has been felt in the automobile and steel industries. The bar chart in Figure 25–2 shows the major products that we import from other countries. Automobiles and parts are the most important part of our total imports. Petroleum products are the next most important.

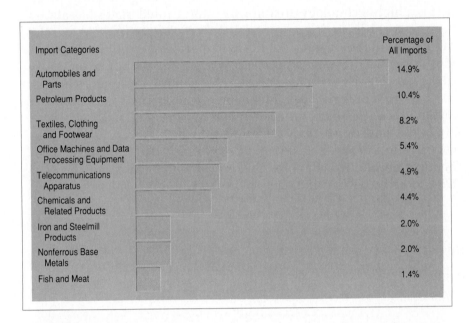

Import Categories	Percentage of All Imports
Automobiles and Parts	14.9%
Petroleum Products	10.4%
Textiles, Clothing and Footwear	8.2%
Office Machines and Data Processing Equipment	5.4%
Telecommunications Apparatus	4.9%
Chemicals and Related Products	4.4%
Iron and Steelmill Products	2.0%
Nonferrous Base Metals	2.0%
Fish and Meat	1.4%

FIGURE 25–2   SOME MAJOR IMPORTS OF THE UNITED STATES
Petroleum products and cars make up the majority of our imports.

Source: U.S. Bureau of the Census, *Statistical Abstract of the United States: 1991*, 111th ed. (Washington, D.C., 1991), 813–814.

PAYING FOR PRODUCTS TRADED BETWEEN COUNTRIES

Trade does not function as simply as Ricardo's model suggests. Labor hours are not accepted as a measure of the costs and prices of goods. Countries do not *barter* their goods in international marketplaces. England and Germany do not simply agree to trade one unit of cloth for one unit of steel. Nations usually set prices and measure costs in terms of their kind of money. The United States uses dollars, England uses pounds, Germany uses marks, Japan uses yen, and so on. Problems arise in trade when nations must compare their different kinds of money. In the history of international trade, many attempts have been made to set the values of these money measures in relation to each other and to some standard.

The Gold Standard

Before 1920, this money problem was not so difficult. Many trading countries of the world tied their money to a gold standard. The **gold standard** is a system in which each nation sets the value of its money in terms of a certain amount of gold. Each nation guaranteed the value of its money by keeping gold to back the money. The system of a gold standard made the bookkeeping for trade between countries much easier. Backing most money by gold allowed for simple comparison of the values of the various kinds of money in terms of gold. For example, what if the American dollar was worth 1/36 ounce of gold, while the English pound was worth 1/18 ounce of gold? Two dollars would equal one pound. The gold standard helped to keep the world money market stable and made international payments easy.

But there were also disadvantages to the gold standard system. The amount or supply of money was tied to the amount of gold a country held. An imbalance in trade had an effect on a country's money supply. For example, suppose the United States had a trade deficit. A **trade deficit** is the result when a country imports more than it exports. In order to pay for its imports, the United States would have had to exchange its dollars for foreign money. Many dollars would have left the country in order to pay for imports. The only way to get these dollars back would be to have foreign countries use them to buy American exports. However, because the United States had a trade deficit, it was not exporting enough goods to get all of its dollars back. Since the United States (before 1920) used the gold standard, it could not add to the supply of dollars. So, there would be too few dollars in the American economy. This could result in lower aggregate demand and perhaps higher unemployment.

Now let's consider the opposite situation. Suppose the United States had a trade surplus. A **trade surplus** is the result when a country exports more than it imports. The United States must pay for its imports by trading its dollars for foreign money. As a result, foreign countries hold many dollars, and they use these dollars to pay for American exports. But if the United States runs a trade surplus, more dollars return to the United States to pay for exports than leave the country to pay for imports. As a result, the number

25–4
25–1
gold standard
A system in which each nation sets the value of its money in terms of a certain amount of gold.

25–1
trade deficit
The result when a country imports more than it exports.

25–1
trade surplus
The result when a country exports more than it imports.

of dollars in the American economy rises. Too many dollars are chasing too few goods, and inflation becomes likely.

Both of these situations show that imbalances in trade under a gold standard system can directly affect domestic economies. Inflation and unemployment at home can be the direct results of trade surpluses or deficits.

Flexible Exchange Rates

25–4

25–1
exchange rate
The rate at which one kind of money can be traded for another.

25–1
flexible exchange rates
A system in which the laws of supply and demand are allowed to set the prices, or exchange rates, between each kind of money.

From 1920 to 1944, the gold standard system slowly broke down. Many forces, including World War II and the United States' monopoly of the gold supply, combined to destroy it. Also, many countries grew unwilling to accept inflation and unemployment in their own economies. During this time, the world could have adopted a flexible system of exchange rates. An **exchange rate** is the rate at which one kind of money can be traded for another. For example, the exchange rate between dollars and German marks might be $1 for 4 marks, or $1 = 4 marks.

Under a system of flexible exchange rates, each country's money is treated like a commodity for sale. **Flexible exchange rates** are a system in which the laws of supply and demand are allowed to set the prices, or exchange rates, between each kind of money. For simplicity, let's consider a two-nation, two-good world.

Our two nations will be the United States and Japan. American money is dollars, and Japanese money is yen. Suppose that the United States makes food, and Japan makes clothes. We will assume that the United States must buy from Japan. Japan will accept only yen (its own money) for payment. Therefore, the United States will demand enough yen to pay for its clothes. Japan must buy food from the United States, but we will accept only dollars as payment. So, Japan will need enough dollars to pay for its food. Suppose that we need 100 million units of clothes, and Japan needs 200 million units of food. Suppose also that a unit of clothes costs 2 yen, and a unit of food costs $1. The United States will need 200 million yen to pay for its 100 million units of clothes. Japan will need $200 million to pay for its 200 million units of food. Each country needs 200 million units of the other's money. So, the exchange rate will be 1:1. They will exchange $1 for 1 yen. This is shown in Table 25–3.

Now suppose that the United States needs 200 million units of clothes and Japan needs 800 million units of food. The prices of clothes and food remain the same. These new commodity demands are shown in Table 25–4. A unit of clothes costs 2 yen, and a unit of food costs $1. The United States will need 400 million yen to pay for its clothes. Japan will need $800 million to pay for its food.

TABLE 25–3

EXCHANGE RATE BETWEEN DOLLARS AND YEN
WHEN EQUAL UNITS OF MONEY ARE NEEDED

United States	Japan
100 million units of clothes needed × 2 yen/unit	200 million units of food needed × 1 dollar/unit
200 million yen needed	200 million dollars needed

Exchange rate:
1 yen = 1 dollar

The exchange rate will be 1 yen to $2. For every dollar, the United States will demand 1/2 yen.

Now let us see what happens if demand changes again but the exchange rate is fixed at 1 yen = 2 dollars. In our two-country system, suppose that our demand for clothes goes up from 200 million units to 400 million units, as shown in Table 25–5. At the same time, Japan's demand for food remains the same. Japan still demands 800 million units of food. However, suppose the exchange rate of 1 yen to $2 stays the same, and the prices of clothes and food stay the same. The United States will need 800 million yen to pay for its clothes. And Japan will need $800 million to pay for its food. But the exchange rate is still 1 yen for $2.

In order to get enough yen to pay for our clothes, we will have to give $1,600 million to Japan. However, Japan can only use $800 million. This leaves a surplus of $800 million. If the exchange rate

TABLE 25–4

EXCHANGE RATE BETWEEN DOLLARS AND YEN
WHEN UNEQUAL UNITS OF MONEY ARE NEEDED—
FLEXIBLE EXCHANGE RATES

United States	Japan
200 million units of clothes needed × 2 yen/unit	800 million units of food needed × 1 dollar/unit
400 million yen needed	800 million dollars needed

Exchange rate:
1 yen = 2 dollars or
1 dollar = ½ yen

TABLE 25–5

EFFECTS OF FIXED EXCHANGE RATE
BETWEEN DOLLARS AND YEN

United States	Japan
400 million units of clothes needed × 2 yen/unit	800 million units of food needed × 1 dollar/unit
800 million yen needed	800 million dollars needed

Exchange rate
fixed at:
1 yen = 2 dollars

United States gives 1,600 million dollars to get 800 million yen.	Japan receives 1,600 million dollars, but only needs 800 million dollars. Trade surplus results.

were fixed at $1 = 1 ounce of gold and 1 yen = 2 ounces of gold (so that 1 yen = 2 dollars), Japan would develop a trade surplus. Inflationary problems would follow.

A flexible exchange rate allows the laws of supply and demand to operate, and a new exchange rate of 1 yen to $1 will bring the system back into equilibrium. The use of a flexible exchange system gets rid of the inflation problem for Japan. But the adjustment is not entirely painless. As the exchange rate adjusts from $1 = 2 yen to $1 = 1 yen, the cost of clothes would appear to rise in the United States. Under the earlier system, the cost of a unit of clothes was 2 yen. Since the people of the United States could get those 2 yen for $1, the cost of clothes to them was $1. Now under the new exchange rate of $1 to 1 yen, the cost of clothes in the United States will rise from $1 to $2. In a flexible exchange rate system, prices are allowed to correct what would be imbalances in trade under a fixed exchange rate system.

The Bretton Woods Agreement of 1944

The world could have adopted a flexible exchange rate system during the period from 1920 to 1944; however, it did not. Many of the countries of the world felt that such a system of flexible rates would not work. They thought that prices would be difficult to set if money exchange values changed. The resulting instability might have cut back on world trade.

After World War II, most of the Western allies tried to set up a new international money system. They wanted to strike a balance between the gold standard and flexible exchange rates. They devised the *Bretton Woods system*. The name comes from Bretton Woods, New Hampshire, where the agreements were reached in 1944.

In the Bretton Woods system, the dollar became the key currency. It replaced gold as a standard. Gold could not be used as a standard because the United States held most of the world's gold. However, the value of the dollar remained tied to gold. The United States continued to sell gold to foreign countries for $35 an ounce. This meant a dollar was worth 1/35 of an ounce of gold.

25–4

The dollar and a few other kinds of money were designated as reserve currencies. A reserve currency acted like gold to support a nation's currency. Each country's currency value was set in terms of the dollar—for example, an English pound was valued at so many dollars. So, exchange rates among different kinds of money were set in terms of dollars. Each country was required to maintain international reserves (usually dollars) in order to back the value of its money. Each had to guarantee that its money's value would change no more than 1 percent upward or downward. If the value of a country's money began to fall, it had to use its reserves to buy up that money. If the value of the money began to rise above 1 percent, it would sell some of it.

The Bretton Woods system also included the creation of an *International Monetary Fund (IMF)*. The IMF made it easier to buy and sell different kinds of money in order to maintain their values. If the reserves of a country ran low, it could borrow reserves up to certain limits. If a country could not maintain the value of its money, it could get permission from IMF directors to change the value of its money up to 10 percent. The system allowed some flexibility but maintained stable exchange rates.

The Bretton Woods system began to break down during the 1950s. In that period the United States began to run large trade deficits. Since dollars were a reserve currency, the United States could run a trade deficit with very little consequence. It was not required to adjust its reserves, since the dollar was a reserve currency. This meant that a surplus of dollars began building up overseas. Foreigners began to trade these dollars for gold. By 1971, the value of dollars held by foreigners was several times larger than the value of gold held by the United States. This meant that we would not have enough gold to meet the potential demand by foreigners who had U.S. dollars.

In August 1971, the United States stopped its sale of gold. It announced that it would no longer buy or sell gold at $35 an ounce. In December 1971, the United States lowered the value of its dollar by about 9 percent. Several other nations also changed the values of their money. In 1972, the United States had the worst trade deficit in history. It again lowered the value of the dollar in February

1973, and several other nations again changed the values of their money. The Bretton Woods system no longer worked.

Since that time, the world has used a system of flexible exchange rates. Despite continued pressure to reestablish an international monetary system, this has not been done.

THE BALANCE OF PAYMENTS AND BALANCE OF TRADE

The term *balance of trade* refers to the relationship between a country's exports and imports. Sometimes the phrase *net exports* is used instead of balance of trade. Both refer to the level of merchandise exports minus the level of merchandise imports. The balance of trade is considered favorable if a country has more exports than imports. If a country has more imports than exports, the balance of trade is unfavorable. In the United States we have had an unfavorable balance of trade in recent years.

Balance of payments is a more comprehensive concept. In addition to merchandise exports and imports, the balance of payments includes:

1. Services we provide to foreigners and the services they provide to us.

2. Travel by U.S. citizens in foreign countries and travel of foreigners in the United States.

3. Income we get from foreign investments and money paid to foreigners for investments they have in the United States.

4. Gold exports and gold imports.

5. Other money movements between countries.

PROS AND CONS OF FREE TRADE

Some people would like to limit free trade while others promote free trade. Before we look at the reasons, let us identify the barriers that are used to restrict trade. One of these *trade barriers* is the tariff. A **tariff** is a tax on imports. A tariff makes imports more expensive for consumers to buy. This happens because producers must charge higher prices to cover the additional cost of the tariff. Another method of restricting trade is to use quotas. A **quota** is a limit on the amount of imports or exports. Quotas make it illegal to import or export more than a certain amount.

Throughout your study of economics, you have seen the advantages of free competition. You also learned that sometimes laws are passed against the restraint of trade. Why, then, would any country

Illustration 25–3
The United States balance of payments is affected by American tourist travel to foreign countries.

25–1
tariff
A tax on imports.

25–1
quota
A limit on the amount of imports or exports.

want to restrict international trade? Several arguments are often presented in favor of such restrictions.

Reasons for Protectionism

Protectionism refers to the idea that we should limit international trade to protect our own self-interest. One of the reasons often stated for restricting international trade is the *national security argument*. This states that some goods are so vital to our national defense and security that we should not depend solely on other countries for them. Steel and aluminum are such goods. The argument is that so much might be imported that our own producers would eventually go out of business. Then, in the event of war, we might not be able to import enough to defend ourselves. We might even be at war with the country upon whose imports we depend. The argument holds that tariffs and quotas should be used to protect defense-related industries. Then these industries will remain strong.

The *infant industry argument* is similar. It says that an industry in its infant or beginning stages may not be able to compete against better organized and more mature foreign industries. Therefore, tariffs or quotas should be used to protect the young industry.

The *diversified economy argument* is also used to justify tariffs and quotas. This argument means that it isn't safe to put all your eggs in one basket. If you rely on just one import source for a particular good, what happens if that source is cut off? This argument holds that domestic producers should be able to supply every kind of good. In other words, an economy should be fully diversified.

Labor leaders frequently argue that we must *protect wages against cheaper foreign labor*. They favor using tariffs and quotas so that domestic workers do not have to compete with foreign workers. They believe that allowing imports produced using cheaper workers will hurt domestic workers' wages. They also believe that imports can cause unemployment in the domestic labor force.

Reasons for Free Trade

Most economists take a stand against the use of tariffs and quotas. First, they point out that tariffs and quotas hurt consumers by causing a rise in prices of goods. A tariff raises the costs for foreign businesses trying to sell products in the United States. When costs rise, businesses will supply a smaller amount of goods at each price than before the tariff. This is because the tariff has the effect of shifting the supply curve up to the left. This is shown in Figure 25–3. If the demand remains constant, the equilibrium price of the good will rise from P_1 to P_2. Also, the equilibrium

25–5

25–1

protectionism
The idea that we should limit trade to protect our own self-interest.

25–6

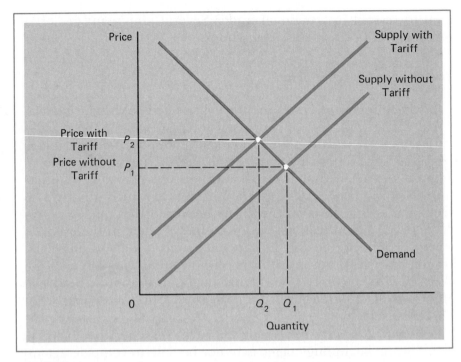

FIGURE 25–3   THE EFFECTS OF TARIFFS
A tariff causes the supply curve to shift up to the left (decrease). If demand does not change, the new equilibrium price, P_2, is higher. Also, the equilibrium quantity decreases from Q_1 to Q_2.

quantity will fall from Q_1 to Q_2. Quotas have a similar effect in that they legislate a decrease in the supply, and so the price rises.

Second, economists point out that tariffs and quotas interfere with the efficient functioning of supply and demand. This may result in the misallocation of valuable resources. Think about the national security argument with respect to oil and petroleum products. Tariffs and quotas allow the domestic prices of oil and petroleum to rise. This encourages more rapid development and depletion of our domestic reserves of oil. As a result, we deplete our domestic supplies and become more and more dependent on foreign supplies in the future. Tariffs and quotas will then have defeated the purpose of protecting our national security.

Third, economists say that some of these protectionist arguments have no validity for the United States. To argue for tariffs and quotas on the basis that the United States must maintain a diversified economy makes little sense. We already have a diversified economy. Labor unions' arguments for tariffs and quotas also sound weak. Members of the labor force think of labor as the only input into production. In reality, the capital supplied by businesses has a lot to do with labor productivity. Think about so-called cheap foreign labor being used to make a product. If a foreign business has less capital equipment than an American business, it will have lower productivity. Higher paid American labor may have better capital equipment and may be more productive. The more expensive and productive labor may well be able to compete with cheaper but less productive foreign labor. In cases where American labor cannot make things as efficiently, it is probably better to let other countries make the product. American labor should be shifted to those areas or industries where it can be most productive. Like all countries, America should apply the law of comparative advantage.

A fourth argument against the use of tariffs and quotas is that they are usually hard to change. For example, an industry may receive the benefit of a tariff or quota during its infant stage. But due to the difficulty of repealing tariffs and quotas, the industry may become quite mature and still receive these protections.

Protective Versus Revenue Tariffs

So far we have discussed tariffs as a means of limiting international trade in order to protect our own self-interest. When tariffs are used in this way they are called *protective tariffs*. Tariffs can also be used primarily to raise money for the government, much like other taxes do. When tariffs are used primarily to raise money for the government, they are called *revenue tariffs*.

A protective tariff will reduce imports only if demand is elastic. When demand is elastic, a given percentage increase in price causes a larger percentage reduction in quantity demanded. So, if we put a tariff on a product which has an elastic demand, we will succeed in reducing imports of that product.

A revenue tariff, on the other hand, can raise money for the government only if the demand is inelastic. When demand is inelastic, a given percentage increase in price causes a smaller percentage reduction in quantity demanded. In such a case the increase in price to the consumer (due to the tariff) has little effect on the amount purchased. The result is that the government can raise a good deal of money. In 1980 President Jimmy Carter advocated a 10 cent a gallon tax on imported oil as a way to help reduce the government's deficit. Oil was a good choice of product to tax, because the demand for oil is quite inelastic. (The price elasticity is about .3).

INTERNATIONAL TRADE COOPERATION

All countries can gain from having free trade. Therefore, it should not be surprising to learn that there is a good deal of cooperation to improve trade. The most important move in the direction of free trade came in 1947. In that year, 23 countries, including the United States, signed the General Agreement on Tariffs and Trade (GATT). The **General Agreement on Tariffs and Trade (GATT)** is an agreement that gave broad international

Illustration 25–4

If American labor cannot produce a good as efficiently as another country's labor, it is probably better to let the other country produce that good. This is an application of the law of comparative advantage.

25–1
General Agreement on Tariffs and Trade (GATT)
An agreement that gave broad international support to improving trade among countries.

25–7

support to improving trade among countries. The countries that belong to GATT, now about 100, meet with each other to lower trade barriers.

The formation of the European Economic Community (EEC) in 1958 also greatly helped to make international trade easier. The main purpose of the EEC was to make trade easier among the member countries by lowering tariffs and reducing nontariff trade barriers. Forming the EEC also helped promote the goals of GATT, since countries like the United States no longer had to deal with each EEC country separately.

The formation of the EEC could have put the United States at a disadvantage in world trade. But the United States took a strong leadership role at the GATT meetings that ended in 1967. The United States led in a new round of tariff reductions and actions to bring a closer working relationship between the United States and the EEC. Movement toward these talks began with the Trade Expansion Act of 1962, which gave American negotiators broad authority to cut tariffs. Another important part of the 1962 Act was a provision for trade adjustment assistance for people hurt by changes in world trade.

In 1974 the Trade Reform Act gave the United States authority to take part in another round of GATT talks in Geneva. These talks aimed mainly to cut nontariff trade barriers (import quotas, licensing requirements, unreasonably strict product quality standards, restrictions on government purchases, and customs procedures that overvalue imports subject to tariffs).

In 1979 a series of Multilateral Trade Negotiations (MTN) were completed in Tokyo as part of GATT. These meetings resulted in agreement to lower tariffs on all industrial goods. There was also agreement to make government purchases more open to foreign businesses. The countries that took part in these MTN meetings also agreed to do away with the use of quality standards that are more strict on foreign products than those made in a domestic economy. Finally, these talks resulted in making it easier to get a license to do business in other countries and also did away with tariffs on most civil aircraft products.

The next round of GATT meetings was called the Uruguay round. This round began in July 1986, with 47 countries setting an agenda of items to be discussed. The formal discussions began in September 1986, in Punta del Este. The Uruguay round included 108 countries. This time the United States was especially interested in issues related to farming, services, and intellectual property. This was the first time services and intellectual property were considered in GATT talks. Progress in this round was slow due to disagreements on agricultural issues and because of these new topics.

Illustration 25–5
The GATT talks in 1974 addressed, among other issues, customs procedures that overvalue imports subject to tariffs.

THINKING
ABOUT ECONOMIC ISSUES

During the 1970s the world became aware of a major problem with its supply of energy. The Arab Oil Embargo of 1973 called the world's attention to how dependent it had become on oil from the Mideast to fulfill its energy needs.

During this "energy crisis," Americans came face-to-face with two important facts. First of all, we realized that we consumed large amounts of energy in our lifestyles. Large gas-guzzling cars and a general lack of concern for the amount of energy we used to heat and cool our homes were commonplace. But more importantly, for the first time, Americans realized that the world's supply of energy is limited.

When the Arab oil embargo ended, the world faced yet another problem with its energy supply—rapidly rising prices. Price increased because the supply of energy was not rising as fast as the demand for energy. In the United States, a home that cost $300 a year to heat with oil in 1970 cost more than $1,300 to heat by 1980. The cost of a gallon of gas went up by almost 400 percent during this period. These price changes meant that people had to spend more income on energy and less on other products and services.

In the 1980s, after about 10 years of rapidly rising energy prices, the cost of energy fell. The primary reason for this related to overproduction by the world's oil-producing countries. The glut of oil caused oil prices to drop. People throughout the world started to substitute oil-based sources of energy for other sources. As a result, the demand for other types of energy dropped. The drop in energy prices had a good deal to do with the lower rates of inflation in many advanced economies during the 1980s.

About 90 percent of the world's energy supply comes from fossil fuels, with about half of that coming from oil alone. Since fossil fuels come from organic deposits within the earth, we know that the supply of these forms of energy is limited. Therefore, we must continue to develop alternate sources of energy (such as nuclear, solar, geothermal, and others) to ensure a supply of world energy in the years to come.

REVIEWING THE CHAPTER

25-2   1. Trade can help two countries even if one of them has the capability to make all goods at a lower cost than another country. This is due to the law of comparative advantage. This law shows that a country should specialize in that activity for which it has the greatest relative cost advantage.

25–3   2. International trade is a very important part of the United States economy. It accounts for about 10 percent of our GNP. Our main exports are chemicals, motor vehicles (mostly auto parts), and aircraft. Our main imports are petroleum and automobiles.

25–4   3. Countries do not use barter to pay for goods that are traded between them, so they must agree upon some other method of exchange. At one time, countries used a gold standard in which each country's money could be exchanged for gold. The gold standard was too rigid, and any imbalance between exports and imports could lead to inflation or unemployment. We now use a flexible exchange system which allows the supply of and demand for a country's money to determine its exchange rate.

25–5   4. Some people argue that trade should be restricted in some situations. These include the following:
1. To protect infant industries.
2. To protect our national security.
3. To keep a diversified economy.
4. To protect American workers from competition by cheap foreign labor.

25–6   5. Economists almost always favor free trade. They realize that trade barriers raise prices for all consumers and interfere with the functioning of the market system. This will reduce efficiency and result in a misallocation of resources.

25–7   6. Since 1947 the General Agreement on Tariffs and Trade (GATT) has been a structure within which countries have been able to lower trade barriers. The result is more world trade and better living standards for all countries.

REVIEWING ECONOMIC TERMS

25–1   Supply definitions for the following terms:

comparative advantage	trade surplus
absolute advantage	exchange rate
exports	flexible exchange rates
imports	tariff
European Economic Community (EEC)	quota
gold standard	General Agreement on Tariffs and Trade (GATT)
trade deficit	protectionism

REVIEWING ECONOMIC CONCEPTS

25–2   1. What law explains why countries trade with each other?

25–3   2. For the United States, how much of the GNP is accounted for by world trade?

25–3   3. What are the major exports of the United States?

25–3   4. What are the major imports of the United States?

25–4   5. How was money valued under the gold standard?

25–4   6. How was money valued under the Bretton Woods system?

25–4   7. How is money valued using flexible exchange rates?

25–5   8. Give four reasons in favor of restricting international trade.

25–6   9. Give four reasons in favor of not restricting international trade.

25–7   10. What was the major reason for forming the European Economic Community?

25–7   11. What was the major reason for the General Agreement on Tariffs and Trade?

APPLYING ECONOMIC CONCEPTS

25–6   1. Why do most economists favor free trade and eliminating tariffs and quotas?

25–7   2. Write an essay in which you discuss the major events since World War II that have led to better world trade. Which of these events seem most important to you? Why?

25–5   3. Recall the four reasons why some people favor trade restrictions. Give an example from the United States economy that you think best fits each reason.

25–2   4. How important is world trade in the United States? Go to the library and find the most recent issue of the *Statistical Abstract of the United States*. Look up both *exports* and *gross national product* in the index. Compare their relative amounts for the most recent year given. As a percentage of GNP, do exports still represent about 10 percent? If there has been a change, can you explain why?

25–3   5. Do you think the law of comparative advantage is as valid between states in the United States as it is between countries in the world? In what kinds of economic activities do you think your state has a comparative advantage? Why?

25–3   6. Use the table below as the basis for answering this question. The table shows the cost in terms of labor hours for making frozen foods and floor tiles in two countries (Country A and Country B). Notice that Country A can make both products with fewer labor hours than Country B. Using the law of comparative advantage, explain why Country A can still benefit from trade with Country B. Would Country B also benefit from trade?

	Cost in Labor Hours	
	One Unit of Frozen Food	One Unit of Floor Tiles
Country A	40	100
Country B	80	120

25–4   7. Assume the country of Alpha trades with the country of Beta and that they both use a gold standard. Alpha's money is called arcs, and Beta's money is called boles. One arc and one bole are each worth one ounce of gold. Suppose Alpha buys 20,000 pounds of steel from Beta for 20,000 boles, and Beta buys 15,000 bushels of corn from Alpha for 15,000 arcs.
(a) Which country will have a trade deficit?
(b) Which country will have a trade surplus?
(c) Which country will be more likely to experience inflation?
(d) Which country will be more likely to experience unemployment?

INTERNATIONAL TRADE PARTNERS MUST UNDERSTAND EACH OTHER

As the economic world becomes smaller, more U.S. businesses trade with foreign businesses. For this international trade to be successful, the people involved must understand one another. Knowing more than just one language will become increasingly important, but even that may not be enough. Consider doing business in England. Do we speak the same English? Consider the following:

In the United States	In England
Apartment house	Block of flats
Newsstand	Book stall
Bathroom	Closet (or water closet)
Suspenders	Braces
Car trunk	Boot of your car

Source: Philip R. Cateora, "You Say You Speak English?" in *International Marketing*, 7th ed. (Homewood, IL: Richard D. Irwin, 1990), 118–119.

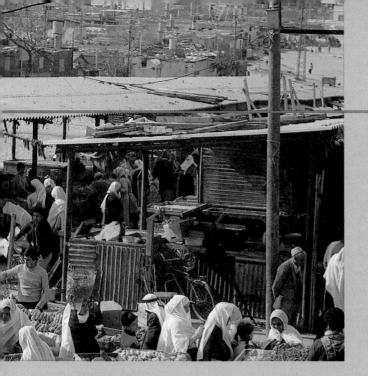

CHAPTER 26

LESS-DEVELOPED COUNTRIES

Learning Objectives

26–1 Define terms related to less-developed countries.

26–2 Identify some conditions in the countries considered to be less-developed.

26–3 Identify several countries that are less-developed.

26–4 Explain some of the effects of poverty in less-developed countries.

26–5 Explain five barriers to economic development in less-developed countries.

26–6 Explain why more advanced countries provide foreign aid to the less-developed countries.

LESS-DEVELOPED COUNTRIES: AN OVERVIEW

Living in the United States, you are among the richest of all the people in the world. You may not come from a family that is wealthy by United States' standards, but in comparison to the entire population of the world you are rich. You almost surely wear shoes to school. You probably have at least one full meal each day. It is likely that someone in your family has a car. Somewhere in your home there is probably a television and one or more radios. Most people in the United States take these luxuries for granted. However, for much of the world's population, adequate food and clothing are not readily available. Cars, televisions, and radios are either unknown or only something heard of but never experienced.

Most of the poorest countries in the world are in Asia, Africa, and Latin America. These countries are often referred to as *less-developed countries* or LDCs. (See the yellow areas in Figure 26–1.) In this chapter you will learn about the LDCs, their people, their economic problems, and their prospects for improvement.

Less-Developed Countries Defined

26–1

less-developed country

A poor country with a relatively low level of education and a largely rural population.

26–2

A **less-developed country** is generally defined as a poor country with a relatively low level of education and a largely rural population. Sometimes less-developed countries are referred to as *third-world countries*. Economists often define a country as being less developed if the annual income level per person averages $3,000 or less.

To help you see how little that is, let us compare it to income per person in the United States. We will use real gross national product (GNP) per person as the measure of income. In the most recent year for which comparable data are available, real GNP was about $19,000 per person in the United States. That equals over six times the $3,000 upper end of the per-person level of income in the LDCs.

26–3

Look at the first column of numbers in Table 26–1 on page 532. You see that many countries have a level of income per person far below the $3,000 level. In Ethiopia the yearly income is only $114 per person. In India income per person is only $329. The countries listed in Table 26–1 are not the only LDCs, but they are representative. You see that they are mostly Asian, African, or Latin American countries.

Many People Live in the LDCs

26–2

You also see in Table 26–1 that the LDCs represent more than just a few very small countries. Some have quite large populations.

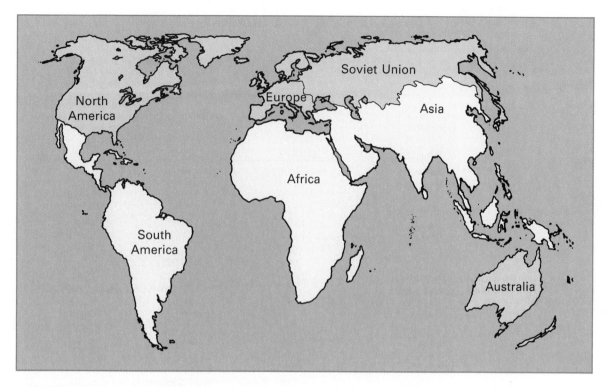

FIGURE 26–1 LESS-DEVELOPED COUNTRIES
Most less-developed countries are located in Asia, Africa, and Latin America. Latin America includes the continent of South America and all other countries south of the United States in the Western Hemisphere.

Look especially at Bangladesh, China, India, Mexico, Nigeria, and Pakistan. It should be clear to you that a great many people live in countries with very low income per person.

The third column of numbers in Table 26–1 shows the population density in these less-developed countries. Population density means the number of people per square mile. The United States has 69 people per square mile. You see that many LDCs are much more crowded than this. Bangladesh is the most crowded of the countries listed, with 2,130 people per square mile. That is almost 31 times more people per square mile than in the United States.

Being crowded is not the reason these countries are poor, however. Japan (860 people per square mile) and the United Kingdom (609 people per square mile) also seem crowded compared to the United States. But both Japan and the United Kingdom are relatively wealthy countries. Japan's GNP per person is $23,290; and in the United Kingdom GNP per person is $14,080. However, being both poor and crowded magnifies the problems in the less-developed countries.

TABLE 26–1

PER CAPITA GNP AND POPULATION FOR THE UNITED STATES
AND TWENTY LESS-DEVELOPED COUNTRIES

	1988 GNP per Person	1990 Population	1990 Population per Square Mile
United States	$19,840	250,410,000	69
Afghanistan	214	15,862,000	63
Bangladesh	172	118,433,000	2,130
China (Mainland)	501	1,118,163,000	302
Colombia	1,168	33,076,000	75
Egypt	1,455	54,706,000	141
Ethiopia	114	51,667,000	110
India	329	849,746,000	669
Kenya	354	24,639,000	110
Mexico	2,076	87,870,000	115
Myanmar (Burma)	278	41,277,000	158
Nepal	173	19,146,000	352
Nigeria	256	118,819,000	333
Pakistan	338	114,649,000	369
Peru	1,846	21,906,000	44
Sri Lanka	415	17,196,000	679
Sudan	306	26,425,000	27
Tanzania	118	25,971,000	71
Thailand	1,031	55,116,000	277
Turkey	1,263	56,704,000	188
Uganda	271	17,960,000	197

Source: U.S. Bureau of the Census, *Statistical Abstract of the United States: 1991*, 111th ed. (Washington, D.C., 1991), 830–832, 841.

Illustration 26–1
Being both poor and crowded magnifies the problems in the less-developed countries.

EFFECTS OF POVERTY IN LESS-DEVELOPED COUNTRIES

As you might expect, the poverty in the LDC's has an important impact on people's lives. Poverty can also weaken the political stability of the country. In addition, the poverty that exists in LDCs can affect those of us who live in the richer countries of the world. As you read about these three results of poverty in LDCs, keep in mind how little income people have in these countries.

Individuals Are Less Well Off

The lives of people in less-developed countries are very different from yours. The depth of their poverty is hard for us to fully understand. Many people do not have the basic food and clothing that we take for granted. Items such as televisions and radios, common in our households, rarely belong to households in LDCs. Table 26–2 illustrates this.

26–4

TABLE 26–2

AVAILABILITY OF SELECTED PRODUCTS
IN THE UNITED STATES AND
SOME LESS-DEVELOPED COUNTRIES

	Persons per Car	Radios per 1,000 People	Televisions per 1,000 People
United States	1.8	2,120	812
Bangladesh	NA	41	4
China (Mainland)	10,220	184	24
Colombia	NA	170	110
Egypt	NA	312	84
Ethiopia	NA	193	2
India	740	78	7.3
Kenya	NA	91	6
Mexico	15	241	124
Nigeria	125	164	6
Pakistan	289	86	13
Peru	NA	241	85
Sri Lanka	NA	191	32
Sudan	NA	233	53
Thailand	NA	177	104
Turkey	59	161	172

NOTE: NA—Not available.

Source: U.S. Bureau of the Census, *Statistical Abstract of the United States: 1985* (p. 844–845) and *1991* (p. 845), (Washington, D.C.).

Illustration 26–2
The Chinese, who share one car between every 10,220 people, rely heavily on bicycles for transportation.

26–1

infant mortality rate
The number of deaths of children under one year of age per 1,000 live births.

The first column of numbers in Table 26–2 shows how many people there are per car in the United States and some of the less-developed countries. The United States has so many cars that on average there is a car for every 1.8 people. Mexico has only one car for 15 people. China shares only one car between every 10,220 people! Think for a moment about how different your life would be if cars were not as readily available as they are in the United States.

The other two columns in Table 26–2 provide information about the availability of radios and televisions. In the United States there are 2,120 radios and 812 televisions for every 1,000 people. The numbers in Table 26–2 show that these items, common to people in the United States, are very rare in LDCs. You probably own your own radio. Perhaps you own more than one. But if you lived in India that would be unlikely. In India there are only 78 radios for every 1,000 people. This equals about 8 radios for every 100 people.

Similar comparisons can be made for televisions. You see that in some of the countries listed in Table 26–2, there are less than 10 televisions for every 1,000 people. Think about how different your life would be if cars, televisions, and radios were not common.

The three goods discussed here act only as examples to help you understand how poor many of the world's people are. If you lived in one of the LDCs, you would not have many other goods you now enjoy: no cassette player, no skateboard, no telephone, no watch, no movie theaters, no new school clothes. You would be lucky to have shoes, basic clothing, and one full meal a day.

In the less-developed countries poverty goes beyond material goods. People generally suffer poor health as well. The level of health care available in the United States far exceeds what is found in the LDCs. As shown in the first column of numbers in Table 26–3, the infant mortality rate is much higher in the LDCs than in the United States. The **infant mortality rate** is measured as the number of deaths of children under one year of age per 1,000 live births. In our country only about 1 percent of children born each year die within their first year. But look, for example, at Ethiopia. There, 116 of every 1,000 children born die in the first year. That is nearly 12 percent.

The rest of the information in Table 26–3 also supports the idea that people in the LDCs have low levels of health care. Compared to the United States they have fewer hospital beds and fewer medical doctors. Let us look at some examples. The United States averages 171 people per hospital bed. Mexico has 863 people per hospital bed, and in Bangladesh that number is 4,545. If you were hurt or very sick you can see that you would be more likely to find hospital care available in the United States than in the LDCs.

TABLE 26–3

HEALTH-RELATED DATA FOR THE UNITED STATES
AND TWENTY LESS-DEVELOPED COUNTRIES

	Infant Mortality*	People per Hospital Bed	People per Medical Doctor	Life Expectancy
United States	10	171	549	76
Afghanistan	154	3,470	14,471	47
Bangladesh	136	4,545	8,908	54
China (Mainland)	34	493	1,769	68
Colombia	38	609	1,969	71
Egypt	90	509	760	60
Ethiopia	116	2,787	72,582	51
India	89	634	2,545	58
Kenya	60	601	10,136	65
Mexico	33	863	2,136	72
Myanmar (Burma)	97	1,140	4,940	55
Nepal	99	5,271	28,767	50
Nigeria	119	1,251	9,591	49
Pakistan	110	1,731	2,911	56
Peru	67	547	1,480	64
Sri Lanka	31	350	7,464	70
Sudan	86	1,091	8,714	53
Tanzania	107	464	16,282	52
Thailand	34	658	6,870	67
Turkey	74	471	1,527	66
Uganda	107	689	22,291	49

NOTE: *Number of deaths of children under 1 year of age per 1,000 live births.

Source: U.S. Bureau of the Census, *Statistical Abstract of the United States: 1987* (p. 822) and *1991* (pp. 834–835), (Washington, D.C.).

The United States has one medical doctor for every 549 people. In comparison, look at the numbers for the LDCs in the third column of Table 26–3. In Thailand one doctor serves 6,870 people and Ethiopia has one doctor for every 72,582 people.

The last column of Table 26–3 shows the life expectancy of people born in these countries. The **life expectancy** is the average age the people in a country live to be. In the United States people live an average of 76 years. Some die much earlier and some at a much older age. As you look down the far-right column of numbers you see that in the LDCs the average life span is less. In Afghanistan, for example, you see that it is only 47 years.

The life expectancy of people may be the best overall measure of the population's general health. Based on this measure you see that people in the less-developed countries suffer from poor health. This is due to many factors. Part of the reason is that they

26–1

life expectancy

The average age the people in a country live to be.

have neither a nourishing diet nor adequate clothing or shelter. In addition, they do not have the level of medical care that exists in more-developed countries.

Political Problems Are Magnified

26–4   We enjoy living in a fairly stable social and political environment. Less-developed countries often generate social and political instability. Government control may rest in the hands of small groups of wealthy people. Corruption among political leaders emerges all too often. People with large amounts of money have a great deal of influence over policies formed by government officials. As different groups of wealthy citizens press for policies that favor them, conflict frequently results.

You may be asking yourself where these wealthy people come from since we have stressed the poverty that exists in these countries. Even though the average income is low, some people are quite rich. The distribution of income is very uneven in many LDCs. There are a few very rich people and many, many very poor people. Unlike the United States, almost no middle class exists in the less-developed countries. As the rich segments push for government policies that favor them, the poor may be nearly forgotten.

The poor tend to stay poor, often living a life no better than their ancestors of a thousand years earlier. Meanwhile the rich get richer. The result is what may be called a dual economy. A **dual economy** is one in which a modern market economy exists side by side with a primitive subsistence economy. In such a dual economy the modern sector may resemble more-advanced countries. Factories, retail shops, and restaurants may line urban streets. At the same time, in the subsistence sector, crude technologies are used in rural areas where goods are exchanged in a barter system. Almost no one advances into the wealthy sector. If you are born poor, you stay poor.

26–1

dual economy

An economy in which a modern market economy exists side by side with a primitive subsistence economy.

Since the poor have the least education and mobility, they tend to be largely ignored. The political system favors the wealthy few, while the subsistence economy continues as it has for decades.

Poverty in LDCs Affects Advanced Countries

26–4   The low level of income in LDCs has an adverse affect on advanced countries such as the United States. There are several reasons why this is so. First, poverty in the LDCs is an opportunity cost for advanced economies. If the buying power of the less-developed countries were greater, there would be larger markets for products that we export. People in the LDCs would purchase

Illustration 26–3
If incomes in the LDCs were greater, there would be larger markets for products — such as washing machines — that the United States exports.

clothing, appliances, computers, cars, and other products that are produced in the more-developed countries.

A second way that countries like the United States are adversely affected relates to the LDCs' failure to repay loans. Many banks and other financial institutions have made large loans to the governments of less-developed countries. Often when these loans are due for repayment the countries do not have enough money to meet their obligations. This is a very real concern. Because of the complexity of international finance it is difficult to judge the seriousness of this problem. Some economists believe that the stability of our domestic financial structure weakens when we lend money to LDCs.

A third way in which the low level of income in LDCs affects us relates to foreign aid. **Foreign aid** is the money that more-advanced countries provide to help the LDCs in their economic development. We will discuss foreign aid in more detail later in this chapter. But it deserves attention here because the money that we give to LDCs could be used to help solve domestic economic problems.

As a country we recognize how wealthy we are in comparison to the LDCs. For years we have been willing to share part of that wealth with them in the form of foreign aid. While this may be a good thing to do, we need to recognize the opportunity cost involved. We do give up the ability to use that money to improve education, to reduce domestic poverty, or to solve other economic problems in the United States.

26–1

foreign aid
The money that more-advanced countries provide to help the LDCs in their economic development.

BARRIERS TO ECONOMIC DEVELOPMENT

26–5

26–1

barriers to economic development
Economic, social, and political characteristics that prevent an economy from developing.

Economic, social, and political characteristics that prevent an economy from developing are called **barriers to economic development**. Five main barriers to economic development exist in the LDCs. These are limited natural resources, low human capital, shortage of investment capital, rapid population growth, and unfavorable political environment. We will look at each of these in the remainder of this section. Every less-developed country may not be faced with all five barriers, but it is not unusual to see all five operating at once.

Limited Natural Resources

Most of the LDCs have very limited natural resources. The resources they have are usually agricultural. Often even these resources are very specialized. For example, in Uganda coffee production is a major industry that accounts for about 98 percent of the country's exports. As another example, in Colombia the major industries are textiles, food processing, clothing and footwear, beverages, chemicals, metal products, and cement. Most of these are based on agricultural processing. The major exports from Colombia are coffee, fuel oil, cotton, tobacco, sugar, textiles, cattle and hides, bananas, and flowers. You see again that these originate from the agricultural sector.

While LDCs do have some useful natural resources, the base of those resources is usually narrow. They do not have the diversity of resources that we see in the United States; nor do they develop their resources effectively. The result for many LDCs is that the narrow and ill-developed resource base acts as a barrier to sustained economic development.

Low Level of Human Capital

A second barrier to economic development is the low level of human capital in the LDCs. By *human capital* we mean the level of education and training that people have. In most of the less-developed countries the level of public spending on education is quite low. Look at the first column of numbers in Table 26–4. These numbers represent the level of public expenditures for education as a percent of GNP. Consider how low those percentages are as compared to the 6.7 percent level for the United States. Also, think back to the GNP per person numbers in Table 26–1. Not only do these countries spend a small part of GNP

Illustration 26–4
Two of the barriers to economic development in the LDCs are limited natural resources and low levels of human capital.

TABLE 26–4

EXPENDITURES ON EDUCATION AND URBANIZATION
FOR THE UNITED STATES AND
TWENTY LESS-DEVELOPED COUNTRIES

	Public Expenditure For Education as a Percent of GNP[1]	Percent Literacy[2]	Percent of Total Population Living in Urban Areas[1]
United States	6.7	99.5	74
Afghanistan	NA	12	15
Bangladesh	2.2	25	15
China (Mainland)	2.7	75	21
Colombia	2.7	81	64
Egypt	5.5	40	44
Ethiopia	4.2	15	11
India	3.4	36	23
Kenya	7.0	47	13
Mexico	3.4	74	66
Myanmar (Burma)	1.6	78	24
Nepal	2.8	20	4
Nigeria	1.4	28*	16
Pakistan	2.1	24	28
Peru	3.3	72	65
Sri Lanka	3.8	87	22
Sudan	4.3	20	20
Tanzania	4.1	79	14
Thailand	3.6	84	17
Turkey	1.7	70	44
Uganda	3.9	52	8

NOTES: NA—Not Available.
        *Midpoint of range.

Sources: 1. U.S. Bureau of the Census, *Statistical Abstract of the United States: 1986* (p. 839, 841) and *1990* (p. 839), (Washington, D.C.).
         2. Central Intelligence Agency, *The World Factbook, 1985* (Washington, D.C., 1985), various pages.

on education, but they also have low levels of GNP. In combination these two factors mean that little support exists for education.

Look also at the second column of numbers in Table 26–4. These numbers show the percent of the adult population that is literate—that is, the percent that can read and write at a very basic level. In the United States 99.5 percent of the adult population is literate. But you see that the percent of literate adults is much lower in nearly all of the LDCs listed.

People with low levels of education and training tend to have low productivity. They cannot do jobs that require them to read and understand written instructions. Often the skills of the labor force in LDCs are appropriate only to an agricultural economy. They are not suited to the kinds of economic activities that will likely lead to substantial economic development.

Illustration 26–5
Without proper training and education, people tend to have lower levels of productivity.

In part, this agricultural orientation is reflected in the rural living patterns we see in less-developed countries. Compared to the more-advanced economic countries, fewer people in LDCs live in urban areas. Instead, they live in rural areas where they use what little skill and education they have to earn a subsistence income. Compare the percentage of people living in urban areas of the United States to the percentage in the LDCs by looking at the right-hand column of Table 26–4.

Shortage of Investment Capital

The third barrier to economic development is that the less-developed countries have a shortage of investment capital. You have learned that in order to invest in capital equipment (like machinery and factories), there must be savings. But, people with very low incomes need all of that income just to provide the basics of survival. There is no chance for them to save money. Typically they live what is called a "hand-to-mouth" existence. When they earn money, it is spent immediately for food or other necessities.

Some investment does take place in the less-developed countries but not nearly enough to promote development. Money available for investment in capital usually comes from the government or from foreign-aid programs sponsored by countries like the United States. Unfortunately the projects undertaken with these monies often do not represent the best interests of the majority of people in the LDCs. Often money is spent on the latest technological processes available when what is needed is an increase in the most basic technologies. The phrase "you need to learn to walk before you can run" is appropriate here. The less-developed nations need to develop basic production methods and human skills before trying to use the most modern and most difficult forms of production.

Rapid Population Growth

The fourth barrier to economic development for many of the less-developed countries is rapid growth of their populations. The number of people grows faster than the rate of growth in GNP. The result is that GNP per person stays very low or even falls despite all efforts at economic development. Look at Figure 26–2 which shows the rate of population growth for our representative LDCs. The rate of population growth for the United States is also shown for comparison. The number of years it would take for each country's population to double is also shown. These numbers should help you to see how rapidly populations are growing in many LDCs. This rapid growth in the number of people living in a country is sometimes referred to as a **population explosion**.

26–1
population explosion
Rapid growth in the number of people living in a country.

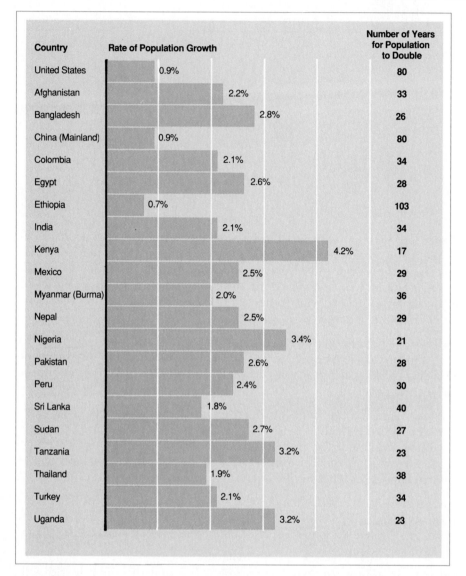

FIGURE 26–2 PERCENTAGE GROWTH RATES FOR POPULATION AND NUMBER OF YEARS FOR POPULATION TO DOUBLE

Source: Central Intelligence Agency, *The World Factbook, 1985*, (Washington D.C., 1985), various pages. (This source for percentages only. Number of years for the population to double are based on the author's estimates.)

Such rapid growth in the number of people coupled with low productivity means that many people live on the brink of starvation. An early economist, Thomas Malthus, predicted that populations would increase so fast that people would be kept at a subsistence level in the long term. He was wrong for the United States and other advanced nations, but for the LDCs he may have been correct. People living in many of the LDCs today are no better off in economic terms than their ancestors of centuries past.

WILLIAM ARTHUR LEWIS

The Nobel prize committee chose Sir William Arthur Lewis as its 1979 recipient for economics because of his deep concern about the need and poverty in the world and efforts to find ways out of underdevelopment. Lewis actually was born in a third-world country, on the island of St. Lucia in the British West Indies, in 1915. Early in his life, however, his family moved to London.

Lewis studied at the London School of Economics and then remained to teach for ten years. Already he had launched a career as a "development specialist," looking for practical economic strategies to help poor countries out of their poverty.

For Lewis, the way to help has been to study how *successful* economies develop. He believes that, before an industrial revolution can take place, a country must undergo an agrarian (agricultural) revolution. All along, Lewis has emphasized the importance of education, of investment in "human capital" through improved health and education programs.

Lewis served as an official for the University of Guyana. For his service to the University of the West Indies, Queen Elizabeth II knighted Lewis in 1963. As a United Nations consultant and advisor, Lewis worked in Ghana, Jamaica, and Nigeria.

Refusing to accept the usual economic belief that the third world will always remain poor and dependent on the charity of wealthy nations, Lewis has preferred to focus on human problems rather than statistics or mathematical models. Yet he is respected as an economic pragmatist in his approach to this specialized problem solving.

Lewis's many books and articles emphasize the need for agricultural and educational development. He has written on politics in South Africa, third-world development theory, and economic conditions of countries as they are transformed from poor to rich. Two better-known books, *Theory of Economic Growth* (1955) and *The Evolution of the International Economic Order* (1978), explain his strategies for helping poor countries achieve economic independence. Lewis has more than ten honorary degrees from universities and has taught at Princeton University in Princeton, New Jersey, since 1963.

Unfavorable Political Environment

The unfavorable political environment in some less-developed countries is a fifth barrier to economic development. Often political leaders are corrupt and/or incompetent. They tend to follow policies that favor a small but elite ruling class. These policies may not promote economic advancement for the masses.

However, the best hope for economic development must rest in proper governmental action. The provision of better education, for example, is probably best accomplished by the government. Further, the government can act as a strong guiding force in providing investment capital. To do so the governments of less-developed countries often turn to the advanced countries for aid.

FOREIGN AID CAN PROMOTE DEVELOPMENT

Foreign aid is the money that more advanced countries provide to help the LDCs in their economic development. One reason that countries like the United States provide foreign aid to the LDCs is that we believe in the morality of sharing a part of our wealth. A second reason is actually based on our own economic interest. If our aid can help less-developed countries become more prosperous, we may reap long-term benefits. Their development will open up more markets for the goods that we produce and thereby increase our own prosperity.

26–6

Table 26–5 shows the amount of money that flows from thirteen developed countries to the LDCs. You see that the United States is the major source of such aid. Other countries such as Japan and France also provide large amounts of money.

The **World Bank** also is a source of aid to the less-developed countries. The World Bank was established in 1944 to help finance reconstruction after World War II. Now the main function of the World Bank is to provide aid to LDCs. The World Bank borrows money from richer nations of the world that is, in turn, lent to less-developed countries.

26–1
World Bank
A source of aid to the less-developed countries.

THE FUTURE OF LESS-DEVELOPED COUNTRIES

The future is not bright for most of the less-developed countries. Some of these countries are not very different today from how they were a thousand years ago. However, as we learn more about how economies work, the prospects for LDCs improve. Applying the "economic way of thinking" to the problems of economic development may provide insights that will lead to more economic progress for the LDCs in the years to come.

TABLE 26–5

NET FLOW OF MONEY TO DEVELOPING COUNTRIES
FROM TEN MAJOR DEVELOPED COUNTRIES IN 1984
(In Billions of U.S. Dollars)

	Billions of U.S. Dollars
United States	28.6
Australia	1.6
Canada	2.8
Denmark	0.6
Finland	0.3
France	8.9
Germany (Fed. Rep. of)	6.5
Italy	2.0
Japan	9.4
Netherlands	2.0
Norway	1.6
Sweden	1.3
United Kingdom	3.8

NOTES: 1. These data do not include military aid.
2. Data for the U.S.S.R. were not available.

Source: U.S. Bureau of the Census, *Statistical Abstract for the United States: 1986*, 106th ed. (Washington, D.C., 1985), 861.

REVIEWING

THE

CHAPTER

26–2 1. Countries are considered to be less developed if their level of income averages less than $3,000 per person per year. In the United States income per person averages about $19,000.

26–2 2. The less-developed countries are not just small countries. Many are very large in terms of population, and many are very crowded.

26–4 3. People living in the less-developed countries do not enjoy the same kinds of goods that we take for granted. Few people have such luxuries as cars, televisions, or radios.

26–4 4. People in the less-developed countries have little available health care. As a result these countries have high infant mortality and low life-expectancy rates.

26–4 5. Less-developed countries often have an unstable political environment. Further, those in power tend to promote policies that favor the few rich people at the expense of the majority of people, who are poor.

26–4   6. Rich countries like the United States are affected by the poverty in LDCs because:
  a. Our export markets are more limited.
  b. Loans from the private sector of our economy are sometimes not repaid.
  c. We provide large amounts of financial aid to the LDCs.

26–5   7. There are five major barriers to economic development in the LDCs:
  a. limited natural resources
  b. low level of human capital
  c. relatively little investment capital
  d. explosive population growth
  e. unfavorable political environment.

26–6   8. Many of the world's most wealthy countries provide substantial money to the LDCs in the way of foreign aid. The World Bank also provides monetary support for economic development.

REVIEWING ECONOMIC TERMS

26–1   Supply definitions for the following terms:

less-developed country

infant mortality rate

life expectancy

dual economy

foreign aid

barriers to economic development

population explosion

World Bank

REVIEWING ECONOMIC CONCEPTS

26–1   1. What is meant by the term *less-developed country?*

26–2   2. Describe the conditions which exist in less-developed economies.

26–4   3. Explain how poverty affects people in less-developed economies.

26–4   4. Explain how poverty in LDCs affects people in the United States.

26–5   5. How does each of the following act as a barrier to economic development?
  a. low resource base
  b. low levels of human capital
  c. low levels of investment capital
  d. rapid population growth
  e. unfavorable political environment

26–6   6. Why does the United States provide foreign aid to less-developed countries?

APPLYING ECONOMIC CONCEPTS

26–2,
26–4

1. Write a one-page essay in which you describe what you think life is like for someone your age in an LDC.

26–6

2. Do you think the United States should continue to provide foreign aid to LDCs? Explain your answer.

26–3

3. Pick one of the less-developed countries listed in Table 26–1 and look up information on that country concerning its:
   a. natural resources
   b. population level
   c. economy
   d. government
   Write a paragraph about each of these four areas for the country you selected.

26–3

4. Use the most recent issue of the *Statistical Abstract of the United States* to update either Table 26–1, 26–2, 26–3, or 26–4. Have the countries listed in the table become more developed in recent years?

THE EXPECTATION GAP

You have certain expectations about your economic future. All of your expectations may not be realized, but for most people in the United States, there is a good chance that many of our expectations will come true. Overall, there is not much of a gap between expectations and reality.

In less-developed nations, this is not true. Modern communications make people in less-developed countries aware of many goods that they are unlikely to ever have. The gap between expectations (hopes) and reality is often very large. This can create great discontent.

This discontent can be overcome in two ways. One way is to promote sufficient economic growth so that standards of living can rise to the level of expectations. This, however, can take a long time. Second, an effort can be made to reduce expectations to a level that can be realized. This could be a desirable short-term measure. A combination of approaches is probably best.

APPENDIX I
ECONOMIC MEASUREMENT CONCEPTS

In Chapter 1 we briefly discussed the concept of opportunity costs. We used a graph of the various combinations of T-shirts and movies you could buy with a fixed income of $12. In effect, we drew a picture of the *relationship* between the two variables, T-shirts and movies. This type of analysis is very important in economics.

We also learned in Chapter 1 that theory gives us a simplified picture of reality. It reduces the complex parts of reality to a manageable piece of information. For example, you could memorize all the possible combinations of T-shirts and movies you could buy. But this would require a lot of work and you probably would not remember them for long. When you look at this information in graph form, however, you see that as the number of T-shirts you can choose goes up, the number of movies you can buy at the same time goes down. Learning this relationship enables you to store important information in your mind more easily. The information also lasts longer in your memory in this form.

Economists use several types of measurement tools to get the information they need into a manageable form. You may already have learned some of these concepts in your mathematics classes. We will refresh your memory and show you how they are used by economists. In this appendix, you will learn to use the following *economic measurements*: tables, charts, and graphs; averages and distributions of data; ratios and percentages; rates and absolute numbers; index numbers; and real and nominal values.

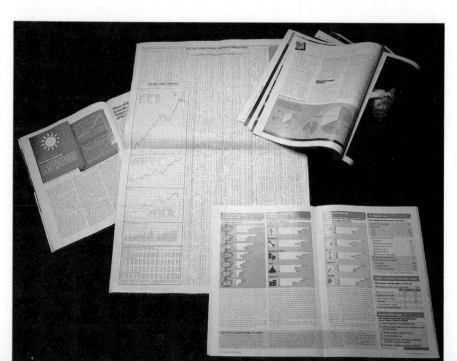

Illustration 1
Tables, charts, and graphs enable economists to get the information they need into a manageable form.

TABLES, CHARTS, AND GRAPHS

Newspapers and magazines present economic information in the form of tables, charts, and graphs. People find information communicated in these ways to be useful. Just pick up the newspaper or such popular publications as *Time, Newsweek*, or *U.S. News & World Report.* You will find examples in nearly every issue.

Presenting economic information in either tables, charts, or graphs is clearly an attempt to get the data into a manageable form that means something to the reader. Perhaps we want to gather data on the distribution of income in your class. Let's assume that you have every class member write on a piece of paper the income they receive each week. You could collect this data and look at it piece by piece. However, the individual pieces of data would not, by themselves, tell you much about how income is distributed in your class.

Tables

table
A simplified arrangement of numbers that makes comparisons among them much more meaningful.

If you were to look at this data in table form, your results would be much more meaningful. A **table** is a simplified way of showing numbers. The weekly income data or information for your 20 classmates is given in Table A–1.

TABLE A–1

STUDENT INCOME DATA

Student No.	Income	Student No.	Income	Student No.	Income	Student No.	Income
1.	$6.00	6.	$ 8.00	11.	$10.00	16.	$13.00
2.	6.00	7.	9.00	12.	11.00	17.	14.00
3.	6.00	8.	9.00	13.	11.50	18.	14.00
4.	7.00	9.	9.50	14.	12.00	19.	15.00
5.	8.00	10.	10.00	15.	12.00	20.	16.00

You could analyze this data by first setting up some groups or categories of income into which you wanted to classify your classmates. For example, you might arrange the incomes into the groups shown in Table A–2.

TABLE A–2

CATEGORIES OF STUDENT INCOME DATA

Category Number	Income Category	Number of Students in Category
1	$ 6.00–$ 8.00	6
2	8.01– 10.00	5
3	10.01– 12.00	4
4	12.01– 14.00	3
5	14.01– 16.00	2

Charts and Graphs

From the information given in Table A–2, we can draw a **chart** or what is sometimes called a **bar graph**. Using a bar graph, we can see the general relationship between the variables we are studying. In the bar graph shown in Figure A–1, the variables are "number of students" and "income group." So we will label the left side of the graph "number of students" and the bottom of the graph "income group." The left side of the graph is the *vertical axis* and the bottom, the *horizontal axis*.

The bar graph in Figure A–1 gives us several pieces of information at a glance. First, we know that more students in your class have incomes in the $6.00 to $8.00 range than any other income category. Second, we know that the fewest number of students have incomes in the $14.01 to $16.00 group. Finally, we can see that the general relationship between income and the number of students who receive it is an inverse relation-

chart
A diagram that shows relationships between variables.

bar graph
A graph in which the general relationship between variables is represented by the length of the bars.

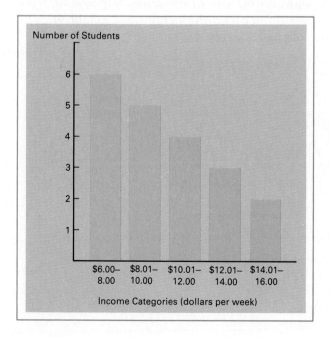

FIGURE A–1 BAR GRAPH OF STUDENT INCOME DATA

line graph
A diagram in which the relationship between variables is represented by a line.

ship. That means that, as income goes up, the number of students receiving incomes in that category goes down. And, as income goes down, the number of students receiving income in that category goes up.

We can convert this bar graph into a rough approximation of a **line graph** simply by plotting in a point at the top of each bar and connecting the dots. This is shown in Figure A–2.

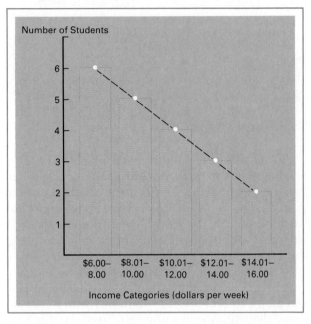

FIGURE A–2   LINE GRAPH OF STUDENT INCOME DATA

Let's now examine another type of graphical relationship. We will look at two variables which clearly depend on each other. That is, the value or size of one variable depends on the size of the other. Suppose we were going to graph a relationship between the height and weight of your classmates. Assume you collected the information given in Table A–3.

TABLE A–3

STUDENT HEIGHT AND WEIGHT DATA

Student No.	Height Inches	Weight Pounds
1	60″	105
2	61″	110
3	62″	117
4	64″	121
5	66″	128
6	67″	140
7	70″	152
8	72″	180
9	73″	192
10	75″	265
Totals	670″	1,510 lbs.

You should set up the vertical axis of your graph showing height and the horizontal axis showing weight and plot in the points for the data you have collected. It will look like the graph in Figure A–3. From this graph, you can *see* a mathematical relationship which you knew existed all along. You can see that weight depends on height. In general, the taller a person is, the heavier he or she is. While this is not always true, it does tell us the general relationship or rule.

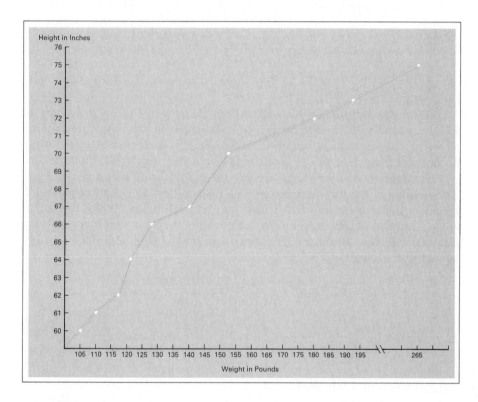

FIGURE A–3   LINE GRAPH OF STUDENT HEIGHT AND WEIGHT DATA

AVERAGES AND DISTRIBUTIONS

From the previous example, we can develop some measurements which will give us more general, but quite valuable, information. You might not be able to remember exactly the height and weight of each class member, for example. You could benefit from knowing a smaller number of measurements which might describe the members of your class in general terms.

The data are more useful when organized in a **distribution**, which is a list of the observations in order from lowest to highest. Table A–3 shows a distribution of the heights and weights for all students.

distribution

An arrangement of data that lists observations in order from the lowest to the highest.

average

A single value that summarizes a series of numbers by dividing the sum of the numbers by the number of figures in the series.

One way of summarizing this data is to calculate the **average**. To calculate the average (or *mean*) height and weight, simply add up the individual heights and the individual weights and divide this sum by the total number of students measured.

$$\text{Mean height} = \frac{\text{Total height}}{\text{Total students}} = \frac{670}{10} = 67''$$

$$\text{Mean weight} = \frac{\text{Total weight}}{\text{Total students}} = \frac{1510 \text{ lbs.}}{10} = 151 \text{ lbs.}$$

The mean height, then, is 67 inches (5'7") and the mean weight is 151 pounds. These average measurements would be one way of describing all ten of the students at one time. However, it is important to notice that no particular student in the group is 5'7" tall and weighs 151 pounds.

The median and the range are two other important measures of data. The **median** is the middle number in a distribution. One half of the total numbers fall above the median, and one half fall below. When there are an odd number of observations in the list, the median is simply the middle number when the numbers are listed from low to high. Consider the following five numbers:

median

A number that represents the middle number in a distribution.

$$\underline{\overset{\text{M}}{20}}$$
$$13 \quad 16 \quad 20 \quad 28 \quad 35$$

As indicated by the <u>M</u>, the median is 20, the middle number.

To find the median when the number of observations is even, we first list the numbers from low to high. This is done below for the heights and weights given in Table A–3.

					M					
Height:	60	61	62	64	66	67	70	72	73	75
Weight:	105	110	117	121	128	140	152	180	192	265

In this case the midpoint for both measures is between two students, as indicated by the line maked <u>M</u>. The median is usually taken as the average of the two numbers on either side of the line <u>M</u>. For our example, then, the median height and weight are

$$\text{Median height: } \frac{66 + 67}{2} = \frac{133}{2} = 66.5 \text{ inches}$$

$$\text{Median weight: } \frac{128 + 140}{2} = \frac{268}{2} = 134 \text{ pounds}$$

Note that the median height and weight are a little below the average, or mean, height and weight. Can you look at the data and guess why this is true? If you can, you will know something very important about averages. Note that the tallest student is 6'3" (75 inches) and weighs 265 pounds. This person is much taller and much heavier than the rest of the class. Obviously, the mean is very sensitive to a single piece of information that is greatly different from the rest. This single tall person pushed the mean height and weight of the class beyond the median, or middle, weight and height of the class. There is a moral to this story: Averages can be misleading without looking at the other measures of the data.

The **range** is simply the largest number in the data minus the smallest number. The range of height would be 75 inches minus 60 inches, or 15 inches. The range on the weight data would be 265 pounds minus 105 pounds, or a range of 160 pounds. There is quite a wide range on both height and weight here. If the ranges were lower, what do you think would happen to the difference between the mean value and the median value? They would probably be closer to each other since there would not be individual pieces of data that were so much higher or lower than the rest.

When thinking about the concepts of mean, median, and range, it is important to understand how they are applied to economics. For example, you might see in the newspapers or on television that the median family income in the United States is approximately $35,000. Ask yourself, why did they choose to report the median income and not the mean income? The answer is simple. The range of family incomes in our economy is relatively large (from several hundred to many millions of dollars per year). If the mean were reported, it might not give an accurate picture of what the "average" family earned. Since we have a large middle class in America, the median of $35,000 tells us that about one half of the families earns more and one half earns less. The median gives us a more descriptive picture of family income in our economy.

range
The largest number in a distribution minus the smallest number.

RATIOS AND PERCENTAGES

Ratios are really nothing more than a way of showing the proportion between two numbers. A ratio shows the relationship of one numerical value to another numerical value. Ratios are often expressed in a form such as 5:1, which is pronounced "5 to 1." A ratio is calculated by expressing two numbers as a fraction and then reducing the fraction to its lowest terms.

For example, we know that consumers can do only two things with their incomes. They can spend (consume) or save them. In other words, consumers use their incomes for consumption and savings. Suppose that the average American family earned $10,000 and consumed (spent) $8,000. Savings, then, would be $2,000. The proportion between these two activities is very important. In this case we know that Americans spend four times as much as they save:

ratios
A way of expressing the proportion between two numbers.

$$\frac{\text{Consumption}}{\text{Savings}} = \frac{\$8,000}{\$2,000} = \frac{4}{1}$$

That gives a consumption to savings ratio of 4:1. Another way of stating this proportion is that on the average, for every one dollar Americans save, they spend (consume) four dollars. This concept of ratios can be extended to include income. Question: What is the ratio of spending to income in the United States? The answer is $8,000/$10,000 or 8:10 or 4:5. On the average, for every $5 earned, Americans may spend $4 and save $1.

percentages

Ratios that have been converted into a base of 100 equal parts.

Percentages simply convert ratios into a base of 100 equal parts. To get a percentage from a ratio, you simply divide the denominator of a ratio into its numerator and multiply the result by 100. For example, what percentage of its income does the average American family consume? We divide consumption ($8,000) by income ($10,000) and multiply the result by 100. We then know that the average family consumes 80 percent of its income.

$$\frac{\$8,000}{\$10,000} = .80 \qquad .80 \times 100 = 80\%$$

Percentages can also show how much a number has changed. For example, suppose your present salary is $5.00 and you get a raise so that your new salary is $7.50. The percentage change in your salary would be figured by dividing the difference between your old and new salary by your old salary and converting it to a percentage.

$$\frac{\$7.50 - \$5.00}{\$5.00} = \frac{\$2.50}{\$5.00} = .50 \qquad .50 \times 100 = 50\%$$

Your new salary then would be 50 percent greater than your old salary. To check your understanding of percentages, answer the following questions and check your results against the answers provided on page 560.

1. What percentage of the number $10,000 is the number $2,000?

2. If the price of a house went up from $100,000 to $150,000, what was the percentage increase?

3. If the price of a house went down from $200,000 to $150,000, what was the percentage decrease?

RATES AND ABSOLUTE NUMBERS

Economic reports in the news media can be confusing because so many numbers are used. One of the most frequent mixups concerns percentage rates and absolute numbers. For example, you might hear that inflation is up 3 percent; or the money supply is growing at an annual rate of 5 percent; or the economy grew at 21 percent last year. The basic difference between rates and absolute numbers is that *rates tell you how fast absolute numbers are changing*. If you drive your car at 50 miles per hour, then 50 mph is the rate at which you are travelling. It may or may not have anything to do with how far you travel. If you travel ten miles, it may take you ten minutes or it may take you ten hours. In both cases, you travel the same distance, but in the first case your rate of travel is much higher.

The classic example of rate versus absolute numbers involves the rate of inflation. The rate of inflation tells us how fast, on an annually adjusted basis, prices are rising. When the headlines in a newspaper say "inflation increases to 15 percent," they mean that prices are going up at a rate of 15 percent per year. If, in the next week, the same newspaper had headlines reading "inflation falls to 10 percent," it does not mean that, in general, absolute prices are falling. What it does mean is that absolute prices are rising at a slower rate (i.e., going up more slowly) than before.

To more fully understand the relationship between rates and absolutes, look at the various functions plotted in Figure A–4 and read over the descriptions of what is happening to the rates and absolutes.

The slope of a graph line or function is really just the amount of change in whatever is measured on the vertical axis divided by the amount of change in whatever is measured on the horizontal axis. In short, slope is really *the rise over the run*. In our graph of Figure A–3, as student height increases from 60 to 61 inches, weight increases from 105 to 110 pounds. This means that our function over this range has a slope of 1/5 (61 − 60/110 − 105). The slope tells us the rate at which weight increases as height increases. For each 1 inch increase in height, weight increases by 5 pounds.

INDEX NUMBERS

Index numbers are frequently used by economists to show relative changes in factors such as the consumer prices and gross national product. These types of measurements first set up a base period and measure the changes from the base period to the present. The base period is usually considered to have an index value of 100 (or 100 percent). The other numbers such as prices in the current year are then expressed as a percentage of the prices in the base period. For example, for a typical market basket of goods in the 1982–1984 base period, the price index is set at 100. The remaining years' price indexes then show the percentage by which prices have increased over the base period. Shown at the top of page 559 is the price index of the same market basket of goods for the years 1985 through 1990.

index numbers
Numbers used by economists to show relative changes.

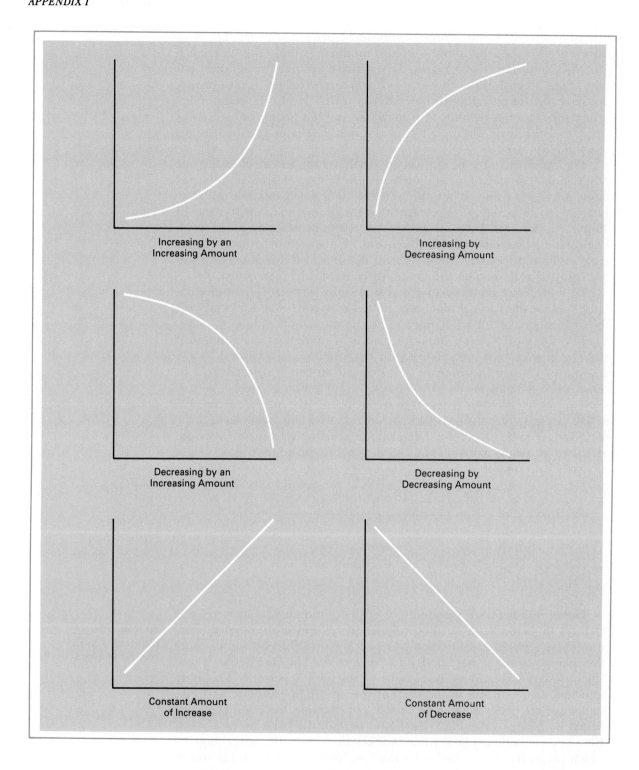

FIGURE A–4   RATES AND ABSOLUTE NUMBERS

Year	Price Index
1985	107.6
1986	109.6
1987	113.6
1988	118.3
1989	124.0
1990	130.7

The 1987 price index of 113.6 shows that 1987 prices were higher than prices in the base period. The values shown above indicate that the average level of prices rose each year from 1985 to 1990. Index numbers are a quick and relatively accurate way to measure increases or decreases in any variable relative to a base period. These indexes also are very valuable in allowing economists to adjust nominal values to real values, as discussed in the next section of this appendix.

NOMINAL AND REAL VALUES

Many measurements in economics have both nominal and real values. For example, you may get paid a salary of $100 per week. In this case, your nominal income would be $100 per week or $5,200 per year. If you received the same salary next year, you would earn another $5,200. But, let's take a closer look at your real income. If prices went up over the year by 10 percent and you get the same $5,200 nominal income, you will not be able to buy as much in the second year. In fact, it will buy 10 percent less. Your nominal income was the same $5,200, but your real income declined by 10 percent to $4,680 ($5,200 − $520 = $4,680). Your nominal income is your income measured in dollars for this year. Your real income is the buying power of your nominal income. A real value in economics is a nominal value adjusted for changes in prices.

An additional example involves the concept of gross national product (GNP). GNP is the total of the market value of all the goods and services produced in the economy in one year. Suppose for a simplified example that we only make three goods in our economy: houses, automobiles, and food. Then GNP would be equal to the sum of the price of each house times the number of houses produced plus the price of each car times the number of cars produced plus the price of each unit of food times the number of units produced. We could compute this as shown below:

	Price per Unit		Units Produced	
Houses	$50,000	×	100,000	= $ 5,000,000,000
Automobiles	$10,000	×	4,000,000	= $40,000,000,000
Food	$ 1	×	100,000,000	= $ 100,000,000
				$45,100,000,000 = GNP

The prices we used might have been this year's prices. If, however, prices go up, you realize that GNP could go up without the economy producing any more goods or services. This means that while nominal GNP went up, real GNP stayed the same: 100,000 houses were built and the same amount of cars and food were produced.

Economists use the concept of index numbers, which we discussed previously, to adjust nominal values to real values. Recall that the price index for a market basket of goods in 1985 was 107.6, and for the same market basket in 1990, it was 130.7. We can use this price index to adjust GNP or income figures. Suppose that GNP in 1985 was $1,000,000 ($1 million) and that GNP in 1990 was $2,000,000 ($2 million). At first glance, it might look like GNP doubled. This might imply that the economy was producing twice as much in 1990 as in 1985. We already know, however, that over that same period of time prices went up. To adjust both values of GNP to constant dollars—that is, dollars with the same buying power—we divide GNP for each year by that year's price index. (Note that the price index is divided by 100 when used in this equation.)

$$1985 \text{ Real GNP} = \frac{1985 \text{ Nominal GNP}}{1985 \text{ Price Index}} = \frac{\$1,000,000}{1.076} = \$929,368$$

$$1990 \text{ Real GNP} = \frac{1990 \text{ Nominal GNP}}{1990 \text{ Price Index}} = \frac{\$2,000,000}{1.307} = \$1,530,222$$

As the calculations show, real GNP did not double: after we adjusted for inflation, it only went up by about 65 percent.

To apply the same concept to earned income, just remember that what cost $1.00 in the 1982–84 base period cost $1.307 in 1990. Dividing your 1990 income by 1.307 would give you your real income measured in terms of the purchasing power of the base period (1982–84). Keep a keen eye out for nominal and real values as you move through this book. They are indeed very important economic concepts.

Answers to questions on page 556.

1. $\dfrac{\$2,000}{\$10,000} \times 100 = 0.2 \times 100 = 20\%$

2. $\dfrac{\$50,000}{\$100,000} \times 100 = 0.5 \times 100 = 50\%$

3. $\dfrac{\$50,000}{\$200,000} \times 100 = .25 \times 100 = 25\%$

APPENDIX II
SUPPLY AND DEMAND FORCES AT WORK: Health Care in the Economy

The health care industry in the United States is big and grows bigger every year. In 1950 Americans spent $40.1 billion on medical care. By 1960 medical care spending had increased to $66.5 billion, and by 1970, it had grown to $120.4 billion. Few people thought that such a rapid increase could continue. But by 1980, medical care spending had risen to $200.6 billion, and by 1990, medical care spending had increased another $100 billion to $301.7 billion. Each year spending on health care continues to rise.

The rise in health care prices creates a major problem in our economy. But are rising prices the real problem? You know that prices act as signals that give information to buyers and sellers. When we see that health care prices are rising quickly, that signal tells us that there may be an imbalance between demand and supply. With rising prices we should expect that demand may be increasing more than supply. So, the problem may be that we are demanding too much health care or that too few health care services are available. Rising health care prices are just a symptom of the real problem.

SUPPLY OF HEALTH CARE SERVICES

The two most important parts of the health care industry are health care workers (such as doctors and nurses) and hospitals. Recent increases in the number of schools for training health care workers should help raise the supply. The number of physicians in the United States has risen from 275,000 in 1960 to well over 600,000 now. The number of nurses has increased by more than 300 percent. In 1950 there were just 375,000 nurses in the United States. By the late 1980s, the number had grown to over 1,627,000.

The number of hospital care facilities has not changed very much in the last 25 years. Although there has been a trend toward larger hospitals (which usually contain more than 100 beds), the total number of hospital beds in the United States has actually dropped since the mid-1960s. The number of beds per 1,000 people has fallen from almost ten in 1960 to less than six. Looking just at these figures, we might say that there has been no change or even a decrease in the supply of hospital care. But hospitals offer much higher quality health care today than they have in the past. Also, more routine procedures are now performed in doctors' offices or in outpatient clinics so that no hospital space is needed.

The most important reason for the slow growth or decrease in the supply of hospital services is rising costs. New medical equipment is expensive; labor costs have risen; and supplies cost more each year. Rising costs tend to lower the amount of a good or service that will be supplied.

DEMAND FOR HEALTH CARE SERVICES

As the population increases, the demand for health care goes up. In addition to the *number* of people, the *age* of people is also important. Each year there are more people in the 65 and older age group. Older people often need more health care than younger people do. As more of our population moves into the higher age group, the greater the demand will be for health care services.

Health care is a normal good: As income rises, people will have more demand for health care. While the demand for health care may be income inelastic, the demand for health services does increase some as income rises. For the whole economy, incomes have gone up fairly steadily since 1950 and so has the demand for health care.

One of the most important reasons for the rising demand for health care services is the change in attitudes toward health care. We have come to expect more and better health care in the United States. Today when we are sick or hurt, we usually think of going to a doctor. Medical science has improved so rapidly that we think there must be a quick cure for nearly every possible ailment. We expect a lot more, and this shows in our demand for health care.

Doctors influence our demand for health care by deciding whether we need to have surgery and even how much surgery to have. In many ways, a doctor not only supplies health care but also influences the quantity of health care we will demand. Also, to guard against accusations of malpractice, doctors may do more tests and see patients more often than might really be needed. This contributes to the overall rise in demand for health care services.

Illustration 1
Doctors influence our demand for health care by deciding whether we need to have surgery and even how much surgery to have.

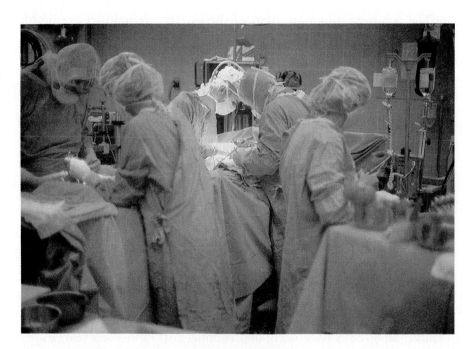

Attempts to control rising health care prices often fail due to price elasticity of demand and the effect of third-party payments. To illustrate the price elasticity of demand, suppose that you have a ruptured appendix. You would need a fairly simple operation and would be back on your feet in a few days. Without the operation, however, you would most likely die. So, price would not be important. You would pay as much as needed if you could find the money. Other people would behave in the same way in this situation. So, for the whole society, demand for this operation would be very inelastic.

But what if you fall and twist your ankle? You think it isn't badly hurt, but you aren't sure. If it costs $10 to have a doctor check it, you probably would do it. But if the doctor's price is $100, would you have it checked? The price you would pay would depend partly on how much pain you have. This demand would then be less inelastic than the demand for the appendix operation. There are many kinds of health care that can be put off without causing death. So, the demand for health services tends to be more elastic for minor health problems than it is for more serious health problems. Overall, the amount of health care services we demand is not likely to change very much when price goes up or down.

When it comes time to pay a doctor or hospital, patients rarely pay the full bill directly. This is because much of the cost of health care is paid for by third parties. In health care services, the third party may be a private insurance company or a public agency such as Medicare or Medicaid. Third parties pay about 90 percent of hospital costs and more than 60 percent of doctor bills in the United States. This means that the direct price to the buyer is far less than the true price of the health care. The law of demand tells us, that for most products and services, more will be bought at lower prices than at higher prices. So, as more of our medical costs are covered by insurance, we will want to use a greater amount of health care services.

Population growth, rising incomes, changing attitudes, and third-party payments all cause an increase in demand for health care services. When all of these factors are combined, demand increases by a large amount. But two factors may help slow the rise in demand in the future. First, the rate of growth of the population has slowed. So, the overall number of people demanding health care will not go up as fast as it has been. Also, the rate of growth in the number of people covered by insurance is slowing. However, the other causes of increasing demand are expected to continue. Therefore, demand will probably stay high in the future.

Illustration 2
Patients rarely pay the full bill for medical services. Generally much of the cost of health care is paid for by third parties.

SUPPLY AND DEMAND OF HEALTH CARE

If nothing else changed, you would expect that if supply went up, price would fall. The supply of health care services has gone up. But prices have not fallen because demand has gone up even more. This is shown in the figure on the next page. The rise in supply is shown by the shift from the first supply curve to the second supply curve. At the same time the rise in demand is from the first demand to the second demand. Demand is shown to have gone up by more than supply.

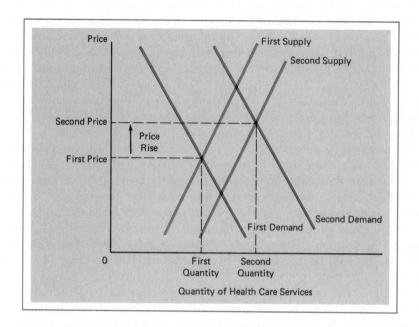

FIGURE A–5   HEALTH CARE SUPPLY AND DEMAND TOGETHER

These changes in supply and demand have caused the price of health care services to rise. Look at the axis that measures price at the left side of the figure. You see that price rises from the first price to the second price. A careful look at the forces of supply and demand has helped explain why the price of health care has gone up.

The amount of health care services we have consumed is also important. From the graph you see that the amount consumed has gone up from the first quantity to the second quantity, even though price rose. Price and quantity have both gone up due to the rise in both demand and supply.

From your understanding of supply and demand, you know that there are two general ways to slow and maybe stop the rise of health care prices. One way would be to keep demand from going up. But, with health care, there really are not many ways to do this. We could also try to help supply increase more. Maybe changing the way doctors work could help increase supply. For instance, one-doctor practices may not be very efficient. So, group practices would make it possible for doctors to make better use of equipment, nurses, and other staff.

Anything that increases supply will help to slow the rise in health care prices. Since the demand for health care is not easily controlled, we need to concentrate on the supply side of the market to slow the rise in health care costs.

GLOSSARY

A

Ability-to-pay principle of taxation. The concept that those who can best afford to pay taxes should pay most of the taxes.

Absolute advantage. The economic advantage which exists in the production of a good when one country can produce that good more efficiently than another country.

Advertisements. Messages from producers of goods which attempt to influence consumers' attitudes favorably toward those goods.

Aggregate demand. The total demand of all people for all goods and services produced in an economy.

Aggregate supply. The total supply of all goods and services in an economy.

Allocation. The process of choosing which needs will be satisfied and how much of our resources we will use to satisfy them.

Alternative. A possible course of action.

Articles of incorporation. A written application requesting permission to form a corporation.

Asset demand for money. The demand for money in order to hold wealth in the form of money.

Average. A way of summarizing the data in a distribution. The most common average is the mean.

Average product. The number of units of output produced per unit of input.

B

Balance of payments. The relationship between all of a country's exports and imports, including goods, services, travel, investments, gold, and all other money movements.

Balance of trade. The relationship between a country's merchandise exports and imports.

Bar graph. A graph showing the general relationship between the variables being studied where the length of each bar represents the number of occurrences for each value.

Barriers to economic development. Economic, social, and political characteristics that prevent an economy from developing.

Barter.   A direct trade of goods or services.

Benefit principle of taxation.   The concept that those who benefit from the spending of tax dollars should pay the taxes to provide the benefits.

Bond.   A certificate stating the amount the corporation has borrowed from the holder of the bond and the terms of repayment.

Budget constraint.   The mix of goods that can be purchased, given a limited amount of income.

Business cycles.   The ups and downs in levels of employment, prices, income, consumption, and production.

C

Capital.   Goods that are produced and can be used as inputs for further production.

Capitalism.   An economic system in which most of the means of production are owned by private individuals.

Cartel.   A formal organization of firms in the same industry acting together to make decisions.

Charter.   The legal authorization to organize a business as a corporation.

Check.   A written order to pay money from amounts deposited.

Civilian labor force.   The total number of people in the working age group (16 years and over) who are either employed or actively seeking work. This excludes people in the armed services or in institutions such as prisons or mental hospitals.

Closed shop.   A business which agrees to hire only those who are members of a union.

Collective bargaining.   The process of having the union negotiate with management to determine the terms of employment for all workers rather than having each worker negotiate separately.

Collusion.   The situation of firms acting together rather than separately.

Command economy.   An economy in which the three economic questions are decided by government.

Commodity Credit Corporation (CCC).   The part of the Department of Agriculture that makes loans to farmers using crops as security.

Common stock.   Stock that gives the holder a partial ownership of the corporation.

Communism. An economic system based on equality and public ownership of goods.

Comparative advantage. The principle that a country benefits from specializing in the production at which it is relatively most efficient.

Competition. The rivalry between two or more parties to gain benefits from a third party.

Complementary products. Products that are used together.

Conglomerate merger. A merger of two companies which are in different businesses.

Conglomerates. Firms made up of many divisions and/or subsidiaries that do not have much in common in their lines of business.

Constant dollar GNP. The value of gross national product after taking out the effect of price changes.

Constituents. The individual citizens or voters in a democracy who are represented by a particular public official.

Consumer goods. Items that are made for final consumption.

Consumer Price Index (CPI). A number used to compare the average level of prices for a number of typical items bought by urban families.

Consumer protection. Activities by government or private agencies which police the interests of consumers in the marketplace.

Consumption. The act of using economic goods in satisfying wants and needs or in producing goods or services.

Contract. A legally binding agreement between two or more competent persons.

Cooperative. A business owned and run by a group with a common interest.

Corporate bond rate. The interest rate paid on corporate bonds.

Corporate income tax. A tax on the earnings of corporations.

Corporation. An organization of people legally bound together by a charter to conduct some type of business.

Cost-push inflation. A rise in the general level of prices that is caused by increased costs of making and selling goods.

Credit union. A financial intermediary formed around something that its members have in common.

Criteria. The characteristics of a group of alternatives that will be judged to make a choice.

Crowding out. The effect on private businesses when increased government borrowing raises interest rates and reduces private borrowing.

Currency. Coins and paper money.

Cyclical unemployment. Unemployment resulting from too low a level of aggregate demand.

D

Decision matrix. A table showing comparisons of alternative decisions.

Deflation. A decline in the average level of prices.

Demand. The quantities of a good that consumers are willing and able to purchase at various prices during a given period of time.

Demand curve. A graphic illustration of the relationship between price and the quantity purchased at each price.

Demand deposit. Money that must be paid upon demand by the holder of a check.

Demand for labor. The amount of labor that firms would want to hire at each wage rate.

Demand-pull inflation. A rise in the general level of prices caused by too high a level of aggregate demand in relation to aggregate supply.

Demand schedule. A listing of the quantities that would be purchased at various prices.

Deposit expansion multiplier. The number that expresses the relationship between a change in bank reserves and the change in the money supply.

Depression. A severe and prolonged decline in the level of economic activity.

Derived demand. A demand for factors of production which is dependent on the demand for the product.

Determinants of demand. The factors that determine how much will be purchased at each price.

Differentiated oligopoly. An oligopoly in which the product is differentiated.

Diminishing marginal productivity. The principle that as more of any variable input is added to a fixed amount of other inputs, the rate at which output goes up becomes less and less.

Diminishing marginal utility. The principle that as additional units of a product are consumed during a given time period, the additional satisfaction becomes less and less.

Direct tax. A tax paid by the person against whom the tax is levied.

Discount rate. The interest rate that banks must pay to borrow from the Federal Reserve System.

Disposable income. The income that is left after deducting tax payments.

Distribution. A list of observations in order from the lowest to the highest.

Distribution effect. The way the benefit or inconvenience of a social issue is distributed among the members of a society.

Dividends. A part of corporate income paid to owners of the corporation's stock.

Dual economy. An economy in which a modern market economy exists side by side with a primitive subsistence economy.

Durable goods. Goods that can be used over and over again and that last for a relatively long time.

E

Economic growth. The change in the level of economic activity from one year to another.

Economic incentive. The increase in our personal satisfaction that may result from some economic activity.

Economic institutions. Organizations in the public and private sectors (such as businesses, government agencies, and households) which are involved in the satisfaction of economic wants and needs.

Economic measurements. Mathematical tools economists use to get the information they need into a manageable form.

Economic profit. The difference between the money you obtain from selling a product and the cost of producing the product.

Economic questions. Decisions a society must make on what, how and for whom to produce goods and services.

Economics. The social science that deals with how society allocates its scarce resources among its unlimited wants and needs.

Economic system. The combination of social and individual decision making a society uses to answer the three economic questions.

Economies of scale. The concept that some economic activities become more efficient when done on a large scale.

Efficiency. Using a given amount and combination of resources to get the maximum amount of benefit.

Elasticity. The ratio of the percentage change in quantity to the percentage change in some factor that stimulated the change in quantity.

Entrepreneurs. Individuals who organize a company to produce a product for a profit.

Equilibrium. The condition in which two forces exactly balance one another.

Equilibrium price. The price at which the quantity demanded equals the quantity supplied.

Equilibrium quantity. The quantity that is both demanded and supplied at the equilibrium price.

Equilibrium wage. The wage rate at which the demand for labor equals the supply of labor.

Equity. Equality of opportunity.

Estate and gift taxes. Taxes levied on wealth (money and property) passed from one person to another either at death or as a gift.

European Economic Community (EEC). A group of European countries that have joined together and agreed on ways to improve trade among themselves.

Excess reserves. The difference between actual reserves and required reserves.

Exchange. The giving of one thing in return for some other thing.

Exchange rate. The rate at which one kind of money can be traded for another.

Excise tax. A sales tax levied only on specific items.

Exclusion principle. The principle that one person can keep others from benefiting from a private good.

Expansionary fiscal policies. Fiscal policies that cause the economy to run more rapidly by increasing aggregate demand.

Explicit costs. Payments made to others as a cost of running a business.

Exports. Goods and services that one country sells to another country.

External debt. The part of the national debt that is owed to people or governments outside the United States.

Externalities. Costs or benefits passed on outside of the market system.

F

Factor of production. Anything used to produce a good or service.

Federal Deposit Insurance Corporation (FDIC). The agency that insures bank deposits of individuals and businesses for up to $100,000 in the event of bank failure.

Federal funds rate. The interest rate banks pay to borrow from each other on a short-term basis.

Federal Reserve System. The central banking system in the United States.

Financial intermediary. An organization that helps the flow of money from people with money to save to people who need to borrow money.

Fiscal policy. The changing of government spending and taxes in order to control the level of economic activity.

Fixed income. Income that is set and does not change from year to year.

Flexible exchange rates. A system in which the laws of supply and demand are allowed to set the prices, or exchange rates, between each kind of money.

Foreign aid. The money that more-advanced countries provide to help the less-developed countries in their economic development.

Fractional reserve banking system. A system in which banks must keep some fraction or part of their deposits in the form of reserves.

Freedom of choice. The individual power to choose and receive both the costs and the benefits of a choice.

Free rider. A person who benefits from a public good without sharing its cost.

Frictional unemployment. Unemployment of people who are temporarily between jobs.

Full employment. The employment of about 95 percent of the labor force.

Functional distribution of income. The way in which income is divided by economic functions.

G

General Agreement on Tariffs and Trade (GATT). An agreement that gave broad international support to improving trade among countries.

Gold standard. A system in which each nation sets the value of its money in terms of a certain amount of gold.

Government-assisted capitalism. An economic system in which most economic decisions are made in the marketplace, and government enacts policies to assist individual decision making.

Gross national product (GNP). The total dollar value of all final goods and services produced in the economy during one year's time.

H

Homogeneous products. Products that vary little from producer to producer.

Horizontal merger. A merger of two companies in the same business.

Human resources. The people who work or may be able to work.

I

Imports. Goods and services that one country buys from another country.

Incentives. Factors which may cause an increase in our personal satisfaction.

Income effect. The effect of increasing or decreasing prices on the buying power of income.

Income elasticity of demand. The percentage change in quantity divided by the percentage change in income that caused the change in demand.

Index numbers. The numbers used by economists to show relative changes.

Indirect tax. A tax that can be shifted, at least in part, to a party other than the one on whom the tax is levied.

Individual choice. Decisions made by individuals acting separately.

Infant mortality rate. The number of deaths of children under one year of age per 1,000 live births.

Inferior goods. Goods for which demand goes down as income goes up.

Inflation. The economic condition in which the average level of prices goes up.

Inflationary bias in fiscal policy. The natural tendency for Congress to favor expansionary policies over restrictive policies.

Injunction. A court order to stop doing something (or *to* do something).

Inside time lag. The time it takes to decide on a policy.

Interdependence. Dependence between different sectors of the economy such as between households, businesses, and government.

Interest. The price paid for the use of money.

Investment. An increase in the amount of productive capital in an economy.

Invisible hand. The incentive that guides individuals to choose in the best interest of society by pursuing their own self-interest.

Irregular economy. The economy consisting of economic activity that purposely avoids the market system in order to avoid reporting income for tax purposes.

J

Job discrimination. The refusal to hire certain people because of their gender, race, or other characteristics that have nothing to do with their ability to do a job.

L

Labor union. An organization of workers formed to give workers greater bargaining power in their dealings with management.

Law of demand. The rule that people will buy more at lower prices than at higher prices, if all other factors are constant.

Less-developed country (LDC). A poor country with a relatively low level of education and a largely rural population.

Life expectancy. The average age the people in a country live to be.

Limited liability. The concept that owners of a corporation are only responsible for its debts up to the amount they invest in the business.

Limited resources. There are never enough resources to fulfill all wants and needs.

Lobbying. The act of communicating with government representatives to influence their votes on a specific issue.

Long run. A period during which the amounts of all inputs used can be changed.

Loose monetary policy. A policy of the Fed that causes the money supply to rise.

Lorenz curve of income distribution. A graphic method showing the amount of income inequality that exists in society at any point in time.

M

Macroeconomics. The branch of economics that examines the behavior of the whole economy at once.

Marginal private benefit (*MPB*). The added benefit that individuals directly involved in an activity get from increasing the activity by one unit.

Marginal private cost (*MPC*). The added cost individuals directly involved in an activity pay to increase the activity by one unit.

Marginal product. The amount that total product increases or decreases if one more unit of an input is used.

Marginal social benefit (*MSB*). The added benefit that society gets from increasing an activity by one unit.

Marginal social cost (*MSC*). The added cost that society pays to increase an activity by one unit.

Market. Exchange activities between buyers and sellers of goods and services.

Market demand. The quantities of a product or service that the total of all consumers are willing and able to purchase at various prices.

Market economy. An economy in which the economic questions are decided mostly by individuals in the marketplace.

Market organization. The way participants in markets are organized and how many participants there are.

Market supply. The quantities of a product or service that the total of all firms will make available for sale at various prices.

Mean. The average in which the total value of the items in a distribution is divided by the number of items in the distribution.

Median. The middle number in a distribution.

Merger. The combining of one company with another company it buys.

Microeconomics. The branch of economics that examines the choices and interactions of individuals concerning one product, one firm, or one industry.

Minimum wage law. A law which sets the lowest wage that can be paid for certain kinds of work.

Mixed economy. An economy in which the three economic questions are decided by a combination of market decision making and government decree.

Model. A simplified form of reality which shows the relationship between different factors.

Monetary policy. The changing of the amount of money in the economy in order to reduce unemployment, keep prices stable, and promote economic growth.

Monopolistic competition. A market organization in which many firms produce products that are different, but similar enough to be substitutes.

Monopoly. A form of market organization in which there is only one seller of a product.

Monopsony. A market in which there is only one buyer.

Multiplier effect. The concept that any change in fiscal policy affects total demand and total income by an amount larger than the amount of the change in policy.

Mutual savings banks. Banks that were first formed for the same reason as savings and loan associations and which promote thrift by their members.

N

National debt. The amount of money that the federal government owes.

Natural monopoly. A monopoly which exists in an industry in which it is not practical to have competition.

Natural resources. The total raw materials supplied by nature.

Negative externality. The result when *costs* are shifted to people who are not directly involved with the production or consumption of a good.

Negative income tax. Poverty programs in which a person or family below some income level receives a payment from the government rather than paying some amount of tax to the government.

Nominal value. The face value of a measurement.

Nondurable goods. Goods that do not last a long time.

Normal goods. Goods for which demand goes up as income goes up.

NOW account. An account that earns interest on deposits and from which amounts can be withdrawn easily using a negotiable order of withdrawal.

O

Objectivity. Ruling out aspects of a problem which seem important only because of strong emotions or feelings about them.

Oligopoly. A form of market organization in which there are relatively few firms.

Open market operations. The buying and selling of United States government securities by the Federal Reserve.

Opportunity benefit. What is gained by making a particular choice.

Opportunity cost. The value of any alternative that you must give up when you make a choice.

Outside time lag. The time it takes for the effects of a policy change to be completely felt in the economy once the policy has been determined.

P

Parity price. A price that changes as prices of other goods change so that the income of producers can purchase the same amount of these goods as in some base year.

Partnership. A type of business organization in which two or more people form a business.

Patent. A legal protection for the inventor of a product or process which gives that person or company the sole rights to produce the product or use the process for up to 17 years.

Payment of rent. The payment made in exchange for land.

Per capita income. The average income per person.

Percentage. A ratio converted to a base of 100 equal parts.

Perfect competition. A form of market organization in which a great many small firms produce a homogeneous product.

Personal distribution of income. How income is shared among people in our society.

Personal income tax. A tax on the income of individuals.

Population explosion. Rapid growth in the number of people living in a country.

Positive externality. The result when *benefits* are shifted to people who are not directly involved with the production or consumption of a good.

Poverty. The condition in which people do not have enough income to provide for their basic needs, such as food, clothing, and shelter.

Price ceiling. A maximum price set by government that is below the market equilibrium price.

Price elasticity of demand. The ratio of the percentage change in quantity demanded to the percentage change in price that caused the quantity demanded to change.

Price elasticity of supply. The ratio of the percentage change in the quantity supplied to the percentage change in the product's price.

Price floor.   A minimum price set by the government that is above the market equilibrium price.

Price index.   A number that compares prices in one year with some earlier base year.

Price setter.   A firm that has some control over the price at which its product sells.

Price support program.   A government program designed to keep prices from falling below some level the government decides is fair.

Price taker.   A firm that takes a price determined by forces outside of the firm's control.

Prime rate.   The interest rate that banks charge their best corporate customers.

Private enterprise.   A system in which private individuals take the risk of producing goods or services to make a profit.

Private goods.   Goods that are privately owned and used to benefit only their owners.

Private sector.   The part of an economy which is owned by private individuals and operated for their personal benefit.

Product differentiation.   The concept that the product of one firm can be distinguished from the products of other firms.

Production possibilities curve.   A graphic illustration of the combinations of output an economy can produce if all of its resources are utilized and utilized efficiently, given the state of technology.

Profit.   Total revenue minus total costs.

Progressive tax.   A tax that takes a larger percentage of higher incomes and a smaller percentage of lower incomes.

Property rights.   The rights which define who owns what rights to property and how individuals or groups may use their property.

Property tax.   A tax levied on real estate, such as a home, land, and buildings.

Proportional tax.   A tax that takes the same percentage of income from all taxpayers.

Proprietorship.   A form of business in which one individual owns the entire business.

Protectionism.   The idea that we should limit trade to protect our own self-interest.

Psychic income.   The nonmonetary reward we get from taking some action.

Public goods.   Goods and services available to the whole society.

Public goods rationale.   The argument that some public goods can be produced more efficiently by social choice.

Public institutions.   Publicly owned organizations established by government to serve the wants and needs of a whole society.

Public sector. The part of an economy which is owned by and operated for the benefit of the whole society.

Pure oligopoly. An oligopoly in which the products are the same for all firms.

Q

Quota. A limit on the amount of imports or exports.

R

Range. The largest number in a distribution minus the smallest number.

Rate of growth. The percentage change in the level of economic activity from one year to the next.

Rates. Indicate how fast absolute numbers are changing.

Ratio. A way of showing the proportion between numbers.

Real GNP. The value of gross national product after taking out the effect of price changes.

Real GNP per person. The real value of the total output of goods and services divided by the number of people in the economy.

Real value. A nominal value that has been adjusted for changes in prices.

Recession. The condition in which unemployment is high and GNP falls for two or more quarters.

Redistributing income. In an effort to provide equity, the public sector gives to people who do not work, money collected from taxing the incomes of those who do work.

Regressive tax. A tax that takes a larger percentage of lower incomes and a smaller percentage of higher incomes.

Research and development (R&D). The activities undertaken to find new and more efficient methods of production.

Reserve ratio. The fraction of deposits that the Fed determines banks must keep on reserve.

Reserve requirement. The dollar amount banks must keep on reserve.

Restrictive fiscal policies. Fiscal policies that cause the economy to run more slowly by reducing aggregate demand.

Returns to scale. The relationship between changes in scale of production and changes in output.

S

Sales tax. A tax on goods that are bought.

Savings and loan association. A financial intermediary that mainly provides a place for people to save money and then lends that money to people to buy houses or other things.

Scale of production. The overall level of use of all factors of production.

Scarcity. The condition that occurs because people's wants and needs are unlimited, and the resources needed to produce goods and services to meet these wants and needs are limited.

Seasonal unemployment. Unemployment of people who are out of work because of factors that vary with the time of year.

Set aside program. A government program that reduces the supply of farm products by keeping land out of production.

Share draft account. An account with a credit union from which withdrawals can be easily made using a draft.

Shortage. The condition in which demand is greater than supply at a certain price.

Short run. Any period during which the usable amount of at least one input is fixed, while the usable amount of at least one other input can change.

Slope. The description of a graphical curve; the amount of change (in what is being measured) on the vertical axis divided by the amount of change on the horizontal axis. "The rise over the run."

Social benefits. The benefits received by a society from a social choice or some other action.

Social choice. Decision making by government in the interest of society.

Social costs. The cost to a society of a social choice or some other action.

Social economy. An economy in which the major economic questions are determined by the government representing the interests of the entire society.

Social goals. The goals of an entire society.

Socialism. An economic system in which most of the basic industries are government owned and operated.

Social security tax. A tax that provides disability and retirement benefits for most working people.

Special interest group. An organized subgroup of society bound together by a common cause.

Specialization. In producing goods and services, an economic entity produces only those products which it can produce with some advantage.

Stock. Shares of ownership in a corporation.

Structural unemployment. Unemployment resulting from skills that do not match what employers require or from being geographically separated from job opportunities.

Subsidy. A payment made by government to encourage some activity.

Substitute products. Products whose uses are similar enough that one can replace the other.

Substitution effect. The effect of increasing or decreasing relative prices on the mix of goods purchased.

Supply. The quantities of a product or service that a firm is willing and able to make available for sale at different prices.

Supply curve. A graphic representation of the quantities that would be supplied at each price.

Supply of labor. The amount of labor that would be available at each wage rate.

Supply schedule. A table showing quantities that would be supplied at each price.

Surplus. The condition in which supply is greater than demand at a certain price.

T

Table. A simplified way of showing numbers.

Tariff. A tax on imports.

Technology. The body of knowledge that is used for the production of goods and services.

Theory. A simplified description of reality.

Tight monetary policy. A policy of the Fed that causes the money supply to decrease.

Total product. All the units of a product produced in a given period of time, such as one year.

Total revenue. The amount of money a company receives from sales of a product.

Trade barriers. Methods of restricting trade between countries.

Trade deficit. The result when a country imports more than it exports.

Trade-offs. Decisions among alternatives in allocating economic resources.

Trade surplus. The result when a country exports more than it imports.

Traditional economy. An economy in which the three economic questions are decided mainly by social customs.

Transaction demand for money. The demand for money to make exchanges.

Transfer payments. Public expenditures made for reasons other than paying for goods and services.

U

Unemployment. The condition of those who are willing and able to work and are actively seeking work, but who are not currently working.

Unemployment rate. The percentage of the civilian labor force that is considered unemployed.

Union shop. A business that requires workers to join a union shortly after taking a job.

Unlimited liability. The concept that an owner's personal assets can be used to pay bills of the proprietorship or partnership.

Unlimited wants and needs. The human characteristic of never feeling that all wants and needs have been satisfied.

Util. The unit of measure for utility.

Utility. The satisfaction one receives from the consumption, use, or ownership of a good or service.

V

Vertical merger. A merger of two companies which are at different stages in the same production process.

W

Wage and price controls. Government controls on the levels of wages and prices.

Wage rate. The price paid for each unit of labor.

World Bank. A source of aid to the less-developed countries.

Y

Yellow-dog contract. A contract workers had to sign before they were hired saying that they would not join a union.

BIBLIOGRAPHY

Chapter 1   The Economic Way of Thinking

Amacher, Ryan, and Holley H. Ulbrich. *Principles of Economics.* 3d ed. Cincinnati: South-Western Publishing Co., 1986, Chapters 1 and 2.

Boulding, Kenneth Ewart. *Economics As a Science.* New York: McGraw-Hill Book Co., 1970.

Bowden, Elbert V. *Economic Evolution: Principles, Issues, Ideas — Through the Looking Glass of Time.* 2d ed. Cincinnati: South-Western Publishing Co., 1985.

Hough, Robbin R. *What Economists Do.* New York: Harper & Row, Publishers, Inc., 1972.

Koopmans, T. C. "Economics Among the Sciences." *American Economic Review* (March 1979): 1–13.

Lange, Oskar. "The Scope and Method of Economics." *Review of Economic Studies* 13 (1945–46): 19–32.

Norton, Hugh. *The World of the Economist.* Columbia, SC: University of South Carolina Press, 1973.

Tollison, Robert D. "Economists As the Subject of Economic Inquiry." *Southern Economic Journal* 52, no. 4 (April 1986): 909–922.

Chapter 2   Making Personal Decisions

Amacher, Ryan and Holley H. Ulbrich. *Principles of Economics.* 3d ed. Cincinnati: South-Western Publishing Co., 1986, Chapter 2.

Clark, J. R., Richard Stroup, and James D. Gwartney. *Essentials of Economics.* New York: Academic Press, Inc., 1982, 34–37.

Gilder, George. *Wealth and Poverty.* New York: Basic Books Inc., Publishers, 1981.

Heyne, Paul T. *The Economic Way of Thinking.* 5th ed. Chicago: Science Research Associates, Inc., 1987.

Smith, Adam. *An Inquiry into the Nature and Causes of the Wealth of Nations.* Edited by Edwin Cannon. Chicago: University of Chicago Press, 1976.

Chapter 3   Making Social Decisions

Bowden, Elbert V. *Principles of Economics.* 4th ed. Cincinnati: South-Western Publishing Co., 1983, Chapters 4 and 5.

Clark, J. R., Richard Stroup, and James D. Gwartney. *Essentials of Economics.* New York: Academic Press, Inc., 1982, 34–37, 66–79.

Marx, Karl. *Capital [Das Kapital].* New York: The Modern Library, 1936.

McKenzie, Richard B. *Economics.* Boston: Houghton Mifflin, 1986.

Miller, Roger L., and Douglas C. North. *The Economics of Public Issues.* 6th ed. New York: Harper & Row, Publishers, Inc., 1983.

North, Douglas. "The Growth of Government in The United States: An Economic Historian's Perspective." *Journal of Public Economics* 28, no. 3 (December 1985): 383–399.

Chapter 4 Private Sector Decisions: Consumers and Businesses

Friedman, Milton. *Capitalism and Freedom.* Chicago: University of Chicago Press, 1962.

McKenzie, Richard B., and Gordon Tullock. *Explorations into the Human Experience.* 4th ed. Homewood, IL: Richard D. Irwin, Inc., 1985, Chapters 1 and 12.

Peterson, Willis, and Yoav Kislev. "The Cotton Harvester in Retrospect: Labor Displacement or Replacement?" *Journal of Economic History* 46, no. 1 (March 1986).

Radford, R. A. "The Economic Organization of a P.O.W. Camp." *Economica* (November 1945).

Smith, Robert F., and Michael W. Watts. *Free Enterprise and the American Economy.* Baton Rouge: Louisiana State University, 1977, Chapters 3, 4, 5, and 6.

Trivoli, W. W. "Has the Consumer Really Lost His Sovereignty?" *Akron Business and Economic Review* (Winter 1970).

Chapter 5 Public Sector Decisions: Public Goods and Services

Bowden, Elbert V. *Principles of Economics.* 5th ed. Cincinnati: South-Western Publishing Co., 1986, Chapters 26, 27, 28, 29, 30, and 31.

Haveman, Robert Henry. *The Economics of the Public Sector.* New York: John Wiley and Sons, Inc., 1970.

McKenzie, Richard B. *Economics.* Boston: Houghton Mifflin, 1986.

McKenzie, Richard B., and Gordon Tullock. *The New World of Economics: Explorations into the Human Experience.* 4th ed. Homewood, IL: Richard D. Irwin, Inc., 1985.

Musgrave, Richard, and Peggy Musgrave. *Public Finance in Theory and Practice.* 4th ed. New York: McGraw-Hill, 1984.

Smith, Robert F., and Michael W. Watts. *Free Enterprise and the American Economy.* Baton Rouge: Louisiana State University, 1977, Chapter 9.

Chapter 6   Demand: Achieving Consumer Satisfaction

Berkovec, James. "New Car Sales and Used Car Stocks: A Model of the Automobile Market." *Rand Journal of Economics* 16, no. 2 (Summer 1985): 195–214.

Foster, H. S., Jr., and Bruce R. Beattie. "Urban Residential Demand for Water in the United States." *Land Economics* (February 1979): 43–58.

Jung, J. M., and E. T. Fujii. "The Price Elasticity of Demand for Air Travel." *Journal of Transport Economics and Policy* (September 1976): 257–262.

Kiechel, Walter, III. "Two-Income Families Will Reshape the Consumer Markets." *Fortune* (March 10, 1980): 110–120.

Schmenner, Roger W. "The Demand for Urban Bus Transit: A Route by Route Analysis." *Journal of Transport Economics and Policy* (January 1976): 68–86.

Taylor, L. D. "The Demand for Electricity: A Survey." *The Bell Journal of Economics* 6, no. 1 (Spring 1975): 74–110.

Chapter 7   Supply: Producing Goods and Services

Barnett, Robert. "The Problems of Productivity: Running on Empty." *The Wharton Magazine* 6, no. 3 (Spring 1982): 54–59.

Dugas, Christine. "Marketing's New Look: Campbell Leads a Revolution in the Way Consumer Products Are Sold." *Business Week* (January 26, 1987): 64–69.

Mansfield, Edwin. *The Economics of Technical Change.* New York: W. W. Norton & Company, Inc., Publishers, 1968.

Meadows, Edward. "How Three Companies Increased Their Productivity." *Fortune* (March 10, 1980): 92–101.

Rothschild, Emma. "Robots Join the Labor Force." *Business Week* (June 9, 1980): 62–76.

Chapter 8   Demand, Supply, and Prices

Bell, Frederick W. "The Pope and the Price of Fish." *American Economic Review* (December 1968): 1346–1350.

Brozen, Yale. "The Effect of Statutory Minimum Wage Increase on Teenage Unemployment." *Journal of Law and Economics* (April 1969): 109–122.

Friedman, David D. *Price Theory: An Intermediate Text.* Cincinnati: South-Western Publishing Co., 1986.

Friedman, Milton. *Capitalism and Freedom.* Chicago: University of Chicago Press, 1962.

Levi, Maurice. *Economics Deciphered: A Layman's Guide.* New York: Basic Books, Inc., Publishers, 1981, Chapters 9, 10, and 11.

Chapter 9   **Business Firms in the Economy**

Adams, Walter. *The Structure of American Industry*. 6th ed. New York: Macmillan Publishing Co., Inc., 1982.

Albrecht, Karl, and Ron Zemke. *Service America: Doing Business in the New Economy*. Dow Jones-Irwin, 1985.

Breyer, Stephen. *Regulation and Its Reform*. Cambridge, MA: Harvard University Press, 1982.

Lynn, Robert Athan, and J. P. O'Grady. *Elements of Business*. Boston: Houghton Mifflin Co., 1978, Chapter 3.

Mandell, Steven L., Scott S. Cowen, and Roger LeRoy Miller. *Introduction to Business:* Concepts and Applications. St. Paul: West Publishing Co., 1981, Chapter 3.

Chapter 10   **Perfect Competition and Monopoly**

Eckert, Ross D., and George W. Hilton. "The Jitneys." *Journal of Law and Economics* (October 1972): 293–325.

Fisher, F. M. "Diagnosing Monopoly." *Quarterly Review of Economics and Business* (Summer 1979): 7–33.

Leftwich, Richard H., and Ansel M. Sharp. *Economics of Social Issues*. 6th ed. Plano, TX: Business Publications, Inc. 1984, Chapter 7.

Levi, Maurice. *Economics Deciphered: A Layman's Guide*. New York: Basic Books, Inc., Publishers, 1981, Chapters 12 and 13.

MacDonald, James M. "Entry and Exit on the Competitive Fringe." *Southern Economic Journal* 52, no. 3 (January 1986): 640–652.

Malmgren, H. B. "Notes for a U.S. Industrial Policy." *Challenge* (January/February 1981): 19–23.

Chapter 11   **Monopolistic Competition and Oligopoly**

Adams, Walter. "Mega-Mergers Spell Danger." *Challenge* (March/April 1982): 12–17.

Marvel, H. P. "Competition and Price Levels in the Retail Gasoline Market." *The Review of Economics and Statistics* 60, no. 2 (May 1978): 252–258.

Moritz, Michael, and Barrett Seaman. *Going for Broke: The Chrysler Story*. Garden City, NY: Doubleday & Co., Inc. 1981.

Nightingale, J. "On the Definition of 'Industry' and 'Market'." *Journal of Industrial Economics* (September 1978): 31–40.

Plaut, S. E. "OPEC Is Not a Cartel." *Challenge* 24, no. 5 (November/ December 1981): 18–24.

Smith, L. "A Superpower Enters the Soft-Drink Wars." *Fortune* (June 30, 1980): 76–77.

Wolinsky, Asher. "The Nature of Competition and the Scope of Firms." *Journal of Industrial Economics* 34, no. 3 (March 1986): 247–259.

Chapter 12   Improving the Market Economy

Arrow, K. J. "The Limitations of the Profit Motive." *Challenge* (September/ October 1979): 23–27.

Butler, Richard V., and Michael D. Maher. "The Control of Externalities: Abatement vs. Damage Prevention." *Southern Economic Journal* 52, no. 4 (April 1986): 1088–1102.

Edel, Matthew. *Economies and the Environment.* Englewood Cliffs, NJ: Prentice-Hall, Inc., 1973.

Leftwich, Richard H., and Ansel M. Sharp. *Economics of Social Issues.* 6th ed. Plano, TX: Business Publications, Inc., 1984, Chapter 6.

Mills, Edwin Smith. *The Economics of Environmental Quality.* New York: W. W. Norton & Co., Inc., Publishers, 1978.

Weidenbaum, Murray Lew. *Business, Government, and the Public.* 2d ed. Englewood Cliffs, NJ: Prentice-Hall, Inc., 1981.

Chapter 13   The Labor Market and Personal Income

Elliott, J. Walter, and Keith R. Sherony. "Employer Search Activities and the Short-Run Aggregate Labor Supply." *Southern Economic Journal* 52, no. 3 (January 1986): 693–705.

Feldman, R., and R. M. Scheffler. "The Supply of Medical School Applicants and the Rate of Return to Training." *Quarterly Review of Economics and Business* (Spring 1978): 91–98.

Ginzberg, Eli. "The Mechanization of Work." *Scientific American* (September 1982): 67–75.

Piore, M. J. "American Labor and the Industrial Crisis." *Challenge* (March/ April 1982): 5–11.

Reder, M. W. "An Analysis of a Small, Closely Observed Labor Market: Starting Salaries for University of Chicago MBA's." *Journal of Business* 2, no. 2 (April 1978): 263–297.

Sabel, C. F. "Marginal Workers in Industrial Society." *Challenge* 22, no. 1 (March/April 1979): 22–32.

Wilson, M. "Big Labor Faces Reality." *Dun's Business Month* 119, no. 2 (February 1982): 37–43.

Chapter 14   Agriculture in the Economy

Brown, L. R. "Global Food Prospects: Shadow of Malthus." *Challenge* (January/February 1982): 14–21.

Duncan, Marvin, and C. E. Harshbarger. "A Primer on Agricultural Policy." *Monthly Review, Federal Reserve Bank of Kansas City* (September/October 1977).

Hayden, F. Gregory. "Family Farmland Reserve: A State Government Program for Restructuring Farm Debt." *Journal of Economic Issues* 20, no. 1 (March 1986): 179–190.

Rasmussen, Wayne D. "The Mechanization of Agriculture." *Scientific American* (September 1982): 76–89.

Schultz, T. W. "Knowledge Is Power in Agriculture." *Challenge* (September/October 1982): 4–13.

Chapter 15   Measuring Economic Activity

Galbraith, John Kenneth. "The Coming of J. M. Keynes." *Business and Society Review* (Fall 1975): 32–38.

Hom, J. "Adhesive Bandages to Zippers." *Across the Board* 14, no. 6 (June 1977): 45–53.

Meadows, E. "Tracking the Ever-Elusive Gross National Product." *Fortune* (May 22, 1978): 100–104.

Sommers, Albert T. *The U.S. Economy Demystified: What the Major Economic Statistics Mean and Their Significance for Business.* Lexington, MA: Lexington Books, 1985.

Stewart, Kenneth. "National Income Accounting and Economic Welfare: The Concepts of GNP and MEW. *Review, Federal Reserve Bank of St. Louis* (April 1974): 18–24.

U.S. Department of Commerce. *The Economic Accounts of the United States: Retrospect and Prospect,* 1971.

Chapter 16   The Distribution of Income

Blumberg, Paul. *Inequality in an Age of Decline.* Oxford, England: Oxford University Press, 1981.

Danziger, S., et al. "Poverty, Welfare, and Earnings: A New Approach." *Challenge* (September 1979): 28–34.

Fichtenbaum, Rudy. "Consumption and the Distribution of Income."*Review of Social Economy* 43, no. 2 (October 1985): 234–244.

Leftwich, Richard H., and Ansel M. Sharp. *Economics of Social Issues.* 6th ed. Plano, TX: Business Publications, Inc., 1984, Chapters 11 and 12.

Leontief, Wassily W. "The Distribution of Work and Income." *Scientific American* (September 1982): 188–204.

Chapter 17   **Unemployment**

Buss, Terry F. "Assessing the Accuracy of BLS Local Unemployment Rates: A Case Study." *Industrial and Labor Relations Review* 39, no. 2 (January 1986): 241–250.

Finegan, T. A. "Should Discouraged Workers Be Counted as Unemployed?" *Challenge* (November/December 1978): 20–25.

Fritz, S. "The Human Tragedy of Unemployment." *U.S. News & World Report* (June 23, 1980): 68–69.

Haveman, R. H. "Creating Jobs: More Than a Dead End Street." *The Wharton Magazine* 4, no. 3 (Spring 1980): 26–33.

Peterson, Wallace C. *Our Overloaded Economy: Inflation, Unemployment, and the Crisis in American Capitalism.* Armonk, NY: M. E. Sharpe, Inc., 1982.

Weintraub, Sidney. *Capitalism's Inflation and Unemployment Crisis.* Reading, MA: Addison-Wesley Publishing Co., Inc., 1978.

Wilson, Marilyn. "Unemployment's Uneven Pain." *Dun's Business Month* (June 1982): 35–37.

Chapter 18   **Inflation**

Dunson, Bruce H., and Peter Jackson. "The Distributional Aspects of Inflation." *The Quarterly Review of Economics and Business* 2, no. 4 (Winter 1986): 62–73.

Minarik, J. J. "Who Wins, Who Loses from Inflation?" *Challenge* (January/February 1979): 26–31.

Nulty, L. E. "How Inflation Hits the Majority." *Challenge* (January/February 1979): 32–38.

Peterson, Wallace C. *Our Overloaded Economy: Inflation, Unemployment, and the Crisis in American Capitalism.* Armonk, NY: M. E. Sharpe, Inc., 1982.

Robinson, J. "Solving the Stagflation Puzzle." *Challenge* (November/December 1979): 40–46.

Weintraub, Sidney. *Capitalism's Inflation and Unemployment Crisis.* Reading, MA: Addison-Wesley Publishing Co., Inc., 1978.

Chapter 19   **Money and Banking**

Cook, Timothy Q., and Bruce J. Summers, eds. *Instruments of the Money Market.* 5th ed. Federal Reserve Bank of Richmond, 1981.

Levi, Maurice. *Economics Deciphered: A Layman's Guide.* New York: Basic Books, Inc., Publishers, 1981, Chapter 3.

Massaro, V. G. "Toward a New Financial Structure for the United States." *Conference Board Record* (February 1976): 18–21.

Ritter, Lawrence S., and William L. Silber. *Money.* 3d ed. New York: Basic Books, Inc., Publishers, 1977.

Rose, S. "More Bang for the Buck: The Magic of Electronic Banking." *Fortune* (May 1977): 202–205.

Chapter 20   **Monetary Policy**

Bluinder, A. S. "Monetarism Is Obsolete." *Challenge* (September/October 1981): 35–41.

Board of Governors of the Federal Reserve System. *The Federal Reserve System — Purposes and Functions.* Washington, D.C., 1974.

Friedman, Benjamin M. "Lessons from the 1979–82 Monetary Policy Experiment." *American Economic Review* (May 1984): 382–387.

Friedman, Milton. "Lessons from the 1979–82 Monetary Policy Experiment." *American Economic Review* (May 1984): 397–400.

Solomon, A. M. "New Strategies for the Federal Reserve?" *Challenge* (March/April 1982): 18–24.

Wilson, M. "Monetarism Under Fire." *Dun's Business Month* (May 1982): 34–39.

Chapter 21   **Taxes**

Aaron, H. J. "Social Security Can Be Saved." *Challenge* (November/December 1981): 4–9.

Allingham, M. "Inequality and Progressive Taxation: An Example." *Journal of Public Economics* (April 1979): 273–274.

Guthrie, R. S. "Measurement of Relative Tax Progressivity." *National Tax Journal* (March 1979): 93–95.

Lawler, Patrick J. "Payroll Taxes: A Two-Edged Sword?" *Voice, Federal Reserve Bank of Dallas* (May 1980): 1–12.

Mills, Gregory, and John Palmer, eds. *Federal Budget Policy in the 1980s.* Washington, D.C.: Urban Institute, 1984.

Chapter 22   **Fiscal Policy**

Galbraith, John Kenneth. "Keynes, Roosevelt, and the Complementary Revolution." *Challenge* (January/February 1984): 4–8.

Grayson, C. Jackson. "Controls Are Not the Answer." *Challenge* (November/December 1974): 9–12.

Leftwich, Richard H., and Ansel M. Sharp. *Economics of Social Issues.* 6th ed. Plano, TX: Business Publications, Inc., 1984, Chapters 15 and 16.

Levi, Maurice. *Economics Deciphered: A Layman's Guide.* New York: Basic Books, Inc., Publishers, 1981, Chapter 5.

Mills, Gregory, and John Palmer. *The Deficit Dilemma: Budget Policy in the Reagan Era.* Washington, D.C.: Urban Institute, 1983.

Chapter 23   Economic Growth

Denison, E. F. "The Puzzling Setback to Productivity Growth." *Challenge* 23, no. 5 (November/December 1980): 3–7.

Gordon, Robert J. "Economic Growth and the Open Economy." *Macroeconomics.* 4th ed. Boston: Little Brown & Company, 1987, 565–594.

Leipert, Christian. "Social Costs of Economic Growth." *Journal of Economic Issues* 20, no. 1 (March 1986): 109–131.

Mansfield, E. "Innovation, Investment and Productivity" *The Wharton Magazine* 5, no. 4 (Summer 1981): 36–41.

Mason, E. S. "Natural Resources and Environmental Restrictions to Growth." *Challenge* 20, no. 6 (January/February 1978): 14–20.

Schumacher, E. F. *Small Is Beautiful: Economics As If People Mattered.* New York: Harper & Row, Publishers, Inc., 1976.

Thurow, L. C. "The Implications of Zero Economic Growth." *Challenge* (March 1977): 36–43.

Chapter 24   Alternative Economic Systems

Abouchar, Alan J. "Western Project-Investment Theory and Soviet Investment Rules." *Journal of Comparative Economics* 9, no. 4 (December 1985): 345–362.

Bowden, Elbert V. *Principles of Economics.* 4th ed. Cincinnati: South-Western Publishing Co., 1983, Chapter 43.

Gwartney, James D., and Richard Stroup. *Economics: Private and Public Choice.* 2d ed. New York: Academic Press, Inc., 1980, Chapter 36.

Heilbroner, Robert L. *The Worldly Philosophers.* 5th ed. New York: Simon & Schuster, 1980.

McConnell, Campbell R. *Economics: Principles, Problems, and Policies.* 8th ed. New York: McGraw-Hill, 1980, Chapter 45.

Miller, Roger L. *Economics Today.* New York: Harper & Row, Publishers, Inc., 1982, Chapter 40.

Palash, Carl J. "Tax Policy: Its Impact on Investment Incentives." *Quarterly Review, Federal Reserve Bank of New York* (Summer 1978): 30–36.

Rivlin, A. M. "Congress and the Budget Process." *Challenge* (March/April 1981): 31–37.

Chapter 25   **International Trade**

DeVries, R. "Urgent Tasks on the International Scene." *Challenge* 24, no. 1 (March/April 1981): 42–49.

Levi, Maurice. *Economics Deciphered: A Layman's Guide.* New York: Basic Books, Inc., Publishers, 1981, Chapter 14.

Rostow, W. W. "Working Agenda for a Disheveled World Economy." *Challenge* 24, no. 1 (March/April 1981): 5–16.

Schott, J. J. "Can World Trade Be Governed?" *Challenge* 25, no. 1 (March/April 1982): 43–49.

Solomon, Robert. *The International Monetary System.* New York: Harper & Row, 1982.

Chapter 26   **Less-Developed Countries**

Brada, Josef C., and José A. Méndez. "Economic Integration Among Developed, Developing and Centrally Planned Economies: A Comparative Analysis." *Review of Economic Statistics* 67, no. 4 (November 1985): 549–556.

Dolan, Edwin G. *Economics.* 4th ed. Dryden Press, 1986, Chapter 36.

Gaiha, Raghav. "Poverty, Technology, and Infrastructure in Rural India." *Cambridge Journal of Economics* 9, no. 3 (September 1985): 221–243.

Herrick, Bruce, and Charles Kindleberger. *Economic Development.* 4th ed. McGraw-Hill, 1983.

VonWitzke, Harold. "Poverty, Agriculture, and Economic Development: A Survey." *European Review of Agricultural Economics* 11, no. 4 (1984): 439–453.

Appendix II   **Supply and Demand Forces at Work: Health Care in the Economy**

Christianson, Jon B., and Walter McClure, "Competition in the Delivery of Medical Care." *The New England Journal of Medicine* (October 11, 1979): 812–818.

Finkler, S. A., S. V. Williams, and J. M. Eisenberg. "R_x for Rising Hospital Costs." *The Wharton Magazine* 5, no. 1 (Fall 1980): 34–41.

Lamberton, C. E., W. D. Ellingson, and K. R. Spear. "Factors Determining the Demand for Nursing Home Services." *The Quarterly Review of Economics and Business* 2, no. 4 (Winter 1986): 74–90.

Shapiro, E. "Controlling Health Care Expenditures." *Challenge* (September/October 1980): 40–44.

"The Spiraling Costs of Health Care R_x: COMPETITION." *Business Week* (February 8, 1982): 56–64.

Wood, Charles T. "Relate Hospital Charges to Use of Services." *Harvard Business Review* (March/April 1982): 123–130.

INDEX

ACKNOWLEDGMENTS

Cover Photo	Hale Photography, Inc.
Contents	p. xii, Camerique; p. xiv, © Nancy Bundt, 1984; p. xvi, Photo Courtesy of ALCOA; p. xviii, Carolina Power & Light
Part I Opener	p. xxvi, Camerique
Chapter 1	p. 2, B. Gerald Cantor Art Foundation; p. 5, Combustion Engineering; p. 9, USDA Photo/Fred A. Witte; p. 11, (top) California Canning Peach Association, (bottom) USDA Photo; p. 13, Courtesy of The Standard Oil Company; p. 15, (fourth photo) Photo Courtesy of The Christ Hospital, (fifth photo) TWR Inc.
Chapter 2	p. 18, Courtesy of Lazarus Department Store; p. 20, Courtesy of JMB Realty Corporation; p. 23, Disabled Children's Computer Group; p. 25, © Clifford W. Hausner/LEO de WYS Inc.; p. 26, Courtesy of Lazarus Department Store
Chapter 3	p. 34, Aetna Life & Casualty Co.; p. 35, © C. Niedenthal/SYGMA PHOTO NEWS; p. 36, L. S. Williams/H. ARMSTRONG ROBERTS; p. 39, Photo by W. R. Grace & Company; p. 46, Owen Franken/STOCK, BOSTON, INC.
Chapter 4	p. 52, © Chas. R. Pearson, 1974/WEST STOCK; p. 56, Burger King Corporation, Mobile Restaurant Divison; p. 61, U.S. Postal Service; p. 63 WIDE WORLD PHOTOS, INC.
Chapter 5	p. 67, © Jeff Zaruba/FOLIO, INC.; p. 69, Kerr-McGee Corporation; p. 73, USDA Photo; p. 75, UNITED NATIONS; p. 78, Sierra Club
Part II Opener	p. 84, © Nancy Bundt, 1984
Chapter 6	p. 86, Dean Foods Company; p. 88, George Catlin, WINNEBAGO SHOOTING DUCKS ON WISCONSIN RIVER, 1836. National Museum of American Art, Smithsonian Institution. Gift of Mrs. Joseph Harrison, Jr.; p. 99, Courtesy of Levi Strauss & Co., San Francisco, California
Chapter 7	p. 114, Photo Courtesy of Brockway, Inc.; p. 119, RJR Nabisco, Inc.; p. 124, Courtesy Michigan Travel Bureau
Chapter 8	p. 141, © Harry Gruyaert/MAGNUM PHOTOS, INC.; p. 146, Photo Courtesy of The May Department Stores; p. 152, USDA Photo; p. 155, (left) Photo Courtesy of Sperry Corporation, (right) Photo Courtesy of Apple Computer, Inc.

Chapter 9	p. 166, The First Boston Corporation; p. 169, (left) The Kroger Co.
Chapter 10	p. 186, Courtesy of Parker Hannifin Corporation; p. 191, USDA Photo; p. 192, USDA Photo; p. 196, Tennessee Valley Authority; p. 197, Photo Courtesy of ALCOA
Chapter 11	p. 208, W. R. Grace & Co.; p. 213, Bethlehem Steel Corporation; p. 217, WIDE WORLD PHOTOS, INC.
Chapter 12	p. 223, © Matt Brown/WEST STOCK; p. 226, General Motors Corporation; p. 235, IUPUI Publications; p. 238, (left) Ford Aerospace & Communications Corporation/Aeronutronic Division
Chapter 13	p. 245, Photo courtesy of R. R. Donnelley & Sons Company; p. 247, (left) Courtesy of The Cincinnati Historical Society, (right) General Motors Corporation; p. 250, (right) Campbell Soup Company; p. 257, WIDE WORLD PHOTOS, INC.; p. 264, Figgie International, Inc.
Chapter 14	p. 268, Allis-Chalmers Corporation; p. 269, Grant Wood, *American Gothic*, 1930, oil on beaverboard, 79.5 × 63.5 cm., Friends of American Art Collection, 1930.934 © The Art Institute of Chicago. All rights reserved.; p. 272, Sperry Corporation; p. 276, (top) USDA Photo, (middle) USDA Photo, (bottom) USDA Photo; p. 280, USDA Photo/Russell Forte; p. 281, © Ellis Herwig/STOCK, BOSTON
Part III Opener	p. 290, Photo Courtesy of ALCOA
Chapter 15	p. 292, New York Convention & Visitors Bureau; p. 294, (left) New York Convention & Visitors Bureau; p. 296, Union Camp Corporation; p. 298, (left) WORLD BANK PHOTO, (right) Austria Information Service, New York; p. 301, USDA Photo; p. 304, TRW Inc.; p. 313, (left) New York Convention & Visitors Bureau, (center) Washington D.C. Convention & Visitors Association
Chapter 16	p. 322, WIDE WORLD PHOTOS, INC.; p. 323, Renate Hiller/MONKMEYER PRESS; p. 326, Sperry Corporation; p. 336, © Glen Donahue/CLICK/CHICAGO
Chapter 17	p. 346, © MCMLXXX Simon Nathan/THE STOCK MARKET; p. 348, USDA Photo; p. 356, © Jeff Smith; p. 358, © Bob Perry/Killington Ski & Summer Resort, Killington, VT
Chapter 18	p. 366, (left) © Steve Leonard/CLICK/CHICAGO LTD., (right) © Jay Lurie, 1982/BLACK STAR; p. 376, Bethlehem Steel Corporation
Chapter 19	p. 388, Reprinted with permission of the Federal Reserve Bank of Cleveland; p. 390, (left and right) Bureau of Engraving and Printing; p. 393, Photo courtesy of Ford Motor Company

Chapter 20   p. 399, American Petroleum Institute; p. 401, Photo courtesy of Walgreen Company; p. 404, Reprinted with permission of the Federal Reserve Bank of Cleveland; p. 413, (top) XTRA CORPORATION, (bottom) P. Conklin/MONKMEYER PRESS PHOTO SERVICE, INC.

Chapter 21   p. 426, Florida Division of Tourism; p. 431, Photo courtesy of Walgreen Company; p. 434, Photo courtesy of Klosterman's Baking Co.

Chapter 22   p. 444, American Petroleum Institute; p. 451, Photo courtesy of Ford Motor Company; p. 452, © Mickey Osterreicher/BLACK STAR; p. 457, The Bettmann Archive, Inc.

Chapter 23   p. 473, Photo courtesy of Unocal Corporation; p. 474, American Petroleum Institute; p. 475, Kerr-McGee Corporation; p. 478, Standard Oil of California; p. 483, © Tom Hollyman, 1987. All Rights Reserved.

Part IV Opener   p. 488, Carolina Power & Light

Chapter 24   p. 490, M. Koene/H. ARMSTRONG ROBERTS, Inc.; p. 492, WORLD BANK PHOTO; p. 494, Zenith Electronics Corporation; p. 499, © G. Rancinan/SYGMA PHOTO NEWS; p. 503, © John Phillips/PHOTO RESEARCHERS, INC.

Chapter 25   p. 509, The Dun & Bradstreet Corporation; p. 515, Photo courtesy AMAX, Inc., Greenwich, CT; p. 520, Taiwan Visitors Association; p. 523, Photography by Milt and Joan Mann/CAMERAMANN INTERNATIONAL, LTD.; p. 524, Dept. of Treasury/U.S. Customs Service

Chapter 26   p. 529, UNRWA; p. 532, UNRWA; p. 534, M. Miller/H. ARMSTRONG ROBERTS, Inc.; p. 537, WORLD BANK PHOTO by Ed. Huffman; p. 538, WORLD BANK PHOTO; p. 539, WORLD BANK PHOTO

Appendix   p. 562, Photo Courtesy of The Christ Hospital

Economist portraits by Pete Harritos